Paul and Paulinism

Essays in honour of C. K. Barrett

edited by

M. D. Hooker and S. G. Wilson

LONDON
SPCK

First published 1982
SPCK
Holy Trinity Church
Marylebone Road
London NW1 4DU

Printed in Great Britain at
the Alden Press, Oxford

ISBN 0 281 03835 X

CONTENTS

Contents

CHARLES KINGSLEY BARRETT

The Reverend Professor C. K. Barrett, DD, has been Professor of Divinity in the University of Durham since 1958, a position he is relinquishing in 1982.

He is a Fellow of the British Academy (1961), and holds honorary degrees from Hull (DD 1970), Aberdeen (DD 1972) and Hamburg (Doctor of Theology 1981). He was awarded the Burkitt Medal for Biblical Studies in 1966.

A list of his published works appears on pages 373–81.

THE CONTRIBUTORS

MARKUS BARTH	Professor of New Testament, Faculty of Theology, University of Basel
P. BENOIT OP	Professor of New Testament, École Biblique et Archéologique Française, Jerusalem
ERNEST BEST	Professor of Divinity and Biblical Criticism, University of Glasgow
MATTHEW BLACK	Emeritus Professor of Divinity and Biblical Criticism, and formerly Principal of St Mary's College, University of St Andrews. Fellow of the British Academy
PEDER BORGEN	Professor of New Testament, Department of Religious Studies, University of Trondheim
F. F. BRUCE	Emeritus Professor of Biblical Criticism and Exegesis, University of Manchester
J.-M. CAMBIER	Professor of St Paul, Faculty of Theology, University of Louvain-Leuven
P. MAURICE CASEY	Lecturer in Theology, University of Nottingham
JOHN M. COURT	Lecturer in Theology, University of Kent
C. E. B. CRANFIELD	Emeritus Professor of Theology, University of Durham
NILS ALSTRUP DAHL	Formerly Professor of New Testament Criticism and Interpretation, Yale University
DAVID DAUBE	Director of the Robbins Hebraic and Roman Law Collections, and Professor-in-Residence at the School of Law, University of California, Berkeley. Emeritus Regius Professor of Civil Law, University of Oxford. Fellow of the British Academy
W. D. DAVIES	Ivey Professor Emeritus of Christian Origins, Duke University, Durham, North Carolina. Bradford University Professor, Texas Christian University, Forth Worth, Texas. Fellow of the British Academy
JACQUES DUPONT OSB	Director of Research at the Istituto per le Scienze Religiose, Bologna, and formerly Professor at the Istituto Biblico, Rome. Now at Monastère Saint-André, Ottignies

ix

The Contributors

M. E. Glasswell	Senior Lecturer in New Testament, and Head of the Department of Religion, University of Nigeria, Nsukka
Ferdinand Hahn	Professor of New Testament, University of Munich
Martin Hengel	Professor of New Testament and Early Judaism, and Director of the Institute for Ancient Judaism and Hellenistic Religion in the Protestant Theological Faculty in the University of Tübingen
Morna D. Hooker	Lady Margaret's Professor of Divinity, University of Cambridge, and Fellow of Robinson College
A. F. J. Klijn	Professor of New Testament, University of Groningen
K. H. Kuhn	Reader in Coptic, University of Durham
John McHugh	Senior Lecturer in Divinity, University of Durham, and Tutor at the Ushaw College, Durham
I. Howard Marshall	Professor of New Testament Exegesis, University of Aberdeen
Robert C. Morgan	Lecturer in New Testament, University of Oxford, and Fellow of Linacre College
John Painter	Chairman of Religious Studies, La Trobe University, Melbourne
Harald Riesenfeld	Emeritus Professor of Biblical Exegesis, University of Uppsala
R. Schnackenburg	Professor of New Testament Exegesis, University of Würzburg
E. Schweizer	Emeritus Professor of New Testament Theology and Exegesis, University of Zürich
U. Wilckens	Bishop of Holstein-Lübeck, and formerly Professor of New Testament, University of Hamburg
R. McL. Wilson	Professor of Biblical Criticism, St Mary's College, University of St Andrews. Fellow of the British Academy
S. G. Wilson	Professor of New Testament, Department of Religion, Carleton University, Ottawa

PREFACE

In compiling this volume of essays in honour of C.K. Barrett we have inevitably had to be selective. We have chosen a small group of colleagues, former pupils and other friends to represent the much larger circle of New Testament scholars who join with us in wishing him well on his sixty-fifth birthday.

Professor Barrett's scholarly interests are so wide that it would have been appropriate to offer him a volume of essays covering virtually every aspect of New Testament research. In the interests of producing a volume with a unified theme, however, it seemed best to limit ourselves to one area of study, and we therefore chose the topic *Paul and Paulinism*. We are grateful to those contributors who agreed to write within this area, even though this was not the natural choice for them all. We have allowed only one exception to this rule. Professor Daube was prevented by illness from writing on our theme, and rather than offering Kingsley a volume without a contribution from a friend of such long standing, we have included an essay on another topic from his pen, a bonus for those who expect to find in these pages only what our title promises.

M. D. Hooker
S. G. Wilson

TABULA GRATULANTIUM

Prof. Paul J. Achtemeier, Union Theological Seminary, Richmond, Virginia.

Rev. Dr James B. Adamson, First Presbyterian Church, Santa Rosa, California.

Lic. Dr Barbara Aland, Universität Münster.

Prof. Dr Kurt Aland, Universität Münster.

Prof. Dr John E. Alsup, Austin Presbyterian Theological Seminary, Texas.

Rev. Prof. George W. Anderson, University of Edinburgh.

Rev. Prof. Hugh Anderson, University of Edinburgh.

Prof. Jean-Louis d'Aragon, Université de Montréal.

Prof. Dr Sasagu Arai, University of Tokyo.

Rev. Eric Ashby, Settle, North Yorkshire.

Prof. Dr David E. Aune, St Xavier College, Chicago, Illinois.

Prof. Dr T. Baarda, Free University of Amsterdam.

Prof. J. Arthur Baird, Wooster College, Ohio.

Prof. William Baird, Texas Christian University, Fort Worth.

Prof. Dr David L. Balch, Linfield College, McMinnville, Oregon.

Dr Robert John Banks, Australian National University, Canberra.

Rev. Prof. R. S. Barbour, University of Aberdeen.

Dr S. Scott Bartchy, University of California.

Rev. Dr G. R. Beasley-Murray, Southern Baptist Theological Seminary, Louisville, Kentucky.

Rev. Brian E. Beck, University of Cambridge.

Prof. J. C. Beker, Princeton Theological Seminary, New Jersey.

Prof. Johannes Bentley, Phil.-Theol. Hochschule St Georgen, Frankfurt.

Prof. Hans Dieter Betz, University of Chicago, Illinois.

Rev. Prof. J. Neville Birdsall, University of Birmingham.

Prof. Dr Hendrikus Boers, Emory University, Atlanta, Georgia.

Gerald Bonner, University of Durham.

Dr G. H. Boobyer, University of Newcastle-upon-Tyne.

Prof. M. Eugene Boring, Phillips University, Enid, Oklahoma.

Prof. Michel Bouttier, Faculté de Théologie, Montpellier.

Prof. Dr G. Bouwman, University of Tilburg.

Prof. Dr François Bovon, Université de Génève.

Rev. Prof. John Bowman, University of Melbourne.

Rev. Prof. Raymond E. Brown ss, Union Theological Seminary, New York.

Prof. Dr N. Brox, Universität Regensburg.

Prof. Harry M. Buck, Wilson College, Chambersburg, Pennsylvania.

Prof. Dr P. Joseph Cahill, University of Alberta.

Rev. Prof. George B. Caird, University of Oxford.

Rev. Dr Muriel M. Carder, Oxford Regional Centre, Woodstock, Ontario.

Monsieur l'Abbé Jean Carmignac, Paris.

Rev. Dr A. Casurella, Emmanuel Bible College, Birkenhead, Merseyside.

Dr David R. Catchpole, University of Lancaster.

C. H. Cave, University of Exeter.

A. Chapple, Seminari Theoloji, Malaysia.

Rev. Prof. J. H. Charlesworth, Duke University, Durham, North Carolina.

Dr A. Chester, University of Durham.

Prof. Max-Alain Chevallier, Université de Strasbourg.

Prof. Dr James T. Clemons, Wesley Theological Seminary, Washington D.C.

Prof. Dr Raymond F. Collins, Katholieke Universiteit te Leuven.

Prof. Dr C. Colpe, Free University of Berlin.

Dr H. J. B. Combrink, University of Stellenbosch.

Prof. James I. Cook, Western Theological Seminary, Holland, Michigan.

Mgr Peter M. Cookson, Ushaw College, Durham.

Prof. Dr Bruno Corsani, Facoltà Valdese di Teologia, Rome.

Abbé Prof. Edouard Cothenet, Institut Catholique de Paris.

Prof. Charles B. Cousar, Columbia Theological Seminary, Decatur, Georgia.

Very Rev. H. Crichlow, Dean of Barbados.

Prof. Dr Oscar Cullmann, Universities of Paris and Basel.

Prof. Dr Alan Culpepper, Southern Baptist Theological Seminary, Louisville, Kentucky.

Rev. Prof. W. J. Dalton sj, Pontifical Biblical Institute, Rome.

Prof. Dr Gerhard Dautzenberg, Justus Liebig-Universität, Giessen.

Rev. Dafydd G. Davies, South Wales Baptist College, Cardiff.

Rev. D. P. Davies, St David's University College, Lampeter.

Prof. Dr Willis P. DeBoer, Calvin College, Grand Rapids, Michigan.

Dr Donald S. Deer, Crozer Theological Seminary, New York.

Prof. D. G. Delling, Martin-Luther-Universität, Halle-Wittenberg.

Margaret R. Diffenderfer, University of Durham.

Prof. Dr Erich Dinkler, Universität Heidelberg.

W. R. Domeris, University of Durham.

Rev. Prof. John R. Donahue sj, Jesuit School of Theology, Berkeley, California.

Rev. Prof. Karl Paul Donfried, Smith College, Northampton, Massachusetts.

Very Rev. Fr G. D. Dragas, University of Durham.

Dr John W. Drane, University of Stirling.

Prof. Marcel Dumais, St Paul University, Ottawa, Ontario.

Rev. Prof. David L. Dungan, University of Tennessee, Knoxville.

Dr James D. G. Dunn, University of Nottingham.

Dr J. K. Elliott, University of Leeds.

Prof. E. Earle Ellis, New Brunswick Theological Seminary, New Jersey.

Rev. Prof. S. Ifor Enoch, United Theological College, Aberystwyth

Prof. Eldon Jay Epp, Case Western Reserve University, Cleveland, Ohio.

Rev. Prof. Christopher F. Evans, University of London.

Rev. Owen E. Evans, University College of North Wales, Bangor.

Prof. William R. Farmer, Southern Methodist University, Dallas, Texas.

Rev. Prof. G. D. Fee, Gordon-Conwell Theological Seminary, Hamilton, Massachusetts.

Rev. Prof. Montagnini Felice, Seminario Vescovile, Brescia, Italy.

Rev. Canon J. C. Fenton, University of Oxford.

Dr Karl Martin Fischer, Karl-Marx-Universität, Leipzig.

Rev. Prof. Joseph A. Fitzmyer sj, Catholic University of America, Washington D.C.

Rev. Prof. R. T. Fortna, Vassar College, Poughkeepsie, New York.

Prof. Dr D. Fraikin, Queen's Theological College, Kingston, Ontario.

Right Rev. Eugene M. Frank, Bishop of the United Methodist Church, USA.

Dr W. Susan Frank, Trent Polytechnic, Nottingham.

Prof. Edwin D. Freed, Gettysburg College, Pennsylvania.

Prof. Dr G. Friedrich, Christian-Albrecht-Universität, Kiel.

Dr M. J. Fućak, Katolički bogoslovni fakultet, Zagreb.

Prof. V. P. Furnish, Southern Methodist University, Dallas, Texas.

Prof. Harry Y. Gamble Jr, University of Virginia, Charlottesville.

Prof. Dr W. Ward Gasque, New College, Berkeley, California.

Rev. G. D. Geddes, Ruskin School, Crewe.

Rev. A. Gelston, University of Durham.

Prof. A. S. Geyser, University of the Witwatersrand, Johannesburg.

Rev. Prof. J. Giblet, Katholieke Universiteit te Leuven.

Rev. Prof. Charles Homer Giblin sj, Fordham University, New York.

Rev. Dr T. Francis Glasson, University of London.

Rev. P. A. Glendinning, St Mary's College, Merseyside.

Prof. Dr J. Gnilka, München.

Rev. Prof. Michel Gourgues op, Collège dominicain de philosophie et de théologie, Ottawa, Ontario.

Rev. Prof. Holt H. Graham, United Theological Seminary of the Twin Cities, New Brighton, Minnesota.

The Librarian, Grand Séminaire, Namur.

Prof. David Granskou, Wilfrid Laurier University, Waterloo, Ontario.

Prof. Dr Erich Grässer, Universität Bonn.

Rev. Prof. K. Grayston, University of Bristol.

Rev. Prof. Prosper Grech osa, Patristic Institute, Rome.

Rev. Canon E. M. B. Green, St Aldate's Church, Oxford.

Prof. Dr D. Heinrich Greeven, Ruhr-Universität, Bochum.

Prof. Pierre Grelot, Institut Catholique de Paris.

Rev. F. X. H. Gresham op, University of York.

Prof. Joseph A. Grispino, California State University, North Ridge.

Prof. Dr Aileen Guilding, University of Sheffield.

Prof. Dr Klaus Haacker, Kirchliche Hochschule, Wuppertal.

Prof. D. Y. Hadidian, Pittsburgh Theological Seminary, Pennsylvania.

Prof. Dr Donald A. Hagner, Fuller Theological Seminary, Pasadena, California.

Prof. Paul L. Hammer, Colgate Rochester Divinity School, New York.

Rev. Canon Dr. R. J. Hammer, Treasurer *Studiorum Novi Testamenti Societas*.

Prof. R. G. Hamerton-Kelly, Stanford University, California.

Rev. John M. Hancock, Church of St John the Evangelist, Hebburn, Tyne and Wear.

Rev. Prof. A. T. Hanson, University of Hull.

Prof. D. R. A. Hare, Pittsburgh Theological Seminary, Pennsylvania.
Prof. Mattier E. Hart, Flagler College, Florida.
Prof. Dr Lars Hartman, Uppsala University.
Prof. Dr Günter Haufe, Ernst-Moritz-Arndt-Universität, Greifswald.
Prof. Dr David J. Hawkin, Memorial University of Newfoundland, St John's.
Prof. Paul T. Hayami, Rikkyo University, and Central Theological College, Tokyo.
Dr C. T. R. Hayward, University of Durham.
Prof. Dr Harald Hegermann, Universität München.
Rev. Prof. G. Henton Davies, University of Oxford.
Prof. Dr James D. Hester, University of Redlands, California.
Prof. J. Heywood Thomas, University of Nottingham.
Rev. C. J. A. Hickling, University of London.
Rev. Prof. A. J. B. Higgins, St David's University College, Lampeter.
Prof. Dr Franz Hildebrandt, Drew University, Madison, New Jersey.
Prof. Dr Earle Hilgert, McCormick Theological Seminary, Chicago, Illinois.
Rev. Dr David Hill, University of Sheffield.
Dr Harold W. Hoehner, Dallas Theological Seminary, Texas.
Prof. Robert G. Hoerber, Concordia Seminary, St Louis, Missouri.
Prof. Dr Paul Hoffmann, Universität Bamberg.
Prof. Dr Otfried Hofius, Universität Tübingen.
Prof. Carl R. Holladay, Emory University, Atlanta, Georgia.
Prof. F. G. T. Holliday, University of Durham.
Rev. Paul W. L. Holt, Church of St Francis, Frimley, Surrey.
Prof. Dr T. Holtz, Martin-Luther-Universität, Halle-Wittenberg.
Rev. Canon J. L. Houlden, University of London.
Prof. Dr W. Ivan Hoy, University of Miami, Florida.
J. H. Hughes, Wellfield Comprehensive School, Wingate, Durham.
Rev. Prof. Philip E. Hughes, Trinity Episcopal School for Ministry, Ambridge, Pennsylvania.
Prof. Dr Claus-Hunno Hunzinger, Universität Hamburg.
Prof. Dr Arland J. Hultgren, Luther-Northwestern Theological Seminary, St Paul, Minnesota.
Prof. J. C. Hurd, Trinity College, Toronto.
John P. T. Hunt, University of Durham.
Rev. Dr M. E. Isaacs, University of London.
Prof. Dr Dom Augustyn Jankowski OSB, Pontifical Faculty of Theology of Cracow.

Rev. David Jasper, University of Durham.

Prof. Dr Gert Jeremias, Philipps-Universität, Marburg.

Rev. Prof. Richard L. Jeske, Lutheran Theological Seminary, Philadelphia, Pennsylvania.

Prof. Robert Jewett, Garrett Evangelical Theological Seminary, Evanston, Illinois.

Prof. Delobel Joël, Katholieke Universiteit te Leuven.

Rev. P. F. Johnson, The King's School, Canterbury.

Rev. Canon Prof. D. R. Jones, University of Durham.

Dr Elwyn Jones, Rydal School, Clwyd, Wales.

Rev. Ivor A. Jones, Wesley College, Bristol.

Prof. Dr M. de Jonge, University of Leiden.

Prof. Dr Ernst Käsemann, Universität Tübingen.

Dr B. N. Kaye, University of Durham.

Dr L. E. Keck, Yale Divinity School, New Haven, Connecticut.

Prof. Dr Karl Kertelge, Westfälische Wilhelms-Universität, Münster.

Dr René Kieffer, Lund, Sweden.

Rev. H. P. Kingdon, University of Oxford.

Prof. Dr Jack Dean Kingsbury, Union Theological Seminary, Richmond, Virginia.

G. W. Kingsnorth, Shebbear College, North Devon.

Prof. Dr Otto Knoch, Universität Passau.

Prof. Dr Robert A. Kraft, University of Pennsylvania, Philadelphia.

Prof. Dr Jacob Kremer, Universität Wien.

Prof. Edgar M. Krentz, Christ Seminary-Seminex, St Louis, Missouri.

Prof. Dr Georg Kretschmar, Universität München.

Prof. Dr Gerhard Krodel, Lutheran Theological Seminary, Gettysburg, Pennsylvania.

Prof. Th. C. de Kruijff, KTHU, Utrecht.

Prof. Dr Heinz-Wolfgang Kuhn, Universität Heidelberg.

Prof. Dr Werner Georg Kümmel, Universität Marburg.

Prof. Dr J. Lambrecht sj, Katholieke Universiteit te Leuven, Belgium.

Prof. Dr Friedrich Lang, Universität Tübingen.

Rév. Père Prof. Paul-Emile Langevin sj, Université Laval, Québec.

Prof. William J. Larkin Jr, Columbia Graduate School of Bible and Missions.

Dr Edvin Larsson, Free Faculty of Theology, Oslo.

Prof. B. C. Lategan, University of Stellenbosch.

Dr Michael Lattke, Universität Augsburg.

Sophie McK. Laws, University of London.

Rev. Thomas W. Leahy sj, Jesuit School of Theology at Berkeley, and Graduate Theological Union, California.

Rev. Prof. A. R. C. Leaney, University of Nottingham.

Rév. Prof. S. Légasse, Institut Catholique de Toulouse.

Prof. Dr Ragnar Leivestad, University of Oslo.

Prof. Dr F. Lentzen-Deis, Phil.-Theol. Hochschule St Georgen, Frankfurt.

Prof. Xavier Léon-Dufour sj, Faculté de Théologie de la Compagnie de Jésus, Paris.

Prof. Dr Herbert Leroy, Universität Augsburg.

Dr Judith M. Lieu, The Queen's College, Birmingham.

Rev. Prof. Barnabas Lindars ssf, University of Manchester.

Prof. Dr Gösta Lindeskog, Abo Akademi, Turku.

Dr Ann Loades, University of Durham.

Landesbischof Prof. Dr Eduard Lohse, Hannover.

Prof. Richard N. Longenecker, University of Toronto.

Fr. Prof. Lorenzo De Lorenzi, Colloqui Ecumenici Paolini, Rome.

Prof. R. W. Lyon, Asbury Theological Seminary, Wilmore, Kentucky.

Rev. Prof. George W. MacRae, Harvard Divinity School, Cambridge, Massachusetts.

Prof. H. K. McArthur, Hartford Seminary Foundation, Connecticut.

Rev. Dr J. D. McCaughey, University of Melbourne.

Rev. Prof. Edgar V. McKnight, Furman University, Greenville, South Carolina.

Rev. Fr Martin McNamara msc, Milltown Institute of Theology and Philosophy, Dublin.

Rev. Dr Robert Maddox, United Theological College, and Sydney University.

Rev. Dr C. S. Mann, St Mary's Seminary and University, Baltimore, Maryland.

Rev. Dr John Marsh, University of Oxford.

J. P. Martin, Principal, Vancouver School of Theology.

Prof. Ralph P. Martin, Fuller Theological Seminary, Pasadena, California.

Prof. J. Louis Martyn, Union Theological Seminary, New York.

Deaconess Margaret Mascall, Herne Bay Parish Church, Kent.

Rev. John G. Mason, Canberra College of Ministry.

Rev. B. A. Mastin, University College of North Wales, Bangor.

Rev. Prof. Kikuo Matsunaga, Tokyo Union Theological Seminary.

Prof. Dr Christian Maurer, Universität Bern.

Prof. Ulrich Mauser, Pittsburgh Theological Seminary, Pennsylvania.

Rev. Prof. John S. Mbiti, Ecumenical Institute, Bossey, Geneva.

David L. Mealand, University of Edinburgh.

Prof. Dr Helmut Merkel, Universität Erlangen.

Prof. Bruce M. Metzger, Princeton Theological Seminary, New Jersey.

Dr Robert P. Meye, Fuller Theological Seminary, Pasadena, California.

Prof. Ben F. Meyer, McMaster University, Hamilton, Ontario.

Prof. Paul W. Meyer, Princeton Theological Seminary, New Jersey.

Prof. Paul S. Minear, Yale University.

Rev. Dr C. L. Mitton, Handsworth College, Birmingham.

Rev. M. J. Moreton, University of Exeter.

Rev. Dr W. G. Morrice, University of Durham.

Rev. Dr Leon Morris, University of Melbourne.

A. T. Morrison, Rarongo Theological College, Papua New Guinea.

Rev. Prof. C. F. D. Moule, University of Cambridge.

Rev. H. K. Moulton, United Theological College, Bangalore, and New College, London.

Dr Elisabeth J. Munck, Aarhus.

Rev. Prof. J. Murphy-O'Connor OP, École Biblique, Jerusalem.

Rev. Fr R. Murray SJ, University of London.

Prof. Dr Franz Mussner, Universität Regensburg.

Prof. Dr F. Neirynck, Katholieke Universiteit te Leuven.

Rev. Dr Poul Nepper-Christensen, Aarhus University.

Rev. Dr J. A. Newton, West London Mission.

Prof. Dr Kurt Niederwimmer, Universität Wien.

Rev. Prof. D. E. Nineham, University of Bristol.

J. L. North, University of Hull.

Editorial staff of *Novum Testamentum*, Leiden.

Rev. Dr P. T. O'Brien, Moore Theological College, Newtown, New South Wales.

Rev. G. O'Grady, Ushaw College, Durham.

Rev. Prof. A. P. O'Hagan OFM, Yarra Theological Union, Victoria.

Rev. Dr J. C. O'Neill, University of Cambridge.

Dom J. B. Orchard OSB, Ealing Abbey, London.

Rev. Prof. E. F. Osborn, University of Melbourne.

Prof. Dr Peter v.d. Osten-Sacken, Kirchliche Hochschule, Berlin.

Dr Margaret Pamment, University of Bristol.

Rev. Dr T. H. L. Parker, University of Durham.

Rev. Vincent Parkin, Edgehill College, Belfast.

Prof. Dr Frederico Pastor-Ramos, Universidad Pontificia Comillas, Madrid.

Rev. Prof. Joseph Pathrapankal, Dharmaram Pontifical Institute, Bangalore.

Prof. Daniel M. Patte, Vanderbilt University, Nashville, Tennessee.

Right Rev. Geoffrey Paul, Bishop of Bradford.

Prof. Dr Henning Paulsen, Universität Mainz.

Prof. B. A. Pearson, University of California.

Rev. Dr Romano Penna, Rome.

Prof. J. R. C. Perkin, Acadia University, Wolfville, Nova Scotia.

Prof. C. Perrot, Institut Catholique de Paris.

Venerable M. C. Perry, Archdeacon of Durham.

Prof. Inc. Dr Mauro Pesce, Università di Bologna.

Prof. Dr Rudolf Pesch, Albert-Ludwigs-Universität, Freiburg.

Prof. Dr Josef Pfammatter, Theologische Hochschule, Chur.

Prof. Dr I. J. du Plessis, University of South Africa, Pretoria.

Prof. Dr P. Pokorný, Comenius Faculty of Protestant Theology, Prague.

Rev. Prof. T. E. Pollard, Knox College, Dunedin.

Dr Wiard Popkes, Theologisches Seminar, Hamburg.

Prof. James L. Price, Duke University, Durham, North Carolina.

M. F. Proud, University of Durham.

Right Rev. and Right Hon. Lord Ramsey of Canterbury.

Rev. Dr C. Rand, Ushaw College, Durham.

Prof. Dr Bo Reicke, Basel.

Prof. Dr J. Reiling, University of Utrecht.

Prof. Dr K. H. Rengstorf, Westfälische Wilhelms-Universität, Münster.

Very Rev. C. Raymond Renowden, St Asaph, Clwyd.

Prof. Dr Martin Rese, Universität Münster.

Rev. Prof. John Reumann, Lutheran Theological Seminary, Philadelphia, Pennsylvania.

Prof. Richard J. Reynolds, Regent College, Vancouver.

Right Rev. J. R. Richards, St David's University College, Lampeter.

Dr Peter Richardson, University of Toronto.

Prof. Béda Rigaux OFM, Katholieke Universiteit te Leuven.

Prof. Dr J. H. Roberts, University of South Africa, Pretoria.

Dr R. H. Roberts, University of Durham.

Right Rev. D. W. B. Robinson, Parramatta, Sydney.

Right Rev. Dr J. A. T. Robinson, University of Cambridge.

Rev. Dr Cyril S. Rodd, Editor *Expository Times*.

Janice Roe, Cheltenham Ladies' College, Gloucestershire.

Right Rev. W. G. Roe, Bishop of Huntingdon.

Rev. Prof. J. W. Rogerson, University of Sheffield.

Prof. Wayne G. Rollins, Assumption College, Worcester, Massachusetts.

Prof. Dr Eugen Ruckstuhl, Theological Faculty of Lucerne.

Rev. Prof. Y. Herman Sacon, Tokyo Union Theological Seminary.

Principal and staff of St John's College, University of Durham.

Rev. Dr A. P. Salom, Avondale College, Cooranbong, New South Wales.

Rev. Dr E. P. Sanders, McMaster University, Hamilton, Ontario.

Prof. Dr Akira Satake, University of Hiroshima.

Rev. Canon Prof. H. A. E. Sawyerr, University of Sierra Leone.

Prof. M. H. Scharlemann, Concordia Seminary, St Louis, Missouri.

Dr Wolfgang Schenk, Berlin.

Prof. Dr W. Schneemelcher OFM, Universität Bonn.

Rev. Dr Bernardin Schneider OFM, Studium Biblicum Franciscanum, Tokyo.

Prof. Dr Wolfgang Schrage, Universität Bonn.

Prof. David Schroeder, Canadian Mennonite Bible College, Winnipeg, Manitoba.

Prof. Dr Heinz Schürmann, Phil.-Theol. Studium, Frankfurt.

Prof. John H. Schütz, University of North Carolina.

Prof. Dr Benedikt Schwank OSB, Faculty of Theology, Jerusalem.

Prof. Robin Scroggs, Chicago Theological Seminary, Illinois.

Rev. Prof. Giuseppe Segalla, Facoltà Teologica dell' Italia, Milan.

Rev. Prof. O. J. F. Seitz, Gambier, Ohio.

Prof. Dr Jaak Seynaeve, Faculté de Théologie, Limete-Kinshasa.

Prof. Dr J. Smit Sibinga, University of Amsterdam.

Prof. J. B. Skemp, University of Durham.

Rev. Michael J. Skinner, University of Cambridge.

Rev. Canon Stephen S. Smalley, Coventry Cathedral.

Rev. Prof. Charles W. F. Smith, Episcopal Theological School, Cambridge, Massachusetts.

Prof. D. Moody Smith, Duke University, Durham, North Carolina.

Rev. Dr Norman H. Snaith, Wesley College, Headingley, Leeds.

Rév. Père C. Spicq, Université de Fribourg.

Rev. Dr David Stacey, Wesley College, Bristol.

Prof. Dr Gustav Stählin, Johannes-Gutenberg-Universität, Mainz.

Rev. Prof. David Stanley sj, Toronto School of Theology, Ontario.
Prof. Graham N. Stanton, University of London.
Prof. Dr Hartmut Stegemann, Georg-August-Universität, Göttingen.
Rev. Graham Stephenson, London.
Very Rev. Prof. James S. Stewart, University of Edinburgh.
Prof. Dr Georg Strecker, Georg-August-Universität, Göttingen.
Prof. Dr Peter Stuhlmacher, Universität Tubingen.
Rev. G. M. Styler, University of Cambridge.
Alan M. Suggate, University of Durham.
Prof. Dr Alfred Suhl, Westfälische Wilhelms-Universität, Münster.
Rev. J. P. M. Sweet, University of Cambridge.
Rev. Canon Prof. S. W. Sykes, University of Durham.
Rev. Prof. Theophilus M. Taylor, Pittsburgh Theological Seminary, Pennsylvania.
Prof. T. W. Thacker, University of Durham.
Rev. Dr A. C. Thiselton, University of Sheffield.
Dr M. E. Thrall, University College of North Wales, Bangor.
Prof. David L. Tick, Luther-Northwestern Seminary, St Paul, Minnesota.
Dr S. H. Travis, St John's College, Bramcote, Nottingham.
Dr Kurt Treu, Akademie der Wissenschaften der DDR, Berlin.
Rev. Canon Prof. H. E. W. Turner, University of Durham.
Prof. Joseph B. Tyson, Southern Methodist University, Dallas, Texas.
Prof. Dr Baseiaan Van Elderen, Calvin Theological Seminary, Grand Rapids, Michigan.
Rev. Prof. A. Vanhoye sj, Pontifical Biblical Institute, Rome.
Rev. Prof. Ugo Vanni, Gregorian University, and Pontifical Biblical Institute, Rome.
Prof. Dr Antonio Vargas-Machuca, Universidad Pontificia Comillas, Madrid.
Prof. J. L. de Villiers, University of Stellenbosch.
Rev. Dr John J. Vincent, Urban Theology Unit, Sheffield.
Prof. Dr Günter Wagner, Baptist Theological Seminary, Ruschlikon.
Prof. A. F. Walls, University of Aberdeen.
Dr Nikolaus Walter, Katechetisches Oberseminar, Naumburg/Saale.
Dr Charles A. Wanamaker, University of Cape Town.
Rev. Canon Dr R. A. Ward, University of Toronto.
Prof. Roy Bowen Ward, Miami University, Oxford, Ohio.
Rev. Dr A. J. M. Wedderburn, University of St Andrews.
Rev. Dr G. A. Weir, Huron College, London, Ontario.

Rev. J. W. Wenham, Allington, Wiltshire.

Prof. Dr W. A. Whitehouse, University of Kent at Canterbury.

Rev. D. E. H. Whiteley, University of Oxford.

Prof. David J. Wieand, Bethany Theological Seminary, Illinois.

Prof. Dr Wolfgang Wiefel, Martin-Luther-Universität, Halle-Wittenberg.

Prof. Max Wilcox, University College of North Wales, Bangor.

Prof. Amos N. Wilder, Harvard Divinity School, Cambridge, Massachusetts.

Rev. Dr R. Williamson, University of Leeds.

Rev. Prof. Walter Wink, Auburn Theological Seminary, New York.

Rev. Fr M. T. Winstanley SDB, Ushaw College, Durham.

Rev. Ben Witherington, University of Durham.

Dr Christian Wolff, Theologische Ausbildungsstätte, Berlin.

Dr Wilhelm Wuellner, Pacific School of Religion, Berkeley, California.

Rev. Dr John E. Yates, University of Leicester.

Dr Frances M. Young, University of Birmingham.

Dr Norman H. Young, Avondale College, Cooranbong, New South Wales.

Rev. Dr J. A. Ziesler, University of Bristol.

ACKNOWLEDGEMENTS

Biblical quotations from the Revised Standard Version of the Bible, copy-righted 1946, 1952 © 1971, 1973 by the Division of Christian Education of the National Council of the Churches of Christ in the USA, are used by permission.

Biblical quotations from the New English Bible, second edition © 1970, are used by permission of Oxford and Cambridge University Presses.

ABBREVIATIONS

ABR	*Australian Biblical Review*
An.Bib.	Analecta Biblica
AThANT	Abhandlungen zur Theologie des Alten und Neuen Testaments
AV	Authorized Version
BBB	Bonner Biblische Beiträge
BETL	Bibliotheca Ephemeridum Theologicarum Lovaniensium
BEvTH	Beiträge zur Evangelische Theologie
BJRL	*Bulletin of the John Rylands Library*
BNTC	Black's New Testament Commentaries
BT	Babylonian Talmud
BWANT	Beiträge zur Wissenschaft vom Alten (und Neuen) Testament
BZ	*Biblische Zeitschrift*
CBQ	*Catholic Biblical Quarterly*
CD	*Damascus Rule*
CQ	*Church Quarterly*
CSEL	Corpus Scriptorum Ecclesiasticorum Latinorum
DBS	*Dictionnaire de la Bible, Supplément*
Did.	*The Didache*
DJD	*Discoveries in the Judean Desert*
DUJ	*Durham University Journal*
EKK	Evangelisch-Katholischer Kommentar
ET	English translation
ET	*Expository Times*
ETL	Ephemerides Theologicae Lovanienses
EvTh	*Evangelische Theologie*
FRLANT	Forschungen zur Religion und Literatur des Alten und Neuen Testaments
Ges. Aufs.	Fuchs, *Gesammelte Aufsätze*

HNT	Handbuch zum Neuen Testament
HThK	Herders Theologischer Kommentar
HTR	*Harvard Theological Review*
ICC	International Critical Commentary
IEJ	*Israel Exploration Journal*
JB (= BJ)	Jerusalem Bible
JBL	*Journal of Biblical Literature*
JJS	*Journal of Jewish Studies*
JSJ	*Journal for the Study of Judaism*
JTS (ns)	*Journal of Theological Studies* (new series)
JTSA	*Journal of Theology for South Africa*
KEK	Kritisch-exegetischer Kommentar
LQR	*London Quarterly and Holborn Review*
LXX	The Septuagint
M	Mishnah
MNTC	Moffatt New Testament Commentaries
MS, ms	Manuscript, minuscule
NAB	New American Bible
NEB	New English Bible
NtAbh	Neutestamentliche Abhandlungen
NTD	Das Neue Testament Deutsch
NTS	*New Testament Studies*
Nov. Test.	*Novum Testamentum*
OED	*Oxford English Dictionary*
OGIS	Dittenberger, *Orientis Graeci Inscriptiones Selectae*
PG	Migne, *Patrologia Graeca*
PL	Migne, *Patrologia Latina*
PW	Pauly-Wissowa, *Real-Encyclopädie der classischen Altertums-wissenschaften*
RB	*Revue Biblique*
RechScR	*Recherches de Science Religieuse*
RHR	*Revue de l'Histoire des Religions*
Riv. Bib.	*Rivista Biblica*
RSV	Revised Standard Version
RV	Revised Version

SANT	Studien zum Alten und Neuen Testament
SBL	Society of Biblical Literature
SJT	*Scottish Journal of Theology*
SNTS	Studiorum Novi Testamenti Societas (Society for New Testament Studies)
SNTSMS	Society for New Testament Studies Monograph Series
SOTS	Society for Old Testament Studies
ST	*Studia Theologica*
StD	*Studies and Documents*
SThU	*Schweizerische Theologische Umschau*
StNT	Studien zum Neuen Testament
Str.-Bill.	Strack-Billerbeck, *Kommentar zum Neuen Testament aus Talmud und Midrasch*
TDNT	*Theological Dictionary of the New Testament* (ET of *TWNT*)
Th.Forsch.	Theologische Forschung
Th.Lit.	*Theologische Literaturzeitung*
Th.Rev.	*Theologische Revue*
Th.St.	Theologische Studien
Th.W.	*Theologische Wissenschaft*
TOB	Traduction oecuménique de la Bible
TR	Textus receptus
TU	Texte und Untersuchungen zur Geschichte der altchristlichen Literatur
TWNT	Kittel und Friedrich, *Theologisches Wörterbuch zum Neuen Testament*
TZ	*Theologische Zeitschrift*
UBS	United Bible Societies
V.Chr.	Vigiliae Christianae
WMANT	Wissenschaftliche Monographien zum Alten und Neuen Testament
WTJ	*Westminster Theological Journal*
WUNT	Wissenschaftliche Untersuchungen zum Neuen Testament
ZNW	*Zeitschrift für die Neutestamentliche Wissenschaft*
ZST	*Zeitschrift für Systematische Theologie*
ZThK	*Zeitschrift für Theologie und Kirche*

Introduction

K. H. Kuhn

To Charles Kingsley Barrett on his 65th birthday.
To pay homage to a man who may, I fear, in spite of all his achievements, be too austere to enjoy receiving it, is no easy task, but his many friends are determined not to let the occasion of Kingsley Barrett's 65th birthday pass without offering him this *Festschrift* and their best wishes for his retirement.

Kingsley Barrett has spent most of his working life at Durham where he became a university lecturer in 1945. There is no need to trace his career step by step; suffice it to say that, although he has attained international eminence over the years, his first loyalty has always been to the University of Durham, for which we here at Durham are deeply grateful. As a one-time pupil of his, I can testify to the profound influence which he has exerted over generations of students, undergraduates and research students alike. To have had him as a tutor was an experience that none of his pupils would have missed. He did not only impart knowledge but challenged and stimulated all who came into contact with him. Under his guidance we did not only learn facts but we also learned to analyse and to assess evidence, and to distinguish between fact and surmise. It would hardly be an exaggeration to say that he taught a way of life which was freely adopted and adapted by many of his students. That some of them have become teachers of the New Testament in universities and colleges in various parts of the world must be a source of particular satisfaction to him.

One institution at Durham to which he has contributed much is the New Testament seminar for members of staff and research students. This is a gathering of theologians and others interested in New Testament exegesis. When I was granted the privilege of joining it as a research student many years ago, Kingsley Barrett was a prominent member; now he has been its chairman for a very long time. The seminar meets weekly in term time and devotes its energies to reading a book of the New Testament, or part of it, as far as possible with an

1

unprejudiced mind and with an eye for every detail, each contributing his own expert knowledge. Not infrequently a term's 'bag' consists of no more than a few verses, but the exercise is well worth while and owes much to Kingsley Barrett who enjoys and stimulates this meeting of minds.

His international reputation rests, in the first place, on his published work. His many books and articles are devoted to the interpretation of the New Testament. His outstanding knowledge of the relevant languages, Greek, Hebrew and Aramaic, as well as his mastery of the history of the period, gives them their very special value. But his scholarship has become influential in other ways as well. He has lectured in many parts of the world: Europe, the United States, Australia, South Africa; and he has enjoyed these visits, as travelling for him is not a strain but rather a welcome relaxation. His faithful attendance at meetings of *Studiorum Novi Testamenti Societas*, and particularly his term of office as the society's president, will not be forgotten by his colleagues. His services to scholarship are indeed too many to enumerate. Although he is happiest in his study, he has given willingly and most generously of his time to serve on all manner of committees furthering the causes of scholarship. Special mention should be made here of his participation in the work of the British Academy.

Kingsley Barrett's life and work has another component of which I am ill qualified to speak but which, nevertheless, is of great importance: his service as a Methodist minister. He entered the ministry in 1943 and, in spite of his many academic commitments, he has given unstinting service here too. Ever since I have known him, hardly a Sunday goes by without some preaching engagement, often in the city or county of Durham. This frequently involves long and tedious journeys, yet all this has been undertaken readily and gladly. As part of his Christian ministry he also takes on speaking engagements for the British and Foreign Bible Society whose activities he supports. He is moreover often consulted by teachers of Religious Knowledge and by ministers and local preachers and does much to help them make their biblical teaching more effective and alive. It would be fair to say, I think, that his work as a Christian minister and his activities as an academic theologian are welded together into one harmonious whole by his strong and positive character.

But I cannot end this brief and altogether insufficient appreciation of Kingsley Barrett without mentioning the friendship he inspires in both his students and his colleagues. As a friend of his of some thirty years' standing, I can speak here with authority. Kingsley is always available when needed. Advice and help are freely given. No trouble is ever too much for him. And there must be literally hundreds of us who have spent many happy hours in his home at 8 Princes Street, where Margaret presides over the domestic scene while Kingsley enjoys nothing better than talking shop with his friends. And let me add that Margaret's role has been much more than that of a marvellously generous hostess. It is she who has provided and, we hope, will go on providing for very many years the well-ordered and peaceful domestic background so essential to Kingsley's busy life as a minister and scholar.

This *Festschrift* is a token of our gratitude to a teacher, a scholar, and a friend. Our best wishes accompany it. We know that Kingsley's retirement will be an active one. May it also be long, happy and fruitful.

1

Paul and the Law
Reflections on Pitfalls in Interpretation

W. D. Davies

Because of its importance not only in his epistles and in other parts of the New Testament but also in the encounter between Roman Catholicism and Protestantism, the treatment of the Law by Paul has been and is one of the most discussed subjects in Christian theology and particularly in New Testament studies. In the course of this discussion Paul's view has frequently been misunderstood. Before we consider this matter, two preliminaries have to be noted. To begin with, there are few strictly 'legal' discussions in Paul. This is highly significant. Of necessity our treatment of the Law in the Apostle's writings has to be only tangentially legal and has to be centred in his understanding of the nature of the life 'in Christ', by which all aspects of life, including the legal are, for him, to be informed. The concentration of the new life 'in Christ' is of the essence of Paul's approach to the Law, which comes not to be dismissed by him but transposed to a new key. As will appear, Paul related all law to religion.

And then, it is important to note that the term *Torah*, or law, has for Paul a broad range of meanings at least four of which have to be borne especially in mind: first, commandments (*mitzwoth*) which have to be obeyed; second, the accounts of Israel's history and the prophetic and wisdom literature; third, in connection with the figure of Wisdom, the cosmic function of *Torah* in creation and redemption; and fourth, *Torah* as the expression of a total culture, the whole of the revealed will of God in the universe, nature and society. Neglect of the complexity of Paul's view of *Torah* has led interpreters, concentrating on one aspect to the exclusion of others, to oversimplify his response to it. We shall try to indicate certain considerations that should be operative in any adequate discussion of Paul and the Law by pointing out pitfalls in interpretation which have led to distortion.[1]

4

Interpretation of the Law simply as commandment

First, there has been a tendency to treat Law as if it simply meant commandment. Many Protestant theologians especially, but not only they, have often misunderstood *Torah* as commandment (*mitzwoth*) and interpreted the Jewish tradition as one requiring obedience to the commandments as the ground of salvation. This diminution of the scope of *Torah* has had momentous historical consequences. The traditional Protestant interpretation of the Pauline polemic against the Law in Judaism and Jewish Christianity is familiar and need not be repeated here,[2] but it has so coloured the minds of Protestants and even Catholics that it has been difficult for them to give the Law its due place in the corpus of revelation.[3] The doctrine of justification by faith, with its corollary of the inadequacy of the Law, has been taken as the clue to Paulinism. The appeal of that doctrine and, to many, its truth for a broken and sinful humanity is altogether natural and should be fully recognized, but it should not be allowed to govern our interpretation of Paul as a historical figure. The traditional picture of Paul as suffering from pangs of conscience under the Law has recently been severely criticized and dismissed.[4] The dismissal cannot be unqualifiedly accepted, but even if pangs of conscience and moral scrupulosity are universally human and Paul experienced them too it would be wrong to make this the source of his criticism of the Law. Paul refers to himself as blameless under the Law and in his own conscience (Phil. 3.6).

Torah in Judaism, moreover, is always seen in the context of God's gracious action. The Exodus precedes Sinai (Exod. 20.1–2). The duties of the decalogue arise out of a deliverance, a deliverance of the unworthy. The precedence of grace over Law in Israelite religion persisted, despite some neglect, in Judaism. The Law and the recognition of the need for obedience to it are not the means of salvation for Judaism but the consequences or accompaniment of it. True, the commands of the Law are often isolated in Judaism and their covenantal ground in the grace of God muted, but the relation of the demands to the grace of God in freeing Israel from Egypt was not severed.

Thus the opposition of the Law to grace which has marked so much of Protestantism, grounded as it is in individualism, that is, in the emphasis on the sinner standing alone before the awful demands of God, is a distortion of Paul. And it is as well to note that, although a

5

profundity, Paul was not a peculiarity in the early Church. His understanding of Christian experience was widespread. The primitive Church understood its experience to be covenantal in character and parallel to that of the Jewish people. The emergence of the Church was, if not the emergence of a new Israel,[5] at least the entrance of Israel on a new stage of its history; and the structure of early Christianity is in at least some respects modelled upon, or grows out of, the structure of Judaism. This means that the Law is as integral to the gospel of the New Testament as it was for the Old.[6] Thus Paul's background in early Christianity, no less than in Judaism, demands that we cease to interpret his relation to the Law solely in individualistic or moralistic terms and recognize that Pauline Christianity is not primarily an antithesis to Law.

To do so is, however, difficult. Between us and Paul stands the Protestant Reformation. Moreover, Paul's conviction that Jesus was the Messiah led to a radical reassessment of current messianic ideas and a vivid contrast between the new order in Christ and the old order under the Law. His sharp antitheses are familiar. From his earliest epistle on, Paul lashed out unrestrainedly at certain Jews. Two things, however, should be borne in mind in assessing Paul's violent criticism. First, the discussion of Judaism and Jews in Paul is intramural. It is criticism of the faith, law, institutions and worship of Judaism not from without, but from within. Though differentiated in some respects, Christians were not separated from Judaism. Indeed, prior to 70 AD, Christianity probably did not exist as a separate religious movement.[7] Second, the Judaism of which Paul was a part was a remarkably fluid and tolerant phenomenon. The Qumran sectarians bitterly attacked the authorities in Jerusalem and cut themselves off from their fellow-Jews, but did not thereby see themselves as forsaking Judaism. Even the assertion that Jesus was Messiah was not for Paul tantamount to a rejection of Judaism, or the founding of a new religion, but rather expressed the profound conviction that the final expression and intent of Judaism had been born.[8]

Why has recognition of this fact been so difficult and tardy? Apart from the weight of scholarly tradition and conservatism, two historical factors are important. On the one hand, the catastrophic effects of the Jewish War led Jamnian Judaism to close its own ranks against dissidents and elevate *Torah* as *the* way of Jewish life. This, and the reaction among Jews and Christians, contributed most to the emergence of what we call Christianity as a distinct religion.[9] But Paul predated Jamnia, and the post-70 separation must not be read back into his time. On the other hand, after Paul's death his letters were read mainly by those who little understood Judaism and were incapable of recognizing their setting in a family dispute. The intensity, and at times ferocity, of Paul's discussions with his contemporaries were endurable when *intra muros*. But once removed from that setting they took on a radically different look. In time, though the process was slow, what was a disruption among Jews came to be spelt out as the denigration and rejection of Judaism and of the people of Israel as a whole.

Isolation of the Law from Paul's Messianic situation

What has been written has by implication pointed to the second pitfall: that of isolating Paul's concept of *Torah* from the total messianic situation in which he believed himself to be living. It is clear from Acts and the epistles that the Law was the point at which Paul met with violent opposition, and it has been easy to suppose that this was the ultimate ground for opposition to him. It was not his messianic beliefs, for Judaism was hospitably tolerant of messianic claimants, but his acceptance of Gentiles without observance of the Law, which passed the limits of Jewish tolerance. But to state the matter thus unqualifiedly is misleading. The immediate cause of Jewish opposition may have been the Law, but Paul's controversial view of the Law was inextricably bound up with the significance which he ascribed to Jesus as Messiah and with the challenge this issued to all the fundamental symbols of Jewish life. To isolate the criticism of the Law from the total messianic situation, as Paul conceived it, is both to exaggerate and to emasculate it. The criticism of the Law was derivative, a consequence of the ultimate place Paul ascribed to Jesus as Messiah.

The messiahship of Jesus was crucial for Paul. He often uses 'Christ' as a personal name and not as a title, but he did not thereby empty it of 'messianic' connotations.[10] That Jesus was Messiah had momentous consequences, for a messianic movement had to come to terms with the Law. Moreover, Paul's reinterpretation of the Law in relation to Christ took place in a world where the role of *Torah* in the present and the future was a burning issue. Despite the firmly entrenched belief that the Law was perfect, unchangeable and eternal, some expected that in the Messianic Age difficulties in the Law would be explained, some commandments changed and, in later Rabbinic passages, that a new *Torah* would be instituted or the old one abrogated.[11] And in the first century, as before and after, the content and character of the Law was a matter of intense debate as is shown by Qumran and the debates between the Houses of Hillel and Shammai.

Two epistles, in particular, discuss this matter. In Galatians 3—4 Paul organizes the history of his people into three epochs: from Abraham to Moses; from Moses to Christ, in whom the promise to Abraham is fulfilled; and the third epoch, introduced by Christ, of true sonship in liberty (Gal. 4.3f; 5.13), a new creation (Gal. 6.5). This radical rewriting of history is Paul's own and gives an eschatological significance to Jesus from which Paul interprets the Law (cf. 1 Cor. 10.11; 2 Cor. 5.17). In Romans Paul presents a similar, but not identical, analysis of history: from Adam to the Law, a lawless era when transgressions were not imputed (Rom. 4.15; 5.13); from Moses to Christ, when Law reigned and transgressions were imputed (Rom. 4.15); and from Christ onwards, when the writ of the Law no longer ran (Rom. 7.6; 10.4).

Thus the proximate cause of Paul's persecution, his view of the Law, points to an ultimate cause, his Christology, which was at the beginning a messianology. In fact, given his Jewish view of the Law, ranging from commandment to an all-encompassing cultural environment and agent of creation, it was only a messianic event of revelatory and cosmic significance that could have induced Paul to reassess the Law as he did.

Failure to recognize variety and change

The third pitfall results from the attempt to treat Paul's view of the Law systematically, making indiscriminate use of his writings without regard to their variety. This attempt to construct a monolithic view of Paul seriously misinterprets him.

In Galatians, where he confronts Judaizers and behind them the Jews, Paul views the Law with the cold eyes of an antagonist. To be under the Law is to be under a curse (3.10); the Law is inferior, given later than the promise, and delivered by angels (3.10–20); to obey the Law is to submit to the elemental and evil cosmic spirits (4.3, 9).[12] The positive function of the Law, as a custodian (3.19f) is recognized only grudgingly. The coming of Christ frees men from the curse and tutelage of the Law (2.21; 3.13, 19; 5.11), so that at best it was a beggarly, passing phenomenon. Christians live under the Spirit and in freedom (5.13), bound to a law of the Messiah, the law of love (6.2).[13]

At Corinth Paul encountered both Jewish-Christian opponents[14] and enthusiasts. In response to the latter he called for restraint and a behaviour governed by his own example (1 Cor 4.16; 11.1) or that of Christ himself (2 Cor. 8.9). There is here, for Paul, a Christian 'way' or 'law', informed by universal Christian practice (1 Cor. 4.17; 11.16; 14.34). Whereas at Antioch (Gal. 2.11f) Paul ignored the scruples of Peter and others, thus ignoring the claims of the weaker brother, in 1 Cor. he urges consideration for them. He can even say that 'keeping the commandments of God is everything' (1 Cor. 7.19) which, while not a reference to Mosaic commands, does show that Christian liberty does not free men from commandments. And in 2 Cor., where he may have faced different opponents, he comes to understand Christian life as life in a covenant, and covenant includes demand or law (2 Cor. 3). The Christian is also constrained by the love of Christ (2 Cor. 5.14f) which, while not a commandment, is a qualification of unrestricted freedom. To Christians in Galatia Paul would have appeared to be an antinomian, but to those in Corinth a disciplinarian if not an incipient legalist!

In Romans, unlike Galatians, Paul is careful to recognize that the Law is holy, righteous and good (7.12, 16), spiritual (7.14), rooted in God (7.22, 25; 8.2, 7), designed for life (7.10), authoritative (7.19) and counts as one of the privileges of Israel (9.4). While some arguments about the Law echo Galatians, in Romans Paul approaches the Law not as if he were viewing it clinically, from outside, but experientially, from the inside. He does consider that Christ is the end of the Law (10.4), the Law, that is, as a means of salvation, but he also gives reasons for this conclusion. The Law was intended to give life (Lev. 18.5), but was unable to do so (Rom. 3.23). It had, in fact, the opposite result from that intended (4.13; 7.13). Romans 7, which is probably a defence of the Law, reveals the problem. The problem is sin, which makes the intrinsically good Law serve its own intrinsically evil ends. The Law reveals sin (3.20), incites it (7.5) indeed brings sin to life, for apart from the Law sin is dead (7.8–9). What was good in itself becomes a power for evil. How is the Law diverted from its original purpose? Not, as in Galatians, because of connections with the 'elemental spirits', but because of the weakness of 'the flesh'. The power of sin and the weakness of the flesh collude to frustrate the purpose of the good and holy Law.

The treatment of Law in Romans is thus different from that in

Galatians. The one is written in the white heat of controversy and the other, perhaps because Paul's view did not prevail in Galatia and because he desired the support of the Christians in Rome,[15] is more conciliatory. In Romans he provides a more positive estimate of the Law even while he still strikes against it. A more subtle and restrained Paul appears. To ignore this, and to present his view of the Law as monolithic, is to misunderstand him.

Neglect of explicit moral demands in the epistles

We have previously connected Paul with early Christian life in general and with the communal aspect of Christian life and we shall do so again. Here we are more concerned with the more directly personal aspects of life in Christ as it is related to the *Torah*.

First, quite simply, Paul places the demands of the *Torah* in the light of Christ. For him, the way of the Law gives place to the law or way of Christ. *Torah* became concentrated in the person of Jesus Christ and its demands informed by the *agape* and, indeed, the very presence of Christ.[16] But what exactly does this mean? First, that the moral life of the Christian bears constant reference to, or is moulded by, the actual life of Jesus of Nazareth.[17] Second, moral teaching has its point of departure not only in the ministry of Jesus, but also in his resurrection. The resurrection was not only a triumph of life over death but also of forgiveness over sin; it was an expression, if not the expression, of God's grace.[18] Third, the mode of the presence of this risen Lord was life in the Spirit, who was the inspiration of the prophets of old, the mark of the new age, and the basis of a new morality (Gal. 5.22; 1 Cor. 13). Thus for Paul, Christian morality had its point of reference in the life, resurrection and living Spirit of Jesus. Putting it geometrically, this was the vertical relation of Christians with the living Lord.

For Christian morality this has three dimensions. First, that those 'in Christ' appropriate and share in Jesus' death and resurrection, so that their moral life is rooted in what they are, new creations in Christ. The moral imperative rests on the indicative.[19] Second, there is the element of imitation in which the life of Jesus becomes the model for moral living. The importance of this theme in early Christianity has been variously assessed, but for Paul, at least, it is an undeniable one (1 Cor. 11.1; Rom 15.3; 2 Cor. 10.1).[20] Third, the Christian life always has an eschatological dimension, which for Paul is most clearly expressed in his apostolic calling. True, his apostolic consciousness may have been more intense than in most, but all Christians believed they were caught up in the counsel of God. Christian morality is rooted in a 'lively hope'. (1 Pet. 1.1) even as it is informed by the earthly Jesus. It is governed by a memory and an anticipation.

But if there was a vertical dimension of Christian life for Paul there was also a horizontal, or human, societary one. Paul knows nothing of solitary religion or individual morality, but rather sees the Christian firmly based in a community. A communal emphasis is probably at the root of Paul's 'Christ mysticism', which issued not in a 'flight of the alone to the Alone', but in the building up of the Church.[21] Along with rationality (1 Cor. 12.8; 14.1f; Rom. 12.2) and respect for personal integrity (Philem. 15–16), Paul sets forth the building up of the Church as *the* criterion of Christian action (Rom. 14.21; 1 Cor. 12—14).

Paul also emphasizes specific moral teaching, sometimes reminiscent of Jesus' words (e.g. Rom. 12.14/Matt. 5.43; Rom. 12.17/Matt. 5.39f; Rom. 13.7/Matt. 22.15–22, etc.), sometimes quoting them directly (1 Thess. 4.15–16; 1 Cor. 7.25). The central command, however, which is the fulfilment of the Law and the principle of cohesion in the Christian community, is the command to love (Rom. 13.8–10; 1 Cor. 8.1, 13; Col. 3.14). In addition, for specific moral teaching Paul could call upon both Jewish and hellenistic sources, the latter perhaps mediated by the Jewish diaspora. Thus in Paul, as in early Christianity in general, not only are the absolutes of Jesus domesticated, but the domestic virtues of the world are also appropriated. That Paul could borrow freely from non-Christian sources suggests that he saw a continuity between the moral awareness of Christians and the non-Christian world, and this in turn was in all probability based on his view of creation.[22] For Paul the good life is the truly natural life. Morality is rooted in creation.

Conclusion

By looking at the historical meaning of *Torah*, the messianic context and the developing theological framework within which Paul worked, we have sought to call in history to readjust the balance of traditional interpretations of his response to the Law.

The antithesis between law and grace which governs much Christian, especially Protestant, thinking would have been alien to Paul. There is little doubt that for him *Torah* was an expression of divine grace. Despite the violent criticisms of the Law that Paul reiterates in his polemical epistles, always there remained in his gospel a demand. The demand, that of *agape*, could be interpreted as even more austere than that of the multitudinous *mitzwoth*, or command-ments, of the *Torah*. 'In Christ' Paul stood under a new Sinai requiring of him universal *agape* such as that called for in the Sermon on the Mount and elsewhere in the New Testament, the infinite demand of the 'Law of Christ'. But this did not mean that he was indifferent to those actualities and intricacies of existence that called for careful legal discrimination, refinement and casuistry. Daube[23] has shown how in dealing with such human problems as marriage Paul stopped short of following the legal logic of his messianic absolutism and squarely faced the social realities of his day. No less than were the Pharisaic sages who taught him, he too was prepared to make concessions to the complexities of the order of society in which he found himself and to human weakness and sinfulness.[24] He was no fanatic unprepared to bend. Under the constraint of the very Christ whom he had called 'the end of the Law', he was ready to be 'all things to all men'.[25] This required, as we have seen, sensitivity in moral direction. Nor again, convinced as he was of standing in the final messianic period of history and, indeed, of participating in the very inauguration of the 'end of the days', was Paul indifferent to the tradition of his people, moral or otherwise. He was no antinomian; for him the Christian dispensation was the fulfilment and not the annulment of that tradition. Distrust of all law, such as is frequently expressed in our time in the counter-culture and elsewhere, and which Protestantism, especially in its Lutheran form, has often fostered, finds no support in Paul.

Notwithstanding this, Paul presents us with a radical and inescap-able challenge. Paul sits lightly to certain specific commandments, and while he elsewhere retains others they do not play an important, and certainly not an independent, part in his thinking. He brings the legal tradition of his fathers before the judgement seat of the *agape* of Christ and thereby achieves an immense and penetrating simplification of it. Moreover, the cause of this simplification, which is at the same time an intensification, is the personalizing of the concept of *Torah* by identifying it with Christ. Such notions challenge not only the concept of *Torah* in Paul's day but also the concept of law in the more restricted sense as it refers to modern legal systems. The problem of rigidity and ossification when laws are treated as absolutes, the oppressive weight and complexity of inherited precedent in legal traditions, and the tendency of the Law to become depersonalized are all matters which Paul's response to *Torah* shed light on.[26] Of course, to move from *Torah* in the sense in which Paul understood it to law as it is understood in modern western societies requires a leap of the imagination. The direct transference of Pauline categories to modern legal systems is inadmissible, not only because the concepts of law are different but also because Paul lived in the fervour of a messianic situation marked by intense eschatological expectation. Moreover, the primary point of comparison between Christianity and any other legal system, as between Christianity and Judaism, lies not in the absolute demands that characterized the early Christian movement in its first fine careless rapture, but in the later developments within Christendom that culminated in Canon Law. Even with these caveats, however, Paul's insights give us much cause for reflection.

There is one further challenge from Paul. Related to this is an apparently paradoxical situation in which society, at least in the West, finds itself. On the one hand, under the impact of the developments of scientific technology, society is faced with perplexities and opportunities that are, apparently, new, and for which there seems to be no direct guidance from the past. On the other hand, this coexists with the sense, born this time of psychological and sociological sophistication and of the brute facts of history, that there are entrenched historical traditions and age-old developments in law, as in other spheres, which hold a dead staying hand over things. There is a fatalism in law, as part of a wider fatalism, which tends to paralyse the belief in the possibility of change. In such a situation Paul is particularly challenging. The closing words of Michael Grant's biography of Paul are apposite:

> The historian's characteristic view that everything which happens has evolved from existing historical tendencies and trends would have seemed to him to be disproved by what, in fact, had happened: the redemptive death of Jesus Christ. Whether one agrees with him or not – Jews, for example, do not – that Christ's death was this total reversal of everything that had taken place hitherto, at all events Paul's general attitude, insisting that such totally world-changing occurrences *can* take place, seems plausible, defensible and right in our own day; the years which lie immediately ahead of us are likely to confirm the cogency of Paul's viewpoint even more insistently.[27]

Paul assumed that the entrenched and oppressive religious, social, political and legal structures of his day, what he refers to perhaps as τὰ

13

στοιχεῖα τοῦ κόσμου, can be decisively challenged and transformed. Certain continuities he honoured, including continuity in law, but he did not allow these to strangle the emerging new creation which he had embraced in Christ. Perhaps it is this daring belief in the possibility of a new beginning – in Law, as in other things – a beginning for him inseparable from Christ, which is Paul's most challenging legacy to mankind.

These reflections are offered to an old friend of now just over forty years, during which 'the Barretts' have been a deep part of our lives. Despite our occasional differences over Paul – so that C.K.B. is not likely to agree with all these reflections – his enthusiastic interest, encouragement and generous praise have never failed.

NOTES

1 This is an abbreviated version of a paper which appeared in *The Hastings Law Journal* 29 (1978), no. 6, pp. 1459–504, and is used with the permission of the editors.

2 E. P. Sanders, *Paul and Palestinian Judaism* (1976), is a brilliant and massive contribution, the true assessment of which will necessarily be a long time in coming. See also D. Patte, *The Faith of the Apostle to the Gentiles: a Structural Introduction to Paul's Letters*, forthcoming.

3 F. J. Leenhardt, *Two Biblical Faiths: Protestant and Catholic* (1964).

4 K. Stendahl, *Paul among Jews and Gentiles* (1976), is especially associated with this view. See W. D. Davies, 'Paul and the People of Israel', *NTS* 24 (1977), pp. 4–39, especially pp. 24–9.

5 P. Richardson, *Israel and the Apostolic Church* (1969), argues that the designation of the Church as the 'New Israel' did not occur until Justin.

6 One of the most illuminating developments in Old Testament studies has been the rehabilitation of the Law. For an account see W. Zimmerli, *The Law and the Prophets: A Study of the Meaning of the Old Testament* (1965), and R. E. Clements, *Prophecy and Covenant* (1965).

7 See E. Trocmé, 'Le Christianisme primitif, un mythe historique?' in *Études théologiques et religieuses*, Revue Trimestrielle (Montpellier 1974), I. 19.

8 The parallel with the seventeenth-century messiah, Sabbatai Svi, is instructive. See W. D. Davies, 'From Schweitzer to Scholem: Reflections on Sabbatai Svi', *JBL* 95 (1976), pp. 529–58.

9 See W. D. Davies, *The Setting of the Sermon on the Mount* (1964), pp. 256–315.

10 See N. A. Dahl, *The Crucified Messiah and other Essays* (1974), pp. 37–47; A. T. Hanson, *Studies in Paul's Technique and Theology* (1974), p. 13.

11 Davies, *Sermon*, pp. 109–90; J. Jervell, 'Die offenbarte und die verborgene Tora. Zur Vorstellung über die neue Tora im Rabbinismus', *ST* 25 (1971), pp. 90–108; P. Schäfer, 'Die Torah der messianischen Zeit', *ZNW* 65 (1974), pp. 27–42; H. Schurmann, 'Das Gesetz Christi (Gal. 6.2): Jesu Verhalten und Werk als Letzgültige Sittliche Norm nach Paulus Neues Testament und Kirche', *Pastoral Aufsatze*, B und 6 (Leipzig 1974), pp. 95–102.

12 Bo Reicke, 'The Law and the World according to Paul', *JBL* 70 (1951), pp. 259–76.

13 The term 'law' in Gal. 6.2 is not to be radically differentiated from the concept of command, or *Torah*, as if it means simply principle or norm rather than demand. See Davies, *Sermon*, p. 353.

14 P. Vielhauer, 'Paulus und die Kephaspartei in Korinth', *NTS* 21 (1974–5), pp. 341–52.

15 cf. J. Jervell, 'Der Brief nach Jerusalem. Über Veranlassung und Adresse des Römerbriefs', *ST* 25 (1971), pp. 61–73; U. Wilckens, *Rechtfertigung als Freiheit: Paulusstudien* (1974), pp. 110–70. Contrast K. P. Donfried, 'False Presuppositions in the Study of Romans', *CBQ* 36 (1974), pp. 332–55.

16 W. D. Davies, *Paul and Rabbinic Judaism* (1948), pp. 147f.

17 Apart from some such assumption, the preservation of the tradition about the words and works of Jesus in the Gospels is difficult to understand. Even granted that much of that tradition is a creation of the primitive community, its attachment to the figure of Jesus is itself significant. On Paul and Jesus, see now the article of Dale C. Allison, Jr, 'The Pauline Epistles and the Synoptic Gospels. The Pattern of the Parallels', *NTS* 28 (1981–2).

18 To connect the resurrection with morality is not usual, but it is implicit in 1 Cor. 15.7f. Note also that the first appearances were to Cephas and the Twelve who had betrayed Jesus. We must assume that Paul knew the tradition about the betrayals.

19 On the 'Indicative-Imperative' motif in Paul see V. P. Furnish, *Theology and Ethics in Paul* (1968), p. 242. Like Furnish, I, too, find the work of M. Goguel especially original and provocative. See M. Goguel, *The Primitive Church* (1964).

20 Furnish, *Ethics*, pp. 217f, discusses the matter acutely and with a wealth of bibliographical detail, though in my view he separates too sharply the historical Jesus and the Son of God, or *Kurios*, thereby making the myth govern the history rather than the history the ground of the myth. I prefer to think of the history as given in the ministry of Jesus and fashioned and transmitted, rather than created, by the Church.

21 This is one of the important insights of A. Schweitzer, *The Mysticism of Paul the Apostle* (1931), p. 105. But caution is necessary in accepting Schweitzer, see Davies, *Rabbinic*, p. 98 n7.

22 See W. D. Davies, 'The relevance of the Moral Teaching of the Early Church', in *Neotestamentica et Semitica: Studies in Honour of Matthew Black* (1969), ed. E. E. Ellis and M. Wilcox, pp. 30–49.

23   D. Daube, 'Pauline Contributions to a Pluralistic Culture: Re-creation and Beyond, Jesus and Man's Hope', in *Jesus the Hope of the World* (1971), ed. D. G. Millar and D. Y. Hadidian, pp. 223–45.

24   D. Daube, 'Concessions to Sinfulness in Jewish Law', *JJS* 1 (1959), pp. 10f, discusses this motif in Rabbinic Law.

25   On 1 Cor. 9.20 see D. Daube, *The New Testament and Rabbinic Judaism* (1956), pp. 336–41; H. Chadwick, 'All Things to All Men', *NTS* 1 (1954–5), pp. 261–75.

26   For fuller discussion of these points see the article in *Hastings Journal* (n1 above), pp. 1495–502.

27   M. Grant, *Saint Paul* (1976), pp. 197–8 (emphasis in original).

2

Statements on the development of Paul's view of the Law

U. Wilckens

Charles Kingsley Barrett, in his commentaries on Romans, 1 and 2 Corinthians and in various other studies, has made an essential contribution to the new understanding of Pauline theology based on his Christian interpretation of the Old Testament. This interpretation appears to be a conception of remarkable inner completeness as well of extremely lively openness to current problems. While this is true, the question still has to be asked whether there are indications of a certain development in Paul's theological thought. It seems to me that this is so and I want to illustrate it by his remarks on the Law. The essay turned out to be too long to be included in the present volume and it will, therefore, soon be published separately.[1] For the present I will summarize the results in a series of brief statements and thus express my affection and respect for Professor Barrett in the form of a contribution to an urgent problem in Pauline exegesis.

Statement 1

Paul focused on the question of the Law from the very beginning.

1.1 Paul persecuted the 'hellenistic' Christians, who enlisted sympathy for their new faith in the Greek-speaking synagogues in Jerusalem (Acts 6.9), for two closely connected reasons: first, they proclaimed someone crucified to be the Messiah which, since the *Torah* curses everyone who hangs upon a tree (Deut. 21.23), was scandalous (1 Cor. 1.23); second, they stated that, on account of the resurrection of the Messiah who had died for the atonement of sinners, any atonement through the cultus (and thereby the *Torah*), had become ineffective – and this was simply blasphemy (Acts 6.11, 14). His fight against this proclamation was a fight for the *Torah* (Phil. 3.6) and his persecution of the Christians as the supposed eschatological congrega-

17

tion of salvation (*Heilsgemeinde*) was a fight for the Israel of God (cf. Gal. 1.14).

1.2 The visionary confrontation with the resurrected One made him understand the eschatological truth of the proclamation of Christ and therefore the implicit end of the *Torah* (cf. Rom. 10.1–4).

1.3 The end of Israel's uniqueness in salvation history was the consequence of the end of the *Torah* caused by the eschatological salvation effected through the atonement and resurrection of the Messiah Jesus. The 'hellenists' in Antioch consequently included the '*goyim*' in the Church (Acts 11.19–21).

1.4 Barnabas and Paul, as Antiochene delegates to the synod in Jerusalem, obtained acceptance of the Gentile mission without circumcision and observance of the *Torah*.

1.5 Paul opposed the demand from Jerusalem that communion between Jewish and Gentile Christians be abandoned to allow Jewish Christians to fulfil the entire Law (Gal. 2.11f). For Paul, this demand meant that the unity of the Church of Jews and Gentiles would be destroyed and the truth of the gospel abandoned.

1.6 Paul left Antioch because he could get no agreement on this point even with the Antiochene leaders. He therefore started a Gentile mission of his own in Macedonia, Achaia and Asia, where the unlimited participation in salvation of Jews and Gentiles, based on the gospel of Christ alone and thus without any obligation to the *Torah*, could be realized.

Statement 2

Paul's opinion in the epistles to the Corinthians is that the Church of believers in Christ is opposed to the synagogue as the institution of the *Torah*.

2.1 Acts correctly reports that all attempts of Paul to convince the synagogues of the gospel of Christ failed because of their opposition (cf. 1 Thess. 2.16). Christian congregations therefore consisted almost exclusively of Gentiles, who had been members of the synagogue before. Everywhere and repeatedly the new truth of Jesus Christ as the end of the Law was realized, as Paul himself had experienced it at his conversion.

2.2   Since the Pauline congregations lived together as a communion of believers, without regard for the *Torah*, the Law is not an issue in the epistles before Galatians. Likewise, the theme of justification by faith, which is central to Romans and Galatians, is also missing in these earlier epistles.

2.3   It is remarkable that Paul reminds us of the suspension of the difference between circumcised and uncircumcised as an effect of baptism (1 Cor. 7.17f) and yet speaks of the purpose of baptism as τήρησις ἐντολῶν Θεοῦ in the same context. Without any doubt this signifies the preservation of those laws of the *Torah* that have not been annulled by Christ. Barrett notes that 'from the Jewish point of view this is a paradoxical, or rather an absurd, statement', but from the position of the gospel of Christ the sentence is entirely clear, i.e. it is a consequence of Christ's atoning death and resurrection. The statement about justification in 1 Cor. 6.11 is in complete agreement: ἐδικαιώθητε signifies the effect of the name of Christ mentioned in baptism – i.e. the effect of his atoning death and resurrection – and the gift of God's Spirit, namely that the unjust have become just.

2.4   The exact formulations in 1 Cor. 9.19–23 can only be understood correctly if the scope of the following dialectic is perceived: on the one hand Paul, in his behaviour as a missionary, corresponds to the effects of the Christ event, since he abolishes the separation of Jews and Gentiles in the history of salvation as it had been established in the *Torah* and signified by circumcision; on the other hand, his behaviour corresponds to the significance of the Christ event in salvation history in that it makes salvation universal by including Gentiles in the sphere of salvation as described by the *Torah*. He states on the one side that, 'to those under the Law I became as one under the Law, though not being myself under the Law', since those 'in Christ' are no longer dominated by the curse of the *Torah*; and on the other side that, 'to those outside the Law I became as one outside the Law, not being without the Law towards God but under the Law of Christ', since the end of the difference between Jews and Gentiles does not mean that all are 'lawless', i.e. unjust, but rather that all become just. Although the function of the *Torah* as a border between those who live within and outside God's sphere of salvation is removed, the *Torah* itself as God's Law is not removed. Christ is not the antipode of the *Torah* but its Lord.

2.5   1 Cor. 15.56 is isolated in its context, for vv. 21f mention the connection of sin and death but never that of sin and Law. This verse, like vv. 21f, probably derives from earlier disputes with the synagogues and is explicated more fully in the later epistles. It has a sharply polemical edge: in view of the sinner the *Torah* is not seen as a power to life, as it is in Judaism, but as a power to death, because it sanctions the fateful connection between sin and death. This is how Paul elaborates the thought later in Rom. 4.15; 5.20; 7.9; 8.2.

2.6   While in 1 Corinthians the Law is mentioned only in passing, 2 Cor. 3.4–18 provides the first passage with the *Torah* as *thema tractandum*. The context is determined by the opposition of the apostolic proclamation of Christ and the proclamation of the Law in the synagogue. Paul elaborates a twofold opposition between the old and the new covenant using Jer. 31.31: first, between the 'letter and the spirit', that is to say the outward *Torah* engraved on stone at Sinai and the word of the spirit in the gospel which fills the heart and changes it; second, between the deadly effect of the 'letter', insofar as the Law condemns the sinner by committing him to death because of the fatal consequences of sin, and the lifegiving power of the spirit, insofar as the spirit as God's power of resurrection (Rom. 8.11) justifies the sinner so that he belongs to life (Rom. 8.6) and is changed into the glory of the resurrection (2 Cor. 3.18). The whole of this 'midrashic' treatise doubtless derives from the dispute with the synagogue. It is a consideration, with a polemical purpose, of the opposition between gospel and Law in the light of salvation history.

2.7   The location of this treatise in 2 Cor. 2.14—7.4 also serves as an apology for the Pauline apostolate and is probably directed at the same Jewish-Christian opponents Paul fights in 2 Cor. 10—13. In 2 Cor. 3 he turns the polemic originally directed towards the synagogue against these opponents within the Church who fought his Gentile mission, which was independent of the Law, by referring to their Jewish advantages (11.22) as servants of Christ (11.15, 23).

Statement 3

In conflict with the Judaizing opponents in Philippi and Galatia Paul sharply defines the proclamation of Christ in such a manner that justification based on faith alone without works of the Law becomes its central subject.

3.1   In Philippi and Galatia Jewish-Christian opponents tried to give Gentile Christians of the Pauline congregations the rank of proselytes who believe in Christ through circumcision and observance of the Law and should thus be integrated into the Church as the 'rest' of Israel.

3.2   In Phil. 3.2f Paul confronts the demand for circumcision with the argument of his own conversion. He had given up his 'own righteousness', as judged by the *Torah*, because he had perceived Christ the resurrected as the source of righteousness given by God and taken up in faith. Thus his own conversion is presented as a representative example of conversion from Judaism to Christianity (cf. the allusion in 2 Cor. 3.16). The Law is part of Judaism which the Christian leaves because of his faith in Christ. As in 2 Cor. 3, Paul fights Jewish-Christian opponents of his Gentile mission independent of the Law against the hermeneutic background of the dispute between Church and synagogue.

3.3   Paul's Galatian opponents argue that the Scripture demonstrates with the normative example of Abraham, the first of the proselytes, that Gentiles only participate fully in the covenant through circumcision (Gen. 17) as well as faith (Gen. 15). Paul confronts this argument with the observation that Abraham became the father of all believing Gentiles (Gal. 3.6f) simply because of his faith, as recorded in Gen. 15. Paul wards off his opponent's further argument that only Isaac and not Ishmael was Abraham's legitimate son with polemically allegorical exegesis: the people of Israel are children of the servant Hagar 'according to the flesh'; and Christians are the children of the free Sarah 'according to the spirit' and therefore the only legitimate heirs of the promise to Abraham (Gal. 4.21f).

3.4   The central argument of both sides is in Gal. 3.10–14. The opponents quote Lev. 18.5, 'By *doing* the Law a man shall live.' They conclude that faith alone is not enough to obtain salvation but that complete observance of the Law is necessary too, and they warn that the curse of the Law will condemn those who are not within the *Torah* (Deut. 27.26). Paul's response is that according to Lev. 18.5 it is precisely the Jews who fall under the curse of the *Torah* because they have been given the Law but have not done what it prescribes. Thus there is nobody whom God recognizes as just and, since the *Torah* grants life only to those who fulfil it, life comes only to those who are justified by faith (Hab. 2.4). For Christ has relieved those justly condemned by the Law as sinners of this curse of the Law by taking it upon himself in his atoning death. The blessing of Abraham is granted to such Gentiles as are 'in Christ Jesus', for only in the effective sphere of Christ's atoning death, in which we participate in spirit and faith, can there be righteousness (cf. 2.19–21).

3.5   Gal. 3.13 is the core of the doctrine of justification in Galatians: it is a matter of *iustificatio peccatorum*, and this is possible not ἐξ ἔργων νόμου but only ἐκ πίστεως Χριστοῦ, i.e. because of faith that engages in Christ's atoning death on which salvation is based. Correspondingly, in Gal. 2.15–21, Paul refers to the death of Christ (v. 21) as the basis of faith, which is in opposition to the works of the Law. We 'through the Law died to the Law' (v. 19) because it is the curse of the Law upon sinners which Christ has vicariously taken upon himself. We live 'to God' because our sin has been absorbed in the death of Christ. We have (ourselves) become just and as such belong to God and to life.

3.6   Paul answers the expected question, 'Why then the Law?' (3.19), with a rough rejection. *First*, the Law has a secondary and not a primary significance in salvation history. God only *added* it in reaction to sin, namely 'because of transgressions', i.e. to condemn them as such (not to cause them!). *Second*, the time of the Law is limited – until the coming of Christ. *Third*, the Law is not even given directly by God but is mediated by angels (3.19f), which shows its inferiority to the promise God had given directly to Abraham. *Fourth*, therefore, Law and promises cannot even be regarded as directly opposed to each other, for the Law is not able to create life like the promises (3.21). On that account, finally and *fifthly*, the function of the Law is to be compared with that of an 'attendant slave' whose time has come to an end: faith in Christ has taken over the position of the *Torah* (3.23—4, 6).

3.7   In the polemical context of Galatians the contrast between Christ and *Torah*, faith and works of the Law, promise and Law, is the centre of attention to such an extent that the argument amounts to a radical *abrogatio legis*. With his exegesis of the gospel of Christ in criticism of the Law Paul has carried the attempts of 2 Cor. 3 and Phil. 3 to extremes.

3.8   Nevertheless the Law as such is not laid aside. Its positive demands, having their heart in the commandment of love (5.14), are of central importance to Christians. For it is love in which faith is realized and, in particular, where the difference between circumcised and

22

uncircumcised has become insignificant: 'in Christ Jesus' (5.6). The Law, under the reign of Christ in the sphere of the spirit, can and should be fulfilled in bearing one another's burdens (6.2).

3.9 How this positive significance of the Law together with its radically negative role are to be seen in the context of justification and the history of salvation cannot be understood from Galatians.

Statement 4

In the Epistle to the Romans Paul reduces the exegesis of the gospel of Christ against the background of the doctrine of justification, which he has gained from the dispute with Judaizers, to a more fundamental level. His exegesis overcomes its antinomistic and anti-Jewish motives and achieves an ecumenical level.

4.1 In Romans Paul wants to overcome the crisis of confidence caused by the conflict with Judaizers. His aim is to get agreement on the theological position of his Gentile mission in all churches. Only when this is the result of his journey to Jerusalem with the collection (15.25f) can he start the planned mission to the west.

4.2 He therefore expounds the doctrine of justification which was marked in Galatians by 'faith alone apart from works of the Law' (Rom. 3.28). Viewing the Law in a general context, the negative function of the Law is granted a positive significance.

4.3 Rom. 1.18—3.20 elaborates the view that because all men have sinned, Jews as well as Gentiles, any justification based on works of the Law is impossible. In 3.21—4.25 it is argued that there is justification in this situation only because Christ has died for sinners. Thus faith in Christ is the only chance of salvation for all, Jews or Gentiles.

4.4 Abraham, the first one justified by faith, already believed in God as the one who justified the ungodly (4.5) and experienced justification as the forgiveness of sins (4.7f). The temporal sequence of Gen. 15 and 17 is therefore of essential importance: *iustificatio peccatorum* applies to all believers, uncircumcised as well as circumcised (4.11f), and the promise of its obtainment is not given by the Law, which 'causes wrath' (4.13f).

4.5 In 5.13f the thought of Gal. 3.19 is elaborated: sin controls all men from Adam onwards and the Law was only 'added' after sin had

23

entered the world in order to 'increase' it. It had to make effective the condemnation of sinners and thus, first of all, to confirm the *power* of sin over all men, which could in turn only be broken by the *predominance* of grace.

4.6   The pointed question whether the Law is sin (7.7) is indignantly rejected. Indeed it is the Law alone which reveals the fatal effect of sin, namely death, and allows the sinner to perceive sin as a dominant force. By exposing sin as the transgression of a commandment that should have protected human life the Law thus proves to be God's holy, just and good word (7.12) and only sin proves to be the cause of the sinner's disorder (7.13). But as sin is the deed of the sinner, the contrast of sin and Law refers to the inside of the sinner himself, where it takes effect through the fatal contradiction of acceptance and rejection of the Law which forms the existential discord of the irredeemable being of the sinner (7.14–22).

4.7   The total inability of the Law to effect its life-giving purpose (8.3, cf. Gal. 3.21) corresponds to the existential dilemma caused by sin. God resolved the sinner's dilemma by the atoning death of his Son so that, being justified, he can fulfil the demands of the Law; and he overcame the inability of the Law to give life, by granting lifegiving power in the spirit, in order to transform the negative effect of the Law in connection with sin and death into the positive effect of the deliverance of the sinner (8.2).

4.8   From this point of view the assessment of Israel's situation is different from Galatians. Righteousness based on the Law, which Israel pursues, and righteousness based on faith are directly contrasted: the former refers to Lev. 18.5 (cf. Gal. 3.12), the latter to Christ, the 'end of the Law' (10.4). But Israel, in pursuing righteousness based on the Law, misses the aim of the Law itself (9.31) which is given in Christ. What is said in Scripture (Deut. 30) in regard to the Law is only realized in righteousness based on faith (10.6f). Israel, having thus failed to recognize Christ and having rejected faith, will finally be saved by God's righteousness in the same way that God is presently saving the believers in Christ (11.25f), namely by mercy through the *iustificatio impiorum* (11.28–31).

4.9   The train of thought throughout the epistle proves that the Law is on no account removed by the proclamation of faith. It is rather fulfilled (3.31), being realized in love (13.8–10; cf. Gal. 5.14).

Statement 5

In summary the following picture is drawn of the development of Paul's understanding of the Law. Paul experiences a 'revelation' in his conversion (Gal. 1.15). Consequently the *Torah* of the cult was removed because of Christ's atoning death and resurrection. He concluded – as did other hellenistic leaders in Antioch – that his mission had to go beyond Israel's borders and that the Gentiles could be included in the Church as God's eschatological congregation of salvation. The synod of Jerusalem accepted this, but the consequence, full communion of Jews and Gentiles, was denied on the Jewish-Christian side. Paul therefore separated from Antioch and founded his own Gentile mission independent of the Law. At first, independence of the Law was approved to the extent that in Paul's early letters the Law is mentioned only incidentally, with reference to conversion. Only with the start of Jewish-Christian opposition does the Law become a central topic of inner-Christian discussion. In 2 Cor. 3 Paul expounds the contrast to opponents against the background of the opposition to the synagogue. In Phil. 3 he intensifies the argument by pointing to his own conversion as the norm for the Christian break with Jewish legal piety.

In Galatians he develops a doctrine of Christian justification by faith alone in opposition to Jewish justification based on works of the Law. This takes place in an actively polemical situation. Thus he proves the truth of his own proclamation of the gospel by setting it over against that of his opponents. At the same time he intensifies the contrast between the Church and Israel by an eschatological contrast between the legitimate and illegitimate children of Abraham. The Galatian crisis led to a crisis throughout the Church concerning Paul's mission. To overcome this Paul submits a new version of his doctrine of justification in the course of Romans. He revises the tendency in Galatians for the gospel of Christ to become totally antinomistic and anti-Jewish and presents a broader conception which includes the Law as God's Law and which brings together Jews and Gentiles under the judgement of God. Although the elements of this conception – especially the christological foundation of righteousness based on faith and independent of the Law – were important from the beginning, the conception as such only became distinct in the context of the dispute with the Judaizers. In this context the danger was that the interpretation of the gospel could lead to a narrow ecclesiology within the confines of an exclusively Gentile Christian Church in opposition to

Israel. When the crisis in Galatia threatened to become a crisis throughout the Church, Paul responded with a more comprehensive presentation of his gospel in Romans, which is thus the astounding result of an extreme historical provocation.

NOTE

1   In *NTS* 28 (1982).

3

The Curse of the Law

F. F. Bruce

The 'curse of the law', an expression occurring in Gal. 3.13, refers in its context to the curse pronounced by the Old Testament Law on the law-breaker. Taken out of its context, however, it might be thought to sum up Paul's estimate of the Law itself in the argument of Galatians. The Law could indeed be regarded as a curse if Hans Hübner rightly interprets Gal. 3.19 to mean that it was introduced by angelic powers hostile to human beings in order to lure them into sin, just as the Satan was permitted, in the course of his divinely appointed service, to expose Job to the strongest temptation to renounce God.[1]

Briefly, Paul's argument in the paragraph Gal. 3.10–14 is that the Law brings no blessing with it, but a curse. Far from justifying men and women in the sight of God, it condemns them. It tells them what to do, but imparts no power to do it, while it pronounces a curse on those who fail to keep it in its entirety. The gospel, on the other hand, tells how men and women may be justified by faith; it puts them in the way of receiving the blessing which God promised to Abraham and, through him and his offspring, to all the nations. It is by faith in Christ that they are justified; it is through Christ, Abraham's offspring *par excellence*, that Gentiles receive the promised blessing. If the Law imparts no power to keep it, the gospel tells how men and women of faith receive the Spirit of God, who bestows on them, and maintains within them, new life in Christ. As for the curse which the Law pronounces on the law-breaker, this has been neutralized for believers by Christ's enduring it himself, through the very manner of his death.

The First Curse Text

Paul warns his Galatian friends not to rely on Law for justification before God because all those who rely on Law expose themselves to the curse which the Law itself pronounces: 'all who are of works of law (ὅσοι . . . ἐξ ἔργων νόμου εἰσίν) are under a curse' (Gal. 3.10). The

27

phrase ἐξ ἔργων νόμου has occurred earlier in Gal. 2.16: 'No human being is justified ἐξ ἔργων νόμου, but only through faith in Jesus Christ.' From its force there we may infer that Gal. 3.10 means that 'all who rely for justification before God on works of law (legal works) are liable to a curse' instead of the blessing which they hope to receive. It is straining Paul's language to understand it as though ἔργα νόμου meant the legalistic misinterpretation of the Law: every one who transgresses the Law by trying to keep it legalistically is under a curse.[2] Paul does not mean that to try to keep the Law legalistically is to transgress it; he means simply that it is a hopeless business to seek justification by the Law – by doing the things it prescribes. This he supports by quoting Deut. 27.26, the concluding curse of the 'Shechemite dodecalogue'.

The 'Shechemite dodecalogue' comprises twelve curses, which were probably repeated in Israel as part of a covenant-renewal ceremony. The first eleven curses were directed against specific religious or social misdemeanours.[3] When a curse was pronounced on each of these, one after another, the members of the congregation responded with an 'Amen' by which they dissociated themselves from such behaviour; the curse involves exclusion from the covenant-community. The twelfth and final curse is more comprehensive, especially in the LXX wording which amplifies it with a twofold πᾶς. 'Cursed is he who does not confirm the words of this law by doing them', says the Masoretic text; the LXX reading is more emphatic: 'Cursed is *everyone* who does not persevere in *all* the words of this law by doing them.' The quotation in Gal. 3.10 replaces the LXX expression 'all the words of this law' by another, equally deuteronomic, phrase: 'all things that are written in the book of the law'.[4]

To Paul, the 'Law' of Deut. 27.26 was not only the Shechemite dodecalogue, not only, even, the code of Deuteronomy, but the entire corpus of pentateuchal law, with its 248 positive commands and 365 prohibitions (if that was the calculation accepted in the school which he attended). To fail to keep one of these was to incur 'the curse of the law'. Paul's argument may thus be supposed to do inadequate justice to the original context of Deut. 27.26. In the opinion of no less an Old Testament exegete than Martin Noth, however, Paul's argument does not misrepresent the original intention of the passage: while the dodecalogue speaks of blessing for the law-keeper as well as cursing for the law-breaker, the blessing is not to be earned by good and meritorious works, but is something 'freely promised. On the basis of this law there is only one possibility for man of having his own independent activity: that is transgression, defection, followed by curse and judgement. And so, indeed, "all those who rely on the works of the law are under a curse".'[5]

More particularly it may be asked: does liability to the curse, according to Paul, arise for all who rely on legal works for justification (*a*) simply because no one keeps *everything* prescribed in the Law or (*b*) because the mere seeking of justification by the Law is misguided, even if one attains full marks in law-keeping? Probably the latter of these two alternatives represents Paul's thinking. Looking back on the time before his conversion from the perspective of mature Christian experience, Paul could say that, 'as regards righteousness under the law', he was 'blameless' (Phil. 3.6). Yet it was not on this ground that he knew himself justified before God, but because of the righteousness which is granted 'through faith in Christ, the righteousness from God on the ground of faith' (Phil. 3.9).

It might well seem to follow from the language of Deut. 27.26 that everyone who does persevere in all that the Law prescribes is exempt from the curse pronounced on everyone who does not so persevere. This indeed is implied in Lev. 18.5 ('the one who does them will find life thereby'), which Paul quotes in Gal. 3.12. But he quotes Lev. 18.5 only to set it aside in favour of the principle of faith (as contrasted with works) which he finds laid down in Hab. 2.4b, 'It is the one who is righteous *by faith* (not the one who perseveres in doing the whole law) that will find life.'[6]

Paul's confrontation with the risen Christ on the Damascus road after his grounding in Judaism, together with the new appreciation of salvation-history which sprang from that confrontation, compelled him to see the legal path to salvation closed by a barrier (which he would not have refused to identify with the cross) carrying the notice: 'No road this way'.

But, according to the Law itself, the condition of those who failed to keep it in its entirety was not hopeless. The Law held out to them a way of rehabilitation, provided they remained within the covenant-community – the way provided by the regular sin-offerings and especially by the great national sin-offering presented annually on the day of atonement.[7]

If, while Paul was developing the argument of Gal. 3.10–14, someone had interposed – ἀλλ' ἐρεῖ τις – with a reminder of the Law's own provision for the law-breaker, what would Paul have said? Presumably the Jewish sacrificial cultus played no part in the arguments of the men who were disturbing the Galatian churches, and therefore Paul does not take up this subject as the writer to the Hebrews does, but Paul's reply might have been not dissimilar to his, if one may judge by what is said in Rom. 3.21–6. Until the coming of Christ some token 'passing over' (πάρεσις) of sins might have been conceded in the forbearance of God, but now (νυνὶ δέ), with the coming of Christ, the true and perfect ἱλαστήριον had been set forth.

The argument of Rom. 3.21–6 is not identical with that of Gal. 3.10–14, although there is some affinity between the ἀπολύτρωσις 'in Christ Jesus' of Rom. 3.24 and the ἐξαγοράζειν of Gal 3.13. But it is difficult to imagine how Paul would have dealt with an objection to his application of Deut. 27.26 based on the provision of the day of atonement otherwise than along the lines which he was later to lay down in Rom. 3.21–6. If the Law as such was inadequate as a way to salvation, that part of the Law which prescribed sin-offerings was *ipso facto* inadequate.

The Second Curse Text

The liability to the curse which is incurred by all who look to the Law for justification is removed from those who are united by faith to Christ. For Christ took on himself the curse which the Law pronounces on the law-breaker: he 'has redeemed us from the curse of the law by becoming a curse on our behalf' (Gal. 3.13). For this last statement Paul invokes the authority of Deut. 21.23, which he quotes in the form: 'Cursed is everyone who is hanged on a tree' (ἐπὶ ξύλου, which may denote a tree or any wooden erection such as a gibbet). He relates this text to Deut. 27.26 by the exegetical device of *gezerah shawah* ('equal category'), which depends on the presence of a common term in the two texts brought together. In the present instance the device is applicable only to the Greek version of these two texts – in the Masoretic text of Deut. 21.23 the hanged man is not said to be ארור (the word rendered 'cursed' in Deut. 27.26) but קללה (קללת אלהים, 'a curse of God' or 'an affront to God'). (Yet Paul probably reveals his awareness that the Hebrew text of Deut. 21.23 shows a substantive meaning 'curse' rather than a participle meaning 'cursed' when he speaks of Christ as γενόμενος . . . κατάρα.) In LXX קללת אלהים is rendered κεκαταραμένος (κεκατηραμένος) ὑπὸ Θεοῦ, whereas Paul uses ἐπικατάρατος, the same verbal adjective as LXX employs to translate ארור in Deut. 27.26 – the connection between the two texts is thus made closer.[8]

To be born under Law, as Christ was (Gal. 4.4), involved no curse in itself. By his lifelong obedience[9] (cf. Rom. 5.19; 2 Cor. 5.21), Christ remained personally immune from the curse of the Law; yet the manner of his death brought him unavoidably under its curse. The context of Deut. 21.23 shows that the original reference was to the exposure of the corpse of a criminal executed by some other means than hanging (e.g. stoning): it was to be removed and buried out of sight before sundown, because otherwise it was offensive to God and a source of defilement for the land. An early instance of this practice in Old Testament history is Joshua's treatment of the body of the king of Ai (Josh. 8.29; cf. also 10.26f). Its extension to those who had been executed by crucifixion is illustrated in the Johannine passion narrative, where the bodies of Jesus and of the two men who were crucified with him are said to have been taken down before sunset at the instance of the Jewish authorities, who were specially concerned that the sanctity of the ensuing sabbath should not be violated.

An earlier instance of this extension is found in the Qumran commentary on Nahum, where the hanging of men alive 'on a tree' (על העץ) is described as something '[never done] before in Israel'[10] – a reference, probably, to Alexander Jannaeus' crucifixion of defeated rebels. The statement that this practice was unprecedented in Israel implies that hanging (impalement, crucifixion) as such was not a mode of capital punishment sanctioned by legal tradition. But towards the end of the Second Commonwealth it became sufficiently common to be mentioned as a matter of course in the Qumran Temple Scroll. In this document provision is made for 'hanging a man on a tree, that he may die', as well as for hanging a dead body on a tree, and both forms of hanging are related to Deut. 21.23, קללת אלהים being amplified to מקוללי אלהים ואנשים, 'cursed by God and men'.[11]

The penalty of being hanged on a tree until one dies is prescribed in the Temple Scroll for an Israelite who has wronged his people by informing against them and delivering them up to a foreign power, or who has cursed (קלל) his fellow-Israelites – in other words, he has been guilty of breaking the covenant-bond.

To be exposed 'in the sun' was judged in Old Testament times a fitting punishment for Israelites who were guilty of covenant violation, like the 'chiefs of the people' who led the apostasy of Baal-peor (Num. 25.4) or the seven descendants of King Saul who had to expiate his breach of the covenant with Gibeon (2 Sam. 21.6, 8f).[12] Since the comprehensive curse of Deut. 27.26 sums up the penalties for a variety of covenant violations, it could be argued that there is more than a merely verbal link between it and being 'hanged on a tree' (Deut. 21.22f). Paul gives no indication, however, that he had this sort of connection in mind.

Paul omits ὑπὸ Θεοῦ after ἐπικατάρατος in his quotation of Deut. 21.23, perhaps to avoid the suggestion that Christ on the cross was actually cursed by God. It would be difficult to square any such suggestion with Paul's conviction that Christ's endurance of the cross was his supreme act of obedience to God (Rom. 5.19) and that 'in Christ God was reconciling the world to himself' (2 Cor. 5.19). (The statement in 2 Cor. 5.21 that Christ was 'made sin' for us by God will be looked at briefly below; Paul's choice of words in varying contexts depends on varying turns of argument.)

It may well be that the argument of Gal. 3.10–14 was worked out in Paul's mind quite early in his Christian career. As soon as he came to acknowledge the crucified Jesus as the Son of God, the problem why the Son of God should have died under a curse clamoured for a solution. Previously, the very manner of Jesus' death had been sufficient to prove to Paul that he could not be what his followers claimed him to be; now that he manifestly was all that they claimed him to be, and more, his being 'hanged on a tree' could not be left unexplained. The collocation of Deut. 21.23 and Deut. 27.26 pointed the way to an explanation.

This explanation, however, is not repeated in Paul's later letters. There is, perhaps, a certain accidental quality about it, as though the redemption effected by Christ in his death depended on the external form of his death – death by crucifixion. True, there was something about the preaching of Christ crucified, with its inevitable σκάνδαλον, which was peculiarly appropriate to the genius of the gospel – the power and wisdom of God were set in greater relief because the work of redemption was accomplished through a death which, by all secular standards, spoke emphatically of weakness and foolishness. True, the disgrace of the cross stood in impressive contrast to the glory of Christ's exaltation by God. But the saving essence of the death of Christ lay in the spirit in which he accepted it. Once he accepted it with his 'Not my will, but thine, be done', the precise form which it took was of secondary importance. Hence, in his later exposition of the redemptive work of Christ in relation to human need Paul passes over matters of secondary importance and affirms that God 'set him forth as ἱλαστήριον, an agent (or means) of atonement' (Rom. 3.25), that God

32

sent him 'περὶ ἁμαρτίας, as a sin-offering' (Rom. 8.3), that God, in fact, made him 'sin' on our behalf (2 Cor. 5.21).

Possibly, when Paul says that Christ 'became a curse for us', he has more in mind than the formal argument based on *gezerah shawah* – he may be thinking of the inner experience of Christ crucified, his sense of alienation from God as his people's sin-bearer. But this is expressed more adequately in the statement that Christ was 'made sin' for us – 'that is', as Professor Barrett puts it, 'he came to stand in that relation with God which normally is the result of sin, estranged from God and the object of his wrath.'[13]

Blessing instead of Curse

The blessing which the gospel holds out in place of the curse of the Law is the blessing assured to Gentiles in God's promise to Abraham. 'Christ has redeemed us from the curse of the law . . . that the blessing of Abraham might come upon the Gentiles.' The pronoun 'us' in this statement denotes not only Jewish believers, who were directly under Law, but Gentile believers also, whose conscience, accusing or excusing them, bore witness to their inward knowledge of what the Law required (Rom. 2.15).

Whatever may be said of the niph'al or hithpa'el conjugations of the verb *brk* in the Hebrew formulations of the promise to Abraham,[14] the Greek version, which Paul is expounding, has the unambiguous passive: ἐνευλογηθήσονται . . . πάντα τὰ ἔθνη (Gen. 18.18; 22.18). It is uncertain if the occurrence of one of these promises as the immediate sequel to the 'binding of Isaac' (Gen. 22.18) should suggest that Paul had the sacrifice of Isaac in mind as an anticipation of the sacrifice of Christ.[15] What is certain is his conviction that Gentiles as well as Jews share in all the benefits secured by Christ's redemptive work to men and women of faith, and among those benefits he includes the greatest boon possible for the people of God on earth – the gift of the Spirit.

The two ἵνα clauses of Gal. 3.14 – ἵνα εἰς τὰ ἔθνη ἡ εὐλογία τοῦ Ἀβραὰμ γένηται and ἵνα τὴν ἐπαγγελίαν τοῦ πνεύματος λάβωμεν διὰ τῆς πίστεως – are probably co-ordinate: that is to say, the 'blessing of Abraham' which Gentiles receive 'in Christ Jesus' is incomparably greater than the sum of all the blessings which in Deut. 28.1–14 are set over against the curses of the preceding chapter; it is their reception of the Spirit through faith.

The redemptive work of Christ receives explicit mention again in

Gal. 4.4f: 'When the time had fully come, God sent forth his Son . . . to redeem those who were under law' – and once again the main clause is followed by two ἵνα clauses (ἵνα τοὺς ὑπὸ νόμον ἐξαγοράσῃ and ἵνα τὴν υἱοθεσίαν ἀπολάβωμεν). This time the second ἵνα clause is probably dependent on the first ἵνα clause: that is to say, if in Gal. 3.13f the purpose of the redemptive work was that we (Jewish and Gentile believers alike) should receive the Spirit, in Gal. 4.5 it is that we should receive our instatement as sons of God, and this instatement carries the gift of the Spirit with it: 'Because you are sons, God has sent the Spirit of his Son into our hearts, crying "Abba! Father!"' (Gal. 4.6).

For the Son of God to be born under Law involved his delighting to fulfil that Law, but (in Paul's eyes) it also involved his voluntarily taking on himself the curse which others, by their failure to keep it, had incurred and so redeeming them from their bondage under Law. This redemption does not imply the payment of a price to someone entitled to exact it. The verb ἐξαγοράζειν is probably used in Gal. 3.13 and 4.5 because of its appropriateness to emancipation from slavery. Moreover, in Gal. 4.5 it is not simply from the curse of the Law but from existence under Law as such that believers have been redeemed. There is no comparison between the religious life conceived as a species of 'working to rule' and the new life of liberty in the Spirit which is sustained through faith in Christ. By contrast with the blessing of this new life, existence under Law might well be regarded as existence under a curse in a more general sense than that pronounced in Deut. 27.26 and reasserted by Paul in Gal. 3.10.

Justification by faith plays a central part in the argument of Galatians, but justification by faith is inevitably accompanied by the gift of the Spirit: it is the gateway to the new life of liberty enjoyed by sons and daughters of God. The argument that justification by faith cannot be so central to Pauline thought as has often been held, because Paul never uses it as a basis for ethical teaching,[16] loses much of its force when the vital association between justification and the gift of the indwelling Spirit is borne in mind. The letter to the Galatians is pre-eminently a manifesto on behalf of spiritual liberty. Paul, with his own exhilarating experience of liberation from existence under Law, found it difficult to understand how any one, having tasted the liberty of the Spirit, could willingly submit all over again to the yoke of bondage. It is nevertheless a fact of life that some people actually feel more comfortable under a yoke of bondage than in the way of liberty.

As scholar and churchman Professor Barrett has consistently pursued and recommended the way of liberty. This paper is offered as a sincere, though inadequate, token of admiration and gratitude to a colleague who, both in academic study and in its practical application, has shown himself to be unsurpassed as a disciple and interpreter of Paul.

NOTES

1   H. Hübner, *Das Gesetz bei Paulus* (Göttingen 1978), pp. 28ff.

2   cf. the argument of R. Bring, *Commentary on Galatians*, ET (Philadelphia 1961) pp. 120–5.

3   cf. A. Alt, 'The Origins of Israelite Law', ET in *Essays on Old Testament History and Religion* (Oxford 1966), pp. 114f.

4   cf. Deut. 30.10; Josh. 1.8.

5   M. Noth, ' "For all who rely on works of the law are under a curse" ', ET in *The Laws in the Pentateuch and Other Studies* (Edinburgh 1966), p. 131.

6.   cf. Rom. 10.5–10, where he sets Lev. 18.5 aside in favour of the principle of faith which he finds expressed in Deut. 30.12–14, significantly omitting from the latter passage its closing words αὐτὸ ποιεῖν.

7   cf. the description of Jewish religion as 'covenantal nomism' in E. P. Sanders, *Paul and Palestinian Judaism* (London 1977), pp. 75, 157ff, *et passim*.

8   cf. M. Wilcox, ' "Upon the Tree" – Deut. 21.22–3 in the New Testament', *JBL* 96 (1977), pp. 85–99, especially p. 87.

9   K. Barth, *Church Dogmatics* II/2, ET (Edinburgh 1957), p. 245, followed by C. E. B. Cranfield, *The Epistle to the Romans*, ICC, ii (Edinburgh 1979), pp. 521f, holds that 'the man who has done them' in Gal. 3.12 and Rom. 10.5 (quoting Lev. 18.5) is Christ. Cranfield argues that this interpretation is exegetically necessary in Gal. 3.12f for Christ's 'becoming accursed . . . would have no redemptive power, were He not Himself the altogether righteous One' (op. cit., p. 522, n2).

10   4Qp Nah 1.7f.

11   11Q Temple 64.6–13. The Temple Scroll adds על העץ after תלוי in quoting Deut. 21.23, as Paul adds ἐπὶ ξύλου after κρεμάμενος. cf. further Y. Yadin, 'Pesher Nahum (4QpNahum) Reconsidered', *IEJ* 21 (1971), pp. 1–12; J. A. Fitzmyer, 'Crucifixion in Ancient Palestine, Qumran Literature, and the New Testament', *CBQ* 40 (1978), pp. 498–513, especially pp. 498–507, 510–12.

12   The Palestinian Targum inserts על צליבא in Num. 25.4, thus relating the incident to Deut. 21.22f. See A. T. Hanson, *Studies in Paul's Technique and Theology* (London 1974), p. 6.

13   C. K. Barrett, *The Second Epistle to the Corinthians*, BNTC (London 1973), p. 180. M. D. Hooker adduces both 2 Cor. 5.21 and Gal. 3.13f as examples

of the motif of interchange in Christ ('Interchange and Atonement', *BJRL* 60 [1977–8], pp. 462f, 470f).

14 Niph'al (נברכו) in Gen. 18.18; hithpa'el (התברכו) in Gen. 22.18. J. Schreiner, 'Segen für die Völker in der Verheissung an die Väter', *BZ* 6 (1962), p. 7, tries to bring out the force of the Hebrew conjugation by translating '(für) sich Segen erwerben, sich Segen verschaffen' ('acquire blessing for themselves').

15 cf. N. A. Dahl, 'The Atonement – An Adequate Reward for the Akedah?', *Neotestamentica et Semitica, Studies in Honour of M. Black*, ed. E. E. Ellis and M. Wilcox (Edinburgh 1969), p. 23; M. Wilcox, '"Upon the Tree" . . .', *JBL* 96 (1977), p. 97; C. H. Cosgrove, 'The Mosaic Law Preaches Faith: A Study in Galatians 3', *WTJ* 41 (1978–9), pp. 146–71.

16 cf. A. Schweitzer, *The Mysticism of Paul the Apostle*, ET (London 1931), pp. 220–6, 294–7.

4

Paul Preaches Circumcision and Pleases Men

Peder Borgen

Gal. 5.11

In Gal. 5.11 Paul says: 'And I, brethren, if I am still preaching circumcision, why am I despite this fact persecuted? In that case the stumbling-block of the cross is done away with.'[1] The conditional clause has the form of a real case. Thus, Paul's opponents had evidently been saying that he himself was still preaching circumcision. Commentators have had difficulties in defining on what basis the opponents made this claim.

H. Schlier and others refer to Acts 16.3, according to which Paul had circumcised Timothy.[2] Paul performed this observance from piety or out of convenience, without regarding circumcision as necessary for salvation. Paul's opponents misinterpreted such actions, and claimed that he still preached circumcision.

Many scholars find this understanding to be unsatisfactory. F. Mussner states that even if Paul had circumcised Timothy, as said in Acts 16.3, such an isolated act did not give sufficient basis for the accusation that he preached circumcision. 'Paul stellt vielmehr aus zorniger Erregung heraus in dem εἰ-Satz einen schlechthin unwirklichen Fall als wirklich hin, *um auf die Konsequenzen dieses "Falles" aufmerksam machen zu können.*'[3]

Before resorting to such psychological speculations, one should make further attempts to take at face value the grammatical form of a real case. Thus, G. Howard tries to picture the situation presupposed. He suggests that the Judaizers out of ignorance actually thought that Paul practised circumcision. They considered Paul to be their ally, not an enemy.[4] This stress on the ignorance of the Judaizers does not harmonize well, however, with their accusation that Paul still *preaches* circumcision. Thus, they must have based their argumentation on the message presented by Paul in his missionary preaching to the Galatians.

There is good reason for raising anew the question whether the context of Gal. 5.11 can yield more information about Paul's preaching of circumcision. The question may be formulated in this way: Does Paul in the context reiterate ideas from his missionary preaching in Galatia, ideas which the opponents have misunderstood and misused in support for their circumcision campaign?

In Gal. 5.19–21 Paul states explicitly that he repeats points from his previous preaching to the Galatians: 'Now the works of the flesh are manifest, such as fornication, etc, respecting which I tell you beforehand, as I have already previously told you, that they who do such things will not inherit the Kingdom of God.' In his missionary preaching to the pagan Galatians Paul spoke against the works of the flesh. With some variation in wording Paul repeatedly stresses this point in his missionary preaching:

Gal. 5.13	εἰς ἀφορμὴν τῇ σαρκί
5.16	ἐπιθυμίαν σαρκός
5.17	ἡ . . . σὰρξ ἐπιθυμεῖ . . .
	κατὰ τῆς σαρκός
5.24	τὴν σάρκα . . .
	σὺν τοῖς παθήμασιν καὶ ταῖς ἐπιθυμίαις

Against this background the following hypothesis can be formulated: Paul refers so pointedly to this topic from his previous preaching, because his opponents have claimed that in this way he preached circumcision as the removal of the passions and desires. On what basis could they make this claim? The reason was that among the Jews of that time circumcision was understood to portray the removal of passions and desires and the evil inclination.

In the works of Philo of Alexandria this interpretation of circumcision is very common, and he uses terminology similar to that which Paul uses in Gal. 5.13, 16, 17, 19, 24:

De Migratione Abrahami 92: τὸ περιτέμνεσθαι ἡδονῆς καὶ παθῶν πάντων ἐκτομήν . . . ἐμφαίνει (receiving circumcision portrays the excision of pleasure and all passions).

De specialibus legibus I.9 ἡδονῶν ἐκτομῆς (excision of pleasures).

De specialibus legibus I.305 περιτέμνεσθε τὴν σκληροκαρδίαν (Lev. 26.41, cf. Deut. 10.16), τὸ δέ ἐστι, τὰς περιττευούσας φύσεις τοῦ ἡγεμονικοῦ, ἃς αἱ ἄμετροι τῶν παθῶν ἔσπειράν τε καὶ συνηύξησαν ὁρμαί ('Circumcise the hardness of your hearts', that is, the superfluous overgrowths of the mind, which the immoderate appetites of the passions have sown and raised).

Of special interest is *Quaestiones in Genesis* III.52, since here the term 'flesh' – central to Paul – symbolizes the passions: 'The flesh of the foreskin, symbolizing those sensual pleasures and impulses (= ἡδονὰς καὶ ὁρμάς) which afterwards come to the body'.[5]

Although Philo has a dichotomic anthropology, in these passages he does not employ a sharp dualism between body and soul. He applies circumcision at both levels, so that both the body and also the soul/mind/heart must be circumcised.

In a similar way we read in the Qumran writings, in 1Qp Hab 11.13, that the foreskin of the heart is to be circumcised in addition to the circumcision of the body, which seems assumed. A parallel to the thoughts of Paul and Philo also occurs in 1QS 5.5–6, where it says that the foreskin of the evil inclination is to be circumcised.[6] It is of importance that in 1Qp Hab 11.13–14 the evil inclination leads to drunkenness, a vice which Paul includes among the works of the flesh in Gal. 5.21 (μέθαι, κῶμοι).

In *Migr. Abr.* 92 Philo shows that such ethical interpretations of circumcision might lead to different attitudes and practices. Philo criticizes some Jews who, although they have the right understanding of the ethical meaning of circumcision, nevertheless ignore the external observance. Philo himself, however, stressed that the ethical ideas were of necessity tied to the external observance of bodily circumcision. Although Philo, according to *Quaestiones in Exodum* II.2, gave heathens the status of proselytes on the basis of ethical circumcision of the pagan pleasures, he meant that the observance of bodily circumcision was to follow.[7] In a similar way Paul's opponents have linked Paul's preaching against (pagan) fleshly desires closely to bodily circumcision: ethical circumcision was to be followed by obedience to the commandment of bodily circumcision.

This idea that the observance of circumcision should follow and complete the ethical circumcision is supported by Gal. 3.3, where Paul writes: 'Having begun with the Spirit, will you now complete with the flesh?' A. Oepke suggests that Paul's opponents in Galatia have argued that the Galatians needed a supplement, needed a completion by obeying the Law of Moses.[8] Circumcision played a basic role in this complete submission to the Law. In this way Paul's opponents – who appeared as his followers – said that he preached circumcision, Gal. 5.11.

In Gal. 5.11 there is another point which Paul comments upon, namely the stumbling-block of the cross. In 5.11 Paul formulates an 'either-or' between circumcision and the stumbling-block of the cross.[9] If in his preaching against the pagan vices of desire and the passions he has preached bodily circumcision, then the stumbling-block of the cross ceases to exist.

The idea of the cross is elaborated upon in 5.24. Against the background of 5.11, how is this elaboration to be understood? In 5.24 Paul writes: 'And they who belong to Christ (Jesus) have crucified the flesh together with the passions and desires.' Since Paul in 5.11 formulated an 'either-or' between circumcision and the cross, it is probable that Paul in 5.24 has made the believer's crucifixion with Christ replace the function of bodily circumcision: crucifixion with Christ and not bodily circumcision has removed the passions and desires.

Philo gives support to this understanding, since to him, as we have seen, circumcision has the role of removing the passions and desires, a role which Paul in Gal. 5.24 attributes to the crucifixion with Christ. As an example, *Migr.Abr.* 92 might be quoted again: '... receiving circumcision portrays the excision of pleasure and all passions ...' The role of circumcision, removing pleasures and passions, has thus by Paul been transferred to the believer's crucifixion with Christ, to the exclusion of the observance of bodily circumcision itself.[10]

In a similar way the role of circumcision in Col. 2.13 is transferred to the believer's resurrection with Christ, and reinterpreted on that basis: 'For though you were dead in your trespasses, and in the uncircumcision of your flesh, he made you live with Christ.'[11] Moreover, in Col. 2.11 we read about the circumcision not made by hands, the circumcision of Christ, ἐν τῇ περιτομῇ τοῦ Χριστοῦ. The meaning is the circumcision which belongs to Christ, and is brought about by union with him.[12]

At this point there is a basic difference between the anti-circumcision-Jews criticized by Philo in *De Migratione* 86–93, and Paul. Those Jews accepted and practised the ethical meaning of circumcision, but ignored the observance of bodily circumcision itself. Paul, on the other hand, transferred the role of circumcision to another event, namely the believer's crucifixion (and resurrection) together with Christ. Paul also rejected the observance of bodily circumcision, but gave the ethical life a new and eschatological foundation in the death and resurrection of Jesus Christ.

In this way we have reached the following conclusion: When Paul preached that the heathen Galatians should depart from the desires of the flesh and enter the society of those who serve and love each other, then his opponents claimed that this was the ethical meaning of circumcision. Paul still preached circumcision, and their task was to persuade the Galatians to make bodily circumcision follow upon their ethical circumcision. By obedience to the commandment of circumcision they would make evident that they lived under the Law of Moses. Paul objected to this misunderstanding and misuse of his missionary preaching to the Galatians. For him their transition from the (pagan) desires of the flesh to a communal life in love was in an exclusive way tied to the believer's crucifixion with Christ, not to bodily circumcision and the jurisdiction of the Law of Moses.[13]

Gal. 1.10b and 6.12–13

The Judaizers, who worked among the Galatians, claimed that Paul preached circumcision, as they did themselves. This claim implied that they meant that Paul, like themselves, wanted the Christian congregations to conform with the Jewish community.

In Gal. 1.10 Paul seems to deal with this matter: εἰ ἔτι ἀνθρώποις ἤρεσκον, Χριστοῦ δοῦλος οὐκ ἂν ἤμην, 'If I still tried to please men, I would not be the slave of Christ.'

H. Schlier, F. Mussner and others rightly understand the sentence to be 'biographical': ἔτι, 'still', is then understood to refer to the time after Paul's call, 1.13ff.[14] When Schlier and Mussner define what Paul refers to when he talks about pleasing men, their interpretations become more problematic. They maintain that Paul's opponents criticized him for pleasing men when he proclaimed a gospel free from circumcision and the other requirements of the Law.[15] This understanding of the opponents' criticism cannot be correct, however, since according to Gal. 5.11 they maintained that Paul still preached circumcision.

It must be remembered that Paul and the Judaizers formulate the same point in different ways. Hence, what Paul in a derogatory sense would call pleasing men, they would evaluate in a positive way: Paul wished to be accepted by the Jewish community after he had heard the call to be an apostle.

When Gal. 5.11 and 1.10 are seen together, they give clues to the way in which the Judaizers claimed that Paul represented their own cause. They claimed that Paul continued (cf. ἔτι) to preach and practise circumcision after he received his call. In this respect there was continuity between his teaching before and after he became an apostle. As has been shown in our analysis of Gal. 5.11 the conformists had reason for their claim: Paul continued to draw on traditions about circumcision and related Jewish tradition. Accordingly, they drew the conclusion that he wanted to be accepted by the Jewish community and please men by still advocating circumcision.

Paul's characterization of his opponents in Gal. 6.12–13 supports this interpretation. So does Philo's treatment of an analogous situation in *Migr. Abraham*, 86–93. In Gal. 6.12–13 Paul states the purpose of the Judaizers in the two ἵνα clauses: v.12: ἵνα τῷ σταυρῷ τοῦ Χριστοῦ['Ἰησοῦ] μὴ διώκωνται, and v.13: ἵνα ἐν τῇ ὑμετέρᾳ σαρκὶ καυχήσωνται. According to Paul the Judaizers wanted to avoid persecution, and to boast over the circumcision of the Galatians.

The point about persecution has been estimated differently in recent research. Some scholars, who mention it, have difficulties in making it part of their hypotheses. They believe that Paul's opponents were Jewish Christian gnostics. If so, why should they seek to avoid persecution, presumably from the Jews?[16]

On the other hand, scholars such as R. Jewett and A. Suhl place much emphasis on the point about persecution, Gal. 6.12. They maintain that Paul's opponents were Judaizers from Judea who sought to escape from persecution by persuading the Galatians to be circumcised. This threat of persecution was, in their view, due to pressures from zealot circles in Judea.[17] Jewett and Suhl are right when they take seriously Paul's own stress on this aspect of circumcision. Their theory about pressure from the Zealots in Judea must, however, be discussed as only one possible background, since Philo, for one, testifies in *Migr.* 86–93 to the fact that in the Jewish communities in the Diaspora also there was a general threat of persecution against non-conformists who ignored or rejected the external observances.

In order to understand Gal. 6.12–13 one has to realize that Paul here states his own polemical view. The Judaizers themselves would have formulated the same points in a positive way. Schmithals has ignored this distinction, and he maintains therefore that Paul's opponents worked for tactical reasons to avoid persecution and gain praise. Schmithals then draws the conclusion that the opponents cannot have been Judaizers, because these fought for circumcision out of conviction, not from expediency.[18]

Philo, in *Migr.* 86–93, shows that the aim of avoiding persecution and gaining acceptance/fame can be given positive evaluation as part of scriptural Jewish convictions. It is a gift from God when people receive 'a great name' and fame because they conform to the Law of Moses and thereby accept and keep the customs, fixed by divinely inspired men in the past. Those who ignore the observances of the feasts and circumcision are taught by the sacred word to have thought for good repute. In this way they can avoid being subject to censure and hostile plotting against them from the Jewish community.

The Judaizers whom Paul criticizes have reasoned along similar lines in their own self-understanding. There is, however, one detail in Gal. 6.13 which seems to speak against this view. Here Paul accuses the 'circumcision people' of not keeping the Law themselves. Many commentators understand this to mean that the 'circumcision people' were selective in their keeping of the Law of Moses, and therefore did not represent a proper Jewish attitude, nor had a regular Jewish community as background.[19]

A closer analysis of Gal. 6.13 suggests that the explanation of Paul's accusation is that he and the Judaizers give different appraisal of the fame they seek. With this question in mind, we see how the statement in Gal. 6.13 places circumcision in sharp focus. In the first half, introduced by οὐδὲ γάρ, the term οἱ περιτεμνόμενοι[20] occurs, and in the second half, introduced by ἀλλά, we find περιτέμνεσθαι. There is then reason for interpreting the verse as an antithetic parallelism: the accusation that members of the circumcision party do not themselves keep the Law means that they have illegitimate reason for wanting the Galatians to be circumcised: they do it for the sake of their own fame.[21] As such Gal. 6.13 is then a word about wrong intentions in connection with the conversion of proselytes. This question receives much attention in rabbinic sources, although there it is the wrong intentions of the prospective proselytes that are discussed, not, as here, the wrong intentions of those who seek to win proselytes.[22]

In Gal. 6.14 Paul moves into a more basic evaluation of this boast. Fundamentally speaking it is not a question of right or wrong intentions behind the circumcision of proselytes. The alternatives are rather whether one puts one's trust in flesh, in this particular case in circumcision, or in the cross of Christ. Paul puts his trust in the cross of Christ (cf. 5.11, 24) to the exclusion of putting his trust in the flesh (namely in circumcision) and thereby in the works of the Law.[23]

It has been rightly pointed out that in Gal. 6.12 Paul does not mention any danger of persecution for the Galatian Christians. This threat existed only for the group advocating circumcision.[24] The explanation is probably that the circumcision party (the conformists) came from a Jewish community, while the Galatian congregations were not Jewish communities.[25] The Judaizers went to the Galatian congregations to take care (in their own view) of proselytes already won by Paul. Thus, Paul does not picture them as missionaries, but as persons who in good Jewish manner sought to care for the proselytes.[26]

Conclusion: when Gal. 5.11 and 1.10 are seen together, the following picture of the Galatian situation emerges: the Judaizers claimed that Paul continued to preach (and practise) circumcision after he received his call to be an apostle. Thus, in their opinion, Paul wanted to be accepted by the Jewish community and to please men by continuing to advocate circumcision. In his letter Paul objects to this misunderstanding and misuse of his missionary preaching to the Galatians. His preaching did not imply that bodily circumcision ought to follow, and thus his service to Christ meant conflict with the Jewish communities: 'If I still tried to please men, I would not be the slave of Christ' (Gal. 1.10).

NOTES

1   See E. de Witt Burton, *A Critical and Exegetical Commentary on the Epistle to the Galatians*, ICC 1921, p. 287.

2   H. Schlier, *Der Brief an die Galater* ([13]Meyer, Göttingen, 1971), pp. 238–9; R. Bring, *Pauli brev til Galaterna* ([2]Stockholm 1969), pp. 259f; E. Haenchen, *Die Apostelgeschichte* ([14]Meyer, Göttingen, 1968), p. 421.

3   F. Mussner, *Der Galaterbrief* (Herder, Freiburg, 1974), pp. 358–9. J. Becker, *Der Brief an die Galater*, Das Neue Testament Deutsch, 8 (Göttingen 1976), pp. 63–4, thinks that Gal. 5.11 does not refer to accusations made by the Judaizers: 'Der Ausdruck "die Beschneidung predigen" ist kein Vorwurf an Paulus, sondern von Paulus selbst polemisch in Antithese zur Wendung "Christus verkündigen" . . . gebildet. Sie soll den Inhalt der gegnerischen Verkündigung in Kontrast zu seiner eigenen kennzeichnen.' Becker does not take seriously, however, the fact that Paul in Gal. 5.11 has given the conditional clause the form of a real case.

4   G. Howard, *Paul: Crisis in Galatia*, SNTSMS 35 (Cambridge 1979), pp. 8–10, 39, 44, 91.

5   R. Marcus, *Philo, Suppl.* I (Loeb Classical Library), p. 253 and n1.

6   See E. Lohse, *Die Texte von Qumran* (Darmstadt 1971), ad loc. cf. R.

Meyer, 'περιτέμνω,' *TWNT*, vi, 78–9. J. J. Günther, *St. Paul's opponents and their background, Nov. Test.* Suppl. 35 (Leiden 1973), pp. 87–8; cf. H. A. Wolfson, *Philo*, II (Cambridge, Mass., 1948), pp. 225–37, who connects the concepts of desire and evil inclination.

7   See P. Borgen, 'Observations on the theme "Paul and Philo"', in S. Pedersen, ed., *Die Paulinische Literatur und Theologie* (Århus 1980), p. 88.

8   A. Oepke/J. Rohde, *an die Galater*, p. 101; so also H. Schlier, *an die Galater*, pp. 123f.

9   H. Schlier, *an die Galater*, pp. 239f: 'περιτομή und σταυρός stehen sich für ihn als einander ausschliessende Mittel und Zeichen des Heiles entgegen . . .'

10 In Gal. 6.13–14 there is another example where Paul makes the cross of Christ replace circumcision: the circumcision people place their boast in the flesh of circumcision, while Paul, accordingly, boasts in the cross of Christ.

11 cf. E. Lohmeyer, *Die Briefe an die Philipper, an die Kolosser und an Philemon* (⁶Meyer, Göttingen, 1964), pp. 113–14: 'Nicht jedes menschliche, sondern alles heidnische Leben ist "tot". So wäre also das Dasein in der "Beschneidung" vor Gott "lebendig" und gerecht?' E. Lohse, *Die Briefe an die Kolosser und an Philemon* (²Meyer, Göttingen, 1977), p. 161: 'Die ἀκροβυστία an die Heidenchristen erinnert werden, ist durch die περιτομή ἀχειροποίητος (2.11) beseitigt worden. In der Taufe ist die Wende vom Tod zum Leben vollzogen worden; Gott hat euch lebendig gemacht mit ihm (Vgl. 2.12).' cf. that according to Phil. 3.2ff the believers are the circumcision (ἡμεῖς γάρ ἐσμεν ἡ περιτομή) who serve by the Spirit of God, who place their boast in Christ Jesus, and put no trust in flesh, as do those who mutilate themselves by bodily circumcision. Here also circumcision is transferred to the union with Christ and life in the Spirit.

12 See E. F. Scott, *The Epistle of Paul to the Colossians, to Philemon and to the Ephesians*, Moffatt NT Com., (⁹London 1958) pp. 74ff.

13 See P. Borgen, *Die Paulinische Literatur und Theologie*, pp. 92–101 for an analysis of Gal. 5.12—6.10.

14 Contra the theological interpretation of ἔτι in A. Oepke/J. Rohde, *an die Galater*, p. 54. The conditional clause has the form of a condition contrary to fact. Thus, Paul's own understanding and evaluation is expressed in the formulation, and not the understanding of the Judaizers. They regarded it as a fact that Paul wanted to please men.

15 H. Schlier, *an die Galater*, p. 42: 'Und Ihr Vorwurf mag darauf gezielt haben, dass er die Freiheit vom Gezetz bzw. der Beschneidung und des Kalenders verkündigte.' F. Mussner, *Der Galaterbrief*, p. 63: 'Es geht Paulus bei seiner ganzen Verkündigung eines gesetzfreien Evangeliums nur um billigen Erfolg, und deshalb auch seine falsche Rücksichtnahme auf die Menschen.'

16 W. Marxsen, *Einleitung in das Neue Testament* (Gütersloh 1964), pp. 52ff; W. Schmithals, *Paulus und die Gnostiker*, Th. Forsch., 35 (Hamburg 1965), p. 28. The point on persecution is ignored to an even larger extent in W.

Schmithals, *Paulus und Jakobus* (Göttingen 1963), p. 90; K. Wegenast, *Das Verständnis der Tradition bei Paulus und in den Deutero-Paulinen* (Neukirchen 1962), pp. 34–49; D. Georgi, *Die Geschichte der Kollekte des Paulus für Jerusalem* (Hamburg/Bergstadt 1965), pp. 35–8; D. Lührmann, *Das Offenbarungsverständnis bei Paulus und in den paulinischen Gemeinden* (Neukirchen 1965), pp. 67–73; E. Güttgemanns, *Der leidende Apostel und sein Herr* (Göttingen 1966), pp. 178–85; E. E. Ellis, *Prophecy and Hermeneutic*, WUNT 18 (Tübingen 1977), pp. 110, 230.

17   R. Jewett, 'The agitators and the Galatian congregation', *NTS*, 17 (1970/1), pp. 198–212; id., *Paul's anthropological terms* (Leiden 1971), pp. 19f, 95ff; A. Suhl, *Paulus und seine Briefe*, StNT 11 (Gütersloh 1975), pp. 15–25.

18   W. Schmithals, *Paulus und die Gnostiker*, p. 28.

19   H. Schlier, *an die Galater*, p. 281; J. Eckert, *Die urchristliche Verkündigung im Streit zwischen Paulus und seinen Gegnern nach dem Galaterbrief* (Regensburg 1971), pp. 34f.

20   For the meaning of οἱ περιτεμνόμενοι and discussion of variant reading, see H. Schlier, *an die Galater*, p. 281; A. Oepke/J. Rohde, *an die Galater*, pp. 201–2; F. Mussner, *Der Galaterbrief*, pp. 412–13.

21   cf. the similar interpretation in A. Oepke/J. Rohde, *an die Galater*, p. 202.

22   See B. J. Bamberger, *Proselytism in the Talmudic Period* (1st edn 1939, repr. New York 1968), pp. 32f. See also Matt. 23.15, where the Pharisees are criticized for their wrong aims in their work for winning proselytes.

23   On the interpretation of boast as trust, see R. Bultmann, καυχάομαι, *TWNT*, iii, 649, n37.

24   See A. Suhl, *Paulus und seine Briefe*, pp. 15f; R. Jewett, *NTS*, 17 (1970–1), pp. 203–6.

25   Against R. Jewett, *NTS*, 17 (1970–1), p. 209. This observation well fits the theory that Paul's letter was addressed to the North Galatian congregations.

26   See B. J. Bamberger, *Proselytism*, p. 24 etc; R. Jewett, *NTS*, 17 (1970–1), p. 200, has overlooked this point when he writes: 'Why would Jewish Christians suddenly lose their traditional disinterest in the Gentile mission and embark on a circumcision campaign in Galatia?'

5

Paul and 'Covenantal Nomism'

Morna D. Hooker

In the introduction to his monumental work on *Paul and Palestinian Judaism*, E. P. Sanders discusses the problems of comparing two religions, and warns against the dangers of picking out similarities in particular elements within them. It is safer, he argues, to compare entire religions, by analysing two 'patterns of religion' and comparing the ways in which these two religions are believed by their adherents to function.[1]

Beginning with Palestinian Judaism, Sanders argues persuasively against the very negative view of Judaism which has dominated much Christian biblical scholarship. His conclusion is that Judaism is not a 'legalistic' religion, since salvation is seen as a matter of God's grace, not of works: the 'pattern of religion' which emerges from the great majority of Jewish writing of the period 200 BC–AD 200 is that of 'covenantal nomism'. Whether Sanders is correct in his definition as to what constitutes a 'legalistic religion', and whether his assessment is therefore true, are questions which we must leave on one side. Possibly his attempt to redress the balance in assessing Judaism goes too far. However, the balance certainly needed to be redressed, and we may be grateful to Sanders for his careful analysis of the material.

We must leave it to experts in Judaism to judge the accuracy or otherwise of Sanders' picture of Judaism. What is of interest to Pauline scholars is the close similarity between the 'pattern of religion' which emerges from his study of Palestinian Judaism and what is commonly believed to be the religion of Paul. No doubt many will have thought that they recognized Paul in the pages of the first part of Sanders' book, and will have concluded, as they turned to Part 2: 'So Paul is thoroughly Jewish after all.' Yet it is at this point that Sanders springs his surprise, and argues that the pattern of Paul's religion, also, is quite different from what we had imagined: we end with Paul and Palestinian Judaism as far apart as they have ever been.

In a short article it is obviously impossible to consider the many

47

questions raised by Sanders' book. With much that he says we would wish to agree. Here we can discuss only this central question as to whether or not Paul's 'pattern of religion' is, as Sanders claims, essentially different from the 'covenantal nomism' of Palestinian Judaism. In contrast to this pattern, Sanders sets out the pattern of 'participation theology': it is by dying with Christ that one obtains new life, and by being a member of the body of Christ that one belongs to the redeemed community.

Sanders' insistence on the central role of 'participation theology' is more than welcome: many will endorse his conviction that this is the heart of Paul's understanding of salvation. But is he right when he sets this in opposition to what he terms 'covenantal nomism'? Are the two approaches necessarily mutually exclusive? May they not perhaps to some extent overlap? By comparing what he terms 'patterns of religion' Sanders hopes to avoid the danger of distortion which comes through drawing parallels between ideas which in fact play very different roles in the two religious systems. But has he himself avoided this danger? In contrasting Jewish 'covenantal nomism' and Pauline 'participation theology', is he in fact comparing like with like?

Before we attempt to answer this question, however, we need to consider whether the idea of 'covenantal nomism' is, after all, in any sense appropriate for an understanding of Paul's view of religion. Now insofar as Paul is protesting against a religious system based on fulfilment of the Law, and arguing that man is justified in Christ *apart* from the Law, and that those who are so justified are not required to keep the Law – and indeed, that Gentiles must not attempt to keep it – he clearly *cannot* be maintaining covenantal *nomism*. In Gal. 3 he describes the Law as something which came 430 years after the agreement with Abraham, and which therefore cannot annul it. Certainly, for Paul, the Law cannot be the proper response of man to God's gracious act in Christ.

On the other hand, just as Palestinian Judaism understood obedience to the Law to be the proper response of Israel to the covenant on Sinai, so Paul assumes that there is an appropriate response for Christians who have experienced God's saving activity in Christ. Those who now partake in the blessings brought by Christ are expected to respond in certain ways. The demands are spelt out in a series of imperatives. They are not *the Law*, but they are *the law of Christ* (Gal. 6.2), and they can even be described as a fulfilling of the Law (Rom. 13.8–10). When Paul speaks about 'the obedience of faith' in

Rom. 1.5, he is clearly thinking about man's *response* to God's grace. The demands upon God's people are no less because they are now understood in terms of living in the Spirit instead of living under the Law. In many ways, the pattern which Sanders insists is the basis of Palestinian Judaism fits exactly the Pauline pattern of Christian experience: God's saving grace evokes man's answering obedience. If one were to ask Paul, 'How is one saved?', his answer would no doubt be framed in terms of what Sanders terms 'participation theology'. It is in Christ that one is justified, and it is by baptism into Christ that one responds to God's call; it is those who are in Christ who belong to the community of God's people, and who therefore behave in accordance with his Spirit; it is those who belong to Christ who will be saved by him from wrath on the day of judgement. Yet clearly this participation language is in no way incompatible with an understanding of Christian experience which can be set out in terms of divine initiative→human response→obedience or adherence to the divine will→final judgement.[2] Sanders argues in the first part of his book that the Jewish emphasis on judgement according to works does not exclude the belief in salvation by grace; it is equally true – as Sanders himself recognizes – that Paul's insistence on salvation by grace does not exclude belief in a final judgement according to works.

In Judaism, the pattern is that of 'covenantal nomism'. The response demanded to God's electing grace was obedience to the Law, and the Law was therefore the means of staying within God's covenant people. If salvation depends on God's election and covenant, reward and punishment are dependent on obedience to the Law. There is an interesting parallel here with the apparent anomaly in Paul's thought whereby, alongside his insistence on justification by grace, he continues to hold a belief in judgement according to works. There are plenty of references in his epistles to future reward and punishment as dependent on one's deeds – and this recompense will be no light affair. Indeed, in Phil. 3, the critical nature of this judgement is such that Paul envisages the possibility of missing out on future salvation altogether. References to future judgement are found in Rom. 2.1–16; 14.10–12; 1 Cor. 3.10–15; 4.1–5; 2 Cor. 5.10. The day of judgement is a day of wrath – from which Christ will save those who belong to him (1 Thess. 1.10; Rom. 5.9f). But in order to escape this wrath it is necessary for Christians to be what they are – God's holy people. The fact that Paul understands response to God's grace in terms of Spirit rather than Law, therefore, does not do away with the idea of final judgement. If the pattern of Israel's religious experience, as it is expressed in Judaism, can be seen in terms of God's election and salvation of Israel→Israel's response to the covenant at Sinai→life within the covenant, in obedience to the Law→final judgement→reward and punishment, this is remarkably close to the pattern which emerges from Paul's writings: God's gracious act in Christ→response to this act through baptism→life in Christ, in accordance with the Spirit→final judgement→reward and punishment. Although 'nomism' may not be the appropriate term for Paul's 'pattern of religion', therefore, it is clear that his understanding of how salvation 'works' is not so far from that of Judaism as his rejection of the Law might suggest. Indeed, one might well sum up his approach in the words of Leviticus: 'Be holy, for I am holy.'[3]

But what of Sanders' other term – the adjective 'covenantal'? Is he right in arguing that the idea of the covenant is not a central one for Paul? Now it is true that the word διαθήκη occurs rarely in Paul's writings, and that on the one occasion when he deals at length with the theme of the contrast between the old and new covenants he is concerned with ministers of the covenant, and it is not Christ who is compared with Moses, but Paul himself. Christ is so much superior to Moses that he is seen as the source of the covenant, not its minister. In Rom. 9.4 there is a reference to the fact that God made covenants with his people Israel,[4] and in Rom. 11.27 we find a quotation from Jer. 31.33 referring to the future establishment of God's covenant with his people. In 1 Cor. 11.25 the death of Christ is described as 'a new covenant in his blood' in a clear contrast with the covenant on Sinai, but this is the only use of this particular idea in Paul, and even that may be a quotation of traditional material. The contrast between the two covenants is made with the help of an allegory in Gal. 4, but the terms 'old' and 'new' are not used, perhaps because both covenants are here traced back to Abraham. It is his descendants through Ishmael, not Isaac, however, with whom the covenant on Sinai was made, and the true sons of Abraham – the children of Isaac – are those who have inherited the promises made to Abraham through the other covenant. Paul does not spell out his allegory here, but presumably he is referring to the covenant ratified in Christ's blood. However, by tracing the line of descent through Isaac, he reminds us that what happens in Christ is the fulfilment of the covenant made with Abraham.

The term διαθήκη is used also in the argument in Gal. 3, once again in connection with Abraham, but here it seems to have the meaning 'will' rather than covenant,[5] though presumably Paul is playing on the word's double meaning. Once again, the emphasis is on the superiority of the promises made to Abraham over the Law given to Moses. The provisions of the Mosaic Law could not annul the provisions of the earlier agreement with Abraham.

This meagre evidence might perhaps suggest that Sanders is right in concluding that the idea of the covenant is not central for Paul. Yet it is clear that Paul is far from suggesting that God has withdrawn from the covenant. The provisions of a διαθήκη – whether it is a 'will' or a 'covenant' – cannot be annulled once ratified, and any suggestion that God's promises have failed is met by Paul with an indignant μὴ γένοιτο! If the idea of the covenant is in any sense played down by Paul, it is only by contrast with the 'new covenant' which fulfils the promises made to Abraham before the Law was given. When Sanders writes that *'Paul in fact explicitly denies that the Jewish covenant can be effective for salvation'*,[6] he is right only if by 'Jewish covenant' he means the covenant on Mt Sinai, which Paul regards as being of temporary validity, an interim measure until God's original promises are fulfilled. What is perhaps surprising is that Paul does not speak of these original promises in terms of a covenant, even though, as we have seen, he twice uses the word διαθήκη in discussing them. In Gal. 3 he does indeed describe the agreement with Abraham as a διαθήκη, but almost certainly in the sense of 'will', not 'covenant', and in Gal. 4 the διαθήκη is made with the descendants of Isaac, though of course it has its origins in the promise made to Abraham. Now it may well be pure chance that Paul never describes God's promise to Abraham as a 'covenant'. But possibly it is because he in fact prefers to speak of it in terms of promise, and to use the term 'covenant' for what happens in Christ. The emphasis in both Gal. 3 and 4 is on the future fulfilment in Christ.[7] God's promises to Abraham are promises for the future, and it is in Christ that the promised blessing comes.[8]

Although Paul refers to the agreement with Abraham in terms of promise rather than covenant, the term used in this connection by Sanders himself – 'covenantal promises' – is certainly an appropriate one. Moreover, these 'covenantal promises' refer forward to a covenant which proves 'effective for salvation'. Paul certainly does not deny that God's covenant with his people is effective for salvation – quite the reverse, for much of his argument is aimed at demonstrating that God's covenantal promises remain sure. Rather he is concerned to show that it is *not the covenant on Mt Sinai* which brings salvation. Possibly this is why he does not make a great deal of use of Exodus typology. For the conversion of Gentiles has, in Paul's view, demonstrated the temporary nature of the Mosaic Law. It is the promises to Abraham which are primary in the divine scheme.

Once again, then, Sanders' assertion that Paul's understanding of religion is far removed from the covenantal nomism of Judaism seems misleading. The term itself may not be an appropriate one for Paul's view, but the basic approach is very similar. The 'covenantal nomism' which Sanders traces in Judaism is only one form of a more fundamental pattern, in which divine election and promise lead to human acceptance and response. Certainly Paul's pattern is more complicated, since what is begun in Abraham is completed only in Christ. The covenant on Sinai and the Mosaic Law, which form the heart of Judaism, are now seen as an interlude, sandwiched between the promises and their fulfilment. But the election of Abraham, and the promises made to him – which cannot fail – are part of God's covenant with Israel, and come to their conclusion with the 'new' covenant in Christ's death. The pattern begins with Abraham, who believed the promises of God, absurd though they appeared; it reaches fulfilment in Christ, the true son of Abraham, and in those who live 'in Christ'. In contrast to Judaism, however, what marks out this community as God's people is faith, not acceptance of the Law, and what governs their behaviour is life in the Spirit, not obedience to the Law's commands. This pattern of covenant/promise→fulfilment/faith embraces both Abraham and those who are now, in Christ, his children and heirs.

It is not the 'pattern of religion', then, that separates Paul from Judaism, but the pieces which make up the pattern. Clearly we cannot speak of 'covenantal nomism' in Paul's case, since that would run counter to Paul's basic quarrel with the Law. But the point is that for Paul, the Law has been replaced by Christ – or rather, since the Law was an interim measure, it has been shown in its true character as a stand-in, now that the reality has arrived. The questions 'Who belongs to the covenant?, and 'How does one respond to the covenant?', are answered by Paul in terms of Christ, by Judaism in terms of the Law.

Almost without noticing it, we have arrived at the notion of 'participation theology', which Sanders not only sees as the heart of Paul's religion, but sets in opposition to 'covenantal nomism'. The two ideas are, he argues, quite different, since[9] in one case 'one ratifies and agrees to a covenant offered by God', in the other 'one dies with Christ, obtaining new life'; the former involves 'becoming a member of a group with a covenantal relation with God and remaining in it on the condition of proper behaviour', the latter means 'that one is a member of the body of Christ and one Spirit with him, and that one remains so unless one breaks the participatory union by forming another'. The problem with this analysis, however, is that we are not really comparing like with like. The differences are partly due to the fact that the covenant ratified on Sinai was an agreement with a group, the call of Israel to be the people of God, whereas what Paul describes in his 'participation' language is the way in which men and women are included in a group which already exists in the person of Christ. What Paul has to say about participation is, as Sanders himself argues, primarily 'transfer terminology':[10] it describes how one is transferred from the power of sin to the dominion of Christ, from bondage to liberty. The question with which Paul is wrestling is: 'How does it come about that Gentiles are responding to the gospel, and are receiving the blessings promised to Abraham, while Jews remain outside the Christian community?' Clearly the normal Jewish understanding as to who belonged to God's chosen people must be wrong. It was not, after all, those who had accepted the Sinaitic covenant and who obeyed the Mosaic Law.

But if Gentiles were now found enjoying the covenantal promises, how had this come about? The answer was that they were there because they had been transferred into God's covenant people through union with Christ, and were now sons of Abraham and inheritors of the promises made to him. Sanders is right to stress the fundamental importance of 'participation theology' in Paul. But it is important precisely because it is an integral part of his understanding of the activity of God. The notion of participation explains how the promises made to Abraham can be relevant to Gentiles, and how the salvation which is effected through the 'new' covenant in Christ's death is worked out in the lives of particular individuals.

It would seem that Sanders has fallen into the very trap which he attempted to avoid, in that he has taken something which is only a part of Paul's theology – central though that may be – and compared and contrasted it with a pattern of religion which he has traced in Judaism. But if this notion of participation is emphasized by Paul, it is because it is his solution to the question that preoccupied him: *How* can one receive the promises of God? Participation in Christ explains how it is that one particular group of people – namely those who believe in

Christ – are members of God's covenant people. Jesus has been raised from the dead and declared righteous, acknowledged as God's Son. But this has taken place *apart from the Law*. This means that it is not, after all, on the basis of obedience to the Law that one is declared righteous. The inclusion of the Gentiles goes hand in hand with the demotion of the Law. The promises of the covenant are not confined to those to whom the Law was given. These promises were made to Abraham's seed, and Abraham's seed turns out to include all those who are in Christ. Gentiles are therefore included in the covenant from which the Law had excluded them. The idea of participation in Christ explains how it is that God's saving grace is not confined to Israel. But we must understand this participation in Christ within the context of the covenant with Abraham and the promises made to him.

There is another way in which Sanders, by contrasting Judaism's 'covenantal nomism' with Paul's 'participation theology', is not comparing like with like. For one very important difference between Judaism and Paul's theological understanding is that, for Paul, history has moved on a stage with the life, death and resurrection of Christ. The Messiah has come: what belongs in Jewish thinking to the End of days has in a sense already taken place. This is why, in contrast to Judaism, Paul thinks of Christians as those who have *already* been declared righteous. This explains what Sanders regards as an important difference between Paul and Judaism, namely that 'righteousness in Judaism is a term which implies the *maintenance of status* among the group of the elect; in Paul it is a *transfer term*. In Judaism, that is, commitment to the covenant puts one "in", while obedience (righteousness) subsequently keeps one in. In Paul's usage, "be made righteous" ("be justified") is a term indicating getting in, not staying in the body of the saved.'[11] But it is precisely this concern with 'getting in, not staying in the body of the saved', which we have already seen to be central in Paul's thinking. And the reason why righteousness is associated with this initiatory act, rather than with what follows, is that by incorporation into Christ, men and women share the status of Christ, who has already been raised from death. If the verdict of acquittal has already been pronounced, then it is not surprising if 'being made righteous' is a 'transfer' term describing the process of removal into the sphere of salvation, namely Christ. Logically, we might perhaps expect there to be *less* similarity between Paul's understanding and the pattern of covenantal nomism than there is! For if eschatology were fully realized, then the resurrection of Christ, which declares him to be righteous, and enables those who are in him to be sharers in his righteousness, would be the final act in the drama. But the End is *not* yet; the day of judgement still lies in the future – which means that there is an interim period between what has happened in Christ and what will happen in the future, an interim period which is in many ways parallel to the present age in Jewish thought. The redemption which takes place in Christ must inevitably be interpreted more in terms of the initial act establishing man's status before God, rather than as the final declaration of his condition. If there is still room in Paul's thinking for a future judgement on the basis of men's deeds, this is the result of the uncomfortable fact that what happens in Christ is not, after all, the end of salvation history but a new beginning, so that we go on living in this present age, as well as in the age to come. This means that something more must be said about man's response to God's grace than the fact that it is made ἐκ πίστεως. Inevitably, Paul must say something about the manner of life which is appropriate for God's people, and the obedience which springs from faith. As long as Christians continue to live in this present aeon, their religion will inevitably bear many similarities to covenantal nomism.

Finally, we may note that in spite of his contrast between Paul's understanding of 'participation theology' and Judaism's 'covenantal nomism', Sanders fails to explain how Paul relates the two views of salvation. For Paul, he says, 'righteousness *cannot* be by law, *since it is by faith* ... If the death and resurrection of Christ provide salvation ... *all other means are excluded by definition.*'[12] But *why* is it 'by definition'? What is it about the death and resurrection of Christ which *excludes* salvation by the Law? What Sanders fails to bring out is the inner logic which leads Paul to argue that the death and resurrection of Christ mean the end of the reign of the Law. Granted that Sanders is right in maintaining that there is nothing in Jewish thought to explain why the coming of the Messiah should dethrone the Law, why have the *death and resurrection* of Christ done so? The answer is surely that the inadequacy of the Law is seen in the fact that one who was *condemned by the Law* has been *pronounced righteous by God*. Christ has been declared righteous, not only *apart from the Law*, but *in spite of the Law*. In the resurrection, the Law's verdict has been overthrown. This is why the righteousness of the Law is not an alternative route to salvation but a blind alley. The death and resurrection of Christ are therefore a demonstration of the fact that the Law is powerless to save.

The features in Paul's thought which Sanders has investigated, and the surprising rarity with which he employs Moses typology, are surely explained by this fact: that Paul sees the Mosaic Law as an interlude, which limited God's mercies to Israel until the time came for all men to be saved. But this does not mean that covenantal nomism is totally foreign to Paul's approach: only that, for him, there is a different covenant and a very different kind of law. The key figures in Paul's plan of salvation are therefore Adam—Abraham—Christ, and Moses is only a subsidiary figure. It is this which leads Professor Barrett to ask the apparently strange question: 'Why does [Moses] appear in Paul's story?'[13] Strictly, Moses does not belong to Paul's scheme. He appears, of course, because he is the mediator of the Jewish Law and cannot be ignored, but it is well to remember that he is, for Paul, primarily a negative figure. To that extent, Sanders is right to stress the difference between Paul and Judaism. But as far as Paul's basic understanding of religion is concerned, Paul is surely right when he claims to be a Hebrew of the Hebrews, and a true interpreter of the Law itself.

NOTES

1   E. P. Sanders, *Paul and Palestinian Judaism* (London 1977), pp. 1–24.

2   cf. G. M. Styler's analysis of Paul, 'The basis of obligation in Paul's Christology and ethics', in *Christ and Spirit in the New Testament*, essays in honour of C. F. D. Moule, ed. B. Lindars and S. S. Smalley (Cambridge 1973).

3   Lev. 11.44f.

4   cf. also Eph. 2.12.

5   cf. E. Bammel, 'Gottes διαθήκη (Gal. 3.15–17) und das Jüdische Rechtsdenken', *NTS* 6 (1960), pp. 313–19; cf. J. Behm, *TDNT* ii, διαθήκη, pp. 129f (*TWNT* ii, p. 132).

6   op. cit. p. 551.

7   Perhaps this explains Paul's use of the verb προκυρόω in Gal. 3.17, a term which seems to fit the legal vocabulary of this passage, but which J. Behm (*TWNT* iii, p. 1099; *TDNT* iii, p. 1099) describes as 'legally meaningless'. It is usually interpreted as meaning that the διαθήκη with Abraham was ratified before the giving of the Law; perhaps, however, it signifies its ratification before it came into force – in Christ.

8   cf. the phrase 'covenants of promise' used in Eph. 2.12.

9   op. cit. p. 514.

10   op. cit. pp. 463–72.

11   op. cit. p. 544.

12   op. cit. p. 484.

13   C. K. Barrett, *From First Adam to Last* (London 1962), p. 46.

6

Paul and the Apocalyptic Pattern

John M. Court

There has already been one opportunity in recent years for me to place on public record my personal indebtedness to Professor Barrett. But I welcome the further opportunity in contributing to this *Festschrift*, not least because it provides a truly collective expression of our communal sense of appreciation and obligation. Professor Barrett will also recognize the starting point of this article, and probably date it exactly to the autumn of 1972. I hope that he might feel that the idea was good and be prepared to overlook any weakness in its execution!

The Little Apocalypse of Mark 13 represents 'a very complete summary of the apocalyptic views spread among the Jewish Christians of the first century, such as we know them by John's book'. At least so Timothée Colani thought when he wrote *Jésus Christ et les croyances messianiques de son temps*, published in 1864. Two features of the text provided the basis for his conclusion: the threefold structure of expectations, recognized in Mark 13 by many other scholars in the century since Colani, but apparently adopted by him from the work of H. J. Holtzmann (cf. *Die synoptischen Evangelien* 1863); and secondly the use of three technical terms, ὠδῖνες, θλῖψις and τέλος, corresponding to this threefold structure.

These terms are found in Mark 13 at verses 8 (ὠδῖνες); 19, 24 (θλῖψις); 7, 13 (τέλος). H. J. Holtzmann divided the discourse into three sections: 5–13, the ἀρχαὶ ὠδίνων (depicted in their *welthistorischen* character and in their significance for the development of the Kingdom of God, verses 5–9 and 9–13 respectively); 14–23, the climax of θλῖψις, associated with the destruction of Jerusalem; and 24–37, the Parousia represented as the τέλος. Since Holtzmann many other sub-divisions and modifications have been proposed. I have already indicated elsewhere my reasons for preferring a different ordering of these events of the 'Little Apocalypse'.[1]

But the combination of triple structure and triple terminology, which first attracted interest, it seems, in the work of Holtzmann and

Colani, remains a significant feature in this material. The reasons for this nineteenth-century interest would repay closer investigation; but meanwhile I should like to test out the possibility that this threefold apocalyptic summary had a wider currency in the New Testament world. The importance of eschatological ideas in the thought of Paul is now undeniable. Are there any traces of these three technical terms, if not of a threefold structure, in his letters?

The first term for our consideration is the feminine noun ὠδίν (more usually spelt ὠδίς outside the New Testament). Of four New Testament occurrences the only one in the Pauline letters is at 1 Thess. 5.3. Although this is classified as a literal use meaning 'birth-pain', it is noteworthy that we have here a simile where 'travail' is compared with 'sudden destruction'. The context refers to the coming of 'the day of the Lord' 'like a thief in the night', a theme clearly related to the closing verses of Mark's Little Apocalypse. While the Thessalonians are watchful 'sons of light', 'those who sleep' 'in darkness' will be surprised by the 'day of the Lord' and 'sudden destruction will come upon them, as travail comes upon a woman with child, and there will be no escape.' In such a context the simile occurs naturally as part of the traditional language of expectation; there is a close and recurrent correlation between the imagery of childbirth and the imagery of the messianic woes תבלי המשיח (as represented by ὠδῖνες in Mark 13.8 and Matt. 24.8). The development of this theme can be observed in Isa. 7.14; 9.2–7; 26.16–19; 66.7–14, and Qumran Hodayoth 3 (1QH3).

Does the use of the cognate verb ὠδίνειν offer any support for the suggestion that Paul may be revivifying the traditional imagery of childbirth in an eschatological context? Two of the three New Testament instances of this verb are found in Gal. 4.19, 27. The latter is a direct quotation from the Septuagint of Isa. 54.1; 'this passage in its context is a song of triumph anticipating the deliverance of God's afflicted people Israel.'[2] Paul applies it to the 'allegory' of the two women, the present Jerusalem and the Jerusalem above. The apocalyptic tradition of the heavenly Jerusalem as a counterpart to the earthly city is well known, and so it is reasonable to conclude that one aspect of Paul's complex juxtaposition is to anticipate God's eschatological deliverance in the light of Israel's history. The fact that Paul's only use of ὠδίνειν outside of a quotation occurs eight verses previously may be coincidental, but it may rather be an echo from one text to the other. At 4.19 the imagery of motherhood illustrates the intensity of Paul's concern for his church, even more vividly than the imagery of fatherhood at 1 Cor. 4.15. In both passages Paul's attitude is emphasized by contrast with other teachers or 'guides'. In Galatians the added urgency is that Paul must go through the birth process again with his converts to ensure their proper development. E. P. Sanders comments on this passage under the heading of 'new creation' transfer terminology in his treatment of Pauline soteriology: 'Paul apparently means that the possibility that the Galatians will accept the law means that Christ is not really "in" them and that the transformation to the new creation (Gal. 6.15) or the transfer from slavery to sonship (Gal. 4.1–7) is threatened with cancellation.'[3]

The second stage – both of this terminological investigation and of the apocalyptic structure – is the largest in scope. The word θλῖψις occurs forty-five times in the New Testament, twenty-four of which are in the Pauline writings. It is necessary to attempt a classification by content. The noun denoted a variety of physical pressures and had a widespread figurative use in the Septuagint; the effect of representing fourteen Hebrew words by the same Greek word is to produce a synthesis of afflictions, both external and internal, including acute distress and anxiety, and the particular context must be studied to see the shades of meaning. Gen. 42.21 is an interesting example because θλῖψις there represents Joseph's anguish and his brothers' distress.

In Paul's usage it may not be possible to discover the actual nature of the 'suffering' or 'affliction', just as one cannot identify Paul's own 'thorn in the flesh', but the references can be classified firstly by the recipients or location of the θλῖψις. It belongs to Paul himself according to 2 Cor. 2.4; Phil. 1.17; 4.14; Col. 1.24; one might add Eph. 3.13. The context suggests or states that it is 'our suffering' in Rom. 5.3; 8.35; 2 Cor. 1.4, 8; 4.17; 6.4; 7.4; 1 Thess. 3.3, 7 (probably also 1.6 as the Thessalonians in their circumstances are μιμηταί of us). The affliction is either 'yours' or belongs to some other distinct group of people in Rom. 2.9; 12.12; 1 Cor. 7.28; 2 Cor. 1.4; 8.2, 13; Phil. 4.14; 1 Thess. 1.6; 2 Thess. 1.4, 6. The reference is to Christ's sufferings in Col. 1.24; probably in 1 Thess. 1.6, as the Thessalonians are μιμηταί 'of the Lord'; in 2 Cor. 1.5 Christ's 'sufferings' are παθήματα but the immediate context has three uses of θλῖψις and one of the cognate verb, which might suggest a stylistic variation.[4] Certainly passages such as 2 Cor. 1.4ff; Phil. 4.14; 1 Thess. 1.6; and Col. 1.24 demonstrate that these classifications are not mutually exclusive; at the least, suffering is a shared experience of Lord, apostle and new convert.

Paul shares the widespread New Testament view that such affliction is necessary (1 Thess. 3.2f: 'you yourselves know that this is to be our lot.'). 'The constant tribulation of Israel in the OT has become the necessary tribulation of the Church in the NT. The former is thus an indication of the latter.'[5] This is one way in which Old Testament texts provided a guide-book for the early Christian. The Christian context was strictly eschatological. While the Jewish expectation for the future might be a continuation of an experience of suffering and its culmination in a period of messianic afflictions, for the Christian such a necessary experience of eschatological suffering had begun already. As the Messiah had come and suffered, so the afflictions which are the Christian's lot are a shared experience of what Christ had suffered.

Paul makes clear the eschatological character of these sufferings in a number of passages already mentioned. Perhaps the most unexpected instance of this comes in the discussion of 'marriage difficulties' at 1 Cor. 7.26ff. The context is established as eschatological by the use of ἀνάγκη in verse 26; 'distress' is 'an apocalyptic term . . . and an established motif of apocalyptic expectation'.[6] This distress is 'impending' or 'imminent' ('woes that are impending over the world, and are already anticipated in the sufferings of Christians')[7]; the translation of ἐνεστῶσαν as 'present' could be preferred, on the grounds that Paul does use the word unambiguously in this sense (cf. 1 Cor. 3.22; Rom. 8.38; Gal. 1.4). Paul's advice on marriage is conditioned by the immediacy 'of the outward menace of these "last evil times".'[8] 'With his awareness of the shortening of the time, Paul obviously sees the afflictions of the last time breaking into the present, and his advice is designed to lessen the related θλῖψις for his community.'[9]

A further instance of precise eschatological timing is provided in 2 Cor. 6.2ff where θλῖψις is connected to καιρὸς εὐπρόσδεκτος and ἡμέρα σωτηρίας. Whatever the problems for exegesis of reconciling *Heilsgeschichte* with the 'now' of existential decision, we can still agree with Oscar Cullmann when he writes: 'Paul finds himself right at the point where in the execution of his plan God brought in the "welcome time" by reconciling the world to himself through Christ (2 Cor. 5.18). Just at this point in time the apostle received his precise calling, his "ministry of reconciliation" (5.18), and therefore must show himself as a "servant of God" on this "day of salvation" through all the tribulations which he enumerates.'[10]

The eschatological perspective for Paul's usage of θλῖψις is also clearly established in two passages referring to the last judgement: according to Rom. 2.5, 9 'on the day of wrath when God's righteous judgement will be revealed . . . there will be tribulation (θλῖψις) and distress for every human being who does evil.' And in 2 Thess. 1.5ff, 'This is evidence of the righteous judgement of God . . . since indeed God deems it just to repay with affliction (θλῖψις) those who afflict you, and to grant rest with us to you who are afflicted.' By the use of cognate noun and verb in this latter passage, it is made explicit that what Christians are now suffering for the duration of the messianic age will become the ultimate punishment for the evildoer on the day of judgement. The same duality of function can be observed in the sequences of plagues within the Book of Revelation; what begins as contemporary sufferings in the Asian churches becomes the final judgement poured upon Babylon from the bowls of God's wrath.

Whereas ὠδίν represents a precise and vivid metaphor of childbirth, and θλῖψις, although covering a variety of afflictions, is defined by a context of eschatological understanding, the third word, τέλος, which must be considered now, has an unprecedented versatility. It is not necessarily used in a technical sense where to talk of eschatology would be tautologous. It can refer to an immediate 'aim' or objective (1 Tim. 1.5), to the finishing or cessation of something ('the fading splendour' – 2 Cor. 3.13), or to the specific discharging of financial duties in the form of 'taxes' (Rom. 13.7). So out of forty occurrences of τέλος in the New Testament and fourteen instances in the Pauline writings, we are concerned selectively with perhaps ten passages.

At least half of these references are clearly eschatological. The parallelism between the clauses of 1 Cor. 1.8 would justify the equation of 'the end' with 'the day of our Lord Jesus (Christ)' – the Old Testament 'day of Yahweh' reapplied in Christian tradition to the Parousia of Jesus. The preferred reading ἕως τέλους can then be translated 'to the end of the world', although it may be recognized that the pressures to diminish the strictly temporal sense, by translating as 'completely',[11] are also present in the variant reading τελείους in P46. The same expression, ἕως τέλους, also occurs at 2 Cor. 1.13; again it is balanced by the reference in verse 14 to 'the day of the Lord Jesus'. Bauer supports the comparable, eschatological, translation here too ('to the end = until the Parousia') and there are excellent reasons for this consistency. It is therefore necessary to resist the RSV's attractive-sounding but inconsistent rendering: 'I hope you will understand fully', despite the support of Lietzmann's commentary. Rather, as C. K. Barrett comments on this verse: 'It points to the future; Paul hopes that recognition will not be withdrawn, though he has some reason to fear that it may be.'[12]

Another instance, possibly with far-reaching implications for the understanding of Paul's eschatology, is 1 Cor. 10.11. Most commentators are agreed that Paul's lesson from the Old Testament has an eschatological application, but the use of the plural expression τὰ τέλη τῶν αἰώνων creates a problem for precise exegesis. This is no reason to avoid the eschatological interpretation, either by substituting sacramental language (as M. M. Bogle suggested with the translation 'to whom the eternal Mysteries have come down' or 'who are the heirs of the Mysteries of the ages', understanding τέλος in the sense of a sacred rite)[13] or by developing a metaphorical use related to the literal use of Rom. 13.7 (A. Souter proposed the translation 'the (spiritual) revenues of the ages').[14] Neither suggestion is justified adequately either by Pauline usage or by the requirements of the contexts. Hardly more convincing is G. Delling's[15] translation 'the aims of the times'; he relies on the formal parallel of Wisdom 8.8 (ἐκβάσεις καιρῶν καὶ χρόνων: RSV 'the outcome of seasons and times'), although neither Heb. 13.7 nor 1 Cor. 10.13 with their different applications of ἔκβασις seem to justify this. He can link this with the present context of 1 Cor. 10.1–10 by saying: 'of these times an especially prominent one was the wilderness age of Israel.' But it is not certain whether he sees τέλος as the immediate objective of Paul's teaching method (cf. 1. Tim. 1.5), or as the promised 'fulfilment in the present events determined by Christ', or, perhaps, both.

According to Oscar Cullmann αἰών ('age') is used in 1 Cor. 10.11 in the sense of 'limited time' – 'with Christ the final phase of the limited world period has dawned.'[16] The two plurals in Paul's expression are not obvious in this interpretation, but one can presumably explain the plural 'ages' with reference to the apocalyptic convention of dividing world history into a number of epochs. What, then, are the 'ends' of these epochs? J. Weiss understood the expression thus: 'we in whom the ends of the aeons meet'. The Christian stands on a narrowing strip of land; the incoming tide, representing the new age of the messianic kingdom, moves ever closer to where he stands; he feels that he is being edged ever closer to the waves by the sense of completeness and fulfilment of past history; the present is a rapidly diminishing, increasingly insecure foothold. This spatial reinterpretation might convey the sense of the meeting of the ends of the ages and how it is meaningful to speak of the ages meeting *us* rather than one another;

but is it possible for the Greek word τέλος to refer, like the English word 'end', to the 'front-end' as well as the 'back-end', to the beginning as well as the end? If we are speaking of periods of time, measured by something like an hour-glass, then the end of one period is the beginning of the next and the same grains of sand may be measuring both. But there is no indication in Greek usage, apart from the present context, which clearly supports this idea. Equally, while the image of the hour-glass and the turning point between ages might suit Paul's eschatology, did he employ it, unless he did so here?

If the plural τῶν αἰώνων refers to the epochs of world history, does the plural τὰ τέλη rather suggest more than one goal or objective of this process of world history? This raises all kinds of difficulty and is presumably the reason for Robertson and Plummer's 'notion that each epoch has the quintessence of the preceding one transmitted to it' – a notion which Conzelmann describes as 'completely mistaken'. A similar desire to resist a proliferation of goals may underlie Conzelmann's own assertion that 'the plural τέλη is to be understood in a singular sense of the end of a unity.'[17] This is making theological capital out of the observation that the plural is sometimes found in a singular sense; in the examples listed by Bauer[18] (Arndt and Gingrich) the partitive genitive is singular not plural, so there is no evidence for the attraction of the plural from αἰώνων. As for αἰώνων, this plural 'is often purely formal'. 'The plural designates simply the world-age, from the point of view of its limitation.' Comparisons are then drawn with the singular use of τέλος in Sibylline Oracles 8.311 and with the plural τέλη in Testament of Levi 14.1. The Qumran Commentary on Habakkuk (1Qp Hab) 7.13 is variously quoted as a parallel, but its usefulness is limited by uncertainty as to whether it refers to the order of ages or the climax of God's appointed times.

It does not seem that there are sufficient grounds for excluding either the possibility that Paul is expressing in these words his sense of the Christians' living between two crisis points, or the view that Paul's plural is formal, representing a singular, so that he is speaking of a single crisis. What seems much clearer is that he regards this situation as one already being experienced. Whether καταντάω with a preposition is used of someone coming to something (Eph. 4.13; Phil. 3.11), or of something coming to someone (1 Cor. 14.36), it is clear that a past tense indicates arrival or attainment or reception, and in this sense a realized eschatology. I venture to suggest that the emphasis is misplaced in the statement: 'Paul believes that he and his correspondents are living in the last days of world history *before* the breaking in of the messianic age.'[19] In a sense this last age *has* come.

This understanding must be in a certain tension with the next example (1 Cor. 15.24), although such tension is not unusual in eschatological contexts. For τὸ τέλος here indicates the third and last stage, which has not happened yet (15.25–8); this is true irrespective of whether the word is used explicitly of the last things (so Héring), adverbially meaning 'finally' (Hofmann, Burkitt, Barth), or as a military metaphor for the 'remainder' – cf. τάγμα (J. Weiss, Lietzmann), i.e. a second or general resurrection, cf. Revelation 20.5ff. This apocalyptic passage, contributing to the sequence of arguments about the resurrection, contains a threefold pattern of expectation which is of a different kind from the sequence of woes that we are examining. It is more broadly based than the signs of the end and relates Christ's resurrection to his Parousia (and a resurrection of Christians) and finally to the conclusive establishment of the Kingdom of God. It is clear that the context is of futurist eschatology.

A group of passages use τέλος in the context of the last judgement or its anticipation. In 1 Thess. 2.16 'God's wrath has come upon' the Jews who have filled up the cup of God's wrath by their sins. As William Neil wrote: 'Two ideas seem to be involved – one, that God's Judgement – the Wrath of God (cf. 1.10), the inevitable retribution for sin – is already at work upon the Jews, their doom is sealed; and two, that the climax of that retribution – the Day of Judgement – is at hand.'[20] In such a context it seems reasonable to understand εἰς τέλος as referring to the ultimate decision ('forever' or 'decisively'), however temptingly the sense 'at last!' might fit with Paul's exasperation. Similarly Paul uses τέλος in Rom. 6.21 in the context of his pronouncement that 'the wages of sin is death' (6.23). The 'outcome' of such enslavement to sin 'is death, here for Paul, not only the consequence of evildoing, but the final judgement of God upon it.'[21] A third explicit statement of punishment, using τέλος is found at Phil. 3.19: 'For many . . . live as enemies of the cross of Christ. Their end is destruction.' Again Paul 'mentions . . . those who will be destroyed on the Day of the Lord.'[22] Finally in 2 Cor. 11.15 Paul refers to those 'false apostles' whose 'end will correspond to their deeds'. 'Men are rewarded at the judgement according to what they have done.'[23]

Taken out of its immediate context, this becomes a statement of the principle of ultimate reward or punishment. So those who have been 'set free from sin' are told: 'your fruit proves to be sanctification, and the ultimate result' (τέλος) 'will be eternal life'[24] (Rom. 6.22). The Jewish inheritance, the scheme of two ways, is set out clearly ('for everything is set under the TELOS either of death or of life, determined by what we were or what we are').[25] What is different for Paul is the sense of freedom, of being released from a route-march down the way of sin. 'It agrees with the view that the death of Christ provides for a transfer of Lordship that Paul can express the transfer in terms of liberation or freedom from bondage. One is free from the power of sin (or the law) and free to live for God.'[26] So the last example of the use of τέλος, at Rom. 10.4, is also intelligible in terms of Paul's eschatology. Christ's death represents this decisive change or liberation: 'for Christ is the end of the law, that every one who has faith may be justified.' '"Christ" means God's act in history, by which he introduced the Age to Come, and brought to an end the old order of relations between God and man.'[27] But having recognized the importance of this eschatological understanding, one can also see the way Paul has exploited the versatility of the word τέλος. For the ultimate goal of the Law, defined as εἰς δικαιοσύνην, has been made possible of achievement by Christ.

We have now examined the occurrences of all three terms from the apocalyptic summary within the letters of Paul. It is clear that the passages discussed gain immeasurably by being understood in the context of eschatological thought. Other vocabulary in these contexts makes a contribution to the eschatological understanding, but it appears reasonable to suggest that our three terms import much of the apocalyptic colouring. Although Paul's explicit reference to three stages of expectation is in rather different terms (1 Cor. 15.24), must we not conclude that Paul uses the technical language of traditional apocalyptic, and may be echoing the formula of a threefold structure, when he speaks of ὠδῖνες, θλῖψις and τέλος?

NOTES

1 J. M. Court, *Myth and History in the Book of Revelation* (London 1979), ch. 3.

2 J. B. Lightfoot, *Saint Paul's Epistle to the Galatians* (London 1890), p. 182.

3 E. P. Sanders, *Paul and Palestinian Judaism* (London 1977), p. 469.

4 Although H. Schlier mentions the distinction drawn by A. Steubing, *Der paulinische Begriff Christusleiden* (1905), p. 10.

5 H. Schlier, Kittel *TWNT* iii, p. 143.

6 H. Conzelmann, *1 Corinthians* (Hermeneia) (Philadelphia 1975), p. 132 n13.

7 C. K. Barrett, *The First Epistle to the Corinthians* (London 1968), p. 175.

8 H. Conzelmann, op. cit., p. 132.

9 H. Schlier, op. cit., p. 145.

10 O. Cullmann, *Salvation in History* (London 1967), p. 255.

11 As A. Schlatter, *Paulus der Bote Jesu* (1962), quoted in C. K. Barrett, op. cit., p. 39.

12 C. K. Barrett, *The Second Epistle to the Corinthians* (London 1973), p. 73.

13 *ET* 67 (1955/6), pp. 246f.

14 *Pocket Lexicon of the New Testament* (1916); cf. P. Macpherson, *ET* 55 (1943/4), p. 222.

15 G. Delling, Kittel *TWNT* viii, p. 54.

16 O. Cullmann, *Christ and Time* (London 1951), p. 48 n22.

17 H. Conzelmann, op. cit., p. 168.

18 *A Greek-English Lexicon of the New Testament* (Chicago 1957), p. 27 (αἰών 2b).

19 C. K. Barrett, *The First Epistle to the Corinthians* (London 1968), p. 228.

20 W. Neil, *The Epistle of Paul to the Thessalonians* (Moffatt) (London 1950), p. 54.

21 M. Black, *Romans* (New Century) (London 1973), p. 99.

22 E. P. Sanders, op. cit., p. 473.

23 C. K. Barrett, *The Second Epistle to the Corinthians* (London 1973), p. 287.

24 C. K. Barrett, *The Epistle to the Romans* (London 1957), p. 134.

25 K. Barth, *The Epistle to the Romans* (London 1933), p. 227.

26 E. P. Sanders, op. cit., p. 468.

27 C. K. Barrett, *The Epistle to the Romans* (London 1957), p. 197.

7

1 Thessalonians 4.13–18
and its Background in Apocalyptic Literature

A. F. J. Klijn

In a Seminar organized by the Department of Theology of the University of Newcastle upon Tyne, May 1979, I had the privilege to say something about 1 Thess. 4.13–18 and apocalyptic in the presence, among others, of Professor Barrett. Stimulated by a discussion of my ideas and suggestions made by the participants, I should like to go into the subject again.

In this well-known passage Paul writes to the Thessalonians that he does not wish them to remain in ignorance about the dead (περὶ τῶν κοιμωμένων) and that they should not grieve like those who have no hope since those left alive until the coming of the Lord will not forestall those who have died. The passage contains a number of exegetical difficulties which we will not discuss in this contribution.[1] Here we should like to deal with the background of the question in Thessalonica and Paul's answer. We should like to show that viewing this passage against an apocalyptic background results in a better understanding.

With regard to the passage a consensus has been reached on several key questions. In the first place it is agreed that the grief of the Thessalonians is not due to Paul's failure to preach the resurrection of the dead.[2] Although in this letter Paul emphasizes vigilance with regard to the coming of Jesus (1. 9–10 and 5. 1–10), it is impossible to conclude that he left out any mention of a resurrection of the dead. In the second place it is accepted that the grief of the Thessalonians has to do with some supposed inequality between those who have died and those who would still be alive at the coming of the Lord. This supposition could have resulted from a belief in some messianic kingdom before the final judgement, although Paul apparently knew of no such kingdom.[3]

Other questions have not been definitely answered. For example, did the grief come about because of influence from outside or did it originate spontaneously within the Thessalonian community, because of perhaps a number of deaths? At the moment some tend to assume a background in Thessalonica similar to that in Corinth where the resurrection of the dead was called into question.[4] Other scholars have remarked that this seems doubtful since Paul approaches the Thessalonian trouble quite differently from that in Corinth.[5] We may add that, if this were the case, it is striking that Paul omits every opportunity to speak about the resurrection of the dead. For example, in 4.14 he mentions Jesus' death and resurrection but continues speaking about those who 'have fallen asleep', introduced by the word οὕτως, neglecting to mention the idea of a resurrection: καὶ ὁ Θεὸς τοὺς κοιμηθέντας διὰ τοῦ Ἰησοῦ ἄξει σὺν αὐτῷ. Apparently not the resurrection but being 'with Christ' is the main point of discussion. This emphasis is repeated in 4.17 which summarizes Paul's argumentation and in 5.10 where 'being with Christ' is the culminating point of Paul's admonition. For these reasons we conclude that a questioning of the resurrection of the dead does not form the background of this passage.[6]

Something which has been generally ignored is that the passage must not be seen in the light of some doctrinal discussion but parenesis. The passage ends with the words: 'admonish each other with these words' (παρακαλεῖτε ἀλλήλους ἐν τοῖς λόγοις τούτοις). In the New English Bible we find: 'Console one another . . .' This is possible and seems in agreement with Paul's remark in v. 13 that one must not be sorrowful, but it is extremely doubtful whether this translation should be accepted. We have to take into consideration that 4.13–18 belongs to that part of the letter in which Paul started to admonish his readers, cf. 4.1: Λοιπὸν οὖν, ἀδελφοί, ἐρωτῶμεν ὑμᾶς καὶ παρακαλοῦμεν ἐν κυρίῳ Ἰησοῦ. Then we have to look at 5.11, where we meet exactly the same words as in 4.18, also at the end of a pericope, which certainly requires a translation in the sense of 'to admonish'. This means that the problem in 4.13–18 is one of parenesis. It seems that parenesis has been frustrated by a question about the dead in Thessalonica. Since the question has to do with the end of time, we can assume that the call to vigilance (cf. 5.1–11) was undermined by the particular ideas in Thessalonica. However, what caused the unhappy situation in Thessalonica?

We have already said that in Thessalonica grief existed about some question related to the status of the living and the dead at the end of time. Apparently the living were thought to be in a more advantageous position.[7] This is a familiar problem in apocalyptic literature.

Already a long time ago, Volz, in his classic book about apocalyptic wrote that the apocalyptic literature did not solve the problem of the status of the living and the dead at the end of time and that the discussion about this subject went on during the first century.[8]

One may raise the objection that this question was unique to an apocalyptic frame of reference and that it cannot be explained in those terms here since it has arisen in a Gentile-Christian Church. Against this objection we may remark that some knowledge of apocalyptic imagery cannot be denied the Thessalonians. In the first place it appears that Paul answers the Thessalonians in 4.16 with a word of the Lord of a purely apocalyptic nature and that in 5.1–2 Paul assumes a thorough knowledge among the Thessalonians with regard to the day of the Lord and its sudden arrival.

Before going into details we can say that difficulties with regard to the living and the dead at the end of time are the result of the merging of two different ideas about the end of time, viz. that of a coming happy future for those who are living at the time, the so-called prophetic eschatology, and that of a resurrection of all men followed by a judgement, the apocalyptic idea, which can be found for the first time explicitly in the Book of Daniel. It appears that apocalyptic has never been able to reconcile the two ideas. In what follows we will discuss this problem in the apocalyptic literature itself.

In the Book of Daniel 12.12–13 we meet both the idea of survival and of the resurrection: 'Blessed is he, who keeps on waiting and reaches 1335 days. But you, go to the end and you will rest and rise.' In this passage a difference between those left alive and those who will rise at the end is certainly noticeable. The first group belong to the 'blessed'. Here two words are especially important, viz. 'who keeps on waiting', המחכה, and 'he reaches', ויגיע. These words have been rendered in the Greek translation of Theodotion with the words ὑπομένειν and φθάνειν εἰς. The last word shows the typical sense of 'arrive at' which should be taken as 'being present at'. We meet the same word in a similar context in 1 Thess. 4.15. More important is the word 'Blessed'. This introduction seems to point at some fixed expression, as is corroborated by a number of other passages. In the Psalms of Solomon 17.50 we read: μακάριοι οἱ γενόμενοι ἐν ταῖς ἡμέραις ἐκείναις ἰδεῖν τὰ ἀγαθὰ Ἰσραὴλ ἐν συναγωγῇ φυλῶν . . . and in 18.7: γενόμενοι ἐν ἡμέραις ἐκείναις, ἰδεῖν τὰ ἀγαθὰ κυρίου . . . Finally in the Sibylline Oracles III.370: ὦ μακαριστὸς ἐκεῖνος ὃς ἐς χρόνον ἔσσεται ἀνὴρ ἠὲ γυνή.

69

Leaving aside the question of the fate of those who will rise, we can conclude that survival until the end was a special privilege.

The reason for it being a privilege to survive is clear since the sources are unanimous. In the Psalms of Solomon it is said that the survivors will witness the ἀγαθά of Israel (Ps. of Sol. 17.50, but 18.7: τοῦ κυρίου). In other words they will be present at the final justification of Israel, cf. 4 Ezra 6.25: 'Et erit omnis, qui derelictus fuerit ex omnibus istis, quibus praedixi tibi, ipse salvabitur et videbit salutare meum et finem saeculi mei'; 7.27: 'Et omnis, qui liberatus est de praedictis malis, ipse videbit mirabilia mea'; and 9.8: '(credidit), is relinquetur de praedictis periculis et videbit salutare meum in terra mea et in finibus meis quas sanctificavi mihi a saeculo.'[9] A few particulars should be noted. We meet here the word *derelictus* which can be compared with περιλειπόμενοι in 1 Thess. 4.15 and 17. Next we see that the joy of survival is even greater since it means that the difficult time coming before the end has been overcome. Then we see that sometimes the happiness at the end is connected with the land of Israel. This is a peculiarity which is not uncommon.[10] Finally we should emphasize that the tradition of being blessed because one is present at the moment of God's acts of salvation goes back to prophetic times as can be seen in Isa. 52.10. This tradition is present in the New Testament in connection with those who have the privilege to see God's salvation in Jesus (Luke 2.30 and 10.24).

Since a tradition existed according to which the survivors were praised, it is to be expected that it was necessary to go into the question of the relation of these with those who died before the end of time. This resulted into a number of discussions about this subject in 4 Ezra.

In 4 Ezra 13.16 we read: 'Vae qui derelicti fuerint in diebus illis, et multo plus vae his qui non sunt derelicti.'[11] Here the relation between the survivors and the dead is discussed. The author comes to his conclusion because the survivors will have to face innumerable horrors. But while he is able to say that the survivors will have a most difficult time, he concludes that the dead are still disadvantaged: 'Qui enim non sunt derelicti, tristes erunt, intellegentes quae sunt reposita in novissimis diebus et non occurrentes eis' (vv. 17–18).[12] The writer continues saying that the survivors will see dangers, but the dead will pass away like clouds and not see 'quae contigerunt in novissimo' (v. 20). The passage ends with the remark: 'Scito ergo quoniam magis beatificati sunt, qui derelicti super eos qui mortui sunt' (v.24).

In this discussion we see that the two groups are compared and that the conclusion is that the survivors are in a much better position than those who die before the end.

This situation can be compared with that of the Thessalonians at the time Paul reacts to their ideas. It is remarkable that here nothing is said about the possibility of rising from the dead, especially since this idea is generally accepted in 4 Ezra.

However, in 4 Ezra we also meet another approach to the question of the relation between those left alive and those who died before that time. In 4 Ezra 5.41–5 we read: 'Sed ecce, domine tu praees his, qui in fine sunt, et quid facient qui ante nos sunt aut nos, aut hi qui post nos?' Here a question is asked which was omitted in the passage before. No problem appears to exist with regard to those 'in fine', contrary to the others. The answer is: 'Coronae adsimilabo iudicium meum; sicut non novissimorum tarditas, sic nec priorum velocitas.' The answer is clear: those coming earlier or later arrive at the judgement at the same time. We may compare this with 1 Thess. 4.15: οὐ μὴ φθάσωμεν (scil. οἱ περιλειπόμενοι) τοὺς κοιμηθέντας. The author, however, is not yet satisfied with the answer. He wonders why it is necessary at all to distinguish between the two groups: 'Nec enim poteras facere qui facti sunt et qui sunt et qui futuri sunt in unum, ut celerius iudicium tuum ostendas? (v. 43).' The answer is: 'Non potest festinare creatura super creatorem, nec sustinere saeculum qui in eo creati sunt in unum (v. 44).' This answer does not satisfy the author, and he replies: 'Quoniam vivificans vivificabi[s] a te creatam creaturam in unum, (si ergo viventes vivent in unum) et sustinebit creatura, poterit et nunc portare praesentes in unum (v. 45).'[13] The answer is that for everything a time is fixed. For our purpose it is important to see that the revivification is spoken of 'in unum'. This is the same word as ἅμα which we meet in 1 Thess. 4.17 and 5.10. The idea is important, since it is also found in other passages in connection with the end of time. In the Apocalypse of Baruch 30.2b we read that the treasuries of the righteous ones will be opened and that the souls will come out and will appear 'at the same time, of one mind and one crowd'. We find a similar idea in the same Apocalypse in 51.13 where it is stated with regard to righteous ones: 'The first shall receive the last, those whom they were expecting, and the last them of whom they used to hear that they had passed away.' In 4 Ezra, again, we read in 6.20 that the books will be opened 'et omnes videbunt simul'. Finally in Ps. Philo, *Antiquit.* 19, 20, it is said that God says to Moses that nobody will be able to find his grave, until he will visit the earth. Then God will raise Moses and the fathers from the earth 'et invenietis simul et inhabitabitis habitationem inmortalem quae non tenetur in tempore'.

From this we see that repeatedly it is said that at the end the particular events will be simultaneous for all people involved.

1 Thess. 4.13–18 can be explained entirely against the background of apocalyptic thinking. That applies to the question asked and the answer given. The question arose from the emphasis laid upon the end of time and the fate of those arriving at this end. All of the attention was given to the people who would experience this last period. They had to be vigilant and to persevere. 1 Thess. 5.1–11 for example is devoted entirely to being vigilant with a view to the coming of Jesus. However, this point of view did not give sufficient attention to the question of what would happen to those who died before that time, although their resurrection was supposed. This neglect caused a number of questions with regard to the dead, for example whether they would or would not be witnesses of God's salvation. But the parenesis is also affected. The question arose whether the same instruction must be given to those who are supposed to die before the end as to those who will survive. According to Paul this has to be assumed, since those 'waking and sleeping' (5.10, where he uses the two words in a sense different from that in 5.6 and 7) will be living ἅμα with Jesus.

Furthermore, as soon as this question came up, the unanimous answer was that at the end all people involved would partake in the events at the same time. With regard to God's judgement there was no earlier and later. Everything would happen simultaneously.

We should like to end with a few words regarding the question whether the problems in Thessalonica arose under influence from outside. Most likely in this situation where emphasis was laid upon the end of time, the question about those dying before that time was bound to arise. The problem is unavoidable given the existence of the prophetic eschatology and the addition of the idea of a resurrection of the dead. Paul's answer is traditional. It is the answer of the apocalypses.

NOTES

1 They can be found in the well-known commentaries of which I particularly mention B. Rigaux, *Saint Paul. Les Épîtres aux Thessaloniciens*, in Études Bibliques (Paris-Gembloux 1956).

2 We refer among others to W. Schmithals, *Paulus und die Gnostiker. Untersuchungen zu den kleinen Paulusbriefen*, in Th. Forsch. XXXV

(Hamburg 1965), p. 118; and U. Luz, 'Das Geschichtsverständnis des Paulus', in *BEvTH.* 49 (1968), p. 321–2.

3 cf. H.-A. Wilcke, 'Das Problem eines messianischen Zwischenreichs bei Paulus', in *Abhandl. z. Theol. des A. u. N.T.* 51 (Zürich 1967), p. 119; and W. Harnisch, 'Eschatologische Existenz. Ein exegetischer Beitrag zum Sachanliegen von 1 Thessalonicher 4.13—5.11, in *FRLANT* 110 (Göttingen 1973), pp. 21–2.

4 Schmithals, op. cit., p. 119.

5 U. Luz, op. cit., pp. 321–2.

6 See already J. E. Frame, *Epistles of St Paul to the Thessalonians,* ICC, p. 164; and also W. Marxsen, 'Auslegung von 1 Thess. 4. 13–18', in *ZThK.* 66 (1969), pp. 22–37, esp. p. 30.

7 We may say that this is a general opinion, although the idea of a messianic kingdom, defended in the past by R. Stähelin, 'Zur paulinischen Eschatologie', in *Jahrbücher für Deutsche Theologie* 19 (1874), pp. 177–237, is rejected in this connection. Usually one speaks about 'the great events at the coming of the Messiah', cf. E. Haack, 'Eine exegetisch-dogmatische Studie zur Eschatologie über 1 Thessalonicher 4.13–18', in *Zeitschr. f. system. Theol.* 15 (1938), pp. 544–69, esp. p. 548; Wilcke, op. cit., p. 119; and Rigaux, op. cit., p. 527.

8 P. Volz, *Die Eschatologie der jüdischen Gemeinde im neutestamentlichen Zeitalter* (Tübingen 1934), pp. 232–5.

9 In the MSS we meet readings like *credidistis, -disti, -dit* and *-derit.* We followed the text of Bensly, Gry and the vg. reading *credidit, is.* Instead of *quas* the MSS show *quem, quod* or *quos.*

10 See also Apocalypse of Baruch 29.2; 40.2 and 71.1; and J. M. Myers, *2 Esdras,* The Anchor Bible (Garden City, New York, 1974), pp. 248–9.

11 See A. Oepke, *Der erste Brief an die Thessalonicher,* Das Neue Testament Deutsch 8 (Göttingen 1949), p. 137, who refers to this passage.

12 The word 'occurrentes' may be a translation of φθάνειν εἰς; cf. Dan. 12.12–13, quoted above.

13 The word 'vivificabi[s]' is necessary, but the MSS read '-cabit' and '-cabitur'. The words between brackets are not in Latin manuscripts, but are present in Ethiopic, Syriac and Arabic (ed. Ewald). They have been added to the Latin text by Bensly and Violet.

8

Πᾶσαι ἐξουσίαι αὐτῷ ὑποταγήσονται

Matthew Black

In his influential little book *According to the Scriptures: the Sub-structure of New Testament Theology*[1] – an early look at the theological use of Old Testament testimonia in the New Testament – C. H. Dodd drew attention to the frequency with which Ps. 110.1 (LXX 109.1) appears, in a variety of passages and combinations. It was 'one of the fundamental texts of the kerygma, underlying all the various developments of it, and cited independently in Mark, Acts, Paul, Hebrews and 1 Peter'.[2] One of the best known of these testimonia is the linked proof-texts of Ps. 110.1 with Dan. 7.13 at Mark 14.62, providing the 'sub-structure' of a fundamental piece of Christian doctrine, the session of Christ at God's right hand and the prediction of his Parousia.[3]

Among other 'echoes of the Psalm' in the New Testament, which do not seem to have been so thoroughly explored, three occur at 1 Cor. 15.24–7; Eph. 1.20–1; and 1 Pet. 3.22.[4] What is of special interest in these passages is that, in addition to their use of the same basic proof-text, all three associate Christ's ascension or session at God's right hand and his victory over his enemies (Ps. 110.1) with his destruction or subjugation of angelic 'powers', 'principalities and powers', evidently, in all three passages envisaged as man's arch-enemies, although at 1 Cor. 15.26 death is listed with them as 'the last enemy' (cf. Rom. 8.38–9).

1 Cor. 15.24–5 reads (in the NEB but my italics): (v. 20 '. . . Christ was raised to life . . .') v. 24 'Then comes the end (τὸ τέλος), when he delivers up the kingdom to God the Father, after abolishing every kind of *domination, authority* and *power* (πᾶσαν ἀρχὴν καὶ πᾶσαν ἐξουσίαν καὶ δύναμιν). v. 25 For he is destined to reign *until God has put all enemies under his feet* (ἄχρι οὗ θῇ πάντας τοὺς ἐχθροὺς ὑπὸ τοὺς πόδας αὐτοῦ Ps. 110.1b); v. 26 and the last enemy to be abolished is death.' Eph. 1.20–1: '. . . when he raised him from the dead, when he *enthroned him at his right hand* in the heavenly realms (καθίσας ἐν δεξιᾷ αὐτοῦ ἐν τοῖς ἐπουρανίοις) far above all *government and authority, all power and dominion,*

74

and any title of sovereignty that can be named (ὑπεράνω πάσης ἀρχῆς καὶ ἐξουσίας καὶ δυνάμεως καὶ κυριότητος καὶ παντὸς ὀνόματος ὀνομαζομένου), not only in this age but in the age to come.' I Pet. 3.22: '. . . it brings salvation through the resurrection of Jesus Christ, who entered heaven after receiving *the submission of angelic authorities and powers*, and *is now at the right hand of God* (ὅς ἐστιν ἐν δεξιᾷ τοῦ Θεοῦ, πορευθεὶς εἰς οὐρανόν, ὑποταγέντων αὐτῷ ἀγγέλων καὶ ἐξουσιῶν καὶ δυνάμεων).'

The common element in these three passages, next to the proof-text Ps. 110.1, is the thought of Christ's destruction of or superiority to and subjugation of these angelic 'powers'. Clearly we have here to do with an early Christian ascension 'theologoumenon' or 'christologoumenon', in which Christ's victory predicted at Ps. 110.1 is to be over all 'principalities and powers'; it is a theological tradition common to Paul and Peter, and one to be further elaborated in Ephesians and Colossians (see below, p. 77f).

Ps. 110.1 is linked with Dan. 7.13 at Mark 14.62: here, in the testimony pattern behind these three passages in the epistles, Ps. 110.1 is combined with Dan. 7.26–7, which reads (NEB): 'Then the court shall sit, and he (the fourth beast) shall be deprived of his sovereignty, so that in the end (ἕως τέλους) *it may be destroyed and abolished*. The kingly power, sovereignty and greatness of all the kingdoms under heaven shall be given to the people of the saints of the Most High. Their kingly power is an everlasting power, and *all sovereignties shall serve* them (LXX πᾶσαι(αἱ)ἐξουσίαι αὐτῷ ὑποταγήσονται, Theod. πᾶσαι αἱ ἀρχαὶ αὐτῷ δουλεύσουσιν) and obey them.' At 1 Cor. 15.24 the τέλος and the destruction of the sovereignty of the last of Daniel's four kingdoms has been developed by a Christian interpretation (*pesher*) into the destruction of 'every kind of domination, authority and power'. 1 Pet. 3.22 contains a further similar development, using the same verb as Dan. 7.27 ὑποτάσσεσθαι for the 'subjugation' of these 'powers'. Eph. 1.21 underlines Christ's superiority over all such 'powers'. In all three passages, moreover, it will be noted that Christ's ascension and victory over the 'powers' are always prefaced by a statement about his resurrection. The words on which the Christian *pesher* is based are πᾶσαι ἐξουσίαι αὐτῷ ὑποταγήσονται, where, in the version of the LXX it is to God and not to the 'saints of the Most High' that the kingdoms of the world are to be subjected; and it is this interpretation of the LXX which the New Testament is following, only substituting Christ for the Danielic 'Most High'.

75

The writer of Daniel had clearly in mind the subjugation of earthly powers: the ἐξουσίαι or 'empires' of verse 27, parallel to the βασιλεία or מלכות which will supersede them, are the kind of tyrannies described in the earlier chapters. The identity, on the other hand, of the 'principalities and powers, dominions and authorities etc.' in the New Testament, is not in doubt: in the company of ἄγγελοι at 1 Pet. 3.22 and Rom. 8.38 (see below) they are unmistakably angelic 'evil powers' or rather celestial 'potentates' or 'tyrants', for the abstract, in most cases, stands for the concrete 'wielders of power' (cf. 1 Cor. 15.24 with 2.6, ἄρχοντες). They are cosmic or celestial potentates whose empires are among the 'hosts of heaven', κοσμοκράτορες τοῦ σκότους τούτου, Eph. 6.12, and most probably the astral deities of hellenistic religions accommodated within a Jewish-hellenistic angelology.[5] It would seem that this pre-Pauline testimony tradition, shared with 1 Peter and Ephesians, is a kind of eisegetic *pesher*, a super-imposed interpretation, reflecting current hellenistic – and no doubt also Christian – dualistic conceptions of the nature of the cosmos, ruled or rather dominated by angelic ἐξουσίαι. Whether the 'powers that be' in the Roman Empire, with their claims to divine status, were included in this order of 'imperialist' angels is a much debated issue (cf. the discussion of Rom. 13); certainly so far as 1 Cor. 2.6 and 15.24 are concerned (and perhaps other similar passages) the terms employed can be construed as not necessarily excluding the kingdoms of this world.[6]

Rom. 8.38–9 develops the theme further, but the general pattern of the underlying testimony tradition is the same: the resurrection and ascension (verse 34) precede the 'hymnic' rhetorical conclusion of verse 38. After the seven afflictions in verse 35, a list of ten 'powers', mostly arranged in pairs, follows.[7] That death comes first may be partly suggested by verse 36, but, as at 1 Cor. 15.26, it ranks along with the 'principalities and powers'. Whether this means that Paul regarded it as another 'demonic power' (Michel) may seem doubtful, since it is coupled with 'life'. 'Death and life' are no doubt here viewed together as 'eschatological' events for the Christian, and 'things present' and 'things to come' in this context are more than the mere present or future:[8] persecution, danger and even death were the present and imminent realities that confronted Paul's readers. The last pair οὔτε ὕψωμα οὔτε βάθος has been variously explained, including the theory that ὕψωμα is an astronomical term along with ταπείνωμα to describe proximity and distance to a star from the North Pole; βάθος is the region of heaven which is below the horizon. Thus Lietzmann supposes that 'astral forces' (*Sternenmächte*) are intended, which rule in the heights of heaven and in the depths beneath the horizon.[9] This explanation would certainly fit in well with the view that 'principalities and powers' are astral powers or potentates. An explanation from Hebrew cosmology has hitherto not been widely mooted. Hebrew and Aramaic רום, רומא and in particular Hebrew מרום are regularly used for the 'heights of heaven', and their opposite תהום = ἄβυσσος, lit. 'the primeval deep' but also 'the depths of the earth (Ps. 71.20 Sheol?). This would be supported by the terminology of Phil. 2.10, ἵνα ἐν τῷ ὀνόματι Ἰησοῦ πᾶν γόνυ κάμψῃ ἐπουρανίων καὶ ἐπιγείων καὶ καταχθονίων (cf. Eph. 3.10 ἐξουσίαι ἐν τοῖς ἐπουρανίοις). The last term, 'nor any other created thing' (οὔτε τις κτίσις ἑτέρα) is inclusive of the entire creation, heaven, earth and beneath the earth, but also implies that the 'principalities and powers' are no less created, not uncreated, beings.

The spatial concept is clearly intentionally prominent throughout these verses, in the idea of cosmic potentates no less than in the contrast between the heights of heaven and the deeps of earth. The believer is separated by an immensity of space and by angelic beings with cosmocratic powers from God who is in heaven above them all, with Christ seated at his right hand (verse 34). Nevertheless, these cosmic powers and immensities shall not have the power (δυνήσεται) to sever the bond of the love of God which is in Christ (cf. Rom 5.4f). Here it is the love of God in Christ which is the stronger 'power'.

The theme of 'principalities and powers' is further pursued and developed in the deutero-Pauline epistles. Col. 1.16 seems to be a 'pre-Gnostic' pericope insisting, as at Eph. 1.31, on the superiority of Christ to all such powers but adding the thought that they were in fact created by him. Similarly at Eph. 3.20 the many-faceted wisdom of God in the gospel is said to have been disclosed 'through the church' to these angelic potentates; and at Eph. 6.10 the nature of the Christian warfare is defined in terms of a battle with these powers of darkness.

There are several further unresolved problems connected with the terminology for these angelic 'powers'. Simply to say that they are 'originally terms of Jewish speculation' explains little.[10] What evidence is there elsewhere for such a cosmic angelology and to what, if any, Hebrew or Aramaic background can these terms be traced? How are we to differentiate between the different terms, especially where, in some cases, they are virtually synonymous (ἀρχαί, ἐξουσίαι, κυριότητες)?

The prominence accorded these cosmocratic powers at 1 Cor. 2.6; 15.24 and Rom. 8.38, and the central place they occupy in the theology of the deutero-Paulines shows clearly that they represent an important dimension in the hellenistic thought-world of the first century – one that was to be further developed in the gnosticism of the second – as well as in the thought of Paul and Paulinism. The situation was no different in the Palestinian Judaism of the first century. The Qumran scrolls have provided us with ample evidence of a similar highly developed angelology, *on a cosmic scale*, which goes far beyond the Old Testament, though it clearly builds on Old Testament angelology. The cosmos is ruled by angelic agents or agencies, good and bad, *'elim* (lit. 'deities', θεοί), 'sons of heaven', 'holy ones', 'angels' (lit. 'messengers'), 'spirits', 'spirits of eternity', as well as the named potentates, Michael, Prince of Light, Belial, Prince of Darkness, Mastema.[11]

In spite of the general cosmic character of the two angelologies, the Pauline hellenistic and the Qumran Palestinian, they appear to have no elements in common which could explain the abstract Pauline terminology.[12] Moreover, while it is usually assumed that Paul is dependent on contemporary Jewish, presumably hellenistic Jewish nomenclature, the evidence for this, so far as contemporary sources are concerned, is extremely exiguous and could be ambivalent, consisting mainly of a single verse from 1 Enoch (61.10) (from the Book of the Parables, now allegedly Christian[13]) and another isolated verse in the Testaments of the Twelve Patriarchs (Levi 3.8, itself possibly deriving from Enoch). The terminology of the Slavonic Enoch (20.1), like that of the Christian Testament of Solomon,[14] seems also to reproduce traditions from the older Enoch apocalypse.

The question of the character and date of the Parables of Enoch is still *sub judice*,[15] and I have argued elsewhere for a pre-Pauline date for its semitic (in my opinion Hebrew) *Vorlage* or *Urschrift*,[16] so that the evidence of 1 Enoch 61.10 cannot be ignored, and indeed becomes all the more important in view of the paucity of other evidence from this period; and Test. Levi 3.8 could also preserve ancient Jewish angelological tradition from other parts of Enoch or even independently of 1 Enoch. In addition, 2 Macc. 3.24, a piece of evidence apparently hitherto unnoted in this connection, deserves to be considered. But more important, in some respects, than any of these verses for our problem is an astronomical (or calendrical) fragment preserved at 4QEnastr[b] 28 (Milik, *The Books of Enoch*, p. 295), which offers a reasonable explanation of the origins of at least three of these Pauline terms, while at the same time supporting the older evaluation of 1 Enoch 61.10.

Ethiopic Enoch 61.10 is still universally regarded by commentators and others as our main ancient authority for the terms, in particular the 'principalities and powers' at Rom. 8.38.[17] Sanday and Headlam (followed by Cranfield) quote the entire verse from the 1897 translation of R. H. Charles: 'And he will call on all the host . . . of God, the Cherubim, the Seraphim, and Ophanim, and all the angels of power, and all the angels of principalities, and the Elect One, and the other powers on the earth, over the water, on that day . . .' In the 1912 edition Charles states: 'These are exactly St Paul's "principalities and powers".' If we are to be guided, however, by the Ethiopic version of Col. 1.16 and Rom. 8.38, the second expression corresponds to κυριότητες ('dominions') not to ἀρχαί ('principalities'), and the text reads 'angels of power' and 'angels of dominions', and not *ḫayl* (δυνάμεῖς Rom. 8.38) or *'aga'ezet* (κυριότητες as at Col. 1.16). The Ethiopic version could of course be simply translating Greek δυνάμεῖς and κυριότητες; but it is not exactly 'St Paul's "principalities and powers"'.

At 2 Macc 3.22f we learn that Antiochus Epiphanes dispatched his grand vizier Heliodorus to Jerusalem to ransack the Temple treasury: 'But at that very moment when he arrived with his bodyguard at the treasury, the Ruler of spirits and of all the powers (ὁ τῶν πνευμάτων καὶ πάσης ἐξουσίας δυνάστης) produced a mighty apparition so that all . . . were . . . striken with panic at the power of God . . .' (NEB) There then appeared an angelic warrior, clad in golden armour and of terrible aspect, accompanied by two young men 'of surpassing strength', and Heliodorus was struck down on the spot. We should probably take ἐξουσία as abstract for concrete; God is described as 'Ruler of spiritual beings and of all (celestial) potentates'. It is by an apparition of three such 'spiritual beings' that Heliodorus is overpowered. The title used here for God is almost certainly an interpretation of the Hebrew 'Lord of hosts' (LXX κύριος τῶν δυνάμεων);[18] and the meaning of ἐξουσίαι for spiritual 'powers' or 'potentates' is not in doubt in such a context.

In the astronomical section of 1 Enoch there are several references to 'powers' (*šeltanat*) of the heavenly bodies, e.g. Enoch 72.1; 82.10. It is this last verse which is preserved in the Aramaic fragment 4Q Enastr[b] 28 where 'in their powers and in their positions' of the Ethiopic text is represented by בשלטנהון לכול מסרתהון 'in their powers with regard to all their positions'. The astronomical meaning of the term is not certain but in its contexts referring to the heavenly bodies the term would seem to refer either to the 'power' of the stars over the division of the year, the seasons and the epagomenal days[19] or the periods or places over which each star 'exercises dominion', i.e. when it is visible or ascendant or the places in the sky where it 'rules' (cf. Gen. 1.16 4Q Enastr[b] 7 iii.4, 8 (Milik, *The Books of Enoch*, pp. 279, 280)).

A synonymous term in Hebrew is used in the same connection: 1QH 1.11 speaks of the winds as 'angels', 'eternal spirits' 'in their dominions' (בממשלותם), and 1QM 17.6–7 refers to the 'authority' (משרה)[20] of Michael (for the noun, cf. Isa. 9.6). Either the Hebrew or the Aramaic noun could lie behind the Pauline terminology; as we have seen, at Dan. 7.27 כל שלטניא 'all dominions' is rendered by πᾶσαι (αἱ) ἐξουσίαι in the LXX and by πᾶσαι αἱ ἀρχαί in Theodotion.

Is it to this astronomical or calendrical usage that the abstract terms ἐξουσίαι, ἀρχαί, κυριότητες are ultimately to be traced, all deriving from synonymous translations of the semitic term?

The term δύναμις is well attested in hellenistic sources in the sense of a 'super-terrestrial being', but in its meaning of a cosmic angelic force or agency, personalized as an 'astral angel', it may also owe something to semitic tradition. It is the Aramaic and Syriac חיל equivalent of the Hebrew צבא for the 'hosts' of heaven, the stars, e.g. Targum 1 Kings 22.19; cf. Test. Levi 3.3 αἱ δυνάμεῖς τῶν παρεμβολῶν 'the hosts of the armies (of angels)' which are ordained for the day of judgement'. (Cf. 3.5 αἱ δυνάμεῖς τῶν ἀγγέλων.) For the Hebrew mind these are the 'forces' of heaven in this military sense; blended, however, with Greek usage, 'powers' convey the idea of miracle-working agencies or agents.

The term θρόνοι seems best explained as a case of synecdoche, where a personal subject is again intended. It comes as the first of the 'powers' at Col. 1.16, no doubt as implying the dignity of a monarch or a judge; cf. Origen, *de Princ.* i.53; i.62 'iudicandi vel regendi . . . habentes officium'. Origen may be right in putting the office of judge first in view of Dan. 7.9; the word is also used for the 'seat' of a governor (Neh. 3.7). There does not appear, however, to be any Hebrew or Aramaic usage which could account for the term – unless, again, we have simply another version of שולטניא. Suggestions that there is a reference to 'throne-angels', the Cherubim who bear the throne of God, should be rejected.[21]

The fact that all of these Greek words were in common use for earthly powers and authorities (with the possible exception of θρόνοι) would make all of them readily applicable to 'higher powers' and comprehensible as such in a hellenistic world which did not hesitate to multiply deities or angels. If they are all derived from the same semitic expression, attempts to differentiate between them, none of which has hitherto proved very successful,[22] seem unnecessary. It is certainly clear that Paul and Peter did not invent these terms; they were already there in the tradition. We are still left with the problem of the paucity of their occurrence in contemporary hellenistic sources, but here the Slavonic Enoch together with Gnostic and rabbinical traditions[23] may well have preserved expressions which have all but disappeared in the earlier period.

NOTES

1 London 1952.

2 op. cit., p. 35.

3 cf. Norman Perrin, 'Mark xiv. 62: the End Product of a Christian Pesher Tradition' in *NTS* 13 (1965–6), pp. 150f.

4 For a brief discussion of them, cf. J. Daniélou, 'La Session à la droite du Père' in TU, Bd 73 (1979), pp. 694f.; B. Lindars, *New Testament Apologetic* (London 1961), pp. 50f.

5 See the excellent discussion of this cosmic dimension of St Paul's thought by G. H. C. Macgregor: 'Principalities and Powers: the Cosmic Background of Paul's Thought' in *NTS* 1 (1954–5), pp. 17f. It was preceded by two equally percipient studies, by William Manson 'Principalities and Powers', SNTS *Bulletin* III, pp. 7f; and J. S. Stewart, 'On a Neglected Emphasis in New Testament Theology', in *SJT* iv (1951), pp. 293f.

6 See the discussion in A. T. Hanson, *The New Testament Interpretation of Scripture* (London 1980), p. 23.

7 The position of δυνάμεις in the best texts in this verse is unexpected: normally it would follow ἀρχαί (and does so in the TR) (the variant reading ἐξουσία(ι) preceding or following it has probably been imported by a scribe from the parallels elsewhere). Sanday and Headlam (p. 223) think of a possible primitive error where δυνάμεις has been first accidentally omitted by a scribe and then reinserted in a wrong place. The order elsewhere at 1 Cor. 15.24; Eph. 1.21 certainly favours the reading of the TR.

8 cf. C. E. B. Cranfield, *The Epistle to the Romans*, ICC (Edinburgh 1975), p. 442.

9 *Commentary on Romans*, Handbuch zum NT III.1, p. 46.

10 J. A. Robinson, *St Paul's Epistle to the Ephesians* (London 1904), on 1.21; cf. B. F. Westcott, *The Epistle to the Hebrews* (London 1889), on 2.5–8.

11 See Y. Yadin, *The Scroll of the Sons of Light against the Sons of Darkness* (Oxford 1962), 'The Angelology of the Scroll', pp. 229f.

12 With '*elim*, cf. 1 Cor. 8.4–6 (λεγόμενοι θεοί); for ἄγγελοι and πνεύματα Heb. 1.7 (Ps. 104.4).

13 cf. J. T. Milik, *The Books of Enoch: Aramaic Fragments of Qumran 4* (Oxford 1976), pp. 89f.

14 Ed. C. C. McCown (1922), *TWNT*, ii, p. 568, n50; E. Schürer, *History of the Jewish People* (Edinburgh 1902), Division II, vol. iii, p. 153.

15 cf. J. Fitzmyer, 'Implications of the New Enoch Literature from Qumran', *Theol. Studies*, vol. 38(2) (1977), pp. 341f.

16 M. Black, 'The Composition, Character and Date of the "Second Vision" of Enoch', *Text-Wort-Glaube: Studien zur Uberlieferung, Interpretation und Autorisierung Biblischer Texte Kurt Aland Gewidmet*, herausgegeben von Martin Brecht (Berlin 1980), pp. 19–30.

17 cf. Bousset-Gressmann, *Die Religion des Judentums* ([4]Tübingen 1966), p. 326.

18 See my article 'Two Unusual *Nomina Dei* in the Second Vision of Enoch', in the Bo Reicke Festschrift (Brill, Leiden, forthcoming).

19 A suggestion made to me by Professor O. Neugebauer, of the Institute for Advanced Study in Princeton, who has made a special study of the Enoch calendar: *Ethiopic Astronomy and Computus* (Vienna 1979). See also 'The "Astronomical" Chapters of the Ethiopic Book of Enoch: Translation and Commentary by Otto Neugebauer, with Additional Notes on the Aramaic Fragments by Matthew Black', *Det Kongelige Danske Videnskabernes Selskab Matematisk-fysiske Meddelelser* 40 (10), Copenhagen 1981, pp. 10, 34.

20 At 1QM 17.5 Belial is referred to as 'the prince of the dominion of wickedness' (שר ממשלת רשעה).

21 cf. J. Lightfoot, *Colossians* (London 1897), p. 152. For στοιχεῖα in this connection, see G. H. C. Macgregor, op. cit., pp. 21f.

22 cf. C. K. Barrett, *The First Epistle to the Corinthians*, BNTC (London 1968), p. 357.

23 See *TWNT* ii, pp. 568f.

9

Ἅγιοι en Colossiens 1.12: Hommes ou Anges?*

P. Benoit

Vers le début de sa lettre aux Colossiens, Paul, que j'en crois l'auteur,[1] exhorte ses lecteurs à 'rendre grâces au Père de ce qu'il les a rendus capables de participer au sort des saints dans la lumière' (Col. 1.12). On est au terme de l'introduction, formulée comme à l'ordinaire par mode d'action de grâces (vv. 3–8) et de prière (vv. 9 s); εὐχαριστοῦντες se rattache matériellement aux participes précédents, des vv. 10 et 11. En fait ce participe de force impérative (comparer Rom. 12.9–13) amorce une modulation qui va déboucher sur le grand thème de l'oeuvre rédemptrice du Christ (vv. 14–22).

Ce verset 12 pose plusieurs problèmes. D'une part, le sens exact de chacun de ses termes, surtout de ἅγιοι et de φῶς; d'autre part, leurs connexions: comment entendre le lien génitif de τοῦ κλήρου avec τὴν μερίδα, et à quoi se rattache ἐν τῷ φωτί? A ἁγίων? ou à τοῦ κλήρου τῶν ἁγίων? ou à τὴν μερίδα τοῦ κλήρου τῶν ἁγίων? ou même à τῷ ἱκανώσαντι?

Disons, pour commencer, que le sens de ce verbe ne devrait pas faire difficulté. Ἱκανός signifiant 'suffisant, convenable', le verbe ἱκανόω, qui en dérive, peut exprimer une suffisance quantitative: au passif, 'avoir assez', 'être satisfait', 'se contenter' de ce qu'on reçoit ou fait; ou une suffisance qualitative: 'être rendu capable de, qualifié, accrédité, habilité'. Je dis 'au passif' car c'est en cette voix seulement que le verbe est utilisé chez les écrivains profanes et par les Septante. L'actif n'apparaît que chez Paul, ici et 2 Cor. 3.6, au sens qualitatif de 'rendre capable de, apte à', mais non pas 'rendre digne': *dignos* de la Vulgate est inexact, mieux *idoneos*. Ce verbe a paru difficile à certains copistes, qui l'ont remplacé par le banal καλέσαντι, peut-être sous l'influence de 1 Pet. 2.9: ὑμᾶς καλέσαντος εἰς τὸ θαυμαστὸν αὐτοῦ φῶς: ainsi D* G 33 d g arm go. Le codex B a une leçon confluente: τῷ καλέσαντι καὶ ἱκανώσαντι ὑμᾶς.

Ceux qui sont ainsi 'qualifiés', sont-ils Paul et tous les chrétiens en général (ἡμᾶς)? ou particulièrement les Colossiens (ὑμᾶς)? La confu-

* See English summary on p. 100

sion entre ces deux formes est facile et fréquente (iotacisme), et ici les autorités textuelles s'équilibrent, sinon par la quantité des témoins, plus nombreux pour ἡμᾶς, du moins par la qualité: en face de A C PΨ D G K L 33 vetlat vg pes sy^h bo pour ἡμᾶς, on a B S (P^46 deest) 1739 sa sy^hmg arm go eth pour ὑμᾶς. Les Pères sont partagés, comme aussi les éditeurs et les commentateurs modernes. Aussi le choix doit-il se faire plutôt d'après les exigences du contexte. Et alors beaucoup dépend du sens que l'on donnera à τῶν ἁγίων. S'il s'agit des chrétiens en général, ou plus particulièrement des judéo-chrétiens de Jérusalem, ὑμᾶς paraît préférable: les païens qu'étaient les Colossiens doivent remercier le Père de les avoir associés à la destinée lumineuse du peuple élu. Mais si les ἅγιοι sont les anges, ἡμᾶς semble mieux convenir, car ce sont tous les chrétiens, d'origine juive ou païenne, que le Père a rendus capables de participer à la condition bienheureuse de ces êtres célestes.

Avant de rechercher le sens précis de ἅγιοι, ce qui sera notre principal problème, il convient de déterminer celui de μερίς et de κλῆρος, ainsi que l'enchaînement de ces deux termes. Etymologiquement ils se distinguent. Μερίς évoque l'idée de division, de partage: d'où 'part', 'portion'. Κλῆρος connote l'idée de tirage au sort, d'où l'effet qui en résulte, 'lot', 'sort', 'destin', avec la nuance de gratuité qu'implique l'intervention supérieure, voire divine, dans le tirage au sort.[2] Les deux mots μερίς et κλῆρος se rencontrent fréquemment dans les Septante, en particulier à propos des portions de territoire que Josué assigna à chaque tribu par tirage au sort; cf. par exemple, Num. 26.55s.; 34.13; 36.2, etc.; Jos. 14.2; 18.6. Celle de Lévi, toutefois, n'avait pas pour portion un territoire, mais Yahweh lui-même (Num. 18.20; Deut. 10.9; 18.1s., etc.; Ecclus. 45.22). De fait, à partir du sens premier, matériel, s'est développé un sens métaphorique, selon lequel la 'part' désigne le 'sort' de quelqu'un, sa destinée, soit mauvaise (Isa. 57.6; Jer. 13.25; Sag. 2.9; Actes 8.21), soit bonne, et alors cette bonne part est Dieu lui-même ou le salut qu'il assure à ses amis (Ps. 15(16).5; 72(73).26), ou inversement c'est Israël qui est la 'portion' du Seigneur (Zach. 2.16; Ecclus. 17.17; 24.12), son 'lot' (Deut. 9.29).

Μερίς traduit le plus souvent חלק, tandis que κλῆρος rend souvent נחלה dans le Pentateuque, et plutôt גורל dans les Ketuvim postérieurs, les Sapientiaux et les Prophètes. Leur relative équivalence fait qu'ils sont souvent associés comme des synonymes et apparaissent alors, soit accouplés en parallèle tautologique: par exemple Deut. 10.9; 12.12; 18.1; Isa. 57.6; Jer. 13.25; Sag. 2.9; Actes 8.21; avec le terme voisin κληρονομία: Gen. 31.14; Num. 18.20; 2 Rois 20.1 grec; Ecclus. 45.22;

soit reliés au moyen du génitif: Ps. 15(16).5; Ecclus. 24.12. Cette dernière construction nous intéresse particulièrement parce qu'elle est celle de Col. 1.12. Elle peut être entendue d'un génitif partitif: la participation au sort, ou à l'héritage. Ainsi le comprennent un certain nombre de commentateurs.[3] D'autres songent plutôt à un génitif d'apposition: la part qui consiste dans le lot.[4] En faveur de cette dernière option, on pourrait invoquer la tendance de l'épître aux Colossiens (et davantage encore l'épître aux Ephésiens) à accumuler des substantifs, parfois synonymes, en les reliant par le mode de construction génitivale,[5] tour de style sémitisant qui s'observe notamment dans les écrits de Qumrân.[6] Et nous allons précisément reconnaître dans ce passage un vocabulaire familier à la secte de Qumrân. Néanmoins le génitif partitif garde ici de sérieuses chances. Les deux termes qu'il relie ne sont pas parfaitement synonymes et l'on croit sentir dans le substantif μερίδα la force du verbe μερίζεσθαι: le Père les a rendus capables de participer au sort des saints.

Le mot חלק apparaît fort peu à Qumrân, mais le mot גורל y est fréquent, soit au sens de la place assignée à chacun dans la communauté (1 QS 2.23), voire de son admission (1 QS 6.16,18,22; 1 QSa 1.9), soit plus souvent au sens de la destinée dans un des deux partis opposés: le lot de ténèbres (1 QM 1.11), ou des fils de ténèbres (1 QM 1.1), de Béliar (1 QS 2.5; 1 QM 1.5), de la perversion (1 QS 4.24), et le lot de la lumière (1 QM 13.9; CD 13.12), de la vérité (1 QM 13.12), de Dieu (1 QS 2.2; 1 QM 13.5).

Particulièrement intéressants pour nous sont les passages où le lot à partager est celui des 'saints' (1 QS 11.7s.; 1 QH 3.22, 11.11s.). Mais avant d'examiner de plus près ces parallèles importants, il nous faut passer en revue les diverses façons dont on peut entendre les 'saints' de Col. 1.12.

Depuis longtemps et maintenant encore, on a spontanément songé aux chrétiens en général.[7] Déjà dans l'Ancien Testament était 'saint', c'est-à-dire consacré, séparé du profane, tout ce qui appartenait à Yahweh, le Saint par excellence (Isa. 6.3), le 'Saint d'Israël' (Isa. 1.4, etc. *passim*; Ps. 71(70).22; 78(77).41): 'soyez saints, car moi, Yahweh votre Dieu, je suis saint' (Lev. 19.2; 20.26, etc.): d'où l'épithète de 'saint' accordée, non seulement au peuple d'Israël dans son ensemble (Exod. 19.6; Deut. 7.6; Dan. 3.35 grec; 2 Mac. 15.24; Sag. 17.2) ou à certains de ses membres privilégiés (Aaron, Ps. 106(105).16; les prêtres, Lev. 21.6s.; Ecclus. 45.24 grec; les Nazirs, Num. 6.5; le Reste, Isa. 4.3; 62.12), mais encore à tous les Israélites: ils sont 'les saints' (Ps.

34(33). 10;[8] 82.4[LXX]; Dan. 7.8[LXX], 21, 22b, 8.24[9]; Sag. 18.9; Tob. 12.15[BA]; 1 Mac. 1.46.

De l'Ancien Testament cette épithète est passée au Nouveau. Les membres du nouvel Israël, sanctifiés par la foi et le baptême (1 Cor. 6.11) qui les rattachent au Christ, sont 'les saints': cf. Actes 9.13,32,41: 26.10; Rom. 8.27; 12.13; 16.2,15; 1 Cor. 6.1s.; 14.33; 2 Cor. 13.12; Eph. 1.15; 3.18; 4.12; 5.3; 6.18; Phil. 4.22; Col. 1.4; 1 Tim. 5.10; Philém. 5.7; Heb. 6.10; 13.24; Jude 3; Apoc. 5.8, etc.; et dans les adresses des épîtres, 2 Cor. 1.1, etc. Ici Paul exhorterait donc les gens de Colosses, qui étaient des païens (Col. 1.27; 2.13) à remercier Dieu de les avoir intégrés au salut chrétien. La 'lumière' est alors la connaissance de la Vérité qui fonde et baigne la foi chrétienne.[10] Jadis donnée à Israël par la Loi (Ps. 119(118).105; Prov. 6.23) et promise aux nations païennes (Isa. 49.6; 51.4; 60.1–3), cette lumière de la révélation brille désormais sur la face du Christ et resplendit par l'Evangile (2 Cor. 4.4–6). On peut donc dire que les chrétiens vivent 'dans la lumière' (1 Jean 1.7; 2.10), ou encore que le sort que Dieu leur accorde se situe 'dans la lumière', selon qu'on rattache les mots ἐν τῷ φωτί à τῶν ἁγίων,[11] ou bien à τοῦ κλήρου,[12] ou même à toute l'expression τὴν μερίδα τοῦ κλήρου τῶν ἁγίων.[13] Les rattacher à ἱκανώσαντι comme d'aucuns l'ont voulu,[14] ne convient guère: ce participe est déjà quelque peu éloigné; par ailleurs la valeur instrumentale de la préposition ἐν n'est pas ici spontanée; elle est plutôt locale: φῶς qui s'oppose à σκότος du verset suivant évoque l'idée d'un domaine où l'on réside plutôt que celle d'un moyen dont Dieu se serait servi pour convertir.

Au fait, ce problème de construction n'est pas très important. Ce qui l'est davantage, c'est la façon dont on entend la lumière. Si elle désigne le domaine où règne la clarté de Dieu, on entrevoit une autre perspective de la situation eschatologique des 'saints', même entendus au sens de chrétiens. On se sent invité, en effet, à envisager le domaine céleste où cette lumière s'épanouit définitivement. Alors que les exégètes que nous venons de citer pensent plutôt à l'eschatologie commencée,[15] terrestre, où la lumière de l'Evangile se répand dans le monde d'ici-bas, les exégètes récents songent davantage à l'eschatologie consommé, où les hommes Bienheureux baignent dans la lumière céleste. Nous retrouverons plus loin cette interprétation à propos des 'saints' Anges, au sort desquels les 'saints' hommes Bienheureux sont associés.

Avant d'en venir à cette autre interprétation, il faut relever une nuance qui peut être apportée au sens de ἅγιοι entendus comme chrétiens. Il s'agirait plus précisément des chrétiens d'origine juive, ceux de Jérusalem, les premiers appelés au salut du Christ.[16] Cette application restrictive du terme s'observe dans plusieurs lettres de Paul, notamment quand il s'agit de la collecte qu'il organise dans ses églises en faveur des pauvres de la Judée.[17] 'La Macédoine et l'Achaïe ont bien voulu prendre part aux besoins des saints de Jérusalem qui sont dans la pauvreté'[18] (Rom. 15.26; cf. 15.25,31; 1 Cor. 16.1,15; 2 Cor. 8.4; 9.1,12). La même nuance se retrouve en Eph. 2.19,[19] où le contexte montre clairement que les saints, dont les païens de jadis (2.11–12) sont devenus les 'concitoyens', sont les chrétiens originaires de la 'cité d'Israël', fondés sur les apôtres et les prophètes avec le Christ comme pierre d'angle (v.20). Cette nuance plus précise du terme ἅγιοι pourrait convenir à Col. 1.12. En fait, rien dans le contexte ne l'exige. D'ailleurs elle ne change pas substantiellement l'exégèse qui voit dans les ἅγιοι les chrétiens en général.

Il en va autrement de l'opinion qui reconnaît dans les ἅγιοι des Anges.[20] Cette opinion ne manque certes pas de bons appuis dans les textes. Autant et plus que les hommes, les anges sont associés au Dieu très saint, comme étant sa cour céleste, ses messagers.[21] D'où, dans plusieurs textes de l'AT, l'épithète 'saints', accolée au substantif 'anges' (Job 5.1 grec.; Tob. 11.14; 12.15a[BA]) et le mot 'saints', employé lui-même comme substantif pour désigner des anges, ainsi que cela ressort, soit du contexte (Ecclus. 42.17 [hb.gr.], 45.2[gr.]; Tob. 8.15[BA]; Zach. 14.5; Dan. 4.14(17) [Theod.]; 34(37)a [LXX]; 8.13), soit du parallélisme avec des désignations explicites telles que 'anges' (en Dan, 4.10(13) et 20(23) קדיש est traduit par ἅγιος chez Theodotion et par ἄγγελος, dans les Septante) ou 'fils de Dieu' (Ps. 89(88). 6–8; Sag. 5.5) ou 'les cieux' (Job 15.15). Il est possible que 'la science des saints' en Prov. 9.10; 30.3; Sag. 10.10 soit celle des anges.

Dans le NT l'expression 'saints anges' se retrouve en Marc 8.38 et Luc 9.26; Apoc. 14.10; Actes 10.22. Les 'saintes myriades' de Jude 14 sont assurément angéliques comme dans Hénoch i.9, qu'il cite. Mais l'usage du substantif ἅγιοι au sens d' 'anges' y est beaucoup plus rare; il est même douteux. Les textes pauliniens, où il pourrait se rencontrer, outre celui que nous étudions à présent, sont Eph. 1.18; 1 Thess. 3.13; 2 Thess. 1.10.[22] Dans ce dernier texte, le parallèle de ἐνδοξασθῆναι ἐν τοῖς ἁγίοις αὐτοῦ avec θαυμασθῆναι ἐν πᾶσιν τοῖς πιστεύσασιν pourrait inviter à voir, dans les deux compléments, des hommes qui ont cru et qui sont devenus des 'saints' en qui le Seigneur se glorifie.[23]

Mais il semble préférable de reconnaître ici un parallèle antithétique, selon lequel le Seigneur sera 'glorifié' dans ses saints, les anges (cf. Ps.89(88).8), et 'admiré' dans ses fidèles, les hommes.[24] L'interprétation de 1 Thess. 3.13 est très discutée. D'une part il est certain que les anges font normalement partie du cortège du Seigneur lors de la Parousie: cf. Matt. 16.27 par.; 24.30–1 par.; 25.31; 1 Thess. 4.16; 2 Thess 1.7; et voir encore Matt. 13.41; Apoc. 3.5. D'autre part il est vrai que d'anciens textes chrétiens ont repris Zach. 14.5 en voyant dans les 'saints' qui accompagnent le Christ dans sa parousie, des hommes ressuscités. Ainsi la Didachè 16.7, reprise par les Constitutions apostoliques 7.32,4, l'Ascension d'Isaïe 4.14–16; peut-être l'Apocalypse de Pierre 1. Mais ces textes, que le P. Rigaux (*comm. ad loc.*) invoque pour défendre le même sens en 1 Thess. 3.13, représentent une imagerie de la Parousie, développée en milieu chrétien, qui ne se rencontre pas encore dans le NT, pas même chez Paul (voir les textes cités plus haut; 1 Thess. 4.14–17 est différent) et que rien n'autorise à introduire en 1 Thess 3.13. Il semble donc préférable de reconnaître des anges dans les 'saints' de ce passage, comme déjà en ceux de 2 Thess. 1.10, ... à moins encore qu'une extension du terme n'autorise à y voir à la fois des anges et des hommes devenus leurs compagnons célestes, hypothèse que nous allons retrouver.

Eph. 1.18 est une reprise parallèle de Col. 1.12 et nous intéresse donc particulièrement ici. La perspective y est nettement celle de l'eschatologie céleste,[25] où s'épanouit 'la richesse de la gloire de l'héritage de Dieu dans les saints'. Qui sont ces 'saints'? On invoque ordinairement une réminiscence littéraire de Deut. 33.3s.; mais, même si elle est fondée, elle n'éclaire pas grand-chose. Dans le texte massorétique, corrompu et obscur, les קדשים (LXX ἡγιασμένοι) semblent être les Israélites; ainsi l'entend le Targum d'Onqelos. Quant à la מורשה (LXX κληρονομία), elle ne figure qu'au verset 4 et désigne la Loi de Moïse donnée en 'héritage' à l'assemblée de Jacob. Existait-il un autre état du texte, ou quelque adaptation d'un florilège qui aurait été utilisé par Eph. 1.18, ainsi que par Actes 20.32? Quoi qu'il en soit d'un tel chaînon très hypothétique, le texte actuel de Deut. 33.3s, en hébreu comme en grec, n'apporte vraiment aucun éclairage au problème qui nous occupe. Nous ne pouvons qu'interroger en lui-même le texte de Eph 1.18 et, en soulignant à nouveau son atmosphère d'eschatologie céleste (ἡ ἐλπὶς τῆς κλήσεως αὐτοῦ), reconnaître que les ἅγιοι peuvent y représenter aussi bien les anges que les hommes béatifiés. Pourquoi pas les deux? c'est-à-dire toute la société des êtres célestes, anges et hommes devenus leurs compagnons de béatitude?

C'est à cela que nous mène peut-être l'examen de l'usage de ce terme dans les pseudépigraphes, surtout Hénoch, et dans les écrits de Qumrân.

Un tel examen approfondi a été occasionné, dans les années récentes, par un débat engagé autour des 'Saints du Très-Haut' de Daniel 7.18, 22, 25, 27. A la suite de O. Procksch et de M. Noth,[26] L. Dequeker[27] et J. Coppens[28] ont voulu voir là des anges, tandis que C. H. W. Brekelmans[29] maintenait qu'il s'agit des hommes membres du peuple élu. La thèse de Noth a été critiquée également par R. Hanhart[30] et par G. F. Hasel.[31] Mais ces derniers, et aussi J. J. Collins,[32] ont fait remarquer que le dilemme, anges ou hommes, doit être assoupli. En fait, si les membres du peuple élu sont appelés 'saints', c'est souvent dans la mesure où ils sont associés au sort des anges, soit dès leur vie cultuelle et combattante d'ici-bas, soit dans la béatitude du ciel. En sorte que dans plus d'un texte le terme 'saints' peut désigner aussi bien les anges que les hommes qui leur sont associés.[33]

Les débats que j'évoque ont donné lieu à des listes utiles où sont rassemblés les textes des Pseudépigraphes, en particulier d'Hénoch, et ceux de Qumrân, où figure le terme 'saints'. Signalons notamment celles de Brekelmans, p. 307 ss.,[34] qui répartissent les textes en trois groupes: ceux où les 'saints' sont certainement des anges, ceux où ils sont certainement des hommes, et ceux dont l'interprétation est douteuse.

Dans le livre des Jubilés, les 'saints' désignent des anges, comme dans les écrits tardifs de l'AT et pour les mêmes raisons: ministres de Dieu et membres de sa cour céleste, ils sont consacrés par cette appartenance au Saint par excellence. 'Saint' est une épithète parallèle de 'ange' en 17.11; 31.14. Voir encore 33.12. Mais en 2.24 Jacob et sa descendance sont également 'bénis et saints' parce que Dieu les a choisis et sanctifiés, en leur confiant la loi du sabbat.

Le Testament de Lévi, 3.3 songe à des anges, quand il situe des 'saints' au-dessus des armées célestes du deuxième ciel. En revanche, les 'saints' de Test. Lévi, 18.11, 14; Test. Issachar, 5.4; Test. Dan, 5.11,12 désignent des hommes dans un contexte eschatologique de retour aux origines, du paradis terrestre et des Patriarches. On ne doit pas oublier toutefois que les Testaments des Douze Patriarches sont suspects d'interpolations chrétiennes.

Ce sont encore des hommes pieux de la race d'Israël qui sont ainsi désignés en 3 Mac. 6.9 (si le mot ἁγίοις, présent dans le seul codex A, y

est original). Mais on retrouve le sens d' 'anges' en Ps. Sal. 17.43 (49).
Quand à Ps. Sal. 11.1, le texte est trop obscur pour autoriser une
décision. Dans l'Apocalypse de Baruch (Bar. syr.) 66, 2, les 'saints',
dont Josias 'éleva la corne' sont évidemment des pieux Israélites, mis
en parallèle avec les 'justes', les 'sages', les 'prêtres'. De même dans les
Oracles Sibyllins, 5.161, les 'nombreux saints fidèles des Hébreux' et
432 où le triomphe du bien sur le mal marque 'le dernier temps des
saints'.

Rien ne se dégage de ces textes qui éclaire vraiment notre problème,
sinon le fait certain que, dans la littérature intertestamentaire comme
dans les écrits tardifs de l'AT, 'saints' peut-être dit, soit des anges, soit
des membres pieux du peuple élu.

Le livre d'Hénoch offre une moisson plus riche mais plus complexe.
Que les 'saints' dans Hénoch désignent,[35] tantôt des anges vivant au
ciel, tantôt des hommes vivant encore sur terre et appelés à vivre eux
aussi au ciel, ou y vivant déjà, la chose n'est pas douteuse. Qu'il suffise,
pour confirmer le premier sens, de renvoyer aux passages où se
rencontrent les 'saints anges', surtout dans le partie II, 20.1–8; 21.5,9;
22.3; 23.4; 27.2 (mais voir aussi 93.2), ou bien les 'anges saints', un peu
dans toutes les parties du livre: II, 24.6; 32.6; III, 46.1; 69.5; 71.1,8,9;
IV, 72.1; 74.2: VI, 100.5; VII, 108.5. Le substantif 'saints' semble bien
désigner des anges, surtout dans le livre des Paraboles: 47.2; 57.2; 60.4;
61.8,10; 69.13; 71.4, mais aussi dans celui de la 'chute des anges', II,
9.3; 12.2; 14.23,25; 15.4,9; et voir encore en I, 1.9; IV, 81.5. Quant au
deuxième sens, de 'saints' désignant des hommes vivant sur terre, il
paraît s'imposer dans plusieurs passages des Paraboles: 43.4; 50.1b;
58.5; 65.12b. Voir aussi en VI, 93.6; 99.16; 100.5.

Mais il se trouve, dans le livre des Paraboles, de nombreux passages
d'une interprétation plus malaisée, où les 'saints' sont juxtaposés aux
'justes' ou aux 'élus', ou aux deux à la fois, selon un ordre variable où
les 'saints' figurent tantôt en tête, tantôt en deuxième, ou même en
troisième place. On voit mal dans quelle mesure ce sont là des
accumulations de synonymes ou des énumérations de catégories
distinctes. Il semble bien que les 'justes' soient des hommes. C'est déjà
moins clair pour les 'élus', car on lit par exemple en 39.1: 'Les enfants
des élus et des saints descendront du haut du ciel, et une sera leur race
avec les enfants des hommes': allusion probable aux anges descendus
du ciel pour s'unir charnellement aux filles des hommes. Quant aux
'saints' de ces expressions bi- ou tripartites, ils peuvent encore parfois
désigner des anges, ainsi en 39.1 et peut-être en 47.4; mais le plus

souvent ils désignent des hommes, ainsi en 38.4,5; 41.2; 48.1,7,9; 50.1s; 51.2; 58.3; 62.8; 65.12b. Le texte 34.4–5 est caractéristique de l'ambivalence du terme:

> 4. Et là je vis une autre vision: les habitations des saints, et les lits de repos des justes. 5. Là mes yeux virent leurs habitations au milieu des anges de sa justice, et leurs lits de repos au milieu des saints.

La marche du texte semble requérir que les 'saints' de 4 soient des hommes (justes) et ceux de 5 des anges (de justice).

En plusieurs cas on ne sait vraiment que choisir: ainsi 45.1; 61.12; 65.12a, et aussi 103.2, 106.19, 108.3, où les tablettes du ciel, livres des saints, peuvent être en possession des saints (anges), ou contenir les noms des saints (hommes). Mais faut-il toujours choisir? Ne lit-on pas en 51.4: 'tous les justes deviendront des anges dans le ciel', ou en 104.4, 'vous jouirez d'une grande joie comme les anges dans le ciel'; 104.6, 'vous aurez part au sort de l'armée du ciel'? Dès lors, le même terme 'saints' ne peut-il pas, dans certains textes, inclure à la fois et des anges et des hommes associés à leur bienheureux sort? et cela non seulement au ciel, mais déjà sur la terre? Nous allons retrouver cette possibilité d'ambivalence dans les textes de Qumrân.[36]

A Qumrân on se préoccupe beaucoup de 'sainteté'.[37] De fondation sacerdotale, la communauté pratique la pureté lévitique et se consacre au service de Dieu, par la prière, l'ascèse et l'étude. L'observation intégrale de la Loi de Moïse et l'accomplissement des oracles prophétiques doivent, selon l'appel de Dieu, les introduire dans une Nouvelle Alliance qui prépare le triomphe définitif du bien sur le mal, de la lumière sur les ténèbres. Pour exprimer cet idéal et ce programme de vie, le mot 'sainteté' (קודש) se rencontre sans cesse dans leurs écrits, en toutes sortes de combinaisons: ils sont une 'maison / demeure / édifice de sainteté', dans une 'alliance de sainteté'; 'hommes de sainteté', ils suivent une 'voie de sainteté', produisent des 'fruits de sainteté', etc. etc.

Parmi ces expressions figurent les 'anges de sainteté' (1 QSa 2.8s; 1 QSb 3.6; 1 QM 7.6; 10.11). Car ils accordent une grande importance aux Anges. Avec ceux de leur parti de lumière, ils combattent les anges du parti adverse, des ténèbres (1 QM *passim*). Ils leur sont associés, non seulement dans le combat de la guerre eschatologique, mais aussi et surtout dans le service cultuel de la sainte liturgie (1 QSb 4.25–6).[38] Les anges sont présents dans leur communauté (1 QSa 2.8s; 1 QM 7.6;

12.7s; 4 QFlor (174) 1.4). Par la révêlation des mystères du plan divin de salut, ils participent à leur connaissance (1 QS 4.21–2; 1 QSb 1.5; 1 QH 3.22–3).[39] Cette association s'épanouit dans la vie éternelle du ciel, mais elle est déjà commencée ici-bas.[40]

On comprend, dans ces conditions, que le nom 'saints' se rencontre lui-même assez souvent dans ces écrits, et qu'il y désigne tantôt des anges, tantôt les membres de la communauté, tantôt les deux à la fois. Plusieurs d'entre eux expriment leur association dans une même destinée (גורל), future ou/et déjà présente; ces textes sont évidemment les plus intéressants pour notre propos.[41]

C'est dans le rouleau de la Guerre que les *Qedoshîm* apparaissent le plus souvent. Ils y sont, tantôt les hommes pieux de Qumrân, 'élus du peuple saint' (1 QM 12.1b), 'saints de son peuple' (6.6; 16.1), 'le peuple des saints de l'alliance' (10.10), qui guerroient contre les fils de ténèbres; et tantôt les anges, habitants du ciel (10.12; 12.1a), qui combattent avec les saints de la terre (12.4,7,8.; 15.14; cf. 1 QSb 3.5–6) pour vaincre les troupes de Bélial. On hésite, non seulement pour 1.16, trop fragmentaire, mais pour 3.5, 'les camps de ses saints', inscrits sur des trompettes, et 18.2, 'la clameur des saints': ces 'saints' sont probablement les hommes combattants, mais ne peuvent-ils inclure les anges qui participent à leur combat?[42]

Ce sont assurément des anges, mis en relation avec la connaissance, que désignent les 'saints' de 1 QSb 1.5; 4 QSl 39; I, 1.24. Mais on peut hésiter pour 1 QSb 3.26; 4.23: les 'saints' de l'assemblée liturgique au milieu ou à la tête desquels le prêtre officie ne sont-ils que les pieux fidèles de Qumrân, ou ne comprennent-ils pas les anges qui participent à leur assemblée? Quant aux 'saints du Très Haut' qui ont maudit l'essénien infidèle (Doc. Damas 20.8), on sait de quelle chaude discussion ils ont été l'objet: anges pour Rabin,[43] Dequeker,[44] hommes pour Nötscher,[45] les uns et les autres pour Lambgerits,[46] Jaubert.[47] Une fois encore, on se demande s'il faut choisir. 'Facile solution', dit Dequeker,[48] que d'associer ainsi saints anges et saints hommes. Je ne le pense pas, étant donnée l'étroite association qui les lie dans bien des textes.

Dans les *Hodaiot* 'l'assemblée des saints' (1 QH 4.25) groupe tous ceux qui ont entendu l'appel du 'Maître de justice' et sont entrés dans l'alliance. Ce sont donc encore les hommes membres de la communauté. Mais c'est d'anges qu'il s'agit en deux autres passages, soit des anges déchus (1 QH 10.35; cf. 1 QGenAp. 2.1), soit des 'fils du ciel' dont les hommes purifiés sont appelés à partager le destin éternel de

louange (1 QH 3.22s.). C'est ce thème qui nous intéresse particulièrement. Pour exprimer ce 'destin', nous avons ici le même terme גורל
que nous avons soupçonné derrière le κλῆρος de Col. 1.12. Et nous le
retrouvons encore dans le même contexte d'idées, avec 'saints' (anges)
en 1 Q36 1.3; 4 Q 181.1.4; avec 'anges de la Face' en 1QH 6.13; 1 QSb
4.26.

1 QH 11.10–13 pose un problème particulier:

> 10. tu as purifié l'homme du péché . . . afin qu'il se sanctifie . . .
> 11. afin qu'il soit uni avec tes fils de vérité et dans un [même] lot avec
> 12. tes saints; afin d'élever cette vermine qu'est l'homme de la
> poussière vers ton secret [de vérité] et de l'esprit pervers vers ton
> intelligence; et afin qu'il se tienne en faction devant toi avec l'armée
> éternelle et les esprits [lacune] et qu'il se renouvelle avec tout
> [lacune] et avec les Connaissants dans une commune jubilation.

Dans la fin de ce texte on retrouve clairement le même thème que dans
les textes précédents, et il paraît spontané de voir des anges dans les
'saints' du début de la ligne 12. Ainsi font plusieurs auteurs. Mais
H.-W. Kuhn[49] me semble avoir prouvé que 1 QH 11.10–13 est une
reprise de 1 QH 3.20–3, où l'entrée dans la communauté a été
introduite selon l'énumération suivante: purification, sanctification,
entrée dans la communauté, résurrection, et enfin communion avec
l'armée céleste. Dans cette perspective les 'saints' de la ligne 12 ne sont
pas encore les anges, mais les membres de la communauté. Sens
parfaitement possible, nous l'avons vu, et ici meilleur car 'fils de vérité',
qui lui fait parallèle, est toujours dit des hommes: cf. 1 QS 4.5–6; 1 QM
17.8; 1 QH 6.29; 7.29s; 9.35?; 10.27. Que le rédacteur de 1 QH 11.12
ait pu reprendre, en les déplaçant, les 'saints' (anges) de 1 QH 3.22 au
sens de saints hommes, rien ne montre mieux à quel point le terme était
à ses yeux ambivalent.

Le seul texte de la Règle de la Communauté où figure le substantif
'saints',[50] à savoir 1 QS 11.8, reprend ce terme avec le même sens et
dans le même contexte que les textes qui viennent d'être examinés.

'A ceux qu'il a élus' Dieu 'a accordé un partage avec le lot des Saints
et avec les Fils du ciel il a réuni leur assemblée.'

N'en déplaise à R. Hanhart,[51] il paraît clair que les 'Fils du ciel', et
donc les 'Saints' qui leur sont mis en parallèle, sont des anges. Ainsi que
nous l'avons vu plus haut, וינחילמ בגורל correspond fort bien à εἰς τὴν
μερίδα τοῦ κλήρου de Col. 1.12. Or il est remarquable que dans les

autres textes où גורל signifie un destin où l'homme est introduit, et même quand ce destin est celui des anges (1 QH 3.22; 1 QSb 4.26), l'expression employée est ordinairement 'faire tomber' le lot sur quelqu'un, ou 'faire tomber' quelqu'un dans le lot, expression figurée qui se ressent de l'image originelle des sorts que l'on tire (cf. Actes 1.26). L'association du 'lot' avec 'partager', commune à 1 QS 11.8 et à Col. 1.12—fréquente, il est vrai, dans l'AT (*supra* p. 84s) mais rare à Qumrân—représente donc une analogie littéraire notable. Elle est d'ailleurs renforcée par d'autres analogies thématiques dans le contexte de Col. La lumière (ἐν τῷ φωτί) est un thème favori de l'essénisme, qu'elle soit communiquée dès ici-bas par le don de la connaissance et de la révélation des mystères accordée aux 'fils de lumière' (voir dans le contexte immédiat 1 QS 11.3,5; et 1 QS 3.20; 1 QSb 4.27; 1 QH 4.5,27, etc.) ou qu'elle rayonne dans la vie éternelle (1 QS 4.8; 1 QH 7.24; 18.29). On peut hésiter ici entre ces deux domaines, de l'eschatologie commencée sur terre ou consommée dans le ciel. Mais une autre perspective s'ouvre par l'opposition manifestement voulue en Col. entre φῶς et σκότος. De l'empire des ténèbres Dieu nous a transférés dans le royaume de son Fils (v.13). Cette opposition entre les deux 'empires' (ממשלה) de lumière et de ténèbres (ou plus souvent de Bélial) est encore un thème typiquement qumrânien. Voir en particulier 1 QS 3.20–2; et aussi 1 QM 13.10–12, etc. On ne trouve pas, me semble-t-il, dans les textes de Qumrân une expression aussi catégorique du transfert d'un empire à l'autre; mais on y rencontre un peu partout l'idée que Dieu purifie ses élus et les délivre de la perversité pour les introduire dans son alliance éternelle: 1 QS 3.24–5; 4.18–23; 11.2–9; 1 QM 13.9; 18.11; 1 QH 3.19–23; 6.4–14; 7.29–31, etc.

Cet ensemble d'analogies invite à reconnaître en Col. 1.12 une influence de la littérature qumrânienne, et particulièrement de 1 QS 11.7–8. Ce n'est d'ailleurs pas le seul indice d'une telle influence. Déjà J. B. Lightfoot avait pressenti le caractère essénien des doctrines et des pratiques rencontrées par Paul à Colosses, et la découverte des documents de Qumrân n'a fait que renforcer cette intuition.

On se sent donc invité à reconnaître des anges dans les 'saints' de Col. 1.12 comme dans ceux de 1 QS 11.7–8. Sans doute n'est-ce pas l'usage habituel du terme dans le vocabulaire paulinien, qui réserve d'ordinaire le nom de 'saints' aux chrétiens (*supra*, p. 86). Mais l'influence qumrânienne sensible dans cette épître aux Colossiens peut expliquer un élargissement du sens. Et puisque, nous l'avons vu, dans

les écrits de Qumrân comme dans les Pseudépigraphes, notamment
Hénoch, le terme 'saints' peut inclure à la fois les anges et les élus
humains qui leur sont associés, je croirais volontiers qu'il en va de
même ici. Ce n'est pas là une solution 'facile', qui refléterait seulement
une incapacité de décider; c'est une solution positive, qui se croit
appuyée sur les faits littéraires.

Les exégètes procèdent trop souvent par mode de choix qui
s'excluent: *vel . . . vel . . .*, alors qu'il vaut mieux laisser au texte la
souple richesse d'aspects complémentaires qui ne s'excluent nullement
et que la pensée de l'auteur a bien pu vouloir embrasser.

Pour la même raison, j'hésiterais à choisir ici entre eschatologie
commencée et eschatologie consommée. Les païens de Colosses
viennent d'être associés au sort des anges et des hommes déjà chrétiens:
arrachés à l'empire des ténèbres, ils vivent dès maintenant dans la
lumière du royaume du Christ, qui s'épanouira un jour dans la gloire.
Cette perspective céleste sera plus accentuée en Eph. 1.18[52] par le
disciple paulinien qui reprendra la pensée de Col. en la développant;
mais ce sera légitime, car cette perspective est déjà implicite dans la
formulation très large de Col. 1.12.[53]

NOTES

1 Voir mon introduction dans le fascicule des épîtres de la captivité, dans la
  Bible de Jérusalem, Paris, 3e édn 1959; et l'article 'Colossiens' dans le
  Supplément au Dictionnaire de la Bible, vii (Paris 1966), col. 157–70.

2 De nombreux exégètes, notamment parmi les anciens Pères, Chrysostome
  et d'autres, soulignent ici cet aspect de gratuité de la brillante destinée de
  salut que le Père céleste offre aux hommes.

3 Ainsi Cornelius a Lapide, Oltramare, Abbott, Haupt, Knabenbauer.

4 Ainsi Lightfoot. Dans le même sens, E. Percy, *Die Probleme der Kolosser- und
  Epheserbriefe* (Lund 1946), p. 195.

5 Percy, op. cit., p. 26.

6 cf. K. G. Kuhn, 'Der Epheserbrief im Lichte der Qumrantexte', *NTS* 7
  (1960–1), pp. 334–46, à la page 335.

7 Ce sens est implicitement admis par les exégètes qui n'envisagent pas le
  sens de 'anges'. Ainsi, parmi les anciens: Chrysostome, Thomas d'Aquin,
  Cajetan; et encore Lightfoot, Oltramare; d'autres, tels que Haupt,
  Ewald, Knabenbauer, rejettent explicitement le sens de 'anges'; de même
  Percy, op. cit., p. 378 n22*, qui opte pour 'die für das Messiasreich
  Auserwählten'.

8 Ceci est le seul passage de la Bible *hébraïque* où se rencontre avec certitude

(Deut. 33.3 étant douteux, parce que corrompu) le substantif *Qedošîm*: les 'saints' dit des Israélites et non des Anges.

9   En Dan. 7.18,22a,25,27 les 'Saints du Très Haut' sont un cas spécial, dont nous reparlerons.

10 Ainsi Chrysostome, Théod. Mops., Théophylacte, Cajetan, Cornelius a Lapide, Oltramare.

11 Ainsi les commentaires de Klöpper, Oltramare; et R. Asting, *Die Heiligkeit im Urchristentum* (Göttingen 1930), pp. 104–5.

12 Ainsi Haupt, Beare, dans leurs commentaires.

13 Ainsi Cornelius a Lapide, Bengel, Lightfoot, Ewald, Lohmeyer; cf. Percy, op. cit., p. 61.

14 Ainsi Meyer, à la suite de Chrysostome et d'autres anciens.

15 Cependant Chrysostome écrivait déjà: Δοκεῖ δέ μοι καὶ περὶ τῶν παρόντων καὶ περὶ τῶν μελλόντων ὁμοῦ λέγειν; de même, à sa suite, Théophylacte (*PG* 62 col. 312; 124 col. 121).

16 Certains exégètes pensent même, de façon générale, aux 'saints' du Peuple élu de l'AT (cf. Matt. 27.52), dont les chrétiens sont les héritiers, l''Israël de Dieu', qui entrent en possession de la Terre promise spiritualisée. Ambrosiaster (*PL* 17, col. 422): 'Inducere gentes in promissionem Iudaeorum'. Dans le même sens, Procksch, *TWNT*, i, pp. 108–9; Bruce, Moule dans leurs commentaires.

17 cf. R. Asting, op. cit., pp. 151–9; L. Cerfaux, *La théologie de l'Église suivant saint Paul* (2ᵉ édn, Paris 1965), pp. 112–20, 373–5.

18 Ainsi traduisent la BJ et la TOB. Littéralement, 'aux besoins des pauvres des saints qui sont à Jérusalem'. La traduction proposée *supra* prend 'des saints' pour un génitif partitif. Si on voit là un possessif, il s'agit des pauvres qui appartiennent aux—qui relèvent des—saints de Jérusalem: ceux-ci sont alors les chefs de la communauté, les apôtres et les prophètes. Ainsi L. Cerfaux, op. cit., p. 116s., qui veut trouver ce sens restreint de 'saints' en plusieurs textes de Paul. Cette interprétation me semble probable pour Rom. 15.26, 31, possible pour Col. 1.26; Eph. 3.5, 8; 4.12, improbable pour 1 Cor. 14.33; Eph. 2.19; 3.18. Cerfaux (p. 118, n2) envisage même ce sens restreint pour notre texte Col. 1.12, ainsi que pour Eph. 1.18; ceci encore me semble improbable. Il offre d'ailleurs, p. 299, une interprétation plus large.

19 Contre Asting, op. cit., pp. 106–8, qui voit des anges dans les 'saints' de Eph. 2.19; 3.18.

20 Peut-être déjà Sévérien de Gabala (voir K. Staab, *Pauluskommentare aus der griechischen Kirche*, Münster 1933, p. 317): ἡ μετ' ἀγγέλων διαγωγή. Parmi les modernes: Klöpper, *comm.*; Asting, op. cit., p. 105; E. Käsemann, *Leib und Leib Christi* (Tübingen 1933), pp. 142, 147; F. Nötscher, *Vom Alten zum Neuen Testament* (Bonn 1962), p. 152; E. Lohse, *comm.* Lohmeyer, *comm.*, englobe les anges et les élus: 'die himmlischen Gestalten, Engel, "Gerechte und Auserwählte" des ATs, die schon in Gotteslanden mit Gott ewig wohnen'. Dans le même sens, J. Ernst, *comm.*

Ceux qui soutiennent cette exégèse entendent ἐν τῷ φωτί au sens local du domaine céleste, où règne la lumière divine dans laquelle baignent les anges (et les Elus); et ils renvoient à Col. 1.5. Cf. *supra* p. 86. Ce sens correspond bien à l'opposition des deux empires (φῶς/σκότος).

21 Selon L. Dequeker, *ETL* 36 (1960), pp. 374–6, le mot *qedošîm* aurait désigné primitivement les dieux cananéens formant la cour du dieu El, et des vestiges de cette acception mythologique subsisteraient dans les plus anciens textes de la Bible: Os 12.1; Ecclus. 42.17; Job 15.13–15; Ps. 16.3.

22 On pourrait encore songer à Col. 1.26, 'ce mystère resté caché depuis les siècles et les générations et qui maintenant vient d'être manifesté à ses saints'. En effet, Eph. 3.9–10 nous dit que le mystère longtemps caché a été révélé maintenant aux Puissances et aux Dominations (voir encore 1 Pet. 1.12). Mais il est plus naturel, et même imposé par le contexte (v. 27) ainsi que par le parallèle Eph. 3.5, d'y voir les hommes à qui est révélé le mystère de la gloire qui est promise à leur espérance, soit qu'il s'agisse des chrétiens en général, soit que les 'saints' soient plus particulièrement les apôtres et les prophètes, chargés de connaître et de faire connaître le mystère, ainsi que le veut Cerfaux (*supra*, n18).

23 Ainsi Rigaux, *comm. ad loc.*

24 Ainsi Procksch, *TWNT.*, i, p. 111, lignes 14–19.

25 J'emploie ce terme pour distinguer de l'eschatologie commencée sur la terre.

26 M. Noth, 'Die Heiligen des Höchsten', *Norsk teologisk Tidsskrift*, 56 (1955), pp. 146–61 = *Gesammelte Studien zum AT* (München 1957), pp. 274–90.

27 L. Dequeker, 'Daniel vii et les Saints du Très-Haut', *ETL* 36 (1960), pp. 353–92; Idem, 'The "Saints of the Most High" in Qumran and Daniel', *Oudtestamentische Studiën* 18 (1973), pp. 108–87.

28 J. Coppens et L. Dequeker, *Le Fils de l'Homme et les Saints du Très-Haut en Daniel 7, dans les Apocryphes et dans le Nouveau Testament* (2ᵉ édn, Louvain, 1961). J. Coppens a consacré de nombreux articles aux questions que pose le ch. 7 de Daniel: L. Dequeker en donne la liste, art. cit., 1973, p. 108, n4. Ajouter *ETL* 54 (1978), pp. 301–22.

29 C. H. W. Brekelmans, 'The Saints of the Most High and their Kingdom', *Oudtestamentische Studiën* 14 (1965), pp. 305–29.

30 R. Hanhart, 'Die Heiligen des Höchsten', *Supplements to Vetus Testamentum* 16 (1967), pp. 90–101.

31 G. F. Hasel, 'The Identity of "the Saints of the Most High"', in Daniel 7', *Biblica* 56 (1975), pp. 173–92.

32 J. J. Collins, 'The Son of Man and the Saints of the Most High in the Book of Daniel', *JBL* 93 (1974), pp. 50–66.

33 Cerfaux, op. cit., p. 107: 'Ce n'est point par un pur hasard que la littérature apocalyptique nous laisse souvent indécis sur le sens à donner au terme 'saints'. Tantôt il s'agit des anges, tantôt des élus. . . . Les élus sont des saints au même titre que les anges, ils forment comme eux la cour

97

du Seigneur ... Les élus des temps messianiques retrouvent au ciel une communauté de saints préexistants, des ancêtres, des Patriarches.'

34 Voir aussi la liste de S. Lambgerits, 'Le sens de QDWŠYM dans les textes de Qumrân', *ETL* 46 (1970), pp. 24–39, aux pp. 24–28.

35 Je m'appuie, pour ces relevés, sur la traduction et les notes de François Martin, *Le livre d'Hénoch* (Paris 1906). Pour la commodité, j'adopte la numérotation suivante des parties de l'Hénoch éthiopien: I. Introduction (i–v). II. Chute des anges et assomption d'Hénoch (vi–xxxvi). III. Livre des Paraboles (xxxvii–lxxi). IV. Livre des Luminaires (lxxii–lxxxii). V. Livre des Songes (lxxxiii–xc). VI. Livre de l'Exhortation et de la Malédiction (xci–cv). VII. Appendice (cvi–cviii). Cette division est celle de F. Martin. Il est bien entendu qu'elle recouvre une situation fort complexe, de variantes et d'interpolations.

36 Dans mes citations des écrits de Qumrân j'utilise la traduction de A. Dupont-Sommer, *Les écrits esséniens découverts près de la mer Morte* (Paris 1960).

37 cf. F. Nötscher, 'Heiligkeit in den Qumranschriften', *Revue de Qumrân*, II.6 (Fév. 1960), pp. 163–81; 7 (Juin 1960), pp. 315–44 = *Vom Alten zum Neuen Testament* (Bonn 1962), pp. 126–74.

38 cf. Annie Jaubert, *La notion d'Alliance dans le Judaïsme aux abords de l'ère chrétienne* (Paris 1963), p. 189 ss.

39 cf. Jaubert, *op. cit.*, p. 196.

40 Ceci est und des thèses maîtresses de H.-W. Kuhn, *Enderwartung und gegenwärtiges Heil* (Göttingen 1966).

41 Outre les travaux cités plus haut aux nn27 à 34, voir l'Exkurs i de H.-W. Kuhn, op. cit.; 'Die Gemeinschaft mit den Engeln in den Qumrantexten', pp. 66–73; et l'Exkurs iv: 'Der Ausdruck "die Heiligen" in den Qumrantexten und im sonstigen Spätjudentum', pp. 90–3.

42 En ce sens, Jaubert, op. cit., p. 193, n278; p. 194; S. Lambgerits, op. cit., p. 29.

43 C. Rabin, *The Zadokite Documents* (2 edn, Oxford 1958), pp. 38–9.

44 Voir n27: art. 1960, pp. 385–8; *art.* 1973, pp. 145–51.

45 *Vom Alten z. N.T.*, pp. 127, 153; de même, avec hésitation, Brekelmans, op. cit., p. 323 s.

46 Op. cit., pp. 34–9.

47 Op. cit., pp. 194–5.

48 *Art.* 1973, p. 148.

49 Op. cit., pp. 80–5.

50 Mais on a 'hommes de sainteté' en 1 QS 5.13,18; 8.17; 9.8.

51 Op. cit. à la note 30, pp. 94–6. Les textes qu'il invoque, 2 Mac. 7.34 et 3 Mac. 6.28, sont peu convaincants, et je ne vois pas qu'il cite 1 QS 4.22 où les 'fils du ciel', dont la sagesse mise en parallèle à la connaíssance du Très-Haut, sont certainement des anges.

52 Dans son commentaire (*NTD*, 1976), Conzelmann rapproche, à juste

titre, Eph. 1.18 de Col. 1.12, mais il ajoute: 'doch sind dort die Engel gemeint, hier die seligen Gläubigen'. Son commentaire de Eph. 1.18 ne justifie pas cette décision sommaire et arbitraire.

53   En Actes 20.32 et surtout 26.18, dont les thèmes et les termes sont curieusement parallèles à ceux de Col. 1.12, le participe ἡγιασμένοι (influencé par Deut. 33.3 grec) invite à penser à des hommes plutôt qu'à des anges.

ENGLISH SUMMARY

The term ἅγιοι in Col. 1.12 has generally been understood to refer to Christians. Used in the Old Testament of God's holy people, the adjective ἅγιος was taken over by the Church and applied to its members. Here Paul (who is presumed to be the author) links the term with the light which is given through the gospel. The idea that Christians dwell 'in light' suggests not only an experience in this present world, but also the life in celestial glory which belongs to the consummation.

An alternative explanation of the term is that it means 'angels'. For this meaning, also, there is Old Testament backing. In the New Testament, however, the use of ἅγιοι as a substantive meaning 'angels' is rare, though the term is sometimes applied to them as an adjective. In the Pauline literature, ἅγιοι probably refers to angels in 1 Thess. 3.13, 2 Thess. 1.10 and Eph. 1.18, though the meaning is debatable in all three cases.

A similar discussion has taken place recently about the 'saints of the Most High' in Dan. 7, who are variously understood to be either God's chosen people or his angels. One possibility is that the term 'saints' should on some occasions be understood to include both men and angels; certainly when the former are described as 'saints' it is in contexts which suggest that they are to share the lot of angels. The same ambiguity is found in several passages in the intertestamental literature, while in 1 Enoch there are numerous clear examples of the term being used to mean 'angels', others where it refers to the elect, and a third group where it is not clear whether the term refers to men or angels. If the word can in fact embrace both meanings, it is perhaps wrong to try to decide between them in those cases where the sense appears ambivalent.

The community at Qumran was much concerned with the idea of 'holiness', and the term occurs frequently. So does the term 'saints', which is used sometimes of angels, sometimes of members of the community, and sometimes of both at once. Is it necessary, when the meaning is not clear-cut, to try to choose between these two senses? Of particular interest is 1 QH 11. 10–13, which reinterprets 1 QH 3.20–23; in the earlier passage, the 'saints' are angels, but in the later they are members of the community.

There are similarities with the themes of Col. 1.12 in several passages in the Qumran literature, in particular in 1 QS 11.7–8. The parallels confirm the judgement of J. B. Lightfoot, who argued that the Colossians were influenced by Essene doctrine. This influence explains how the term ἅγιοι could be widened to mean 'angels' in Col. 1.12, even though the normal sense of the word in Pauline literature is 'Christians'. Here, as in the Qumran literature and I Enoch, the term may well include *both* meanings. Exegetes too often choose one solution and exclude another, so losing part of the richness of an author's meaning.

10

Gnosis at Corinth

R. McL. Wilson

Several years ago Erich Fascher ended an article on this theme with the words: 'Die Frage der Gegner des Paulus in Korinth bleibt also weiterhin umstritten.'[1] This may serve as justification for returning to a much-discussed subject, in a field to which Professor Barrett over the years has made some notable contributions. The venture is however not undertaken in the hope of reaching a complete and final answer, of finding a new solution on which all parties to the debate would agree. Entrenched positions on one side and on the other are probably too firmly established for that. Rather is it a matter of trying to see the reasons for the disagreement, to understand why the doctors differ. When this is done, then it may prove that in fact the opposing sides are not so far apart, that a clearer definition of the terms employed will help to reduce the area of disagreement, or at least to remove misunderstanding. Even so it is likely that a fundamental cleavage will still remain, between those on the one hand who believe that there was a pre-Christian gnostic movement which could have influenced Paul or his opponents, or both, and those who hold that there was not.

The fact of the matter is that while on the one hand we are dealing with a well-defined body of material in the form of Paul's Corinthian letters, from which we can extract Paul's own ideas and at least to some extent those of his opponents, on the other side we have to do with something that remains rather vague, nebulous and protean. E. M. Yamauchi distinguishes two divergent views of Gnosticism, and writes: 'Those who will accept only a "narrow" definition of Gnosticism do not find any conclusive evidence of pre-Christian Gnosticism, whereas those scholars who operate with a "broad" definition of Gnosticism find it not only in the New Testament but in many other early documents as well.'[2] Adherents of the 'narrow' view can point to the fact expressed long ago by C. H. Dodd, that 'there is no Gnostic document known to us which can with any show of probability be dated – at any rate in the form in which alone we have access to it – before the period of the New Testament.'[3] Despite new discoveries this remains a fact, for the Nag Hammadi library in its present form dates from somewhere in the fourth century, and even the Greek originals from which the Coptic texts were translated are generally dated to the second century at the earliest. On the other hand several of these texts seem to afford evidence of the Christianization of something that was originally non-Christian (e.g. the Apocryphon of John, the Gospel of Mary, and particularly the Sophia Jesu Christi as a Christianization of the Letter of Eugnostus), and some have been claimed as witnesses to a non-Christian form of Gnosticism.[4] Moreover even adherents of the 'narrow' view admit the presence of trends and tendencies in a gnostic direction in the background of the New Testament.

Another source of difference of opinion lies in the direction of approach. Those who begin with the developed Gnosticism of the second century and go back to Paul's letters have no difficulty in identifying 'gnostic motifs' – terms, concepts and ideas which may legitimately be described as gnostic because they are used as technical terms in the context of gnostic systems. This usage however may be question-begging, since there is no way of showing that these terms and concepts are *already* gnostic in an earlier context. Greek rationalists often regarded religion as 'ein von den Mächtigen zur Beherrschung der Massen erfundenes Mittel',[5] which comes near to Marx's 'opium of the people', as that phrase is commonly understood; but that does not make them Marxists! On the other hand, those who begin at the other end can interpret such terms and concepts without reference to Gnosticism – only to find themselves at a loss to explain how and why this new significance should so suddenly be given to them. The developed gnostic systems of the second century can certainly be classed as Christian heresies, and cannot be understood apart from Christianity, but we now have gnostic material of a non-Christian character, or documents in which the Christian element appears to have been imposed upon something originally non-Christian; all of which suggests that there was something developing alongside of Christianity and to some extent interacting with it. The problem remains that for the earliest stages we have no clear knowledge of it, no documentation that would allow us to trace its development. In regard to the beginnings of this movement we are still in the main reduced to hypothesis.

Reference to 'heresy' raises another point: one may sometimes suspect that it is the heretical associations of *gnosis* that have led some scholars to reject the very thought of gnostic influence on the New Testament. The legacy of Hegesippus is still with us, the idea that the Church remained pure and undefiled so long as the apostles continued at the helm, but that with their departure from the scene the heretics moved in. In point of fact this use of the terms is anachronistic. The distinction between orthodox and heretic is not something that is present from the outset. Rather are we likely to find a variety of ideas and opinions in circulation, which may be more or less compatible with one another. Only when matters come to a head, when there is clear and open conflict, is a decision formally taken – and the heresy of one period may be the orthodoxy of another! At the New Testament stage the issues are not yet clean-cut, and views later to be stigmatized as heretical could be entertained alongside those later considered orthodox. Moreover it is not a case of two opposing and rival points of view, which stand always and at all points in opposition. Part of the complexity of the problem lies in the fact that they could and did share so much. 'Gnostic' and 'Christian' elements are not always easily differentiated, and some are shared by both.

So far as the Corinthian situation goes, the least that can be said is probably the remark of Robert Law some seventy years ago, that Paul's Corinthian correspondence shows 'into how congenial a soil the seeds of Gnosticism were about to fall'.[6] How congenial may be seen from the use the gnostics were to make of it later: 1 Cor. 2.9 appears in logion 17 of the Gospel of Thomas, where it is placed on the lips of Jesus;[7] 1 Cor. 8.1 is quoted in §110 of the Gospel of Philip, and 15.50 in §23;[8] 5.9f appears in the Exegesis on the Soul.[9] In noting such cases, however, we have to bear in mind the warning voiced above: gnostic use of a book does not mean that the book itself is gnostic.

This last point is underlined by a further consideration. Several years ago Dr Barrett wrote: 'The situation Paul deals with in 2 Corinthians is no longer the tendency to division, the free use of the terms wisdom and gnosis, the libertinism, and the misunderstanding of the resurrection that mark 1 Corinthians. The second epistle must not be interpreted in terms of the situation presupposed by the first.'[10] He goes on to argue that 'the intruders were Jews, Jerusalem Jews, Judaizing Jews, and as such constituted a rival apostolate to Paul's, backed by all the prestige of the mother church.'[11] Yet 2 Corinthians also was known to and used by the gnostics: 2.14 is echoed in the Gospel of Truth (34.4); 3.6 in the Exegesis on the Soul (134.1f), while

12.4 according to patristic sources was quoted by Basilides, the Cainites and the Naassenes.[12] If Dr Barrett is right, this would be another case of gnostic use of an originally non-gnostic document. It would of course be possible to take the whole Corinthian correspondence together and claim that Paul is confronting the same gnostic opposition throughout, as is done by Schmithals, but as Dr Barrett says, 'there is fairly wide agreement that he was wrong.'[13] Or one may think with Kümmel of 'Palestinian opponents of the Pauline mission' who 'joined themselves with the Gnostic opposition against Paul recognizable in 1 Corinthians, or already before his coming to Corinth assumed Gnostic-pneumatic features',[14] although it must be said that his reference to 'a definite Gnostic, Palestinian, Jewish-Christian opposition created by new additional opponents' seems more difficult than the idea of a 'double front' (Lietzmann-Kümmel, Wikenhauser) or Dr Barrett's case for Judaizing Jews from Jerusalem.

At all events, it is clear that there is some difference in the situation reflected in these two letters, and that it is primarily in the first that the 'gnostic' element is to be found. We may therefore confine our further consideration to this. It is not of course possible in a short paper to cover every aspect, to deal exhaustively with every point of detail, the more especially since the modern literature on the subject is so extensive. All that will be attempted is to single out a few of the areas which come into consideration.

At the outset, reference may be made to two quite recent articles. In a study of 1 Cor. 1.18–25[15] Ernest Best contrives to discuss the passage almost without reference to Gnosticism, and where it is mentioned it is almost always as one of a number of possibilities.[16] One of the key concepts here is wisdom, which inevitably recalls the gnostic Sophia; but we must look more closely. The Sophia of the gnostic systems is an aeon, a figure of the supra-mundane world, whose fault is ultimately responsible for the creation of the world and consequently for the woes that afflict mankind. There are no grounds whatever for seeing any such Sophia-myth in the background to 1 Corinthians.[17] Paul's concern is to set on the one side a merely human wisdom of this world, and over against it Christ as the wisdom of God. 'The wise man is nowhere because God has made his wisdom foolish, and he has done this in the cross . . . it is in the cross that the wisdom of the world is first judged and made to be folly.'[18] It is of course possible to see in the background the Jewish wisdom theology represented by Ecclesiasticus, the Wisdom of Solomon and Philo, which 'offered the possibility

105

of an interpretation of Christ as the pre-existent agent of creation and of the government in the world, and as the agent of revelation of religious truth',[19] but if the gnostic Sophia also goes back to the wisdom tradition we have two quite different lines of development. It is also well to bear in mind D. E. H. Whiteley's warning about speaking of 'identifying' Christ with an 'hypostatized' wisdom: 'When St Paul speaks of Christ in terms of Wisdom his intention is not to identify him with an hypostatisation of Wisdom, but to ascribe to him the function of being God's agent in creation, revelation and redemption. In fact, the "Wisdom Christology" of St Paul may be summed up in these words: What Wisdom meant to the Jews was part of what Jesus Christ meant for St Paul.'[20]

The second article mentioned above, by Ulrich Wilckens,[21] is devoted to 1 Cor. 2.1–16, and includes a statement and discussion (pp. 517–24) of four criteria for the identification of 'Corinthian theology'. Of more immediate relevance for present purposes is the ensuing discussion of four points which have been claimed to show gnostic influence: the concept of σοφία in 2.6; the reference to the ἄρχοντες of this world in 2.6, 8; the use of τέλειος in 2.6, and the contrast of ψυχικός and πνευματικός in 2.14f. The ἄρχοντες are not gnostic archons or demonic powers, but rather the Jewish leaders of the passion story (see pp. 508–10). The direction of Paul's polemic, according to which the Corinthian wisdom was a merely human wisdom, a wisdom of this world in opposition to the wisdom of God, does not permit the assumption that the Corinthians conceived their wisdom as a divine and spiritual Wisdom; nor can we interpret it as the redeeming 'knowledge' possessed by the pneumatic (pp. 524 ff). Τέλειος does occur in gnostic sources as a description of the redeemed pneumatic, but almost always in late texts to some extent based on 1 Corinthians itself (p. 526). Moreover in Paul as in primitive Christianity generally the Jewish ethical and eschatological significance of the term predominates, whereas for the gnostic understanding of the word the ethical criterion plays no part. Paul stands closer to Philo, but neither of them is gnostic (nor are the Corinthians). 'Was Paulus, Philo und die Gnosis verbindet, sind lediglich gewisse hellenistische Mysterienvorstellungen, die aber eine dominierende Wirkung allein in der Gnosis gewonnen haben' (p. 528).

The contrast of ψυχικός and πνευματικός has long been the subject of debate. 'By far the most important set of terms involved in the argument (sc. about Gnosticism in Corinth) is the πνευματικός –

106

ψυχικός terminology, the allegedly 'gnostic' differentiation between the πνεῦμα of man and his ψυχή and between the πνευματικός man and the ψυχικός.'[22] As Wilckens notes (pp. 528f), the antithesis is often to be found in gnostic sources, but the dualism of soul and spirit rarely occurs in a pure form. 'Ungleich häufiger findet sich eine trichotomistische Anthropologie, in der die Seele zwischen Körper und Geist eine vermittelnde Funktion hat. Diese wurde überall dort vertreten, wo die platonische Leib-Seele-Differenz durch die gnostische Pneuma-Lehre lediglich überboten werden sollte.' This as it happens could be a quite important pointer to a stage in the development of Gnosticism proper: when and where was the element of Greek philosophy introduced into gnostic thought? At the very outset, or only in the course of time?

The texts which present this anthropology are mostly from Christian Gnosticism, where 1 Corinthians was known and sometimes expressly used. 'Deshalb kann ohne überzeugende Nachweise nicht behauptet werden, es handle sich um gnostisches Traditionsgut, das im Ursprung vorchristlich und also von Paulus bzw. den Korinthern übernommen worden sei.' Like Pearson, but apparently independently, he now finds the origin of the contrast in hellenistic-Jewish exegesis of Genesis 2.7. As Pearson writes, 'One can perhaps term that sphere of ideas "Hellenistic-Jewish speculation" or "Hellenistic-Jewish speculative mysticism"' (p. 82), an interesting suggestion in view of a more recent contribution to be noted later.

Wilckens concludes (p. 537) by saying: 'Man kann darum vielleicht sagen, dass die Gnosis die Ansätze jener von Paulus bekämpften protologischen Christologie und Anthropologie aufgenommen und "gnostisch" umgedeutet habe. Aber weder die korinthische noch die paulinische Theologie sind gnostisch beeinflusst gewesen. Die Gnosis ist vielmehr überlieferungsgeschichtlich eine spätere Bewegung, in der zweifellos sowohl die urchristliche Tradition wie auch die breit rezipierte jüdische massiv hellenisiert worden sind.'

This position is in broad agreement with the views advanced in two earlier articles, in one of which it was argued that at Corinth we have 'at most only the first tentative beginnings of what was later to develop into full-scale Gnosticism', while in the other the Japanese scholar Sasagu Arai summed up by saying 'Die Gegner des Paulus in Korinth wären also geneigt gewesen, "gnostisch" zu sein, sie waren aber noch nicht gnostisch.'[23] It is also in keeping with what appears to be a developing tendency to distinguish in some measure between the classic gnostic systems of the second century and the trends and tendencies in a gnostic direction which preceded them in the first. It seems however to stand in flat contradiction to the view advanced in the latest full monograph on Gnosticism, by Kurt Rudolph.[24]

Professor Rudolph writes that Paul's letters 'enthalten wiederholt eine leidenschaftliche Frontstellung gegen falsche Lehrmeinungen, die sich in den meist von ihm gegründeten Gemeinden breitmachten und zu denen auch gnostische gehörten. Am deutlichsten ist dies in Korinth der Fall gewesen . . . Aus der Polemik geht die gnostische Herkunft der Gegner deutlich hervor.' Here a footnote refers to the work of Schmithals and Wilckens, the latter of whom, as already indicated, has now changed his mind.

The evidence adduced demands more detailed discussion than space will allow, and only a few comments can be made here. 'Es sind Pneumatiker und "Vollkommene", die auf ihre "Erkenntnis" stolz sind und denen "alles erlaubt ist"; daher schauen sie auf die "Schwachen" ab.' This needs for a start to be considered in the light of the discussion of the πνευματικός terminology by Pearson and Wilckens (see above). 'Als Geistbesitzer haben sie schon die Auferstehung' – which presupposes a particular interpretation of 1 Corinthians 15 in the light of 2 Tim. 2.17–18, which is not held by all scholars. 'Die Gemeindeversammlung wird zu einer Demonstration gnostischer Geistbesessenheit, Frauen sind dabei aktiv tätig' – but is spirit-possession necessarily gnostic? 'Das Abendmahl wird zu einem Sättigungsmahl degradiert'; what is gnostic here? 'Der irdische Jesus wird offenbar zugunsten des himmlischen Christus verachtet, was später von den so-genannten Ophiten berichtet wird': 1 Cor. 12.3 is admittedly often regarded as referring to a gnostic slogan, but need this be so?[25] And can we enlist a reference in Origen in this way for the interpretation of a passage in the New Testament?

This summary treatment, verging on demolition by the gentle art of ridicule, is of course not entirely fair to Rudolph.[26] It is merely intended to indicate that the evidence is not so clear and unambiguous as could be wished. That in fact is the problem! As he himself remarks on an earlier page, we cannot dispense with hypotheses, particularly where the beginnings of Gnosis are concerned. It is a matter of some importance, however, to distinguish such hypotheses from what is clearly backed by evidence, to separate firm knowledge from what is at most speculation.

What is more striking is the continuance of Rudolph's discussion on the following page (320), where he writes that Paul himself was not without responsibility, 'denn auch seine eigenen Auffassungen sind nicht frei von Anklängen an gnostische Lehren, und noch spätere Gnostiker haben sich häufig auf ihn als Zeugen berufen.' In fact, on this showing Paul was more gnostic than his opponents![27]

Once again, however, it is necessary to look more closely at the points adduced. For one thing, gnostic appeal to Paul does not make Paul himself a gnostic. The contrast of psychic and pneumatic has already been referred to. The idea that this world is ruled by Satan and by demonic powers is known to Jewish apocalyptic, and should be so described. It was indeed taken over by the gnostics, but to describe it as gnostic at this stage, without more ado, is to beg the question. That the Jewish Law derives from angelic powers is true both for Paul and for Gnosticism, but the way in which this motif is used is different. If 'eine weltablehnende Haltung' is dominant, and marriage regarded as a danger, a closer examination of the context in each case will reveal that there are differences which should not be overlooked. So one might go on: the similarities are certainly present, but when we examine each in its context, in Paul on the one hand and in the gnostic literature on the other, then the differences emerge. Since the gnostics admittedly appealed to Paul, the inference is that they are the borrowers, and that the material has undergone some *Umdeutung* at their hands. To prove gnostic influence on Paul (or his opponents) we should require to find independent evidence for the existence of something which could be clearly recognized as Gnosticism in the background to Paul's ministry. This we may suspect, but we cannot prove; nor have we any means of defining its nature and character with any degree of precision. All too often a 'pre-Christian gnosis' is postulated on the basis of the evidence we have, then to provide firmer contours and give it substance the main features of second-century Gnosticism are projected into the first century, and we end with the hypothetical influence upon Paul and early Christianity of a 'pre-Christian Gnosticism' for which there is no real evidence and which results from reading first-century documents with second-century spectacles.[28]

At the beginning of his article (p. 281) Fascher writes 'Doch ist Gnosis nicht, wie die vorige Generation meinte, eine kirchliche Verfallserscheinung.' On the other hand Wilckens (p. 524) says 'mit der einfachen Arbeitshypothese einer vorchristlichen gnostischen Religion, die aus dem Osten in den vorderen Orient eingedrungen sei, kann heute keinesfalls mehr gearbeitet werden.' In his commentary on 1 Corinthians, Professor Barrett says without qualification, 'There was

109

for example Jewish gnosticism in Corinth,'[29] whereas Alan Richardson writes, 'The objection to speaking of Gnosticism in the first century AD is that we are in danger of hypostatizing certain rather ill-defined tendencies of thought and then speaking as if there were a religion or religious philosophy, called Gnosticism, which could be contrasted with Judaism or Christianity. There was, of course, no such thing.'[30]

What are we to make of this variety of conflicting opinions (which could easily be multiplied)? On the surface we appear to have at least two diametrically opposite views, yet it is not impossible to bring them fairly close together. For one thing, Fascher is correct in that it is no longer possible to treat the Gnosticism of the second century in isolation as a merely Christian heresy; there are affinities and anticipations already in the first century. Even Richardson admits, although as the most that could be said, that certain notions were 'in the air' in the latter part of the first century, such as subsequently crystallized into the doctrines of the gnostic sects. On the other hand the tendency today is no longer (if it ever really was) to think of a full-scale developed gnostic religion in confrontation with primitive Christianity. Rather it is to think of a movement that grew and developed, more or less contemporary with Christianity and interacting with it. James M. Robinson for example speaks of 'a trajectory that led from wisdom literature to Gnosticism', and sees in Q 'one of the connecting links between the hypostatizing of Sophia in Jewish wisdom literature and the gnostic redeemer myths attested in the second century systems'.[31]

As for Professor Barrett's 'Jewish gnosticism', the striking feature of the articles and books discussed is the number of references to the Jewish or hellenistic Jewish wisdom tradition. To these may be added yet another article, which suggests that it is possible 'to determine with some degree of precision the nature and background of the "proto-Gnosticism" in Corinth: hellenistic Jewish religiosity focused on *sophia* and *gnosis*'.[32] Here it is argued that the Corinthian *gnosis* can be explained from 'a hellenistic Jewish religion of enlightenment' which can be documented from the Wisdom of Solomon and Philo, an 'enlightened wisdom-theology' in response to which Paul asserts 'his own apocalyptic perspective on the demonic powers which rule the world' (p. 50).

This is a salutary reminder that Judaism in the New Testament period was not uniform or monolithic, and that concentration upon one aspect of the contemporary background to the exclusion of others may simply distort the picture. Reference has already been made to the way in which Professor Best adduces a number of possibilities,[33] and Horsley notes the three listed by Conzelmann, to which he himself adds a fourth. We must take account of *all* the relevant possibilities, observing both the similarities and the differences, and noting where possible which is the more significant at any given point. Only so shall we be able to do justice to the variegated New Testament background, to understand the manifold influences which have operated in the development of Christianity. Sweeping generalizations based on superficial similarities can be dangerous and misleading. It is not enough to label something as 'Jewish' or 'gnostic' and have done with it. We must ask in what sense, to what tradition does the element belong, to what extent it has been modified in the transition from one tradition to another. To speak in general terms of the Jewish origins of Gnosticism, for example, is to beg a whole series of questions: does this mean apocalyptic Judaism or the wisdom tradition, rabbinic Judaism or Hekhaloth mysticism? Does it imply that the originators of the movement were themselves Jews, or that Jewish material was taken over and possibly adapted by non-Jews? That there is a substantial Jewish contribution is not in question – one need only refer to the gnostic use of the early chapters of Genesis – but Alexander Böhlig years ago, in his studies of the Jewish and Jewish-Christian background of some Nag Hammadi texts, drew attention to the *Umdeutung* which has taken place.[34] The gnostics not only adopted, they also adapted.

In sum, the quest for a developed pre-Christian Gnosticism, even a Jewish one, which could be said to have influenced the Corinthians, or Paul himself, has not yet yielded any conclusive results. Philo of Alexandria, for all the affinities with Gnosticism which can be found in his writings, is not yet a gnostic in the full second-century sense.[35] Nor is Gnosticism in the full sense to be found at Qumran. If we adopt the programmatic statement of Hans Jonas, 'A Gnosticism without a fallen god, without benighted creator and sinister creation, without alien soul, cosmic captivity and acosmic salvation, without the self-redeeming of the Deity – in short: A Gnosis without divine tragedy will not meet specifications',[36] then we must probably wait for the second century. On the other hand there can be little doubt that something was already in process of developing in the first century which may properly be described as at least a kind of *gnosis*. In the same volume as Jonas' article, Helmut Koester wrote 'For the historical

111

dating of the emergence of Gnosticism I would maintain that it cannot be dated later than Simon Magus, that it is a presupposition of Philo's philosophy, and that many aspects of Pauline theology (not to speak of Paul's opponents in 1 Corinthians) cannot be explained, unless we recognise that a considerable formation of Gnostic thought had already taken place before Paul' (p. 191). If this referred to a developed Gnosticism in the second-century sense, it would in the light of the discussion above be open to question. If however what is meant is an incipient Gnosticism, the 'kind of *gnosis*' referred to above, that would be another matter. More important for present purposes is a remark on the previous page: 'If there are close relations between Gnosticism on the one hand, and Jewish mysticism and wisdom theology on the other, it is necessary to determine and to localize with more precision the decisive turning point in the line that leads from such Jewish predecessors into Christian and pagan Gnosticism.' It is precisely to mark the existence of this turning point (even if we cannot yet localize it exactly), to give due weight both to the continuity and to the discontinuity in the development, that some of us have suggested a differentiation in the use of terms, reserving 'Gnosticism' for what Yamauchi called the 'narrow' definition, the developed Gnosticism of the second century. What we have at Corinth, then, is not yet Gnosticism, but a kind of *gnosis*.

NOTES

1 E. Fascher, 'Die Korintherbriefe und die Gnosis', in *Gnosis und Neues Testament*, ed. K. W. Tröger (Berlin 1973), pp. 281–91.

2 *Pre-Christian Gnosticism* (London 1973), pp. 13f.

3 *The Interpretation of the Fourth Gospel* (Cambridge 1953), p. 98.

4 cf. G. W. MacRae in *Gnosis*, Festschrift Hans Jonas (Göttingen 1978), pp. 147ff.

5 P. Wendland, *Die hellenistisch-römische Kultur* (Tübingen 1912), p. 102.

6 *The Tests of Life* (Edinburgh 1909), p. 28.

7 For other citations of this text, cf. P. Prigent in *TZ* 14 (1958), pp. 416–29; cf. also U. Wilckens, in *Theologia Crucis-Signum Crucis* (Tübingen 1979), p. 510 n25: 'Dass das Zitat vielfach in gnostischer Literatur vorkommt beweist nicht seinen gnostischen Ursprung, sondern – wenn nicht Kenntnis der Stelle 1 Kor. 2.9 – die Verbreitung apokalyptischer Tradition in der Gnosis.'

8 See also the references in the index to W. Foerster, *Gnosis* vol. 2 (ET Oxford 1974), p. 355.

9   Foerster, vol. 2, p. 105.

10   *NTS* 17 (1971), p. 236.

11   op. cit., p. 251.

12   See the references in the index to Foerster vol. 2, p. 355. It is worthy of note that none of the patristic references is to Irenaeus, and none of the references to 2 Corinthians in the index to Harvey's edition of Irenaeus relates to Book 1 where he discusses the gnostic systems.

13   op. cit. 236. See W. Schmithals, *Die Gnosis in Corinth* (Göttingen 1956, ²1965; ET Nashville 1971). For criticism of Schmithals, cf. H. M. Schenke and K. M. Fischer, *Einleitung in die Schriften des Neuen Testaments 1* (Berlin 1978), pp. 104f.

14   *Introduction to the New Testament* (ET London 1966), p. 209.

15   'The Power and the Wisdom of God', in *Paolo a una Chiesa divisa* (Rome 1980), pp. 9–39.

16   e.g. p. 30: 'There is nothing at this point to help us to determine what significance we should give to wisdom in relation to content; it could be philosophical understanding, the practical wisdom of Jewish wisdom theology, the esoteric wisdom of Gnosticism, or spiritual revelation in mystic cult or enthusiastic trance.'

17   It is worthy of note that K. Rudolph in his list of the gnostic elements in Paul's Corinthian letters does not even mention this chapter (*Die Gnosis* (Leipzig 1977), pp. 319–20).

18   Best, p. 22 (see n15 above).

19   R. H. Fuller, *The Foundations of New Testament Christology* (London 1965), p. 75 (see pp. 72ff).

20   *The Theology of St. Paul* (Oxford 1964), p. 111 (quotation from p. 112). As Dr Best notes (27), it is surprising to find the Jews introduced in 1 Cor. 1.22 as asking for signs, and not considered under the heading of 'wisdom': 'it is hard to believe that he (Paul) could have excluded Jewish wisdom theology from his consideration of wisdom' (op. cit. 25).

21   'Zu 1 Kor. 2.1–16', in *Theologia Crucis – Signum Crucis*, Festschrift E. Dinkler, ed. Carl Andresen and Günter Klein (Tübingen 1979), pp. 501–37. At certain points this constitutes a revision and correction of Wilckens' earlier views.

22   B. A. Pearson, *The Pneumatikos-Psychikos Terminology*, SBL Dissertation Series 12 (Missoula 1973), p. 1; cf. also R. A. Horsley in *HTR* 69 (1976), pp. 269ff.

23   Wilson, *NTS* 19 (1973), pp. 65–74; Arai, ib., pp. 430–7 (quotation from p. 437).

24   *Die Gnosis* (see note 17), pp. 319–20.

25   cf. Pearson, *JBL* 86 (1967), pp. 301ff, against which Schmithals (*Gnosticism at Corinth*, p. 350) adduces Brox, *BZ* 12 (1968), pp. 103ff.

26   It may suffice to remark that I value Professor Rudolph's book enough to be glad to have had a hand in the preparation of an English translation.

27   Wilckens, as it happens, writes of 1 Cor. 2.1–16: '*Wenn* also gnostische Motive in diesem Abschnitt nachweisbar sind, so betreffen sie allein die Argumentation des Paulus', citing Scroggs, *NTS* 14 (1967/8), p. 54.

28   cf. A. Richardson, *Introduction to the Theology of the New Testament* (London 1958), pp. 42f: 'Those scholars who readily find Gnostic influences at work in the NT argue that the beginnings of this type of thought must have been fairly well defined in the first century; they then set out to look for evidence of it in the NT, and are thus in peril of interpreting the earlier by the later writings.'

29   *The First Epistle to the Corinthians* (London 1968), p. 55.

30   op. cit., p. 41.

31   Robinson and Koester, *Trajectories through Early Christianity* (Philadelphia 1971), p. 43.

32   R. A. Horsley, 'Gnosis in Corinth: 1 Corinthians 8.1–6', *NTS* 27 (1980), pp. 32–51.

33   See n16 above.

34   *Mysterion und Wahrheit* (Leiden 1968), pp. 80–111 (e.g. p. 83: 'Die Umdeutung von jüdischem Traditionsgut in gnostische Gedankengänge wird besonders deutlich an der Neuinterpretation von Bibelstellen und heilsgeschichtlichen Grössen').

35   cf. M. Simon in *Le Origini dello Gnosticismo*, ed. U. Bianchi (Leiden 1967), pp. 359f.

36   *The Bible in Modern Scholarship*, ed. J. P. Hyatt (Nashville 1965), p. 293.

11

Paul's Christology and Gnosticism

E. Schweizer

In Rome, in 1968, C. K. Barrett emphasized that Paul's Christology was certainly not formed in direct continuation of what Jesus himself preached, but that the essential question was 'whether in his theology he affords a valid interpretation of the total event of Jesus Christ'.[1] I shall try to deal with that very problem in a context in which I think Barrett might also be interested. He pointed to an 'incipient gnosticism' behind the Corinthian theology,[2] to the Son of Man figure in John with its descent from and ascent to heaven (John 6.53, cf. vv. 51, 62), very similar to a gnostic redeemer,[3] and to the gnosticizing opponents of Ignatius.[4] In doing so he showed in the first case the influence of Platonism, in the second the roots in a pre-Johannine tradition of the Lord's supper which, in its part, may be influenced by Mark 10.45, and in the third the accommodation of Judaism to its environment. In the Cato lecture of 1969, he defines Gnosticism as 'an atmosphere, a fashion, a habit of thought . . . so like Christianity and, at the same time, so radically different'.[5] He consequently includes the gnostic Poimandres in his *Selected Documents*.[6] This still leaves the question open, however, whether or not what we usually call Gnosticism was, in the time of Paul, essentially more than judaizing Platonism or platonizing Judaism. By contributing some thoughts to this problem I shall try to reopen the question about Paul's Christology which C. K. Barrett put to us in San Paolo fuori le mura in Rome, in the hope that my discussion will remind him of the discussion there and of the many occasions when we tried together to learn from Paul and to strive after the truth proclaimed by the apostle as the source of all real life.

I *Christ, the Word of God*

In Rom. 10.6–7 Paul reinterprets what Deut. 30.12–14 says of the Mosaic commandment. He agrees with that passage, and also with

4 Ezra 4.8, i.e. that since no man is able to ascend to heaven or descend to the abyss, God approaches man in his word. This is strikingly similar to what 1 Bar. 3.29–30, also a reinterpretation of Deut. 30, applies to God's Wisdom who is, according to 4.1, identical to the Law of Moses. This is probably dependent on a saying of Sirach about Wisdom, also identified with the Law of God (24.4–5, 23), taking her seat in the height and going to the depths of the flood of chaos (in that order!). Like Sirach and Baruch, Paul speaks of a figure separate from God and yet, in its action, essentially God himself; but, unlike them, he cannot identify it with the Law. Does this presuppose the gnostic myth of the redeemer-revealer descending from heaven and ascending there again? Obviously not in the case of Sirach and Baruch, as long as one does not call the Wisdom myth gnostic; very probably not in the case of Paul. 'To bring Christ down' seems to refer to the resurrected Lord, of whom verses 7 and 9 speak. Even if Paul had thought of the pre-existent Christ, he would be close to the idea of Wisdom descending from heaven; but in fact he wishes only to emphasize Christ's nearness in the kerygma. Also, Christ's ascent would be that from the tomb which, of course, would be anti-gnostic. But neither descent nor ascent are mentioned. On the contrary, ascending (mentioned first as in Deuteronomy, Baruch and Sirach)[7] or descending (not to the earth but to the abyss) would be senseless, since Christ is present in the word. If there is a polemical overtone it is not against a gnostic myth but, as in John 3.13 and 4 Ezra 4.8, against 'prophets' who claimed to have ascended to heaven.

Actually, Paul's interpretation stands much closer to what we find in Q and Matthew, differing from them of course in its understanding of the kerygma as being the word about Jesus Christ, not the teaching of Jesus. We read in Wisd. 7.27 that 'from generation to generation Wisdom passes into pious souls and equips friends of God and prophets.' According to Q, John the Baptist and Jesus were such friends of God and prophets in whom Wisdom, vindicated by her 'children' and rejected by the masses (Luke 7.35; 11.49–51), definitively spoke. Matthew even identified Wisdom with the Christ.[8] This enabled him to understand Jesus as the incarnation of the Law and, hence, to construct the antithesis 'But I say to you . . .' Matthew could have written 'the Word became flesh' without thinking of a pre-existent Christ but rather of God's electing and redeeming word in the Law and the prophets which was finally spoken in Jesus, who 'will be with' all nations as long as they are taught to 'observe all that he has commanded' (28.20, cf. Heb. 1.1–2).

2   *Christ in the Old Testament*

1 Cor. 10.4 is not far from this view. In Wisd. 11.4–8, Wisdom's relationship to the 'friends of God and prophets' is explained in terms of the intervention of God's wisdom in the history of Israel, e.g. in her provision of water out of the rock. Philo and Pseudo-Philo show a much higher degree of personification, even suggesting that the rock accompanies Israel on its journey (*Leg.All.* II.86; *Det.Pot.Ins.* 115–18; *Ant. Bibl.* X.7).[9] Again Paul replaces Wisdom with Christ, but he teaches neither one decisive descent of a saviour nor a continuous relationship between the saviour and man's innermost self. Rather, it is a case of the word of God coming from outside, in an historic event, to the whole people of God (and not just to some gnostics) and bringing them water (which was lacking and which they did not possess within them).

3   *Christ the agent of creation and redemption*

1 Cor. 8.6 presupposes a pre-existence of Christ, even in the act of creation. This is again parallel to Prov. 3.19; 8.30; Wisd. 7.22; 9.2–4, etc. and again contrary to a gnostic devaluation of creation. The historical (baptismal?)[10] experience of redemption as the restoration of creation may have led to the belief in Christ as the agent of creation and redemption – the more so since 2 Cor. 4.6 shows how the Wisdom image facilitated the comparison of first and new creation.[11] This comparison is expanded in Col. 1.15–20, where parallels to Wisdom literature are again obvious[12] and nothing is said about the descent/ascent of the redeemer. His role in creation is seen positively and not simply as a past stage. He *is* both the agent of creation and the agent of redemption. Finally, Heb. 1.3 combines Christ as the Wisdom-image of God in creation with his glory in his exaltation. In both cases the reference to the cross has probably been added by the author of the letter to a tradition which said nothing about the earthly Jesus.[13] Even if this were not so, it is an historical event rather than the pattern of descent/ascent which is mentioned, and this is inconceivable for gnostic thinking.

4   *Christ incarnate*

All this shows a curious fact. There are Pauline concepts which presuppose that Christ existed in heaven when the world was created,

117

that he was on earth during his ministry (especially on the cross), and that he is now again sitting at the right hand of God – and yet the pattern of descent/ascent is totally lacking. Does it go unmentioned because Paul and his churches were familiar with it? And is there a gnostic myth at its roots? If so, we should expect at least some hint of it. Is there such a hint in the prologue of the Fourth Gospel? The Pauline references to Christ's co-operation in the creation of the world are here greatly expanded. C. H. Dodd long ago collected the parallels in the Wisdom literature and Philo and they are indubitable.[14] In contrast to 1 Cor. 8.6; Col. 1.15–18; and Heb. 1.3, John does speak of incarnation. The dwelling among us of the Logos forms the analogy to his work in creation and not his sitting at the right hand of God. On the one hand, this is parallel to Q and Matthew who see the word of God incarnated in the earthly ministry of Jesus; on the other hand, it is precisely in the incarnation that his glory is to be seen (John 1.14). Again, nothing is said about his descent, let alone his ascent. On the contrary, v. 18 sees Christ as still being 'in the bosom of the Father'. The descent/ascent pattern appears in 3.13, but in reverse order. The main point is that 'nobody has ascended to heaven except the one who descended from heaven, the son of man'. This clearly contests the claims of apocalyptists, a background to which the Son of man title also points.[15] The emphasis lies on the ascent, which will take place on the cross. The descent is mentioned not in order to describe a saving event, but to express the dimension in which Jesus, ascending to the cross and thus to heaven, is to be seen.[16]

5   *Christ, Son of God sent to earth*

The phrase 'God sent his son in order to . . .' (Gal. 4.4–5; Rom. 8.3–4; also John 3.16–17; 1 John 4.9) points to what one may call a descent, but only God's action is emphasized and not the redeemer's act of descending. Again, parallels in the Wisdom literature and Philo are overwhelming. Only there do we find the parallelism of sending Wisdom and sending the Spirit (Wisd. 9.10–17, expressed with the same, otherwise un-Pauline, verb as in Gal. 4.4, 6); a verb of sending with the 'son (of God)' as its object (e.g. Philo, *Agric.* 51); and the idea that *the* son creates other sons (e.g. Philo, *Conf. Ling.* 145–8).[17] Conversely, the phrase appears only in Paul and John, where a pre-existence of the son is taught, and the goal of the sending of the son is in all four instances his death on the cross.[18] His ascent is never mentioned, as it is in Tobit 12.20 ('I ascend to the one who sent me', cf. ἐγώ εἰμι v. 15). Thus, this phrase stands much closer to the concept of Wisdom sent by God (like an angel) as redeemer-revealer, as we find it in Wisd. 10–12, than to a gnostic myth.

6   *Christ humiliated and exalted*

There is one text which seems to be related to a gnostic myth: Phil. 2.6–11. I do not exclude the possibility of such a relation. Hellenistic Judaism was not 'holier' than Gnosticism. Both adapted many non-Israelite ingredients as well as genuinely Israelite ideas. Thus the discussion should remain as little influenced by one's prejudices as possible. Having stated this, I may say that this hymn does not literally speak of a descent, but of a self-humiliation;[19] and not of an ascent, but of Christ being exalted by God in response to his obedience. Much depends on the interpretation of the subjection of all beings in heaven, on earth and under the earth. For Paul, it is at the Parousia that this will happen – cf. 1 Cor. 15.24–8 and, especially, the same Old Testament quotation in Rom. 14.11 referring to the last judgement of God. Personally, I think this is also true for the pre-Pauline author of the hymn, since the closest parallel is the eschatological theophany, as Judaism expected it.[20] The theological insight which seems to be at the root of these verses is that of 2 Cor. 8.9,[21] i.e. an interpretation of the whole ministry of Jesus, to which Phil. 2.9–11 adds the vindication by God and the ultimate effect on the destiny of the universe. If the gnostic redeemer myth is in the background, which I consider improbable, the hymn uses gnostic language in order to stress the total difference between the abstract idea of a revelation which brings knowledge of man's divine innermost self, and the incarnation of one who had been 'equal with God', became obedient even to the extent of death on a cross, and was vindicated by God.

7   *Christianity and Gnosticism*

There is no doubt about the importance of Wisdom literature for both New Testament Christology and Gnosticism. However, I think that their roads separated early. By and large, Wisdom literature speaks of God's gift to man, teaching him what he does not find in himself and what he would consider folly. Wisdom is the word from 'outside', foreign to his own reasoning, and not merely waking up some sleeping, or digging up some buried, original wisdom. It is, therefore, given only to the 'friends of God and the prophets' (Wisd. 7.27; also Ecclus. 1.6, 10–14, 20). There are also other trends (Ecclus. 1.9, 10a) and they become effective in Philo's identification of God's Wisdom or Logos with the human mind. However, his difficulties become obvious when he distinguishes between the Logos of God as the original image of God (the 'coining die') and its copies (the *logoi* of men), or even introduces a further intermediate entity, an ideal human 'mind' or 'reason'.[22] Anyway, this is platonizing Judaism, not Gnosticism.

Developed from a Greek background the Colossian 'philosophy' was not very different. A Pythagorean text (1st century BC) uses the same terms as Col. 2: the divine soul has to be separated from the four elements of this world by an ascetic life (according to Pythagorean *dogmata*) and participate in baptisms and adoration of God and angels in order to enable it to ascend to the world above after death. This is judaizing Platonism, not Gnosticism. The ascent is that of the soul and the divine revealer is, for this group, their philosopher, as for the Colossians it is Christ. He is already sitting above, but the problem remains: is the soul purified enough by asceticism to ascend to him?[23]

Gnosticism proceeds on this road and identifies Wisdom of God and ideal mind. God then becomes Man ("Ανθρωπος with a capital 'A), and the redeeming act the coming of Man to man, reminding him merely of what he actually is in his innermost self. This may happen at any time and in any place on earth, and the mythical language of a descent and ascent of Wisdom and Logos serves only to describe what happens time and time again. Hence, one myth may easily be substituted for another one, the Attis myth being as helpful as the Christ myth.

Christianity, on the contrary, picks up the threads of the Jewish statements that Wisdom enters the souls of friends of God and prophets and becomes manifest at one place only – in Israel, in Jerusalem, in the Law of Moses (Ecclus. 24.7–8, 23; 1 Baruch 3.37; 4.1; cf. Prov. 8.17). It also proceeds on this road and identifies Wisdom or Logos with the one in whom God's word became flesh. While Gnosticism took up and radicalized a notion which had, perhaps, been at the root of Jewish Wisdom literature, the idea of a divine order inherent in all things and particularly in man's mind, Christianity, on the contrary, did so with the typically Jewish idea of Wisdom as the gift of God to his elect people, manifest in the vocation of the prophets, in the written Law and definitively, 'eschatologically' (Heb. 1.2) in Jesus Christ. This is where one has to throw the switch to one track or to the other.

With Paul, the starting point is not the detection of the otherness of the human mind or spirit over against the mere physical existence of man, to which the Wisdom myth gives expression, but the life and, especially, the death and resurrection of Jesus Christ which attracted Wisdom language. The Jewish description of Wisdom as rejected by all nations fitted Paul's interpretation of Jesus, the one crucified by the Romans. It had merely to be radicalized: Israel also rejected God's wisdom. She became a folly for the Gentiles and a stumbling block for the Jews. In contrast to the Synoptic writers, Paul and John no longer speak of God sending prophets or angels, because the Old Testament concept of God sending his angels, his prophets, his word or his wisdom to man has now been focused on the one event – Jesus Christ.

What parts of the Wisdom myth attract the Christian reinterpretation?

(*a*) The myth enables man to speak of the presence of God among men without confining him within the created world. It is his word in which he is present and the definitive, eschatological word is the kerygma of Jesus Christ, either preached by Jesus himself or by the apostles (point 1 above).

(*b*) The myth emphasizes the creative power of God manifested in the creation of the world and again in his redeeming acts in the history of Israel. Christianity sees the definitive act of God in the resurrection (points 2, 3) or the incarnation (point 4) of Jesus Christ, by whom the new creation was brought into being.

(*c*) The myth proffers the image of a decisive movement from God to man, a coming or sending. What gives the Christ event its distinction is the incarnation, or even the cross, in which this movement came to its goal (point 5). In all these points the descent is neither combined with an ascent nor described, e.g. as a passing through the different spheres of heaven.

(*d*) The resurrection of Jesus Christ and the experience of his continuing lordship had to be interpreted from the beginning, independently from any concept of a pre-existent Christ. This was done by reference to Ps. 110.1, to imagery of the suffering righteous exalted and vindicated by God, to Old Testament descriptions of the lordship of God and theophanies etc. Since the crucifixion and resurrection of Jesus were combined very early, the ideas of his becoming poor for the sake of man and of being vindicated and exalted

121

to continuing lordship up to the Parousia were also combined (point 6). To be sure, Phil. 2.6–11 in and of itself could be related to a gnostic redeemer myth. Yet what one might call a descent is actually a manifestation of self-humiliation, of obedience and self-sacrifice, for which the concept of God sending his word to earthly men gives the means of linguistic expression, and what one might call an ascent is rather a description of vindication, in which only the exalted place of the Lord (given by God himself!) and the final triumph which is still to be brought about by God's eschatological action are essential and not the act of ascending itself.

Thus I may close with C. K. Barrett's statement that Gnosticism is indeed 'an atmosphere' which forms the background of the New Testament. I might even say that its redeemer myth is 'so like Christianity and, at the same time, so radically different',[24] that I interpret it as a myth rooted in the same area of Jewish Wisdom literature as the Christian statements about the pre-existence, incarnation and exaltation of Jesus, but developed independently. I even think that, as far as the redeemer myth (and not merely the gnostic atmosphere) is concerned, cross-fertilization started by and large only in the period after the New Testament and that the New Testament has scarcely been influenced by it.

NOTES

1 'I am not ashamed of the Gospel', in *Foi et salut selon S. Paul*, An.Bib. 42 (1970), p. 30, cf. p. 50. Also idem, *Jesus and the Gospel Tradition* (London 1967), pp. 17–19.

2 *The Second Epistle to the Corinthians* (London 1973), p. 39.

3 'Das Fleisch des Menschensohns', in *Jesus und der Menschensohn*, Festschrift for A. Vögtle, ed. R. Pesch and R. Schnackenburg (Freiburg 1975), pp. 351, 354.

4 'Jews and Judaisers in the epistles of Ignatius', in *Jews, Greeks and Christians*, Festschrift for W. D. Davies, ed. R. Hamerton-Kelly and R. Scroggs (Leiden 1976), pp. 235, 240–2.

5 *The Signs of an Apostle* (London 1970), p. 97, cf. p. 137 n241. Here the problem of the gnostic redeemer-revealer is explicitly left aside; cf. also idem, *The Gospel according to St. John* (London 1978), pp. viii, 38–9, 140–1, 204, etc.

6 *The New Testament Background: Selected Documents* (London 1956), pp. 54, 80–90, esp. p. 81.

7   The order is reversed in 4 Ezra 4.8; but its context shows how this happens without any influence of a gnostic myth.

8   M. J. Suggs, *Wisdom, Christology and Law in Matthew's Gospel* (Cambridge, Mass., 1970), pp. 30–97; also E. Schweizer, *Matthäus und seine Gemeinde* (Stuttgart 1974), pp. 54–7; cf. the personified Wisdom in 11QPsa 154, *DJD* iv (Oxford 1965), pp. 64–5.

9   C. K. Barrett, *The First Epistle to the Corinthians* (London 1968), pp. 222–3. He refers also to *Leg.All.* III.162, where Philo thinks of a permanent relation between God and man. The rock is for Paul not a mere allegory, but the scene of Christ's activity (cf. Barrett, *Second Corinthians*, pp. 223–4); God's power manifested there appeared definitively in Christ.

10 R. Kerst, '1 Kor. 8.6 – ein vorpaulinisches Taufbekenntnis?', *ZNW* 66 (1975), pp. 130–9; cf. R. A. Horsley, 'The Background of the Confessional Formula in 1 Cor. 8.6', *ZNW* 69 (1978), pp. 130–5.

11 There may be a polemical usage of 'gnostic' (i.e. Corinthian) terms (Barrett, *Second Corinthians*, p. 135).

12 E. Schweizer, *Der Brief an die Kolosser* (Einsiedeln/Neukirchen 1976), pp. 56–9 (English edition by SPCK, London 1982).

13 ibid., pp. 53–4; also G. Theissen, *Untersuchungen zum Hebräerbrief* (Gütersloh 1969), pp. 51–2 n51.

14 *The Interpretation of the Fourth Gospel* (Cambridge 1953), pp. 274–7; also Barrett, *John*, pp. 153–7; M. D. Hooker, 'The Johannine Prologue and the Messianic Secret', *NTS* 21 (1974), esp. pp. 52–8.

15 cf. Barrett, *Jesus*, pp. 30–2, 89–99; and *John*, pp. 72–3, 181.

16 cf. Barrett, *John*, pp. 212–3 (stressing both descent and ascent).

17 Cornut. *Theol.Graec.* 16 (contemporary with Paul) is an allegorization of Hermes myths, which may also go back to Hermetic Logos speculations in Egypt.

18 cf. Gal. 4.5 with 3.13; περὶ ἁμαρτίας (Rom. 8.3) is the term for atoning sacrifice; John 3.16b runs parallel to v. 15, suggesting that v. 14 is parallel to v. 16a; 1 John 4.9 is interpreted by v. 10.

19 Ταπεινοῦν means 'to lower' and can be used to contrast with 'to exalt', but is used only in a spiritual sense, and no longer in its originally local sense (Liddell-Scott, s.v.).

20 O. Hofius, *Der Christushymnus Philipper 2.6–11* (Tübingen 1976), pp. 41–55.

21 cf. Barrett, *Second Corinthians*, pp. 222–4 (with his cautious reference to a gnostic myth) and the descent/ascent of the word (Isa. 55.10–11), the angel (Tobit 12.20), and the wisdom (Eth.Enoch 42.2).

22 E. Schweizer, *TWNT* ix, pp. 464–5; idem, *Heiliger Geist* (Stuttgart 1978), pp. 57–8.

23 E. Schweizer, *Kolosser*, p. 104, and 'Christianity of the Circumcised and Judaism of the Uncircumcised', in *Jews, Greeks and Christians*, Festschrift for W. D. Davies, esp. pp. 249–55.

24 Barrett, *Signs*, p. 97.

12

Chronology and the Development of Pauline Christology

Maurice Casey

Less than thirty years after the death of the historical Jesus, St Paul wrote the first surviving Christian work in which Jesus is very probably termed Θεός (Rom. 9.5).[1] Moreover, this occurrence may be seen as the natural culmination of an observable process of development which had already raised Jesus to a unique status as a pre-existent divine being hardly more than twenty years after his death.[2] Why did Pauline Christology develop so quickly?

We may begin by using the pre-Pauline material embedded in the epistles to bridge the large gap between the Christology of the historical Jesus and that of St Paul.[3] In this material we find the titles Κύριος and Χριστός, both evidently very old: while we cannot be precise about their age, it is evident that both originated in their full sense much less than twenty years after the death and resurrection of Jesus. Κύριος is found in the confessions of Rom. 10.9; 1 Cor. 12.3; Phil. 2.11; and perhaps Rom. 1.4, as well as in the early tradition of 1 Cor. 11.23, while the Aramaic *maranatha* at 1 Cor. 16.22 (cf. *Did.* 10.6; Rev. 22.20) shows that the Aramaic-speaking church already addressed the risen Jesus as 'Lord'. Χριστός occurs in the confession of Phil. 2.11, as perhaps in the confession of Rom. 1.4, and in the early tradition of 1 Cor. 15.3: Paul's use of it as virtually a name of Jesus further confirms that it is early (cf. Acts 2.36; 11.26). Rom. 1.3 adds belief in Jesus' descent from David, a belief which may be inaccurate but early. The term 'Son of God' is also pre-Pauline in a sense which goes beyond that current in Jesus' lifetime, but Rom. 1.3f appears to show an intermediate state of development when Jesus was believed to have been appointed 'Son of God' after the resurrection (cf. Acts 2.36; 5.31; 13.33). The absence of the virgin birth from this tradition, and from developed Pauline Christology, is notable.

The ancient piece of tradition preserved at 1 Cor. 15.3–5 shows the development that Jesus' death was 'for our sins', while his resurrection is attested 'on the third day according to the Scriptures' (1 Cor. 15.4), and a list of appearances attests the fundamental importance of the resurrection of Jesus to the Church in the pre-Pauline period. Very early belief in the second coming of Jesus is also attested by the Aramaic formula *maranatha* (1 Cor. 16.22). Rom. 6.3ff, without using any pre-Pauline formula, seems to assume not only the development of Christian baptism as the normal and unquestioned mode of initiation into the Christian community, but also that baptism was understood in the pre-Pauline community as baptism into Christ's death. Considerable further development is to be found in the pre-Pauline hymn of Phil. 2.6–11. Here the death of Jesus, like his incarnation, is treated chiefly as obedient humiliation, and the complexity of atonement theology found elsewhere in Paul is absent, while the status of Jesus has risen to be almost divine. Before the incarnation Jesus was pre-existent ἐν μορφῇ Θεοῦ, and after his exaltation he received the name of God. Col. 1.15–20 may also be a pre-Pauline hymn, and here too Jesus is seen as in some sense divine, for ἐν αὐτῷ εὐδόκησεν πᾶν τὸ πλήρωμα κατοικῆσαι (Col. 1.19). In this hymn Jesus is the pre-existent agent of both creation and redemption εἰκὼν τοῦ Θεοῦ τοῦ ἀοράτου and ἡ κεφαλὴ τοῦ σώματος τῆς ἐκκλησίας. His cosmic role also includes that of sustaining the universe.

This pre-Pauline material demonstrates that Pauline Christology is not the work of a single mind, nor is it a single entity whose sudden appearance must be accounted for; it is the result of a detectable process of development. To this process, the development of intermediary figures in intertestamental Judaism provides useful parallels of explanatory significance.[4] The parallel material has two aspects which I call 'static' and 'dynamic'. By 'static' parallels I mean discrete items of known Jewish belief about intermediary figures which are found also as beliefs about Jesus: these items may have been simply transferred from one intermediary figure to another. For example, at Wisd. 7.21 Wisdom is the agent of creation: at 1 Cor. 8.6; Col. 1.16, the same belief is predicated of Jesus: thus Wisd. 7.21 contains a static parallel to an item of Pauline Christology. By a 'dynamic' parallel I mean evidence that an intermediary figure was involved in a process which increased its status and/or function. The existence of such parallels will enable us to fit the development of Pauline Christology into a broader pattern.

We may consider static parallels first. Of the titles of Jesus found in the Pauline epistles, κύριος has a very wide range, running from the equivalent of 'sir' up to the designation of God, and this is true also of the Aramaic מר which was occasionally used to address the historical Jesus, though it was not a term which his closest disciples normally used. The early formula *maranatha* (1 Cor. 16.22) shows how easily the content of the term could slide upwards if the community did no more than continue to address Jesus, whom they believed to be alive in heaven. There are Jewish parallels to addressing angels in similar fashion, using the equivalent Hebrew אדני or the Greek κύριε (cf., e.g., Zech. 4.4, 5; 4 Ezra 4.3, 5; 3 Baruch 4.1). Χριστός, though apparently not yet in use as a full title, was developed from משיח which was already in use as applied to major intermediary figures, of whom the expected Davidic king and the expected Levitical priest were especially important, and it seems probable that the crystallization of this expectation into a single figure was the only necessary condition required for the emergence of the title. 'Son of God' was already in use during the ministry of Jesus, as occasionally in Jewish documents, to indicate an exceptional human being. Jewish parallels include its use of an exceptionally righteous man (cf., e.g., bT *Taan.* 24b//bT *Ber.* 17b//bT *Hull.* 86a), and its application to Levi (Test.Levi 4.2) and to a Hasmonean king (4Q ps-Dan). Wisdom is described in terms which begin to approach divine status (Wisd. 7.21ff), and in 11Q Melchizedek OT passages containing the terms אל and אלהים (Ps. 82.1) are interpreted of Melchizedek, while Paul's single description of Jesus as Θεός is most closely paralleled by Philo's description of Moses as ὅλου τοῦ ἔθνους θεὸς καὶ βασιλεύς (*de Vit. Mos.* I. 158).

Pre-existence is easiest to parallel in hellenistic Judaism, where all men's souls were believed to exist before they entered bodies (e.g. Wisd. 8.19–20; cf. also Josephus, *B.J.* II. 154–5), and this belief is probably to be found predicated of all the righteous in the Similitudes of Enoch (1 Enoch 70.4; cf. 39.4f). Pre-existence in a stronger and more relevant sense was attributed to Enoch himself, who was named and hidden not merely before his earthly life but before the creation of the world (1 Enoch 48.3, 6; cf. 62.7). The most significant material concerns Wisdom, who was created before everything else, before earth itself, already at Prov. 8.22f (cf. Ecclus. 1.4; 24.3, 9); while at Wisd. 7.21 she is the agent of creation. Pre-existent beings which subsequently dwell on earth necessarily become candidates for descent-ascent patterns. The clearest examples are angels who live in heaven but who descend temporarily for a specific purpose, as does for example the archangel Raphael in the Book of Tobit.[5] The pattern must be deduced in the case of Enoch in the Similitudes, and it is explicit for Wisdom at 1 Enoch 42, while elements of it are applied to Wisdom elsewhere (cf., e.g., Wisd. 9.10, Baruch 3.37–8). The presence of these partial elements reflects the fact that the complete pattern may be made up of similar elements in the case of another intermediary, and need not be taken over in one piece.

When we look for parallels to Jesus' fundamental role in salvation history, we must note that in different ways the Davidic king, Michael, Melchizedek, Moses, Enoch and Wisdom were believed to play a fundamental role in bringing salvation to Israel. The Davidic king was generally expected to achieve this by military and political means, in accordance with normally current concepts of kingship (cf. esp. Ps. Sol. 17—18), while Michael and Melchizedek appear to have been expected to act in a supernatural manner (cf. Dan. 12; 11Q Melch). Moses had already played a fundamentally significant role as the lawgiver (e.g. Philo, *de Vit.Mos.* II. 8ff). Enoch was expected to perform as an eschatological judge, and in the Similitudes this role was regarded as so important that it could be said that the righteous are saved in his name (1 Enoch 48.7). Wisdom may be given the major role in the salvation of Israel (Wisd. 10—11, cf. Baruch 3.9—4.4), or in the lives of men (Wisd. 9.18). Thus the performance of a major role in salvation history may appropriately be predicated of an intermediary figure, while the details of such a role differ from one figure to another.

For parallel material to Paul's assessment of the death of Jesus, we must turn primarily to the martyrs. The death of martyrs was believed to have atoning significance (cf. esp. 2 Macc. 7.37–8; 4 Macc.17.20–2). Sacrificial terminology is used of it, thus providing sufficient parallel to explain the creative application of sacrificial terminology to the death of Jesus: the death of the martyrs was considered effective in bringing about the removal of the wrath of God. Faith in the Teacher of Righteousness also functioned, alongside the suffering of the Qumran community, as a reason for deliverance by God (1QpHab 8. 1–3). There is some evidence that martyrs were believed to have gone straight to heaven, not having to wait for the general resurrection of the dead. Abel, Elijah, Enoch, Melchizedek, Michael, Moses, Wisdom and others were variously believed to be in heaven: Enoch, later Metatron, was enthroned there (cf., e.g., 1 Enoch 62; 3 Enoch 10), as was Abel (Test.Abr. 13) or David (R.Akiba, bT *Hag.* 14a//bT *San.* 38b), while Ezekiel portrayed Moses as dreaming that he sat on the throne of God (Eusebius, *Praep.Ev.* IX.29; cf. also Wisd. 9.10). Prayer is addressed to Moses at Philo, *De Somn.* I. 164–5, and the kings and mighty were expected to supplicate Enoch at the last day (1 Enoch 62.9). Prayers addressed to the sun still survived among the Essenes (Josephus, *Wars* II.128). The Davidic king, the Levitical High Priest, a prophet, Elijah, Enoch and Moses were variously expected to come at the last day (cf., e.g., 1 Enoch 90.31; 1QS 9.11; 4 Ezra 13.52; Tg Ex. 12.42): at this time Abel (Test.Abr. 13) or Enoch (1 Enoch 62; 69.26f) was expected to play an active role as an eschatological judge. The application of OT passages to Jesus (cf. esp. Phil. 2.10–11; 2 Thess. 1.8f; 1 Cor. 15.25–7; 2 Cor. 3.16; Eph. 1.20–2) is paralleled by the application of OT passages to messianic and intermediary figures in rabbinical literature and at Qumran, where it includes the application of Hab. 2.4b to the faithfulness (אמנתם) of appropriately observant Jews to the Teacher of Righteousness (1QpHab 8.1–3), and the application of Ps. 82.1 and Ps. 7.7–8 to Melchizedek, who is thus seen as אלהים and אל (11Q Melchizedek). The transference to Wisdom of actions explicitly those of God in a scriptural narrative is to be found in Wisd. 10—11.1.

These static parallels to Pauline Christology are substantial and extensive. It is also important that the more outstanding intermediary figures are significantly unique, and that the elaboration of these intermediaries bears witness to the existence of a dynamic creative process in intertestamental Judaism. The variety and extensive elaboration of these figures is remarkable: the Davidic king, an eschatological High Priest, an eschatological prophet, Abel, Elijah, Enoch, Melchizedek, Michael, Moses, Wisdom, all these were held by some Jews in this period to be of unusually elevated status and to have performed or to be about to perform some function of evident significance. The ascription of significant new functions to these figures, and the dynamic parallels thus provided, are of greater importance than the static parallels already discussed, because they testify to the existence of a developmental process whose variability shows that when another intermediary figure is elaborated we should not expect it to conform to any existing figure. The following are some of the more striking developments.

The expected Davidic king becomes increasingly righteous until at Ps.Sol. 18.36 he is to be καθαρὸς ἀπὸ ἁμαρτίας: eventually he receives the title מלכא משיחא or simply משיחא (in Hebrew, המשיח). The expectation of a Levitical high priest evidently developed in the post-exilic period, and in passages such as 1QSa 2.11ff and Test. Judah 21 he is evidently superior in status to the Davidic king: at

Test.Levi 18.12 he is expected to bind Belial. Enoch, already translated to heaven in Gen. 5.24 and presumably the object of more attention than this brief report tells us, appears to have become, as early as the third century BC, a supernatural scribal figure who receives and transmits revelations, and at 1 Enoch 13—14 he conveys the message of judgement to the Giants. In the Similitudes, however, he has become the eschatological judge himself. At the beginning of the intertestamental period Michael appears as the angel who stands up for Israel (Dan. 12.1), and in 1QM 17 he is so exalted that the angelic world can be designated the kingdom of Michael in contrast to the kingdom of wickedness or the realm of Israel. At Test.Levi 5.6–7 he intercedes for the people of Israel and for all the righteous, and at 1 Enoch 54.6 he, with Gabriel, Raphael and Phanuel; executes judgement on the hosts of Azazel at the last day. In 11Q Melchizedek, Melchizedek, having figured briefly in the OT (Gen. 14.18–20; Ps. 110.4), suddenly appears as the eschatological redeemer, so exalted that OT texts containing the terms אל and אלהים are applied to him. 2 Enoch adds his miraculous birth, without any biological father. Abel, an early patriarch, was deemed worthy of mention at 1 Enoch 22 because his spirit was making accusation against Cain, and at Test.Abr.13 he has become an eschatological judge.

Wisdom is a pre-existent abstract figure at Prov. 8.22: in passages such as Ecclus. 24, Wisd. 7 and 1 Enoch 42 she is the agent of creation, while the succeeding verses build an almost divine status for her. At Wisd. 18.14f the Word of God is also portrayed like a separate entity of great power, and Philo can describe the λόγος as δεύτερος θεός (*Qu. in Gen.* II.62; cf. *Leg.All.* III.207; *De Somn.* I.229–30, 238–9). Martyrdom theology did not begin until the Maccabean revolt, and it developed so that the death of the martyrs was believed to be an effective atoning sacrifice which removed the wrath of God and thereby delivered the people of Israel. Moses was already a fundamentally significant intermediary in the OT, and further developments occurred in the intertestamental period. At Ass.Mos. 1.14 he is pre-existent at least in the sense of being foreseen, Ezekiel portrayed him dreaming that he sat on the throne of God (Eusebius, *Praep.Ev.* IX.29), Josephus has him disappear in a cloud rather than merely die (*Ant.* IV.48), and continued development in the rabbinical period includes the expectation that he will return at the end (e.g. Tg Ex. 12.42). Josephus reports that the Essenes venerated him most after God himself, and punished blasphemy against him with death (*Wars* II.145; cf. 152).

Prayer is addressed to him at Philo, *De Somn.* I.164–5, and Philo's lengthy, detailed and idealized portrayal of him includes the assertion that God gave him the whole world as a possession fit for an heir so that all the elements obeyed him (*de Vit.Mos.* I.155) and the description of him as ὅλου τοῦ ἔθνους θεὸς καὶ βασιλεύς (*de Vit.Mos.* I.158). Later developments include the application to him of Isa. 53.12 (R.Simlai, bT *Sot.* 14a).

Continued development in the rabbinical period is especially striking in the case of Elijah and *Torah*. Elijah was already a significant prophet, and as early as Mal. 3.23f we find the development that he will return in a significant role, an expectation taken up at Ecclus. 48.1–12. Justin retails a Jewish belief that Elijah will anoint the Messiah (*Dial.* 49), and M.*Sot.* IX.15 says that the resurrection of the dead will come through him. He was also expected to solve some outstanding halakhic disputes (cf., e.g., M.*Eduy.* VIII.7). The Law lay at the centre of Judaism, and it was expected to continue to exist for ever (Philo, *de Vit.Mos.* II.14). In the rabbinical period it came to be thought of as pre-existent, and even as the agent of creation (e.g. R. Akiba, *Pirqe Aboth* III.19). These developments, together with continued speculation about other figures such as Metatron, show that despite the drastic effects of the disaster of AD 66–70, the tendency of intermediaries to rise in status and increase in function continued into the rabbinical period.

A basic limitation to the rise in status of these intermediaries was provided by the now traditional Jewish monotheism. One after another, these intermediaries could take over some of the functions of God, but they could not take fully divine status because belief in one God alone was not only well established – it was a distinguishing mark of the Jewish community (e.g. Ps-Aristeas 134, cf. 137). When Christianity spread to the Gentile world, this restraining factor was removed. In Paul, the outstanding facilitator of this spread, Christology has begun to break through the limitations imposed by its Jewish origins. Jesus is uniquely Son of God, the combined functions of Jesus have surpassed those of any single Jewish intermediary, and the thrust continues upwards, so that we have both monotheistic belief and the single description of Jesus as Θεός. In the author of the Fourth Gospel we meet a Gentile who has allowed the deity of Jesus to assume consistently expounded ontological status.

Thus Judaism at the time of St Paul bears witness to the development of intermediary figures to a sufficient extent for the development of Christology to be seen as falling into a more general pattern. Moreover, so many of the items of secondary christological development are already to be found in Jewish intermediary figures as to make a rather rapid development intelligible; it need not take long to decide that what was already believed of Enoch or of Wisdom was in fact true of Jesus. In the case of Jesus, however, a further factor came into play: it was he who constituted the identity of the whole early Christian community. This is true of him in a sense which goes beyond anything found in contemporary Judaism: even Moses and the Davidic king, important as they were to many Jews, were not as fundamental as Jesus to the Christians. Perhaps the nearest parallels are Enoch and Wisdom, who appear to constitute significant identity factors for the sub-groups which elevated them to such a high position. Already at 1 Enoch 93.10 the elect group are chosen from the eternal plant of righteousness, and these can hardly be any other than the Enoch circle within Judaism. In the Similitudes of Enoch, where Enoch is the eschatological judge, the identification of the supreme figure as Enoch constitutes the final climax of the whole work (1 Enoch 71.14): eternal bliss can be described in terms of being with him (1 Enoch 71.16–17; cf. 62.14), and the community is sufficiently identified with reference to him to be able to say that he has preserved the lot of the righteous and in his name they are saved (1 Enoch 48.7); the kings of the earth on the other hand denied him as well as the Lord of Spirits (1 Enoch 48.10), and it is he whom they will petition at the last day (1 Enoch 62.9). Thus this community formed a sub-group distinguished from most Jews by its attitude to Enoch.

The author of the Wisdom of Solomon evidently regarded his learning as being of fundamental significance for both himself and his group of wise men. The passage in which Wisdom is given a role in creation and her virtually divine nature is expounded at some length (Wisd. 7.21ff) is immediately preceded by a list of branches of knowledge which are included within the purview of wisdom (Wisd. 7.17ff). One of the descriptions of the wicked man is he who despises wisdom and instruction (3.11), while kings should learn it (6.9); at the group level, πλῆθος δὲ σοφῶν σωτηρία κόσμου (6.24). Both of these communities, however, were groups within Judaism as a whole, and neither regarded salvation as denied to other Jews. At 1 Enoch 45.2 the sinners are defined as those who have denied the name of the Lord of Spirits, and at 46.6–8 their sins are of a general kind, including the persecution of the faithful who hang upon the name of the Lord of

Spirits. The Book of Wisdom asserts the oneness of God (12.13), and assumes that the righteous man reproaches the wicked for sins against the Law (2.12); Sirach follows his lofty personalized picture of wisdom by identifying Wisdom with the Law (Ecclus. 24.23). To this extent these intermediary figures are of secondary importance even to their sub-groups: they are something less than the main focus for groups primarily devoted to the one God and his Law, that is, to the mainstream markers of Judaism.

In this respect, Pauline Christianity differs from its parent Judaism: once the gospel was spread in such a manner that Gentiles could be accepted who did not take upon themselves obedience to the Law, the new community needed a focus of identity which was not a distinguishing mark of the orthodox Judaism which they declined to take on. As Paul put it, οὐκ ἔνι ᾽Ιουδαῖος οὐδὲ ῞Ελλην . . . πάντες γὰρ ὑμεῖς εἷς ἐστε ἐν Χριστῷ ᾽Ιησοῦ (Gal. 3.28; cf. 1 Cor. 12.12–13; Col. 3.11). From the theological point of view, this change necessitated the working out of the function and status of Jesus at an intellectual level. This task was begun in Christian communities before and apart from Paul, but Paul's grounding in hellenistic Judaism, his conversion on the Damascus road and the deep commitment to Jesus which he always maintained, his personal vigour and intellectual ability, all fitted him ideally for the task of further development. As a faithful Jew, he went no further than a single worshipful description of Jesus as Θεός, with other expressions on the verge of deity. Once he had so facilitated the spread of the gospel to the Gentiles, other Christians who were Gentiles could go further, even reinterpreting the Jewish monotheistic tradition to which Paul had also adhered (cf. Rom. 3.30; 1 Cor. 8.4–6; Gal. 3.20) to ensure that the community was not dissipated by adherence to a plurality of Gods, a situation in which it would not have been clearly marked off from the rest of the Gentile world.

Furthermore, if Jewish parallels enable us to see how some christological development could take place quickly, the position of Jesus as the focus of the community's identity means that christological development *had* to take place quickly, because no community can form itself as a separate entity and yet have a focus of identity which is of insufficient status and function. From this perspective, twenty or thirty years is not a short time. Finally, it should be noted that certain christological developments are a necessary adjunct to Jesus' position as the focus of the community's identity. Two of these are especially notable. Firstly, if Jesus was elevated to this position in a community which admitted Gentiles and ceased thereby to observe the Law, the fact that the Law need not be observed was bound to be attributed in some sense to him (cf., e.g., Rom. 10.4; Gal. 3.13–14 and, independently, Heb. 7ff). Secondly, it became easy to use incorporative language of Jesus: πάντες γὰρ ὑμεῖς εἷς ἐστε ἐν Χριστῷ ᾽Ιησοῦ (Gal. 3.28), not least because otherwise you could not be one at all. Thus Jesus has two significant functions which could hardly be those of a purely Jewish intermediary.

The following hypothesis may therefore be suggested. Two aspects of Judaism at the time of St Paul are important in explaining the rapid rise of Pauline Christology. The first is that of static parallels: these enable us to see how certain discrete items could be taken over from existing Judaism into Christology. The second is that of dynamic parallels: these show us intermediary figures increasing in function and status so as to produce several different unique figures, and Jewish monotheism is the only limiting factor that can be detected. Any new intermediary may therefore be expected to differ from existing figures: there is no discernible limit to the functions it may have, and the only limit to its status is that of monotheism, which would not operate in a Gentile community. The next fundamental factor is then the spread of the gospel to the Gentiles: in Paul, brought up and trained as a strict Jew, this has not quite resulted in the removal of the limitation of monotheism. It has however already had the fundamental consequence that the focus of the community's identity is Jesus rather than God or the Law, and this is the factor which necessitated rather than merely permitted rapid christological growth.

NOTES

1   B. M. Metzger, 'The Punctuation of Rom. 9.5', in *Christ and Spirit in the New Testament*, in honour of C. F. D. Moule, ed. B. Lindars and S. S. Smalley (Cambridge 1973), pp. 95–102.

2   For definition and discussion of the chronological problem, cf. M. Hengel, 'Christologie und neutestamentliche Chronologie', in *Neues Testament und Geschichte*, Festschrift für O. Cullmann zum 70 Geburtstag, ed. H. Baltenweiler und B. Reicke (Zürich/Tübingen 1972), pp. 43–67.

3   For an exposition of what the Christology of the historical Jesus was, and a description of the subsequent development, with full bibliography, cf. P. M. Casey, 'The Development of New Testament Christology', in *Aufstieg und Niedergang der Römischen Welt*, ed. H. Temporini und W. Haase, vol. ii. 26 (forthcoming).

4 For discussion of these figures, cf. *TWNT*, s.v. Ἡλείας (J. Jeremias), Μωυσῆς (J. Jeremias), σοφία (G. Fohrer, U. Wilckens), χρίω κτλ (F. Hesse, M. de Jonge, A. S. van der Woude); M. Smith, 'What is implied by the Variety of Messianic Figures?', *JBL* 78 (1959), pp. 66–72; J. Starcky, 'Les quatre étapes du messianisme à Qumran', *RB* 70 (1963), pp. 481–505; R. E. Brown, 'J. Starcky's Theory of Qumran Messianic Development', *CBQ* 28 (1966), pp. 51–7; M. de Jonge, 'The Use of the Word "Anointed" in the Time of Jesus', *Nov. Test.* 8 (1966), pp. 132–48; id., 'The Role of Intermediaries in God's Final Intervention in the Future according to the Qumran Scrolls', in *Studies in the Jewish Background of the New Testament*, ed. O. Michel et al. (Assen 1969), pp. 44–63; E. Schürer, rev. and ed. G. Vermes, F. Millar and M. Black, *The History of the Jewish People in the age of Jesus Christ*, vol. ii (Edinburgh 1979), ch. 29; P. Grelot, 'La Légende d'Hénoch dans les Apocryphes et dans la Bible: Origine et signification', *RechScR* 46 (1958), pp. 5–26, 181–210; P. M. Casey, 'The Use of the Term "son of man" in the Similitudes of Enoch', *JSJ* VII (1976), pp. 11–29; id., *Son of Man. The Interpretation and Influence of Daniel 7* (London 1980), pp. 99–107; M. Delcor, 'Melchizedek from Genesis to the Qumran Texts and the Epistle to the Hebrews', *JSJ* II (1971), pp. 115–35; F. Horton, *The Melchizedek Tradition* (SNTSMS 31 (Cambridge 1976); W. L. Knox, 'The Divine Wisdom', *JTS* 38 (1937), pp. 230–7; J. W. Wood, *Wisdom Literature* (London 1967), chs 5—7; G. W. Macrae, 'The Jewish Background of the Gnostic Sophia Myth', *Nov. Test.* 12 (1970), pp. 86–101; E. Stauffer, *New Testament Theology* (ET London ⁵1948), App. I; C. K. Barrett, 'The Background of Mark 10.45', in *New Testament Essays. Studies in Memory of T. W. Manson*, ed. A. J. B. Higgins (Manchester 1959), pp. 1–18; J. Downing, 'Jesus and Martyrdom', *JTS* NS XIV (1963), pp. 279–93; W. H. C. Frend, *Martyrdom and Persecution in the Early Church* (Oxford 1965), ch. 2; T. F. Pollard, 'Martyrdom and Resurrection in the New Testament', *BJRL* 55 (1972), pp. 240–51; R. Williamson, 'Philo and New Testament Christology', *ET* xc (1979), pp. 361–5.

5 cf. C. H. Talbert, 'The Myth of a Descending-ascending Redeemer in Mediterranean Antiquity', *NTS* 22 (1975–6), pp. 418–40; Talbert has further examples, but his syncretistic use of mostly late evidence does not seem to me to have established that 'A myth of a heavenly redeemer who descended and ascended in the course of his/her saving work existed in pre-Christian Judaism and alongside first- and second-century Christianity', ibid. 430. The gnostic material still seems too late to utilize here; cf. in general, C. Colpe, *Die religionsgeschichtliche Schule* (FRLANT 78, Göttingen 1961); E. M. Yamauchi, *Pre-Christian Gnosticism* (London 1973).

13

Erwägungen zum Sprachgebrauch von Χριστός bei Paulus und in der 'vorpaulinischen' Überlieferung*

Martin Hengel

Unter den Appellativa und Namen, die der Apostel in seinen echten Briefen (Röm.; 1 und 2 Kor.; Gal.; Phil.; 1 Thess.; Philem.) verwendet, steht Χριστός[1] in der Häufigkeit seines Vorkommens hinter Θεός an zweiter Stelle. Nach der Konkordanz zur 26. A. des Nestle-Aland erscheint es insgesamt 270mal (Θεός 430mal),[2] d.h. zugleich: mehr als die Hälfte der 531 Belege für Χριστός in Neuen Testament begegnen uns in dem Briefcorpus des frühesten christlichen Autors. Bei den anderen christologischen Namen und Titeln ist die Relation zwischen dem paulinischen Sprachgebrauch und dem der späteren neutestamentlichen Schriften bei weitem nicht so einseitig. Ἰησοῦς findet sich bei Paulus 143mal (919); κύριος 189mal (719)[3]; υἱὸς Θεοῦ (bzw. absolutes υἱός) nur 15mal (105).[4] Da gerade bei den christologischen Titeln und Namen des Corpus Paulinum eine nicht geringe Zahl von Textvarianten besteht, sind die genannten Zahlen nach oben oder unten leicht variabel, was auch ein Vergleich mit der Statistik Morgenthalers[5] zeigen kann, am Gesamteindruck ändert sich dadurch jedoch kaum etwas. Auch in den Deuteropaulinen setzt sich diese Vorliebe für die Bezeichnung Χριστός—freilich in erheblich abgeschwächter Weise—noch fort, mit Ausnahme des Titusbriefs, dessen Christologie, wie der auffallend häufige Gebrauch von σωτήρ zeigt, ein besonders hellenistisches Gepräge besitzt.[6] Die Apostelgeschichte, die umfangreichste Schrift des Neuen Testaments, hat dagegen nur 26 Belege,[7] das Corpus Johanneum (Evangelium und Briefe) 30.[8] Beide sind in ihrem Umfang nur etwa 20% kürzer als die echten Paulusbriefe. Die Apokalypse steht mit sieben Stellen hinter den acht des Philemonbriefes zurück, Heb. (12) und 1 Pet. (22) haben wesentlich weniger Christosstellen als der kürzere Phil. (37).

Dieser eindeutige Befund ist wohl kaum ein blosser Zufall, sondern bedarf der Erklärung. Auf der anderen Seite darf diese nicht

* See English summary on p. 159

vorschnell in den unbestreitbaren Tatbestand eine theologische Begründung hineinlesen. Darum zögere ich, ohne weiteres der Bemerkung von L. Cerfaux zu folgen: '"Christus" ist das Schlüsselwort der paulinischen Briefe.'[9] Das gilt sicherlich für die *Person* Jesu Christi, kann dann aber von den allermeisten Schriften des N.T.s ebenfalls gesagt werden. Bei dem blossen Namen Χριστός muss es erst begründet werden. Die auffallende häufige Verwendung des Wortes zur Bezeichnung Jesu bei Paulus scheint zunächst eher ein Rätsel als ein 'Schlüssel' zum besseren Verständnis der paulinischen Christologie zu sein.

Das Rätsel wird noch grösser, wenn wir bedenken, dass nach der ältesten Evangelientradition, d.h. dem Markusevangelium und der Logienquelle, Jesus den Messiastitel nie expressis verbis unmittelbar für sich selbst beansprucht hat. In Q erscheint er überhaupt nicht, und bei Markus wird er—wenn wir von 9.41 absehen, wo schon der typische christliche Sprachgebrauch als Name vorliegt—immer von anderen an Jesus herangetragen.[10] Es erhebt sich hier sofort die Frage, die das Grundproblem der frühesten Christologie überhaupt darstellt: Wie wurde Jesus zum Messias, und wie kam es dazu, dass in einer—für religiöse Entwicklungen in der Antike—relativ kurzen Zeit der Messiastitel so fest mit dem Namen Jesu verbunden wurde, dass er nicht nur diesem als Cognomen beigefügt werden, sondern sogar an dessen Stelle treten konnte, und darum schon beim ersten christlichen Autor als die häufigste Bezeichnung Jesu verwendet wurde?[11]

Der älteste Brief des Apostels an die Thessalonicher um 50 n. Chr. setzt diesen Sprachgebrauch in der auch sonst in den echten Paulusbriefen üblichen Vielfalt[12] und in festgeformten Wendungen bereits voraus. D.h. derselbe muss sich schon geraume Zeit zuvor verfestigt haben. Wir begegnen dort der liturgisch klingenden Formel κύριος Ἰησοῦς Χριστός im Briefeingang,[13] häufiger noch erscheint die erweiterte Fassung ὁ κύριος ἡμῶν Ἰησοῦς Χριστός, vor allem am Ende des Briefes (5.9,23,28; vgl. 1.3),[14] weiter das einfache ἐν Χριστῷ (4.16) wie das erweiterte ἐν Χριστῷ Ἰησοῦ (2.14; 5.18),[15] und schliesslich das ebenfalls geprägte εὐαγγέλιον τοῦ Χριστοῦ (3.2).[16] Dabei macht der christologische Sprachgebrauch des ersten erhaltenen Paulusbriefes im Vergleich mit den anderen Schreiben des Apostels fast einen atypischen Eindruck. Denn hier finden wir Χριστός nur 10, dagegen κύριος 24 und Ἰησοῦς 16mal. Dies mag damit zusammenhängen, dass in diesem Brief in besonderer Weise das Thema der Parusie Jesu im Mittelpunkt steht, das von frühester Zeit an aufs engste mit dem

Kyrios-Titel verbunden war. Bereits die Formel *maranatha* 1 Kor. 16.22 weist auf dieses besondere Junktim hin. Die Bezeichnung 'Herr' findet sich darum allein in den beiden entscheidenden Kapiteln 1 Thess. 4 und 5 insgesamt 15mal. Man muss daher nicht annehmen, dass sich der christologische Sprachgebrauch und damit die Verkündigung des Apostels in den wenigen Jahren zwischen dem ersten Brief und dem an die Galater bzw. dem 1 Korintherbrief grundsätzlich verändert haben.

Dass Paulus die Reihenfolge des Jesusnamens in den Briefeingängen der späteren Briefe gegenüber 1 Thess. 1.1 und Gal. 1.1 ändert und statt des traditionellen 'Jesus Christus' (s.u.S. 143) zu Beginn von 1 Kor., 2 Kor., Phil., Philem. und Röm. 'Christus Jesus' schreibt, hat keine grundsätzliche Bedeutung, sondern hängt mit der jeweils besonderen Form des Briefeingangs zusammen.[17] Die Kommentare trugen hier im Zusammenhang mit Röm. 1.1 häufig unbegründete Vermutungen vor,[18] und es spricht für die besonnene Nüchternheit des Jubilars, dass er diese Scheinfrage in seinen Römerbriefkommentar als unwesentlich übergeht. Schon die zahlreichen unsicheren Textvarianten bei der Wortstellung 'Jesus Christus' oder 'Christus Jesus' sollten uns hier vor einer Überbewertung warnen.[19] Dem Urteil von E. v. Dobschütz in seinem Kommentar zu 1 Thess. ist grundsätzlich recht zu geben: 'Christus ist für Paulus so gut Personenname wie Jesus, womit er es bald promiscue braucht, bald zu einem Doppelnamen verbindet'. Die umgestellte Form Χριστὸς Ἰησοῦς mag ursprünglich titulare Bedeutung besessen haben, bei Paulus wird diese jedoch nicht mehr sichtbar, ihre Verwendung hat vielmehr in der Regel eindeutige sprachliche Ursachen[20] (s. o. A. 15). Der These von Cerfaux wird man so den Satz entgegenhalten müssen, 'κύριος Ἰησοῦς, nicht Ἰησοῦς ὁ Χριστός ist das paulinische Grundbekenntnis'.[21] Die sorgfältigen Untersuchungen von N. A. Dahl und W. Kramer haben die These von Dobschütz' bekräftigt und präzisiert. Die vier grundlegenden philologischen Beobachtungen von Dahl sprechen hier für sich:[22]

(*a*) Χριστός ist bei Paulus nicht mehr blosses Appellativum, sondern immer nur Bezeichnung *einer* einzigen konkreten Person, d.h. Jesu.

(*b*) Χριστός hat nirgendwo prädikative Bedeutung. Paulus muss, im Gegensatz zur Darstellung seiner Predigt in der Apg., in den Briefen nirgendwo mehr bekräftigen: 'Jesus ist der Messias' (s.u.S. 138).

(*c*) Es wird – im Unterschied zur vorchristlichen alttestamentlichen und jüdischen Tradition[23] – nie durch einen Genitiv (θεοῦ, κυρίου, etc.) oder ein Possesivpronomen bestimmt.

(*d*) Auch die appositionelle Form 'Ιησοῦς ὁ Χριστός sucht man in den Paulusbriefen vergebens.

Man könnte noch hinzufügen, dass Paulus nirgendwo den *Beweis* führt, dass Jesus der in den Texten des Alten Testamentes verheissene Gesalbte und Heilbringer sei. Dass Jesus der davidische Messias ist, setzt er zwar unter Verwendung einer älteren Bekenntnisformel selbstverständlich voraus,[24] benützt es jedoch nie im Zusammenhang seiner Argumentation. Die traditionellen messianischen Belegstellen des Alten Testamentes spielen in seinen Briefen keine unmittelbare, wesentliche Rolle, das gilt auch für jene Belege, die für den christlichen Schriftbeweis der Messianität Jesu von Bedeutung sind. 'Natürlich weiss der Jude und Rabbi Paulus, dass Χριστός der Gesalbte = Messias heisst',[25] doch er hat in seinen Briefen keine Veranlassung, dieses selbstverständliche Wissen zu begründen oder zu entfalten. Die wenigen möglichen Hinweise darauf sind zufällig und untypisch. So deutet er in 2 Kor. 1.21 dieses Wissen in einer Art von Wortspiel an: ὁ δὲ βεβαιῶν ἡμᾶς σὺν ὑμῖν εἰς Χριστὸν καὶ χρίσας ἡμᾶς Θεός: 'Der uns aber mit euch (zusammen) auf Christus gegründet und uns gesalbt hat, das ist Gott (selbst)'.[26] Bezeichnend ist dabei, dass der Apostel entgegen dem übrigen Sprachgebrauch des N.T.s das Verbum χρίειν nicht auf die 'Salbung' Jesu, sondern die der Glaubenden bezieht,[27] die durch den Geist in der Taufe geschieht (vgl. 1 Johannes 2.20). Schlatter bemerkt dazu: 'Die Salbung weiht zum königlichen Handeln I. 4,8. Sie ist in der Gleichgestaltung der Gemeinde mit dem Christus enthalten.'[28] Es steht hinter der Formulierung wohl ein ähnlicher Gedanke wie Röm. 8. 14–17, 29, dass uns Gott aufgrund der Vermittlung des einen Sohnes durch den Geist zu seinen Söhnen gemacht hat. Aber mehr als eine Anspielung für den Kundigen ist es nicht. Auch wenn hier und an einigen anderen Stellen, v. Dobschütz nennt Röm. 9.5; 2 Kor. 5.10; Phil. 1.15; Dahl ausserdem 1 Kor. 10.4; 15.22; 2 Kor. 11.2f; Phil. 1.17; 3.7,[29] die alte Bedeutung als Würdetitel noch 'irgendwie mitschwingt',[30] so ändert dies doch nichts an dem eindeutigen paulinischen Sprachgebrauch, bei dem es, um den Apostel zu verstehen, 'niemals notwendig [ist] zu wissen, dass "Christos" ein inhaltlich gefüllter, bedeutungstragender Begriff ist. Alle Aussagen der Briefe ergeben einen guten Sinn auch für denjenigen, der nichts anderes weiss, als dass Christus ein Beiname Jesu ist'.[31]

Diese feste Ausformung des Namens Jesu in sehr früher Zeit hat von der äusseren Form her klare Parallelen in der römisch-hellenistischen Umwelt. Denn die traditionelle Namensform, die Paulus gerne in feierlichen Zusammenhängen, etwa in den Briefeingängen und am Ende verwendet, ὁ κύριος Ἰησοῦς Χριστός (s.o.A.13), hat eine ähnliche Gestalt wie die des römischen Herrschers:

Imperator Caesar Augustus
Αὐτοκράτωρ Καῖσαρ Σέβαστος[32]

oder hellenistischer Könige

Βασιλεὺς Πτολεμαῖος Σωτήρ
Βασιλεὺς Ἀντίοχος Ἐπιφανής.[33] Jesus war der eigentliche Eigenname, 'Christos' das Cognomen und 'Kyrios' der Titel.[34] Weitere Würdebezeichnungen konnten hinzugefügt werden, so vereinzelt 'Sohn Gottes' (τοῦ υἱοῦ αὐτοῦ Ἰησοῦ Χριστοῦ τοῦ κυρίου ἡμῶν 1 Kor. 1.9; vgl. 2 Kor. 1.19), oder auch 'Soter' (1 Tim. 1.10; Titus 1 1.4; 2.13; 3.6; vgl. Phil. 3.20). In analoger Weise waren auch die Namen und Titulaturen der hellenistischen Herrscher und römischen Kaiser variabel und konnten verkürzt oder ergänzt werden.

Dass Paulus sich bei alledem wohl *bewusst* blieb, dass 'Jesus' das eigentliche nomen proprium und 'Christos' *ursprünglich* ein Appellativum war, zeigt sich daran, dass das Bekenntnis der paulinischen Gemeinden κύριος Ἰησοῦς bzw. κύριος Ἰησοῦς Χριστός[35] lautete, die Formel κύριος Χριστός uns dagegen nie begegnet. Die scheinbar einzige Ausnahme Röm. 16.18 erklärt sich aus dem Kontext des falschen Dienstes: οἱ γὰρ τοιοῦτοι τῷ κυρίῳ ἡμῶν Χριστῷ οὐ δουλεύουσιν ἀλλὰ τῇ ἑαυτῶν κοιλίᾳ[36]. Bei der Namensform 'Christus Jesus' kann entsprechend das 'Kyrios' nie voran-, sondern nur nachgestellt werden.[37]

Auf die wesentlichen sprachlichen Besonderheiten haben N. A. Dahl und W. Kramer hingewiesen. Am häufigsten erscheint das einfache 'Christos', insgesamt *ca.* 150mal, davon *ca.* 60mal mit Artikel. Ähnlich wie κύριος hat es relativ oft die Position des Subjekts im Satz, so vor allem in der bei Paulus häufigen Sterbeformel, die aus vorpaulinischer Tradition stammt.[38] Gegen die Meinung von H. Conzelmann kann dabei weder die determinierte Form noch auch die Stellung als Subjekt als Hinweis auf eine titulare Bedeutung gewertet werden.[39] Erscheint 'Christos' in einer Genitivverbindung als Nomen rectum, hat es immer den Artikel, auch wenn das Nomen regens

139

determiniert ist, so etwa in dem relativ häufigen formelhaften τὸ εὐαγγέλιον τοῦ Χριστοῦ, das aus vorpaulinischer Tradition stammt.[40] Nach Präpositionen wie bei den häufigen Formeln ἐν Χριστῷ,[41] ὑπὲρ Χριστοῦ[42] und εἰς Χριστόν[43], folgt in der Regel kein Artikel, bei διά mit Genitiv und Akkusativ gibt es determinierte und artikellose Formen.[44]

In anderen Fällen mag die Determination wie bei dem Eigennamen Jesus durch anaphorischen Gebrauch bedingt sein. Auch dort, wo das determinierte 'Christos' im Nominativ steht, ist 'ein sachliches Motiv für die Determination . . . in keinem Fall zu entdecken'.[45]

Gerade auch bei Texten, wo eine mögliche titulare Bedeutung noch im Hintergrund stehen könnte, scheint der Artikel im Grunde zufällig zu sein. Wir finden ihn zwar in Röm. 9.3,5 nicht aber in 10.4,6f., er begegnet uns in 15.3,7, dagegen nicht in dem wichtigen Text 15.8, wo Paulus auf Christus als den διάκονος περιτομῆς hinweist, der die Verheissungen gegenüber den Vätern erfüllt. Hier kann nur der 'messianische Dienst' Jesu gegenüber seinem Volk gemeint sein. M.a.W., zwischen dem Gebrauch des Artikels und einer rudimentären titularen Bedeutung besteht keinerlei nachweisbarer grundsätzlicher Zusammenhang.[46]

Auch andere feine Differenzierungen im Sprachgebrauch lassen sich schwer erklären. So etwa, warum das einfache 'Christos' mit und ohne Artikel in 2 Kor. am häufigsten erscheint.[47] Hängt es damit zusammen, dass in diesem persönlichsten von allen Briefen alles liturgisch-formelhafte Reden von Christus stärker zurücktritt? Auch warum die Relationen zwischen 'Christos' und 'Kyrios' in den einzelnen Briefen relativ stark variieren, ist, ausser in dem Sonderfall 1 Thess. mit dem Hauptthema der Parusie (s.u.S. 136), im Grunde rätselhaft. Nur in 1 Kor. sind beide Bezeichnungen fast gleich (64:66), in 2 Kor. überwiegt Christos bei weitem (47:29), ebenso in Röm. (66:44), besonders schroff ist das Verhältnis in Gal. 38:6. Hier könnte man sich fragen, ob dieses 'Missverhältnis' mit der Heraushebung des Kerygmas vom gekreuzigten 'Christos' bei der Auseinandersetzung mit den Judaisten zusammenhängt? Dagegen kann man von Phil. mit der Relation 37:15, abgesehen von der auffallenden Verbindung des Christusnamens mit Parusieaussagen, kaum behaupten, dass gerade dort ' "Christos" mehr und mehr in Sachzusammenhänge eingefügt (werde), in denen ursprünglich der Kyriostitel beheimatet war'.[48] Noch weniger darf man dieses Wechseln der Zahlenverhältnisse als Argument zur Datierung der Briefe verwenden.

Die Verwendung von Christos umfasst im Grunde *das ganze Heilsgeschehen*, wobei das stellvertretende Sterben und die Auferstehung Jesu zwar gewiss im Zentrum stehen, sich aber darüber hinaus eine breite Vielfalt dieses Namens ergibt, so dass sich einzelne Schwerpunkte nicht so eindeutig klar abgrenzen lassen wie etwa bei der Verwendung von Kyrios (Parusie, Herrenmahl, Sklavenfrage und Ehe in 1 Kor. 7, etc.), oder bei dem sehr viel selteneren Sohn Gottes (Sendungsaussagen). Am ehesten kann man dort von einer Konzentration des Namens 'Christos' sprechen, wo er in älterer 'vorpaulinischer' Überlieferung fest verankert ist, so bei Substantiven und Verben der Verkündigung und des Glaubens, in Verbindung mit der Sterbensformel, dem Kreuz Christi, ja überhaupt Aussagen über die Passion und Auferstehung Jesu, schliesslich auch im Zusammenhang mit der typisch paulinischen Formel ἐν Χριστῷ ('Ιησοῦ),[49] und im Bereich der Verpflichtung des Einzelnen.[50] Dennoch wird man sagen müssen, dass 'Christos' in seinem Gesamtgebrauch wegen seiner vielseitigen Verwendung unter den christologischen Namen und Titeln bei Paulus am wenigsten ein eindeutig erkennbares 'Profil' besitzt.

Ein weiterer grundlegender Gesichtspunkt besteht darin, dass 'Christos' für Paulus ähnlich wie βασιλεία τοῦ Θεοῦ oder die Auferstehung von den Toten ein *eschatologischer Begriff bleibt*.[51] Durch den Tod und die Auferstehung des 'Christos' wird das Endgeschehen eingeleitet. Sein Sterben ist für Paulus *das entscheidende 'eschatologische' Heilsereignis*. Eben darum ist er zugleich der Erfüller der alttestamentlichen Verheissung.[52] Die missionarische Verkündigung des εὐαγγέλιον τοῦ Χριστοῦ bestimmt die gegenwärtige Wirksamkeit des Paulus als ἀπόστολος Χριστοῦ 'Ιησοῦ (1 Kor. 1.1; 2 Kor. 1.1; vgl. 1 Thess. 2.7; 2 Kor. 11.13)[53] bis zur Parusie, die er Röm. 11.26 mit Jes. 59.20 als Kommen des 'Erlösers von Zion her' umschreibt. Die traditionelle Verbindung des Kyrios-Titels mit Parusieaussagen schliesst nicht aus, dass Paulus auch den Christus-Namen in diesem Zusammenhang verwenden kann. Die formelhafte Verwendung von ἡμέρα Χριστοῦ in Phil. 1.10 und 2.16 zeigt, dass dieser Begriff mit dem vom AT her vorgegebenen ἡμέρα κυρίου praktisch austauschbar geworden war.[54] Man sollte daher mit dem Urteil vorsichtig sein, dass die Verwandlung des Titels 'Christos' in einen Eigennamen zugleich ein klares Indiz für die Abschwächung der endzeitlichen Erwartung beim Übergang zur Heidenmission gewesen sei.[55]

Welche Schlüsse kann man nun aus diesem eigenartigen Sprachgebrauch ziehen? Versuchen wir, der Reihe nach einige grundsätzliche Fragen zu beantworten.

1 Warum hat Paulus gerade 'Christos' als Einzelwort, aber auch im Zusammenhang mit anderen Bezeichnungen, so auffallend häufig verwendet, ganz im Gegensatz zum übrigen neutestamentlichen Sprachgebrauch? Man wird sich doch sehr fragen müssen, ob dies auf blosser Konvention oder Zufall beruhte, und ob nicht vielmehr 'Christos' für Paulus als die bei ihm häufigste Bezeichnung Jesu entscheidende bleibende theologische Bedeutung besass und behielt.

2 Sollte dies zutreffen, ergibt sich daraus sofort die nächste Frage: Warum tritt dann aber die ursprüngliche titulare Bedeutung in seinen Briefen so wenig deutlich – man könnte auch sagen: nie eindeutig – hervor, obgleich sie ihm doch selbstverständlich wohl vertraut sein musste? Der pharisäische Gelehrtenschüler war ja nicht zuletzt deshalb zum Verfolger der jungen Gemeinde geworden, weil er die Verkündigung des gekreuzigten Jesus als Messias Israels für eine Blasphemie gehalten hatte. Darauf weisen noch Aussagen wie Gal. 3.13 hin, dass der gekreuzigte 'Christus' aufgrund von Deut. 21.23 "für uns zum Fluch" wurde. Auch die formelhafte Rede vom σταυρὸς τοῦ Χριστοῦ[56] oder vom Χριστὸς ἐσταυρωμένος[57] ist ein Indiz für diesen Sachverhalt. Nach allem, was wir wissen, erwarteten gerade die Pharisäer den einen Messiaskönig aus dem Geschlecht Davids als die zentrale eschatologische Heilsgestalt. Die Volkstümlichkeit dieser Erwartung demonstrieren die späteren jüdischen Gebete und die Targumim. Für den Gelehrtenschüler und Pharisäer Paulus war offenbar der 'gekreuzigte Messias' Jesus von Nazareth selbst höchstes 'Ärgernis' (vgl. 1 Kor. 1.23; Gal. 5.11) gewesen, ein schwerer religiöser Anstoss, der nur durch die Verfolgung der Gotteslästerer (vgl. Gal. 6.12) und die Zerschlagung ihrer Gemeinden[58] beseitigt werden konnte. Die Erscheinung des Auferstandenen vor Damaskus brachte ihm die Gewissheit, dass der Gekreuzigte wirklich der verheissene Messias und sein Tod das entscheidende Heilsereignis sei.[59] Dass Paulus in Gal. 1.15f davon spricht, dass Gott ihm damals 'seinen Sohn' geoffenbart habe, deutet u.a. darauf hin, dass der Titel 'Sohn Gottes' nach urchristlichem Verständnis den Messiastitel interpretierte und präzisierte. Ansätze waren dazu schon im zeitgenössischen Judentum vorhanden.[60] Die überaus vielseitige Verwendung des 'Christus*namens*' in den späteren Briefen zeigt so dort vermutlich das nach wie vor bestehende *Interesse* des Apostels an *dieser* Bezeichnung,

zugleich aber auch, dass in den Briefen, die christlichen Gemeinden geschrieben wurden, die Frage der *Messianität* Jesu überhaupt *nicht mehr* zur Diskussion stand, sondern ganz selbstverständlich vorausgesetzt wurde. Wenn Paulus von 'Christus', 'Jesus Christus' oder 'Christus Jesus' spricht, gebraucht er weder einfach den traditionellen jüdischen 'Messias-*Titel*', aber auch nicht einfach einen neuen, *beliebigen*, zusätzlichen Namen für Jesus von Nazareth, sondern er statuiert eben damit, ohne dass es jeder weiteren Erörterung oder besonderer Hinweise bedarf, dass *allein* dieser Jesus—und d.h. zugleich kein anderer—der von den Propheten des Alten Bundes verheissene[61] Erlöser ist. Die erstaunliche Variabilität in der Verwendung von 'Christos' zeigt, dass es dabei nicht entscheidend darauf ankommt, ob man in einzelnen Zusammenhängen oder gewissen grammatikalischen Formen noch Spuren einer möglichen oder wahrscheinlichen titularen Bedeutung entdecken kann, sondern dass *'Christos' gerade als 'Eigenname' die Einzigartigkeit Jesu als 'endzeitlicher Heilbringer' zum Ausdruck bringt.*[62]

3   Nun gilt freilich nach einer verbreiteten Ansicht diese enge Verbindung des ursprünglichen Titels 'Christos' mit dem Eigennamen Jesus zu einem Doppelnamen als 'Erstarrung',[63] in der 'das Eschatologisch-Messianische in der Gestalt Jesu mehr und mehr zurücktritt'.[64] Den Vorgang selbst versetzte man unter Hinweis auf Apg. 11.26 in die frühe antiochenische Gemeinde, wo die Jünger zum ersten Mal 'Christianer' genannt werden. Die heidnische Bevölkerung habe in Christus 'eine Art von Parteihaupt' gesehen, und seinen Anhängern entsprechend einen 'Parteinamen' gegeben.[65] Diese Ereignisse setzen dabei die fest etablierte Verwendung von 'Christos' als 'Eigennamen' über einen längeren Zeitraum hin bereits voraus. Offenbar wurde dabei der für griechische Ohren ungewohnte 'Name' Χριστός als Χρῆστος missverstanden, darauf weist nicht nur die berühmte Suetonnotiz,[66] sondern auch die ursprüngliche Lesart Chrestiani bei Tacitus, *Ann.* xv.44.2 hin.[67] Die Verwendung des Verbaladjektivs mask. χριστός als Bezeichnung für einen Menschen findet sich als sprachliche Neuerung erst in der Septuaginta, die griechische Umgangssprache kannte nur das Neutrum, so z.B. als Substantiv τὸ χριστόν in der Bedeutung von 'Salbe' oder 'Aufstreichmittel'[68] für medizinische oder magische Zwecke.

Die aus der Entwicklung in Antiochien erschlossene Folgerung, dass im dortigen 'Heidenchristentum' 'Christos' seine titulare und damit zugleich eschatologische Bedeutung 'ziemlich vollständig verloren' habe, und dass Paulus dort diesen Gebrauch von 'Christos' als Eigennamen vorgefunden und übernommen habe,[69] ist aus verschiedenen Gründen extrem unwahrscheinlich. Ist die Konstruktion einer frühen überwiegend 'heidenchristlichen' Gemeinde, in der die Entwicklung der Christologie durch das Unverständnis der neugewonnenen Nichtjuden entscheidend geprägt worden sei, eine unglaubwürdige Fiktion.[70] Denn einmal wurde das theologische Denken in diesen frühesten 'heidenchristlichen' Gemeinden, so weit wir sehen, weiterhin von den judenchristlichen Wortführern bestimmt, zum anderen waren die sogenannten 'Heiden', die in Antiochien oder auch später in Rom für die neue messianische Botschaft gewonnen wurden, zunächst ganz überwiegend Gottesfürchtige und Sympathisanten im Umkreis der Synagoge, denen die neue jüdische Sekte durch den Verzicht auf die Beschneidungsforderung volle religiöse Gleichberechtigung gewährte.[71] Im Blick auf das baldige Kommen des gekreuzigten und zu Gott erhöhten Messias und Herrn hatte das Ritualgesetz seine exkludierende Bedeutung verloren. In diesem (eingeschränkten Sinne) war schon für die unbekannten ersten judenchristlichen Missionare aus dem Kreis der 'Hellenisten' von Apg. 6 'Christus des Gesetzes Ende'.[72] Nicht zuletzt um diese 'Gottesfürchtigen' zu erreichen, suchte Paulus auf seinen Missionsreisen zunächst die Synagogen auf. Darum konnte diesen ersten 'Heidenchristen', die aus dem Kreis der nichtjüdischen Sympathisanten und Synagogenbesucher kamen, der von der Septuaginta und der jüdischen Messiaserwartung vorgegebene Begriff Χριστός nicht so unbekannt sein, dass sie ihn—gar noch vor Beginn der paulinischen Mission[73]—nicht mehr verstanden und zu einem bedeutungslosen Eigennamen verfälscht hätten. Die Entfaltung der Christologie war auch an den Orten, wo die früheste heidenchristliche Mission getrieben wurde, weiterhin an judenchristliche oder zumindest gottesfürchtige 'Opinionleaders' gebunden.[74] Durch sie erfuhr der so ganz ungriechische jüdische Begriff Χριστός gewiss eine fortlaufende *interpretatio christiana*, wobei jedoch zu fragen ist, ob diese Interpretation in ihren Anfängen nicht bereits auf die erste Gemeinde in Jerusalem, ja vielleicht gar—ich selbst bin davon überzeugt—auf Jesus selbst zurückzuführen ist, der in seiner 'messianischen Vollmacht' dem Titel 'Messias' eine ganz neue Auslegung gegeben hatte, die von den zeitgenössischen jüdischen Messiasbildern erheblich abwich. Aber diese Frage würde den Rahmen unserer Erwägungen sprengen.

Halten wir zunächst nur fest, dass das paulinische und 'vorpaulinische Heidenchristentum' der 'eschatologisch-titularen' Bedeutung
von 'Christos' nicht verständnislos oder gleichgültig gegenüberstand.
Eine eigenständige spezifisch *'heidenchristliche'* Christologie, die Paulus
in seinen Briefen bereits voraussetzen soll, gab es nicht. Wenn die vier
Evangelisten, aber auch Lukas in seiner Apg., der Autor von
1 Johannes und der Apokalypse das Wissen um die titulare Bedeutung
von 'Christos' selbstverständlich voraussetzen,[75] so muss dies auch für
die wesentlich älteren Gemeinden gelten, an die die Paulusbriefe
gerichtet sind. Lukas berichtet—sachlich m.E. durchaus zutreffend—
dass Paulus als Missionar in den Synagogen verkündigt habe, dass
Jesus der Messias sei und dass er leiden müsse.[76] Dass dieses Motiv in
den Paulusbriefen keine Rolle spielt und bestenfalls durch die
Sterbeformel Χριστὸς ἀπέθανεν ὑπέρ . . . angedeutet wird, zeigt nur,
dass wir von der paulinischen *Missionspredigt* herzlich wenig wissen.
Die Briefe des Apostels umfassen durchaus nicht seine ganze Verkündigung und Lehre. Immerhin hat Paulus diesen Kernsatz des neuen
Glaubens vom Sterben des 'Christos' für uns in Korinth (und
sicherlich auch in anderen Gemeinden) ἐν πρώτοις als das εὐαγγέλιον
τοῦ Χριστοῦ verkündigt, und man muss annehmen, dass er den
Korinthern und allen anderen neugegründeten Gemeinden erklärte,
was es mit dem Namen 'Christos' auf sich hat.[77] Denn auf der anderen
Seite zeigen die Paulusbriefe in eindrücklicher Weise, welch gründ-
liche Kenntnis der alttestamentlich-jüdischen Tradition der Apostel
bei seinen 'heidenchristlichen' Gemeinden voraussetzte. Wer eine so
schwierige typologische Auslegung wie 1 Kor. 10.1–11 versteht, wird
wohl auch die wahre Bedeutung des 'Namens' ὁ Χριστός kennen,
dessen Träger mit dem 'geistlichen Felsen' des Wüstenzugs identisch
ist. Es wäre abwegig zu vermuten, die paulinischen Gemeinden hätten
nicht gewusst, dass 'Christos' kein vulgärer Sklavenname, sondern
eine Bezeichnung von einzigartigem eschatologischem Rang ist, die
Jesus allein zukam. Die Verwechslung mit Χρηστός können wir getrost
ausschliesslich den Nichtchristen, d.h. den wirklichen 'Heiden',
überlassen.

4 'Christos' erschien ja als ein Wort von völlig eigenem Charakter. Es
war weder ein Name unter vielen wie 'Jesus' noch ein im Griechischen
gebräuchliches Appellativum, ein Würdetitel wie βασιλεύς, κύριος
oder δεσπότης. Auch wenn es im zeitgenössischen Judentum eine
relativ vielfältige 'Messiaserwartung' gab, so wurde, wenn wir von

145

dem priesterlichen und davidischen Messias in Qumran absehen, in der Regel doch nur *eine* beherrschende 'messianische' Gestalt erwartet, die freilich recht verschiedene Züge tragen konnte. Ähnlich wie das verwandte κύριος brachte Χριστός gerade die 'unverwechselbare Einzigartigkeit' Jesu zum Ausdruck.[78] Im Gegensatz zu dem zur Zeit Jesu ausserordentlich beliebten Namen *Ješuᵃᶜ*, der Kurzform von *Jᵉhošuᵃᶜ*,[79] dem religiös-nationalen Heros der Landnahme, der wie die beliebten Makkabäernamen Judas, Simeon, Eleazar oder Jonathan das hochgespannte religiös-nationale Bewusstsein der Zeit zum Ausdruck brachte, war der 'Name' 'Christos' einmalig, ja einzigartig. Schon aus diesem Grund musste er dem Allerweltsnamen Jesus zur Seite treten, ihn näher bestimmen, ja teilweise ersetzen. Die Grenze zwischen bestimmten biblischen Appellativa und Eigennamen ist ja fliessend: 'Ein in seiner Art einziges Wesen bezeichnen auch θεός und κύριος (=jhwh, aber auch Christus), und diese Wörter (vor allem κύριος) kommen dem Eigennamen sehr nahe'.[80] Aus diesem Grund konnten (ὁ) Χριστός und ὁ κύριος sowie vor allem das formelhafte ἐν Χριστῷ und ἐν κυρίῳ fast auswechselbar gebraucht werden. Wie G. Dalman,[81] K. H. Rengstorf[82] und vor allem J. Jeremias[83] gezeigt haben, erhielt selbst im späteren rabbinischen Sprachgebrauch das artikellose mašîᵃḥ teilweise die Bedeutung eines Eigennamens. Das Alter dieser Sprachform bleibt umstritten, es könnte vielleicht schon in der Damaskusschrift in der Wendung *mšyḥ m'hrwn wmyśr'l*[84] vorliegen. Überhaupt ist in diesem Zusammenhang auffallend, dass gerade im semitischen Bereich die Verwandlung von ursprünglichen Appellativa in 'Eigennamen' innerhalb des religiösen Sprachgebrauchs nicht selten ist. Das Phänomen begegnet uns bei *śāṭān*,[85] *bᵉlijjaᶜal* und *maśṭemā*,[86] aber auch bei 'Marnas', dem Stadtgott von Gaza, dessen Bezeichnung ursprünglich 'unser Herr' bedeutete (aram *mr'* und Suffix 1. Plur) und den man in hellenistischer Zeit mit Zeus identifizierte,[87] dem syrischen *Baᶜal šamem*, der ebenfalls zum Zeus wurde, dem phönizischen Adonis und der Gottesbezeichnung *ᶜäljon-*ὕψιστος.[88] Klaus Berger verweist in diesem Zusammenhang auch auf den Beinamen *kepha'*- Πέτρος für Simon.[89]

5 Dass 'Kyrios' seine titulare Bedeutung in Verbindung mit dem Jesus-Namen stärker behielt und als κύριος Ἰησοῦς zum akklamatorischen Bekenntnis der paulinischen Missionsgemeinden wurde, hängt damit zusammen, dass bereits im ältesten Bekenntnis der palästinischen Gemeinde in der Formel *ješûᵃᶜ mᵉšîḥā* (oder [*ham-*]*māšîᶜᵃḥ*)

'Jesus' und 'Messias' untrennbar verbunden worden waren, beide sich also von Anfang an näher standen als Kyrios und Jesus. Weiter spielt eine Rolle, dass für die griechischsprechende Synagoge 'Kyrios' schon längst als *q^{e}rê* anstelle des unaussprechbaren Tetragramms zum liturgischen Gottesnamen geworden war. Kyrios hatte so durch den gottesdienstlichen Gebrauch den höheren Rang. Dass dieser auf Gott selbst bezogene 'Name, der über jedem Namen ist' auf den Gekreuzigten übertragen und der Erhöhte von allen Geschöpfen als κύριος Ἰησοῦς Χριστός akklamiert wird (Phil. 2.9, 11), bedeutete eine zusätzliche Steigerung der Würde Jesu, die über das eschatologische *maší^{a}ḥ* Χριστός hinausging. Sie wurde bereits in der palästinischen Gemeinde vorbereitet,[90] wo schon die Anrede *mārān* bzw. das absolute *mareh* in Verbindung mit Ps. 110.1 das rätselhafte unkerygmatische *bar $^{\textit{a}}$nāšā* verdrängt hatte, aber damit noch nicht jene grundsätzliche— man darf wohl schon sagen—'göttliche' Bedeutung erhielt wie in den paulinischen Gemeinden.[91] Solange sich die urchristliche Mission vornehmlich jüdischen Hörern zuwandte, blieb das Bekenntnis zu Jesus als dem Messias im Mittelpunkt und sorgte eben dadurch dafür, dass spätestens bei der Übertragung der neuen Botschaft in den griechischen Sprachbereich beide 'Namen' sich zu einer untrennbaren Einheit verschmolzen. Dem Pharisäer Paulus in Jerusalem wird bei den Hellenisten der bekenntnishafte Doppelname Ἰησοῦς Χριστός bereits schon begegnet sein, er erhielt seine für ihn so anstössige Spitze durch die Formel Χριστὸς ἀπέθανεν ὑπὲρ ἡμῶν.[92] Denn, wenn wir auch nicht eindeutig wissen, ob es eine feste Tradition vom leidenden Gottesknecht und Messias im Judentum vor Jesus gegeben hat,[93] so kann man doch mit gewisser Sicherheit sagen, dass die Botschaft von dem *gekreuzigten* Messias Jesus aufgrund Deut. 21.23 in gesetzestreuen Kreisen äusserstes Ärgernis erregen musste. Für Paulus wurde der bisherige Anstoss zur tragenden Mitte jenes εὐαγγέλιον τοῦ Χριστοῦ, das er δι' ἀποκαλύψεως Ἰησοῦ Χριστοῦ empfing.[94]

6   Der historische Grund für diese überragende, zentrale Bedeutung des Bekenntnisses zu Jesus als dem Messias in der frühesten Gemeinde, das sich in veränderter Sprachform, genauer in der so auffallend häufigen Verwendung von Χριστός als einzigartigem 'Eigennamen' Jesu selbst noch bei Paulus durchgehalten hat, liegt einerseits in der historischen Tatsache, dass Jesus auf Anstiften der Volksführer von Pilatus als messianischer Prätendent hingerichtet worden war. Der Prozess Jesu bis hin zum Titulus mit der *causa poenae* und der

Verspottung des Gekreuzigten (Markus 15.26–32) offenbarte seinen 'messianischen' Anspruch öffentlich und endgültig.[95] Es ist kein Zufall, dass dieser Anspruch den ältesten Prozessbericht des Markus wie ein roter Faden durchzieht. Die radikale Kritik, die ihn eliminieren will, zerstört zugleich die Möglichkeit, die Anfänge der Christologie historisch zu verstehen. Die Gemeinde wusste, dass Jesus aufgrund seines 'guten Bekenntnisses' (1 Tim. 6.13) vor Pilatus als Messias in den Tod gegangen war und dass sich Gott durch die Auferstehung zu seinem messianischen Dienst und seiner Würde bekannt hatte. Zugleich hatte Jesus als der sündlose Gesalbte Sühne für die Sünde des Volkes gewirkt. Durch die unauflösliche namensartige Verbindung *ješûᵃᶜ mᵉšîḥā* Ἰησοῦς Χριστός wurden gleichzeitig alle Ansprüche anderer jüdischer Messiasprätendenten—die offenbar gar nicht so selten waren—zurückgewiesen und festgehalten, dass das 'Wesen' des Messias nicht von irgendwelchen traditionellen Messiaserwartungen her zu definieren war, sondern 'ein für allemal' durch Jesus, seinen sühnenden Tod am Kreuz, seine Auferweckung durch Gott, seine Erhöhung zur Rechten Gottes und seine Parusie als Richter und Erlöser bestimmt ist. Wie sehr diese Verschmelzung wirksam war, selbst dort, wo man die eschatologische Würde Jesu ablehnte, zeigt sich bei Josephus, der *Ant.* XX.200, 'Jakobus, den Bruder Jesu, des sogenannten Christus' nennt (τὸν ἀδελφὸν Ἰησοῦ τοῦ λεγομένου Χριστοῦ).[96]

Fassen wir das Ergebnis kurz zusammen. Die so erstaunlich vielseitige Verwendung von 'Christos' bei Paulus, dem häufigsten Namen Jesu in den Briefen des Apostels, ist nicht Zufall oder gedankenlose Konvention, blosse Angleichung an einen heidenchristlichen Sprachgebrauch. Auf der anderen Seite hat es wenig Sinn, bei Paulus noch eine titulare Bedeutung des Namens entdecken zu wollen. 'Christos' ist mit Jesus untrennbar verschmolzen, wobei die Heilsbedeutung des Namens im Blick auf den Kreuzestod Christi für den Apostel selbstverständlich präsent ist. Diese 'Namenswerdung' von Christos ist schon in Antiochien als abgeschlossen vorauszusetzen, sie geht selbst auf die vorpaulinische Gemeinde der Hellenisten in Jerusalem zurück und wurde von Paulus bereits nach seiner Berufung vor Damaskus übernommen. Es kam darin zum Ausdruck, dass der gekreuzigte Jesus und kein anderer der eschatologische Heilbringer ist. Bereits in der ältesten palästinischen Gemeinde war *ješûᵃᶜ mᵉšîḥā* das wichtigste missionarische Bekenntnis, das schon in der aramäischen Form die

Tendenz hin zum Doppelnamen zeigte. Es ist historisch begründet durch die Hinrichtung Jesu am Kreuz auf Grund seines messianischen Anspruchs.

ANMERKUNGEN

1 Lit: F. Kattenbusch, *Das apostolische Symbol*, II, 1900, S. 541–62; vgl. 491f; E.v. Dobschütz, *Die Thessalonicherbriefe*, *KEK* 1909 (Nachdruck 1974), 60f; ders., κύριος 'Ιησοῦς, *ZNW* 30 (1931), S. 97–123; J. Weiss, *Das Urchristentum*, 1917, S. 127–30; W. Bousset, *Kyrios Christos*, [2]1921, S. 3ff, 77f; H. Lietzmann, 'An die Römer', *HNT*, [4]1933, S. 23; L. Cerfaux, *Le Christ dans la théologie de Saint Paul*; Paris 1951, [2]1954, S. 361–74 (Ich zitiere die deutsche Übersetzung, *Christus in der paulinischen Theologie*, 1964, S. 294–305); V. Taylor, *The Names of Jesus*, London 1953, S. 18–23; N. A. Dahl, 'Die Messianität Jesu bei Paulus', *Studia Paulina: in honorem Johannis de Zwaan*, Haarlem 1953, S. 83–95 (durch Literaturhinweise ergänzte englische Übersetzung: 'The Messiahship of Jesus in Paul', *The crucified Messiah*, Minneapolis 1974, S. 37–47); B. Rigaux, *Saint Paul: les Épîtres aux Thessaloniciens*, Bruxelles 1956, S. 171f, 351; F. Neugebauer, *In Christus*, 1961, S. 44–64; F. Hahn, 'Christologische Hoheitstitel', *FRLANT* 83, 1962 ([2]1964); W. Kramer, 'Christos Kyrios Gottessohn', *AThNT* 44, 1963, S. 15–60, 131–53, 203–14; K. Berger, 'Zum traditionsgeschichtlichen Hintergrund christologischer Hoheitstitel', *NTS* 17 (1970–1), S. 391–425; M. Hengel, 'Christologie und neutestamentliche Chronologie', *Neues Testament und Geschichte. Festschrift O. Cullmann z. 70. Geburtstag*, 1972, S. 43–67; W. Grundmann, Artik. χρίω ..., *TWNT* ix, 1973, S. 532–50; C. F. D. Moule, *The Origins of Christology*, London 1977, S. 31ff, 47ff. Grundlegend sind nach wie vor die Untersuchungen von Dahl und Kramer.

2 K. Aland (Hg.), *Vollständige Konkordanz zum griechischen Neuen Testament*, 1978, S. 300f, 130f. Θεός ist im NT mit 1318 Belegen mit Abstand das häufigste Substantiv.

3 Op. cit., S. 136f; 166; bei κύριος wurden Belege mit der Beziehung auf Gott selbst oder mit profaner, soziologischer Bedeutung nicht ausgeschieden. Bei Paulus würde sich *der christologische Gebrauch auf ca. 184 verringern*, wobei Textvarianten eine gewisse Unsicherheit bewirken.

4 S. dazu M. Hengel, *Der Sohn Gottes*, S. 19ff. Dieses zahlenmässige Missverhältnis wird dadurch etwas gemildert, dass Paulus vom 'Sohn Gottes' an besonderen Höhepunkten seiner Briefe spricht. Dennoch muss es beachtet werden.

5 *Statistik des neutestamentlichen Wortschatzes*, 1958, S. 156: 266 zu 529.

6 Op. cit., S. 167, für das gesamte *Corpus Paulinum*; Θεός, 548; Χριστός, 379; κύριος, 275; 'Ιησοῦς, 213. Zieht man die echten Paulusbriefe ab, ergibt sich nach Morgenthaler für Eph.; Kol.; 2 Thess. und Past: Θεός, 118; Χριστός, 113; κύριος, 91; 'Ιησοῦς, 70. Im Titusbrief erscheint Χριστός nur

4mal jeweils formelhaft im Genitiv als 'Ἰησοῦ Χριστοῦ 1.1; 2.13; 3.6 bzw.
Χριστοῦ 'Ἰησοῦ 1.4 dagegen 6mal σωτήρ, dreimal auf Gott (1.3; 2.10;
3.4) und dreimal auf Christus (1.4; 2.13; 3.6) bezogen. Der vielfältige
lebendige Sprachgebrauch des Paulus ist hier weitgehend durch liturgische Formeln ersetzt.

7 Vgl. dazu nach der Statistik von Aland (o.A.2): κύριος, 107 (Gott und
Jesus); 'Ἰησοῦς, 70; Θεός, 168.

8 Vgl. κύριος, 53 (nur im Evg.); 'Ἰησοῦς, 258; υἱός (absolut und mit Θεοῦ),
79; Θεός, 150; πατήρ, 154.

9 Op. cit. (A.1), S. 294.

10 Markus 12.35–7 ist ein messianisches Lehrgespräch, das sich kritisch mit
der Messiaslehre der 'Schriftgelehrten' auseinandersetzt, bei dem aber
die Lösung der Rätselfrage offen bleibt. Sie gibt Jesus erst 14.62 als
Antwort auf die Messiasfrage des Hohenpriesters, wobei er auch dort das
Wort χριστός nicht in den Mund nimmt. Dies ist alles kein Zufall. Der
Messiastitel wird bei Markus, obwohl der Evangelist selbstverständlich
voraussetzt, dass Jesus der 'Christus' ist,—aus welchen Gründen auch
immer—problematisiert. Es geht ihm um mehr als nur um diesen Titel.
Umso mehr fällt die Häufigkeit und Selbstverständlichkeit auf mit der
Paulus 'Christos' verwendet.

11 S. M. Hengel *Christologie* (A.1), S. 43ff; *Sohn Gottes* (A.4), S. 9ff, 95ff.

12 E. v. Dobschütz, *Thess.* (A.1), 60, 'Paulus ist in den Formeln ungemein
beweglich'. In 1 Thess. finden sich allein vier Formeln, die Gott und den
'Herrn Jesus Christus' (o. ä.) verbinden, und 14 verschiedene Spielarten
von Kyrios, Christos und Jesus. Dementsprechend ist die wesentlich
einfachere stereotyper klingende christologische Ausdrucksweise von 2
Thess. ein Indiz dafür, dass es sich hier um eine sekundäre Imitation des
ersten Briefes handelt. Von den 15 'christologischen Formeln' und
Begriffen, die v. Dobschütz aus 1 und 2 Thess. anführt, sind sechs exklusiv
im ersten Brief zu finden, dagegen nur eine im zweiten.

13 1 Thess. 1.1: ἐν θεῷ πατρὶ καὶ κυρίῳ 'Ἰησοῦ Χριστῷ. Nachgeahmt in 2
Thess. 1.1; 3.12; vgl. 1.2, 12. Zu den anderen Paulusbriefen vgl. Röm. 1.7;
15.6; 1 Kor. 1.3; 8.6; 16.23; 2 Kor. 1.2; 13.13; Gal. 1.3; Phil. 1.2; 2.11;
3.20; 4.23; Philem. 3; es findet sich vor allem in Salutatio und Schluss des
Briefes. Zur Form S. W. Kramer, op. cit. (A.1), 149–53.

14 Vgl. 2 Thess. 2.1, 14,16; 3.16; Röm. 5.1, 11; 13.14; 1 Kor. 1. 2, 8; 6.11;
2 Kor. 1.3; 8.9; Gal. 6.14.

15 Nach F. Neugebauer, op. cit. (A.1), S. 48, erscheint ἐν Χριστῷ in den
echten Briefen 25mal, ἐν Χριστῷ 'Ἰησοῦ 27/28mal. Im Zusammenhang
mit der Präposition ἐν und bei Genitivverbindungen bevorzugt Paulus
etwas mehr den Doppelnamen. Vgl. dazu auch die Statistik bei W.
Kramer, op. cit. (A.1), S. 204f.

16 Röm. 15. 19; 1 Kor. 9. 12; 2 Kor. 2.12; 9.13; 10.14; Gal. 1.7; Phil. 1.27; 2
Thess. 1.8 τῷ εὐαγγελίῳ τοῦ κυρίου ἡμῶν 'Ἰησοῦ fällt dagegen ganz aus
der Reihe und zeigt wieder den sekundären Charakter von 2 Thess. Zur
vorpaulinischen Formel s. W. Kramer, op. cit. (A.1), S. 46ff. Bei der

Formel τὸ εὐαγγέλιον τοῦ Χριστοῦ handelt es sich um einen Genitivus objectivus im Gegensatz zu dem Gen. auctoris bei der Parallelformel τὸ εὐαγγέλιον τοῦ θεοῦ, die im Gegensatz zum sonstigen Sprachgebrauch im 1 Thess. häufiger erscheint (2.2, 8, 9). Vgl. dazu W. Kramer, op. cit., S. 46ff, und P. Stuhlmacher, *Das paulinische Evangelium*, I. Vorgeschichte (*FRLANT* 95) 1968, S. 258ff, 266, die zu Recht darauf hinweisen, dass dieser formelhafte Sprachgebrauch vorpaulinisch ist. Vgl. auch Markus 1.1 und 1 Pet. 4.17. Wenig aufschlussreich und weiterführend sind dagegen die Ausführungen von G. Strecker, 'Das Evangelium Jesu Christi', *Jesus Christus in Historie und Theologie: Festschrift H. Conzelmann*, 1975, S. 503–48, die nur alte Thesen wiederholen.

17   In 1 Thess. 1.1 (und seiner Imitation im 2 Thess. 1.1 s.o.A. 13) stellt Paulus—wie auch sonst gerne—'Gott den Vater' und den 'Herrn Jesus Christus' zusammen. Vermutlich handelt es sich um eine Gebetsformel; vgl. die Grussformeln, Röm. 1. 7; 1 Kor. 1.3; 2 Kor. 1. 2f (2x); Phil. 1.2; Philem. 1,3. Auch in Gal. 1.1 mag das atypische διὰ 'Ιησοῦ Χριστοῦ durch das nachfolgende καὶ θεοῦ πατρός und die damit verbundene liturgische Gewöhnung bedingt sein. In den späteren Briefen erscheint dagegen die Genitivform, bei der in der Regel Χριστός vorangestellt ist: Röm. 1.1; δοῦλος Χριστοῦ 'Ιησοῦ; vgl. Phil. 1.1; 1 Kor. 1.1, ἀπόστολος Χριστοῦ 'Ιησοῦ; vgl. 2 Kor. 1.1; Philem. 1.1, δέσμιος Χριστοῦ 'Ιησοῦ; s. dazu auch in A. 53.

18   W. Sanday & A. C. Headlam, *The Epistle to the Romans*, *ICC*, [1]1895 ([5]1902), S. 3f; E. Kühl, *Der Brief des Paulus an die Römer*, 1913, S. 7: 'Christos' wird 'noch in seiner eigentlichen Bedeutung (= 'der Messias') empfunden', da 'der Apostel in der Grussüberschrift . . . von dem im AT verheissenen "Messias" Jesus als dem Inhalt des Evangeliums zu reden weiss'; O. Kuss, *Der Römerbrief*, 1963, S. 3: 'lässt die ursprüngliche Bedeutung von "Christus" (Messias) als Würdename noch durchscheinen'. Ähnlich C. E. B. Cranfield, *The Epistle to the Romans*, *ICC*, I, 1975, S. 51; H. Schlier, *Der Römerbrief*, HThK, 1977, S. 19f; U. Wilckens, *Der Brief an die Römer*, EKK I, 1978 S. 61, A. 24; O. Michel, *Der Brief an die Römer*, KEK [5]1978, S. 66: 'Wahrscheinlich klingt das Messiasbekenntnis nach'. Zurückhaltender unter Zitierung von E. v. Dobschütz H. Lietzmann op. cit. (A.1), S. 23, dort auch Hinweise auf den späteren 'von Paulus abhängigen' Sprachgebrauch in 1 Clem. und den Ignatiusbriefen.

19   Der neue Text des Nestle-Aland 26. A. hat bei mehreren Stellen die Wortfolge des bisherigen Textes geändert, so 2 Kor. 1.19; 4.5; Gal. 2.16; 3.14; Phil. 2.21. Bei allen diesen Stellen ist ein endgültiges Urteil ausserordentlich schwierig. Nach W. Kramer op. cit. (A.1), S. 204 sind von den 60 Fällen mit Doppelnamen bei Paulus nur 42 wirklich gesichert. Zum Problem der Umstellung s. auch S. V. McCasland, 'Christ Jesus', *JBL* 65 (1946), 377–83: 'I am unable to say why 48 of the 91 examples of "Christ Jesus" are in the dative and why 102 of the 127 instances of "Jesus Christ" are in the genitive. It is difficult, if not impossible, to explain how or why idiomatic expressions in any language arise and survive' (p. 383). Die genannten Zahlen betreffen das ganze NT.

20 O. Cullmann, *Christologie des Neuen Testaments* [3]1963, S. 135 sieht in der 'gelegentlichen Voranstellung des Christustitels vor "Jesus" einen Beweis, dass für Paulus 'das Wort "Christus" kein Eigenname ist'. Auch G. Bornkamm, *Das Ende des Gesetzes, Paulusstudien*, 1952 (= *Ges. Aufs.* I, [2]1958), S. 40 vertritt eine ähnliche Auffassung: 'Die Tatsache, dass Paulus den Christusnamen gelegentlich als *nomen proprium* verwenden kann, hat die verbreitete Auffassung veranlasst, der Christustitel sei für ihn fast bedeutungslos geworden und durch den κύριος-Titel ersetzt. Das trifft jedoch keineswegs zu. Beide Namen haben bei ihm allermeist titularen Sinn und eine durchaus verschiedene Funktion.' Vgl. auch F. Hahn, op. cit (A.1), S. 213f, der sich auf Bornkamm beruft.

21 E. v. Dobschütz, op. cit. (A.1), S. 61. Vgl. die die These von Dobschütz' bestätigende ausführliche Untersuchung von W. Kramer, op. cit., S. 199ff, 203ff 'Die Bezeichnungen "Jesus", "Christos" und "Jesus Christos" sind innerhalb des corpus Paulinum sachlich gleichbedeutend' (202). Nur wenn man diese Voraussetzung anerkennt, kann man weiter fragen, ob nicht doch zuweilen sprachliche Reminiszenzen an den titularen Gebrauch zu finden sind und warum Paulus so gerne den Namen Christus verwendet. Dazu u.S. 145.

22 Op. cit. (A.1), S. 83f.

23 Der absolute Gebrauch von Χριστός —*mašiᵃḥ* ohne Genitivattribut ist in vorchristlichen jüdischen Texten ausserordentlich selten: Dan. 9.25 '*ad mašiᵃḥ nāgîd* = Theodotion ἕως χριστοῦ ἡγουμένου, vermutlich auf Kyros, Serubabel oder auf den Hohepriester Josua zu beziehen. 9.26: *jikkaret mašiᵃḥ* ein Hinweis auf die Ermordung des Hohepriesters Onias III. Die determinierte Form *ham-mašiᵃḥ* findet sich möglicherweise 1 QSa 2.12 s. A.S. v.d. Woude, *TWNT* ix, S. 509f.

24 Dazu M. Hengel, *Sohn Gottes*, S. 93ff; U. Wilckens (A.18) I, S. 56ff; J. D. G. Dunn, *Christology in the Making*, 1980, S. 33–5; 138f.

25 E. v. Dobschütz, op. cit. (A.1), S. 61.

26 Übersetzung und Deutung nach H. Lietzmann & W. G. Kümmel, *An die Korinther* I/II, *HNT*, [4]1949, S. 102f.

27 Lukas 4.18; Apg. 4.27; 10.38; Heb. 1.9; vgl. 11 QMelch 3 II, Zeile 18: *hw('h) mšyḥ hrw(ḥ)*, dazu Jes. 61.1 und J. T. Milik, *JJSt* 23 (1972), S. 98, 107f.

28 *Paulus der Bote Jesu*, 1934, S. 482; vgl. W. Grundmann, op. cit. (A.1), S. 549f, der die 'Salbung' im Sinne der Eingliederung in den Leib Christi versteht.

29 E. v. Dobschütz, loc. cit.; N. A. Dahl, op. cit. (A.1), S. 86.

30 Loc. cit. Dahl betont jedoch A. 2 ausdrücklich: 'Χριστός mit "Messias" übersetzen darf man aber bei Paulus auf keinen Fall.'

31 Op. cit., S. 84; W. Kramer, op. cit. (A.1), S. 209f, möchte überhaupt nur noch in Röm. 9.5 und 1 Kor. 11.3 eine titulare Deutung gelten lassen, und auch dort nur als Möglichkeit.

32 Vgl. etwa die kaiserlichen Edikte in Cyrene bei V. Ehrenberg & A. H. M.

Jones, *Documents illustrating the reigns of Augustus and Tiberius*, ²1955, Nr. 311, S. 139, die stereotyp mit dieser Formel eingeleitet werden. Häufig wurde zwischen Caesar und Augustus ein *divi filius* (Θεοῦ υἱός) eingeschoben oder nach Augustus angefügt. Augustus-Sebastos wurde dann auf alle Nachfolger im kaiserlichen Amt übertragen. D.h. der ursprünglich individuelle Beiname erhielt allmählich fast titulare Bedeutung.

33 Vgl. *OGIS* 19.1; 25.1; 249.1; 250.1. Auch hier waren Ergänzungen möglich: z.B. Σωτὴρ καὶ Θεός, 16.2.3; Θεὸς ἐπιφανής, 246.10; 253.5.

34 W. Grundmann, op. cit. (A.1), S. 534f zu Augustus s. A. 324 den Hinweis von Risch.

35 κύριος Ἰησοῦς: Röm. 10.9; 14.14; 1 Kor. 12.3; 2 Kor. 4.14; 11.31; Phil. 2.19. Zu 1 Thess. s.o.A. 12 und 13. κύριος ἡμῶν Ἰησοῦς (oder Ἰησοῦς ὁ κύριος ἡμῶν): Röm. 4.24; 16.20; 1 Kor. 5.4; 9.1; 2 Kor. 1.14; κύριος Ἰησοῦς Χριστός Phil. 2.11; vgl. o.A. 13.

36 W. Kramer, op. cit. (A.1), S. 214, A. 744 möchte darin eine 'unerklärliche Ausnahme sehen'; vgl. jedoch N. A. Dahl, op. cit. (A.1), S. 84, der noch auf das deuteropaulinische Kol. 3.24, τῷ κυρίῳ Χριστῷ δουλεύετε verweist. Zu beachten ist, dass Röm. 16.16 ein τοῦ Χριστοῦ vorausgeht, und in den Versen 7–12 ἐν Χριστῷ und ἐν κυρίῳ in gleicher Bedeutung erscheint. Röm. 14.18 spricht Paulus von einem δουλεύειν τῷ Χριστῷ, 12.11 hat er den Imperativ τῷ κυρίῳ δουλεύετε. Dieser mehrfache Wechsel zwischen κύριος und Χριστός sowie das Motiv von Herrsein und Dienst mag die ungewöhnliche Ausdrucksweise bewirkt haben, wobei das Genitivpronomen ἡμῶν die Kluft zwischen τῷ κυρίῳ und Χριστῷ abschwächte.

37 Vgl. Röm. 6.23; 8.39; 1 Kor. 15.31; Phil. 3.8.

38 Dazu W. Kramer, op. cit. (A.1), S. 22ff; K. Wengst, *Christologische Formeln und Lieder des Urchristentums*, 1972, S. 78ff; M. Hengel, *Atonement*, London 1981, S. 34ff.

39 In *Theologie als Schriftauslegung: Aufsätze zum Neuen Testament*, 1974, S. 110 (= 'Was glaubte die frühe Christenheit?' *SThU* 25 [1955], S. 65): ' "Christus" hat da titularen Sinn, wo der bestimmte Artikel steht, aber auch da, wo "Christus" (ohne den Namen "Jesus") Subjekt eines Satzes ist'.

40 S.o.A. 16.

41 Ähnlich wie bei ἐν κυρίῳ. Ausnahmen: 1 Kor. 15.22 abhängig von ἐν τῷ Ἀδάμ; 2 Kor. 2.14; F. Neugebauer, op. cit. (A.1), S. 47; W. Kramer, op. cit. (A.1), S. 208f.

42 2 Kor. 5.20; 12.10; Phil. 1.29.

43 Röm. 16.5; 1 Kor. 8.12; 2 Kor. 1.21; Gal. 3.27; Philem. 6; 2 Kor. 11.3 ist der Text unsicher. Die 26. A. des Nestle-Aland hat gegenüber der 25. A. den Artikel eingefügt.

44 διὰ τοῦ Χριστοῦ, 2 Kor. 1.5; 3.4; διὰ Χριστοῦ, 2 Kor. 5.18; διὰ Χριστόν, 1 Kor. 4.10; διὰ τὸν Χριστόν, Phil. 3.7.

45 W. Kramer, op. cit., S. 209; vgl. N. A. Dahl, op. cit., S. 85.

46 Vgl. W. Kramers grundsätzliche Feststellung, op. cit., S. 211 '. . . ist die Unmöglichkeit der generellen Verquickung der Artikelfrage mit der Titelfrage erwiesen'.

47 Im absoluten Gebrauch 39mal, zusammengesetzt 8mal. Kyrios begegnet dagegen nur 29mal, davon 21mal im absoluten Gebrauch; Ἰησοῦς nur 19mal, davon 7mal absolut. Das Verhältnis zwischen absolutem Gebrauch von 'Christos' und dem in zusammengesetzten Formeln ist in den anderen Briefen wie folgt: Röm. 36:30; 1 Kor. 40:24; Gal. 20:18; Phil. 17:20; Philem. 3:5.

48 Gegen W. Kramer, op. cit., S. 146.

49 S. die minutiösen Analysen von W. Kramer, op. cit., S. 15–60, 131ff. Zur Sendung des Sohnes s. M. Hengel, *Der Sohn Gottes,* ²1977, S. 112ff. Zu ἐν Χριστῷ s. F. Neugebauer, op. cit. (A.1), S. 65ff; W. Kramer, op. cit., S. 131ff.

50 W. Kramer, op. cit., S. 134ff.

51 N. A. Dahl, op. cit., S. 92.

52 Röm. 9.3–5; 15.8; 1 Kor. 5.7; 10.4, 9; 15.3f; Gal. 3.13f, 16, 22, 24. Vgl. W. Kramer, op. cit., S. 146.

53 Op. cit., S. 41–60; s.o. A. 17.

54 Man wird dies kaum mit Ph. Vielhauer, *Aufsätze z. N. T., ThB* 31, 1965, S. 183f., dadurch erklären können, dass Phil. der 'späteste Brief' des Paulus sei. Er könnte sehr wohl auf der '3. Reise' von Ephesus aus geschrieben worden sein. Vgl. auch 1 Thess. 5.24; 1 Kor. 1.7–8 mit einer kombinierten Formel, weiter 1 Kor. 15.22—3. 2 Kor. 5.10. Das Fazit von Vielhauer, loc. cit., 'der Terminus "Christos" hat seine ursprüngliche Heimat nicht in der Eschatologie, sondern in der Soteriologie', schafft einen falschen Gegensatz, beides lässt sich nicht trennen. Was sollte Χριστός für Paulus anderes bedeuten als den 'eschatologischen Erlöser', auch wenn er bei Parusietraditionen den Titel Kyrios besonders häufig verwendet. Gewiss, der Kyriostitel hat eine 'Domäne' in Zusammenhang mit der Parusietradition. Das mag—wie der Gebetsruf *Maranatha* zeigt—damit zusammenhängen, dass die Erwartung des erhöhten Herrn (vgl. Ps. 110.1) an die Stelle der Hoffnung auf den Menschensohn getreten war. Aber auch dieser Bereich war für den Christus-Titel bzw. Namen keineswegs verschlossen. Nur als Träger des 'Christos'-Namens bzw. Titels war Jesus zugleich der Kyrios. Es gab im Urchristentum keine Kyrios-Christologie, die unabhängig war von der Messianität Jesu.

55 Auch das abgegriffene Klischee der Parusieverzögerung sollte in diesem Zusammenhang nicht mehr verwendet werden, es ist zu schlicht, um den komplizierten Vorgang der Entfaltung der Christologie auch nur teilweise erklären zu können. Es enthält zudem nichts spezifisch Christliches; s. A. Strobel, *Untersuchungen zum eschatologischen Verzögerungsproblem, Nov.Test.Suppl,* 2, 1961.

56 1 Kor. 1.17; Phil. 3.18; vgl. Gal. 6.12, 14.

57 1 Kor. 1.23; 2.2; Gal. 3.1.

58 Das harte Verb πορθεῖν Gal. 1.13, 23; Apg. 9.21: 'vernichten, verwüsten, zerstören', 'vertilgen', ausrotten, s. W. Bauer, *Wörterbuch*, sub voce, ist ernstzunehmen und darf nicht abgeschwächt werden. Dies legt eine Verfolgung in Jerusalem nahe, wo die Möglichkeiten eines gerichtlichen und aussergerichtlichen Vorgehens gegen die neue messianische Lehre am günstigsten waren. Auch das Pharisäertum des Paulus und sein Torastudium sind nur sinnvoll zu erklären, wenn man von einer vorchristlichen Wirksamkeit und Verfolgertätigkeit in Jerusalem ausgeht (Phil. 3.5; Gal. 1.14). Im Pharisäismus vor 70 war das vertiefte Torastudium im Zusammenhang mit der Ausbildung als Schriftgelehrter aus religiösen Gründen in Jerusalem konzentriert. Die Heilige Stadt war das einzigartige Zentrum der Schriftgelehrsamkeit. Wenn Markus (3.22 vgl. 7.1) von den 'Schriftgelehrten aus Jerusalem' spricht, gibt er einen durchaus historischen Sachverhalt wieder.

59 Dazu M. Hengel, *Atonement* 1981, S. 44ff.

60 *Der Sohn Gottes*, ²1977, S. 71f.

61 Röm. 1.2; 3.21, 31; 4.14ff; 9.4f; 15.8; 2 Kor. 1.20f; Gal. 3.14–29.

62 Vgl. W. Grundmann, *TWNT* ix, S. 533.

63 O. Cullmann, *Christologie des Neuen Testaments*, ³1957, S. 135 'zum Eigennamen erstarrt'; F. Hahn, op. cit. (A.1), S. 223 'die relativ bald einsetzende Erstarrung des titularen Gebrauchs und die Verwendung... als *Eigenname*'; W. Kramer, op. cit. (A.1), S. 39 ' "Christos" ist blosser Eigenname, ohne Eigenglanz und eigenmächtiges Strukturschema'.

64 J. Weiss, *Das Urchristentum*, 1917, S. 127.

65 Op. cit., S. 128.

66 Claudius 25.4. Dazu W. Bauer, *Wörterbuch* sub voce χρηστός und K. Weiss, *TWNT* ix, S. 473 A.11. Zum Eigennahmen χρῆστος S. W. Pape und G. E. Benseler, *Wörterbuch der griechischen Eigennamen*, ³1911, S. 1690; F. Preisigke, *Namenbuch*, 1922, S. 478.

67 Dazu Harald Fuchs, *VChr*. 4 (1950) S. 65–93, und die Ergänzungen *Mus. Helv.* 20 (1963) 221ff. Einen Forschungsüberblick gibt P. Keresztes, *The Imperial Roman Government and the Christian Church* I, From Nero to the Severi, *ANRW* II. 23,1 (1979), S. 247–57 (250 A 12). Vgl. auch A. Wlosok, *Rom und die Christen*, 1970, S. 8f. Sie weist im Anschluss an H. Hommel darauf hin, dass Tacitus mit der Formulierung 'quos per flagitia invisos vulgus Chrestianos appellabat' ein ironisches Wortspiel bildet: 'Die das Volk, wiewohl sie durch Schandtaten verhasst waren, die "Biedermänner" nannte', S. 10.

68 W. Grundmann, *TWNT* ix, S. 485; C. F. D. Moule, *The Origin of Christology* 1977, S. 32 A 37.

69 W. Kramer, op. cit. (A.1) S. 39f: 'Seine eschatologische Stellung lässt sich nicht mehr an der Bezeichnung 'Christos' ablesen, sondern hängt allein an den Akten, von welchen die Aussagen der Pistisformel sprechen', S. 39. Dem wäre entgegenzusetzen: Der Name Χριστός hatte für Paulus—wie auch sein Evangelium—eo ipso 'eschatologische' Bedeutung. Durch

diesen ihm allein exklusiv geltenden einzigartigen Namen war die Person Jesu 'eschatologisch' qualifiziert.

70 S. M. Hengel, *Chronologie* (A.1), S. 56f.

71 S. dazu die zutreffende These von W. Schmithals in seinem sonst freilich allzu phantasievollen Werk *Der Römerbrief als historisches Problem*, 1975, S. 76: 'Man muss . . . die These wagen, dass die frühen heidenchristlichen Gemeinden sich überhaupt im wesentlichen aus ehemaligen Gottesfürchtigen zusammensetzten, . . . und dass erst in langsam wachsendem Masse vorwiegend in nachapostolischer Zeit solche Heiden zur Gemeinde fanden, die zuvor noch in keiner Verbindung zur Synagoge gestanden hatten'. Zu den 'Gottesfürchtigen' s. die Studie meines Schülers F. Siegert, "Gottesfürchtige und Sympathisanten", *JSJ* 4 (1973), S. 109–64; vgl. auch G. Delling, 'Die Altarinschrift eines Gottesfürchtigen in Pergamon', *Nov. Test.* 7 (1964) S. 73–80 = *Studien zum NT und zum hellenist. Judentum*, 1970, S. 32–38.

72 Freilich darf man dort noch keine grundsätzliche theologisch völlig durchreflektierte Gesetzeskritik wie bei Paulus voraussetzen. S. dazu *Zwischen Jesus und Paulus*, *ZThK* 72 (1975), S. 151–206 (190ff).

73 Dies ist schon aus chronologischen Gründen schwierig. Paulus begann nach Gal. 1.15f seine Heidenmission bald nach seiner Bekehrung ca. zwei-fünf Jahre nach dem gemeindegründenden Urgeschehen, wenn auch noch nicht exklusiv und in weltweitem Masstab. G. Lüdemann, *Paulus der Heidenapostel*, Bd. I, *Studien zur Christologie*, 1980, S. 23 A 14 verfälscht durch sein Zitat meine Aussage in *Zur urchristlichen Geschichtsschreibung*, 1979, S. 100. Es ist keine Frage, dass für Paulus das sog. Apostelkonzil und die Vorgänge in Antiochien, die zur Trennung von Barnabas führten, einschneidende Bedeutung im Blick auf seine weltweite Missionsstrategie besassen. Nichts spricht in Gal 1.12–21 dafür, dass Paulus schon in dieser Zeit—getrennt von Barnabas—nach Makedonien und Griechenland vorgestossen ist. Es ist eigenartig, dass gerade solche radikalen Kritiker, die Lukas vorwerfen, eine Art von 'Paulusroman' geschrieben zu haben, selbst der romanhaften Ausgestaltung der Quellenaussagen schwer widerstehen können.

74 Vgl. den Katalog der Sieben Apg. 6.5f, der fünf 'Propheten', Apg. 13.1 in Antiochien, die Namen, die 18.2,7f in Korinth aufgeführt werden, die Namensliste Röm. 16.3ff und selbst noch Kol. 4.10ff.

75 Markus 8.29; 12.35; 14.61; 15.36; Lukas 2.11, 26 u.ö; Matt. 1.17; 11.2; 16.16; 1 Johannes 2.22; 5.1; Johannes 1.25, 41; 3.28; 4.25,29; 7.26f. u.ö; Apok. 1.5; 12.10; dieses Wissen kommt, wie Justin zeigt, vor allem im Dialog mit Juden zum Vorschein. Dies schliesst nicht aus, dass Χριστός nicht der einzige und nicht der wichtigste 'Würdename' Jesu ist. Markus, Matt. und Johannes schätzen Sohn Gottes höher ein, Lukas stellt neben 'Christos' zumindest gleichberechtigt Kyrios; vgl. Lukas 2.11; Apg. 2.36. Zum frühchristlichen Gebrauch von 'Christos' im 2. Jhdt s. F. Kattenbusch, op. cit. (A.1), S.553–60. Selbst im römischen Symbol πιστεύω . . . καὶ εἰς Χριστὸν ’Ιησοῦν τὸν υἱὸν αὐτοῦ τὸν μονογενῆ τὸν κύριον ἡμῶν hat nach K. 'Christos' noch den Klang einer Würdebezeich-

nung: 'Die Gemeinde, die R. (d.h. das Romanum) geschaffen hat, bewegt sich noch durchaus selbst in der messianischen Denkkategorie und hat ihr Pathos daran, dass sie begriffen habe, der Messias sei eine gegebene, in Jesu erschienene Grösse.' (S. 541)

76 Apg. 9.22; vgl. 20; 17.3; 18.5; vgl. 26.23 und Apollos, 18.26. Die schematisierende Berichterstattung des Lukas bedeutet noch nicht, dass sie die geschichtliche Wirklichkeit hinter sich lässt. Zum Gebrauch von 'Christos' bei Lukas s. F. Bovon, *Luc le théologien*, 1978, 201f., 207ff.

77 Zu dem alten Streit um das artikellose Christos 1 Kor. 15.3 s. abschliessend J. Jeremias, *ZNW* 57 (1966), S. 211–15; 60 (1969), S. 214–19, ausserdem die Kritik von I. Plein *EvTh* 29 (1969) S. 222f an E. Güttgemanns, *EvTh* 28 (1968) S. 533–54.

78 W. Grundmann, *TWNT* ix, S. 533.

79 A. Schalit, *Namenwörterbuch zu Flavius Josephus*, 1968, S. 6of zählt 19 Namensträger auf, Tcherikover-Fuks, *Corpus Papyrorum Judaicarum*, vol. III, 1964, S.180 weitere 10. J.-B. Frey, *Corpus Inscriptionum Judaicarum* II, 1952 aus Palästina J^ehošu^{ac} Nr. 897; 1196; J^ešû^{ac} Nr. 1317; 1345; 1365; Ἰησοῦς Nr. 1231; 1327. B. Lifshitz, *Donateurs et fondateurs dans les synagogues juives*, 1967, Nr. 73a Ἴσουος. Umsomehr fällt auf, dass bald nach 70 die Kurzform Ješû^{ac} als Name in den jüdischen Quellen praktisch völlig verschwindet. Ješû^{ac} han-nôṣrî hatte ihn für Juden unmöglich gemacht.

80 F. Blass und A. Debrunner, *Grammatik des neutestamentlichen Griechisch*, ¹¹1961. §254 S. 158.

81 *Die Worte Jesu*, ²1930 (Nachdr. 1965) S. 239ff unter Verweis auf F. Delitzsch.

82 *Die Auferstehung Jesu*, ⁵1967, S. 129ff.

83 *ZNW* 60 (1969) S. 214–19.

84 CD 20, 1. Vgl. K. H. Rengstorf op. cit. (A. 80), S.131; J. Jeremias, op. cit. (A. 83), S. 219.

85 Indeterminiert 1 Chr. 21.1; vgl. I. Plein, op. cit. (A. 72), S. 223.

86 Die Grenzen zwischen Appellativum und Eigennamen sind dabei fliessend s. W. Foerster, *TWNT* vii, S. 153f.

87 S. dazu Preisendanz, *PW*, 14.2, 1930, 1899.

88 M. Hengel, *Judentum und Hellenismus*, ²1973, S. 542–46.

89 Zum Hintergrund christologischer Titel, *NTS* 17 (1970/71), S. 391–425 (391f). Man sollte freilich 'Christus' und 'Petrus' als 'eschatologische Eigennamen' nicht einfach auf eine Ebene stellen.

90 Grundlegend dazu J. A. Fitzmyer, 'Der semitische Hintergrund des neutestamentlichen Kyriostitels', in *Jesus Christus in Historie und Theologie: Festschrift H. Conzelmann*, 1975, S. 267–98.

91 Immerhin ist der Satz Fitzmyers zu bedenken op. cit., S. 297: 'Aber dennoch kann man nun nicht mehr einfach den Gedanken beiseite schieben, dass der auf Jesus angewandte Kyriostitel eine Transzendenz impliziert, die Jesus mit Jahwe zusammenstellt, in einer Art "Gleichheit",

Martin Hengel

wenn auch nicht als "Identifizierung", denn er ist ja nicht *'abbā'* "Vater".' Ich würde eher von einer durch Ps. 110.1 geförderten 'Angleichung' des Erhöhten an Gott sprechen.

92 Dazu W. Kramer (A. 1), S.15–40 zur 'Pistisformel' und einschränkenden Kritik von K. Wengst, *Christologische Formeln und Lieder des Urchristentums* 1972, 78ff, 92ff. M. Hengel, *Atonement*, 1981, 33ff.

93 *Atonement*, S. 57ff.

94 Gal. 1.12 dazu P. Stuhlmacher, op. cit. (A. 16), S.71.

95 Dazu N. A. Dahl, 'Der gekreuzigte Messias', H. Ristow & K. Matthiae (Hg.), *Der historische Jesus und der kerygmatische Christus*, 1961, S. 149–69 = *The crucified Messiah and other Essays*, Minneapolis 1974, S. 10–36, 161ff, 167–69.

96 Vgl. dagegen das christlich interpolierte sog. Testimonium Flavianum, *Ant.* XVIII.63: ὁ Χριστὸς οὗτος ἦν. Zur Überlieferungsgeschichte der verschiedenen Rekonstruktionsversuche s. A.-M. Dubarle, 'Le témoignage de Josèphe sur Jésus', *RB* 80 (1973), S. 481–513. Er folgt der Version des Hieronymus und des Michael Syrus (495–511): *credebatur esse Christus.* Zur Bibliographie s. A. Schalit, *Zur Josephus-Forschung*, Darmstadt 1973, S. 417–19; zusammenfassende Darstellung von P. Winter in E. Schürer, *The History of the Jewish People in the Age of Jesus Christ*, I, Edinburgh 1973, S. 428–41.

ENGLISH SUMMARY

Paul's letters contain over fifty per cent of the New Testament uses of *Christos* and it is by far his most frequent designation for Jesus. This remarkable fact, made the more puzzling by Jesus's apparent refusal to call himself Messiah, requires an explanation. It poses, in fact, the central problem of early christology: how was it that in such a short span of time the title *Christos* was so firmly linked to Jesus that it became his surname and in such a way that it is the most frequent designation for him in the earliest Christian writer? The strictly titular sense of *Christos* is not to be found in Paul and he shows not the slightest interest in demonstrating Jesus' Messiahship by the use of proof-texts. The various formulaic usages of *Christos* are already evident in Paul's earliest letter, 1 Thessalonians. Both the number and the type of usages differs from one epistle to another, as does the relative frequency in relation to other terms such as *Kyrios*, but only rarely is there any apparent explanation for this. Rather, Paul's use of *Christos* is both promiscuous and undifferentiated, although it is noticeable that it is more frequent when he is anchored in pre-Pauline tradition and when he refers to the eschatological significance of Jesus' death, resurrection and parousia.

The manner and the frequency with which Paul uses *Christos* is the result neither of chance nor mere convention. The widely held view that the use of *Christos* as a surname has its roots in an early form of Gentile Christianity which no longer understood its messianic sense is as improbable as the view that Paul and his readers were in the same position. It cannot be doubted that both Paul and his readers understood the messianic significance of the term, although clearly it was not a matter of controversy for them. For Paul, *Christos* continues to have a decisive theological meaning: it is neither simply a Jewish messianic title nor merely a surname; rather it is tied inseparably to the notion that Jesus is the one who, through his death and resurrection, has become the sole bringer of eschatological salvation. This use of *Christos* was common in Antioch, goes back to the preaching of the Hellenists, and was known to Paul immediately after his call. Although we know little about Paul's *missionary* preaching, there is no reason to doubt that in this context he did preach the Messiahship of Jesus in a manner not unlike that recorded in Acts. Indeed, the conviction that Jesus was Messiah was central to the preaching of the Palestinian communities and was historically grounded in the crucifixion of Jesus as a messianic pretender.

159

14

Christ and All Things

Markus Barth

I *The State of a Discussion*

Does it make sense to speak of a cosmic rule of Jesus Christ and of the reconciliation of all things, the whole universe, through him? Or are his person and work related only to the salvation of humankind?

Among the numerous recent publications on this issue, three may be mentioned which come by various routes to the same conclusion: the talk of a 'cosmic Christ' contradicts the intentions and witness of the whole New Testament or essential parts of it; therefore, a Christ-centred theology must abstain from statements that sound cosmological. Rather it must deal only with the salvation of individuals, the Church, and society.

A. Vögtle[1] examines passages from the whole of the New Testament. Employing the current historical-critical methods of interpretation, he forms the thesis that all New Testament utterances regarding the universal power and effect of Christ pertain only to the salvation of mankind from its corruption. The new creation is the eschatological community: the Church. What the Fourth Gospel calls κόσμος and what in the letters is named κτίσις means people, not things. The concern and care for the material universe and its future may therefore be left to the natural scientists.

E. Schweizer[2] crowns the impressive number of his earlier published treatises on Col. 1 by trying to show that only the application of the modern methods of form, tradition, and redaction criticism can solve the issue between a wider cosmic and a narrower anthropocentric soteriology. First, out of the present text of Col. 1.15–20 an original, religio-cosmological, almost naturalistic creator-saviour hymn is reconstructed.[3] Second, the assumption is made that under Paul's influence the author of Colossians (perhaps Timothy during Paul's lifetime) drastically changed the meaning of the original hymn: he added to it the ecclesiastical and missionary, introductory and concluding framework of verses 12–14, 21–3, and he interpolated

Pauline phrases into the wording of the original hymn. Third, the conclusion is drawn that the present text of Colossians proclaims solely the reconciliation and new creation of Christians, together with their worldwide missionary responsibility. In his comments on Col. 2, Schweizer presents additional arguments for his conviction that Christ must not be understood as a quasi-natural power, process, or event, and that nature is neither the beneficiary nor a means of salvation. Only the Colossian philosophers, influenced by neo-Pythagorean notions as they were, held the opinion that the inclusion of 'world-elements' in the process of salvation and worship would liberate people from their *Weltangst*. For the author of Colossians, however, Jesus Christ's death and the reception of baptism are the exhaustive and perfect means of salvation, pacification, reconciliation; there is no need of anything natural. The 'bodily' presence of the deity in Jesus of which Col. 2.9 speaks does not mean, according to Schweizer, a presence in (physical) substance, but only a manifestation through functional power.

Finally, J. Murphy-O'Connor[4] discusses one single Pauline verse with the following result: whenever in a Pauline sentence τὰ πάντα are mentioned in connection with God or Christ, then exclusively the salvation of 'all' Christians is meant – a salvation which is performed by 'all' instruments chosen by God for his specific action, and despite 'all' obstacles. The mention of τὰ πάντα never means that heaven and earth, spiritual and material powers are being saved, or that God or Christ are in any relation to them for their own sake. This author thus virtually suggests the eviction of all non-human creatures from Christ's care, and a human monopoly on divine mercy and salvation.

Two of the great fathers of New Testament form criticism and its later refinements had prepared the way for these exegetical 'discoveries'. According to R. Bultmann,[5] the 'cosmic meaning' of Jesus Christ's death is restricted to the effect of that death on people alone, and to the relevance of that one hour for ever new historical moments in human existence. M. Dibelius followed E. Norden[6] when he compared the New Testament confessions related to 'all things' with a 'hellenistic formula' which is usually called the 'Stoic omnipotence formula', and which directly relates the creation, sustenance and purpose of all sticks and stones, plants and animals, powers and virtues to a supreme deity. He argued that this formula was taken up and endorsed by early Christian authors – but not without incisive changes. Its 'Christianization' presupposed a 'narrowing of the horizon', that is, 'the transfer of a formula which originally meant the cosmos onto the church'. Dibelius considered hellenistic Judaism to be 'the mediator between the creeds of hellenistic culture and those of early Christianity'. Bultmann, however, offered another explanation: 'In both John and Paul, Christology is formed after the pattern of the Gnostic redeemer-myth.' Because the residues of that myth in the New Testament communicate the message of salvation in cosmic-naturalistic terms, the New Testament language of salvation must be purged of all naturalistic elements by modern interpreters. Demythologizing and existential interpretation are the scholarly names of the task and art of this purging process. The cosmic Christ and universal salvation are among its prime victims.

No one among such interpreters of the New Testament would contest the weight, relevance, and beauty of those Jewish and Christian credal statements that call God the creator of heaven and earth. Neither would they obliterate in Marcionite fashion any and all connections between the first and the new creation. But while they promote or, at least, tolerate a *Theo*logy of creation, they shun a *Christo*logy which goes beyond statements on sin and forgiveness, death and life, justification and sanctification, faith, hope, and love – in short, beyond those things which people experience as members of the human community and the Church. The creation may still be permitted to form the background or theatre, an occasion or an obstacle, perhaps at times even a mirror of the sinners' salvation and new creation, but itself seems to be excluded from the reconciliation and peace brought by Jesus Christ.

While there have been occasional protests against the restriction of salvation to human persons,[7] and while a few New Testament scholars[8] have made a beginning in this area, in general the views sketched above seem to represent a current consensus. It is not the purpose of this paper to scrutinize and test individual exegetical arguments; we ask rather what might be the underlying theological and non-theological factors which contribute to the western neglect of or opposition to the extension of Jesus Christ's creative, sustaining, judging and saving functions over *all* things. Because biblical exegetes are not immune from the temptation to choose or to create methods which lead to predetermined results, this question can and must be posed.

II *The Challenge of New Testament Texts*

The reticent or negative attitude toward a cosmic and universal
salvation through Jesus Christ cannot be caused by a lack of New
Testament references to the omnipotence of Jesus Christ. There are the
miracle accounts of the Gospels. There are the apocalyptic descriptions of the present and the end-time in the Synoptic Gospels, in several
letters, and in the Book of Revelation. Finally there are, spread over
the whole of the New Testament and representing the most diverse
traditions, many explicit affirmations concerning Jesus Christ's
mighty and beneficial lordship over all created powers and things.[9]
Descriptions of *Christ's* dominion usually refer to the *eschaton*: in the
future all creatures will pay homage to him. But the eschatological
affirmations are occasionally matched by 'protological' statements: it
is said of τὰ πάντα that they owe their very existence to Christ in
almost all passages that contain the 'high' doctrine of the Son's
pre-existence. Besides the eschatological and protological confessions a
third group is found which might be called extended-protological or
realized-eschatological: all things subsist in him, are upheld by his
word, are kept alive and illuminated by him, from whom and for
whom they also are created and destined (Col. 1.16–17; Heb. 1.2–3;
John 1.3–4, 10).

Other texts refer to the Father alone as creator, sustainer and
perfecter of heaven and earth.[10] Do they contradict or at least stand in
tension with all that is said about Jesus Christ's relation to all created
things? Is it really the case that the *theo*logical praises of God Almighty
are no more than Jewish and Christian copies of Stoic omnipotence
formulae, while there are two elements of the *christo*logical hymnic
confessions which reveal their specifically Christian origin: (1) the
completely un-Stoic affirmation that Father *and Son* have all things in
their hands, and (2) the narrowing down of the meaning of 'all things'
to the sense 'all believers'? It is most likely that these differentiations
and explanations fail to do justice to the New Testament texts in
question. For in both, some of the *theo*logical and some of the
*christo*logical confessions, the words πάντα, κόσμος, and κτίσις sometimes refer only to 'people' but more frequently include also all created
spirits and things.

The sharing of the Son of God in the Father's omnipotence is not a
novel idea that contradicts the testimony of the Old Testament. It is
rather to be explained by utterances indicating that the Father and

Creator has 'given' his own unique and universal power to the Son. The harmony of this transfer with the 'monotheistic' experience and faith of Israel is indicated for instance by New Testament references to Ps. 8.7 and 110.1[11]: the God of Israel had promised that he would put 'all things', including victory over demonic, psychical, and political 'enemies', at the disposition and into the hands of 'the Royal' Man, the Son of God, the Messiah. In the Fourth Gospel, the common omnipotence of the Father and the Son is described in utmost brevity: what the Father works, this also the Son does (5.17–19). According to the Book of Revelation (chs. 5ff) the 'sealed book' entrusted to the slaughtered lamb contains more than just the names of the people who will inherit eternal life.

Not even the atoning character of Christ's death and resurrection is mentioned more frequently and praised more highly in the New Testament than is Christ's glory as eternal *kosmokrator*. For this reason the prime exponent of narrow anthropocentric thinking, that is, the neglect, concealment, limitation or crude negation of Jesus Christ's creative and redemptive omnipotence, must have its basis somewhere other than simply in the careful study of New Testament texts.

III   *The Problem of Hidden Persuaders*

1   *A Mechanical Concept of Nature*   E. Kant is the spiritual father of W. Herrmann's theology, W. Herrmann of R. Bultmann's anthropocentrism, R. Bultmann of, e.g., E. Schweizer's aversion to a naturalistic description of Jesus Christ and salvation. All of them repudiate and abhor the notion that the spiritual and liberating work, message, and effect of Christ the saviour should in any way resemble a natural event, affect nature itself, or make use of natural means. Unshaken and unquestioned appears to be Kant's creed according to which nature is the existence of things insofar as it is determined by general laws, and only the realm of the spirit is governed by freedom.[12]

But since the second quarter of the twentieth century, changes have taken place in both camps of what C. P. Snow called 'the two cultures'. There were and are theologians who renounce the nineteenth-century alliance with idealism and emphasize the materialistic dimension of the incarnation of the Logos. In the fields of the humanities, many scholars gladly make use of methods made available by natural science. Natural scientists no longer speak of 'natural laws' as objective principles that make the universe tick, but rather as working hypotheses fabricated by the human mind because they prove useful for looking at nature, for describing it, and – in a limited sense – for explaining it. Scientists and humanists together raise warnings against unlimited extension of research and ruthless exploitation of nature. Thus, avenues have been opened to a new dialogue, perhaps even to community and solidarity between the various university faculties. Only when these and other changes are ignored can New Testament exegetes continue to struggle as unreconstructible idealists against the very idea of a cosmic Christ and universal salvation. Actually, the blunt exclusion of everything natural from christological research and proclamation is neither true to the substance of the New Testament nor does it meet any needs of modern man.

2   *The Language of Imagination*   When the Bible speaks of trees clapping their hands, of mountains that jump with joy, of stars that sing, of sparrows that live and lilies that blossom in praise of the Lord and of his deeds of salvation, then it uses poetic language. For biblical scholars the temptation is great to call these personifications of natural elements and events at best artistic, at the worst mythical or fictitious. In any case, utterances of this type are considered totally distinct from the realistic sense and value of historical or ethical biblical statements. Because of the lack of analogy and evidence in daily experience, affirmations pertaining, for example, to an end of all suffering among the totality of creatures, or to a new heaven and a new earth, are ascribed to subjective visionary gifts, to wishful thinking or to exaggerated enthusiasm.

However, while modern exegesis owes much to the period of Enlightenment, even to its call for perspicuity and sobriety, and to its battle against omnivorous credulity and sinister practices, biblical interpretation is not forced to criticize, eliminate or 'existentially' recast everything that the Book says in artistic forms of imagination about the will and the power of the Lord. More ultimate truth than in rationalistic interpretations and demythologizations may be found in statements about the mysterious sufferings and the unabatable yearnings which torment not only human beings but also the elements, plants, animals and spirits at the present time. In the Bible, nature is more than just the background of salvation. It also suffers from God's judgement, it also serves as God's instrument, and finally it is also a beneficiary of God's goodness. When the New Testament speaks of Jesus Christ's omnipotence, it points to something beyond human grasping and experience, and it uses the language of adoration and imagination. Only a very limited openness to and sense of reality can urge a biblical interpreter to disregard what is said in that language.

3 *Deterrent Precedents*   The identity of God and nature is an accepted fact in so-called primitive religions and societies as well as in sophisticated philosophical systems. Examples of the latter are the religious halo surrounding the ancient ἓν καὶ πᾶν formula, Spinoza's *deus sive natura*, and the search and theses of various other significant figures.[13] Since the New Testament agrees with the Old Testament in rejecting all identifications of God and nature, a carefully developed New Testament Christology and soteriology can never result in an apotheosis of nature. As little as God can Christ form a part – not even the most noble force – of a comprehensive 'world-view'. Opponents of the confession of a cosmic Christ are reacting to the idolatry inherent in monism. But their alternative, the 'Christ-for-people-and-the-Church-only', may well be no less dangerous. For a dualistic world-view which in gnostic or idealistic form simply separates God, Christ, and the Spirit from all 'beings that have no soul', is no nearer the witness of the New Testament than its monistic sister. When the intention prevails to avoid the pitfalls of old and new religions and world-views, then it makes little sense to escape Scylla only to be devoured by Charybdis.

There may also be an overreaction to certain christomonistic systems of thought as developed by, e.g., P. Tillich and P. Teilhard de Chardin. For Tillich, 'the Christ' is the principle of mediation and community between the spiritual and material universe; 'the Christ' is the one great symbol of true being, inasmuch as it reveals and communicates itself with transforming power to the material world; faith and art, science and reason bear testimony to the same mysterious process and are held together by it. Teilhard, too, speaks of Christ rather than of God when he wants to demonstrate that the subject matter of, and the search for, faith and natural science merge. He avers that out of the many created elements the eternal Christ realizes himself, arising out of the lithosphere, passing through the zoosphere, and culminating in the noosphere – much as the top of a cone embodies the unity and the crown of its many lower levels. While Tillich appears to have been widely ignored by New Testament scholarship, Teilhard has been read – and has encountered its practically unanimous rejection.[14] But who dares decide whether the thought of Teilhard stands closer to that of the Colossian heretics than to the christocentric message of this epistle?

It is not shameful for New Testament scholarship when bold theses and burning contemporary issues, new ways of thinking about nature, more subtle ways of exploring it, and impressive warnings against destroying it, give a new turn to exegetical work. Responsible Bible interpretation is not done in an ivory tower but in awareness of both the dangers and the contributions of contemporary ways of thought. By elaborating constructive alternatives, it faces rather than dodges the risks involved in interpretation.

4 *Spiritual Worship* Because among all creatures only humanity is created in the image of God, and because the Logos took the form of man, not of an angel, animal, plant or dead matter, humankind is given a prerogative. Men, women, and children can know and serve God in a privileged way. They can become conscious of their creation, of God's will, of their sin, of God's forgiveness. While they moan and groan under the burden of the weak and moribund body (Rom. 7.24; 2 Cor. 5.4), the spirit of each one of them can also listen and respond to the inspiration of God's Spirit (Rom. 8.16, 26). When they believe, when they hope, when they love even while they live in the present body, then their worship is 'spiritual'. The Bible appears to condemn as idolatrous or hypocritical all those forms and acts of worship that are based on something other than personal experience of sin and grace, e.g. on the pretension that the relation between God and humanity is based on nature rather than on spontaneity, honesty and ethics. Therefore, a cosmic Christology would seem to contradict the essence of spiritual worship. How should the things and powers that form the cosmos participate in the recognition of grace and the offering of a service to God for which only humankind is elected and equipped?

But such an exclusion and prohibition of non-human creation from spiritual worship ignores essential statements which the Bible makes about the Spirit, the vocation of the manifold creatures, and the actual worship of God and Christ. The Spirit of God gives life not only to the human but to all other creatures (Gen. 2.7; Ps. 104.30). Not only humanity groans and moans under the consequences of sin but also the whole of creation (2 Cor. 5.4; Rom. 8.22). Not only persons but also spirits, living creatures, and dead things are promised liberation (Rom. 8.21); both Christians and the Church are saved not only for their own sake but as the 'firstfruit of God's creation' (James 1.18). The call to worship is therefore extended not only to Israel, the Church, and eventually to all nations, but also to all creatures – and this not in vain.[15]

The dignity of being a living body, and the honour to be offered to God as a spiritual sacrifice (Rom. 12.1–2; Col. 1.22; 2.9) do not prevent or stop a human being from forming a part of nature. Atoms and cells, energies and functions, as it were hardware and software, are not dispensable attributes of humanity. Unless Christ were the saviour of all things, he could not be the saviour of humankind. An idealist's god might do without the material world. The creator, redeemer, and renewer of heaven and earth, however, loved 'the world' so much as to give his only Son. When people fail to speak up in honour of God, the heavenly hosts and the earthly stones will still shout.

The four reasons here collected for a possible explanation of the scholarly recalcitrance against the cosmic Christ are as little exhaustive as the arguments raised against them. The mentioned motivations need not be conscious to the promoters of an anthropocentric Christology and soteriology. Great exegetes, however, have never refused to acknowledge dogmatic and other presuppositions, and to shoulder responsibility for the credal and existential consequences of their exegetical work.

IV *A Great Task at Hand*

A full and persuasive alternative to the traditional, western, restrictive Christology has not yet been developed. A convincing name and title has not yet been found for it. Not even the term 'cosmic Christ' is fully suitable, for it subjugates the unique Son of God to the general concept 'cosmic'. In order to confess the true rank of Christ and to avoid the separation of that which God has joined together, an ever closer integration of Old Testament and New Testament studies is a prime necessity.[16] It cannot be carried out without careful consultation of Jewish intertestamental and later forms of worship, teaching, and literature. The 'creator of heaven and earth', the 'king of the universe' who is proclaimed, adored, and petitioned in Jewish prayers, is the only reliable antidote against the idealistic or naturalistic idolatries to which western teachings on the Spirit, on Christ, and on God have often paid tribute.

Among the many areas of contemporary Old Testament study, three may prove to be of prime importance for the elucidation of the unity and diversity of the Old and the New Testaments, for the rediscovery of the closest possible connection between creation and salvation, and for the proclamation of the omnipotence of Jesus Christ not only over humanity but also over the realm of the unseen spiritual and the visible material beings:

1   *Kingship* in Israel is an institution by which the heavenly and eternal King promises not only protection to the poor and needy and victory over demonical and political enemies, but also a blessing that grants fertility to nature and is beneficial even to the hills, fields, and flocks (see esp. Ps. 72). Enthusiastic voices call the present or the hoped-for king 'Son of God' or 'God' – for he does God's work and ushers in a paradise more glorious than the first.[17] The 'divine kingship' motifs may look mythical and appear incomprehensible to sober historians and rationalistic scholars. Still, the New Testament takes them up when it affirms that Jesus of Nazareth is the royal Son of God, and that all things and powers are placed under his feet.

2   *Wisdom* is in Israel a mystery, a force and a way. It is not only God's beloved child and/or master-worker but also a challenger and a gift to chosen individuals and the elect people. All things and the use of all things and circumstances are directed by it, and it likes to govern human beings to its own as well as to their pleasure. When it is sought and found, it gives life a direction and meaning, and in addition, it conveys blessing, happiness, and rest.[18] No less than the hymnic praises of Israel's king, the personification and praise of Wisdom may look like a mythological residue in the Old Testament, or like sheer poetic imagery. But again the New Testament praises Jesus Christ's relation to God, to mankind, and to all things in the terminology of Wisdom literature.[19]

3   *Eschatology*, including its later apocalyptic shapes, is in Israel's holy literature the sum of the promises and anticipations of future cosmic events, which are keys for actual history and offer standards for a wise conduct in the present. Eschatology does not separate the past and present experience of the elect people, or their threatening or comforting future, from particular or worldwide cosmic events. The New Testament confirms these prophetic visions. If E. Käsemann's thesis is right, that 'apocalypticism is the mother of Christian theology', then it is impossible to separate the New Testament doctrine

and proclamation of Christ from the announcement that the totality of the moaning creatures will be liberated. In the New Testament the Messiah or Son of man is in person the sign and guarantee, the mediator and the sum of the salvation and renewal of all things as well as persons from all nations.

In conclusion, an invitation or a warning needs to be added. Without the confession of Jesus Christ's deity, that is, without the adoration of Jesus as 'my Lord and my God' (John 20.28), it does not make sense to speak of Jesus Christ as the reconciler of 'all things'. If he had come, suffered, and died for no other purpose than to give comfort to sinful people and to reform rebellious societies, then his deity might have been less than essential. Human responses can be evoked by human beings and events, even by a fictitious superman. Because all early testimonies emerge from the confession that Jesus is 'Lord' and converge upon the same praise, a 'Christology from below' cannot be the last word of New Testament research.[20] It is the divine Lord who pities 'Nineveh, that great city in which there are more than a 120,000 persons . . . *and also much cattle*' (Jonah 4.11).

NOTES

1 *Das Neue Testament und die Zukunft des Kosmos* (Düsseldorf 1969); cf. the same author's essay, 'Röm. 8.19–22: Eine schöpfungstheologische oder anthropologisch-soteriologische Aussage', *Mélanges bibliques en hommage au R. P. Béda Rigaux* (Gembloux 1970), pp. 351–66.

2 *Der Kolosserbrief* (Zürich/Neukirchen 1976), esp. pp. 45–80, 106–9, 186–221.

3 Unlike several predecessors, who analysed the hymn and explained it as originally gnostic, Schweizer ascribes the basic hymn to Christian origins, i.e. to an over-enthusiastic eucharistic mood with heretical tendencies.

4 'I Cor. VIII.6: Cosmology or Soteriology?', *RB* 85 (1978), pp. 253–67.

5 *Theology of the New Testament* I (New York 1951), pp. 254–9, 296–307; II (1955), pp. 6, 15–22.

6 Dibelius, *Botschaft und Geschichte* II (Tübingen 1956), pp. 20, 27–8; Norden, *Agnostos Theos* (Leipzig/Berlin 1913), pp. 240–54, 347–54.

7 See e.g. A. D. Galloway, *The Cosmic Christ* (New York 1951), and the work of P. Teilhard de Chardin. Passionate pleas for a widening of the theological horizon were made at meetings of the World Council of Churches by J. Sittler (New Delhi 1961) and C. Birch (Nairobi 1975).

8 Among German scholars, cf. especially M.-A. Wagenführer, *Die Bedeutung Christi für Welt und Kirche*, Studien zum Kolosser- und Epheserbrief (Wigand, Leipzig, 1941); F. Mussner, *Christus, das All und die Kirche;*

Studien zur Theologie des Epheserbriefes (Paulinus-Verlag, Trier, 1955);
O. A. Dilschneider, *Christus Pantokrator* (Käthe Vogt-Verlag, Berlin,
1962); also E. Käsemann's commentary on Romans (1973). Among
French scholars, P. Benoit, 'Corps, tête et plérôme dans les épîtres de la
captivité', *RB* 63 (1956), pp. 5–44 = *Exégèse et théologie* (Du Cerf, Paris, II,
1961), pp. 107–20; and 'L'hymne christologique de Col. 1. 15–20' in J.
Neusner, ed., *Christianity, Judaism and Other Greco-Roman Cults*, Essays in
honour of M. Smith, I (Brill, Leiden, 1975), pp. 226–63; A. Feuillet, *Le
Christ, Sagesse de Dieu, d'après les épîtres pauliniennes* (Gabalda, Paris, 1966).

9   Matt. 11.25par; 28.18–20; John 1.3, 11, 14; Rom. 8.19–23; 1 Cor. 8.6b;
   15.25–7; 2 Cor. 5.17 v.l.; Gal. 6.15; Phil. 2.10–11; 3.21; Col. 1.15–20; 2.9;
   Eph. 1.10, 19–23; 2.14–16; 4.10; Heb. 1.2–14; 2.6–10, 16.

10 For instance, John 17.2; Rom. 8.28, 31–2; 11.32 v.l., 36; 1 Cor. 8.6a;
   11.12; 15.28; 2 Cor. 4.6; 5.19; Eph. 3.9, 15; 4.6; 1 Tim. 6.13.

11 In 1 Cor. 15.25, 27; Eph. 1.19–23; Heb. 1.13; 2.6–9.

12 This conviction, in turn, is part of the dualistic separation of spirit and
   nature, which goes back at least to Plato, was given anthropological
   expression by Augustine's distinction between the inner life and the
   fleshly nature of humanity, and was a commonplace of the medieval
   attempt to consider spirit and matter opposites.

13 Not only mystics and magicians disregarded or contested the dividing line
   between the realms of God and nature, spirit and matter. Great scholars,
   philosophers, and poets such as Nikolaus Cusanus, G. Bruno, T. B.
   Paracelsus, J. W. Goethe, and F. W. Schelling sought to deny or to
   overcome the division. There were also rationalistic theologians and
   Württemberg pietists who questioned such a dualistic separation.

14 See esp. A. Feuillet, *Le Christ Sagesse de Dieu* (Paris 1966), pp. 243 n,
   376–85.

15 Ps. 19 A and B; 29; 104; 147; etc. The apocryphal Song of the Three
   Young Men which supplements Dan. 3 intends to give a list of all
   creatures which is even more exhaustive than the catalogue contained in
   the creation account of Gen. 1.

16 C. K. Barrett's *From First Adam to Last* (London 1962), together with E.
   Hoskyns and N. Davey, *The Riddle of the New Testament* (London 1931),
   and C. H. Dodd, *According to the Scriptures* (London 1952), are pioneering
   works that have not in vain pressed forward in this direction. P.
   Stuhlmacher, *Gottes Gerechtigkeit bei Paulus* (Göttingen 1965) gives an
   elaborate example of the usefulness of this integration, and he also shows,
   in *Vom Verstehen des Neuen Testaments* (Göttingen 1979), that the
   integration of OT and NT research is the key to a NT hermeneutics that
   seeks to avoid philosophical biases. J. A. H. Gunnemann goes even
   further, *Vom Verstehen des Alten Testaments* (Göttingen 1977), pp. 7–8: the
   OT–NT relationship is 'the' problem of Christian theology.

17 Ps. 2; 45; 110; Isa. 9; 11, etc.

18 Prov. 8; Wisd. 7; Ecclus. 24.

19   Matt. 11.19, 25–30; John 1.1–18; 1. Cor. 1.30; Heb. 1.1–3; Col. 1.15–20; 2.3.
20   In the formulation of the Greek Orthodox theologian B. Tsakonas, 'A Comparative Study of the term "Son of God" ', *Theologia* 36–7 (Athens 1965–6), pp. 28f: 'The cosmological significance of the Son . . . leave[s] no doubt about Christ's participation in the divine substance.'

15

Pauline Theology
in the Thessalonian Correspondence

I. Howard Marshall

At a time when interest is being increasingly directed to the problem of unity and diversity in the NT writings[1] it may be appropriate to pay some attention to the question of the distinctive theological outlooks of the individual Pauline writings. It is of course true that one of the reasons offered for regarding certain writings as deutero-Pauline is their alleged differences in theological content. But the question of the theological distinctiveness of the acknowledged Pauline epistles has scarcely been discussed.[2]

The present study is confined to the Thessalonian correspondence. In 1 Thessalonians we have an undisputed Pauline epistle, but the authenticity of 2 Thessalonians stands under some suspicion.[3] A comparison of these epistles with the accepted epistles of Paul may be significant both in order to highlight the theological individuality of 1 Thessalonians and to establish the constant features in the Pauline writings generally, and also to shed some light on the question of the authorship of 2 Thessalonians. We should perhaps expect to find that the contents of an epistle are influenced by its circumstances and purpose, but that there is a basic theological outlook and method of argument common to the several epistles.

I

In his discussion of Pauline theology, *From First Adam to Last*, C. K. Barrett organized his treatment round certain key figures such as Adam and Moses. He comments: 'When I was discussing the subject of this book with a learned friend he suggested to me (and the idea, though not his way of expressing it, had occurred to me also) that it might be interesting and profitable to include a chapter under the heading "Absent Friends". This is a true and valuable observation, and it would be possible to fill many pages with absentees, and with suggested reasons for their non-appearance.'[4] This hint is worth following up with regard to theological concepts absent from the Thessalonian epistles.

1   There is an almost entire omission of material relating to Paul's status as an *apostle*. As in Phil. 1.1 he does not name himself as an apostle in the epistolary introduction. The fact that he associates Timothy and Silvanus with himself as co-authors of the epistles does not explain this omission, since elsewhere he was capable of producing a suitable form of words to get round the fact that Timothy was not an apostle (2 Cor. 1.1). The word 'apostles' is found only once, with reference to Paul and Silvanus[5] as 'apostles of Christ'.[6] The usage is fairly casual, but implies a known and accepted standing and practice (cf. 1. Cor. 9.3–7). This lack of emphasis is surely because Paul's apostleship was not questioned in Thessalonica and there was no need for him to produce 'official' backing for his teaching, although he did have to deal with criticisms of his motives and conduct as a missionary. In 2 Thessalonians the point at issue is not Paul's authority, which is unquestioned,[7] but rather the fact that his teaching has been misrepresented.

2   The concept of *sin* plays little part in the epistles. The noun appears only in 1 Thess. 2.16 with reference to the sins of the Jews who reject the gospel.[8] Paul is not concerned with the sins of his readers, apart from the warning against evil in 1 Thess. 5.22 and the promise of divine help in 2 Thess. 3.2. On the contrary, he is more concerned to give thanks for their spiritual progress, and only in one section does he develop a warning against immorality (1 Thess. 4.1–8). Judgement on sin is likewise not prominent (1 Thess. 4.6). God's wrath is a fate from which the readers have been delivered (1 Thess. 1.10; 5.9) and which is reserved for their opponents (1 Thess. 2.16; 2 Thess. 1.6–9; 2.10–12).

This lack of emphasis on sin may seem surprising, since the ἁμαρτ-word-group occurs some ninety-one times in Paul. However, this impression is considerably modified when we discover that sixty of these occurrences are in Romans; when we compare the Thessalonian epistles with the other Pauline epistles, the lack of emphasis is less surprising.

3   Closely related to this omission is the almost total lack of theological concepts associated with the *Judaizing controversy*. Circumcision, uncircumcision, the Law, works, boasting, justification and

freedom are not mentioned. There is but one word from the δικαιο-word-group (δίκαιος, 1 Thess. 2.10), and it is used of the missionaries' own conduct. The only reference to boasting is to Paul's exultation in his converts. Even grace is scarcely mentioned; apart from its use in epistolary formulae it appears in 2 Thess. 1.12 and 2.16. The whole problem of how a man may be put right with God is simply not mentioned. The reason is surely to be found in the fact that this controversy was absent from Thessalonica, but was very much alive in the Galatian and Roman situations, and to a lesser extent at Corinth and Philippi. Paul could write about the gospel quite easily without using a set of categories that arose only in controversy with Judaizing Christians.[9] This does not mean that the topic was unimportant to Paul, only to be discussed on occasions of controversy. Rather, controversy may serve to sharpen the expression of one's convictions and to bring out the latent presuppositions more explicitly.

4   Other topics which receive little emphasis are *truth* and *wisdom*. The former of these is absent from 1 Thessalonians except for the description of God as 'true' or 'real' in what is probably a piece of traditional phraseology appropriately used in drawing a contrast with idolatry. 'Truth' appears more frequently in 2 Thess. 2.10, 12, 13 with reference to those who follow antichrist and reject the Christian revelation; this fits in with Pauline usage which contrasts the truth of the divine revelation with error.[10] The omission of 'wisdom' is not surprising, since the bulk of the references to this concept in Paul are in the polemical situations reflected in 1 Corinthians and Colossians.

5   Much more remarkable is the almost total absence of *flesh* and *body*. Only the latter term occurs, and that but once, in the difficult phrase in 1 Thess. 5.23.[11] Elsewhere in his epistles Paul uses 'body' with reference to the presence of sin in believers, the resurrection of the body, and the Church as the body of Christ. The first of these topics does not concern him in Thessalonians. The second is a concern, but the problem is not the nature of the resurrection but rather the fact and timing of it. The third topic is likewise not a concern. The absence of 'flesh' is more striking since it comes regularly throughout the Pauline corpus with a variety of uses. One can only comment that its absence is a clear warning against expecting that all of Paul's favourite expressions must occur in any given letter.[12]

175

II

From these omissions we turn to look at some constant factors which are found in the epistles.

1   The use of *christological titles* is similar to that elsewhere in Paul. The same names and titles, 'Jesus', 'Christ', and 'Lord', and the same combinations of these titles are found in the Thessalonian epistles and the other epistles. The description of Jesus as 'Son' is found only in 1 Thess. 1.10, and this usage may rest on tradition (for the connection with the resurrection see Rom. 1.4); the rareness of the word fits in with Pauline usage.[13] One unusual feature, to which W. Trilling has drawn attention, is the way in which 'Jesus' and 'Jesus Christ' always appear combined with 'Lord' in 2 Thessalonians.[14] The combination is thoroughly Pauline. What is strange is its comparative frequency in the epistle. However, Trilling's conclusion that this represents a late stage in the development of Christology when OT divine attributes were being ascribed to Christ is to be rejected, since the same combinations are also present with high frequency in 1 Thessalonians.[15]

2   There is not a lot of *christological information* in the epistles, but it is not Paul's habit to engage in christological discussion for its own sake. The formulae Christ 'died for us' and 'died and rose again' (1 Thess. 5.9f; 4.14) express the basis of salvation and the hope of resurrection in a thoroughly Pauline manner. The present spiritual power of Jesus alongside the Father is assumed (1 Thess. 1.1; 3.11f; 5.28; 2 Thess. 1.2; 3.3–5; 3.16, 18). His Parousia is particularly stressed. These are all features of basic Paulinism. The death and resurrection of Jesus are not mentioned in 2 Thessalonians, but the subject-matter of the epistle did not call for any particular reference to this saving event.

3   The references to the *Spirit* in 1 Thessalonians tie in with Pauline usage. The Spirit is active in the preaching and reception of the gospel (1 Thess. 1.5f). His presence is associated with power and joy (1 Thess. 1.5f). He is God's gift to believers (1 Thess. 4.8) and is associated with holiness; one must beware of disregarding the Spirit by lapsing into sin. Spiritual gifts, such as prophecy, must not be quenched (1 Thess. 5.19). It is easy to parallel these references from Paul's other epistles. W. Trilling characterizes the teaching of 2 Thessalonians on the Spirit as poverty-stricken,[16] but it must be insisted that the silence is explained by the subject-matter of the epistle.[17]

176

4   An extremely important constant is the '*in Christ/Lord/him*' formula. If we set aside the so-called 'cosmic' use (found only in Colossians and Ephesians) we find that of the remaining eight types of usage listed by E. Best[18] no less than five are found in the seven occurrences of the phrase in 1 Thessalonians, and three uses are found in the four occurrences in 2 Thessalonians.[19] The Pauline conviction that the life of the Christian is determined by the Christ-event is fully expressed. The unusual phrase 'in God the (our) Father and the Lord Jesus Christ', which might have aroused suspicion had it been found only in 2 Thess. 1.1, occurs in 1 Thess. 1.1 (cf. Eph. 3.9; Col. 3.3).

5   The *corporate* aspects of the faith are taken for granted. Believers form 'the church' of the Thessalonians (1 Thess. 1.1; 2 Thess. 1.1)[20] and are placed alongside the churches of God in Judea (1 Thess. 2.14) and elsewhere (2 Thess. 1.4). The readers are addressed as members of a community, and it is their communal life as a Christian fellowship with which Paul is concerned.

6   The essence of Christian experience is expressed in the three basic attitudes of *faith, hope and love*. These are grouped as a triad (1 Thess. 1.3; 5.8) which may well be of pre-Pauline origin and is widely found in Paul and elsewhere in the NT.

The readers can be described simply as 'believers' (1 Thess. 1.7; 2.10, 13), a familiar Pauline expression. The same usage is found in 2 Thess. 1.10 (cf. 2.12), although here the aorist participle is used. The usual elements of faith are present in 1 Thessalonians: it is directed towards God (1.8f), it can grow (3.10), it involves acceptance of credal statements (4.14), and it is expressed in action (1.3). The material in 2 Thessalonians is smaller in quantity (1.3, 10, 11; 2.12f) but conveys the same emphases.[21]

Paul speaks of God's love for his people (1 Thess. 1.4; 2 Thess. 2.13, 16)[22] and of the need for believers to love one another (1 Thess. 1.3; 3.6, 12; 4.9; 2 Thess. 1.3), including especially their church leaders (1 Thess. 5.13), but the scope of love must include all men (1 Thess. 3.12). There is an unusual reference to 'loving the truth' in 2 Thess. 2.10; the phrase is unparalleled, but the same thought appears in Rom. 1.18 (cf. Gal. 5.7).

The hope of future salvation distinguishes believers from non-believers and is centred on the coming of Jesus (1 Thess. 1.3; 4.13; 5.8; 2 Thess. 2.16), and the linking of hope with endurance is typically Pauline (1 Thess. 1.3; 2 Thess. 1.4; 3.5; Rom. 5.2–4; 8.25).

·   177

7   The *ethical implications* of the faith are expressed in the same kind of way as elsewhere in Paul. It is because believers are sons of light (indicative) that they can be summoned to show the Christian virtues (imperative, 1 Thess. 5.5–8). Because God has called them to salvation, they are the objects of exhortation (1 Thess. 5.9–11; 2 Thess. 2.13–15). Sanctification is both the work of God, whose Spirit is active in believers and who is petitioned by Paul to complete his work (1 Thess. 3.12f; 4.8; 5.23f; 2 Thess. 1.11; 3.16f; 3.5), and also the task of the believer who is given both general and specific commands regarding his personal way of life (1 Thess. 2.11f; 4.1–12; 5.6–8, 12–22; 2 Thess. 2.15; 3.4, 6–13).

8   Finally, underlying Paul's theology is a linguistic and conceptual basis in the OT. Space forbids discussion of this theme, and it must suffice to comment that, despite the lack of explicit OT quotations, there is a usage of OT language and phraseology which is typically Pauline in both the epistles.[23]

III

Various features stand out as particularly prominent in the epistles.

1   A marked peculiarity of style is the use of the *second person plural* to address the readers. The pronoun ὑμεῖς occurs eighty-four times in 1 Thessalonians and forty times in 2 Thessalonians out of a total of about seven hundred occurrences in the Pauline corpus. This is roughly twice as often as might have been expected, although it must be admitted that the distribution is somewhat uneven; it is low in Romans and 1 Corinthians, and high in 2 Corinthians. In the same connection we may note the high frequency of the address ἀδελφοί (fourteen times in 1 Thess.; seven times in 2 Thess.), especially in 1 Thessalonians. This is symptomatic of the way in which both the letters are very much couched in terms of address to the readers and deal with them and their situation. It also demonstrates the warm feelings of Paul to his readers.

2   Considerable stress is laid in 1 Thessalonians on the *conversion of the readers* and the circumstances surrounding Paul's mission. The term 'gospel' is characteristic of 1 Thessalonians, although it is equally frequent in Galatians and Philippians. Paul dwells on the fact that the message preached by himself and his colleagues really was the word of God accompanied by the power of the Spirit (1 Thess. 1.5; 2.13),[24]

that the Thessalonians received it as such, and that they were prepared to endure suffering for its sake. Similar thoughts are found in 1 Cor. 2.4, but it is 1 Thessalonians which provides the fullest exposition of the theme. This topic is lacking in 2 Thessalonians, which is more concerned with the current problems of the readers.

3   The topic that has come to be known as the '*apostolic parousia*' is found in several epistles, but the treatment in 1 Thess. 2.17—3.13 is particularly extended and rivalled only by the discussion in Rom. 15, i.e. in an epistle whose specific aim was to prepare the readers for Paul's arrival. There is nothing comparable in 2 Thessalonians, although we may note that Paul uses the example of how he behaved during his visit to Thessalonica in his exhortations to the church (2 Thess. 3.7–10).[25]

4   The major distinguishing feature of both epistles is the extent of the teaching about the *Parousia*. The prominence of the actual word[26] reflects the prominence of the concept. The occasion for the extended teaching is the need to correct misunderstandings on the part of the readers, and this in turn reflects the fact that teaching about the Parousia had formed part of Paul's oral message at Thessalonica. This is apparent from 1 Thess. 1.9f where the essence of being a Christian is to serve God and to wait for his Son from heaven, the one who delivers from the wrath to come. The language is probably pre-Pauline, but it fits in with Paul's thinking elsewhere (Phil. 3.20f). The Parousia reference in 2.19 is concerned with Paul's own personal expectation (cf. Phil. 4.1). In 3.13 the purpose of holy living is that the Thessalonians may be unblamable at the Parousia – and therefore not come under judgement. The major discussion in 4.13 — 5.11 appears to arise from problems that were perplexing the church. First, Paul assured the believers who were grieving because some of their number had died that such people would rise first and be reunited with living believers at the Parousia so as to be with the Lord for ever. This misunderstanding could have arisen because Paul's preaching had emphasized the significance of the Parousia for the living. Second, Paul tackled the suggestion that uncertainty about the date of the Parousia could lead to believers being unready for it. He argued that believers should not be caught unready for it, since God had destined them for salvation and in any case they should be living all the time in a manner appropriate for people with such a destiny. The final prayer (5.23) that they might be blameless at the Parousia is contextually appropriate and is in harmony with Pauline thinking elsewhere (1

Cor. 1.8; Phil. 1.6; cf. Rom. 13.11–14). The centrality of the Parousia in 1 Thessalonians thus arises from the fact that it was an integral part of Paul's message and from the misunderstandings which had arisen. The Parousia is treated as an incentive to godly living, but it is not the only incentive, and Paul's exhortations would not completely lose their force if references to the Parousia were dropped.

In 2 Thessalonians Paul begins with a reference to the judgement of God on the persecutors of the Church at the Parousia. This association of the Parousia with judgement is implicit in Phil. 3.19–21 and 2 Cor. 5.10, but 2 Thess. 1 is unique in the amount of detailed description of judgement. The apocalyptic passage in 2 Thess. 2 is certainly unique in the Pauline corpus, although of course it has other NT parallels of a broad nature. It is motivated by the need to correct misunderstanding, and there is no reason to doubt that the misunderstanding really did exist. The discussion thus arises out of the readers' situation, just like the unique extended discussion of the nature of the resurrection in 1 Cor. 15. The problem is whether the answer given to the misunderstanding is in line with Paul's theology elsewhere; here we must confine ourselves to the one observation that Jewish eschatology generally expects a time of troubles before the End, and that it would be surprising if Paul had not shared this expectation.

5   There is a good deal of *exhortation* in both epistles. First, Paul is especially concerned with the need for believers to stand firm in the midst of afflictions. He displays a mixture of confidence, based on the good news which he had received from Timothy, and of concern that the Thessalonians should continue to stand firm. These feelings are entirely natural in an adverse situation, especially when Paul had been unable to spend very long in Thessalonica to establish the church. Second, there is ethical exhortation to purity and love which fits in well with similar instruction elsewhere in Paul (e.g. Rom. 13; 1 Cor. 6) and was natural in epistles directed to Gentile converts. Finally, there are general exhortations to hard work, to orderliness in the church and to the promotion of spiritual gifts. These, and particularly the warnings against idleness in 2 Thess. 3, are appropriate in the situation of the readers.

IV

Our brief discussion has indicated something of the individuality of the Thessalonian correspondence alongside the constant factors that tie it to the rest of the Pauline corpus. We have taken care to consider the evidence as it relates to 1 and 2 Thessalonians separately. In the case of 1 Thessalonians we have been able to observe that despite some interesting omissions the main features of Pauline theology are present. The same is also true of 2 Thessalonians, although the theological content of the epistle is less marked. It is clear in any case that 2 Thessalonians stands closest to 1 Thessalonians in its general outlook.

In his commentary on the epistles E. Best raises the general question of Pauline theology in them with particular reference to 1 Thess. 4.13 — 5.11.[27] He notes the omissions and the additions which constitute 'vast differences' in theology from that of the other epistles. Various relevant factors are summarized: (1) Paul is answering questions arising out of the situation of his readers, and thus omits matters that were not directly relevant. (2) What is written in the letters needs to be supplemented by what Paul said at Thessalonica in his preaching and teaching. (3) The rise of particular problems at a later stage led Paul to formulate his basic theological convictions in answer to them in a way that is not found in the earlier epistles. (4) Despite these omissions various basic structural features of Paul's thought are present in 1 Thessalonians: the new existence of the believer, the association of the indicative and the imperative, and the close relationship of believers to Christ.

The effect of our analysis has been to confirm Best's position. The comparative absence of certain apparently key-concepts from 1 Thessalonians has not prevented us from tracing a basic similarity of structure with Paul's theology as it is expressed elsewhere. At the same time the elements that receive special emphasis in this letter contribute to a fuller picture of Paul's thought and demonstrate specially his pastoral concern for a congregation undergoing affliction and persecution.[28] There is admittedly less of Paul's theology in 2 Thessalonians, but much of the same basic structure is visible. Certain peculiarities of expression have been observed, but we have not observed anything which individually or cumulatively stands in the way of accepting the Pauline authorship of the letter. If 2 Thessalonians is regarded as a kind of explanatory appendix to 1 Thessalonians, the comparative lack of Pauline theology in it receives a satisfactory explanation. It has become all the more apparent that the distinctiveness of the individual Pauline letters is closely related to the differing situations which Paul was addressing. While his theology had a basic content, the actual expression of it could be very varied, and in a real sense it could be said that what he wrote arose out of a creative encounter with his congregations and the problems which they were facing.

If we bear in mind that the Thessalonian correspondence belongs to an earlier date in Paul's missionary work, what C. K. Barrett has written à propos of 1 Corinthians finds some illustration here: 'The practical advice . . . is consciously grounded in theological principles which can usually be detected; and, more important, the problems with which Paul deals seem to have reacted upon his theological views, or at least to have had a catalytic effect in pushing forward developments that might otherwise have taken place more slowly.'[29]

NOTES

1   J. D. G. Dunn, *Unity and Diversity in the New Testament* (London 1977); cf. G. Strecker, ed., *Das Problem der Theologie des Neuen Testaments* (Darmstadt 1975).

2   Various writers have attempted to trace stages in Pauline thought, reflected in his epistles when placed in chronological order. See C. H. Dodd, *New Testament Studies* (Manchester 1953); W. L. Knox, *St Paul and the Church of the Gentiles* ([2]Cambridge 1961); R. Jewett, *Paul's Anthropological Terms* (Leiden 1971); J. W. Drane, *Paul: Libertine or Legalist?* (London 1975).

3   W. Trilling, *Untersuchungen zum 2. Thessalonicherbrief* (Leipzig 1972); J. A. Bailey, 'Who wrote II Thessalonians?', *NTS* 25 (1978–9), pp. 131–45.

4   C. K. Barrett, *From First Adam to Last* (London 1962), p. 22.

5   For the view that Paul is thinking only of Silvanus and himself as apostles here see W. Schmithals, *The Office of Apostle in the Early Church* (London 1971), pp. 23, 65–7.

6   The phrase recurs in 2 Cor. 11.13.

7   The lack of appeal to Paul's authority *as an apostle* in 2 Thessalonians would seem to speak in favour of the authenticity of the epistle. W. Trilling's comments (op. cit., pp. 110–21) lose much of their force when it is realized that 2 Thess. says nothing about Paul being an apostle.

8   Synonyms for 'sin' appear in 1 Thess. 5.22; 2 Thess. 2.10, 12; 3.2f.

9   The lack of mention of this topic in 1 and 2 Thessalonians is thus not an argument against the possibility that Galatians is the first of Paul's extant writings.

10 Trilling's claim (op. cit., pp. 112f) that the concept of truth in 2 Thess. is not Pauline seems weak to me.

11 R. Jewett, op. cit., p. 181, thinks that Paul is combating a gnostic type of view that the body and soul were unimportant in comparison with the spirit of a man.

12 Other characteristic Pauline words which are not found in the epistles include κατά, κόσμος, τοιοῦτος.

13 M. Hengel, *The Son of God* (London 1976), pp. 7–15.

14 W. Trilling, op. cit., p. 128. The phenomenon had been observed by earlier writers.

15

	Jesus	Christ	Lord	Christ Jesus	Lord Jesus	Lord Jesus Christ
1 Thess.	3	3	13	2	6	5
2 Thess.	–	1	9 (10)	–	4 (3)	9

16 W. Trilling, op. cit., p. 130.

17 Πνεῦμα has the meaning 'breath' in 2 Thess. 2.8. In 2.2 it is used of an ecstatic utterance (for the usage cf. 1 Cor. 14.12), and in 2.13 the Spirit is probably the agent of sanctification (as in 1 Pet. 1.2).

18 E. Best, *One Body in Christ* (London 1955), pp. 1–7.

19 1 Thess. 1.1; 2.14; 3.8; 4.1, 16; 5.12, 18; 2 Thess. 1.1, 12; 3.4, 12. W. Trilling's verdict (op. cit., pp. 129f) that the usage is weak and only occasionally influential in 2 Thess. is not justified by the comparative statistics.

20 For the phrasing cf. Gal. 1.2.

21 The use of the aorist participle in 2 Thess. 1.10 and 2.12 is strange, but may be explicable in terms of the writer looking back from the perspective of the last day (E. Best, *The First and Second Epistles to the Thessalonians* (London 1972), p. 265, mentions, but does not adopt, this possibility), cf. Eph. 1.13.

22 It is debatable whether 'the love of God' in 2 Thess. 3.5 is his love for us or our love for him; see E. Best, op. cit., p. 330, and R. Jewett, op. cit., pp. 320–2, for the opposing views.

23 See the references in B. Rigaux, *Saint Paul: Les Épîtres aux Thessaloniciens* (Paris/Gembloux 1956), pp. 94f.

24 Despite the reluctance of commentators to allow it, 1 Thess. 1.5 could refer to miraculous signs accompanying the preaching, as in Gal. 3.1–5.

25 See R. W. Funk, 'The Apostolic *Parousia*: Form and Significance', in W. R. Farmer, et al., *Christian History and Interpretation* (Cambridge 1967), pp. 249–68. W. Trilling, op. cit., pp. 118f, comments that in no text other than 2 Thess. 3.7–10 is imitation of Paul treated so thematically, and his aim said to be the provision of an example for others to imitate. It is hard to see why this should be regarded (as apparently it is) as an argument against Pauline authorship.

26 Παρουσία occurs four times in 1 Thess. and three times in 2 Thess. (once with reference to the man of lawlessness). Its only other Pauline use with reference to Jesus is in 1 Cor. 15.23.

27 E. Best, op. cit., pp. 220–2.

28 For a study of Paul's doctrine, grouped around his doctrine of God, see R. F. Collins, 'The Theology of Paul's First Letter to the Thessalonians', *Louvain Studies* 6 (1977), pp. 315–37.

29 C. K. Barrett, *The First Epistle to the Corinthians* (London 1968), p. 17.

16

Romans 3.9: Text and Meaning

Nils Alstrup Dahl

All exegetes recognize that Rom. 3.9 is a difficult passage, but in spite of the difficulties nearly all modern commentaries and translations end up accepting a common exegetical tradition. The translation in the Revised Standard Version may serve as an example: 'What then? Are we Jews any better off? No, not at all; for I have already charged that all men, both Jews and Greeks, are under the power of sin.' A minority of interpreters prefer to understand οὐ πάντως as a qualified negation to be translated, e.g., 'Not in all respects', but even so they accept the common understanding of Paul's question.[1]

Lexicographers and grammarians have been more hesitant than recent commentators to accept the common opinion. There was no general consensus in Christian antiquity, and commentaries from the nineteenth and early twentieth century show a greater diversity of opinion than the more recent ones.[2] The usual procedure in modern commentaries is first to eliminate textual variants and then to eliminate one exegetical option after another, until only the traditional interpretation is left and accepted, sometimes reluctantly.[3] I have for many years followed the same exegetical procedure myself but have become increasingly sceptical. The traditional exegesis is beset by a number of difficulties.

In order to render προεχόμεθα by 'are we better off?' or 'do we have an advantage?', one has to postulate that Paul uses the middle form προεχόμεθα in the same, or nearly the same, sense as the active verb προέχω. This usage, though conceivable in Koine Greek, is never attested. Another objection against this traditional exegesis is more decisive, namely that it arbitrarily makes the plural subject of the verbs shift from one sentence to the next. E.g., the rsv takes the subject of προεχόμεθα to be 'we Jews' but understands προῃτιασάμεθα as a plural of authorship, meaning 'I', i.e. Paul. This not only presupposes that 3.9 begins a new paragraph but contrasts also with Paul's use of first person plural forms in 3.5–8. In 3.5 ἡ ἀδικία ἡμῶν means the wickedness of all human beings (see πᾶς δὲ ἄνθρωπος in 3.4). The question τί ἐροῦμεν; is part of a dialogical style which, as in the diatribes of Epictetus for example, is used as a pedagogical device to include and engage the audience.[4] To be sure, in 3.8 the plural forms βλασφημούμεθα and ἡμᾶς λέγειν refer primarily to Paul; but these references may include his companions or, more likely, his dialogue partners. In fact, these partners are Christians in Rome and not the Jews about whom Paul speaks in the third person, in 3.1–3 as well as in 3.9b. The assumption, then, that 'we Jews' is the subject of προεχόμεθα in 3.9 does violence to the context and style of the passage.

The exegesis of Rom. 3.9 is not simply a question of word usage, syntax, and exegetical details; even the structure and the logic of Paul's argumentation are at stake. According to the common opinion, Rom. 3.9a is a restatement of the questions in 3.1 about the advantage of the Jew but the answer is the opposite – no longer 'much in every way', but 'not at all' or, possibly, 'not in every respect'. Thus on this reading Paul is made to retract, or at least to qualify, what he has said about the advantage of the Jew and the value of circumcision. This understanding of Rom. 3.9 is in line with a common misunderstanding of Romans 9—11 which makes Paul both affirm and deny that God has rejected the Jews. Moreover, if the question in 3.9 is read as a restatement of the questions in 3.1, the series of questions and answers in 3.5–8, especially vv. 7–8, appear to be an aside.[5] The further consequence is that interpreters lose sight of the inner coherence of the whole argument in Romans 3.

We have to come back to the wider questions later. A fresh examination of Rom. 3.9 has to start at the basic level, with the textual evidence. There is a possibility that the exegetical consensus is based upon a distorted text, but only a somewhat complicated investigation can establish a probability.

The textual evidence

The following list of variant readings is based upon existing editions. As far as possible I have checked separate editions of the most important manuscripts, patristic commentaries, and ancient translations. The apparatus is more complete than can be found in any single edition or commentary, but it cannot claim to be more accurate.[6]

The various forms of text in Rom. 3.9 may best be classified in two

185

categories: (1) variants which include the negation οὐ πάντως and (2) variants which do not. This classification already anticipates a major part of the conclusion because it treats the text of Codex Porfirianus (P/025), an independent form of a text without οὐ πάντως, on equal terms with other variants. The text-critical discussion will explain the reasons for this decision. The following list does not include minor variants in the latter part of Rom. 3.9.[7] Punctuation and accents are left out.

1   *Texts with the negation*

1.1   τι ουν προεχομεθα ου παντως προητιασαμεθα γαρ . . . ℵ B K (9th cent., with 'Chrysostom commentary') 33, 1739 and the great majority of minuscules; commentaries of Photius, Arethas and Theophylact. This text is also attested by the margin of the Harclean Syriac version and, apparently, by the Sahidic version. It is presupposed by the second corrector of the Greek text of Codex Claromontanus (D^2, probably before 500 AD) and by the revised Latin version that became part of the Vulgate (see subvariants 1.2.3 and 1.2.4).

1.2   Subvariants
    1.2.1   Same as 1.1, but προεχωμεθα A L.
    1.2.2   Same, but προερχομεθα, 1734; προσεχομεθα, 489, 1938; προσερχομεθα, 2127; προσευχομεθα, 330; περιεχομεθα, 623.
    1.2.3   Same, but προκατεχομεθα (D^2) E = D^{abs}.
    1.2.4   Same as 1.1, but ητιασαμεθα γαρ, 450, 614; cf. Vulg.

2   *Texts without the negation*

2.0   Exact wording uncertain: Origen, Theodore of Mopsuestia, 'Euthalian' chapter list; Ephraem; Ethiopic version(s).[8]

2.1   τι ουν προεχομεθα προητιασαμεθα γαρ . . . P.

2.2   τι ουν κατεχομεν περισσον . . .
    2.2.0   Continuation uncertain, 'the more accurate and ancient copies' according to a catena manuscript.[9]
    2.2.1   . . . ητιασαμεθα γαρ . . . 2495.
        Quid ergo tenemus amplius? causati enim sumus . . . d g a/61 b/89; Ambrosiaster, etc.
    2.2.2   . . . προητιασαμεθα γαρ . . . Ψ (?) 1108, 1611: Severian of Gabala, Theodoret; Peshitta and Harclean text; possibly Bohairic archetype.[10]

2.3   τι ουν προκατεχομεν περισσον ητιασαμεθα γαρ . . . G F 104:
        Chrysostom.
   2.3.1   Same, but γαρ om. D*.

The last of the subvariants (2.3.1) is without interest; the testimony of
G F and of d (the Latin column of Codex Claromontanus, D) proves
that the common ancestor of these bilingual manuscripts had the
particle γαρ.[11] The subvariants of the text with the negation (1.1)
illustrate some trends in later textual history. Subvariants 1.2.1–2
prove that the verb προεχομεθα caused difficulties. Subvariant 1.2.3 is
due to an erroneous correction of 2.3.1 after 1.1. Subvariant 1.2.4 is
an incomplete substitution of 1.1 for 2.2.1, as is obvious in the case of
the Vulgate version: there 'Quid igitur praecellimus eos?' is a fresh
translation from the Greek text 1.1, but 'causati enim sumus' has been
retained from the Old Latin version.

The various forms of texts without the negation cause more
problems. Editors and commentators have paid most attention to the
form which is attested by the more famous Greek manuscripts (2.3).
This form can be traced back to a fourth-century bilingual edition and
beyond that to the Greek manuscript(s) used at the composition of this
edition.[12] It is also attested by witnesses that are independent of the
bilinguals (104, Chrysostom). Form 2.2 has, however, a broader and,
due to the Old Latin version, also the earlier attestation. The form 2.3
should, probably, be regarded as a third subvariant of 2.2;
προκατεχομεν is to be explained as a partial conflation of κατεχομεν
and προεχομεθα.[13] By analogy with this, the form προητιασαμεθα in
subvariant 2.2.2 is probably the result of a partial correcton of 2.2.1
after 1.1 or 2.1. For the exegesis it makes little difference whether
subvariant 2.2.1 or 2.2.2 is more original.

Having eliminated secondary subvariants we have to deal with
three major forms of the text in Rom. 3.9 (1.1, 2.1 and 2.2). The first of
these is attested by the famous uncials ℵ and B and by the great
majority of minuscules, regardless of whether they represent an
Egyptian or a Byzantine type of text.[14] The form that deviates most
from the majority text (2.2) is attested by only a small number of Greek
manuscripts, all fairly late; but subvariants, translations, and commentaries show that it was at one time widespread, in Syria as well as
in the West. In view of the distribution and the attestation we may call
this form (2.2 with subvariants) the 'Antiochene' rather than the

'Western' text in Rom. 3.9. The text of P shares the verbs προεχομεθα and προητιασαμεθα with the Egyptian-Byzantine manuscripts but omits ου παντως with the Antiochene text. It holds an intermediate position and must be taken into account when we compare the main variants.

Printed editions of the Greek New Testament have always reproduced the Egyptian-Byzantine text in Rom. 3.9, and text critics and commentators have tried to explain the origin of the variants on the assumption that it is original.[15] Their arguments work well up to a point. The history of exegesis as well as the subvariants (1.2.1–2) prove that the form προεχομεθα caused difficulties. It was ambiguous, might be considered an incorrect use of the middle for the active, and was therefore changed to κατεχομεν περισσον. The alteration of προητιασαμεθα to the simpler form ητιασαμεθα may have occurred at the same time. These are fairly characteristic examples of a kind of linguistic and stylistic revision which has left many traces, especially in the 'Western' and Byzantine types of text. It is difficult, not to say impossible, to find any reason for an alteration in the opposite direction (from 2.2 to 1.1).

The explanations given for the deletion of ου παντως are much less convincing. It is unlikely that any corrector or scribe would substitute (προ-) κατεχομεν περισσον for προεχομεθα ου παντως. It is no easier to believe that the unexpected sequence (hyperbaton) caused the omission of ου παντως. A corrector or scribe who found the word order inappropriate would have changed it and not omitted the negation. On most readings, Paul's question called for a negative answer.[16] It is therefore much more likely that ου παντως was added as a marginal gloss or by a corrector, in order to make the implied negation explicit, than that the negation was omitted if part of the primitive text.

It is almost as difficult to explain the Antiochene text in Rom. 3.9 on the assumption that the Egyptian-Byzantine form is original as it is to assume an alteration the other way round. The genealogical relationship is much more easily explained if we assume that the text of P is original. The text τι ουν προεχομεθα προητιασαμεθα γαρ . . . would then have been changed in two different ways, by the addition of ου παντως on the one hand and the alteration of the wording to . . . κατεχομεν περισσον ητιασαμεθα . . . on the other. We have already seen that there would be good reasons for both of these alterations. It is much more difficult to derive the intermediate text of P from one of the two other forms or to explain it as a conflation of both. Why was the negation omitted? Or why was it not added when the text was otherwise corrected?

In general, it is a sound text-critical rule that one ought not to accept the testimony of one single manuscript, be it the most venerable one. There are, however, exceptions to this rule, cases in which a poorly attested variant proves to be the one text which, if original, explains how the other variants came into being and, at the same time, fits the context as well as the style of the author.[17] The assumption that the text of P in Rom. 3.9 may be such an exception needs to be undergirded by an attempt to explain how the original reading can have disappeared almost completely from the manuscript tradition.

Tentative reconstruction of textual history

The widespread assumption that the transmitted text of the Pauline letters goes back to one primitive edition of the entire corpus has proved to be untenable. There must have been at least two early editions, one which did and another which did not include the last two chapters of Romans. The edition without Romans 15—16 probably did not have the local address in Rom. 1.7, 15, did not include the Pastorals, and may have had Ephesians as a letter to the Laodiceans. It became obsolete during the latter part of the second century, but it had served as the basis for Marcion's critical revision and left several other traces, especially in the early Syriac and Latin versions.[18]

The doxology at the end of Romans (16.25–7) was originally added to the short version of the letter, after 14.23, a place which it still has in the majority of minuscule manuscripts. In this case, as in many others, the Byzantine text goes back to an earlier Antiochene form. In most other instances it is difficult to tell exactly which variants go back to the edition which had the short version of Romans. The most likely examples are to be found among 'Western' and/or Byzantine readings which are not due to corrections of language and style and which are supported by some early witnesses, e.g. Clement, Origen, P[46], B, ℵ and/or 1739.[19]

The existence of at least two early editions of the Pauline corpus is relevant to the textual problem of Rom. 3.9 because it turns out that the negation ου παντως is absent only in manuscripts whose ancestry can be traced the edition which had the short version of Romans, without chapters 15—16. Like the majority of the minuscules, Ψ and 2495 (and 1108 and 1611) have the doxology after Rom. 14.23, a position also attested by Chrysostom and Theodoret. In P and 104, as in A 33 pc., the doxology occurs twice, at the end of chapter 14 and after chapter 16. As is clear from G and F, the common archetype of the bilingual manuscripts D, G and F did not have the doxology at all. More important, when the bilingual edition was prepared, the text of Romans 15—16 was taken from a Greek manuscript different from the exemplar used in Romans 1—14. This exemplar must have lacked Romans 15—16, as did the manuscript(s) from which the Latin translation was first made.[20]

On the basis of this evidence we can safely conclude that the short version of Romans had a text without ου παντως in Rom. 3.9, whereas the text with the negation is likely to go back to the edition of the Pauline corpus which included Romans 15—16. The question remains whether the short version had the text of P (2.1) or an 'Antiochene' text in Rom. 3.9. The latter possibility can be excluded since the Antiochene text is an example of a kind of correction that is very unlikely to go back to any of the primitive editions of the Pauline corpus. If the short version of Romans had a text without the negation in 3.9, it can only have read the text preserved in P. The almost complete disappearance of this text can be explained, because the negation was present from the outset in another early edition of the Pauline corpus.

Some of the indirect attestation for a Greek text without ου παντως, listed above under 2.0, may presuppose the text preserved in P. It can be taken for granted that Theodore read the Antiochene text in one form or the other (2.2 or, less likely, 2.3). But the Armenian translation of Ephraem's commentary on Romans seems to presuppose a Syriac text that differed from the Peshitta and might go back to a Greek original that had προεχομεθα but not ου παντως.[21] Even so, a translation of a translation is an uncertain witness to the exact wording of the Greek text. The Ethiopic evidence strengthens the possibility that traces of an ancient variant were preserved at the outskirts after it had become obsolete in the great centres.[22] There are, moreover, indications that Origen used, or at least was familiar with, the text of P.[23] It may be added that the subvariants listed as 2.2.2 and 2.3 are not likely to be corrections made on the basis of the prevailing text 1.1, since the negation was not added. They are more likely to be conflations of the Antiochene text 2.2.1 with a text which had προεχομεθα and προητιασαμεθα but not ου παντως. What is more important, if I am correct, the Antiochene text itself (2.2) is derived from a text like that of P which thus has considerable, albeit indirect, support.

Not only the text of P but also the once widely used Antiochene text of Rom. 3.9 has been so consistently eliminated that only traces are left in Greek manuscripts. This is clear from (a) a comparison of the prevailing Byzantine text with the antecedent texts attested by Antiochene exegetes and Greek chapter lists; (b) a comparison of the corrected text of Claromontanus (D², cf. D^abs or E) with the original text of this codex (D*) and its archetype (cf. G F); (c) a comparison of the Vulgate with the preceding Latin version. The same trend is apparent in the marginal reading of the Harclean version and, probably, in ms. 1739 and its allies over against the original text of Origen's commentary on Romans.[24]

The Egyptian-Byzantine text in Rom. 3.9 prevailed over the Antiochene which, at an earlier date, had suppressed the text of which it was itself a correction. The corrected text with κατεχομεν περισσον or a subvariant must have become common in Antioch, whence it spread both westward and eastward in the second and third centuries. In areas where an Egyptian type of text was predominant, manuscripts which had the same text as P are likely to have been corrected by the addition of ου παντως. If we consider the general trends of the textual history, it is remarkable that this text has survived at all, instead of leaving only some vague and uncertain traces. It is necessary to add some remarks about the general character of the text of ms. P.

The text of P can in general and traditional terms be described as a late Egyptian type, more or less like the texts of A, 33, and some other minuscules, e.g., 81, 1175 and 1881. To a fairly high degree, varying from one part to another, P concurs with the emerging majority text, but in several cases P agrees with one or two ancient 'Egyptian' manuscripts (P⁴⁶ and/or B, or ℵ*, ℵ^c or 1739) and/or with a minority of minuscules against the majority of Egyptian as well as Byzantine witnesses.[25] P has also a considerable number of readings in common with the text of the bilinguals D G F; I have, however, detected few, if any, examples of the corrections of language and style which are one characteristic component of the 'Western' text.[26] There are remarkably few scribal errors. Singular readings in P are in most cases clearly secondary but likely to have originated long before the manuscript itself was written.[27] On the whole, I get the impression that P reproduces a normalized form of a text that has had a prehistory of its own and has preserved a very ancient layer. Eventually, the ancestry can be traced back to the edition which had the short version of Romans.

The result of this part of our investigation is (1) that the prevailing Egyptian-Byzantine text of Rom. 3.9 has a continuous prehistory which goes back to one of the earliest editions of the Pauline corpus of letters, but (2) that the textual history leaves room for the possibility that the text of P, in spite of much poorer attestation, goes back earlier still. The third main variant, which we have called the Antiochene text, is a corrected text which can be dismissed from further consideration except as a witness to the history of interpretation. The choice between the other two texts, which differ only in the inclusion or exclusion of the negation, depends upon exegetical as much as upon text-critical considerations.

Questions of meaning

Several questions are involved in the exegesis of Rom. 3.9, among them the question of punctuation. Τί οὖν can be read as a separate question, as most editors and commentators do. If οὐ πάντως is deleted, it is more natural to connect τί οὖν with the following verb and take Rom. 3.9a to raise only one question. In both cases, however, the punctuation depends also upon the form and meaning of the word προεχόμεθα. There are three main possibilities: προεχόμεθα can be either (1) passive or (2) middle with an active sense or (3) a genuine middle. The choice among these three options is linked, in turn, with questions of word usage and content, including the question of the identity of the subject implied in the predicate. I shall concentrate upon the basic issues and the chief possibilities.

1   The passive understanding of προεχόμεθα is philologically unobjectionable.[28] The meaning can be rendered by a translation like 'Have we been excelled?' or, in free paraphrase, 'Are we worse off?' The problem is that this question does not grow naturally out of the preceding discussion in Rom. 3.1–8; neither is it the question answered in 3.9bff. The interpretation works relatively best if Paul is assumed to ask if 'we Jews' are worse off but, as pointed out in the introduction to this essay, the use of the first person plural in the context makes it extremely unlikely that the same form in 3.9a would mean 'we Jews'. A question 'Are we Christians worse off (than the others)?' would be completely unmotivated in the context.

192

2   The assumption that Paul used the middle προεχόμεθα in the same sense as the active form προέχομεν is not impossible, even though contrary to common usage.[29] As commentators usually point out, already the Vulgate version and the editor who substituted κατέχομεν περίσσον for προεχόμεθα seem to presuppose this understanding. Not even the Vulgate, however, favours the present-day consensus that Paul restates the questions in 3.1 in order to give an opposite or at least highly qualified answer.[30] Dissatisfaction with this interpretation was the starting point for this essay and it is unnecessary to repeat the arguments against it.

The understanding of προεχόμεθα as middle used for active works somewhat better if οὐ πάντως is left out. Paul would in that case raise the question(s) in Rom. 3.9a on behalf of his Christian readers: 'What then? Are we better off?' or 'What advantage do we then have?' He would first give the negative answer that all human beings are under the power of sin and then proceed to explain that the justifying grace of God in Christ makes all the difference. This is how the Antiochene exegetes interpreted their corrected text and the underlying text of P might be understood in a similar way.[31] The problem is that if Paul had wanted to set Christians off from Jews and Greeks as a third group, he ought to have made it clear and could have easily done it. The whole notion of Christians as a third group is alien to Paul's argumentation in Romans 1—4. While possible, the understanding of προεχόμεθα as middle used for active is loaded with difficulties in all its variations.

3   The view that προεχόμεθα is a genuine middle has had relatively few spokesmen and never been set forth in a form that carried conviction. There are several reasons for this. The basic meaning of προέχεσθαι, mid., is 'to hold, have, set or put something before oneself', e.g. a shield. It is, apparently, used only as a transitive verb, and this has caused difficulties for the syntactical analysis of Rom. 3.9. If τί οὖν is read as a separate question, the verb would have no object; if τί οὖν προεχόμεθα is read as one question, the answer should have been οὐδέν and not οὐ πάντως. The difficulty has been even further compounded because there are only a few examples of προέχεσθαι (mid.) used in a figurative sense, and those that are known led to the assumption that the meaning was to pretend or to allege something as a pretext.[32] In the context of Romans 3 this meaning makes little sense. The idea that Paul was putting forth a pretence or an excuse for himself and his

brethren, whether Christians (3.7–8) or Jews (3.1–8), is too farfetched to call for any denial. There is, however, no reason to limit the meaning of the verb to an alleged pretext or an excuse; it simply means to hold something before oneself, either literally or in speech. In the latter case, what one sets forth may be an argument or a defence as well as a pretence or an excuse. This is now clear from a passage from the last chapters of Enoch to which commentators have so far failed to pay sufficient attention.

A series of threats and woes against the wicked oppressors is followed by an exhortation: 'Then prepare yourselves, you righteous, and hold your supplications before you, that they may be remembered (προέχεσθε τὰς ἐντεύξεις ὑμῶν εἰς μνημόσυνον); make them a solemn testimony before the angels, that the angels may bring the sins of the wicked ones before the Most High God that they may be remembered; and then they [the sinners] shall be terrified on the day when unrighteousness is destroyed' (1 Enoch 99.3–4).[33] The passage suggests forensic imagery; the righteous sufferers are to put forth their supplications as a plea for their own vindication; their lamentations will function as an accusation when the angels bring them to the attention of God who will then inflict the judgement. In a quite different way, Rom. 3.4–6 (and 19–20) also suggests the idea of a lawsuit between God and humanity, Jews and Gentiles alike. Especially προητιασάμεθα (3.9b) suggests that προεχόμεθα also (3.9a) has legal connotations. Under these circumstances a translation like the following is most appropriate: 'What, then, do we plead as a defence?'[34]

The great advantage of this interpretation is that it eliminates the necessity of assuming that Paul vacillates between different ways of using first person plural forms. The use of the more or less inclusive forms in Romans 3 consistently reflects a diatribal style in which Paul includes his dialogue partners and occasionally all human beings with himself. In Rom. 3.1–9 Paul is engaged in a dialogue with himself and his audience rather than with an imaginary opponent, so that it is not only difficult, but also unnecessary, to decide which questions and answers should be attributed to a respondent rather than to Paul himself. The dialogue style serves a didactic purpose; Paul wants to engage his Roman audience and make them partners in his argumentation.

The question in Rom. 3.9a brings the preceding 'dialogue' to its conclusion. It marks neither a return to the questions in 3.1 nor a fresh start, nor does it add another deliberative question. The question 'What, then, are we to set forth (as a defence) in our discourse?' would have required the subjunctive mood. If προεχόμεθα is a genuine middle, Rom. 3.9a is best understood as a rhetorical question that does not call for an answer or for further deliberation. To raise the question: 'What, then, do we hold before us as a defence?' is to answer it: We human beings have nothing that we can plead as a defence or an excuse before God.

This solution to the semantic problem would be preferable to other proposals even if the Egyptian-Byzantine text in Rom. 3.9 had to be retained. The syntax would be awkward, whether τί οὖν is read as a separate question or not, but there are several ways in which one can try to come to terms with it.[35] My explanation works more smoothly, however, if we follow the text of P.[36] As the textual history leaves room for this option, we ought to regard οὐ πάντως as a very early gloss. It was intended to make the implied negative answer explicit, but obscured syntax and meaning and diminished the persuasive power of Paul's condensed rhetorical argument. By leaving the answer unstated, Paul takes it for granted that his readers already agree that human sinners have nothing to hold before themselves in a contest with their creator and judge; thus he persuades them to consent. In v. 9b and in the following catena of quotations, vv. 10ff, Paul states the reason for his rhetorical question and the implied answer. Even here he uses the first person plural form, including the audience that has followed his argument (see 3.19).[37]

The apparent lack of patristic support is no real objection against the proposed interpretation. The meaning of προεχόμεθα given in ancient Greek lexicons tends to support it.[38] There is no early evidence for the traditional exegesis of Rom. 3.9; the earliest known commentaries offer an interpretation which comes closer to my own. Ambrosiaster understands the Latin text 'Quid ergo tenemus amplius?' as a rhetorical question which terminates the preceding discussion ('Why continue?') and provides the transition to Paul's restatement of his charge and the supporting quotations.[39] That is, indeed, the function of the question in Rom. 3.9a; but the forensic connotations were lost in the Latin translation, as already in the corrected Greek text upon which it was based.

Origen's interpretation must have been along the same line. The Greek text of his commentary on Rom. 3.9a has been lost, and Rufinus' Latin translation is abbreviated. What is clear from the evidence at hand is that Origen maintained Paul acted like an umpire; in alternating parts of Rom. 1.18—3.8 he argued the case of the Jews against the Gentiles and vice versa, and the question in 3.9a terminated this procedure. Origen may have read the text of P or the Antiochene text, or have been familiar with both variants. In any case, he must have taken Rom. 3.9a to contain a rhetorical question which functioned as a conclusion and transition, without much theological significance of its own.[40] It is not possible to tell how close Origen's interpretation came to my own but it must have been along the same lines, like that of Ambrosiaster.

The context

It is, finally, time to relate our findings to the context in Romans 3 and other parts of the letter. Large portions of Romans are devoted to the demonstration that God is impartial in his dealings with Jews and Gentiles, both when he manifests his wrath and judgement and when he manifests his grace and saving righteousness. In Rom. 2.11 Paul has stated as an axiomatic truth that God shows no partiality. In 2.12–13 he spells out the implications of this axiom and then applies it to Gentiles (vv. 12–16) and to Jews (vv. 17–24), drawing a conclusion that seems to make the distinction between the two groups an external and, ultimately, irrelevant one (2.25–9).[41] Yet, Paul insists, the Jewish privileges are both genuine and manifold (3.1–2a). Paul does not enumerate these privileges in chapter 3, but he does so in 9.4–5 and never retracts his affirmation.

Paul can uphold the two apparently contradictory notions, that there is no distinction and that Israel's privileges are real, because of his conviction that God is both impartial and faithful, absolutely sovereign and always right. Jewish faithlessness does not nullify God's faithfulness but serves, like human sin in general, to vindicate God over against humanity and to make him prevail in his contest because it becomes clear that faithfulness, truth, and rectitude (justice, righteousness) belong to God alone and that man is never right over against God (Rom. 3.3–5a). The positive aspect of this is, as Paul later on explains, that salvation is solely the work of the one God of Jews and Gentiles, who justifies the ungodly and makes the dead alive, and in precisely that way keeps his word and promises to Israel (Rom. 3.21—4.25, 9–11).

196

Paul answers the questions raised in Rom. 3.1–3 by showing that God has manifested his righteousness in Jesus Christ and demonstrated his sovereignty, impartiality, and faithfulness in his dealings with Abraham and with Jews and Gentiles in Paul's own time. But first Paul raises some objections which might be put forward as charges against God or in defence of man: if human falsehood and wickedness serve to vindicate God and make his glory abound, has God, then, any right to punish the sinners? Why am I condemned? Why not do evil that good may come? Paul does not deal with these countercharges and excuses at any length but brushes them aside as senseless or even blasphemous. The rhetorical question in Rom. 3.9a draws the summary: human beings are unable to plead their own case against God. What do they have to hold forth?

It is generally recognized that the questions and answers in Rom. 3.1–8 anticipate in an extremely condensed form issues to which Paul returns in Romans 9—11; already in chapters 6—7 he deals with the question raised in 3.8. We can now add that the rhetorical question in 3.9a anticipates the question which Paul in 9.20 addresses to his imaginary dialogue partner: 'Who are you to answer back to God?' Without any major change of meaning Paul could have written in Rom. 3.9: τί οὖν ἀνταποκρινόμεθα; – and much confusion in the history of text and exegesis would have been avoided.

The passage in 1 Enoch 99.3 which provides a key to Paul's use of προεχόμεθα in Rom. 3.9 also contributes to the interpretation of the following catena of quotations in 3.10–18, because it proves that the lamentations of the righteous functioned as accusations against their oppressors, in an environment not too distant from Paul's. The catena is mostly made up by excerpts from psalms of lamentation, with the exception of 3.15–18 which is drawn from the lament over and indictment of the sins of Jerusalem in Isa. 57. Paul may have been aware of the original context even though his immediate source is likely to have been a florilegium which combined various passages into a coherent complaint over the wickedness of lawless oppressors.[42] In sharp contrast to the customary use of such accusatory lamentations, Paul takes the catena to confirm his charges against Jews as well as Greeks and makes the Law, not righteous sufferers, the speaking subject. Commenting upon the quotations, he even argues that the charges are addressed to those who are 'in the law' and not to wicked outsiders alone.[43] This application of complaints over human wicked-ness is analogous to the sudden change of address in Rom. 2.1 which

197

turns traditional charges against idolaters against anyone who judges, including the Jew.

Within the catena, sins committed by organs of speech loom remarkably large (3.13–14). This feature prepares for the conclusion, that every mouth should be stopped, at the same time as it links back to the preceding emphasis upon human falsehood and lies (3.4, 7). Paul's comments on the catena of quotations restate in negative terms what was expressed positively in words from Psalm 51: God is to be vindicated in his words and prevail when he is sued; every mouth is to be stopped and the whole world to be accountable and guilty before God. The whole section, Rom. 3.3–19, has an inner unity which becomes fully clear when we recognize that the transition from 'dialogue' to 'florilegium' makes the same point. Whether Jews or Greeks, we human beings have nothing to put up to defend or excuse ourselves before God. What Paul has charged in Rom. 1.18—2.25 is not that all Jews and Gentiles are equally gross sinners but that they are without excuse (ἀναπολόγητοι, 1.20; 2.1) because they all have known the will of God but have not done it. Just this inability to do what is recognized as right is the predicament of human beings under the sway of sin (ὑφ' ἁμαρτίαν, 3.9b; 7.14ff).

Paul's further comment in Rom. 3.20 already prepares for the transition to the next step in his argument. The negative statement, that no creature (σάρξ) is justified by works of the Law, and the positive thesis, that now the righteousness of God has been manifested without the Law, form a contrasting pair. There is no sharp break between Rom. 3.1–20 and 21–31, or even between 1.18—3.20 and 3.21—4.25.[44] The theme that God is impartial and that there is no distinction between Jews and Greeks continues when Paul turns to the positive aspect of God's righteousness, his salvific action in Jesus Christ. In grace as in judgement, God is sovereign and will prevail and be vindicated.

In this article it is neither possible nor necessary to follow Paul's argument any further. Interpreters of Romans have gradually liberated themselves from a longstanding exegetical tradition that tended to internalize Paul's doctrine of justification and to isolate it from his dealings with Jews and Gentiles. As a consequence, Romans 9—11 was often considered an appendix, and theological interest in these chapters was made to centre on the problems of predestination and free will. The approach, which was common to both sides in the Catholic-Protestant controversy, could be combined with the popular notion that the privileges of Israel had been taken from the Jews and given to Christians. In Romans 3, Paul's use of the term δικαιοσύνη θεοῦ in 1.17 and 3.21–6 was isolated from his use of the same term in 3.5. The tension which, on the common interpretation, exists between Rom. 3.1–3 and 3.9, as well as within Romans 9—11, was explained as a dialectic between divine election and human responsibility. Most of the solutions offered made the faithfulness of God contingent upon the response of the Jews, in spite of Paul's insistence that it was not.[45]

In this article I have argued that the generally accepted exegesis of Rom. 3.9 is a relic of an approach that has otherwise been abandoned. The common interpretation needs not only reconsideration but outright rejection. Hoping that I have convinced my friend C. K. Barrett and future interpreters of Romans that this is indeed the case, I offer my own text-critical and exegetical proposals for their consideration.

NOTES

1   See e.g. the commentaries of B. Weiss, Lietzmann, Lagrange, Cranfield, Käsemann. (I have deemed it unnecessary to give full bibliographical references for commentaries on Romans and translations of the New Testament.)

2   For the diversity of opinions, see e.g. Meyer (1864), Weiss (1886), Oltramare (1881).

3   See e.g. J. Murray (1959); Fitzmyer in *The Jerome Bible Commentary* (1968), ii. p. 300.

4   See Stanley K. Stowers, *A Critical Reassessment of Paul and the Diatribe: The Dialogical Element in Paul's Letter to the Romans.* Dissertation, Yale 1979 (available from University Microfilms, Ann Arbor, Mich.), pp. 181–234, esp. 233f.

5   Lietzmann explicitly speaks about an excursus.

6   Information provided by the UBS edition and Nestle-Aland[26] has been supplemented with the help of von Soden's and Tischendorf's major editions. K. Staab, *Pauluskommentare aus der Alten Kirche* (Ntl. Abh. 15, Münster 1933) has proved especially valuable for the text of Greek commentators and is simply quoted as Staab.

7   e.g., the addition of πρωτον after τε in A, the form απαντας in G, or υπο in B.

8   The UBS edition lists 'eth Origen Ephraem' in support of 2.1 but caution has prevented me from following their example. It would be especially important to know whether the information about Origen's (Greek) text is based upon solid information or simply derived from von Soden, who might be unreliable. See notes 21–3.

199

9 Cod. Marc. 546, see Staab, p. 654. The fragment is attributed to Arethas (d. 914) but the original source of information is no doubt earlier and the ascription open to doubt since Arethas according to another fragment commented upon the prevailing majority text.

10 The parenthesis in Nestle-Aland[26] suggests that Ψ has the same text as 2495 in 3.9a (against UBS). In the Bohairic version ου παντως (Greek!) may be an insertion.

11 The omission of γαρ in D* is related to the irregular colometric writing in Codex Claromontanus; two commata, ητιασαμεθα [γαρ] and Ιουδαιους τε, are written on one line. Some oriental versions left γαρ untranslated, but any connection with the text of D* is unlikely. The corrector of Claromontanus intended to make the manuscript conform to the prevailing text 1.1 but forgot to obliterate the letters κατ. The scribe of E/D[abs] copied the contaminated form.

12 On the Greek-Latin bilinguals and their fourth-century archetype, see H. J. Frede, *Altlateinische Paulushandschriften* (Freiburg 1964), pp. 15–101, and my article in *Text and Interpretation*, ed. E. Best and R. McL. Wilson (Cambridge 1979), pp. 99–114.

13 Thus already H. J. Vogels in *Amicitiae Corolla*, ed. H. G. Wood (London 1933); and J. N. Birdsall in *Cambridge History of the Bible*, i (1970), p. 431.

14 Unfortunately, P[46] is deficient at this point, as are C, H, I and other fragmentary manuscripts. The early Egyptian text may well have been less uniform than one would think on the basis of the preserved manuscripts.

15 See, e.g., the commentaries of Lietzmann and Cranfield and the report given in B. M. Metzger, *A Textual Commentary on the Greek New Testament* (UBS, London/New York, 1971).

16 A positive answer would be expected, and found in Rom. 3.21ff, if 3.9a is taken to raise the question about the special advantage of Christian believers. But this interpretation, common among Antiochene exegetes (see note 31), is a result, not the cause, of a text without the negation.

17 The most famous example is 1 Cor. 2.4 where all the variants go back to ουκ εν πειθοι σοφιας, a form which is attested only by 35* (omitted in Nestle-Aland[26]) but must also have been intended in the original bilingual edition. Like P[46], G and F have a dittography (εν πειθοις σοφιας) but g and f have 'in persuasione sapientiae'. The ninth century G has preserved an extremely ancient text without local address in Romans, in 1.15 alone, in 1.7 supported by marginal notes about Origen's text in 1739 and 1908. See H. Y. Gamble, Jr., *The Textual History of the Letter to the Romans* (StD 42, Grand Rapids, 1977), esp. pp. 15–33. Gamble's investigation has led to the conclusion that the original letter did not have the doxology but included chapter 16 with two final wishes of grace (16.20b and 24), a form preserved only by ms. 629 (see pp. 129–32).

18 See the works of Gamble, Frede, and myself, notes 12 and 17. On a completely different approach, Aland has recently rejected the idea of a common archetype for the whole Pauline corpus, concluding that there

must have been several early editions. The statistical method runs the double risk that it takes too little account of the activity of correctors, whose diligence in normalizing a text may have varied from one letter to the other and even within one letter, and that it may treat the late 'Majority Text' as a more homogeneous entity than it is. But the data presented by Aland certainly call for further investigations. See K. Aland, 'Die Entstehung des Corpus Paulinum', in *Neutestamentliche Entwürfe* (München 1979), pp. 302–50.

19 In other words, the preliminary results of my own study point in the direction of those components in the 'Western text' which are W^+ in the terminology of G. Zuntz, *The Text of the Epistles* (Oxford 1953). The two (or more) textual traditions must, however, have been conflated at such an early date that we can disentangle them only in exceptional cases.

20 See Gamble, op. cit., p. 29; P. Corssen, *ZNW* 10 (1909), pp. 15–17.

21 J. Molitor, *Der Paulus-Text des hl. Ephraim* (Rome 1938) retranslates the words τι ουν (προεχομεθα) . . . ητιασαμεθα.

22 Oral information from Dr Ephraim Isaac suggests that the later Ethiopic version renders an 'Antiochene' text. The earlier version has simply 'What (therefore) shall we say?' in Rom. 3.9a. That could possibly go back to the text of P.

23 The Tura papyrus published by J. Scherer, *Le commentaire d'Origen sur Rom. III. 5—V. 7* (Cairo 1957), contains neither Origen's text nor his interpretation of Rom. 3.9a. Min. 1739 and its allies (6, 424, 1908), whose text in Romans ultimately goes back to Origen's commentary, have the Egyptian-Byzantine text in Rom. 3.9, as does the lemma of the catena fragment published by Ramsbotham (*JTS* 13 (1912), p. 219). In his translation, Rufinus used the current Old Latin text (2.2.1). He could do so because the interpretation presupposes a text without ου παντως. The text of P would seem to fit better than the Antiochene text, followed by the Old Latin and Rufinus (see below, note 40). I have, however, a suspicion; the note, attributed to Arethas (see note 9), that the most accurate and ancient copies had τι ουν κατεχομεν περισσον rather than προεχομεθα, may ultimately go back to Origen, just like the report of Basilius, *Eunom.* II. 37 (*PG* 29. 612F), that ancient manuscripts omitted εν Εφεσω in Eph. 1.1. In that case, Origen would have considered the Antiochene text to be better attested than that of P; the note makes no reference to the presence or absence of ου παντως. On the chapter list, see note 31.

24 See the preceding note.

25 For some examples, see the apparatus in Nestle-Aland[26] on, e.g., Rom. 10.1; 11.16; 14.4, 12; 15.4, 5; 16.1; 1 Cor. 5.4; 14.12; 15.52; 2 Cor. 7.14; 8.19; Gal. 4.7; Eph. 4.28. Several other examples could be added, e.g. Eph. 5.33 (εκαστος ινα).

26 There are, however, some special agreements between P and the text of the bilinguals D G F, e.g. Rom. 16.5 (omission), and Eph. 4.19 (απηλπικοτες). In several cases the text of P agrees with other Latin witnesses rather than the bilingual manuscripts, d and g (f); see, e.g.,

1 Cor. 14.12 (πνευματικων); 2 Cor. 8.19 (αυτην); Eph. 1.1 (+ πασιν).

27 For singular variants, see, e.g., Rom 2.3; 9.23; 12.16; 1 Cor. 3.4; 2 Cor. 11.23; Gal. 3.26; 6.1; Eph. 1.9. The apparatus in Nestle-Aland[26] shows that several of the variants have some support outside Greek manuscripts. In Eph. 4.28, P, 1739 and 6, 33, 1881 al. may well have preserved the primitive text, εργαζομενος το αγαθον; diverse additions from 1 Cor. 4.12 and/or 1 Thess. 4.11 can have caused the many variants.

28 See, esp., Plutarch, *Mor.* 1038C–D. The passive construction was considered one possibility by Photius (Staab, 486, 21–9). His comments were reproduced by Ps.-Oecumenius (*PG* 118. 378 CD) and paraphrased by Arethas (Staab 654, 16–24). The interpretation was adopted by Wettstein and later, e.g., by Sanday-Headlam, who refer to F. Field and J. B. Lightfoot. It has been accepted in English translations (RV, Goodspeed; RSV and NEB only in footnotes), and has again been found worthy of serious consideration (by Danker?) in the new edition of the Arndt-Gingrich translation of Bauer's *A Greek-English Lexicon* (1979).

29 On the use of the middle for active in Koine Greek, see e.g. Blass-Debrunner-Funk, paragraph 316. In contrast to Blass and Debrunner, Rehkopf in the 14th German edition (1979) has approved the general consensus of the commentators without reservation; see paragraph 433.2 in the various editions of the grammar.

30 It is, in spite of the exegetical tradition, hard to believe that 'eos' in the Vulgate ('praecellimus eos?') should refer to the Gentiles, who are not mentioned in 3.1–8. Even some modern interpreters assume that Paul used middle for active without making Paul ask the question in Rom. 3.9a on behalf of the Jews (e.g. Zahn, Schlatter).

31 Theodore paraphrases Paul's question in Rom. 3.9a: 'Well then, after rebuking them we shall show what makes those who are of our kind great' (Staab, 117). In a similar way, the other Antiochene commentators and homilists took the question in 3.9a to introduce 3.21ff as well as 3.9b–21. See Severian (Staab, 216); Chrysostom, *Hom.* 7 (ed. Field, i. 86); Theodoret (*PG* 82. 41). See also the summary of chapter 4 (Rom. 3.9—4.25) in the common Greek chapter list: 'About the grace through which alone men are justified, not by way of ethnic discrimination but by the gift of God, on equal terms, with Abraham as the prime example.' (Text in L. A. Zacagni, *Collectanea monumentorum veterum ecclesiae graecae* (Rome 1898)); also *PG* 85. 740; von Soden, *Schriften* I. 1, 462. The summary may, possibly, presuppose the text of P (and Origen? see note 23), rather than the Antiochene text. Both the chapter list and the 'Euthalian Edition' of which it became a part are likely to have originated at the library in Caesarea; see L. Charles Willard, *A Critical Study of the Euthalian Apparatus* (Diss. Yale 1970), esp. pp. 64–78, 175.

32 Connotations of an alleged pretext are present in Sophocles, *Antigone*, 80, but hardly in Thucydides, I.40.4, the other text most frequently used to support an analogous interpretation of Rom. 3.9. Among commentators

Meyer, Lipsius, and Jülicher followed this line of interpretation, as did Weiszäcker in his translation.

33 The Greek text was first edited by C. Bonner (*StD* 8, 1937), later re-edited by M. Black (1970). For some comments, esp. on the phrase εἰς μνημόσυνον, see W. C. van Unnik, *Sparsa Collecta* I (1973), pp. 213–58, esp. 230–2. Van Unnik translated ἐν διαμαρτυρίᾳ by 'under oath', but thereby missed the point that the prayers of the righteous are considered a charge as well as a solemn petition.

34 I have found one commentator who advocates the view to which I also had arrived, J. C. O'Neill, who writes: ' "What, then, do we put up as a defence?" is a beautifully apt step in the argument', *Romans* (Harmondsworth 1975), p. 68. O'Neill, however, thinks that Paul by this remark introduces a defence against charges levelled against him, and that parts of the following text are secondary interpolations.

35 There are several possibilities. One can, e.g., assume that Paul intended to ask a deliberative question. Both the meaning and the awkward form could then be rendered in English translation: 'What, then, are we to plead? Not at all, for we have already charged . . .' The subjunctive form in A and L might be a correction of a primitive orthographic error, like the restoration of an intended indicative in Rom. 5.1 and 1 Cor. 15.49.

36 This was recognized already by Lagrange (1916), p. 68, who felt obliged to retain the received text and, as a consequence, the traditional interpretation.

37 Paul fairly often uses γάρ to connect an explication with a preceding rhetorical question, see e.g. Rom. 2.21–3; 4.1–2; 7.1–2; 9.19; 14.20f; also Heb. 11.32. On the didactic purpose of the dialogical style in Romans, see the dissertation of Stowers (note 4), esp. pp. 274–6.

38 Photius, *Lexicon*, ed. Naber (1864), has προεχόμεθα· ὑποβαλλόμεθα ἢ προβαλλόμεθα; thus also Suidas, ed. Adler, IV (1935), 2402 for the subjunctive form and 2917 on Thucydides I.40.2. Hesychius, ed. Schmidt, III (1861), 3440, has only προβαλλόμεθα, but a separate entry 3441 has πλέον κρατοῦνται.

39 The paraphrase varies slightly in the three editions reconstructed by H. J. Vogels (CSEL 81), 104–5: 'quid adhuc latius loquimur?' 'quid adhuc immoramur latius loquentes?' 'quid adhuc iam moramur latius loquentes?'

40 According to K. H. Schelkle, *Paulus, Lehrer der Väter* (Düsseldorf 1956), pp. 101f, Origen read and interpreted Rom. 3.9 in the same way as the majority of modern exegetes. I have found no basis for this view except the lemma of the catena fragment; it is contradicted by the translation of Rufinus which, as a comparison with the papyrus text shows, reproduces the general trend of Origen's interpretation fairly faithfully. The Greek form of the Antiochene text would not easily yield the meaning which Ambrosiaster found in the Latin translation. This observation favours the conjecture that Origen commented upon the text of P, but no certainty is possible; see note 23. Schelkle may have overlooked some other evidence;

if not, Photius is the first Greek proponent of what has become the common exegetical opinion.

41 See esp. Jouette Bassler, *The Impartiality of God: Paul's Use of a Theological Axiom*, Diss. Yale 1979 (to be published in the SBL Dissertation Series).

42 See esp. L. E. Keck, 'The Function of Rom. 3.10–18', in J. Jervell and W. A. Meeks, ed., *God's Christ and His People* (Oslo 1977), pp. 141–57.

43 In contrast to common opinion, the term ὁ νόμος may have its usual meaning even on its first occurrence in Rom. 3.19. The idea might be that the holy Law of God, speaking through the mouth of psalmists and prophets, utters complaints and accusations because not even those who are 'in the law' have done what it commanded; cf. 3.20; 7.7–25; 9.31.

44 See, most recently, R. B. Hayes, 'Psalm 143 and the Logic of Romans 3', *JBL* 99 (1980) pp. 107–15.

45 On my own approach to the interpretation of Romans, see *Studies in Paul* (Minneapolis 1957), chs 5–10. On Romans 9—11, see now Paul E. Dinter, *The Remnant of Israel and the Stone of Stumbling according to Paul (Romans 9—11)*, Diss. Union Theological Seminary 1979.

17

La Liberté du Spirituel dans Rom. 8.12–17*

J.-M. Cambier

La locution initiale de Rom. 8.12, ῎Αρα οὖν' introduit explicitement une conclusion pratique découlant de ce que saint Paul vient de dire et qu'il sera donc utile de résumer ici en guise d'introduction.[1]

Le régime religieux de l'Esprit apporte aux croyants la grâce de la justice, c'est-à-dire la libération du Péché et de la Mort; il leur donne ainsi la possibilité d'obéir aux exigences de l'amour de Dieu (8.1–4), en somme de vivre leur foi ou, comme le dit saint Paul au début et à la fin de sa lettre (cf. l'inclusion que l'on trouve en 1.5; 16.26), 'l'obéissance en laquelle consiste la foi'.

Le péché et la mort étaient l'aboutissement du régime religieux de la Loi. L'Esprit-Saint remplace la puissance Péché, qui nous arrache à Dieu, par la 'paix' (= un résumé des bienfaits messianiques) qui nous unit à Dieu (8.6); il remplace la mort, qui est damnation, par la vie qui est salut définitif; et il remplace aussi le péché par la justice (8.10). L'inhabitation de l'Esprit-Saint dans les croyants conduit ceux-ci à la vie éternelle, participation à la vie du Christ ressuscité (8.11).

Cette situation religieuse nouvelle entraîne des moeurs nouvelles. Libéré de l'esclavage du mal, le croyant est invité à vivre la liberté du spirituel. C'est ce qu'explique la péricope suivante, 8.12–17, que nous allons étudier plus en détail.

Si l'orientation religieuse nouvelle des croyants (8.9, 10a, 11a) est une oeuvre que Dieu a commencée (8.10b) et que seul il achèvera par son Esprit (8.11b), il reste que cette grâce est une tâche, une réalité de grâce à exprimer concrètement. La vie selon l'Esprit (8.12–13 contient trois fois le verbe ζῆν) est celle des enfants de Dieu (8.14–16: υἱοί . . . Θεοῦ, πνεῦμα υἱοθεσίας, τέκνα Θεοῦ, ce qui sous-entend la participation à la vie du Fils de Dieu); ceux-ci sont héritiers de la gloire de Dieu, par participation avec le Christ (8.17: à noter la triple répétition du préfixe συν-).

* See English summary on p. 220

1   *Les exigences de la vie selon l'Esprit: Rom. 8.12s*

L'action de l'Esprit dans le croyant appelle une réponse de celui-ci; d'où la formule de conclusion qui introduit notre péricope 8.12–17: Ἄρα οὖν. L'apostrophe, ἀδελφοί, comme souvent chez saint Paul, ponctue le début de cette conclusion; elle rappelle en même temps le ton et le style de la péricope précédente, 8.9–11, où l'exposé de l'action de l'Esprit-Saint est fait à la deuxième personne du pluriel et s'adresse aux chrétiens de Rome. Dans notre dernière péricope, il y a un mélange de la deuxième et de la troisième personne du pluriel, avec une nette prédominance de cette dernière: l'Esprit-Saint agit dans *tous* les croyants et *tous* se doivent de répondre à son action.

Nous avons ici une précision concrète et pratique sur l'acceptation spirituelle du salut. Celle-ci est principalement donnée en 8.12s., et elle sera suivie d'une raison introduite par un double γάρ (8.14a, 15a), précisant la situation nouvelle qui résulte de l'action de l'Esprit, avec, à la fin (8.17c), un rappel du caractère concret et actuel de notre acceptation spirituelle du salut. L'homme est placé dans une situation de créature et il doit nécessairement manifester cette condition de vie. Nous sommes désormais 'débiteurs' de l'Esprit. L'antithèse formulée en 8.12b–13 rappelle le monde ancien, dans lequel l'homme était dominé par la puissance Péché (cf. Rom. 7): envers celle-ci le croyant n'a plus aucune dette et il ne peut donc plus vivre selon la chair (κατὰ σάρκα), en suivant le φρόνημα de la chair (8.12), dont l'aboutissement est la mort (8.13; cf. 8.6a).[2]

Tout comme à la fin de 8.4, il y a en 8.13 le rappel de la double situation-orientation que l'homme peut toujours prendre pendant sa vie terrestre. L'Esprit n'établit pas l'homme dans une situation acquise définitivement; mais il lui propose continuellement un choix absolu et exclusif, l'exercice de sa liberté chrétienne. Il y a dans la formulation même le rappel de la condition de faiblesse propre à l'homme mortel porté à suivre les convoitises charnelles (cf. Rom. 6.12). En effet, le croyant est réellement justifié et délivré de son péché (le contraire de la situation de l'homme pécheur, avant le Christ, décrite en Rom. 7.14), mais il reste 'charnel'. S'il 'se laisse vivre' (cf. κατὰ σάρκα ζῆν), il mourra (μέλλετε ἀποθνήσκειν). Il lui faut faire un effort positif contre ce qu'il est en son moi déformé et 'faire mourir les oeuvres de son corps' pour accueillir la vie (8.13b) et vivre la liberté de l'Esprit (cf. 2 Cor. 3.17b).

Il sera utile de préciser le sens de quelques termes de nos deux versets et d'illustrer ceux-ci par d'autres passages pauliniens. Le mot σῶμα a une signification qui se rapproche du même terme, dans Rom. 8.11c et plus encore dans 6.12: ces deux versets parlent de 'votre corps mortel', c'est-à-dire du chrétien qui vit encore en ce monde terrestre et attend l'achèvement de son union à la destinée du Christ, après sa mort terrestre, par la résurrection. La coloration péjorative de σῶμα est cependant plus forte en 8.13b qu'en 8.11c, au point de se rapprocher de la signification de σάρξ.[3] Mais le mot σῶμα est bien choisi: il désigne toute la personne de l'homme croyant qui désormais n'est plus 'charnelle', au sens où ce mot est employé en Rom. 7.14b, mais qui, vivant encore dans un corps mortel (cf. 8.11c; 6.12a), doit continuellement choisir la liberté chrétienne, c'est-à-dire renouveler son choix d'être spirituel, et cela activement, en faisant 'mourir les oeuvres de son corps'. Le sens de πράξεις doit se déduire du contexte et peut être illustré par Rom. 6.12b: faire les oeuvres du corps c'est 'obéir aux convoitises du corps'. Πνεύματι, en 8.13b, a le même sens que ce terme en 8.10: c'est le νοῦς de l'homme avant le temps du Christ (cf. Rom. 7.25b), mais maintenant transformé, dans le régime de l'Esprit, en πνεῦμα; c'est le croyant 'spirituel' appelé à réaliser la double tâche décrite en 8.10: en temps qu'homme mortel (σῶμα), il ne peut plus produire de fruits en vue du Péché; en tant qu'homme spirituel (πνεῦμα), il est appelé à 'vivre'. Ce dernier verbe, dans notre texte, a avant tout un sens eschatologique, celui-ci étant encore souligné par la forme verbale du futur: ζήσεσθε; mais cela n'exclut pas une anticipation-réalisation actuelle, comme cela apparaîtra mieux plus loin, en 8.16. Cependant, il est important de valoriser le sens eschatologique de l'oeuvre de l'Esprit. Le croyant ne peut pas réaliser pleinement le don qu'il a reçu—ceci est l'oeuvre finale de l'Esprit en nous (cf. 8.18–25)—mais il peut déjà actualiser l'oeuvre du Christ et de l'Esprit habitant en lui. Notre appartenance au Christ mort et ressuscité,—et nous la faisons vivre en faisant mourir en nous tout ce qui est 'charnel' et qui s'oppose à l'Esprit,—fait que nous produisons des fruits en l'honneur de Dieu (cf. 7.4: ἵνα καρποφορήσωμεν τῷ Θεῷ). C'est seulement dans la mesure où nous acceptons et vivons nos obligations 'spirituelles' (ὀφειλέται ἐσμέν) que nous appartenons au monde-temps nouveau, celui de l'Esprit qui donne la vie, celui de la liberté du spirituel. Dans ce sens, on peut dire qu'il nous faut continuelle-ment quitter 'notre' histoire pour entrer dans l'histoire 'de Dieu' que conduit l'Esprit (cf. 8.14ss). Cette marche, entreprise par notre liberté, nous fait retrouver notre 'vrai moi', notre personnalité profonde créée par Dieu et librement offerte à lui par le croyant. Le parallélisme entre notre passage et Gal. 5, spécialement Gal. 5.1–6, 16s., 25, est éclairant. Des deux côtés on décrit la situation du 'spirituel', libéré par le Christ (Gal. 5.1; cf. Rom. 8.2), mais vivant encore dans ce monde-temps-ci et continuellement placé devant un choix existentiel dont l'absoluité est davantage soulignée dans Gal., ce qui s'explique par le ton polémique de cette épître. Le croyant décide de choisir librement le régime religieux de grâce (Gal. 5.4), celui de l'Esprit qui nous fait attendre l'objet de notre espérance, la justice achevée (Gal. 5.5); et il exprime concrètement ce choix par une vie de foi s'exprimant en charité (Gal. 5.6) Il sait que tout nous vient par grâce, c'est-à-dire en régime de foi, par l'Esprit de Dieu (cf. Gal. 3.2, 5). Dans le cas contraire, l'homme subit la servitude de la Loi (Gal. 5.1): l'opposition absolue entre les deux situations de vie, charnelle ou spirituelle, est fortement soulignée en Gal. 5.16s.; ces derniers versets constituent un bon parallèle de Rom. 8.13.[4] Dans la mesure où nous sommes fidèles à l'Esprit, celui-ci produit en nous des fruits spirituels, c'est-à-dire 'la récolte spirituelle qu'est la charité fraternelle' (Gal. 5.22), signe authentique que 'les exigences de la loi [de Dieu] s'accomplissent en nous' (cf. Rom. 8.4a); ce 'fruit conduit à la sainteté, dont l'aboutissement est la vie éternelle' (cf. Rom. 6.22b). C'est bien le sens premier du dernier mot de nos deux versets, comme dit plus haut: ζήσεσθε, vous vivrez. Ce terme est expliqué dans les versets suivants, 8.14–17, et il constitue le lien entre ces derniers versets et 8.12s.: en vivant selon l'Esprit, nous attendons la vie éternelle et, par anticipation, nous la vivons déjà en régime de grâce et de foi parce que nous sommes les enfants de Dieu. Et le style de cette manière de vivre est la liberté du spirituel.

Nous sommes donc 'des débiteurs' (ὀφειλέται ἐσμέν) vis-à-vis du régime religieux de l'Esprit, tout comme on le serait vis-à-vis de celui de la Loi (cf. Gal. 5.3). Mais le régime religieux introduit par l'Esprit est celui de 'la vie chrétienne' (Rom. 8.2a): nous sommes donc invités à accepter librement la vie de l'Esprit, la liberté spirituelle, fruit du φρόνημα de l'esprit (cf. ζωὴ καὶ εἰρήνη, Rom. 8.6b) et à refuser le fruit du φρόνημα τῆς σαρκός qui est la mort (θάνατος, Rom. 8.6a).

L'acceptation spirituelle du salut est ainsi l'acceptation de la vie de Dieu, vie déjà anticipée en ce monde-temps-ci (8.14–17), mais dont nous attendons l'achèvement: c'est l'objet de notre espérance, de notre liberté et de notre salut achevés, lors de la révélation de la liberté des enfants de Dieu, au temps de la gloire (Rom. 8.21).[5]

2 *Les croyants sont des enfants de Dieu: Rom. 8.14–16*

La vie des croyants (ζήσεσθε, 8.13b), fidèles à l'action de l'Esprit en eux (ὀφειλέται . . . πνεύματι, 8.12s.) est celle des enfants de Dieu, précisément parce qu'ils sont sous la mouvance de l'Esprit de Dieu (8.14) qui les fait participer à l'adoption filiale divine (8.15). L'Esprit, vivant en eux, rend témoignage qu'ils sont réellement des enfants de Dieu (8.16). L'affirmation lapidaire de Gal. 5.25 peut constituer un bon parallèle de Rom. 8.12–17. En effet, Gal. 5.25b, πνεύματι καὶ στοιχῶμεν, résume bien Rom. 8.12s.; et Gal. 5.25a, εἰ ζῶμεν πνεύματι, répond à la description de Rom. 8.14, introduite par le dernier mot de 8.13, ζήσεσθε.

Les trois versets 8.14–16 sont construits sur l'affirmation suivante: l'action de l'Esprit en nous fait de nous des enfants de Dieu. Les trois versets se complètent et il faudra tenir compte de ce fait pour préciser le sens de tel ou tel mot particulier. De plus, la doctrine et les expressions parallèles nous seront d'un grand secours pour l'intelligence de notre texte. On pourrait être tenté, en effet, de comprendre Rom. 8.14ss. en y découvrant le schéma de l'Exode, l'exemple-type de la présentation du salut de Dieu à son peuple. Il faut reconnaître que certaines expressions se prêtent à la formulation de cette hypothèse: 'nous sommes menés par l'Esprit de Dieu' (8.14); nous ne pouvons plus vivre avec une mentalité 'd'esclave' (8.15); nous sommes les 'héritiers de Dieu'. On pourrait ainsi comprendre cette présentation du salut spirituel comme un accomplissement de l'événement de l'Exode où Dieu délivrait son peuple de l'esclavage et le 'menait' vers 'l'héritage' de la terre promise. Il ne nous semble pas que l'on puisse relever, dans Rom. 8, la structure du schéma de l'Exode. L'introduire dans 8.14ss. sans raison suffisante est courir un risque de ne pas donner toute leur valeur aux affirmations de ce passage qu'est 8.12–17.[6]

Il y a peu de passages bibliques qui peuvent éclairer l'expression de 8.14: πνεύματι Θεοῦ ἄγονται. Nous avons l'expression parallèle de Gal. 5.18: εἰ δὲ πνεύματι ἄγεσθε, à laquelle nous reviendrons bientôt. On peut encore citer Luc. 4.1: Jésus, rempli de l'Esprit-Saint, . . . ἤγετο ἐν τῷ πνεύματι ἐν τῇ ἐρήμῳ (avec les parallèles de Marc 1.12: τὸ πνεῦμα αὐτὸν ἐκβάλλει εἰς τὴν ἔρημον, et de Matt. 4.1: ὁ Ἰησοῦς ἀνήχθη εἰς τὴν ἔρημον ὑπὸ πνεύματος). Il s'agit ici du Christ Jésus qui, sous l'impulsion de l'Esprit, commence sa mission messianique. L'expression antithétique de 1 Cor. 12.2s. est fort intéressante: au temps où ils étaient païens, les Corinthiens étaient 'entrainés malgré eux' vers les idoles muettes, avec l'expression: ἤχεσθε ἀπαγόμενοι; or, à ce moment, ils n'étaient pas sous la mouvance de l'Esprit-Saint et ils ne pouvaient pas encore, comme maintenant, confesser que Jésus est Seigneur (1 Cor. 12.3). D'après l'ensemble du contexte général de Rom. 7—8, la Loi n'a pas apporté la vie, mais elle a favorisé la mort (cf. Rom. 7.5, verset introduisant l'explication approfondie de Rom. 7. Voir *supra*, n4), au lieu que l'Esprit a introduit la nouveauté (Rom. 7.6) et la vie chrétienne (Rom. 8.2, 10). Or, c'est notre appartenance à l'Esprit, l'action de l'Esprit en nous qui nous fait participer à la destinée du Christ jusqu'à son achèvement (Rom. 8.9–11). Le sens obvie de Rom. 8.14 est de comprendre l'expression Πνεύματι Θεοῦ ἄγονται comme exprimant la dynamis salvifique que l'Esprit exerce à la suite de l'événement du Christ et à cause de celui-ci en faveur de tous ceux qui y adhèrent par une obéissance en laquelle consiste la foi; c'est ce qu'annonçait déjà le début de l'épître, en Rom. 1.4s. Cette même action de l'Esprit transforme notre νοῦς en πνεῦμα υἱοθεσίας (8.15a), elle nous fait prier Dieu en l'appelant 'Père' (8.15b), elle témoigne que nous sommes les enfants de Dieu (8.16): tout cela est annoncé dans la première phrase (8.14) de l'explication (8.14–17) qui justifie les exigences de la vie selon l'Esprit (8.12s.). Ainsi, le fait que nous sommes sous la conduite de l'Esprit nous constitue enfants de Dieu, et c'est là la raison pour laquelle les croyants doivent renoncer à tout ce qui est charnel pour devenir 'spirituels' en vue de la vie éternelle (le dernier mot de 8.13), laquelle est déjà anticipée dès cette vie, mais non achevée. L'anticipation est soulignée en 8.14–17, l'attente de l'achèvement et la manière de vivre cette attente est décrite en 8.18ss.[7]

Le v. 8.15 est structuré par le couple πνεῦμα δουλείας-πνεῦμα υἱοθεσίας, le second terme conditionnant la formulation du premier. Il nous faut donc brièvement étudier la valeur de δουλεία et de sa conséquence, εἰς φόβον, pour mieux comprendre la valeur de l'υἱοθεσία dont le résultat est le cri de 'Père'. Nous préciserons mieux ensuite la valeur de l'expression ἀλλὰ ἐλάβετε πνεῦμα υἱοθεσίας, laquelle est l'affirmation centrale de 8.15 justifiant le formule finale du verset précédent: υἱοί εἰσιν Θεοῦ.

La formule de 8.15a est calquée sur celle de 8.15b; les termes ἐλάβετε et πνεῦμα ne s'y trouvent que pour accentuer, par le contraste verbal, le vrai propos de Paul, exprimé en 8.15b; par contre, les termes δουλείας πάλιν εἰς φόβον, par l'antithèse très forte qu'ils constituent, doivent éclairer le sens de notre affirmation. L'antithèse fondamentale qui structure la composition de Rom. 7–8, explicitement énoncée en

7.6 (avec le verbe δουλεύειν), et les rappels précédents de l'esclavage du péché, auquel étaient soumis les hommes avant le salut du Christ, obligent à entendre le mot δουλεία de notre verset comme exprimant le régime religieux ancien du Péché et de la Mort dont le Christ nous a libérés (cf. 8.2). Δουλεία désigne l'ancien régime religieux (Rom. 7), dans lequel l'homme n'est pas habité par l'Esprit mais par le Péché (7.17, 20); l'homme charnel, avant le Christ, est 'vendu au Péché', il est son esclave (7.14b) et il ne peut accepter la grâce du salut (7.25b). D'ailleurs, la filiation adoptive achevée sera la libération complète de cette δουλεία, celle de la corruption à laquelle est encore soumis notre corps mortel (cf. 8.21–3).[8] La liberté du 'spirituel', caractéristique des enfants de Dieu (Rom. 8.21), du régime de grâce (cf. Rom. 6.12–23), de l'action de l'Esprit du Seigneur (cf. 2 Cor. 3.17s.) est opposée, en Gal. 5.1, au joug de l'esclavage: καὶ μὴ πάλιν ζυγῷ δουλείας ἐνέχεσθε, formule qui rappelle fortement celle de Rom. 8.15a: πνεῦμα δουλείας πάλιν εἰς φόβον. On peut s'interroger sur le sens de ce dernier terme. L'interprétation de 'la Loi' ne doit pas être retenue: Paul n'oppose pas l'ancien régime religieux au nouveau en parlant d'une loi de crainte et d'une loi d'amour; ce sont là des précisions—qui sont d'ailleurs, souvent présentées d'une manière trop schématique!—ultérieures. Le substantif φόβος, chez Paul, signifie habituellement la crainte de Dieu, ce qui n'est évidemment pas le cas ici.[9] Mais le rappel de Gal. 5.1, fait plus haut, πάλιν ζυγῷ δουλείας, en même temps que le parallélisme entre 8.15a et 15b, peuvent être éclairants. De fait, 'le joug' est le contraire de la liberté; par ailleurs, l'υἱοθεσία qui permet de prier Dieu en l'invoquant comme 'Père' signifie la situation de l'enfant de Dieu, libéré par l'événement du Christ et vivant, dans le régime religieux de l'Esprit, la liberté du spirituel. Ainsi, l'expression πάλιν εἰς φόβον est déjà une annonce implicite du thème de la liberté propre au régime de l'Esprit et qui n'existait pas avant le Christ.

L'expression πνεῦμα υἱοθεσίας est la formule capitale de la péricope 8.12–17 et peut-être même de Rom. 8: elle résume au mieux l'action de l'Esprit-Saint dans les croyants, le résultat de celle-ci qui permet une acceptation spirituelle du salut de Dieu. Elle combine les deux formules de Gal. 3.26s et 4.6. Gal. 3.26s. affirme la qualité d'enfants de Dieu de tous ceux qui ont la foi dans le Christ Jésus et qui sont 'baptisés au Christ'. Gal. 4.6 conclut à la même qualité de tous ceux dans le coeur desquels le Père a envoyé l'Esprit de son Fils; les deux versets précédents, Gal. 4.4s, rappellent d'ailleurs que nous avons reçu l'υἱοθεσία parce que le Père nous a envoyé son Fils pour nous racheter.

Participation ou communion à l'Esprit (πνεῦμα) et participation à la vie du Fils de Dieu (υἱοθεσία) désignent donc la même réalité nouvelle du croyant. Dans la perspective fonctionnelle de l'exposé paulinien, la christologie est aussi pneumatologie et réciproquement. Tout cela est le fruit de la foi, celle-ci étant, selon nous, rappelée par le verbe ἐλάβετε; celui-ci a la même signification qu'en Rom. 5.17; il rappelle ἀπολάβωμεν de Gal. 4.5, tout comme διὰ πίστεως ἐν Χριστῷ 'Ιησοῦ de Gal. 3.26.

La prière, qui est l'expression normale du chrétien racheté par le Christ et devenu 'spirituel', est introduite ici par le verbe κράζειν; ce dernier ne peut exprimer un état extatique, mais le mouvement de foi de tout croyant chrétien. Dans la LXX, κράζειν introduit la prière du fidèle, à laquelle répond le salut de Dieu; ceci est particulièrement vrai dans les psaumes (cf. Ps. 3.4; 21.2; 33.6; 56.2, etc.). Notre salut est que nous puissions appeler Dieu: 'notre Père', dans le sens de 'notre Père bien-aimé'; concrètement, le salut assuré est ici la δόξα du Christ, à laquelle nous sommes appelés à participer dans la mesure où, en cette vie, nous avons 'accepté [en foi] l'esprit d'adoption filiale divine', c'est-à-dire la participation à la destinée du Christ (cf. 8.17). C'est une prière que le croyant fait en fonction même de l'inhabitation de l'Esprit en lui et parce que, par sa foi, il lui appartient (Rom. 8.9). La formule n'est donc pas très différente, pour le sens, de celle de Gal. 4.6, où c'est l'Esprit lui-meme, envoyé dans nos coeurs par le Père, qui 'crie, Abba, Père'. L'Esprit en nous témoigne de la vérité de la situation nouvelle opérée par lui. [10]

Il reste à dire un mot sur la prière suggérée par l'Esprit: 'Abba, Père' que l'on peut traduire aussi par 'Abba, mon Père bien-aimé'. Dans son style direct, l'invocation signifie et l'acceptation de la grâce par le croyant et surtout l'action de grâce et l'adoration rendues par lui au Dieu-Père, c'est-à-dire au Dieu qui sauve: c'est une suggestion-témoignage de l'Esprit en nous. On peut aussi se rappeler 'la grâce' de 'l'accès auprès de Dieu' et 'la paix' que nous a obtenues la foi dans l'événement du Christ et qui nous rend 'certains de l'objet de notre espérance qu'est la gloire de Dieu' (Rom. 5.1s.); cet objet de notre espérance sera développé dans le texte qui suit immédiatement notre péricope, en 8.18–25. Cette prière n'est possible qu'à celui qui a compris le régime religieux de l'Esprit où tout est grâce, parce qu'il est l'enfant du Père par participation avec le Christ Jésus, le Fils de Dieu.[11] La prière suggère que l'Esprit ne fait que souligner le réalisme de son action.

Celle-ci est rappelée, une dernière fois, en 8.16, indiquant et cette action (αὐτὸ τὸ πνεῦμα συμμαρτυρεῖ) et la transformation qu'elle opère en nous (nous sommes devenus πνεῦμα, c'est-à-dire sa signification profonde (ὅτι ἐσμὲν τέκνα Θεοῦ); celle-ci avait déjà été affirmée en 8.14, 15. La locution πνεύματι ἡμῶν ὅτι ἐσμὲν τέκνα Θεοῦ reprend le πνεῦμα υἱοθεσίας du verset précédent et a déjà été expliquée. Dans les versets 8.14–16, on acceptera facilement un triple parallélisme entre les trois termes désignant la réalité nouvelle que l'Esprit opère en nous: υἱοί εἰσιν Θεοῦ (14), πνεῦμα υἱοθεσίας (15), τῷ πνεύματι ἡμῶν ὅτι ἐσμὲν τέκνα Θεοῦ (16). Il y a aussi un parallélisme synthétique entre les trois verbes exprimant l'action de l'Esprit: πνεύματι ἄγονται (14), ἐν ᾧ κράζομεν (15), τὸ Πνεῦμα συμμαρτυρεῖ (16): les trois verbes signifient la présence agissante de l'Esprit dans le croyant; la valeur de la foi, comme dit plus haut, est connotée par le verbe ἐλάβετε. On a souvent expliqué le préfixe du verbe συμμαρτυρεῖ comme signifiant un second témoignage, celui de l'Esprit-Saint qui s'ajouterait à celui de notre propre πνεῦμα, et cela est possible.[12] Mais nous pensons que le préfixe συν- a probablement ici une autre fonction. Il faut se rappeler les nombreux termes pauliniens composés avec le préfixe συν- qui indiquent notre union avec le Christ et notre participation à sa vie, en notant tout particulièrement les trois termes du verset suivant (συγκληρονόμοι, συμπάσχομεν, συνδοξάσθωμεν). A cause du contexte immédiat et aussi du contexte général de 8.1–17, où la vie dans le Christ est l'équivalent concret de la vie dans l'Esprit, on doit admettre ici cette même signification pour συμμαρτυρεῖν. Ce dernier verbe indique et la présence de l'Esprit en nous, témoignant de la nouveauté qu'il crée en nous et signifiant notre participation à la vie du Fils de Dieu par la présence de l'Esprit. Notre κοινωνία avec l'Esprit est une participation à la grâce du Christ, celle-ci étant l'expression de l'amour du Père et du Fils pour tous les hommes (cf. 8.31–9, spécialement 32; cf. aussi 2 Cor. 13.13).

Outre le double parallélisme entre les trois versets 8.14–16, on peut aussi noter une certaine inclusion entre les versets 14 et 16 qui, tous deux, indiquent l'action de l'Esprit: le dernier verset reprend la description du premier, ce qui confirme le sens que nous avons proposé pour ἄγεσθαι. Entre les deux versets, il y a l'apostrophe de 8.15: l'affirmation de 8.15 est la preuve de la vie et de l'action de l'Esprit dans les croyants. L'expression-clé πνεῦμα υἱοθεσίας résume notre condition nouvelle qui s'exprime dans une relation nouvelle avec Dieu à qui, en toute vérité, nous disons, 'Abba, notre Père'!

3 L'héritage des enfants de Dieu: Rom. 8.17

Rom. 8.17 comprend trois affirmations dont les deux premières constituent un raisonnement introduit par τέκνα, repris au verset précédent: la réalité nouvelle, à vivre dans l'Esprit, est le point de départ de ce petit syllogisme. La troisième affirmation rappelle le comportement actuel des enfants de Dieu (συμπάσχομεν) et fait ainsi inclusion avec le début de la péricope (ὀφειλέται ἐσμέν, 8.12); elle affirme aussi notre destinée future prévue par le plan salvifique divin (ἵνα καὶ συνδοξάσθωμεν).

Le théologoumène de l'héritage divin lié à la foi, dans la promesse divine, est proprement paulinien. On ne le retrouve dans aucun autre document du NT.[13] C'est particulièrement dans les deux épîtres exposant la justice de Dieu en régime de foi qu'on rencontre le théologoumène de l'héritage divin à cause de la foi en la promesse divine (cf. Gal. 3.18, 29 et surtout Rom. 4.13). On le rencontre encore dans Eph. 1.13s. Dans notre texte, pas plus que dans son parallèle Gal. 4.6s. (avec le vocabulaire: τὸ πνεῦμα, υἱός, κληρονόμος διὰ Θεοῦ), il n'y a pas le terme ἐπαγγελία; mais il y est supposé et il est même implicitement rappelé, dans Rom. 8.17c, par la conjonction ἵνα rappelant le plan salvifique divin et donc la promesse divine. Dans ce plan, la communion avec l'Esprit-Saint nous rend enfants de Dieu et fait donc de nous des héritiers de Dieu. Il faut souligner la valeur du génitif Θεοῦ: dans l'oeuvre du salut, tout est don exclusif de Dieu. Mais Dieu opère notre salut par le Christ et dans l'Esprit. Nous sommes héritiers de Dieu parce que nous sommes dans la communion de vie avec l'Esprit (cf. le contexte prochain de 8.12–17 et le contexte général de 8.1–30) et aussi parce que nous sommes héritiers du Christ par participation à sa destinée. Cette participation est exprimée ici par le préfixe συν-. Nous participons dès maintenant à la vie du Christ parce que nous avons accueilli la nouveauté de vie de l'Esprit-Saint qui habite en nous. La précision συγκληρονόμοι δὲ Χριστοῦ souligne que la grâce du Père nous est donnée par et dans le Christ. Le thème κληρονόμος est le pendant de l'inhabitation de l'Esprit (cf. peut-être l'expression de l'AT: 'ils habiteront la terre [messianique], leur héritage'); mais il faut d'abord accepter Dieu et son mystère de salut, la communion à la mort et à la vie du Christ: l'υἱοθεσία. La communion achevée à sa vie sera le salut achevé que nous vivons maintenant dans l'espérance (cf. la péricope suivante, Rom. 8.18–25).

La promesse de l'héritage est une affirmation de la réalité, de la continuité et de l'achèvement final du salut de Dieu. Ceux en qui habite l'Esprit ne sont plus seuls, laissés à eux-mêmes et donc sans espoir de salut (cf. Rom. 7.24). Sans doute le monde ancien, hostile ou indifférent à Dieu, existe toujours (8.7s); le chrétien peut encore y retourner, tant qu'il vit dans un corps mortel (6.12) et que celui-ci n'aura pas été transformé par Dieu (8.11). Mais 'cet homme ancien a été crucifié avec le Christ' (6.8): cela implique que le croyant doit actualiser, dans sa vie, cette crucifixion de l'homme charnel (Gal. 5.24). L'acceptation spirituelle de la communion avec le Christ doit toujours être actualisée en vivant selon notre πνεῦμα; la phase finale et l'achèvement du salut sont uniquement l'oeuvre de Dieu. Ces deux aspects de la vie chrétienne sont complémentaires et ils sont assez souvent notés ensemble, chez Saint Paul, comme ici, en Rom. 8.17c (souffrance et gloire); il en est de même en 8.12s ('mortification' de la chair et vie éternelle), en Rom. 5.1–5 (la grâce de l'accès auprès du Père, la patience en cette vie et l'objet de notre espérance future), en 8.18–25 (mêmes thèmes qu'en 5.1–5, mais plus développés), en 2 Cor. 5.7 (le temps de la foi et celui de la vision), etc. Ainsi, en tant qu'enfants de Dieu, nous participerons à l'héritage du Christ parce que nous sommes actuellement unis à la destinée du Christ: εἴπερ συμπάσχομεν.[14] Cette participation à l'héritage de Dieu et du Christ se fait suivant le plan divin; c'est ce que souligne le ἵνα de la dernière proposition de 8.17.

Examinons encore quelques passages parallèles de Gal. 3—5. Gal. 5.1–12; 13–26 constituent deux explications sur la liberté chrétienne, à la suite de la présentation allégorique des passages de la Genèse concernant Sara et Agar, en Gal. 4.21–31. Nous relevons le thème de l'ἐπαγγελία en 4.23, 28, tout comme en Gal. 3 (sept emplois) et en Rom. 4.13ss (quatre emplois). Il y a, dans ces textes, un ensemble de thèmes décrivant le salut comme une libération de l'esclavage de la Loi pour accéder, par le Christ et par l'Esprit, à la liberté des enfants de Dieu: Dieu a envoyé aux hommes son Fils et son Esprit en vue de l'objet de l'espérance qu'est la justice; c'est un salut qui se réalise en régime de foi. Nous retrouvons les mêmes thèmes qu'en Rom. 8; toutefois, ce dernier exposé n'a pas la coloration polémique de Gal., dominé par l'antithèse Loi-grâce du Christ. Rom. 8 parle de la Loi (= régime religieux) 'du Péché et de la Mort' (Rom. 8.2) et de la condamnation du Péché qui avait son siège dans l'homme charnel (8.3).[15]

Il y a, des deux côtés, en Rom. comme en Gal., une exhortation à ne plus vivre 'charnellement', mais 'spirituellement'. Dans Gal. 5.13–26, le premier verset introduit bien l'application pratique dont nous parlons: votre vocation à la liberté, frères, ne peut constituer un prétexte pour vivre charnellement; elle est, au contraire, une possibilité de service mutuel dans l'expression de la charité fraternelle, celle-ci résumant la loi du Christ. Il faut choisir entre les deux régimes religieux: celui de la Loi (assimilée à la chair) ou celui de l'Esprit. Les 'spirituels' sont ceux dans le coeur de qui Dieu a envoyé son Esprit (Gal. 4.6), ceux qui sont menés par l'Esprit (Gal. 5.18). Ayant accepté et choisi l'Esprit, ils ont à vivre 'spirituellement' (Gal. 5.25).

Cette venue de l'Esprit dans les coeurs signifie l'amour de Dieu (cf. Rom. 5.5), se révélant dans la grâce du Christ. L'Esprit nous fait 'communier' à la grâce chrétienne de l'amour de Dieu (cf. 2 Cor. 13.13) qui est la vie des enfants de Dieu (Rom. 8.13: ζήσεσθε) et aussi la liberté des enfants de Dieu dont, pendant cette vie, nous attendons la révélation, dans la patience (Rom. 8.18–25).

Dans Gal., tout comme dans Rom., nous avons une explication centrée sur l'antithèse 'Loi-Esprit' et qui se trouve dans un contexte de salut. Il est peut-être tentant de supposer, dans Gal. 5.18 comme dans Rom. 8.14ss, le schéma de l'Exode. Mais, comme nous l'avons vu, l'ensemble des thèmes utilisés ne sont pas caractéristiques du schéma de l'Exode. Citons surtout celui de l'intervention divine par l'envoi de son Fils et de son Esprit, le couple 'fils-esclaves' comme aussi celui de l'adoption filiale-héritage. Ils suggèrent l'imagerie familiale. Ils expriment bien le salut, mais en partant de l'exemple de la foi d'Abraham à la promesse divine. Ajoutons que, dans Rom. 8, l'horizon s'est élargi, à cause de l'explication antithétique préliminaire de Rom. 7: tous les hommes, tous 'charnels' (= pécheurs) et voués à la mort, ne peuvent être libérés et sauvés, accéder à la vie à cause de la justice, que dans le régime religieux nouveau de l'Esprit qui les rend 'spirituels', enfants de Dieu capables de vivre la liberté du spirituel et appelés à recevoir un jour 'la liberté achevée' des enfants de Dieu en même temps que 'l'adoption filiale divine achevée' (cf. *infra*, la péricope suivante, 8.18–25. Voir n5).

Ainsi, tout comme l'envoi de l'Esprit (Gal. 4.6), l'inhabitation de l'Esprit (Rom. 8.9–11), le fait d'être mûs par l'Esprit de Dieu (Rom. 8.14; Gal. 5.18) ou de recevoir un esprit d'adoption filiale divine (8.15), comme aussi le témoignage de l'Esprit en nous (8.16), tout cela indique l'action salvifique de l'Esprit, au temps eschatologique inauguré par le Christ. Dans Rom. 8.12–17, cette action est intimement liée à son résultat: l'action de l'Esprit de Dieu fait de nous des enfants de Dieu, donc des héritiers de Dieu. Nous avons ici des explications sur le régime religieux de l'Esprit qui suit les articulations du schéma suivant: l'action divine de l'Esprit, l'adoption filiale divine, l'héritage, le tout étant lié à la destinée du Christ, comme le rappelle brièvement 8.17c.

La communion à la vie du Christ et de l'Esprit est l'accueil par l'homme spirituel de la libération-liberté apportée par le Christ et l'Esprit. Sans doute, la communion à la passion du Christ est ressentie par nous, au niveau psychologique, comme une souffrance et un mal: il nous faut la vivre dans la patience eschatologique, c'est-à-dire illuminée par l'espérance. Par la foi, nous savons que notre communion à la passion-mort du Christ (συμπάσχομεν) est déjà une anticipation à la communion de sa gloire, et cela par l'action de l'Esprit qui nous initie progressivement à 'la liberté du spirituel' (cf. 2 Cor. 3.18). L'acceptation de notre participation à la passion-mort du Christ permettra au plan de Dieu (cf. le ἵνα) de s'achever en nous: nous participerons alors à la gloire du Christ (συνδοξασθῶμεν), c'est-à-dire que nous recevrons le salut achevé, l'objet actuel de notre espérance (8.18–25). Avec l'aide de l'Esprit (8.26s.), nous savons que le plan de salut divin s'achèvera dans la glorification des croyants (8.28–30).

NOTES

1 Notre premier projet avait été de présenter une étude de notre thème dans Rom. 8.1–17. Quand les instructions nous sont parvenues de ne pas dépasser les 4,000 mots, nous avons été forcé de limiter notre recherche à Rom. 8.12–17, et aussi de diminuer considérablement le nombre de notes bibliographiques.

2 Après la proclamation d'une 'loi', dans l'AT, suit une exhortation engageant les Israélites à l'observer; le même topique se retrouve dans le NT. Ici, après l'exposé sur la situation du 'spirituel', l'exigence divine est exprimée par le terme ὀφειλέτης.

3 La *lectio facilior*, τῆς σαρκός, de D,G et de la tradition latine est un bon commentaire du texte.

4 Pour la différence de la situation religieuse de l'homme, exposée en Rom. 8.13 et Gal. 5.16, d'une part, et, d'autre part, celle exposée en Rom. 7, cf. J.-M. Cambier, Le 'moi' dans Rom. 7, *The Law of the Spirit in Rom. 7 and 8*, Rome, 1976, pp. 13–44, surtout la conclusion, p. 39–44.

5 cf. J.-M. Cambier, 'L'espérance et le salut dans Rom. 8.24', *Message et Mission*, Louvain-Paris, 1968, pp. 77–107.

6 La présence du schéma de l'Exode en Rom. 8.14 est proposé par I. de la Potterie, 'Le chrétien conduit par l'Esprit dans son chemin eschato-

logique', *The Law of the Spirit in Rom. 7 and 8*, Rome 1976, pp. 209–41. Dans la discussion qui suit l'exposé on relèvera plusieurs auteurs qui ne sont pas d'accord avec l'Auteur. Cette dernière opinion est partagée par C. K. Barrett, *The Epistle to the Romans* (BNTC), London [2]1962, pp. 162–4.

7   Pour l'explication de cette dernière péricope, cf. n8. Par ailleurs, il n'est pas impossible d'interpréter ἄγονται de 8.14 dans le sens d'un moyen: 'car ceux qui se conduisent par l'Esprit de Dieu, ceux-là sont des enfants de Dieu'. Mais le soulignement de l'action de l'Esprit dans la péricope précédente (cf. surtout 8.9–11) et dans la présente (cf. τὸ πνεῦμα συμμαρτυρεῖ, en 8.16), ainsi que l'insistance sur le fait que cette situation nouvelle est le don exclusif de Dieu, tout cela nous fait préférer le sens passif: 'ceux qui sont conduits par l'Esprit de Dieu'. De plus, ce passif peut se rattacher à ce qu'on a appelé 'le passif apocalyptique': le salut final des hommes par Dieu est décrit au passif pour souligner que tout, ici, est l'oeuvre exclusive de Dieu, ce qui est bien une thèse centrale de Rom. Rappelons enfin le parallèle de Gal. 5.18, où la formule πνεύματι ἄγεσθε est placée en antithèse avec la proposition parallèle οὐκ ἐστὲ ὑπὸ νόμον et qui décrit une situation, donc au passif. Signalons que W. Pfister, *Das Leben im Geist nach Paulus*, Fribourg, Suisse, 1963, p. 76, interprète πνεύματι ἄγονται de 8.14 comme un réflexif. C. K. Barrett, *Romans*, pp. 162s., opte pour le passif.

8   Cf. J.-M. Cambier, 'L'espérance et le salut', *Message et Mission*, Louvain-Paris, 1968, pp. 77–107.

9   Sur les treize emplois du mot par Paul, neuf ont la signification de 'la crainte de Dieu, du Seigneur, du Christ', c'est-à-dire que le terme signifie 'le sentiment religieux authentique'; deux autres versets se rattachent d'ailleurs indirectement à cette acception: Rom. 13.3, 7. Il y a deux exceptions: 1 Cor. 2.3 décrit une attitude personnelle de faiblesse de l'apôtre; ensuite, il y a notre cas, 8.15.

10 Selon W. Grundmann, dans *TWNT* iii, pp. 900s, le terme, dans le judaïsme, introduit un texte inspiré tiré de la Bible, donc une vérité révélée par Dieu.

11 cf. J. Jeremias, *Abba: Studien zur neutestamentlichen Theologie und Zeitgeschichte*, Göttingen, 1966, p. 163.

12 Pour la discussion concernant le sens du verbe συμμαρτυρεῖν, cf. O. Kuss, *Der Römerbrief*, Regensburg, 1957–9, pp. 604–6.

13 Dans Héb., on retrouve les deux termes cités ensemble, mais sans lien interne entre l'héritage et la promesse. De plus, ce dernier terme est, dans cette épître, l'équivalent de l'héritage ou du salut. Cf. Héb. 6.12, 15, 17; 11.13, 39.

14 Il y a sept emplois de la conjonction εἴπερ dans le NT, uniquement dans saint Paul: 2 Thess. 1.6; 1 Cor. 8.5; 15.15; 2 Cor. 5.3; Rom. 3.30; 8.9, 17. Le sens est ou hypothétique et concessif ou aussi causal; cette dernière nuance n'est pas signalée dans F. Blass & A. Debrunner, *Grammatik der neutestamentlichen Griechisch*, n°454, 2. Mais il est parfois difficile de préciser s'il faut souligner la nuance du conditionnel (= si du moins) ou celle de la

causalité (= parce que). Il nous semble préférable de comprendre le εἴπερ de 8.17c comme ayant surtout un sens causal, tout comme en 8.9. En effet, après le registre de l'impératif (8.12s.), à partir de 8.14, Paul reprend celui de l'indicatif pour décrire notre condition nouvelle. Par ailleurs, il est possible qu'il y ait un rappel discret de l'obligation, où nous sommes en cette vie, d'accepter notre condition actuelle. L'interprétation d'un conditionnel *réel* est aussi possible.

15 Des deux côtés, cependant, nous retrouvons la même doctrine fondamentale; cf. aussi l'antithèse Loi-grâce [du Christ] en Rom. 6.14b.

ENGLISH SUMMARY

Rom. 8.12–17 spells out the practical consequences of life in the Spirit, which has replaced the law of sin and death (vv. 1–11). In vv. 12–13 Paul reminds his readers of the demands of this new life. Although the believer is justified and delivered from sin, he still lives in a mortal body and is therefore continually confronted with a choice. He must repeatedly choose the path of Christian freedom, renewing his decision to be spiritual and to 'mortify the deeds of the body'. The life which he receives belongs to the time of fulfilment in the future (cf. vv. 18–25) but is experienced already through the work of the Spirit, which is transforming him and continually moving him towards the liberty of the 'spiritual' (the Christian who is becoming increasingly free). Similar ideas are set out more fully in Gal. 5.

Vv. 14–16 are concerned with the work of the Spirit in us which makes us children of God. The contrast between the old regime and the new is summed up in v. 15, in a formula which recapitulates ideas set out in Gal. 3.26f. and 4.6f. Three times in vv. 14–16 Paul tells us what we become through the work of the Spirit, and the three verbs he uses emphasize the active presence of the Spirit in the believer.

In v. 17 we reach the conclusion of this section: those who live in the Spirit and who are thereby children of God will inherit what God has planned for them. If they are united with Christ they will share his destiny: because they suffer with him, they will also be glorified with him. This sharing in the passion of Christ is an anticipation of the participation in Christ's glory which is God's plan for us, and which is achieved through the work of the Spirit in those who believe.

18

Zum Verständnis von Römer 11.26a:
'... und so wird ganz Israel gerettet werden'*

Ferdinand Hahn

I

Röm. 11.26a bzw. der ganze Abschnitt 11.25–32 ist ein in der Exegese sehr umstrittener Text. Es gibt grundsätzlich vier Möglichkeiten des Verständnisses: (a) man deutet πᾶς 'Ισραήλ auf das Gottesvolk aus Juden und Heiden;[1] (b) man versteht πλήρωμα τῶν ἐθνῶν in V.25b im Sinn der Vollzahl, also der Totalität aller Heiden und dementsprechend πᾶς 'Ισραήλ in V. 26a von der Gesamtheit des Volkes Israel;[2] (c) man erklärt πλήρωμα τῶν ἐθνῶν und πᾶς 'Ισραήλ im approximativen Sinn, wonach der grossen Zahl der bekehrten und geretteten Heiden eine vergleichbare Repräsentation ganz Israels am Ende der Zeiten entsprechen wird;[3] (d) man spricht von einem 'Sonderweg' zum Heil für Israel, was besagt, dass unabhängig von Evangeliumsverkündigung und Glauben am Ende der Tage 'ganz Israel' als erwähltes Volk sola gratia das Heil empfangen wird.[4]

Die Entscheidung ist deswegen schwierig, weil eine Lösung sich nicht unmittelbar aus dem Wortlaut der Stelle ergibt, sondern nur aufgrund des Kontextes von Röm. 9–11 und der gesamten paulinischen Theologie. Klar ist von vornherein nur, dass die Erklärung (b) ausscheidet;[5] denn die daraus resultierende Vorstellung von der Allversöhnung widerspricht der paulinischen Heils- und Gerichtsverkündigung.[6] Aber auch die Deutung (a), für die man auf Gal. 6.16 verweisen kann, kommt hier nicht in Frage, da die Verwendung des Namens Israel innerhalb von Röm. 9–11 eindeutig auf das alte Gottesvolk beschränkt ist und ein semantischer Wechsel von V.25b zu V.26a schwer nachvollziehbar wäre.[7] So bleibt das häufig vertretene Verständnis (c). Da neuerdings aber die Lösung (d) mit so grossem Nachdruck zur Diskussion gestellt worden ist, besteht Anlass, dem Problem erneut nachzugehen.

Bei den folgenden Erwägungen kann von dem Zusammenhang des Briefteils nicht abgesehen werden, doch ist es nicht erforderlich, das

*See English summary on p. 235

Gesamtverständnis und die zahlreichen Einzelprobleme von Röm. 9–11 zu erörtern.[8] Es sollen lediglich die Linien in der Gedankenführung des Apostels berücksichtigt werden, die für eine Entscheidung des Interpretationsproblems von Röm. 11.26a von Belang sind.

II

Abgesehen von der persönlich engen Bindung des Apostels an Israel, die trotz seiner Abwendung von der früher angestrebten δικαιοσύνη ἐκ νόμου (Phil. 3.9) und den πατρικαὶ παραδόσεις (Gal. 1.14) weiterhin besteht, ist für Paulus wesentlich, dass Gott Israel seine Verheissungsworte anvertraut hat (Röm. 3.2), dass sein Wort nicht hinfällt (Röm. 9.6a) und dass Gott das Volk, das er einst erwählte, nicht verstösst (Röm. 11.1). Denn Gottes Gnadengaben und seine Berufung sind unumstösslich (Röm. 11.29). Die Israeliten sind und bleiben 'Geliebte' gemäss der Erwählung, und zwar 'um der Väter willen' (Röm. 11.28).

Gerade der Verweis auf die Väter macht nun aber deutlich, dass nicht einseitig die geschichtliche Herkunft von Abraham ausschlaggebend ist, sondern die gleichzeitige Nachfolge im Glauben, weswegen die Beschneidung für die wahren Nachkommen Abrahams über das Zeichen der leiblichen Zugehörigkeit hinaus 'Siegel der Glaubensgerechtigkeit' ist (Röm. 4.9–12). An Glaube und Unglaube entscheidet sich daher das Geschick Israels. Nicht zufällig spielt im Mittelabschnitt von Röm. 9–11 die Frage der Rechtfertigung und des Glaubens ebenfalls eine entscheidende Rolle (9.30—10.21). Was in Abraham als dem 'Vater des Glaubens' typologisch im voraus verwirklicht war, das geht aufgrund der Geschichte Jesu und der Botschaft des Evangeliums in Erfüllung.

Aber nur ein 'Rest' aus Israel hat die Heilsbotschaft angenommen (Röm. 11.1–6), die Mehrheit dagegen verharrt im Unglauben. Was wird mit ihnen geschehen? Droht ihnen das Schicksal Pharaos, da doch der Satz aus Exod. 33.19 gilt: 'Ich schenke Erbarmen, wem ich will, und erweise Gnade, wem ich will' (Röm. 9.14–18; vgl. V.19–24)?[9] In jedem Fall hat Paulus in Zusammenhang mit der ausdrücklichen Feststellung, dass das Wort Gottes nicht hinfällig sei (9.6a), eindeutig gesagt: οὐ γὰρ πάντες οἱ ἐξ 'Ισραήλ, οὗτοι 'Ισραήλ· οὐδ' ὅτι εἰσὶν σπέρμα 'Αβραάμ, πάντες τέκνα, ἀλλ' ἐν 'Ισαὰκ κληθήσεταί σοι σπέρμα (9.6b-7).

So stellt der Apostel nach der Einleitung in Röm. 9.1–5 eine geradezu widersprüchliche Feststellung an den Anfang seiner Erörterungen über Israel.[10] Erst nach langen Ausführungen gibt er in 11.25–32 eine Antwort. Dabei kann er von der weltweiten Verkündigung des Evangeliums unter den Heiden nicht absehen. Vielmehr liegt für ihn gerade darin der Schlüssel zum Verständnis des Weges und der Zukunft Israels.

III

Während Israel sich immer noch weitgehend dem Heilshandeln Gottes verweigert, haben zahllose Heiden das Evangelium im Glauben angenommen. Auch dies ist in der Gestalt und Geschichte Abrahams vorgezeichnet, denn Abraham hat der Gottesverheissung bereits geglaubt, bevor er beschnitten wurde, und das ist ihm zur Gerechtigkeit angerechnet worden; deshalb ist er der Vater der Beschnittenen wie der Unbeschnittenen, der 'Vater vieler Völker' (Röm. 4.9–17a).[11] Darüber hinaus ist in der Verkündigung der alttestamentlichen Propheten das Heilshandeln Gottes unter den Heiden angekündigt worden (Röm. 9.25f; 10.16–20; 15.9–12).[12] Schliesslich ist Paulus selbst von Gott als Apostel Jesu Christi auserwählt und berufen worden, damit er ihn unter den Heiden verkündige (Gal. 1.16: ἵνα εὐαγγελίζωμαι αὐτὸν ἐν τοῖς ἔθνεσιν),[13] und beim Apostelkonvent ist sein εὐαγγέλιον τῆς ἀκροβυστίας von den anderen Aposteln förmlich anerkannt worden (Gal. 2.6–9).

Letzteres bedeutet selbstverständlich nicht, dass er ein eigenes Evangelium verkündigt, sondern das eine Evangelium wird von Paulus als Heilsbotschaft für die 'Unbeschnittenen' weitergegeben, so wie es von Petrus und den anderen Aposteln den 'Beschnittenen' angesagt wird.[14] Dies hat allerdings die Konsequenz, dass die spezifisch jüdische Voraussetzung der Tora eine unterschiedliche Rolle spielt, auch wenn Gesetzesfrömmigkeit in keinem Fall mehr den Weg zum Heil bestimmen kann (Gal. 2.15–21; Röm. 10.5–8). So wenig es ein eigenes Evangelium für die Heiden gibt, so wenig kann es eine eigene Kirche geben, sondern nur die eine Kirche aus Juden und Heiden (Gal. 3.28; 1 Kor. 12.13).

Unter dieser Voraussetzung sind nun aber auch die Heiden an die Geschichte Gottes mit Israel gebunden; denn mit der Erwählung und Führung Israels hat Gott sein endzeitliches Heilshandeln vorbereitet. Die Heiden sind deshalb auf Israel als 'Wurzel' angewiesen, wie dies im Ölbaumgleichnis des Apostels eindrucksvoll veranschaulicht wird (Röm. 11.13–24). Sie partizipieren mit und durch Christus, der seinerseits dem Volk Israel entstammt (Röm. 9.5), an den Vätern und den Verheissungen des alten Bundes. Sie sind damit einbezogen in das von Israel ausgehende Gotteshandeln, und aus diesem Grunde können Juden- und Heidenchristen auch einmal zusammen als das 'Ισραήλ τοῦ θεοῦ angesprochen werden (Gal. 6.16), und zwar unter Berücksichtigung der gesamten in Erfüllung gehenden Erwählungsgeschichte Gottes, in die nun auch die glaubenden Heiden einbezogen sind.

IV

Wenn Paulus von 'Ισραήλ spricht, denkt er stets vom alttestamentlichen Erwählungshandeln Gottes her. Aus diesem Grunde hat er dabei meist nur das alte Gottesvolk im Blick, das noch nicht zum Glauben gekommen ist.[15] Erst recht gilt das überall dort, wo er von 'Ιουδαῖοι spricht, zumal 'Ιουδαῖοι für ihn ein antithetischer Relationsbegriff zu ἔθνη ist, während 'Ισραήλ als Ehrentitel und Erwählungsbezeichnung offen bleibt im Blick auf das weitergehende und noch unabgeschlossene Gotteshandeln, innerhalb dessen das alte Gottesvolk aber eine konstitutive Stellung und Funktion behält.[16] Deshalb spielt der 'Rest' (λεῖμμα) aus Israel eine so bedeutsame Rolle (Röm. 11.1–6), weil dieser Rest die Treue Gottes zu seiner Erwählung und Verheissung erkennbar werden lässt trotz allen Unglaubens auf jüdischer Seite (Röm. 10.16–20).[17]

Warum aber gibt es den Unglauben gerade unter denen, die die Errettung, die Führung und das in die Zukunft weisende Wort Gottes einst erfahren haben? Für Paulus handelt es sich nicht nur um menschliches Versagen; es geht auch nicht allein um das Sich-Abwenden von Gott und das Aufbegehren gegen ihn (1 Kor. 10.1–13), das die Menschen seit Adam in Solidarität miteinander verbindet (Röm. 5.12–19), weswegen ja auch Juden wie Heiden unterschiedslos der Sünde verfallen sind (Röm. 1.18—3.20).[18] Vielmehr ist dieser Unglaube in einer besonderen, zusätzlichen Weise gekennzeichnet. Es ist nicht ausschliesslich die Macht der Sünde, durch die die Juden in ihrer Mehrheit gefesselt sind und sich weiterhin fesseln lassen, es ist ebenso der eigene Wille Gottes, der ihnen für eine befristete Zeit πώρωσις, 'Verstockung', auferlegt hat.[19] Dies ist der entscheidende Inhalt des Mysteriums, das Paulus der Gemeinde in Rom in den Kap. 9–11 deutlich machen will (Röm. 11.25–7).[20]

'Verstockung' aber heisst, dass Israel gerade mit seinem Unglauben eine ganz bestimmte, ihm von Gott auferlegte Aufgabe zu erfüllen hat.

Diese Verstockung ist Israel 'teilweise' (ἀπὸ μέρους) widerfahren, ἄχρι οὖ τὸ πλήρωμα τῶν ἐθνῶν εἰσέλθῃ (Röm. 11.25b). Das 'zuerst den Juden', das aufgrund der Erwählungs- und Verheissungsgeschichte für die Verkündigung des Evangeliums, die Botschaft der Rechtfertigung aus Glauben, gilt (Röm. 1.16), wird somit im Blick auf die Heilsvollendung zu einem 'zuerst den Heiden'.[21] Hieran zeigt sich aber, wie das mangelnde Vertrauen Israels auf seinen Gott, das an dem in Zion aufgerichteten 'Stein des Anstosses' zerbrochen ist (Röm. 9.32f), zusammentrifft mit dem göttlichen Willen zur Verstockung Israels, um der Zuwendung zu den Heiden willen.[22] Darum hat Gott den Israeliten einen 'Geist der Betäubung' (πνεῦμα κατανύξεως) gegeben, so dass sie 'bis zum heutigen Tag' nicht sehen und nicht hören können (Röm. 11.8 im Anschluss an Deut. 29.3; Jes. 6.9f).

Aber damit nicht genug: Die Juden, die umso hartnäckiger an dem Gesetz und der Gesetzeserfüllung als Mittel einer eigenen Gerechtigkeit, mit der sie vor Gott bestehen wollen, festhalten (Röm. 10.2f), sollen erkennen, was Gott allein aus Gnade mit den Heiden tut. Sie sollen begreifen lernen, dass nur rückhaltloser Glaube, der im Handeln Gottes in Christus begründet ist, retten kann. So sollen sie 'eifersüchtig' gemacht werden; denn sie sind nicht gestrauchelt, damit sie zu Fall kommen und des Heiles verlustig gehen, sondern damit durch ihr Versagen das Heil zu den Heiden gelangt (Röm. 11.11).[23] Paulus versteht aus diesem Grunde sein missionarisches Handeln unter den Heiden so, dass er damit in seiner eigenen Gegenwart wenigstens 'etliche' aus Israel eifersüchtig machen und auf diesem Wege retten kann (Röm. 11.13f).[24]

V

Eine zentrale Stellung in der Argumentation des Paulus in Röm 9–11 nimmt das Ölbaumgleichnis ein (11.13–24), sowohl im Blick auf die Heiden als auch im Blick auf die Juden.[25]

Für die Heiden besagt es, dass sie nicht nur von Israel als der 'Wurzel' abhängig bleiben, sondern dass der ganze Ölbaum von dorther seine 'Heiligkeit' bekommt (Röm. 11.16), ein Begriff, mit dem auf das erwählende, zum Heil führende Gotteshandeln verwiesen wird.[26] Sie sind als Zweige eines wilden Ölbaums 'eingepfropft' worden in den edlen Ölbaum, damit sie an seiner kraftspendenden Wurzel teilhaben (11.17: συγκοινωνὸς τῆς ῥίζης τῆς πιότητος τῆς ἐλαίας). Und nach wie vor gilt: 'Nicht du trägst die Wurzel, sondern die Wurzel trägt dich' (11.18b). Das Einpfropfen der Zweige geschah aufgrund des Glaubens der Heiden, während zahlreiche einst zum Ölbaum gehörende Zweige wegen des Unglaubens der Juden herausgebrochen wurden (11.19). Die Zugehörigkeit zum edlen Ölbaum hängt in jedem Fall von dieser Voraussetzung des Glaubens ab, weswegen Paulus vor jeder Überheblichkeit auf Seiten der Heiden warnt (11.18a.19–22); umgekehrt sollen aber auch die Israeliten wieder eingepfropft werden, 'wenn sie nicht im Unglauben verharren' (11.23). Die Heiden werden also gerade im Blick auf ihren Glauben, der ihnen Anteil am Heil ermöglicht hat, auf ihre unaufhebbare Bindung an Israel und an das Gotteshandeln im alten Gottesvolk angesprochen.

Für die Juden dagegen besagt das Gleichnis, dass sie aufgrund der einstigen Erwählung zu dem edlen Ölbaum gehören, zu einem Teil aber ihre lebensnotwendige Verbindung dazu verloren haben. Sie existieren als herausgehauene, tote Zweige, weil ihre Existenz durch den Unglauben an Gottes heilschaffendes Wirken in Jesus Christus bestimmt ist. Aber das wird nicht als Dauerzustand angesehen. Sobald sie nicht mehr im Unglauben verharren, werden sie wieder zu Zweigen dieses Ölbaums (11.23a). Sie sollen wieder eingepfropft werden und erneut an der Lebenskraft der Wurzel teilbekommen, weil Gott die Macht hat, sie wieder mit dem Ölbaum zu vereinen (11.23b) und ζωὴ ἐκ νεκρῶν zu schaffen (11.15), da er der Gott ist, der die Toten lebendig macht und das Nichtseiende ins Sein ruft (4.17b).[27] Es geht jedoch nicht nur um die prinzipielle Möglichkeit, dass auch ausgehaue Zweige wieder eingepfropft werden können, vielmehr vertraut Paulus darauf, dass Gott aufgrund seiner Treue und Verheissung die 'von Natur' zugehörigen Zweige ihrem eigenen Ölbaum dann erst recht wiederum einpfropfen wird, wenn er sogar Zweige aus einem wilden Ölbaum 'gegen ihre Natur' in den edlen Ölbaum eingepflanzt hat (11.24f).

VI

Von hier aus stellt sich nun die Frage: Was heisst in diesem paulinischen Kontext die Aussage von Röm. 11.26a, wonach 'ganz Israel' gerettet werden soll?[28]

Dass das Handeln Gottes an Israel nicht zu Ende ist, ist der erste wesentliche Gesichtspunkt für Paulus, den er nun abschliessend in Röm. 11.25–32 noch einmal ausdrücklich hervorhebt. Wie die einstige Erwählung und die bleibende Bedeutung der Geschichte des alten Gottesvolkes für die Kirche unaufhebbar sind, so auch die Gültigkeit der Israel betreffenden Heilsverheissung. Wie aber wird sie sich nach der Erwartung des Paulus realisieren?

In Röm. 11.32 formuliert der Apostel zusammenfassend: συνέκλεισεν γὰρ ὁ Θεὸς τοὺς πάντας εἰς ἀπείθειαν, ἵνα τοὺς πάντας ἐλεήσῃ. Mit dem zweimaligen οἱ πάντες sind, wie die vorangehenden Aussagen eindeutig zeigen, Juden und Heiden gemeint (vgl. Röm. 3.9).[29] Dass für die Heiden das Erbarmen Gottes im Angebot der Heilsbotschaft, der Verkündigung des εὐαγγέλιον, besteht, ist deutlich. Auch jener 'Rest' aus Israel, von dem in Röm 11.1–6 die Rede ist, hat allein auf diesem Wege das Erbarmen Gottes erfahren und angenommen. Steht es mit jenen, die von der Verstockung betroffen sind, anders?

Klar ist zunächst einmal, dass das Erbarmen mit 'ganz Israel' an das Ende der Zeiten gehört. Mit näheren Angaben ist Paulus äusserst sparsam. Lediglich aus der Verbindung von Röm. 11.25–7 lassen sich einige Beobachtungen gewinnen. Dabei muss zuerst entschieden werden, wie Vv. 25b, 26a und 26b–27 zusammengehören. Die Entscheidung hängt an dem Verständnis von οὕτως. Sieht man in οὕτως—καθώς (V. 26a.b) eine korrelative Wendung,[30] wozu es bei Paulus allerdings kaum Entsprechungen gibt,[31] dann wird V. 26a mit dem Schriftzitat V. 26b–27 begründet; V. 25b ist hierbei Vordersatz, V. 26f ein weiterführender und selbständig motivierter Nachsatz. Versteht man dagegen οὕτως rückbezüglich,[32] dann stellt die Aussage V. 25b die Begründung für V. 26a dar, und V. 26b–27 ist ein zusätzlicher, mit der geläufigen Wendung καθὼς γέγραπται eingeführter Schriftbeweis. Letzteres verdient sprachlich und sachlich zweifellos den Vorzug, was wiederum darauf hindeutet, dass das von Paulus kundgegebene μυστήριον primär in der Erkenntnis der gegenwärtigen, aber befristeten Verstockung Israels besteht, was jedoch die Erwartung zukünftiger Rettung mit einschliesst.[33] Das wird unterstrichen durch die Wendung ἄχρι οὗ τὸ πλήρωμα τῶν ἐθνῶν εἰσέλθῃ, zumal das Verbum εἰσέρχεσθαι im Neuen Testament ein terminus technicus für das 'Eingehen' in die endgültige Gottesherrschaft bzw. Heilsvollendung ist.[34] Für 'ganz Israel' vollzieht sich diese Errettung nach Röm. 11.26b–27 im Zusammenhang mit der Parusie Christi, des 'aus Zion', der himmlischen πόλις, kommenden Erlösers (vgl. 1 Thess. 1.10; Phil. 3.20f). Dementsprechend zielt auch der Schluss des Abschnitts in Röm. 11.28–32 auf die endzeitliche Vollendung des Heils für Heiden wie Juden.[35]

Mit dem Hinweis auf den Zeitpunkt der Errettung ist noch nicht gesagt, *wie* sich das Erbarmen Gottes an Israel vollzieht. In dem mit Röm. 11.26a eng verbundenen Mischzitat aus Jes. 59.20f und 27.9 wird in Röm. 11.26b-27 auf die Abwendung der ἀσέβεια von Israel, auf die Vergebung der Sünden und auf die von Gott realisierte διαθήκη hingewiesen.[36] Das ist eine Umschreibung für das endzeitliche Heil, das Israel widerfahren soll. Wie aber steht es mit Israel selbst? In der Tat ist hier von Bekehrung und Glaube nicht gesprochen. Allein daraus abzulesen, dass es sich um eine Rettung Israels handeln müsse, die ausschliesslich in der Treue Gottes und seinem Erbarmen begründet ist, wäre ein *argumentum e silentio*, sofern man dabei von jedem menschlichen Verhalten meint absehen zu können.[37] Doch schon das Zitat besagt mehr, als auf den ersten Blick zu bemerken ist. Denn die Abwendung der ἀσέβεια von Israel ist doch, wie andere Paulusstellen zeigen, gleichbedeutend mit der Abwendung der ἀπείθεια und der ἀπιστία.[38] Die Vergebung der Sünden begründet ein neues Gottesverhältnis, und die διαθήκη ist eine gemeinschaftsstiftende Setzung Gottes, für die nach neutestamentlichem Verständnis der Glaube der dazugehörenden Menschen konstitutiv ist. Hinzu kommen weitere Stellen des Kontextes, aus denen sich ein noch deutlicheres Bild ergibt.

Die Aussage in Röm. 11.23 ἐὰν μὴ ἐπιμένωσιν τῇ ἀπιστίᾳ, ἐγκεντρισθήσονται hat dabei ein erhebliches Gewicht.[39] Für sich genommen lässt sie neben 11.25-7 allerdings noch keine abschliessende Entscheidung zu; denn sie könnte natürlich auch im Blick auf diejenigen formuliert sein, die sich in der Zwischenzeit als einzelne dem 'Rest' aus Israel anschliessen. Gleichwohl macht diese Stelle klar, welch fundamentale Bedeutung der Glaube im Zusammenhang mit dem eschatologischen Handeln Gottes hat.

Mit Röm. 11.23 stehen aber noch andere Stellen in sachlichem Zusammenhang. Wichtig ist schon die Beobachtung, dass die πώρωσις in Röm. 11.7-10 unverkennbar in Beziehung zu dem Unglauben Israels steht. Diese von Gott verhängte Verstockung, die das Hören und Sehen bei der Verkündigung des Evangeliums unmöglich macht,[40] ist jedoch befristet und wird aufgehoben, 'wenn das πλήρωμα der Heiden eingegangen ist' (11.25fin).[41] Das Erbarmen Gottes widerfährt ihnen ebenso wie den Heiden, und schliesslich werden die Heiden 'mit seinem Volk' jubeln und den Herrn preisen (Röm. 15.10f). Jedes Anrufen des Herrn setzt aber nach Röm. 10.14 voraus, dass die betreffenden Menschen an ihn glauben.[42]

Bevor weiterreichende Konsequenzen gezogen werden, muss jetzt

geklärt werden, wie das Nebeneinander von τὸ πλήρωμα τῶν ἐθνῶν
und πᾶς 'Ισραήλ zu verstehen ist. Berücksichtigt man die paulinische
Gerichtsverkündigung und die Bedeutung des Glaubens für das Heil
der Heiden, dann kann es nicht strittig sein, dass πλήρωμα in Röm.
11.25b die 'Vielzahl', nicht aber die 'Vollzahl' im numerischen Sinne
bedeutet, also die unvorstellbar grosse Menge, jedoch nicht die
Totalität aller Heiden.[43] Um so auffälliger ist daneben das πᾶς
'Ισραήλ, und in Verbindung mit der Tatsache, dass in V. 25b–27 nicht
ausdrücklich vom Glauben die Rede ist, hat man ja erwogen, ob es sich
hier um einen 'Sonderweg für Israel' handeln könne. Das wäre dann
eine Heilszuwendung ohne Bekehrung und ohne Glauben, als Zeichen
der Treue und des Erbarmens Gottes für jeden, der zu Israel gehört.[44]
Aber dem steht doch der Satz aus Röm. 9.6b unüberhörbar entgegen,
dass nicht 'alle aus Israel' in Wahrheit zu 'Israel' gehören.[45]

An dieser Stelle muss nun auch noch Röm. 11.12 herangezogen
werden. Die Aussage über das πλήρωμα αὐτῶν (*sc.* τῶν 'Ισραηλιτῶν)
wird verschieden interpretiert, zum Beispiel im Sinne von πλήρωμα
(τῶν ἐθνῶν) in 11.25b, was bedeuten würde, dass die Formulierung
πᾶς 'Ισραήλ in 11.26a mit der Vorstellung vom πλήρωμα Israels völlig
identisch wäre.[46] Aber näher liegt vermutlich doch, πλήρωμα αὐτῶν
in strenger Relation zu παράπτωμα αὐτῶν und zu ἥττημα αὐτῶν zu
verstehen; dann geht es, im Gegensatz zu der 'Übertretung' und der
'Niederlage' Israels bei der bisherigen Begegnung mit der Botschaft
des Evangeliums, in der Zukunft um die 'Erfüllung' dessen, was
angesichts der Heilszuwendung Gottes von ihnen erwartet wird: um
Umkehr, Vertrauen und Glauben.[47]

Israel wird also noch einmal mit dem Heilsangebot konfrontiert
sein. Dann wird gelten: ἐὰν μὴ ἐπιμένωσιν τῇ ἀπιστίᾳ,
ἐγκεντρισθήσονται (11.23), und Paulus erwartet, dass hierbei 'ganz
Israel' zum Heil gelangt, was aber nicht heissen kann, dass schlechthin
jeder, der leiblich zum Volk Israel gehört, ohne Bereitschaft vertrauenden Glaubens an dieser Rettung teilhat.[48] Das πᾶς ist kompre-
hensiv zu verstehen. Es steht insofern dem Begriff πλήρωμα (τῶν
ἐθνῶν) nahe, aber dem Apostel geht es in Röm. 11.26a darum, dass
Israel am Ende der Geschichte die Heiden prozentual hinsichtlich der
Vielzahl der zum Heil eingehenden Glieder noch übertreffen wird.[49]

VII

Die unverbrüchliche Hoffnung des Apostels auf eine endzeitliche
Rettung Israels lässt ihn Abstand nehmen von seinem Wunsch, selbst

verflucht zu sein zugunsten seiner Brüder (Röm. 9.3). Paulus beugt sich dem Verstockungswillen Gottes und erfüllt sein Werk unter den Heiden, solange ihm dazu Zeit gegeben ist (Röm. 15.14–33). Er vertraut auf eine zukünftige Errettung Israels.

Paulus würde jedoch seiner Erkenntnis der Wahrheit des Evangeliums untreu werden, wenn er davon absehen könnte, dass dem Menschen Rechtfertigung und Heil widerfährt, sofern dieser unter Verzicht auf jede Eigenmächtigkeit und Selbstrechtfertigung das erbarmende Handeln Gottes und dessen Zuwendung vertrauend und glaubend annimmt. Er hätte zudem seine eigenen Prämissen preisgegeben, wenn er in Röm. 11.25–32 die zentralen Aussagen des Mittelabschnitts 9.30—10.17 unberücksichtigt liesse, wo es im Blick auf den in Zion jetzt aufgerichteten λίθος προσκόμματος (Röm. 9.33a = Jes. 28.16a) mit alttestamentlichen Zitaten heisst: ὁ πιστεύων ἐπ' αὐτῷ οὐ καταισχυνθήσεται (Röm. 10.11b = Jes. 28.16b), und weiter: πᾶς γὰρ ὃς ἂν ἐπικαλέσηται τὸ ὄνομα κυρίου σωθήσεται (Röm. 10.13 = Joel 3.5).[50]

Heil ist für den Apostel vom Glauben des Menschen als einer vertrauenden, rückhaltlosen Selbstpreisgabe an den sich erbarmenden Gott unablösbar, und nicht zufällig heisst es in 1 Kor. 13.13a: νυνὶ δὲ μένει πίστις, ἐλπίς, ἀγάπη, τὰ τρία ταῦτα. Denn der Glaube gehört nicht zu den vergänglichen Erscheinungen unseres geschichtlichen Lebens in dieser Welt, sondern ist konstitutiv für jede Beziehung zwischen Mensch und Gott. Darum kann es eine Rettung ganz Israels nur dadurch geben, dass die Juden in ihrer Vielzahl zum Glauben kommen und erkennen, dass Gott in Jesus Christus gehandelt und sein endzeitliches Heilswerk begonnen hat und es in ihm vollenden wird. Jesus ist der erwartete Messias, und den jetzt ungläubigen Israeliten sollen dafür die Augen noch geöffnet werden.[51]

ANMERKUNGEN

1 So J. Jeremias, 'Einige vorwiegend sprachliche Beobachtungen zu Röm. 11.25–36', L. De Lorenzi (Hg.), *Die Israelfrage nach Röm. 9–11* (Monographische Reihe von *Benedictina*, Biblisch-ökumenische Abteilung 3), Rom 1977, S. 193–205, bes. S. 199f. Diese Auslegung wird auch vertreten von K. Barth, *Kirchliche Dogmatik* II/2, Zürich 1942, S. 328ff, bes. S. 330.

2 Dazu vgl. W. Michaelis, *Versöhnung des Alls*, Gümlingen (Bern) 1950, S. 126–9.

3 So z.B. C. K. Barrett, *The Epistle to the Romans* (BNTC), London ²1962, S. 224: 'it seems probable that he [*sc.* Paul] is thinking in representative terms'.

4 F. Mussner, 'Ganz Israel wird gerettet werden' (Röm. 11.26), *Kairos* 18 (1976), S. 241–55 (hiernach im folgenden zitiert); zusammengefasst in ders., *Traktat über die Juden*, München 1979, S. 52–67.

5 Auch das οἱ πάντες in Röm. 11.32 kann dafür nicht in Anspruch genommen werden.

6 Vgl. Liselotte Mattern, *Das Verständnis des Gerichts bei Paulus* (*AThANT* 47), Zürich 1966.

7 Dazu sei verwiesen auf die Diskussion des Beitrags von Jeremias in De Lorenzi, *Israelfrage*, S. 205–16, auch S. 231f. Vgl. auch Mussners Untersuchung des Begriffs 'Ἰσραήλ, aaO., S. 241ff.

8 An neueren Arbeiten ist ausser den Kommentaren zu verweisen auf U. Luz, *Das Geschichtsverständnis des Paulus* (*BEvTh* 49), München 1968, bes. S. 268–300; P. Richardson, *Israel in the Apostolic Church* (SNTSMS 10), Cambridge 1969, S. 126–47; D. Zeller, *Juden und Heiden in der Mission des Paulus* (*Forschung zur Bibel* 11), Stuttgart 1973, S. 202–69; B. Mayer, *Unter Gottes Heilsratschluss* (*Forschung zur Bibel* 15), Stuttgart 1974, S. 167–313; W. G. Kümmel, 'Die Probleme von Römer 9–11 in der gegenwärtigen Forschungslage', De Lorenzi, *Israelfrage*, S. 13–33.

9 Vgl. F. Montagnini, 'Elezione e libertà: grazia e predestinatione a proposito di Rom. 9.6–29', De Lorenzi, *Israelfrage*, S. 57–86.

10 Vgl. E. Käsemann, *An die Römer* (HNT 7a), Tübingen ³1974, S. 250f.

11 Hierzu verweise ich auf meinen Aufsatz: 'Genesis 15.6 im Neuen Testament', *Probleme biblischer Theologie: Festschrift für G. v. Rad*, München 1971, S. 90–107.

12 Ich beschränke mich auf die zentralen Stellen des Römerbriefs.

13 Vgl. die Ausführungen in meinem Buch, *Das Verständnis der Mission im Neuen Testament* (*WMANT* 13), Neukirchen ²1965, S. 82ff.

14 Ebd. S. 65ff.

15 Eingehend untersucht von Mussner, aaO. S. 241ff.

16 Vgl. G. v. Rad-K. G. Kuhn-W. Gutbrod, Art. 'Ἰσραήλ etc., *TWNT* iii, Stuttgart 1938, S. 356–94, bes. S. 382ff, 389ff.

17 Dazu sei verwiesen auf Luz, aaO. S. 8off.

18 Vgl. C. K. Barrett, *From First Adam to Last*, London 1962, S. 15ff.

19 Vgl. K. L. Schmidt, 'Die Verstockung des Menschen durch Gott', *ThZ* 1 (1945) S. 1–17.

20 Der Satz V. 26a darf innerhalb der Aussagen des Paulus über das Mysterium keinesfalls isoliert werden. Er ist lediglich die Konsequenz aus V. 25b. Zu diesem Textabschnitt sei vor allem verwiesen auf P. Stuhlmacher, 'Zur Interpretation von Römer 11.25–32', *Probleme biblischer Theologie: Festschrift für G. v. Rad*, München 1971, S. 555–570.

21 O. Michel, *Der Brief an die Römer* (*KEK* IV), Göttingen ¹⁴1978, S. 355,

Anm. 1: Die Bekehrung der Heiden ist 'nicht nur die zeitliche, sondern auch die sachliche Voraussetzung für die Rettung Israels'.

22 Vgl. C. K. Barrett, 'Romans 9.30—10.21: Fall and responsibility of Israel', De Lorenzi, *Israelfrage*, S. 99–121; ferner E. Dinkler, 'Prädestination bei Paulus', in ders., *Signum crucis* (*Ges. Aufs.*), Tübingen 1967, S. 241–69, bes. S. 254 ff.

23 Hierzu vgl. H. Schlier, *Der Römerbrief* (HThK VI), Freiburg i.B. 1977, S. 327f.

24 Besonders herausgearbeitet bei G. Schrenk, 'Der Römerbrief als Missionsdokument', in ders., *Studien zu Paulus* (*AThANT* 26), Zürich 1954, S. 81–106. Vgl. auch Richardson, aaO. S. 126 ff, 146f.

25 Zuletzt dazu C. E. B. Cranfield, *The Epistle to the Romans* (ICC) vol. II, Edinburgh 1979, S. 563–72.

26 Das entspricht dem alttestamentlichen Begriff, vgl. dazu O. Procksch-K. G. Kuhn, Art. ἅγιος, *TWNT* i, Stuttgart 1933, S. 87–116.

27 Vgl. meinen Artikel, 'The Confession of the One God in the New Testament', *Horizons in Biblical Theology* 2 (1980) S. 69–84.

28 Ausser der bereits genannten Literatur seien noch erwähnt: K. L. Schmidt, *Die Judenfrage im Lichte der Kapitel 9–11 des Römerbriefs* (ThSt 13), Zürich 1943; G. Eichholz, *Die Theologie des Paulus im Umriss*, Neukirchen 1972, S. 284–301; Chr. Müller, *Gottes Gerechtigkeit und Gottes Volk* (FRLANT 86), Göttingen 1964, S. 42–9, 68–72, 93–100; R. Batey, 'So All Israel Will Be Saved': an Interpretation of Romans 11.25–32', *Interpretation* 20 (1966) S. 218–28.

29 Vgl. Käsemann, *Römer*, S. 301.

30 So z.B. Müller, aaO., S. 43; Luz, *Geschichtsverständnis*, S. 294; Stuhlmacher, *Zur Interpretation*, S. 559f; P. Benoit, 'Conclusion par mode de synthèse', De Lorenzi, *Israelfrage*, S. 231f.

31 Vgl. die Übersicht über den Wortgebrauch bei Jeremias, De Lorenzi, *Israelfrage*, S. 198f, 207f.

32 So z.B. Barrett, *Romans*, S. 223f; Michel, *Römer*, S. 354f; Käsemann, *Römer*, S. 300; Mayer, *Heilsratschluss*, S. 284f. Dabei dürfte die modale Bedeutung des καὶ οὕτως allerdings der temporalen vorzuziehen sein; vgl. Jeremias, aaO., S. 198; Mussner, *Kairos* 18 (1976), S. 243f, 249; Schlier, *Römer*, S. 339f; Cranfield, *Romans*, S. 574ff.

33 Zu Röm. 11.25a vgl. G. Bornkamm, Art. μυστήριον, *TWNT* iv, Stuttgart 1942, S. 829; ferner Batey, aaO., S. 222f.

34 Immer noch beachtenswert ist die Untersuchung von H. Windisch, 'Die Sprüche vom Eingehen in das Reich Gottes', *ZNW* 27 (1928), S. 163–92.

35 Zu dem hier nicht im einzelnen berücksichtigten Abschnitt Röm. 11.28–32 sei vor allem auf Barrett, *Romans*, S. 224ff, und Käsemann, *Römer*, S. 301ff, verwiesen.

36 Zum Schriftzitat vgl. Michel, *Römer*, S. 357f; Luz, *Geschichtsverständnis*, S. 294f. Stuhlmacher, *Zur Interpretation*, S. 559ff, will V. 25–7 auch in Zusammenhang mit der modifizierten Vorstellung von der Völkerwall-

fahrt verstehen, doch m.E. klingt dieses Motiv hier nur schwach an. ὁ ῥυόμενος ist auf Christus, nicht auf Gott zu beziehen; gegen Mayer, *Heilsratschluss*, S. 291f. Ferner ist ἥξει futurisch zu erklären und nicht auf das geschichtliche Kommen Jesu zu beziehen; gegen D. Zeller, 'Israel unter dem Ruf Gottes (Röm. 9–11)', *Internat. kath. Zeitschr.* 2 (1973), S. 289–301, dort S. 296.

37 Mussner, *Kairos* 18 (1976), S. 245ff, 250f, beruft sich daher im besonderen auch noch auf den Sprachgebrauch von σῴζειν, σωτηρία, was aber m.E. nichts austrägt.

38 Vgl. ἀσέβεια, ἀσεβής in Röm. 1.18; 4.5; 5.6; ἀπείθεια, ἀπειθεῖν in Röm. 2.8; 10.21; 11.30–2; ἀπιστία, ἀπιστεῖν in Röm. 3.3; 4.20; 11.20, 23.

39 Das wird auch von Mussner, aaO., S. 252f, gesehen.

40 Dazu vgl. Michel, *Römer*, S. 340ff.

41 Jeremias, aaO., S. 201: 'Der Kern des Mysteriums liegt in der Konjunktion ἄχρι οὗ'.

42 Vielleicht kann man aufgrund der Kette 'verkündigen—hören—glauben—anrufen' in Röm. 10.14f sogar darauf schliessen, dass Paulus, der im Blick auf die Heilsvollendung von der Umkehrung der Reihenfolge Juden-Heiden ausgeht, auch hier die Vorstellung von der erneuten endzeitlichen Verkündigung des Evangeliums—des 'ewigen Evangeliums' nach Apk 14.6, das kurz vor dem Ende den heidnischen Völkern vom Himmel her verkündigt werden soll—nun abgewandelt auf das Volk Israel anwendet, ohne im einzelnen zu sagen, welche konkrete Vorstellung er dabei hat. Zu Apk 14.6 vgl. mein Buch über *Mission*, S. 47f. Auf einen Zusammenhang zwischen Röm. 11.6f und Markus 13.10 hat schon O. Cullmann, *Der eschatologische Charakter des Missionsauftrags und des apostolischen Selbstbewusstseins bei Paulus* (franz. 1936), in ders., *Vorträge und Aufsätze 1925–62*, Tübingen 1966, S. 305–36, dort S. 328, hingewiesen; ebenso Käsemann, *Römer* S. 299f.

43 Hierzu vgl. G. Delling, Art. πλήρωμα, *TWNT* vi, Stuttgart 1965, S. 297–304.

44 Ausser Mussner vgl. K. L. Schmidt, aaO., S. 32ff, 38f; Eichholz, aaO., S. 301.

45 Das Problem lässt sich keinesfalls so lösen, dass man Röm. 11.25–7 als sekundären Zusatz ansieht; so Chr. Plag, *Israels Weg zum Heil* (*Arb. z. Theol.* I/40), Stuttgart 1969, vgl. S. 36ff, 66ff. In eine verwandte Richtung gehen die sachkritischen Erwägungen bei C. H. Dodd, *The Epistle of Paul to the Romans* (*MNTC*), London 1932, S. 182f.

46 So G. Delling, *TWNT* vi, S. 303; Barrett, *Romans*, S. 213f; Käsemann, *Römer*, S. 292; mit ausführlicher Begründung Cranfield, *Romans*, S. 556ff.

47 Vgl. W. Bauer, *Griechisch-deutsches Wörterbuch zu den Schriften des Neuen Testaments und der übrigen urchristlichen Literatur*, Berlin ⁵1963, Sp. 691, 1334; ebenso Schlier, *Römer*, S.327f. Vgl. den Sprachgebrauch in Röm. 13.10.

48 Vgl. P. Benoit, 'Israel dans l'histoire du salut', in ders., *Exégèse et Théologie*, vol. III, Paris 1968, S. 400–21, dort S. 418: 'De toute façon il faut observer

que Paul considère ici les collectivités plutôt que les individus . . . le "tout Israel" . . . exprime tout au plus un retour en masse du peuple juif sans affirmer le salut de chaque juif en particulier'. Vgl. auch Luz, *Geschichtsverständnis*, S. 291f; Zeller, *Juden und Heiden*, S. 253ff; Käsemann, *Römer*, S. 300; Schlier, *Römer*, S. 340f.

49 Im Blick auf die Vollendung gilt dann aber, dass alle das Erbarmen Gottes erfahren haben und dass es keinerlei Sonderstellung mehr gibt; vgl. G. Schrenk, *Die Weissagung über Israel im Neuen Testament*, Zürich 1951, S. 36f.

50 Zum inneren Zusammenhang von Röm. 9–11 mit der Rechtfertigungslehre des Paulus vgl. Müller, aaO., S. 106ff; Käsemann, 'Rechtfertigung und Heilsgeschichte im Römerbrief', in ders., *Paulinische Perspektiven*, Tübingen 1969, S. 108–39, bes. S. 134f; Kümmel, 'Probleme', De Lorenzi, *Israelfrage*, S. 22, 28ff.

51 Nachträglich verweise ich noch auf Ulrich Wilckens, *Der Brief an die Römer* Bd. 2, (EKK VI/2), Zürich-Neukirchen 1980, S. 251–68.

In the phrase 'and so all Israel shall be saved' (Rom. 11.26a) it is improbable that 'all Israel' means the church made up of Jews and Gentiles (Gal. 6.16) or the total number of Israelites. It therefore refers either to a representative number of Israelites or to a special way of salvation for all Israelites which is independent of faith and the gospel and rests solely upon their initial election. The latter, currently popular, view is probably wrong. A correct interpretation of this verse depends not only upon the immediate context (vv. 25–7), but also upon its setting in Rom. 9–11 and in Pauline theology as a whole.

For Paul, inheritance of the promise to Abraham comes through faith rather than physical descent, which is why justification is an important theme in Rom. 9.30—10.21. Yet the fate of Israel is closely tied to the question of God's faithfulness. The paradox is set up in 9.6–7—the word of God cannot fail, and yet not all descendants of Israel are true Israelites—and first answered in 11.25f.

'Israel' is for Paul an honorific term, implying election and an ongoing, unfinished plan of God. The election of Israel was the first stage in God's plan, the influx of the Gentiles the second and the return of Israel, moved by jealousy of the Gentiles, the third. The hardening of the Jews, therefore, is not merely a human phenomenon or the result of universal human sin (Rom. 1.18—3.20, 5.12–19) but a specific part of God's plan; and their salvation is not just a possibility, but a certainty based on God's promise.

The saving of 'all Israel', as of the 'fulness of the Gentiles', is an eschatological event (11.25, 28–32) about which Paul is deliberately terse. The temporary hardening of Israel and the admission of the Gentiles are the necessary premiss (οὕτως, v. 26a is retrospective rather than correlative) for the future salvation of Israel (vv. 25b–6a). How will Israel be saved? It is true that the mixed quotation in vv. 26b–7 does not speak of conversion and faith, but we cannot confidently use an *argumentum e silentio*. Moreover, the quotation does speak of the banishment of ἀσέβεια from Israel, which is equivalent to the banishment of ἀπείθεια and ἀπιστία, and implies a new relationship to God, a new covenant based on faith (as in the rest of the NT). The importance of faith for salvation is also clear in Rom. 10.11–14; 11.23 and it is unlikely that Paul would contradict these or his statement that not all from Israel belong to Israel (9.6).

'All Israel' may be equivalent to the 'fulness' of Israel in 11.12 and thus to the 'fulness' (i.e., the great number, rather than the totality) of the Gentiles (11.25). However, 'all' is probably comprehensive, is closely related to the 'fulness of the Gentiles', and implies that in percentage terms the number of Israelites who will be saved will exceed the number of Gentiles. The salvation of the Israelites, like that of the Gentiles, will depend upon conversion and faith.

19

Paul and the
Πνευματικοί at Corinth

John Painter

The problem of the πνευματικοί at Corinth is notoriously difficult and complex. The word, not found in any Greek version of the Old Testament, is almost a Paulinism. It is found only in Rom. (3 times), 1 Cor. (14), Gal. (1), Eph. (3), Col. (2), 1 Pet. (2).[1] In Rom., Eph., Col. and 1 Pet. the word is always used adjectively in such expressions as 'spiritual songs', 'spiritual house', etc., as also in 1 Cor. 10.3–4; 15.44. The absolute use of οἱ πνευματικοί referring to 'the people of the Spirit' is distinctive to 1 Cor. having only Gal. 6.1 as a *formal* parallel. But the Corinthian situation is distinctive as is indicated by the following:

1. The concentration of use in 1 Cor. signals attention.

2. In Gal. οἱ πνευματικοί is Paul's designation for those who manifest the fruit of the Spirit, Gal. 5.16—6.1, while the polemical context at Corinth is clear and Paul is repudiating the claims of the self-styled πνευματικοί, 3.1.

3. At Corinth the πνευματικοί are also called τέλειοι and they refer to others as ψυχικοί and σαρκικοί (σάρκινοι), also called νήπιοι.

4. The self-styled πνευματικοί/τέλειοι claim to possess σοφία, γνῶσις and ἡ φανέρωσις τοῦ πνεύματος.

5. In addition to the *constellation of terms* already mentioned there are other expressions, not common in the *corpus Paulinum*, which fit into the emerging pattern such as μυστήριον; οἱ ἄρχοντες τοῦ αἰῶνος τούτου; τὰ βάθη τοῦ Θεοῦ. This pattern suggests the specific and distinctive nature of the problem encountered at Corinth.[2]

Various solutions have been proposed in response to the problems raised by this material:

I. It is suggested that what we have is wholly a Pauline construction of his own teaching.

II. Alternatively it is suggested that Paul is responding to an immature expression of his own teaching.

III. Paul is countering the teaching of envoys of the Jesusalem church.

IV. Paul is opposing the teaching of Gnosticism or mystery cults.

I *A Pauline Construction?*

The πνευματικοί also appear to be related to the problem of divisions at Corinth. According to Hans Conzelmann what Paul opposed was the Corinthian *penchant* for divisions which did not arise out of any deep-seated theological differences in the community.[3] Thus he suggests that the motifs and terms of I Cor. are Pauline and were not taken over by him from his opponents and that even 2.6–16 is his composition using motifs and terms from Jewish and Christian apocalyptic-wisdom theology.[4] Robin Scroggs recognizes that 'Paul nowhere else in his extant correspondence suggests he has such a teaching (σοφία for the τέλειοι) nor are several words and phrases which appear here repeated elsewhere in Paul', but paradoxically concludes that Paul 'does have an esoteric wisdom teaching in which he instructs only a few' and '2.6–16 must be seen as an expression of Paul's own theological position'.[5] But *general parallels* with the Jewish wisdom literature fail to explain the *specific terminology* which appears to signal gentile influence.[6] Scroggs acknowledges the parallels in Gnosticism but comments, 'Paul never uses the noun ψυχή in a negative sense as do the gnostics.'[7] He also notes that Paul's use of τέλειοι 'is formally similar to that of the mysteries' and 'not prominent in Jewish wisdom literature'[8] but concludes that 'Paul cannot have meant by the word what its strict use in the mysteries was – to denote people who had undertaken certain initiations' and that 'Paul's use of mystery terminology can only be metaphorical in character'.[9] Naturally if Paul used the language of his gnostic or mystery cult *opponents* he could do so only by redefining the mythical language and giving it a metaphorical sense. Thus pagan and Jewish literary characteristics exist[10] side by side in I Cor. and it might well be that the pagan religious characteristics are a reflection of Paul's opponents while the Jewish wisdom characteristics were introduced by Paul in the construction of his response, though this is probably an oversimplification as the opponents also seem to have used 'wisdom' motifs.

II *Paul's Response to his own Earlier Position?*

According to J. C. Hurd Paul was responsible for the position of the πνευματικοί, having taught the Corinthians to practise and value glossolalia.[11] Subsequently he had matured and come to terms with the 'Jerusalem decree' which he communicated to the Corinthians in his 'previous letter' (5.9), modifying his original position. The Corinthians replied expressing bewilderment and anger at his blatant changes (7.1, etc.). Paul's response (1 Cor.) could not directly criticize glossolalia without going back on his original position. 1 Cor. is an attempt to reconcile his original position with the 'previous letter'. John Drane[12] develops this position by arguing that the 'Jerusalem decree' established two levels of Christians, law keepers and partial law keepers. The Corinthians responded with a gentile evaluation in terms of the strong and the weak. He also interprets the Corinthian response as a gnosticizing of Paul's extreme response to Jewish legalism (Galatians) in the pagan context of Corinth while 1 Cor. borders on legalism in response to the gnosticizing Corinthians. The observation of the role of the pagan context at Corinth is important and *seems* to be recognized by Hurd when he asks why Paul began 'his treatment of the Holy Spirit by mentioning first the enthusiasms of idol worshippers', 12.2.[13] This observation does not fit well with the view that Paul introduced glossolalia to Corinth.

III   *Paul's Response to Envoys of the Jerusalem Church?*

Cephas probably visited Corinth (1.12; 3.22) mediating the influence of the Jerusalem church.[14] It is argued that he demanded glossolalia as the manifestation of the Spirit and distinctive mark of the Palestinian mission,[15] and Paul was reluctant to criticize Cephas.[16] Paul's oblique criticism does constitute a problem but the explanation is not to be found in his reluctance to criticize Cephas, see Gal. 2.11.

Gerd Theissen[17] also sees a conflict between the Pauline and Palestinian missions at Corinth. He argues that wandering charismatic prophets from rural, peasant-class Palestinian Christianity portrayed Paul as a faithless missionary because he did not accept payment from the Corinthians, 1 Cor. 9.3–18. But there is no evidence that criticism of Paul comes from outside the Corinthian community until the appearance of the 'intruders' of 2 Cor. and then the problem of the πνευματικοί with their σοφία, γνῶσις and glossolalia had disappeared.[18] But in their opposition to Paul the 'intruders', who perhaps identified themselves with the Cephas party, adopted the 'Corinthian criteria' of spirituality in order to further their own cause, 2 Cor. 12.1–10. These criteria appear to be the expression of the values of an *urban minority élite*[19] which claimed a superior status of σοφία, γνῶσις and the φανέρωσις τοῦ πνεύματος. In 1 Cor. Paul is opposed to those values and criteria without the complication of the 'intruders'. Paul's ironical criticism of those who boasted in their 'natural abilities' and possessions (1 Cor. 4.6ff) fits well in the context of the critique of a privileged élite. But it was with the privileged élite of pagan Corinth that Paul takes issue in 1 Cor.

IV *Paul's Response to Gnosticism or Mystery Cults?*

Recognition of the importance of Paul's conflict with the πνευματικοί in 1 Cor. arises from awareness of the focus on them in chapters 1—4 and 12—14 which are also linked by the use of χαρίσμα, 1.7; 12.4, 9, 28, 30, 31; σχίσμα 1.10; 12.25; the contrast between τέλειος and νήπιος 2.6; 3.1; 13.10—11 (14.20); the use of ζῆλος and ζηλόω in the negative sense of jealousy 3.1; 13.4; μυστήριον 2.1, 7; 4.1; 13.2; 14.2; σοφία sixteen times in chapters 1—4 and in 12.8, nowhere else in 1 Cor. and rarely elsewhere in Paul; σημεῖον 1.22; 14.22; and a general parallelism of argument in the two sections. Thus it appears that chapters 1—4 and 12—14 are Paul's response to pneumatic wisdom at Corinth.[20] The constellation of terms used by the self-styled πνευματικοί, to which attention has been drawn, was also used by certain gnostic sects[21] and in the mystery cults.[22] The use of this language does not in itself prove gnostic influence as it is possible that Paul's language influenced the development of later Gnosticism.[23] But this fails to explain the 'un-Pauline' complex of language, the use of which constitutes a problem. Certainly Paul was not a Gnostic[24] but the language seems to have been drawn from his opponents whose pagan origins are noted, 1.22f; 12.2; 14.23. Could these opponents have been Gnostics?

The problem of the origin of Gnosticism is complex and partly semantic, a problem of definition.[25] But it also concerns the question of whether Gnosticism is a child of Christianity or Judaism or is an intrusion into both. While the evidence is inconclusive it seems probable that Gnosticism is pre-Christian in origin.[26] But it should not be assumed that earlier and later forms were identical. Thus the question arises, what makes Gnosticism gnostic? Is a redeemer presupposed or is redemption guaranteed by origin? If the latter, it is better characterized as an anthropological myth,[27] the redeemer myth being a secondary feature made *common* by the influence of the Christian redeemer.[28] Thus Ulrich Wilckens[29] seems to be right in recognizing the polemical context of 1 Cor. 1—2 and that Paul's language in 2.6–16 was 'intentionally formed according to the language of his opponents' but (*pace* Wilckens) the christological development is probably Paul's in response to the anthropology of his opponents, 1.24, 30. That does not exclude the possibility that the opponents had an unacceptable (to Paul) Christology expressed perhaps in the slogan 'I am of Christ' understood in the mythological sense of the corporate primal man.[30]

A *Wisdom*

Paul's use of σοφία in 1 Cor. 1—2 is varied, but this does not prove that the πνευματικοί did not have a unified mythical use. A mythical use does seem to underlie some uses in this section.[31] Paul's response to σοφία at Corinth is presented in two related stages, 1.18—2.5 and 2.6–16. In the first section Paul sets the kerygma, the word of the cross, in opposition to the Corinthian claim to wisdom. He argues that theirs was not true wisdom, opening the way for the presentation of the true wisdom of God in the second section. The two sections reveal the struggle between two opposed evaluative standpoints, Paul's and the self-styled πνευματικοί.[32] They regarded the preaching of the crucified one as μωρία, 1.18, while Paul *described* their wisdom in terms of persuasive speech, probably ecstatic, 1.17; 2.1, 4, 13, which led to boasting, καυχᾶσθαι, 1.26–31; 4.6–8.[33] In 4.6 the ἃ γέγραπται looks back to the quotation of Jer. 9.24 in 1.31 and the theme which it concludes. The kerygma excludes *boasting* before God, 1.29, and it is in terms of boasting that Paul *evaluates* those who think of themselves as πνευματικοί while regarding others as ψυχικοί or σαρκικοί, 4.6–7. The comparison of Paul and Apollos in 4.6 illustrates the point that boasting arises from an *inflated* pride which causes discrimination of the one against the other and obscures the place of each in the economy of God (3.4–9), that is, the necessary diversity expressed in the χαρίσματα of 12.4ff. The diversity is a manifestation of the manifold *gifts* from the one God, Lord, Spirit. Because these things are *gifts* they should not become the basis of pride and boasting before God, 4.7. The use of φυσιοῦσθε in 4.7 is a Paulinism, used elsewhere only in 4.18f; 5.2; 8.1; 13.4; Col. 2.18 and see also 2 Cor. 12.20. The use of the word links 4.6–7; 8.1; 13.4. This association becomes an argument. The σοφία and γνῶσις of the πνευματικοί are the basis of the pride which divides the community (cf. 1.10–11) whereas ἀγάπη οἰκοδομεῖ the com-

241

munity. This contrast is transferred to the discussion of glossolalia and prophecy, 'he who speaks in a tongue builds up himself, but he who prophesies builds up the church', 14.4. Both 14.4 and 8.1 are linked by the use of οἰκοδομεῖν but the ἑαυτὸν οἰκοδομεῖ of 14.4 falls under the critique of ἀγάπη which οὐ ζητεῖ τὰ ἑαυτῆς, 13.5.

If the πνευματικοί *evaluated* Paul's kerygma as μωρία, 1.23, he *evaluated* their wisdom as the wisdom of the *world*, 1.20f; 2.6; 3.19; which God has made foolish, 1.20. The *world* probably was understood in a negative sense by the Corinthians, and this could be a reversal of their own evaluation of his kerygma which he defended in two ways. He asserts: firstly, if the kerygma is μωρία it is the foolishness of God, which is wiser than men, 1.25; secondly, what the *world* has called foolishness is in fact the wisdom of God, 1.24. This reversal is characteristic of Paul's apologetic method (1 Cor. 9.19–23) because the preaching of the cross as the saving event is the reversal of human values, 2.5; 4.8–13, which leaves no room for boasting before God but only boasting in the Lord whose wisdom and power are manifest in the situation of human suffering and weakness, 1.29–31; 4.8ff.

In 2.6–16 Paul discusses the true wisdom of God which he communicates to the τέλειοι/πνευματικοί[34] amongst whom he cannot include the self-styled πνευματικοί, 3.1. Much of the language is drawn from his opponents but he has reversed their evaluation. Theirs is the wisdom of the world, of this age, while his wisdom is spiritual, taught by the Spirit to the πνευματικοί, 2.13. But the ψυχικὸς ἄνθρωπος rejects the things of the Spirit as μωρία, 2.14, just as the perishing reject his kerygma as μωρία, 1.18. Thus Paul's σοφία is the preaching of the cross[35] which is taught by the Spirit and leads to the fulfilment of νοῦς, ἡμεῖς δὲ νοῦν Χριστοῦ ἔχομεν, 2.16. But glossolalia, according to Paul, involves the negation of νοῦς, 14.14.

B *Glossolalia*

Paul's response to the enquiry[36] about the πνευματικοί[37] runs through chapters 12—14, which are bound together by the discussion of the *evaluation* of glossolalia. The πνευματικοί claimed to manifest the Spirit in some form of ecstatic speech and Paul, who became a proclaimer of σοφία to those who claimed to be wise (2.6–16), here becomes a πνευματικός to the self-styled πνευματικοί, a tongue speaker to those who spoke in tongues.[38] It is not only the constellation of language that draws attention to the mysteries. In 12.2 Paul refers to the background of the Corinthians in the ecstatic religion of paganism, e.g. the Dionysus cult.[39] The language 'suggests moments of ecstasy experienced in heathen religion, when a human being is (or is believed to be) possessed by a supernatural; for example in Lucian's *Dialogi Mortuorum* xix. 1'.[40] Thus the problem of the πνευματικοί is to be understood in the context of pagan ecstatic religion. While ecstasy was commonly expressed in glossolalia the speech was sometimes intelligible. For Paul ecstasy was not an adequate criterion for evaluating the claims of the πνευματικοί. His first criterion concerned content. Those who confess 'Jesus is Lord' do so by the Holy Spirit, whether or not they speak ecstatically and no utterance of 'Ανάθεμα 'Ιησοῦς,[41] however ecstatic, is inspired by the Spirit of God, 12.3. In this way Paul redefines the acceptable meaning of πνευματικός by calling the criterion of ecstasy into question. This is taken a stage further by the introduction of the term χαρίσματα,[42] stressing *gifts*, thus removing the ground for pride and boasting, 12.4 and see 4.6–7. The *plural* is in opposition to the claim that ecstasy, especially glossolalia, was *the* manifestation of the Spirit, revealing those baptized in the Spirit, 12.7, 13. Paul denied the exclusive criterion and argued that many gifts manifest the Spirit so that all believers are members of the one body. The Corinthian πνευματικοί valued ecstasy without distinguishing prophecy from glossolalia (ecstatic = πνευματικός) but Paul distinguished prophecy from glossolalia[43] and the prophet from the Corinthian πνευματικός, 14.37[44] though in 14.1 he used the plural of the Corinthian term in his redefined sense of χαρίσματα, see 12.4ff.

The stress of 12.4–31 is on diversity,[45] the manifold gifts, a stress which makes sense in opposition to the claim that there is a single manifestation of the Spirit possessed by a few people. Diversity suggests equality but the gifts are graded, first . . . second . . . third . . . etc., 12.27–31, and there are greater and lesser gifts, 12.31; 14.5. According to the three lists in 1 Cor. glossolalia is consistently last. It seems that Paul is attempting to modify the Corinthian evaluation of glossolalia by denying that it has an exclusive place and then listing it low in the order of priorities. Glossolalia is mentioned nowhere else in the Pauline letters.[46] Thus it would be a mistake to see the practice as normative in the Pauline communities. Paul wrote about glossolalia because he considered the Corinthian practice to be an abuse.

Chapter 13 is an integral part of the polemic[47] against the Corinthian evaluation of glossolalia. The distinction between the tongues of men and of angels is puzzling. Perhaps the Corinthians claimed that in glossolalia they were 'speaking to God' (14.2) in the language of angels which no man understands and that this was a sign to believers, 14.20–5. This is consistent with their practice of glossolalia 'in church' without interpretation. Contrary to this Paul asserts that αἱ γλῶσσαι are a sign to unbelievers. But the illustration that follows shows the uselessness of the *Corinthian* practice of glossolalia for unbelievers and the effectiveness of prophecy. Perhaps we are to understand an alternative form of tongues (ἐν ἑτερογλώσσοις) in the quotation of Isa. 28.11f in 1 Cor. 14.21 which like Acts 2.4ff ἑτέραις γλώσσαις and ἡμεῖς ἀκούομεν ἕκαστος τῇ ἰδίᾳ διαλέκτῳ ἡμῶν . . . would naturally refer to intelligible human languages. Such a manifestation would be a sign to unbelievers. But the outsider coming into the *Corinthian* church hears only the babble of ecstatic speech and concludes μαίνεσθε,[48] 14.23, equating the practice with pagan ecstasy. Such an interpretation makes sense of 1 Cor. 14.20–5 but involves taking the tradition of Acts 2.4ff at face value without recognizing conflicting details in Luke's account. According to Acts 2.13, 15 the hearers thought the speakers were drunk, which perhaps accords more easily with μαίνεσθε in 1 Cor. 14.23 than the account in Acts 2.4ff. Whether Luke has interpreted the tradition in Acts in terms of the Corinthian practice at this point or theologized the tradition, so that Pentecost becomes the reversal of Babel, perhaps must be left open.[49] But if we exclude such an explanation, Paul's argument in 1 Cor. 14.20–5 must be set out as follows: Tongues are not a sign for believers but for unbelievers. Tongues are ineffective for the conversion of unbelievers but prophecy is effective. Through intelligible prophecy the unbeliever comes to worship God and to confess 'God is certainly among you' (14.25) which presumably the Corinthian πνευματικοί claimed was manifest in glossolalia. The argument so stated is strange but conclusive.

Chapter 13 places all the gifts under the criterion of love. The gifts exist to make love actual in the community.[50] Love is fundamental because ἐκκλησίαν οἰκοδομεῖ, 14.4; cf. 8.1; 13.4. The fact that glossolalia does not build up the church, is not a manifestation of ἀγάπη, raises a serious question concerning its place among the χαρίσματα. While individual statements in chapter 14 can be taken as a recommendation of glossolalia the *drift* of the chapter is contrary to that interpretation. Perhaps Paul did not wish to *exclude* the practice, 14.39, especially in private. He certainly set out to exert some controls and to change the Corinthian evaluation of the practice. His apologetic method is clear in such passages as 14.5, 15f, 18ff. In each case he qualifies what first looks like approval and directs the Corinthians away from the practice.[51] In this way he protected himself against the charge of being 'unspiritual'.

c *Who were the* πνευματικοί?

Paul's treatment of the πνευματικοί and their σοφία was polemical. The polemic is directed against aberrations which arose, in Paul's view, from the pagan background of the Corinthian community. While chapter 1 discusses Jews and Greeks (gentiles), 1.22f, it is the σοφία of the Greeks that is the focus of the discussion, σοφία to the τέλειοι/πνευματικοί. The constellation of terminology peculiar to 1 Cor. draws our attention to Gnosticism and the mysteries. The problem of the πνευματικοί of 12.1ff is related to the background of the Corinthians in pagan ecstatic religion, 12.2, and Paul indicates that an outsider coming into their community would interpret what he saw and heard in those terms, 14.23. The evidence suggests that Paul saw the problem in terms of the influence of the pagan mysteries on Corinthian Christianity. The treatment of baptism and the Lord's supper suggests that the πνευματικοί might have interpreted Christianity as a greater mystery, see 1.14–16; 10.1ff; 11.17ff. But there is no evidence of a Corinthian gnostic redeemer myth. Paul was opposed to their understanding of man and 'spirituality' and their rejection of the proclamation of the cross as the saving event. If 'I am of Christ' was the slogan of the πνευματικοί it is possible that this was understood in a mythological sense indicating participation in the 'heavenly man'. But this is uncertain. Nor is it clear whether the πνευματικοί understood their position as inherent through their origin or as a result of initiation. Perhaps probability lies with the latter in the light of the place of baptism as an initiatory rite at Corinth. If this is true then it would seem that the influence of the mysteries on Christianity at Corinth led to a situation that could be called gnosticizing.[52]

Paul's critique of the situation was complicated by two factors. The language of the πνευματικοί was, in some respects, similar to his own but used with a different meaning. Further, their attitude of spiritual superiority laid him open to the charge of being unspiritual had he rejected their position outright, especially as his own position involved a reversal of typical human values. Thus his argument is sophisticated, subtle and indirect. Nevertheless it is a concerted attack on the status and claims of the self-styled πνευματικοί and an elaboration of criteria of spirituality consistent with the proclamation of the cross as the saving event.

NOTES

1   Even if Eph. and Col. are not by Paul they are in the Pauline tradition.

2   Thus the πνευματικοί and glossolalia are not the norm of the Pauline communities; see Walter Schmithals, *Gnosticism in Corinth* (Abingdon 1971), = *GIC*, p. 175 n89; and my 'The Charismatic Movement and the New Testament', *Journal of Theology for Southern Africa* 7 (June 1974), = 'CMNT', p. 57 n28.

3   *1 Corinthians* (Fortress Press 1975), pp. 14, 32, 34, 212ff, 235. The seriousness of the divisions is minimized also by Johannes Munck, *Paul and the Salvation of Mankind* (John Knox Press 1959), pp. 159–67; J. C. Hurd, *The Origin of 1 Corinthians* (SPCK 1965), = *OIC*, pp. 125, 193, 269.

4   Thus B. C. Johanson, 'Tongues, A Sign to Unbelievers', *NTS* 25 (1979), = 'Tongues', p. 199. E. E. Ellis, 'Spiritual Gifts in the Pauline Community', *NTS* 20, = 'SGPC', p. 130 suggests the activity of a pneumatic Pauline school. Conzelmann, *1 Cor.*, p. 8, also favours Jewish wisdom speculation but notes contact with the mysteries suggesting that *gnosis* was the Corinthian word and *wisdom* was introduced by Paul, p. 57. But outside 1 Cor. *wisdom* is not a characteristic Pauline word. However Conzelmann is not far from recognizing gnostic *gnosis* at Corinth, to which Paul responds with Jewish *wisdom*.

5   'Paul: ΣΟΦΟΣ and ΠΝΕΥΜΑΤΙΚΟΣ', *NTS* 14 (1967–8), = 'Paul', pp. 33–8. On the gnostic character of this complex see Schmithals, *GIC*, pp. 155, and 382 n275.

6   The gentile character of the problem is noted by Paul, 1.22f; 12.2; 14.23. Hurd, *OIC*, p. 227 notes the significance of 12.2, but does not relate it to the πνευματικοί and their practice of glossolalia.

7   'Paul', p. 52. See J. G. D. Dunn, *Unity and Diversity in the New Testament* (SCM 1977), p. 277.

8   'Paul', p. 38 n5 and Conzelmann, *1 Cor.*, pp. 39, 59ff.

9   ibid.

10 Recognized by Conzelmann, *1 Cor.*, p. 8.

11 *OIC*, p. 281.

12 *Paul: Libertine or Legalist* (SPCK 1975), = *Paul*, p. 122. For a brief critique of Drane's position see my review in *JTSA* 18 (1977), pp. 58f.

13 *OIC*, pp. 226f., 281.

14 T. W. Manson, *Studies in the Gospels and Epistles* (Manchester 1962), pp. 197–207; C. K. Barrett, 'Cephas and Corinth', in *Abraham unser Vater* (Leiden 1963), pp. 1–13; J. P. M. Sweet, 'A Sign to Unbelievers', *NTS* 13 (1966–7), = 'Sign', p. 246.

15 Thus Sweet, 'Sign', p. 246.

16 Sweet, 'Sign', p. 252.

17 'Legitimation und Lebensunterhalt', *NTS* 21 (1975), pp. 192–221.

18 C. K. Barrett, 'Christianity at Corinth', *BJRL* 46 (1963) = 'CAC', p. 276 and *2 Corinthians* (BNTC 1973), p. 6. The concentration of this vocabulary in 1 Cor. suggests that Paul took it over from the Corinthians.

19 See Gerd Theissen, 'Soziale Schichtung in der korinthischen Gemeinde', *ZNW* 65 (1974), pp. 232–72; and W. Wuellner, 'The Sociological implications of 1 Cor. 1.26–28', *Studia Evangelica* IV (1977), pp. 666–72.

20 See Johanson, 'Tongues', pp. 198f, and Scroggs, 'Paul', p. 38 n4.

21 E. H. Pagels, *The Gnostic Paul* (Fortress Press 1975), = *TGP*, pp. 53ff; and also *TDNT* ix, pp. 478, 656; and Nag Hammadi Texts (facsimile edn) I. 118, 37; I 19, 21; II. 145, 22; III. 55,3, for the use of πνευματικός ψυχικός ὑλικός.

22 R. R. Reitzenstein, *Die Hellenistischen Mysterienreligionen* (³Berlin 1927), pp. 67, 70f, 325ff, 333ff; and W. Scott, *Hermetica* IV (Oxford 1924), p. 105, 25. The Mysteries are conceived widely as pagan ecstatic religion. Either this is the source of the Corinthian *terminology* or no source is known to us. W. D. Davies, *Paul and Rabbinic Judaism* (SPCK 1955), pp. 193f, draws attention to the sparsity of the linguistic evidence and argues that Paul's terminology 'is best explained in the light of OT anthropology'. But πνευματικός is not found in any Greek version of the OT and it, with other terms, appears in the conflict at Corinth, introduced by Paul's opponents and used by Paul in a redefined sense. In Romans he was able to use it in a different way, not of the threefold division of people. Paul's meaning is perhaps to be understood in terms of OT anthropology but this does not explain the specific use of terms in a polemical context in 1 Cor.

23 Pagels, *TGP*, pp. 162ff, argues that the Gnostics derived the terms from Paul, appealing to Conzelmann, *1 Cor.*, p. 15, as does R. McL. Wilson, 'How Gnostic were the Corinthians?', *NTS* 19 (1972), = 'HGC', pp. 71f. But then how are we to account for Paul's terminology?

24 *Pace* Reitzenstein. Drane, *Paul*, pp. 2–3, 90, 96, 162 n11 *incorrectly* says that for Schmithals 'Paul himself was at heart some sort of Gnostic.' Pagels, *TGP*, p. 162, rightly recognizes Schmithals' rejection of Reitzenstein's position. According to Schmithals Paul derived the language of gnostic mythology through hellenistic Christianity without being aware of the mythological meaning. In the conflict at Corinth his opposition to the gnostic meaning becomes clear, *GIC*, pp. 63, 65, 71. Schmithals (p. 29) criticizes Reitzenstein for mistaking Paul's use of gnostic motifs for genuine Gnosticism.

25 Wilson, 'HGC', p. 74 etc.

26 Wilson, 'HGC', p. 71 points to the lack of evidence. This is explicable according to Schmithals, *GIC*, p. 79. According to J. M. Robinson, 'The Gnostic Library To-day', *NTS* 14 (1967–8), pp. 372ff; and *The Nag*

Hammadi Library (Harper and Row 1977), pp. 6–10, especially 9f, the Nag Hammadi material confirms the non-Christian origin of Gnosticism.

27 So Schmithals, *GIC*, p. 30 n12 who is thus able to refute Colpe's charge that he presents an *undifferentiated* pan-Gnosticism, p. 30 n11. Likewise Bultmann's 'emphasis on "development" and his qualification of "Gnosticism" generally have been ignored'. J. H. Charlesworth and R. A. Culpepper, 'The Odes of Solomon and the Gospel of John', *CBQ* 35 (1973), p. 318 n91.

28 That the redeemer figure was derived from Christianity is argued by R. McL. Wilson, *The Gnostic Problem* (Mowbrays 1958), p. 75; R. M. Grant, *Gnosticism: An Anthology* (Lutterworth 1965), p. 97. Schmithals, *GIC*, p. 82 n219 argues that Christianity was not the primary influence, noting the importance of Marduk and mystery cults, but R. H. Fuller, *The Foundations of New Testament Christology* (Lutterworth 1965), p. 97, quotes Schmithals to the effect that the appearance of an *historical* redeemer was due to Christian influence. Barrett, 'CAC', p. 280 n6, notes the difficulty.

29 *Weisheit und Torheit* (Tübingen 1959), p. 71; and *TDNT* vii, pp. 517–22. E. Schweizer, *TDNT* vi, p. 416, rightly says 'the cross has no place in this (gnostic) conception'.

30 Thus Schmithals, *GIC*, pp. 63–5, 70–1 who argues that this *underlies* (via hellenistic Christianity) Paul's use of ἐν Χριστῷ which Paul uses in a different sense.

31 On the variety see Barrett, 'CAC', pp. 277ff, and on the mythical sense see p. 280.

32 See Barrett, *2 Cor.*, p. viii. In 1 Cor. 15.44, 46 Paul has reversed the gnostic order of first πνευματικός and then ψυχικός. He also speaks of σῶμα πνευματικόν, distinguishing the σῶμα from such physical organs as the κοιλία, much to the confusion of the Corinthians, 6.13ff. See Schweizer, *TDNT* vi, p. 421.

33 On Paul's polemical use of the boasting motif see Bultmann, *TDNT*, iii, pp. 648–52. Paul's *evaluation* of the Corinthians should not be used in the reconstruction of their own understanding of their position, as is done by Scroggs, 'Paul', p. 54.

34 Scroggs, 'Paul', p. 47 n5 rejects the identification of the πνευματικοί with the τέλειοι. But this would be strange in the light of the identification of the σάρκινοις with the νήπιοις in 3.1.

35 Thus Bornkamm, *TDNT* iv, pp. 819f; Schweizer, *TDNT* vi, p. 425; Wilckens, *Weisheit . . .*, p. 220; Sweet, 'Sign', p. 253; but rejected by Scroggs, 'Paul', p. 37.

36 That the περὶ δέ of 7.1, 25; 8.1, 4; 12.1; 16.1, 12 refers back to a letter from the Corinthians is generally recognized, see Conzelmann, *1 Cor.*, p. 204, and Hurd *OIC* p. 63. Both recognize that the subject of 12.1 embraces chapters 12—14.

37 That the reference in 12.1 is to people is confirmed by the 'No one . . .' of

12.3 which takes up 12.1. Elsewhere Paul's use of the neuter is clear in such combinations as 10.3f.

38 Schmithals *JGIC*, p. 217, says Paul 'becomes a Gnostic to the Gnostics ... but only thereby to be heard in his ultimate concern.' See also pp. 264, 272f, and 1 Cor. 9.19–23.

39 Conzelmann, *1 Corinthians*² (BNTC 1971), p. 205 n12.

40 Barrett, *1 Cor.*, p. 278.

41 Barrett, *1 Cor.*, pp. 279ff, lists the main possible interpretations and concludes, 'A similar but more developed situation appears in 1 John 4.1–3, where the simple anathema is displaced by the docetic denial of the human life of the Son of God in the flesh.' See also Schweizer, *TDNT* vi, p. 423, and Schmithals, *GIC*, pp. 126, 350 n120. Perhaps the πνευματικοί distinguished the earthly Jesus from the heavenly Christ enabling them to say Jesus is accursed while confessing the heavenly Christ. This is reversed by Paul who proclaimed *Christ* crucified (1.23) and *Jesus* as Lord, 12.3.

42 D. Moody Smith, 'Glossolalia and Other Spiritual Gifts in a New Testament Perspective', *Interpretation* 28 (1974), p. 311, suggests that *pneumatika* was the Corinthian's word and *charismata* Paul's. This is supported by the use of the latter in Rom. 12.6, but it is probable that the Corinthians thought of a single πνευματικόν.

43 According to Bornkamm Paul was the first to make this distinction. If this is so the contrast of the value of the two in chapter 14 becomes even more significant.

44 *Pace* Schmithals, *GIC*, p. 284, and Schweizer *TDNT* vi, p. 423. 1 Cor. 14.37 reads 'If anyone thinks he is a prophet *or* a pneumatic . . .'

45 Hurd, *OIC* p. 186ff.

46 It does not appear in the lists of Rom. 12.6ff or Eph. 4.7–16. Whether or not Paul elsewhere *alludes* to the practice is debatable.

47 Recognized by Reitzenstein, see N. Johansson, '1 Cor. 13 and 1 Cor. 14', *NTS* 10 (1963–4), p. 383. On the polemical character of chapters 12—14 see Sweet, 'Sign', p. 240; F. W. Beare, 'Speaking with Tongues', *JBL* 83 (1964), = 'SWT', pp. 243f; Hurd, *OIC*, pp. 89 n1, 186–93.

48 The word implies 'You are possessed; it could suggest something like the Bacchic frenzy . . .', C. K. Barrett, *1 Cor.*, p. 326.

49 Some contemporary reports suggest that various languages are sometimes spoken in glossolalia. That contemporary data are relevant has been argued by E. Best, 'The Interpretation of Tongues', *SJT* 28 (1975), p. 52. That glossolalia in the NT refers to various human languages has been argued by J. G. Davies, 'Pentecost and Glossolalia', *JTS* ns 3 (1952), pp. 228–31. See also R. H. Gundry, 'Ecstatic Utterance (NEB)?', *JTS* ns 17 (1966), pp. 299–307, and A. C. Thiselton, 'The "Interpretation" of Tongues', *JTS* ns 30 (1979), pp. 28–31.

50 For an analysis of 1 Cor. 13 in terms of the criterion of love see Karl Barth, *Church Dogmatics* IV, 2 (Edinburgh 1958), pp. 824–40, 'Love alone counts

249

. . . conquers . . . endures.' 'Love is . . . the essence and power of all διακονία.'

51 See my 'CMNT', p. 58, and Beare, 'SWT', pp. 243f. For example: How could Paul know that he spoke in tongues more than any of the Corinthians? This is not the point! The assertion allowed him to continue, 'but . . . ' without laying himself open to the charge of being *unspiritual*.

52 According to Schmithals, *GIC*, pp. 149, 246 the mysteries and Gnosticism had much in common; a pessimistic world rejection arising from a metaphysical dualism where the idea of escape from the evil world is primary, see Barrett, 'CAC', p. 280 n6. Consistent Gnosticism involved salvation by nature whereas the mysteries taught salvation through initiation, Schmithals, *GIC*, pp. 148f. In fact this distinction is blurred, perhaps because of the syncretistic nature of the phenomena. If the redeemer myth was not original and essential to Gnosticism its distance from the mysteries is greatly reduced. Both appear to have understood the pneumatic status in terms of ecstasy. This is well attested in terms of the oracles, e.g. Delphi. On pneumatic ecstasy in Gnosticism see Schweizer *TDNT* vi, p. 432.

20

Faith and Love Promoting Hope
An interpretation of Philemon v. 6

Harald Riesenfeld

Few passages in the New Testament have been interpreted and translated in so many different ways as has been done with Philem. v. 6.

4 I thank my God always when I remember you in my prayers, 5 because I hear of your love and of the faith which you have toward the Lord Jesus and all the saints, 6 and I pray that the sharing of your faith may promote the knowledge of all the good that is ours in Christ. 7 For I have derived much joy and comfort from your love, my brother, because the hearts of the saints have been refreshed through you. (RSV)

6 My prayer is that your fellowship with us in our common faith may deepen the understanding of all the blessings that our union with Christ brings us (*or* that bring us to Christ). (NEB)

6 My prayer is that our fellowship with you as believers will bring about a deeper understanding of every blessing which we have in our life in union with Christ. (Good News Bible)

6 I pray that this faith will give rise to a sense of fellowship that will show you all the good things that we are able to do for Christ. (Jerusalem Bible)

From these examples we can draw the conclusion that there is not the slightest consensus about what Paul really wants to make known to his friend Philemon in this single sentence.

It is obvious that four elements in the sentence, words or groups of words, are in fact being understood, by translators and interpreters in our time, in very different ways. These elements are ἡ κοινωνία τῆς πίστεώς σου, παντὸς ἀγαθοῦ, τοῦ ἐν ἡμῖν/ὑμῖν and εἰς Χριστόν. Only the middle part of the sentence is to a certain extent unambiguous:

251

something should show its efficiency (ἐνεργὴς γένηται) in promoting a thorough knowledge (ἐν ἐπιγνώσει). But there we cannot omit to ask whose knowledge Paul speaks of, and once again the answers differ.

In order to tackle this difficult little piece of Greek text, it might be wise first to take the immediate context, i.e. vv. 4–7, into consideration from the point of view of both form and context.

As usual in his epistles, Paul proceeds from the opening salutation, vv. 1–3, to thanksgiving and prayer, vv. 4–7. The apostle is anxious to thank God every time that he in his prayers remembers the person or the church to whom an epistle is addressed, v. 4. This time he expresses his gratitude because of the report which he has received: Philemon has done excellent work in the Christian congregation which he is in charge of, v. 5. (Probably he lives at Colossae or in some place in the neighbourhood of that town in the inner parts of Asia Minor.) From thanksgiving Paul goes on to a prayer which has the form of a final clause with ὅπως.

There is no verb governing the dependent clause; the idea of prayer can easily be supplemented from ἐπὶ τῶν προσευχῶν μου in v. 4. An explanatory sentence (introduced by γάρ) concludes the thanksgiving: Paul says that he has derived joy and comfort from Philemon's successful work among his fellow Christians. With this statement the wheel has come full circle, and we are back where Paul started in v. 4: information on Philemon's laudable work which he has received is the reason why he thanks God when he remembers his friend in his prayers.

As a general rule concerning the Pauline epistles it can be stated that whenever their author in his introductory thanksgivings remembers distinctive addressees, his thoughts are continuously centred on the Christian life and the needs of precisely these correspondents. In the epistle to Philemon this is particularly justified because the thanksgiving undoubtedly has been worded in view of the main theme of the letter: the appeal in favour of Onesimus. Though being a thanksgiving in their form, the opening verses of the letter are in fact, as regards their content, a *captatio benevolentiae* which is intended to make Philemon favourably disposed in view of the request which is going to be made and which is the main theme of the letter.

This understanding of the function of vv. 4–7 in the framework of the whole letter indicates that the prayer in v. 6 is likewise focused on Philemon and his work among his fellow Christians. Paul prays neither for progress in his own faith as a consequence of his relation to

Philemon nor for progress in Philemon's faith as a result of his fellowship with Paul. The reason for the apostle's thanksgiving is the fact that Philemon's belief in the Lord Jesus has manifested itself in love toward all saints, i.e. Christians in the local church where Philemon is active, v. 5. A source of joy and refreshment for the apostle is the fact that the hearts of the saints have been refreshed through Philemon, v. 7. The context of vv. 4–7 makes it almost certain that v. 6 deals with Philemon and the Christians he is in charge of.

After these considerations we can set about scrutinizing the details of v. 6. The central word in this prayer is ἐπίγνωσις, 'thorough understanding'. Paul prays that a thorough understanding may be promoted. As Lightfoot pointed out in his commentary on Philem. v. 6 and Col. 1.9, Paul's prayer for his correspondents, in the captivity epistles, culminates in this word ἐπίγνωσις, Eph. 1.7; Phil. 1.9; Col. 1.9 and here. Thorough understanding is the result and the reward of faith manifesting itself in deeds of love. But who is the subject in the act of understanding which is envisaged here? It is certainly not Paul, though even this idea has been adopted (Good News Bible). In his opening thanksgivings the apostle does not reflect on the progress of his own faith but concentrates his attention on the growth of Christian life in the community which he addresses. From this point of view it is not even likely that Philemon, and exclusively he himself, is the logical subject of ἐπίγνωσις. The context makes it plausible that Philemon's faith and his love towards the saints, i.e. his fellow Christians, have supported the spiritual growth of his congregation, and the most spectacular sign of this growth is precisely a more thorough understanding. The object of this understanding we shall deal with later.

The crucial point in our passage lies beyond doubt in the words ἡ κοινωνία τῆς πίστεώς σου. What does κοινωνία mean in this passage? And does the pronoun σού belong to τῆς πίστεως or to ἡ κοινωνία (or rather to ἡ κοινωνία τῆς πίστεως as a whole)? Both combinations are possible from the point of view of mere grammar.

The combination of σού with κοινωνία appears in the following translations: 'your fellowship with us in our common faith' (NEB); 'ta participation à la foi' (Traduction oecuménique de la Bible); 'deine Glaubensgemeinschaft' (Dibelius in his commentary, 1953); 'dein Anteil am Glauben' (Lohse in his commentary, 1968); 'deine Teilnahme am Glauben' (Stuhlmacher in his commentary, 1975); 'your sharing of the faith with others' (NAB). A survey of the various translations can be found in C. F. D. Moule's commentary (1957). A rather cryptic wording might be added: 'unser gemeinsamer Glaube in dir' (Einheitsübersetzung der Heiligen Schrift, 1979).

An immediate dependence of σού upon τῆς πίστεως has been supposed in translations like these: 'the sharing of your faith' (RSV); 'die Gemeinschaft deines Glaubens' (Lohmeyer in his commentary, 1929); 'their sharing in your faith' (J. A. Fitzmyer in the Jerome Biblical Commentary, 1969). A somewhat fanciful translation is presented by the Bible de Jérusalem: 'Puisse cette foi (this must be Philemon's faith which has been mentioned) rendre agissant son esprit d'entreaide en l'éclairant pleinement.'

A realistic attempt to solve the difficulties of our problematic sentence will have to start not from our own opinion of Pauline theology, reading into the text what it ought to say, but from a study of the words and expressions in their present context.

The very fact that Paul in v. 5 has praised Philemon because of his faith toward the Lord Jesus makes it more than plausible that τῆς πίστεώς σου in v. 6 refers back precisely to that faith of Philemon which has just been mentioned. And as Philemon's love toward the members of his local church has been stressed in v. 5 (for the chiastic structure of v. 5 see Moule's commentary) it is highly probable that κοινωνία has to do with Philemon's relation to his fellow Christians. But what does ἡ κοινωνία τῆς πίστεώς σου mean in this case?

The noun κοινωνία followed by a genitive denoting a person usually means 'fellowship', i.e. 'the fellowship of his Son', 1 Cor. 1.9; 'the fellowship of the Holy Spirit', 2 Cor. 13.13. A seeming exception is 'your partnership in the gospel', Phil. 1.5, where the sense of κοινωνία is determined not by ὑμῶν, but by εἰς τὸ εὐαγγέλιον. In those cases where κοινωνία is determined by the genitive of a non-personal noun; it usually means 'participation', 'sharing', e.g. 'sharing his sufferings', Phil 3.10; 'taking part in the relief of the saints', 2 Cor. 8.4. In these two examples it is a question of sharing what others give part of. But κοινωνία can also be used in a primarily active sense of sharing one's own means or resources with others, e.g. 'your contribution for them and others', 2 Cor. 9.13; 'doing good and sharing what you have', Heb. 13.16. In Philem. v. 6 the logical subject of κοινωνία can be either Philemon: he lets his fellow Christians take part in his faith; or these fellow Christians: they share in Philemon's faith. It is difficult to decide what Paul has meant in this case; both alternatives make sense, and good sense.

When Philemon shares his faith with his congregation, or when the members of this flock share in Philemon's faith, this sharing has the effect of promoting ἐπίγνωσις, a more thorough understanding, and they who are guided to this understanding are those who share in Philemon's faith, i.e. members of his congregation. As Philemon himself is integrated with this congregation, he is involved in and gets his own part of this understanding.

Once again we have reason to refer to the introductory thanksgivings in the other captivity epistles and to their use of the word ἐπίγνωσις. A thorough understanding is the gift of God, mediated through the spirit of wisdom and revelation, Eph. 1.17. It is the outflow of love which is active in a Christian community and leads to the assessment of what is important in matters of faith, Phil. 1.9f. Having heard of the faith of his Colossian Christian brethren, the apostle prays that his correspondents may be filled with the divine gift of understanding the will of God, so that they are enabled to lead a life worthy of God (Col. 1.9), Faith (Eph. 1.15; Col. 1.4), and love (Eph. 1.15; Phil. 1.9; Col. 1.4), as they are manifest in the life of the congregations, contribute to the promotion of understanding.

The parallel passages in Eph., Phil., and Col., in which the word κοινωνία itself does not appear, make it almost certain that κοινωνία in Philem. v. 6 does not mean Philemon's fellowship with Paul in a common faith, still less Paul's fellowship with Philemon based on the latter's faith, but precisely the circumstance that Philemon's faith is shared by the members of his congregation and thus becomes active in his church.

Our next question concerns the object of ἐπίγνωσις. What will Philemon and his fellow Christians learn by a thorough understanding? In our text ἐν ἐπιγνώσει governs the genitive παντὸς ἀγαθοῦ τοῦ ἐν ἡμῖν/ὑμῖν (there are two different readings in the manuscripts). But it is not obvious what 'all the good' means in this context.

In his commentary Moule quotes two examples of the use of ἀγαθόν in New Testament epistles, and he adds: '(τὸ) ἀγαθόν occurs often elsewhere, but usually as something which is *done* or *performed* (as in v. 14 below), rather than a *possession* or the *object of knowledge*.' We can add that in Col. 1.9f it is said that the understanding of God's will leads to a life marked by 'every good work', ἐν παντὶ ἔργῳ ἀγαθῷ, but this thought does not help us in our present context. More important, or rather decisive, is the argument in Eph. 1.17–19. There we read that the understanding of God leads to the knowledge of what is the hope to which God has called the addressees of the letter: 'what are the riches of his glorious inheritance in the saints, and what is the immeasurable greatness of his power in us who believe'. In the introductory thanksgivings of Eph. as well as of Col., hope is mentioned alongside faith and love. Therefore it is highly probable that ἀγαθόν in our passage denotes the content of Christian hope.

This use of ἀγαθόν is by no means rare in the Septuagint and in the New Testament. It has been treated in W. Grundmann's article ἀγαθός in *TWNT*, i, pp. 13–14: ἀγαθόν stands for all that is implied in salvation in the messianic time, the content of eschatological hope. From Heb. might be quoted τὰ μέλλοντα ἀγαθά, 'the good things to come', 9.11; 10.1. Paul writes: 'We know that in everything God helps those who love him to reach that which is good', Rom. 8.28; cf. 10.15. This interpretation of ἀγαθόν, which fits perfectly into the whole argument of vv. 4–7, is seconded by the parallelism of the supplement τοῦ ἐν ἡμῖν/ὑμῖν as compared with ἐν τοῖς ἁγίοις in Eph. 1.18. In this passage in Eph. the Christian hope is characterized: 'what are the riches of his glorious inheritance in the saints', ἐν τοῖς ἁγίοις. The riches of the final salvation are present among the heavenly saints and belong to them. In Philem. v. 6 Paul speaks of 'all the (eschatological) good that is ours/yours (through anticipation by means of a Christian hope and as the content of that hope)'.

Now it is necessary, in order to solve the spectacular problems of our passage, to make a decision about the two readings: τοῦ ἐν ἡμῖν and τοῦ ἐν ὑμῖν. Does Paul include his proper person, when he mentions those to whom the goods of Christian hope belong? The UBS Greek New Testament (3rd edn, 1975) has opted for τοῦ ἐν ἡμῖν and listed this as a C variant. B. M. Metzger, in his Textual Commentary (1971), remarks that this reading is 'perhaps slightly less well supported'. It was, however, chosen 'because it is more expressive and because, standing amid other pronouns of the second person singular and plural, ἡμῖν was more likely to be changed by copyists to ὑμῖν than vice versa'. Already Lohmeyer, in his commentary, remarked that τοῦ ἐν ὑμῖν must be the original reading. This is evident from the fact that Paul consistently uses the second person in the opening thanksgivings and prayers in his letters. From our comparison of Philem. 6 with Eph. 1 and Col. 1 we can adduce the observation that in Col. 1.5 we read διὰ τὴν ἐλπίδα τὴν ἐπικειμένην ὑμῖν ἐν τοῖς οὐρανοῖς. Above all Paul's argument in v. 6, where he starts from Philemon's faith which is shared by his fellow-Christians, makes it probable that hope is shared by

Philemon and his flock in the same way as is faith. Therefore we prefer τοῦ ἐν ὑμῖν.

There is one more problem left. Where does εἰς Χριστόν belong? Lightfoot connects the words 'not with τοῦ ἐν ἡμῖν, but with the main statement of the sentence ἐνεργὴς γένηται κ.τ.λ.'. As a whole, translations and commentaries differ. The most natural solution of that problem, however, is to take it as an explication, in addition to τοῦ ἐν ὑμῖν, of παντὸς ἀγαθοῦ. The word ἀγαθόν in this position needs in fact a clarification of its eschatological content: 'all your good in view of Christ'. It is Christ who is the final object of Christian hope and the goal of Christian life. We can note the significant difference between πρὸς τὸν κύριον Ἰησοῦν in v. 5 and εἰς Χριστόν in v. 6. Faith is directed towards the earthly Jesus having become Lord because of his resurrection. Hope faces the heavenly Christ. Paul is speaking of 'all the good that is yours in view of Christ'—which precisely sums up the content of Christian hope. A similar outlook in connection with faith can be found in Col. 2.5: τὸ στερέωμα τῆς εἰς Χριστὸν πίστεως ὑμῶν, 'the firmness of your faith in Christ'. In this context faith is not so far from endurance and perseverance in view of a final salvation.

The interpretation of Philem. v. 6 which has been given here differs only slightly from the translation, curiously enough rather solitary, which we find in the RSV. Only in the choice of a variant in the Greek text is there a divergence. We propose finally the following translation: 'May the sharing of your faith promote a thorough understanding of all the good that is yours (i.e. belongs to you and your fellow-Christians) in view of Christ.'

Faith, love, and hope are delightful herbs in the grounds of New Testament, especially Pauline, thought. This little bouquet of the three flowers in a somewhat new combination is dedicated to the dear friend and highly esteemed scholar and colleague Kingsley Barrett.

21

Die Kirche als Bau: Epheser 2. 19–22 unter ökumenischem Aspekt*

R. Schnackenburg

Es gibt im Neuen Testament keine andere Schrift, die eine so explizite Ekklesiologie enthält wie der Epheserbrief. So ist der Themenbereich von Christus und Kirche nach dem Epheserbrief seit den dreissiger Jahren oft behandelt worden. Erinnert sei an die Arbeiten von Heinrich Schlier, Ernst Käsemann, Viktor Warnach, Franz Mussner, Ernst Percy, Stig Hanson, in jüngerer Zeit R. J. McKelvey, Josef Ernst, Helmut Merklein, Karl-Martin Fischer, Andreas Lindemann und anderen.[1] Christsein gibt es schon für Paulus nicht ohne Bindung an die Gemeinde der an Jesus Christus Glaubenden. Für das ökumenische Bestreben in unserer Zeit gewinnt die Kirchenkonzeption des Epheserbriefes eine erhöhte Bedeutung; denn dieses Schreiben, das an einen begrenzten Kreis von Gemeinden etwa im Umkreis von Ephesus gerichtet sein dürfte, stellt den heutigen Kirchen Texte vor Augen, die zum Nachdenken über das jeweilige ekklesiale Selbstverständnis zwingen. Die Interpretation des Epheserbriefes hat schon in der Zeit der Reformation, im Horizont der damaligen Kontroversfragen, eine nicht geringe Rolle gespielt. Für den Abschnitt Eph. 2.11–22 liegt jetzt eine aufschlussreiche exegesegeschichtliche Untersuchung vor: William Rader, *The Church and racial hostility*, Tübingen 1978. Aus dem reichen Material der Auslegungsgeschichte ist für das ökumenische Anliegen viel zu lernen.

Am Ende des Abschnittes Eph. 2.11–22 steht das Bild von der Kirche als Bau, aus dem man in der Reformationszeit erhebliche Folgerungen für das jeweilige Kirchenverständnis gezogen hat. Diese Stelle erfährt auch in der heutigen Exegese noch unterschiedliche Interpretationen. Im Unterschied zu der Vorstellung vom Haupt und Leib (1.22f; 4.11–16) und zum Bild von der Ehe (5.22–33), bei denen die Position Christi eindeutig ist, sind nämlich bis heute die Meinungen darüber geteilt, ob Jesus Christus als der in das Fundament eingelagerte Eckstein oder als der krönende und alles zusammen-

* See English summary on p. 271

258

haltende Schlussstein gedacht ist. Diese Frage, die noch nicht zu einer Einigung geführt hat, ist aber auch mit der anderen verbunden, wie das 'Fundament der Apostel und Propheten' zu verstehen ist. Schliesslich hängt davon das Gesamtverständnis des 'wachsenden Tempels' bzw. 'Gottesbaues' ab, also des ekklesialen Selbstverständnisses, das den Epheser-Autor leitet.

I *Exegese von Eph. 2. 19–22*

19 ἄρα οὖν οὐκέτι ἐστὲ ξένοι καὶ πάροικοι,
         ἀλλὰ ἐστὲ συμπολῖται τῶν ἁγίων
                 καὶ οἰκεῖοι τοῦ θεοῦ,

20 ἐποικοδομηθέντες ἐπὶ τῷ θεμελίῳ
                 τῶν ἀποστόλων καὶ προφητῶν,
         ὄντος ἀκρογωνιαίου αὐτοῦ Χριστοῦ Ἰησοῦ,

21   ἐν ᾧ πᾶσα οἰκοδομὴ συναρμολογουμένη
                 αὔξει εἰς ναὸν ἅγιον
                         ἐν κυρίῳ

22   ἐν ᾧ καὶ ὑμεῖς συνοικοδομεῖσθε
                 εἰς κατοικητήριον τοῦ θεοῦ
                         ἐν πνεύματι.

19 So seid ihr nun nicht mehr Fremde und Anwohner,
                 sondern ihr seid Mitbürger der Heiligen
                         und Hausgenossen Gottes,

20 aufgebaut auf dem Fundament
                 der Apostel und Propheten,
         wobei der ἀκρογωνιαῖος Christus Jesus selbst ist,

21   in welchem der ganze Bau zusammengefügt
                         wächst zu einem heiligen Tempel
                                 im Herrn,

22   in welchem auch ihr mitaufgebaut werdet
                         zu einer Wohnung Gottes
                                 im Geist.

(*a*) Jede Übersetzung ist schon eine Interpretation. Einige Übersetzungsprobleme sind bei dieser Wiedergabe bereits in einem bestimmten Sinn entschieden. Die Passage mit Jesus Christus steht im Griechischen in einem Gen. absol., und das vor den Namen gestellte

Personalpronomen αὐτοῦ ist als betontes '[Jesus Christus] selbst' interpretiert, also nicht, wie es auch möglich wäre, auf 'Fundament' zurückbezogen (Jesus Christus ist sein ἀκρογωνιαῖος). Im letztgenannten Fall wäre entschieden, dass Jesus Christus als Eckstein im Fundament anzusehen ist. Aber der Gen. absol., der betont mit ὄντος einsetzt, will die Rolle Jesu Christi hervorheben, und darum wird auch αὐτοῦ betont auf ihn verweisen. Ferner: Die nach der klassischen Regel für πᾶσα οἰκοδομή zu gebende Übersetzung 'jeder Bau', die von einigen Exegeten festgehalten wird,[2] ist im Kontext kaum möglich, zudem nicht nötig, da nach anderen Beispielen der Artikel in der Bedeutung 'der ganze Bau' auch fehlen kann.[3] Die Übersetzung von ἀκρογωνιαῖος sollte noch offen bleiben.

(*b*) Nun zum Text im Zusammenhang des Abschnitts. Die Ausführung über die früheren Heiden, die damals 'fern' waren und jetzt durch das Blut Christi zu 'Nahen' geworden sind, weil Christus die beiden Menschheitsgruppen der Juden und Heiden durch das Kreuz mit Gott versöhnt hat, gipfelt in V. 18 in dem Satz: 'Durch ihn haben wir, die beiden, in einem einzigen Geist den Zugang zum Vater'. In V. 19 wird die Folgerung für die Heidenchristen gezogen: Jetzt seid ihr nicht mehr Fremde und Anwohner, sondern ihr seid Mitbürger und Hausgenossen Gottes. Ohne auf die darin implizierten Probleme näher einzugehen, ist so viel klar, dass die Angeredeten jetzt Anteil an der Welt Gottes erlangt haben. Ob man 'die Heiligen' auf die Glieder der irdischen Gemeinde oder auf die Engel beziehen soll, ist kontrovers.[4] Nicht möglich erscheint mir die Deutung auf die Angehörigen Israels. Die exegetische Streitfrage ist insofern nicht von sehr grossem Gewicht, als nach anderen Stellen für den Epheser-Autor feststeht, dass die Glieder der irdischen Gemeinde schon Anteil an der himmlischen Welt haben (vgl. 2.6).

Die viel verhandelte Frage, was aus dem Abschnitt für das Verhältnis von Kirche und Israel folgt, kann ich hier nicht aufnehmen.[5] Nur so viel sei bemerkt, dass meiner Meinung nach der Verfasser einen Vorzug Israels für die Zeit vor Christus nach V. 12 anerkennt und die heidenchristliche Kirche an diese Vergangenheit für ihr gegenwärtiges Selbstverständnis erinnern will, im übrigen aber ab V. 18 nur die eine Kirche aus Juden und Heiden in den Blick fasst und zum Verhältnis von Kirche und Synagoge keine Stellung nimmt. Für ihn ist an die Stelle der 'Gemeinde Israels' (V. 12) unter dem Heilsaspekt die Kirche Jesu Christi getreten.

(*c*) Durch den Gedanken der Mitbürger der Heiligen und Hausgenossen Gottes angeregt, führt der Verfasser nun das Bild vom Bau ein, das ihm aus Paulus, aber auch aus breiterer urchristlicher Tradition bekannt ist. Wenn er die Heidenchristen in den Raum Gottes, damit auch in den himmlischen Bereich einbezogen sieht, so ist es höchst bedeutsam, dass er nun ebenfalls auf die irdische Grundlegung der neuen Gottesgemeinde hinblickt. Man muss einmal auf die verschiedenen Tempora in den Versen 20–2 achten. Der Verfasser beginnt mit einem Aorist-Partizip 'ihr seid aufgebaut worden' und bringt dabei das Fundament der Apostel und Propheten in den Blick, das also schon vor den Adressaten gelegt war. Daran schliesst sich der Genitivus absolutus, der von Jesus Christus handelt, mit einem Präsens-Partizip derart an, dass damit eine Gleichzeitigkeit mit dem Fundament der Apostel und Propheten und dem sich darauf erhebenden Bau gemeint sein muss. Jesus Christus übernimmt für den Bau die Funktion eines ἀκρογωνιαῖος, so dass dieser Stein unlöslich und unabdingbar dazu gehört, ja als derart hervorgehobener Stein eine entscheidende Bedeutung für den Bau hat. Nach diesem Satzteil treffen wir nur noch auf Präsensformen: In Jesus Christus wird der ganze Bau zusammengefügt, vielleicht noch deutlicher: zusammengefugt, er wächst zu einem heiligen Tempel, in dem auch die Adressaten mitaufgebaut werden. Es ist also ein gegenwärtiger Bau, aus Menschen bestehend, gleichsam aus lebendigen Steinen (vgl. 1 Pet. 2.5). Das Wachstum mit der Zielpräposition εἰς ist ebenfalls als ein gegenwärtiges zu verstehen, und zwar in einem intensiven Sinn. Zum heiligen Tempel wird der ganze Bau immer mehr durch die von Christus ausgehende Kraft.

Die Frage, ob die Apostel und Propheten schon als Grössen der Vergangenheit erscheinen oder als in der Gegenwart wirkende Personen, lässt sich zwar nicht mit letzter Sicherheit beantworten, dürfte aber im Kontext des ganzen Briefes im ersten Sinn zu entscheiden sein. Denn wenn Eph. ein pseudepigraphisches Schreiben ist, das sich unter der Autorität des grossen Apostels in späterer Zeit (etwa 80–90 n.Chr.) an kleinasiatische Gemeinden wendet,[6] weilt Paulus nicht mehr unter den Lebenden. Er wird jedoch in 3.5 mit den 'heiligen Aposteln und Propheten im Geist' in eine Linie gestellt (vgl. 3.3 mit 5). Gewiss sind diese Männer nicht nur als historische Grössen verstanden, sondern üben auch weiter eine 'fundamentale' Funktion aus; aber das können sie auch, wenn sie bereits gestorben sind. Auch ihre Zusammenstellung mit den 'Evangelisten, Hirten und Lehrern' in

4.11 zwingt nicht dazu, sie noch unter die Lebenden zu rechnen.[7] Im Kontext, in dem die Adressaten auf ihren gegenwärtigen Status (im Präsens) angesprochen werden, legt der Aorist ἐποικοδομηθέντες näher, dass der Verf. bereits auf die Gründergeneration zurückblickt.[8]

(*d*) Eine weitere Beobachtung ist wichtig: Auf die Nennung der Person Jesu Christi folgen zwei Relativsätze, jener, der von der Zusammenfügung des ganzen Baues in ihm handelt, und ein zweiter, der den Adressaten zuspricht, dass sie mitaufgebaut werden. Rein grammatisch könnte sich das zweite Relativpronomen auch auf den davor stehenden Satzteil 'zu einem heiligen Tempel im Herrn' beziehen; aber das ist abzulehnen. Das zweite ἐν ᾧ greift das erste auf, meint also wieder Jesus Christus. Das ergibt sich zwingend aus der Korrespondenz der beiden Relativsätze. Satzlogisch macht καὶ ὑμεῖς im zweiten Relativsatz darauf aufmerksam: In Jesus Christus wird der ganze Bau zusammengefügt, in ihm werdet auch ihr mitaufgebaut. Dem συναρμολογουμένη entspricht das συνοικοδομεῖσθε, und schliesslich stehen die Zielangaben 'zu einem heiligen Tempel im Herrn' und 'zu einer Wohnung Gottes im Geist' parallel. Überdies zeigt der Stil des Verfassers, dass er auch sonst Satzreihungen mit neu aufgegriffenen Relativpronomina bildet, deutlich in der Eingangseulogie mit dem gleichen, auf Jesus Christus bezüglichen ἐν ᾧ (1.7, 11, 13a,b). Daraus ergibt sich die exegetische Erkenntnis: Die Einführung Jesu Christi als ἀκρογωνιαῖος nimmt eine Schlüsselstellung ein und macht im Zusammenhang überhaupt erst verständlich, wodurch die heidenchristlichen Adressaten lebendige Bausteine, in den heiligen Gottesbau eingefügte Menschen sind, die mitaufgebaut werden. Sie werden es durch Jesus Christus, der für die Zusammenfügung und das Wachstum des ganzen Baues sorgt.

(*e*) Erst nach dieser sachlichen Klärung, welche Funktion Jesus Christus, der ἀκρογωνιαῖος, für die angesprochenen Christen ausübt, wenden wir uns der Frage zu: Wird im Bild vom Bau Jesus Christus als Fundament-Eckstein oder als krönender und alles zusammenhaltender Schlussstein betrachtet? Zur Geschichte dieser exegetischen Kontroverse nur so viel: Während man in der alten Kirche nur vereinzelt an den Schlussstein gedacht hat, der—besonders bei einem Portalbau—dem ganzen Bau Halt von oben gibt, hat diese Auffassung aufgrund der Arbeiten von Joachim Jeremias in unserem Jahrhundert nicht wenige Anhänger gefunden. Jetzt ist aber eher wieder eine rückläufige Bewegung festzustellen. Die Anhänger der einen oder anderen Auffassung finden sich übrigens quer durch die Reihen evangelischer und katholischer Exegeten. J. Jeremias hat seit seiner Arbeit 'Der Eckstein' in *Angelos* 1 (1925) für die These, dass es sich um den krönenden Schlussstein handelt, in weiteren Arbeiten neues Material ausgebreitet, und ihm haben sich u.a. Philipp Vielhauer, Alfred Wikenhauser und in ihren Kommentaren Dibelius-Greeven, Schlier, Conzelmann und Gnilka angeschlossen.[9] Zeitigen Widerspruch erhob Ernst Percy, dann folgten u.a. Franz Mussner, Josef Pfammatter, Karl Theodor Schäfer, R. J. McKelvey und Helmut Merklein.[10] Wir wollen nur einmal die Hauptgründe für die beiden Standpunkte gegenüberstellen.

Für die Deutung auf den Schlussstein führt man vor allem an: (i) Es gibt nicht wenige Zeugnisse aus der Literatur des 2. bis 4. Jahrhunderts, die diese Bedeutung von ἀκρογωνιαῖος belegen; (ii) eine Reihe archäologischer Tatsachen und Funde (verzierte Schlusssteine) bekräftigen diese Zeugnisse; (iii) da das 'Fundament' schon durch die Apostel und Propheten besetzt ist, lässt sich Christus als Eckstein nur schwer damit vereinbaren; (iv) Christus als der obere, den Bau krönende und beherrschende Schlussstein entspricht der Vorstellung von Christus als Haupt der Kirche, besonders nach Eph. 4.16.

Die Vertreter der anderen These, dass es sich um den Eckstein handelt, wenden ein, dass die literarischen Zeugnisse zum Teil recht fragwürdig sind. Ferner machen sie darauf aufmerksam, dass bei 'Fundament' an den untersten Bauteil (nicht an den steinernen Grund) gedacht sei und der dort eingefügte Eckstein eine wichtige Funktion hat. Ferner sagen sie, dass der zuletzt eingefügte Schlussstein zum Bild vom *wachsenden* Bau nicht passe. Stärker als diese Gründe scheinen mir die traditionsgeschichtlichen zu sein, die man positiv für die Deutung auf den Eckstein anführt: Die einzige Stelle in der Septuaginta, wo die Vokabel vorkommt, ist Jes. 28.16, die eindeutig einen in die Fundamente eingefügten (kostbaren) Eckstein bezeugt. Diese Stelle, schon im Targum zu Jes. 28.16 messianisch gedeutet, wurde für die Urkirche in Verbindung mit anderen 'Stein'-Worten ein wichtiges messianisches Testimonium für Jesus, vgl. besonders 1 Pet. 2.4–8. Ferner: da in 1 Kor. 3.10f das vom 'Baumeister' Paulus gelegte Fundament Christus ist, legt sich auch für Eph. 2.20 eine Fundament-Funktion Christi nahe. Der Epheser-Autor steht sicherlich der paulinischen Tradition noch nahe, auch wenn er eine andere Terminologie benutzt. Schliesslich führt man auch einen gewichtigen theologischen Grund an, in der Formulierung von Merklein: Wenn

Christus als Schlussstein angesehen wird, bleibt das Verhältnis der Apostel und Propheten zu Christus unklar. Man könnte dann das Fundament der Apostel und Propheten als isolierte Grösse ansehen; aber in Wirklichkeit sind sie ja ganz und gar von Christus abhängig und ohne ihn gar nicht zu denken.[11]

Wägt man alle Gründe für und wider ab, dürften die Argumente für Christus als Eckstein das stärkere Gewicht haben: Der seltene Ausdruck erklärt sich aus der urchristlichen Tradition, welche die einzig verfügbare Stelle Jes. 28.16 im Sinn des Ecksteins auf Christus bezieht. Bildmässig ist das durchaus, wie besonders Pfammatter gezeigt hat, mit dem Fundament der Apostel und Propheten zu vereinbaren: Der eine entscheidende Eckstein wurde als erster für das Fundament, den untersten festen Gebäudeteil gelegt, und nach diesem Eckstein bestimmen sich alle anderen Steine des Fundaments.[12] Theologisch war das dem Epheser-Autor, der die Apostel und Propheten wegen ihrer Bedeutung für die Folgezeit (seine eigene Gegenwart) herausstellen wollte, darum wichtig, weil auch sie noch einen Grund ihrer Existenz und eine Norm für ihre Verkündigung haben: Jesus Christus, auf dem sich der ganze Bau der Kirche erhebt, Halt und Zusammenhalt gewinnt und zum vollendeten Gottestempel emporwächst. Dieses in sich konsistente Bild schliesst nicht aus, dass unter anderem Aspekt, unter dem Bild vom Leib, Christus als das beherrschende Haupt und als das Ziel des Wachstums der Kirche angesehen wird (vgl. 4.11, 13, 15f).

(*f*) Warum aber werden dann die Apostel und Propheten als Fundament des Gottesbaues überhaupt genannt? Warum wird den Adressaten gesagt, dass sie darauf aufgebaut wurden? Hier scheint das Interesse des Verfassers für seine Zeit, die schon beginnende nachapostolische Zeit, durchzuschlagen. Traditionsgeschichtlich kann man an 1 Kor. 3.10f erinnern, wo sich Paulus zwar nicht als Fundament des Baues, aber als den Baumeister bezeichnet, der Christus als Fundament gelegt hat. Inzwischen gehört der Apostel selbst schon zur Gründergeneration. Er hat auf Christus, dem Fundament, aufgebaut und lässt sich—in einer Verschiebung des Bildes—zusammen mit den anderen Aposteln und mit den Propheten als mit Christus verbundenes Fundament der späteren Kirche betrachten. Warum dem Verfasser an dieser Sicht liegt, wird im nächsten Abschnitt offenkundig, wo Paulus als der hervorragende Apostel erscheint, dem das Christusmysterium offenbart wurde, damit er es in seinem ganzen

Reichtum den Heiden verkündige (3.3f, 8f.). Aber auch die heiligen Apostel und Propheten insgesamt werden als Offenbarungsempfänger genannt (3.5), so dass Paulus in diese Gruppe integriert wird, freilich so, dass er als der massgebliche Theologe, dem besondere Einsicht verliehen wurde, und als Künder des Evangeliums hervortritt. Aus der Sicht des Verfassers wird er für die spätere Zeit zum vorzüglichen Traditionsträger, der die Wahrheit des Evangeliums verbürgt und an den man sich zu halten hat. Die apostolische Zeit mit den Erstverkündigern und den vom heiligen Geist erleuchteten Propheten wird zum Fundament und Massstab des Glaubens für die spätere Kirche, in der sich sonst Unsicherheit und gefährliche Abirrungen breit machen können. In dieser Gefahr sieht der Verfasser nach 4.14 offenbar die von ihm angesprochenen Gemeinden. Welche Bedeutung in dieser Hinsicht die zu seiner Zeit tätigen Evangelisten, Hirten und Lehrer haben, von denen in 4.11 die Rede ist, können wir hier nicht erörtern.

(g) Die nachapostolische Perspektive wird schliesslich durch die beiden parallelen Wendungen 'zu einem heiligen Tempel im Herrn' und 'zu einer Wohnung Gottes im Geist' bestätigt. Sie klingen nämlich schon fast formelhaft, wie geprägte Ausdrücke einer Sprache, in der sich das ekklesiale Bewusstsein gefestigt hat. Vergleicht man 1 Kor. 3.16f, so ist auch da vom Tempel Gottes die Rede, vom Geist Gottes, der darin wohnt, vom heiligen Tempel, den die Christen bilden. In Eph. 2.22 wird daraus die Analogiebildung: heiliger Tempel—Wohnung Gottes, und daran schliessen sich die abgeschliffenen Wendungen 'im Herrn'—'im Geist'. Ἐν κυρίῳ, das wie im ganzen Schreiben nur Christus meinen kann, stösst sich sogar mit dem einleitenden Relativpronomen, das sich auch schon auf Christus bezieht, wäre also überflüssig. Aber die Redeweise vom Tempel im Herrn hat sich bereits verfestigt, und ähnlich gilt das für die Wohnung Gottes im Geist. Dennoch steckt dahinter das Bewusstsein, dass der Herr durch den Geist in der Kirche anwesend und wirksam ist, wie auch aus 4.4f hervorgeht.

2   *Wirkungsgeschichte und ökumenische Aspekte*

(a) Aus der reformatorischen Auslegung von Eph. 2.20, die William Rader ausführlich behandelt,[13] sei so viel hervorgehoben: Für Martin Luther und andere Reformatoren wurde die Stelle zu einem Argument gegen Matt. 16.18 und den daraus abgeleiteten Anspruch der römischen Kirche auf den Primat des Papstes. Luther, der keinen Kommentar zum Epheserbrief geschrieben hat, kommt darauf in der Schrift 'Wider das Papsttum zu Rom' zu sprechen: Christus, der Eckstein, kennt nicht zwei Arten von Kirchen, sondern nur eine, wie der Glaube der ganzen Christenheit sagt: 'Ich glaube an eine heilige christliche Kirche.' Die römische Kirche ist und muss sein ein Stück oder Glied der heiligen christlichen Kirche, nicht das Haupt, das allein Christus angemessen ist, dem Eckstein.[14] Deutlicher ist Johannes Calvin in seinem Epheserkommentar: Diejenigen, die die Ehre, der Eckstein zu sein, auf Petrus übertragen, um zu behaupten, dass die Kirche auf ihm begründet sei, missbrauchen schamlos dieses Zeugnis. Sie stellen es nämlich so dar, dass Christus der primäre Stein im Hinblick auf andere genannt werde; daher gebe es mehrere Steine, durch die die Kirche gestützt wird. Das Fundament der Apostel und Propheten erklärt Calvin wie fast alle Reformatoren von ihrer Lehre. Damit stimmt nach Calvin auch 1 Kor. 3.11 überein, wo sich Paulus einen Baumeister nennt, der auf Christus, dem einmal gelegten Fundament, aufbaut; denn eben in Verkündigung und Lehre bestehe die Tätigkeit eines Apostels.[15]

Sehen wir uns nun auch die katholische Position an! Die damaligen katholischen Exegeten unterschieden mit Thomas von Aquin das primäre Fundament, das Christus ist, von dem sekundären Fundament, das die Apostel und Propheten bilden. Deren Fundamentfunktion versteht aber schon Thomas von Aquin mit Berufung auf 1 Kor. 3.11 von der Lehre.[16] Zur Zeit der Reformation schreibt Cajetan, dass wir auf Christus aufgebaut sind, aber nicht unmittelbar, sondern nur insofern, als er die Apostel und Propheten stützt, da die vermittelnde Lehre durch die Apostel und Propheten verwaltet werde.[17] Wir sehen, dass die beiden Standpunkte gar nicht so weit voneinander entfernt sind, nur dass die Protestanten einen scharfen Unterschied zwischen den Aposteln und Propheten selbst und ihrer Lehre oder ihrem Zeugnis machen, während die Katholiken den Aposteln und Propheten selbst eine vermittelnde Funktion zuschreiben. Das geschieht jeweils sicherlich im Interesse der apostolischen Sukzession, die hier und dort anders verstanden wird. Für die protestantischen Theologen wird die Lehre, die rechte Auslegung des Evangeliums gemäss der apostolischen Überlieferung dann zunehmend zum Kriterium für die Kirche. Für die Katholiken wird die apostolische Überlieferung mit der Amtssukzession gekoppelt: In der Nachfolge des Amtes wird auch die apostolische Überlieferung bewahrt. Aber an der einmaligen und unaufhebbaren, für alle Zeiten geltenden und allein massgeblichen Stellung Jesu Christi als des Ecksteins halten beide Seiten fest. Weder wird der Eckstein von den Katholiken auf Petrus übertragen oder dieser auch nur als weiterer Stein neben Christus gestellt, noch wird von den Protestanten die Bedeutung der Apostel und Propheten als Vermittlern der Botschaft Jesu Christi verkannt. Nur die Weitergabe der apostolischen Überlieferung in der darauf folgenden Zeit bleibt kontrovers. Man wird Rader zustimmen müssen, dass es in der Auseinandersetzung der Reformationszeit Missverständnisse und falsche Perspektiven auf beiden Seiten gab.

Doch kehren wir zur Exegese zurück und ziehen wir einige Folgerungen für den heutigen Horizont!

(*b*) Das Bild vom Bau, das in Eph. 2.19–22 für die Kirche entworfen wird, ist nicht eine zeitgelöste theologische Beschreibung der Kirche in symbolischer Sprache, sondern eine Anrede der Adressaten auf ihr ekklesiales Selbstverständnis in ihrer Situation, eine Erinnerung an das, was sie in der Kirche und durch die Kirche geworden sind. Das setzt freilich ein bestimmtes, durch den Glauben vermitteltes Kirchenverständnis voraus, schliesst also eine Theologie der Kirche ein, entwickelt diese aber nicht lehrhaft, sondern in der Applikation auf die heidenchristlichen, schon in vorgerückter Zeit lebenden Adressaten. Darum beginnt der Verfasser mit dem Zugang zu Gott, den sie bereits erlangt haben, gemeinsam mit den Judenchristen: Sie sind Mitbürger der Heiligen und Hausgenossen Gottes. Wie aber haben sie diesen Zugang erlangt? Allein durch Jesus Christus, der sie mit Gott und untereinander versöhnt und ihnen in der Kirche den gemeinsamen Weg zu Gott, dem Vater, erschlossen hat. Das ist des längeren in 2.14–18 dargelegt. Vom erlangten Heilsstand blickt der Verfasser auf die Kirche, in der die Heiden Platz gefunden haben, und hebt nun deren Grundlegung durch die Apostel und Propheten hervor. Aber die alleinige heilsmittlerische Funktion Christi ist ihm so wichtig, dass er Jesus Christus in dieses Bild der Kirche als den Eckstein einführt, der sowohl die Apostel und Propheten trägt und stützt als auch den ganzen Bau so zusammenfügt und zusammenhält, so dass die Adressaten nur in ihm zu dem heiligen Tempel, der Gotteswohnung, aufgebaut werden. Aus dieser theologischen Intention des Verfassers versteht man noch besser, warum er das traditionelle Bild vom Eckstein heranzieht.

(*c*) Wenn man das Zustandekommen des Textes so sieht, schwinden auch die Spannungen zu den anderen Texten, in denen das Bild vom Bau in anderer Weise verwendet wird. In 1 Kor 3.10f liegt Paulus daran, die einmalige, alle Verkündiger gleicherweise verpflichtende Stellung Jesu Christi hervorzuheben, und er gebraucht dafür das Bild von dem ein- für-allemal gelegten Fundament, auf dem die Verkündiger nur je und je aufbauen können. Da er selbst der Hauptverkündiger und Gründer der Gemeinde von Korinth ist, bezeichnet er sich als den Baumeister, der dieses Fundament gelegt hat, schliesst aber andere Verkündiger als Mitaufbauende, darauf Aufbauende nicht aus. Die Verschiebung des Bildes auf das Fundament der Apostel und Propheten in Eph. 2.20 erklärt sich hauptsächlich aus der veränderten zeitgeschichtlichen Perspektive. Der Verfasser blickt auf die Erstverkündiger, die Apostel und Propheten zurück, bringt aber nachträglich im Bild vom Eckstein die unveränderte grundlegende Position Christi ein. 1 Pet. 2.4ff ist deswegen wichtig, weil hier die Christen wie in Eph. 2.22 als die lebendigen Steine am geistigen Tempel betrachtet werden, die mitaufgebaut werden, und weil Christus dabei ebenfalls als der lebendige, kostbare Eckstein genannt wird, zu dem sie hinzugetreten sind. Die menschlichen Vermittler, Apostel und Propheten oder andere Verkündiger, werden hier nicht genannt; ihre Einführung in Eph. 2.20 entspringt einer besonderen Intention des Epheser-Autors. Und was ist zu Matt. 16.18 zu sagen, wo Petrus als der Fels erscheint, auf den Jesus seine Kirche bauen will? In der Perspektive der bisher genannten Texte wird man die Stelle als eine Funktionsbestimmung für jenen auch sonst hervorgehobenen Jünger bezeichnen müssen, aber eine Funktionsbestimmung, die in die übergreifende Konzeption von der Kirche einzuordnen ist. Das heisst konkret, dass Petrus nicht an die Stelle Jesu Christi tritt, sondern ebenso wie die Apostel und Propheten in Eph. 2.20f ganz und gar von ihm abhängig bleibt und nur von Christus her seine Felsfunktion ausüben kann. Das ist auch in Matt. 16.18 durch '*meine* Kirche' angedeutet. Es ist wieder ein anderer Bildgebrauch, der aber sachlich die in den anderen Texten aufleuchtende Konzeption der Kirche nicht in Frage stellt. Das Verhältnis der Verkündiger und Gründer der Gemeinden, wie immer sie jeweils in den Blick treten, zu Christus selbst ist überall das gleiche: Er ist der eigentliche 'Gründer' der Kirche, der unverrückbare Eckstein, der die Kirche trägt und mit seinem Geist weiter durchwaltet.

Damit sind gewiss nicht alle Fragen, die bis heute im ökumenischen Gespräch anstehen, gelöst. Es bleiben so gewichtige Fragen wie die, in welcher Weise die 'fundamentale' Funktion der in Eph. 2.20

genannten Apostel und Propheten fortwirkt, ob und auf welche Weise sich eine apostolische Sukzession ergibt, welche Rolle dabei die schon in Eph. 4.11 genannten kirchlichen Ämter spielen, wie die Amtsweitergabe zustande kommt usw. Aber es dürfte wichtig genug sein, dass wir uns schon einmal im Blick auf Eph. 2.19–22 auf ein Grundverständnis der Kirche als eines unablöslich auf Christus gegründeten und nur von ihm her und auf ihn hin wachsenden Baues einigen können, in dem alle menschlichen Vermittler und Funktionen nur eine untergeordnete und subsidiäre Bedeutung haben.

ANMERKUNGEN

1 Am meisten beschäftigte sich die Forschung mit der Konzeption der Kirche als Leib Christi; vgl. die Bibliographie bei M. Barth, *Ephesians I* (The Anchor Bible) 1974, S. 414–17; hinzuzufügen sind H. Merklein, *Das kirchliche Amt nach dem Epheserbrief*, München 1973, S. 83–97; K. M. Fischer, *Tendenz und Absicht des Epheserbriefes*, Göttingen 1973, S. 48–78. Weitere Vorstellungen sind die vom Pleroma; vgl. dazu die Monographie von J. Ernst, *Pleroma und Pleroma Christi*, Regensburg 1970, und von der Ehe (*Hieros gamos*, Eph. 5.22–33). Einen Gesamtüberblick über die Ekklesiologie des Eph. bietet J. Gnilka, *Der Epheserbrief* (HThK) 1971, S. 99–111. Wir beschränken uns hier auf die Konzeption vom Gottesbau in Eph. 2.19–22.

2 Vgl. T. K. Abbott (*ICC*) S. 74f ('everything that from time to time is builded in'); E. Haupt (Meyers K) S. 96f (jede Einzelgemeinde); E. Percy, *Die Probleme der Kolosser- und Epheserbriefe*, Lund 1946, 462f (ebenso); Ch. Masson (*Comm. du NT*, 1953), S. 171 (eine Teilkonstruktion, die hinzugefügt wird).

3 Vgl. Apg. 2.26, 'das ganze Haus Israel'; 17.26; Röm. 3.20, 'alles Fleisch'; 11.26 u.a. Wahrscheinlich liegt semitischer Einfluss vor, der auch sonst in Eph. zu spüren ist. Vgl. Blass-Debrunner § 275,2, Anm. 4; Moulton-Turner, *Grammar*, III, S. 199f; C. F. D. Moule, *An Idiom Book of NT Greek*, Cambridge 1953, S. 94f.

4 Für Glieder der irdischen Gemeinde Abbott, Haupt, Masson, J. Ernst, *Die Briefe an die Philipper*, usw., Regensburg 1974; Merklein, *Kirchliches Amt*, S. 131f; für die Deutung auf Engel u.a. H. Schlier, *Der Brief an die Epheser*, Düsseldorf ⁵1965, 140f; J. Gnilka, 154; A. Lindemann, *Die Aufhebung der Zeit*, Gütersloh 1975, S. 183. Diese Deutung stützt sich auf Qumran-Texte, vgl. 1 QS 11.7f; 1 QSb 1.5; 3.26; 1 QM 7.6; 12. 1,7; 1 QH 3.21f; 4.25; 4 Qflor I. 4; CD 20.8. Vgl. F. Mussner, 'Beiträge aus Qumran zum Verständnis des Epheserbriefes', *Neutestamentliche Aufsätze*: Festschrift J. Schmid, Regensburg 1963, S. 184–98, hier 188–91.

5 Vgl. meinen Beitrag 'Zur Exegese von Eph. 2.11–22 im Hinblick auf das Verhältnis von Kirche und Israel', der in der Festschrift für Bo Reicke erscheinen soll.

6 Die lange Diskussion, ob Eph. von Paulus selbst stammen kann, scheint jetzt doch zur Annahme eines pseudepigraphischen Schreibens zu führen; vgl. C. L. Mitton, *The Epistle to the Ephesians: its authorship, origin and purpose*, Oxford 1951; W. G. Kümmel, *Einleitung in das Neue Testament*, Heidelberg [17]1973, S. 314–23; A. Wikenhauser & J. Schmid, *Einleitung in das Neue Testament*, Freiburg i.B., [6]1973, 486–96; Merklein, *Kirchliches Amt*, 19–48; Lindemann, *Aufhebung der Zeit*; die meisten neueren Kommentare. Paulinische Verfasserschaft vertreten noch A. van Roon, *The Authenticity of Ephesians*, Leiden 1974; M. Barth, *Ephesians*.

7 Anders G. Klein, *Die zwölf Apostel: Ursprung und Gehalt einer Idee*, Göttingen 1961, S. 66–75; Fischer, *Tendenz und Absicht*, S. 33–9. Den 'nachapostolischen' Ursprung von Eph. vertrat auch C. K. Barrett, 'The Apostles in and after the New Testament', *Svensk Exeg. Arsbok* 21 (1956), S. 30–49, hier 47.

8 Das schliesst nicht aus, dass in Didache 11.3ff noch Apostel und Propheten in den Gemeinden auftreten. Es ist ein anderer Apostelbegriff; könnten diese Wandermissionare, die an äusseren Kriterien überprüft werden sollen, als 'Fundament' der Kirche bezeichnet werden?

9 J. Jeremias in *TWNT* i, S. 792f; derselbe in *ZNW* 36 (1937), S. 154–7; Ph. Vielhauer, *Oikodome*, Karlsruhe 1940, S. 125–8; A. Wikenhauser, *Die Kirche als der mystische Leib Christi nach dem Apostel Paulus*, Münster i.W. 1940, S. 161; M. Dibelius, *An die Kolosser, Epheser, an Philemon*, 3. Aufl. neu bearbeitet von H. Greeven, Tübingen 1953, S. 72; H. Schlier, *Brief an die Epheser*, S. 142 (mit weiteren Autoren); J. Gnilka, S. 158; H. Conzelmann in NT Deutsch 8 (1976), S. 101.

10 Percy, *Probleme*, S. 328–32; F. Mussner, *Christus, das All und die Kirche*, Trier 1955, S. 108–11; J. Pfammatter, *Die Kirche als Bau*, Rom 1960, S. 143–51; K. Th. Schäfer, Zur Deutung von ἀκρογωνιαῖος Eph. 2.20, *Ntl. Aufsätze: Festschrift J. Schmid*, Regensburg 1963, S. 218–24; R. J. McKelvey, 'Christ the Cornerstone', *NTS* 8 (1961/2) S. 352–9; derselbe, *The New Temple*, Oxford 1969, S. 195–204; Merklein, *Kirchliches Amt*, S. 144–52. So jetzt auch H. Krämer in *Exeg. Wörterbuch zum NT* I, Stuttgart 1979, S. 645–8.

11 *Kirchliches Amt*, S. 151; vgl. auch Masson, S. 170, Anm. 1; E. Gaugler, *Der Epheserbrief*, Zürich 1966, S. 121.

12 Pfammatter, *Kirche als Bau*, S. 149; McKelvey, art. cit., S. 354; Krämer (Anm. 10), S. 647.

13 Rader, *Church*, S. 70–8.

14 *Weimarer Ausgabe*, Bd. 54, S. 245f.

15 Corpus Ref., *Calvini opera* 51, col. 174f.

16 *Ad Eph. lect. VI* (ed. Cai, nr. 127–31).

17 *Epistolae Pauli*, Paris 1540, S. 264.

ENGLISH SUMMARY

An exegesis of Eph. 2.19–22 is offered in the conviction that it has an important bearing on ecumenical discussion. The following exegetical conclusions are defended: (a) αὐτοῦ in v. 20 refers to Jesus and not to the 'foundation' and πᾶσα οἰκοδομή in v. 21 means the 'whole building' rather than 'each building.' (b) The 'saints' in v. 19 are either Christians or angels, but not Israelites. (c) The earthly foundation of the ever-growing Church consists of 'apostles and prophets' and, above all, Jesus. The author, writing c. A.D. 80–90, looks back on an earlier generation when the apostles and prophets, including Paul, became the foundation of the Church. They are no longer alive, but their influence is still felt. (d) The relative clauses in vv. 21–22 both refer back to Jesus Christ, by whom the Church is held together and through whom the Gentiles, whom the author addresses, were included. (e) ἀκρογωνιαῖος in v. 20 refers to Christ as the 'cornerstone' rather than the 'capstone' and is based on a messianic use of Isa. 28.16 LXX (cf. 1 Pet. 2.4–8; and especially 1 Cor. 3.10f). All the other stones, including the apostles and prophets, rest on the one cornerstone, Jesus Christ. (f) Among the foundational apostles and prophets Paul is pre-eminent, since it was to him that God revealed the mystery of the inclusion of the Gentiles (Eph. 3.3f, 8f). The apostles and prophets are also the foundation of the present leadership of the Church, who build it up and protect it from the winds of false doctrine (Eph. 4.11–14). (g) The post-apostolic perspective is further confirmed by the advanced ecclesiology of v. 22.

The relevance of this passage for ecumenical discussion is assessed in three ways. First, the Reformation debate in which Eph. 2.19–22 was set over against Matt. 16.18 led to misunderstanding and false perspectives on both sides. In reality they agree on the centrality of Christ, for while Catholics do not replace Christ with Peter, neither do Protestants deny the importance of the apostles and prophets. The dispute centres solely on how the apostolic tradition is to be preserved and transmitted. Second, the image of the Church in Eph. 2.19–22 is not timeless. The author addresses himself directly to his readers to show that their membership in the Church rests solely on Jesus Christ and the foundation of the apostles and prophets. Third, in the light of Eph. 2.19–22, Matt. 16.18 should be seen as a functional definition, which also applies to other apostolic figures and in no way challenges the centrality of Christ (who speaks, in Matt. 16.18, of *my* Church).

271

Many other questions remain, but it is important to have established that the Church has only one cornerstone and that all others are subordinate to him.

22

Ephesians 1.1 Again

Ernest Best

In attempting to determine the original reading of Eph. 1.1 two other problems appear to require simultaneous explanation:

(1) the peculiar position of the phrase τοῖς οὖσιν (ἐν ᾿Εφέσῳ) which makes it refer only to τοῖς ἁγίοις;

(2) the insertion of ἐν ᾿Εφέσῳ and not some other geographical designation, assuming that the reference to Ephesus was not part of the original text.

We know from the evidence of Marcion and 2 Peter that at least by the middle of the second century a recognized collection of Paul's letters existed. But long before this there will have been an informal collection or collections of some, if not all the letters. Many scholars date the first formal collection as early as the end of the first century.[1] Whether this is so or not there were at least by this stage partial collections.[2] When Clement writes from Rome to Corinth he is aware of both Paul's letter to his own church and the first letter to Corinth; a copy of the latter must therefore have arrived in Rome by this time. Col. 4.16 shows awareness of a letter to Laodicea of which the Colossians are to obtain possession; they will then have had at least two letters. Once a number of letters come together problems of identification arise. In the ancient world most letters carried some identification on the outside, usually the name of the recipient or recipients.[3] It is, however, unlikely that Paul's autographs had any such outer address since they were taken by one of his associates to the church or churches to which they were directed; if they did have an external identification this, of course, has now been lost. The identification of letters by some word on the outside would, however, not be strange to the ancient world.

At Rome 1 Corinthians could either have had on the outside 'To the Corinthians' or 'To Corinth'. This would just give sufficient information to distinguish it from any others that might lie in the archive of the church in Rome. The full title, 'To the church of God which is at

Corinth, to those sanctified in Christ Jesus, called to be saints together with all those who in every place call on the name of our Lord Jesus Christ, both their Lord and ours', would have been far too unwieldy and not necessary for identification. In view of later manuscript usage 'To the Corinthians' would seem the most probable, for all the early witnesses corroborate this as the heading to the letter. Once the letter became part of a codex the exterior identification would, of course, appear at the top of the first page.

If with most scholars we reject the view of Goodspeed[4] that Ephesians was written to be the introduction to the first collection of Paul's letters, we still need to enquire at what stage it was brought into association with other Pauline letters. Ignatius apparently knew and made use of both Ephesians and 1 Corinthians, though of course he does not identify either by name. The author of 1 Peter knows the thought of Romans and Ephesians. How then was Ephesians identified as over against the other two letters with which it was associated in different areas?

If the manuscript already contained the words ἐν Ἐφέσῳ then clearly a reference to Ephesians would be put on the outside, almost certainly πρὸς Ἐφεσίους. We cannot determine from its use by the author of 1 Peter (assuming he had used it), whether he knew it under this identification or not. It has, however, been argued that Ignatius knew it as addressed to the Ephesians because he uses it in his own letter to the Ephesians as if the Ephesians would be specially conscious of Paul's letter as a letter addressed to them.[5] We note however: (1) *Smyrn.* 1.1. may show acquaintance with Eph. 2.16; *Polyc.* 1.2 with Eph. 4.2 and *Polyc.* 5.1 with Eph. 5.25. It may therefore only be chance that there are two probable places in Ignatius' *Ephesians* (*the address* which recalls Eph. 1.3ff,[6] and Ignatius, *Eph.* 20.1 which recalls Eph. 2.15; 4.24) showing acquaintance with Pauline Ephesians. (2) Ignatius' *Eph.* equally probably displays acquaintanceship with 1 Cor. (cf. Ignatius, *Eph.* 16.1 with 1 Cor. 6.9f; and Ignatius, *Eph.* 18.1 with 1 Cor. 1.18, 20) and possible acquaintance with Romans (cf. Ignatius, *Eph.* 8.2 with Rom. 8.5, 8; and Ignatius, *Eph.* 19.3 with Rom. 6.4); indeed of all the letters of Ignatius his Ephesians is the one which shows the greatest acquaintanceship with various parts of the Pauline corpus.[7] (3) It is not certain that Ignatius does in fact use Ephesians in his *address*; this and the corresponding passage in Pauline Ephesians are both highly liturgical and may be dependent on a common tradition; Schenk[8] in fact argued that the existence of these two similar passages led someone in the early Church to deduce erroneously that Pauline Ephesians was a letter addressed to the Ephesian church. (4) If Ignatius knew our letter as a letter addressed to the Ephesians, why did he make the very vague reference in his *Eph.* 12.2 to Paul mentioning the Ephesians in all his letters when he could have been much more concrete and recalled them to the letter Paul had written to them? It therefore seems easiest to conclude that Ignatius did not know Pauline Ephesians as a letter addressed to the Ephesian Christians. Yet he knew it and other Pauline letters, so Pauline Ephesians must have had some identification. Of course if there were a number of minor collections which were later formed into a major collection of Pauline epistles it would only have been necessary for Pauline Ephesians to have been so identified in one of these collections for this identification to have been carried into the new total collection.

We may continue our further consideration of the identification given to our letter by beginning with the text of 1.1 [9]

The vast majority of manuscripts read τοῖς ἁγίοις τοῖς οὖσιν ἐν Ἐφέσῳ καὶ πιστοῖς and if this was the original text then it would have been perfectly natural to identify the letter as 'To the Ephesians'. There are, however, few today who contend for this as the original form of the text. [10] Not merely are there good witnesses which do not contain the reference to Ephesus but the position in the text at which it appears renders the text grammatically difficult to construe since by implication it attaches 'Ephesus' only to ἁγίοις and 'in Christ Jesus' only to πιστοῖς. Moreover the letter appears to be a general letter rather than one addressed to the specific situation of a particular church. For these and other reasons we reject this as the original text and therefore do not need to see the original identification as necessarily 'To the Ephesians'.

Codex Vaticanus reads τοῖς ἁγίοις τοῖς οὖσιν καὶ πιστοῖς. The variety of explanations offered for the understanding of τοῖς οὖσιν shows that this text is even more difficult to understand than the previous. If we commence with it we have to assume a stage at which 'in Ephesus' was added. [11]

The text of P[46] τοῖς ἁγίοις οὖσιν καὶ πιστοῖς is also difficult to translate and has little manuscript support. [12]

It has been conjectured that originally there was a gap left in the manuscript at the place where 'in Ephesus' now appears and that this was filled in with the appropriate name by the messenger as he took the letter round a number of churches or that a number of copies were sent

275

with a lacuna in each for the local church to fill in its own name when it received the letter. However, there seems to be no evidence for the latter practice in the ancient world.[13] Even if the letter was taken round by Tychicus and he inserted the name of each church as he came to it, it is still the wrong point in the text at which to do this.

Thus none of the possible text forms which we have examined is easily explicable and only one of them possibly provides the geographical identification which we require.

It is now time that we looked at the nature of the letter. Its content does not suggest a precise geographical address. It is generally agreed that it is written to a wider audience than one church. This wider audience might have been identified as the church or churches in a particular district, e.g. Asia (cf. Gal. 1.2; 1 Pet. 1.1) or have lacked identification altogether (cf. Jas. 1.1). If there had been an original wide address 'The Churches of Asia' which was later reduced to 'Ephesus' this wide address would have appeared at the point where 'Ephesus' appears today in the great majority of manuscripts. But the grammatical difficulty would still exist even for such a wide form of address. It may then be better to assume that originally there was no geographical definition of the addressees. Since the forms of the text which lack geographical definition in Codex Vaticanus and P^{46} are also difficult to construe it might be better to take as the original form of the address τοῖς ἁγίοις καὶ πιστοῖς ἐν Χριστῷ Ἰησοῦ[14] and see if from this we can construct an evolution of the present text forms. It must be admitted that there is no manuscript evidence for this form of the text, but the suggestion we are about to make may account for the disappearance of the original form. Strong support for this as the original form is given if Colossians was the model for Ephesians;[15] if we were to generalize Colossians (i.e. issue a letter based on it but addressed to a wider audience) the first item in the address to disappear would be the reference to Colossae. The difference between the address in Colossians and Ephesians would then amount to the omission from the address in Colossians of the reference to 'Brethren' and the addition of 'Jesus' in Ephesians to the simple 'Christ' of Colossians. Such variations are typical of those we find elsewhere between Ephesians and Colossians.[16] Whether Ephesians is by Paul or not there is clearly some relation between it and Colossians of a general nature.

Sooner or later 'Ephesians' would be brought into contact with other letters of Paul and would need to be identified. The others would be identified with geographical names. Most of those who have discussed the question of identification have assumed therefore that the first identification of Ephesians would have been geographical,[17] but this may be an incorrect assumption. The first significant words relating to the addressees are τοῖς ἁγίοις. This phrase[18] might then have been written on the outside of the roll, or at the head of the page if the collection of letters was first made in the form of a codex. (However it is more probable that in those communities where a number of Pauline letters were beginning to be used these would originally be on separate rolls; only later would they be combined into a codex.) So on the outside of the letter we would find 'To the Saints'. It would be unnecessary to add καὶ τοῖς πιστοῖς for 'To the Saints' would be sufficient to distinguish the letter from other Pauline letters with their geographically oriented identifications ('To the Romans', etc). In either case, however, the identification is through people – 'To the saints' and 'To the Romans (Corinthians, etc.)' – and not simply geographical and non-geographical.

At a later stage[19] in some unknown Christian community and for some unknown reason it was felt that the letter ought to have a geographical destination. For a reason again which is not clear to us and for which we do not now need to seek an answer 'Ephesus' was chosen as the appropriate identification. We suggest that for this purpose τοῖς ἁγίοις was expanded to πρὸς τοὺς ἁγίους τοὺς ὄντας ἐν Ἐφέσῳ. A number of other suggestions are possible:[20] τοὺς ἐν Ἐφέσῳ ἁγίους (cf. Col. 1.2); τοὺς ἁγίους Ἐφεσίων (cf. 1 Thess. 1.1; 2 Thess. 1.1); τοὺς ἁγίους τοὺς ἐν Ἐφέσῳ (cf. Jas. 1.1); τοὺς ἁγίους ἐν Ἐφέσῳ (τοῦ Ἐφέσου cf. Gal. 1.2); but most of the letters of the Pauline corpus employ the present participle of εἰμί (Rom. 1.7; 1 Cor. 1.2; 2 Cor. 1.1; Phil. 1.1).[21] The earliest evidence for the association of Ephesians with other letters comes from 1 Peter where the author may know both it and Romans, and from Ignatius who probably knew both Ephesians and 1 Corinthians. The use of either of these as model would lead to the form we have suggested.

It is now possible to trace the further development of the text.

(*a*) The heading to the letter, probably once the letters had come together in codex form, was now abbreviated to πρὸς Ἐφεσίους.

(*b*) It was felt that the geographical destination should now be placed in the letter itself and so the phrase was carried bodily into the letter

277

and changed to the dative. Thus the text of Alexandrinus came into existence with the unfortunate position of ἐν Ἐφέσῳ.

(*c*) Some scribes however remembered that the original letter had no geographical reference and so when they copied it they simply omitted the reference to Ephesus, thus creating the text of Vaticanus.

(*d*) The text of P^{46} probably arose through the carelessness of a copyist faced with three words ending in οις.

This suggestion is independent of the question of Pauline authorship. Its strength lies in the way it accounts for the present very difficult forms of the text. Its weakness lies in the considerable amount of development, and therefore of time, which is necessary for the whole to be worked out. It does not solve the problem of the identification of the letter with the church at Ephesus but by dissociating this from the first identification of the letter it leaves greater flexibility for a solution to this problem.

NOTES

1   e.g. W. G. Kümmel, *Introduction to the New Testament* (London 1975), p. 480; D. Guthrie, *New Testament Introduction* (Leicester 1976), pp. 654–7; W. Schmithals, *Paulus und die Gnostiker* (Hamburg-Bergstedt 1965), pp. 175–200; C. L. Mitton, *The Formation of the Pauline Corpus of Letters* (London 1955); A. von Harnack, *Die Briefsammlung des Apostels Paulus* (Leipzig 1926).

2   There are good grounds for arguing for a number of informal collections of Paul's letters which were later united to form the present corpus; see most recently, K. Aland, 'Die Entstehung des Corpus Paulinum', in his *Neutestamentliche Entwürfe*, Theologische Bücherei 63 (Munich 1979), pp. 302–50.

3   O. Roller, *Das Formular der paulinischen Briefe*, BWANT IV, 6 (Stuttgart 1933), pp. 45 and n204, 392–4.

4   See, e.g., E. J. Goodspeed, *The Meaning of Ephesians* (Chicago, Ill., 1933), pp. 10f.

5   cf. T. Zahn, *Geschichte des neutestamentlichen Kanons* (Erlangen 1888), I, pp. 816–9. The attempt to deduce Ignatius' knowledge of Pauline Ephesians as addressed to the Ephesians from his *Eph.* 12.2 cannot be sustained; cf. T. K. Abbott, *Epistles to the Ephesians and to the Colossians*, ICC (Edinburgh 1897), pp. ix–xi.

6   e.g. H. Rathke, *Ignatius von Antiochien und die Paulusbriefe*, TU 99 (Berlin 1967), pp. 45f; cf. pp. 21–3.

7   If we take the rating of the Oxford Society of Historical Theology, *The New Testament in the Apostolic Fathers* (Oxford 1965) in respect of knowledge of particular New Testament writings and allocate numerical

values to their ratings (A = 4, B = 3, C = 2, D = 1) and add up the results as a rough guide to the knowledge shown by the various letters of Ignatius of the ten letter Pauline corpus then *Ephesians* makes the highest score at 37 with *Romans* next at 14.

8 W. Schenk, 'Zur Entstehung und zum Verständnis der Adresse des Epheserbriefes', *Theologische Versuche* (Berlin 1975) VI, pp. 73–8.

9 For a fuller discussion of the extant text forms see Best, 'Ephesians i.1' in *Text and Interpretation. Studies in the New Testament presented to Matthew Black*, ed. E. Best and R. McL. Wilson (Cambridge 1979), pp. 29–41, and the literature quoted there.

10 A. Lindemann, 'Bemerkungen zu den Adressaten und zum Anlass des Epheserbriefes', *ZNW* 67 (1976), pp. 235–51. In a review of the Matthew Black *Festschrift* (see n9) J. K. Elliott, *TZ* 35 (1979), pp. 368–70, apparently argues for the originality of this reading. He criticizes me for not observing that the present participle of εἰμί is often followed in Paul by a prepositional phrase and instances 1 Cor. 1.2; 2 Cor. 1.1; Phil. 1.1. This is so but, leaving aside the difficulty that Ephesians may not be Pauline, Elliott has failed to grasp the real difficulty (seen in the multiplicity of unsatisfactory explanations) of the resulting dissociation of ἅγιοι and πιστοί.

11 If a geographical identification had to be given no satisfactory explanation has as yet been offered why Ephesus was chosen.

12 On this reading cf. P. Benoit, *DBS*, VII, pp. 195–211.

13 cf. Roller, op. cit., pp. 199–212, and n382, pp. 520–5.

14 A number of writers have argued for this conjecture, e.g., J. Schmid, *Der Epheserbrief des Apostels Paulus* (Freiburg im Breisgau 1928), pp. 125ff; cf. M. Goguel, 'Esquisse d'une solution nouvelle du problème de l'épître aux Éphésiens', *RHR* 111 (1935), pp. 254ff, and 112 (1936), pp. 73ff, at p. 254, n1; P. Dacquino, 'I destinatari della lettera agli Efesini', *Riv. Bib.*, 6 (1955), pp. 102–10; J. C. Kirby, *Ephesians, Baptism and Pentecost* (London 1968), p. 170.

15 If Paul wrote both Colossians and Ephesians he clearly allowed himself to be influenced in Ephesians by what he wrote in Colossians and our argument would still hold.

16 cf. the addition of καὶ κυρίου 'Ἰησοῦ Χριστοῦ in 1.2 and the alteration of ἁμαρτιῶν (Col. 1.13) to παραπτωμάτων (Eph. 1.7); see C. L. Mitton, *The Epistle to the Ephesians* (Oxford 1951), pp. 279–315.

17 e.g., T. Zahn, *Introduction to the New Testament*, vol. i (ET Edinburgh 1909), p. 481.

18 Or πρός with the accusative.

19 It is difficult to estimate how much later this would be.

20 Assuming πρός in each instance.

21 In the first instance the dative may have been retained and πρός with the accusative appeared only when the identification was reduced to a simple geographical destination; see below.

23

Changes of Person and Number
in Paul's Epistles

C. E. B. Cranfield

A good many of the problems connected with Paul's varying uses of the first, second and third persons singular and plural and the apparent suddenness of his changes from one person to another have, of course, often been noted and studied; but the whole subject strikes us as fascinating, and we cannot help wondering whether a careful, systematic and comprehensive study of it might not make some modest but worthwhile contribution to the exegesis of the epistles – though any one engaging in such a piece of research would be well advised not to take himself too seriously or to try to claim for his 'findings' a greater reliability than could properly be ascribed to them. Such a study is quite beyond the range of a brief paper. All that can be undertaken here is to note just a few of the things which have interested us in this area.

I

It will be convenient to start with Paul's use of the second person plural and his transitions to it from other persons, because the occurrence of the second person plural in itself clearly requires no explanation in letters addressed to communities. Its frequent occurrence is only to be expected. We may notice that Paul occasionally uses it with reference not to the community, to which his letter is addressed, as a whole, but just to a particular section of it. Thus in Rom. 11.13, 25, 28, 30f, the second person plural refers to the Gentiles in the Christian community in Rome, not to the whole community. But what interests us particularly is the question whether it is possible to detect any special significance in Paul's transitions to the second person plural when he has been using another person.[1] We may look at a few examples.

An interesting one is to be seen in 1 Cor. 15.58. In the preceding verse the first person plural has been used ('but thanks be to God, which giveth us the victory through our Lord Jesus Christ').[2] The second person plural has occurred only once (in v. 51: 'Behold, I tell you a mystery') since v. 34 ('Awake up righteously, and sin not; . . . I speak *this* to move you to shame'). Then in v. 58 we have 'Therefore, my beloved brethren, be ye stedfast, unmoveable, always abounding in the work of the Lord, forasmuch as ye know that your labour is not in vain in the Lord'. In this situation the second person plural imperative seems to us to be a good deal more forceful than an exhortation in the first person plural would have been. The effect of the sudden change to the second person plural imperative seems to be to recall the Corinthian Christians with a certain peremptoriness from thoughts of future glory, on which they may well have been too ready to dwell, to the urgent demands of the present for resolute obedience to the Lord Jesus Christ.

In 1 Cor. 10.13 the effect of the return to the second person plural is rather different. The verse is the conclusion of a paragraph which began with this person (v. 1: 'For I would not, brethren, have you ignorant . . .') but is more strongly characterized by the use of the first person plural (vv. 6, 8f, 11) than by use of the second person plural (vv. 7 and 10). After the warning note sounded by the third person singular imperative of v. 12 ('Wherefore let him that thinketh he standeth take heed lest he fall') the return to the second person plural in v. 13 ('There hath no temptation taken you but such as man can bear: but God is faithful, who will not suffer you to be tempted above that ye are able; but will with the temptation make also the way of escape, that ye may be able to endure it') seems to give additional emphasis to the comfort and encouragement which are being offered.

In Rom. 8.9a there is an interesting change from the third persons plural and singular of vv. 5–8 to the second person plural, which is then continued (after the third person singular in the parenthetic v. 9b) in vv. 10 and 11. We suggest that by introducing the second person plural at this point, when it has not been used since 7.4 (though the second person singular was, it is true, used in 8.2, which will be discussed below), Paul is emphasizing the contrast between those whom he thus addresses directly ('But ye are not in the flesh, but in the spirit [RV: but 'Spirit' is surely to be preferred], if so be that the Spirit of God dwelleth in you') and those about whom he says in v. 8, 'they that are in the flesh cannot please God'. The continuation of this direct address in vv. 10 and 11 is natural enough. The extraordinary series of changes of person which follow in vv. 12–18 will be more appropriately discussed

281

under III. It is interesting that in Romans the use of the second person plural, while it is frequent in 1.1–15 and 15.14—16.27, is in the rest of the epistle – apart from the passages in chapter 8 already mentioned in this paragraph – confined to 2.24; 6.3, 11–14, 16–22; 7.1, 4; 11.13ff (the occurrences mentioned above in which the reference is to the Gentile Christians alone); 12.1–3, 9–19; 13.6–8, 11, 14; 14.1, 16; 15.5–7, 13.

II

We turn next to the use of the second person singular. One reason for the relative scarcity of occurrences of the second person plural in Romans is the frequency of the use of the second person singular (see 2.1, 3–5, 17–23, 25, 27; 8.2; 9.19f; 10.6, 8f; 11.17–22, 24; 12.20f; 13.3b–4; 14.4, 10, 15, 20–2). In chapter 2 Paul apostrophizes those who set themselves up to judge others. That from v. 17 to the end of the chapter he has the Jews in mind is clear, but we agree with those who think that Paul has them in mind right from v. 1. It is for the sake of greater forcefulness that the individual is addressed. The use of the second person singular in chapter 11 is not quite the same; for, whereas in chapter 2 Paul is apostrophizing the typical individual member of a group which is neither the community to which the letter as a whole is addressed nor yet a section of that community, so that the use of the second person singular is a somewhat artificial rhetorical device, in 11.17–22, 24, he uses the second person singular as a means of bringing home what he has to say as vividly as possible to each individual in the particular section of the Roman church which he is specially addressing in this passage of his letter (see 11.13).

In Rom. 12.20 ('But if thine enemy hunger . . .') the second person singular belongs to the Old Testament quotation, and the use of the same person in v. 21 ('Be not overcome of evil, but overcome evil with good') is natural enough. The individual Roman Christian is directly addressed. In Rom. 10.6, 8f also Paul is using Old Testament passages, and the second person singular comes with what he takes over ('Say not in thy heart, . . . The word is nigh thee, in thy mouth, and in thy heart: . . . with thy mouth . . . in thy heart'), and again he continues with the same person in his own 'thou shalt be saved' at the end of v. 9. In Rom. 13.3f the individual believer is addressed for the sake of vividness and forcefulness; and in chapter 14 the force of the appeal is greatly strengthened when in vv. 4 and 10a the individual 'weak'

Christian is addressed and in vv. 10b, 15 and 20–2 the individual 'strong' Christian. The second person singular in 9.19f is directed to an objector (cf. 1 Cor. 15.35–7).

The most interesting occurrence of the second person singular in Romans is surely that in 8.2, which is altogether unexpected and isolated. The best explanation of the σε[3] would seem to be that Paul, being very conscious of the amazing and momentous nature of the affirmation he was making and of its apparent incompatibility with what he had just said in the latter part of chapter 7, and fearing that its significance would be likely to be missed, hoped to compel the most alert attention possible by thus suddenly addressing the individual Roman Christian: 'the law of the Spirit of life has in Christ Jesus set thee free from the law of sin and of death' (our translation).

There is an interesting and significant variation between the second person singular and the second person plural in the Epistle to Philemon. In vv. 2, 4–22a and 23, the second person singular is used, the reference being to Philemon himself; but in vv. 3, 22b and 25, where Paul is associating with Philemon the other people mentioned in v. 2 (Apphia, Archippus and the church meeting in Philemon's house), the second person plural is used. The distinction disappears in the modern English versions – without trace.

The disastrously flattening effect of the abandonment of the second person singular in translation may be vividly illustrated by setting side by side the 1611 rendering of 1 Cor. 15.35f ('But some *man* will say, How are the dead raised up? . . . *Thou* fool, that which thou sowest . . .') and the 1881 rendering ('But some one will say, How are the dead raised? . . . Thou foolish one, that which thou thyself sowest . . .'), on the one hand, and the translation in the New English Bible ('But, you may ask, how are the dead raised? . . . How foolish! The seed you sow . . .'), on the other.[4]

III

We turn now to the first person plural. A number of different uses may be distinguished.

The most obvious is that which joins together Paul and those to whom the particular epistle is addressed – though it should be noted from the start that it is often difficult, or maybe impossible, to be sure whether in a particular occurrence of the first person plural the 'we' is thus limited or includes Christians quite generally. This use is frequently alternated with that of the second person plural. Thus in Rom. 8.9–17 we have the second person plural in vv. 9a and 10f (in the parenthetic v. 9b the third person singular is used) followed by the first person plural in v. 12, with which a new paragraph begins. The vocative 'brethren' makes it natural to understand the 'we' to mean just Paul and those addressed (though it does not necessitate it). By using the first person plural Paul takes his place alongside the Roman Christians rather than bringing out the contrast between himself and them. We might perhaps term this 'the first person plural of humility'. While the statement of obligation is not less authoritative, the fact that the authority is the authority of the gospel, to which Paul just as much as those he addresses is bound to submit, is emphasized rather than his own special position as an apostle. But in v. 13 he reverts to the second person plural with the warning and promise, 'for if ye live after the flesh, ye must die; but if by the spirit [RV: better 'Spirit'?] ye mortify the deeds of the body, ye shall live'. We then get a statement in the third person plural (the general statement, 'For as many as are led by the Spirit of God, these are sons of God'). Verse 15 then starts off in the second person plural, but in the middle of v. 15b Paul changes to the first person plural: 'whereby we cry, Abba, Father'. This use of the first person plural is then continued in vv. 16 and 17. While in v. 12 Paul's motive in using the 'we' form was probably (as we suggested above) to get alongside his readers in a brotherly way, it may be suggested that in vv. 15b–17 its use was motivated rather by the desire to acknowledge his own personal involvement – we might perhaps call it a 'confessional first person plural'. In the rest of the chapter the first person plural is predominant. It may well be that the more inclusive 'we Christians' use should be recognized here.

For further examples of the use of the first person plural in which something of a confessional significance is perhaps to be discerned we may compare Rom. 4.24f (in v. 25 a traditional formula is probably present); 5.1–11, 21; 6.1–8; 9.24 (the 'us', which is inserted rather awkwardly as far as the grammar is concerned, seems to have the effect of giving to the statement something of the character of a confession of faith); 15.4 and 7 (if Nestle 25th edn is right as against 26th in reading ἡμᾶς: RV has 'you').

Rom. 13.11–14 shows an interesting alternation between the second and first persons plural. Paul changes from the second person to the first person plural in the middle of v. 11. Then in vv. 12b–13 we have a hortatory use of the first person plural, Paul taking his place alongside the Christians of Rome in the consciousness that he himself too needs to try to do the things indicated. In v. 14 we have a crisp second person plural imperative. The three instances of the first person plural in Rom. 14.10c, 12 and 13a ('for we shall all stand before the judgement-seat of God', 'So then each one of us shall give account of himself to God', and 'Let us not therefore judge one another any more', respectively) may all perhaps, like those in 13.12b–13, be regarded as examples of what we called above 'the first person plural of humility'.

In Rom. 14.7f the first person plural is used in what would seem to be general doctrinal statements concerning all Christians. For some further instances of this usage, in which the 'we' most probably means Christians generally, reference may be made to 1 Cor. 15.19, 49, 51f, 57; Phil. 3.3, 20f; 1 Thess. 4.14f (though here the 'we' of the λέγομεν is different), and 17.

Another use of the first person plural is that to be found in Rom. 15.1, where 'we that are strong' refers to Paul together with one particular section of the Christians to whom the letter is addressed.

Elsewhere Paul uses the same person to associate himself with his fellow-Jews (e.g. Rom. 3.9; 4.1; 9.10).

Two other uses may be mentioned together: first, the special use of οἴδαμεν δέ in Rom. 2.2; 3.19; 8.28; and 1 Tim. 1.8 and of οἴδαμεν γάρ in Rom. 7.14; 8.22; 2 Cor. 5.1, to introduce a statement which the writer can assume will be generally acceptable to those whom he is addressing or whom he has in mind (the use of οἴδαμεν in 1 Cor. 8.1 and 4 may also be compared, though it is somewhat different); and, secondly, the formula τί ἐροῦμεν, which is employed in Rom. 3.5; 6.1; 7.7 and 9.14 to introduce an indication of a possible false inference from what Paul has been saying before rejecting it, in Rom. 8.31 and 9.30 to introduce his own conclusion, and in Rom. 4.1 to introduce the case of Abraham to clinch his argument.

The fact that the superscriptions of a number of the epistles include one or two other names alongside that of Paul[5] raises the question whether some of the first person plurals refer to Paul and persons associated with him in the composition of his letters. But this question cannot be isolated from another question, namely, that of the possible presence in the Pauline epistles of instances of an author's or literary plural with reference simply to Paul himself. So we shall consider the two together. In the case of 1 Thessalonians, which is written in the names of Paul, Silvanus and Timothy, it seems fairly natural to understand the first person plurals as far as 2.16 to refer to the three colleagues (apart from the double 'our' in 1.3 which is more naturally understood to refer to Christians generally or to the three colleagues and the people addressed). The use of the plural 'apostles' in 2.6 [RV: in Nestle 2.7] would seem to be some support for this interpretation. But, when 2.17—3.13 is taken into consideration, doubts arise. Does 'I Paul once and again' in 2.18 just emphasize Paul's own eagerness which was part of the common eagerness of the three colleagues or does it interpret the first person plurals 'we would fain' and 'us' in the same verse? And are we to understand the first person plural 'sent' (ἐπέμψαμεν) in 3.2 as referring to Paul and Silvanus or are we, in view of the use of the first person singular in 3.5 ('For this cause I also, when I could no longer forbear, sent') to take it to refer to Paul alone? And, when we turn to the end of the epistle, what are we to make of 'I adjure' in 5.27? Does it stand in contrast with 'we exhort' in 4.10, 'we would' in 4.13, 'we say' in 4.15, 'we beseech' in 5.12 and 'we exhort' in 5.14, or does it rather interpret these occurrences of the first person plural? In 2 Cor. 1.19, at any rate, it is clear that 'us' refers to Paul, Silvanus and Timothy, since it is explicitly so interpreted; and it seems likely that the first person plural pronouns in the following three verses have the same reference. Another clear instance of a first person plural referring to Paul and a colleague is to be seen in 1 Cor. 4.6 ('Now these things, brethren, I have in a figure transferred to myself and Apollos for your sakes; that in us ye might learn . . .'), and the first person plurals in vv. 1 and 8 may best be explained as having the same reference. Compare 1 Cor. 9.6 ('Or I only and Barnabas, have we not a right to forbear working?') and the possibility that some other first person plurals in the context may also refer to Paul and Barnabas. The expression 'us the apostles' in 1 Cor. 4.9 probably has a wider reference than Paul and Apollos.

That Paul did sometimes use the first person plural with reference simply to himself we regard as almost certain. It has been claimed that no such author's plural is to be found in those epistles of the Pauline corpus the superscriptions of which do not associate one or more persons with Paul.[6] But 'we received' in Rom. 1.5 ('through whom we received grace and apostleship, unto obedience of faith among all the nations') is, we think, most probably to be explained as such a plural;[7] and βλασφημούμεθα and ἡμᾶς in 3.8 and προῃτιασάμεθα in 3.9 of the same epistle are surely also most naturally so explained. In 1 and 2 Corinthians (both of which do have more than one name in the superscription) there are quite a number of first person plurals which it seems most natural to take as referring simply to Paul: for example, those in 1 Cor. 9.11f (in view of the use of the first person singular in the sequel); those in 2 Cor. 1.4–14 and 18 (compare vv. 15–17) and 24 (compare v. 23); 7.5–7 (note the combination of the plural and singular of the first person pronoun in v. 7 and the continuation in the first person singular in vv. 8ff); 7.12—8.8 (note the occurrences of the first person singular in 7.12, 14, 16; 8.3 and 8) and 9.3 ('our glorying on your behalf': cf. 'your readiness, of which I glory on your behalf' in the previous verse).

From what has been said above it is clear, we think, that there is scope for a good deal of further, and more careful, investigation of the occurrences of the first person plural in Paul's epistles.

IV

We must look now briefly at Paul's use of the first person singular. We refer, first, to two points in connection with Rom. 1.8–16. One is the use of the genitive of the first person singular pronoun with 'God' in v. 8. It is something which is not common in Paul's letters, being limited otherwise to Phil. 1.3 and Philem. 4, which are similar contexts to this, and 2 Cor. 12.21 and Phil. 4.19 (it occurs also in some authorities in 1 Cor. 1.4). It strikes a strongly personal note reminiscent of some passages in the Psalms. Compare 'Jesus Christ my Lord' in Phil. 3.8 and 'who loved me, and gave himself up for me' in Gal. 2.20. The other point is just that the contrast between the ordinary use of the first person singular in these verses and the – if we were right about 'we received' – perhaps somewhat formal and official tone of v. 5 may be noted.

A number of places where there is a specially emphatic use may be noted: Rom. 9.3 (ηὐχόμην γὰρ ἀνάθεμα εἶναι αὐτὸς ἐγὼ ἀπὸ τοῦ Χριστοῦ ὑπὲρ τῶν ἀδελφῶν μου τῶν συγγενῶν μου κατὰ σάρκα); 2 Cor. 10.1 (Αὐτὸς δὲ ἐγὼ Παῦλος παρακαλῶ ὑμᾶς . . . ὃς κατὰ πρόσωπον μὲν ταπεινὸς ἐν ὑμῖν, ἀπὼν δὲ θαρρῶ εἰς ὑμᾶς); 1 Thess. 2.18 (διότι ἠθελήσαμεν ἐλθεῖν πρὸς ὑμᾶς, ἐγὼ μὲν Παῦλος καὶ ἅπαξ καὶ δίς . . .). There is a special emphasis also in the first person singular perfect passive (πέπεισμαι) in Rom. 8.38 following the use of the first person plural (referring to Christians generally) in v. 37: it was surely intended to emphasize the character of personal testimony possessed by vv. 38 and 39. Emphatic also are the instances of the first person singular in Rom. 14.14 ('I know, and am persuaded in the Lord Jesus . . . ') and 15.14

('And I myself also am persuaded of you, my brethren, . . .'). Mention may also be made of Rom. 11.1 ('. . . For I also am an Israelite . . .'), where Paul appeals to the evidence afforded by the fact that the chosen apostle of the Gentiles is himself a Jew. We may notice here that, while sometimes Paul seems to use a first person plural with a certain authoritative formality and solemnity (so, we think, in Rom. 1.5), he seems also on occasion to employ the first person singular with a specially solemn effect (e.g. λέγω in Rom. 12.3 and 15.8; παρακαλῶ in Rom. 12.1).

There seems also to be a generalizing use of the first person singular in a number of places in the Pauline epistles. We mention as probable examples Rom. 3.7 ('But if the truth of God through my lie abounded unto his glory, why am I also still judged as a sinner?'); 1 Cor. 6.15b (cf. v. 12); 10.29f; 13.1–3, 11f; 14.11 (cf. vv. 14f); Gal. 2.18. The most discussed passage in this connection is Rom. 7.7–25; but, as we have recently discussed it at some length elsewhere,[8] we refrain from treating it here.

V

The third person singular and plural in Paul's epistles we can do no more here than just touch on. That the occurrences are very numerous goes without saying; but there are some things in particular which we should want to consider, if space permitted, as, for example, the passages of some length which are prevailingly in the third person plural; the characteristics and functions of short third person singular or plural statements introduced in the course of passages marked by the use of another person; and Paul's apparent reference to himself in the third person (2 Cor. 12.2–5).

Perhaps what has been said above may be, in spite of its cursoriness and other very obvious defects, enough to suggest that Paul's uses of the different persons and his sometimes remarkably rapid transitions from one to another (which surely contribute a good deal to the general impression of vivacity which one gets from his epistles) may deserve rather closer attention than they usually receive.

NOTES

1   The possibility that some of these changes were motivated by nothing more serious than a desire for variety or are merely accidental is not to be ruled

out. Textual variants often occur where there are changes of person; but, since the tendency to assimilate was strong, readings which involve a change of person are, other things being equal, probably to be preferred to those which do not.

2   We shall quote the English Revised Version unless we indicate otherwise.

3   On the textual question reference may be made to C. E. B. Cranfield, *A Critical and Exegetical Commentary on the Epistle to the Romans* I (Edinburgh ³1980), pp. 376f.

4   Perhaps it would not be out of place to record here our conviction that the jettisoning of the second person singular in recent English versions has not just resulted in a lessening of accuracy in detail and a considerable literary impoverishment, but has also effected a much more serious and substantial loss. By obliterating what we would call 'the evangelical second person singular', that use of the second person singular which so often, both in the Old Testament and in the New, expresses with pointed directness and haunting appeal the truth that God's grace and judgement concern not just men in general but each individual man in particular, it has obscured something utterly essential to the gospel, which it is always the Church's duty to try to declare as unambiguously as possible. In a day when the individual, unless he happens to belong to a privileged élite of power, wealth or ability, tends to count for less and less, and is often oppressed by his consciousness of the fact, one might have expected the Church to cherish every resource at its disposal for emphasizing the direct appeal of the gospel to the individual. It is, in our view, an extraordinary ineptitude hastily to throw away the means our language possesses for expressing directly that gospel truth which cannot be so readily or effectively expressed without it, on the ground that it seems archaic to our bourgeois taste (it is still to be heard in ordinary use in some parts of the country among manual workers), and to insist on preferring to it the plural of politeness which originated as a servile plural in the rigid class distinctions of a feudal society (the serf addressing his manor lord in the plural while the lord addressed his serf in the singular). (That we also regard the deferential plural as a thoroughly inappropriate form of address to the God whose oneness is fundamental to the faith of Christians, Jews and Moslems alike need hardly be said!)

5   In Gal. 1.1–2 we have 'Paul . . . and all the brethren which are with me'.

6   So, for example, in F. Blass and A. Debrunner, *A Greek Grammar of the New Testament and other early Christian literature*, ET R. W. Funk (Cambridge 1961), §280.

7   See further Cranfield, op. cit., p. 65.

8   op. cit., pp. 340–70 (especially 342–7).

24

La Mission de Paul d'après Actes 26.16–23 et la Mission des Apôtres d'après Luc 24.44–9 et Actes 1.8[*]

Jacques Dupont

Notre image de la personnalité de Paul est celle qui se dégage des lettres que nous reconnaissons provenir de lui. Elle est sensiblement différente de celle que proposent les lettres deutéro-pauliniennes, différente aussi du portrait qui nous est donné de Paul dans les Actes des Apôtres. Cela ne signifie pas que la présentation lucanienne de Paul est sans intérêt et sans valeur. Le Professeur Barrett est revenu récemment sur le fait que l'auteur des Actes n'utilise pas et semble ignorer la correspondance de Paul,[1] mais il a également souligné que, s'il n'y a pas coïncidence entre la pensée exprimée dans un discours comme celui qui est adressé aux Anciens de l'Eglise d'Ephèse (Actes 20.18–35) et celle que traduisent les épîtres certainement pauliniennes, les Actes n'en reposent pas moins sur des traditions dont les épîtres nous permettent de vérifier la qualité.[2]

Sur un point le désaccord est manifeste: Paul revendique avec insistance le titre d'Apôtre de Jésus Christ, alors que les Actes refusent de le lui accorder, au moins dans son sens prégnant. Il est trop clair, et le Professeur Barrett l'a rappelé avec raison,[3] que ce refus n'implique aucune dépréciation: la place que les Actes font à Paul montre assez l'importance décisive qui lui est reconnue. Mais, prenant très au sérieux la tradition qui identifiait les Apôtres aux Douze,[4] Luc devait trouver un autre moyen pour exprimer le rôle unique joué par Paul aux origines du mouvement chrétien, rôle comparable à celui de Pierre et des douze Apôtres et pourtant distinct du leur. La manière dont il s'y est pris a fait l'objet de nombreuses études ces dernières années, et l'attention s'est particulièrement portée sur la qualification de 'témoin' du Christ, reconnue à Paul comme elle l'est aux Douze, même si son contenu n'est pas identique dans les deux cas.[5]

Les limites étroites assignées à cet article ne permettent pas de reprendre l'ensemble de la question. Nous voudrions simplement

* See English summary on p. 300

attirer l'attention sur le passage des Actes qui définit avec le plus de
soin la mission attribuée à Paul, et rapprocher ce passage de celui dans
lequel Luc précise la mission que les Apôtres ont reçue du Christ
ressuscité (Luc 24.44–9; cf. Actes 1.8). Nous pensons que ces textes ont
une importance capitale pour ce qui concerne la pensée christologique
de Luc et la perspective dans laquelle il a voulu prolonger le récit
évangélique par l'histoire racontée dans les Actes;[6] leur portée ne
paraît pas moins grande pour ce qui regarde la manière dont Luc situe
Paul par rapport aux Douze.

Commençons par une remarque sur l'emplacement des textes qui
vont nous occuper. En Luc 24.44–9 et Actes 1.8, il s'agit des dernières
paroles de Jésus avant son enlèvement définitif au ciel. Actes 26.16–23
constitue la finale du dernier grand discours attribué à Paul dans les
Actes, immédiatement avant le départ pour Rome, où il n'y aura plus
de discours proprement dit, mais seulement une déclaration extrême-
ment solennelle destinée à conclure le livre (Actes 28.25–8). On peut
noter aussi que le discours du chapitre 26 contient le dernier des trois
récits de l'apparition de Damas, complété ici par une vue d'ensemble
sur la manière dont Paul a accompli la mission qu'il avait reçue
(26.19–23). Nous nous trouvons ainsi en face d'une sorte de récapitula-
tion générale de la carrière de Paul, terminant l'histoire qui avait été
amorcée à la fin du chapitre 7 (l'épisode de Rome apparaît d'abord
comme la conclusion de l'histoire du procès: 28.17–22).[7] A ce point de
vue aussi, le discours du chapitre 26 fait figure de finale et peut être
rapproché des dernières instructions de Jésus à ses disciples avant son
ascension.

Analyse de Actes 26.16–23

Introduit par un exorde de circonstance (26.2–3), le discours devant le
roi Agrippa commence par un rappel du passé, celui où Paul était
Pharisien et auquel il reste fidèle dans son espérance (v. 4–8), celui
aussi où il s'opposait de toutes ses forces au christianisme (v. 9–11). On
arrive ensuite à l'apparition de Damas: dans un premier temps, Jésus
s'est fait reconnaître (v. 12–15); après quoi, il a dit à Paul ce qu'il
attendait de lui (v. 16–18). Paul achève son discours en rapportant la
manière dont il a rempli la mission qu'il avait ainsi reçue (v. 19–20) et
en précisant ce qui fait l'objet de sa prédication (v. 21–3). Il saute aux
yeux que les trois dernières sections concernent la mission de Paul:
comment elle a été définie par Jésus, comment Paul l'a exécutée, ce qui
en fait le contenu.

Il ne serait pas sans intérêt de comparer ces trois petites sections avec les deux récits antérieurs de l'événement de Damas: plus précisément avec ce que le Seigneur dit à Ananie au sujet de la mission de Paul en 9.15–16, et ce qu'Ananie en dit à Paul en 22.14–15. Dans ce dernier cas, la déclaration d'Ananie est complétée par celle que Jésus lui-même a faite à Paul lors d'une vision ultérieure dans le Temple de Jérusalem (22.18,21). La confrontation des textes prendrait trop de place, et elle ne paraît pas indispensable au but que nous poursuivons. De même, il ne paraît pas nécessaire de s'attarder aux rappels d'Ancien Testament qui forment le tissu des paroles attribuées à Jésus en 26.16–18. Il suffit pour notre propos de caractériser les quatre points auxquels on touche en parlant de la mission de Paul, au moment où elle lui est confiée (v. 16–18), à propos de son exécution (v. 19–20) et de son contenu (v. 21–3).

Le début du v. 16 assure le lien avec ce qui précède: Paul était tombé à terre (v. 14), il est invité à se relever. Jésus commence alors: 'Voici pourquoi je te suis apparu (ὤφθην).' Nous avons affaire à une apparition, à l'irruption d'une réalité céleste dans le monde des hommes: appelons cela le point A. Paul apprend aussitôt en quoi cela le concerne (point B): Jésus veut 'l'instituer ministre et témoin' de ce qu'il a vu et verra encore. Le point C s'intéresse aux destinataires de cette mission: Paul est envoyé 'au Peuple et aux Nations' (v. 17). Il lui est dit enfin (point D) en quoi consiste sa charge: 'leur ouvrir les yeux', c'est-à-dire 'les convertir des ténèbres à la lumière, de l'empire de Satan à Dieu, pour que par la foi en (Jésus), ils reçoivent le pardon des péchés . . .' (v. 18).

Même ordonnance dans ce que les vv. 19–20 disent de l'exécution. Paul ne s'est pas montré indocile 'à la vision céleste' (A). Chargé de faire oeuvre de témoin, il s'acquitte de sa tâche en 'annonçant', ἀπήγγελλον (B). On précise ensuite les destinataires du message (C): 'D'abord à ceux de Damas et à Jérusalem ainsi que dans tout le pays de Judée, puis aux Nations'. Enfin l'objet du message (D): 'je leur ai annoncé de se repentir et de se convertir à Dieu . . .', (v. 20).

Le v. 21 se présente comme un élément de transition; on remarque en même temps qu'il fait inclusion avec le v. 16: le Seigneur était apparu à Paul pour l'instituer (προχειρίσασθαι) témoin; les Juifs ont essayé de le supprimer (διαχειρίσασθαι). Le v. 22 enchaîne: Paul a bénéficié 'de la protection qui vient de Dieu'; c'est encore une intervention céleste dans les affaires terrestres (A), bien que d'un autre type que celle du v. 16. Alors qu'au v. 16 Paul avait été établi 'ministre et témoin' (B), il déclare maintenant: 'jusqu'à ce jour je me suis tenu debout en rendant témoignage (μαρτυρόμενος); alors qu'au v. 20 Paul avait rempli sa mission en 'annonçant' (ἀπήγγελλον), on trouve le verbe correspondant en fin du v. 23: le Christ devait 'annoncer' (καταγγέλλειν) la lumière', ce qu'il fait pratiquement par le ministère de son témoin (B). Pour ce qui concerne les destinataires (C), le v. 22 dit simplement 'devant petits et grands', soulignant l'universalité; mais la précision du v. 17 revient en fin du v. 23: 'au Peuple et aux Nations'. Enfin l'objet du message (D): 'rien en dehors de ce que les Prophètes ainsi que Moïse avaient annoncé devoir arriver' (v. 22). La formulation n'a pas d'équivalent dans les versets précédents, mais elle s'inscrit bien dans le prolongement des allusions que les v. 16–18 faisaient à plusieurs textes prophétiques. Ce qui est dit tout à la fois du contenu des Ecritures et de la prédication de Paul est plus important: 'que le Christ aurait à souffrir et que, le premier ressuscité d'entre les morts, il annoncerait la lumière au Peuple et aux Nations' (v. 23). Cette annonce que l'Ecriture attribue au Christ ressuscité trouve précisément sa réalisation dans la mission de Paul, envoyé par le Christ 'au Peuple et aux Nations' (v. 17) pour 'les convertir des ténèbres à la lumière' (v. 18). En fait, le v. 18 assignait un double objet à la prédication: la conversion et la foi; le v. 20 a repris et accentué l'aspect conversion, tandis que les v. 22–23 insistent sur l'argumentation christologique qui correspond à l'aspect de la foi.

En voilà assez, semble-t-il, pour penser que les v. 16–18, 19–20 et 21–23 recourent trois fois au même schéma de base: (A) intervention céleste, (B) mission confiée au témoin, (C) concernant les Juifs et les Gentils, (D) portant sur un message de conversion et de foi.

Analyse de Luc 24.44–9 et Actes 1.8

En divisant son ouvrage en deux livres, Luc sait qu'il doit soigneusement éviter de faire de cette division une interruption du récit. Le procédé recommandé dans ce cas est celui de 'l'entremêlement des extrémités':[8] la finale du premier livre anticipe sur les événements du second, et le début du second revient sur ce qui a déjà été rapporté dans le premier. Il n'est donc pas étonnant que la fin de l'évangile et le début des Actes mentionnent les paroles par lesquelles, avant son ascension, Jésus a confié aux Apôtres leur mission. Ces paroles reçoivent naturellement deux formes différentes: Luc connaît assez l'art d'écrire pour éviter de se répéter. Nous pouvons donc nous attendre à trouver en Luc 22.44–9 et Actes 1.4–8 deux versions parallèles et complémentaires des termes par lesquels Jésus a pris définitivement congé de ses Apôtres.

Il va de soi que ces dernières paroles sont introduites par le récit de l'apparition (Luc 24.36–43) ou des apparitions (Actes 1.3) au cours desquelles le Ressuscité s'est fait reconnaître. Nous n'avons pas plus à nous attarder sur cette mise en scène que nous ne l'avons fait pour celle d'Actes 26.12–15.

Luc 24.44–9 se présente non pas comme un discours seulement mais comme deux discours, introduits l'un et l'autre par le lemme 'Et il leur dit' (v. 44, 46) et séparés l'un de l'autre par la notice narrative du v. 45: 'Alors il leur ouvrit l'intelligence pour qu'ils comprennent les Ecritures.' Le v. 44 présente les événements qui viennent de se produire comme accomplissant à la fois les paroles de Jésus qui les avait annoncés et les Ecritures qui le concernaient: 'Ce sont là mes paroles que je vous ai dites quand j'étais encore avec vous:[9] il faut que s'accomplisse tout ce qui se trouve écrit de moi dans la Loi de Moïse, les Prophètes et les Psaumes.' Il ne s'agit pas encore directement ici de la mission des Apôtres, mais nous avons affaire déjà à ce qui en fera l'objet.

Les v. 46–7 reprennent en précisant le contenu des Ecritures qui visaient Jésus en sa qualité de Messie: 'Ainsi était-il écrit que le Christ souffrirait et ressusciterait d'entre les morts le troisième jour, et qu'en son nom le repentir et la rémission des péchés seraient proclamés à toutes les Nations, en commençant par Jérusalem.' Le v. 48 ajoute enfin la parole d'institution: 'De ces choses, c'est vous qui êtes les témoins'. Ainsi les Apôtres ne sont établis dans leur mission qu'après la définition de ce qui doit faire l'objet de leur témoignage: l'accomplissement en Jésus de ce que les Ecritures disaient du Messie; après aussi la mention des destinataires de ce témoignage: toutes les Nations, à partir de Jérusalem. Reste le v. 49: la mission des témoins ne commencera vraiment que quand ils auront été 'revêtus de la force d'en haut', par la venue de l'Esprit que Jésus leur enverra d'auprès du Père.

Nous croyons pouvoir découvrir dans ces versets une définition de la mission des Apôtres, même s'il est vrai que les paroles du Ressuscité sont prononcées en présence 'des Onze et de ceux qui étaient avec eux' (v. 33; cf. v. 9).[10] Ce qui n'était peut-être pas parfaitement clair dans la finale de l'évangile devient limpide avec le début des Actes. On y voit d'abord que la dernière instruction de Jésus s'adressait 'aux Apôtres qu'il avait choisis' (Actes 1.2), expression qui rappelle indubitablement la scène du choix des douze Apôtres en Luc 6.13–16. De plus, il faut tenir compte du fait que l'introduction des Actes se termine par une liste nominative des Onze (Actes 1.13), à la suite de laquelle Luc ajoute: 'Tous ceux-là étaient persévérants unanimement dans la prière, avec des femmes et Marie, la mère de Jésus, et avec ses frères' (v. 14). Les Onze ne sont donc pas seuls, mais le texte les distingue nettement de ceux qui les accompagnent. La présence d'autres personnes n'empêche nullement que les instructions du Ressuscité concernent proprement 'les Apôtres', c'est-à-dire ici les Onze, auxquels un douzième sera bientôt adjoint (1.22, 26).[11] C'est aux Apôtres que Jésus a prescrit de ne pas s'éloigner de Jérusalem, là où ils doivent recevoir l'Esprit (Actes 1.4–5 = Luc 24.49) et inaugurer leur ministère (Actes 2.14, 37).

C'est dans ce contexte que notre attention doit se porter sur la définition du ministère apostolique donnée en Actes 1.8. Pour donner à ce verset tout le relief qu'il mérite, Luc l'a pourvu d'une double introduction: d'abord une question des Apôtres sur le moment du rétablissement de la royauté en Israël (v. 6), puis une première réponse, négative, par laquelle Jésus écarte cette fausse perspective (v. 7).[12] Alors seulement vient la déclaration décisive: 'Mais vous allez recevoir la force du Saint Esprit qui viendra sur vous, et vous serez mes témoins tant à Jérusalem que dans toute la Judée et la Samarie, et jusqu'à l'extrémité de la terre.' On reconnaît ici la promesse d'une 'force d'en haut' sur laquelle se terminait l'instruction de Luc 24.49. On retrouve ensuite la manière dont Luc 24.48 définissait la mission des Apôtres comme celle de 'témoins'. Il est enfin question des destinataires de cette mission: par rapport à l'ordre inversé de Luc 24.47, 'à toutes les Nations, en commençant par Jérusalem', Actes 1.8 rétablit la succession normale, mais en adjoignant à Jérusalem la Judée et la Samarie,[13] et en substituant à 'toutes les Nations' l'expression prophétique: 'jusqu'à l'extrémité de la terre' (Isa. 49.6 = Actes 13.47).

Confrontation

Il doit être possible de rapprocher la manière dont Actes 26.16–23 présente trois fois la mission de Paul et ce qui est dit deux fois de la mission des Apôtres en Luc 24.44–9 et Actes 1.8:

A   La mission de Paul suppose une intervention céleste: apparition du Christ en gloire (Actes 26.16, 19) ou protection particulière accordée par Dieu (v. 22). Les Apôtres ne pourront exercer la mission qu'ils ont reçue lors de l'apparition du Ressuscité qu'après avoir été investis de la 'force d'en haut' qui leur sera donnée par l'Esprit (Luc 24.49; Actes 1.8).

B   L'apparition de Damas a pour but d'instituer Paul 'ministre et témoin' de ce qu'il a vu (Actes 26.16);[14] Paul se montrera obéissant en 'rendant témoignage' (v. 22), en 'annonçant' (v. 20) un message qui coïncide avec celui que le Christ devait 'annoncer' (v. 23). Jésus ressuscité institue les Apôtres 'témoins' (Luc 24.48) et les charge d'agir comme 'ses témoins' auprès des hommes (Actes 1.8); ainsi se réalisera ce que l'Ecriture disait de la 'proclamation', qui doit être faite 'au nom' du Christ (Luc 24.47).

C   Destinataires du message: 'le Peuple et les Nations' (Actes 26.16, 23), 'd'abord ceux de Damas et de Jérusalem et tout le pays des Juifs, puis les Nations' (v. 20), 'toutes les Nations, en commençant par Jérusalem' (Luc 24.47), 'tant à Jérusalem que dans toute la Judée et la Samarie, et jusqu'à l'extrémité de la terre' (Actes 1.8).

D   Le contenu du message est explicité par rapport aux Ecritures. Actes 26.16–18 se contente d'accumuler les allusions bibliques, tandis que, dans les v. 22–3, Paul affirme 'ne rien dire en dehors de ce que les Prophètes et Moïse ont annoncé devoir arriver: que le Christ aurait à souffrir et que, le premier ressuscité d'entre les morts, il annoncerait la lumière au Peuple et aux Nations'. C'est le point accentué en Luc 24.44, 46–7: 'Il fallait que s'accomplisse tout ce qui a été écrit à mon sujet dans la Loi de Moïse, les Prophètes et les Psaumes . . . Il était écrit que le Christ souffrirait, qu'il ressusciterait d'entre les morts le troisième jour, et qu'en son nom seraient proclamés le repentir et la rémission des péchés . . .' Au lieu de parler du 'repentir et de la rémission des péchés', Actes 26.18 est une invitation à 'se convertir des ténèbres à la lumière' et à 'recevoir le pardon de ses péchés', tandis que le v. 20 appelle à 'se repentir et se convertir à Dieu'. A noter qu'en Actes 1.8 la référence à l'Ecriture est seulement impliquée dans l'allusion finale à Isa. 49.6; il semble qu'après avoir si fortement souligné ce point dans le finale de l'évangile, Luc a voulu éviter une répétition.

Les observations que nous venons de faire devraient être étendues à un ensemble de textes plus large; elles sont trop limitées pour constituer plus qu'un sondage. Elles sont cependant assez claires pour permettre de penser que Luc applique à la mission de Paul le même modèle que celui qui définit la mission des douze Apôtres. Comme celle des Apôtres, la mission de Paul se rattache directement au Christ: comme eux, il est 'témoin' immédiat et accrédité, même si son témoignage au Ressuscité ne s'étend pas à l'existence terrestre de Jésus. Comme celle des Apôtres, la mission de Paul réalise une tâche qui fait partie intégrante du programme assigné au Messie par les Ecritures: 'annoncer la lumière au Peuple et aux Nations' (Actes 26.23; cf. Luc 24.47).

Il faudrait ajouter que, dans le cadre du récit des Actes, c'est finalement sur Paul que repose la responsabilité principale de cette tâche messianique. Le rôle des Apôtres est strictement confiné à Jérusalem et aux régions qui s'y rattachent, la Judée et la Samarie; Pierre ne va pas plus loin que Césarée, et rien n'est dit du séjour qu'il a fait à Antioche (Gal. 2.11–14). Lors du dernier voyage de Paul à Jérusalem, les Apôtres ne paraissent plus s'y trouver (Actes 21.17–19). Où sont-ils donc? Peu importe aux yeux de Luc: en quittant Jérusalem, ils sortent en même temps de la scène des Actes (cf. 12.17). Pierre et les responsables de l'Eglise de Jérusalem ayant admis le principe (Actes 10.1–11, 18; 15.6–29), c'est à Paul qu'il revient de faire parvenir le témoignage du Christ aux nations païennes (Luc 24.47), jusqu'à l'extrémité de la terre (Actes 1.8). Il apparaît ainsi comme l'exécuteur de la mission confiée aux Apôtres, et cela en vertu du mandat qu'il a reçu directement du Christ, approuvé par les Apôtres et les presbytres de Jérusalem, mais sans avoir besoin d'aucune délégation de leur part.

Dans le rôle qui leur est propre, limité dans l'espace et dans le temps, les Apôtres assurent la continuité entre le ministère terrestre de Jésus et l'Eglise née de la venue de l'Esprit. Mais c'est à Paul qu'a incombé la tâche d'assurer à cette Eglise sa dimension universelle telle que Luc l'a sous les yeux et telle qu'il la voit annoncée par les prophètes. Dans les Actes, Paul apparaît en quelque sorte comme le chaînon unique par l'intermédiaire duquel l'Eglise d'après les Apôtres se rattache à ses origines.

NOTES

1   C. K. Barrett, 'Acts and the Pauline Corpus', *ET* 88 (1976–7), pp. 2–5.

2   C. K. Barrett, 'Paul's Address to the Ephesian Elders', dans *God's Christ and His people: studies in honour of N. A. Dahl*, edd. J. Jervell & W. A. Meeks, Oslo-Bergen-Tromsö 1977, pp. 107–21.

3 C. K. Barrett, 'Pauline Controversies in the Post-Pauline Period', *NTS* 20 (1973–4), pp. 229–45 (240).

4 Tradition qui semble supposée déjà par la rédaction de Marc (6.30; cf. 3.14; et 6.7) et en tout cas clairement présente en Apoc. 21.14.

5 Voir C. Burchard, *Der dreizehnte Zeuge: Traditions- und kompositionsgeschichtliche Untersuchungen zu Lukas' Darstellung der Frühzeit des Paulus*, FRLANT 103, Göttingen 1970, pp. 51–136; G. Schneider, 'Die zwölf Apostel als "Zeugen": Wesen, Ursprung und Funktion einer lukanischen Konzeption, dans *Christuszeugnis der Kirche. Theologische Studien* (edd. P.-W. Scheele & G. Schneider), Essen 1970, pp. 41–65; K. Löning, *Die Saulustradition in der Apostelgeschichte*, NtAbh 9, Münster 1973, pp. 126–64; H.-J. Michel, *Die Abschiedsrede des Paulus an die Kirche, Apg. 20.17–38: Motivgeschichte und theologische Bedeutung*, SANT 35, München 1973, pp. 77–80; V. Stolle, *Der Zeuge als Angeklagter. Untersuchungen zum Paulusbild des Lukas*, BWANT 102, Stuttgart 1973, pp. 140–54; C.-P. März, *Das Wort Gottes bei Lukas: die lukanische Worttheologie als Frage an die neuere Lukasforschung, Erfurter theol. St.* 11, Leipzig 1974, pp. 44–52; U. Wilckens, *Die Missionsreden der Apostelgeschichte: Form- und traditionsgeschichtliche Untersuchungen*, WMANT 5, 3e éd., Neukirchen-Vluyn 1974, pp. 144–49; C. Burchard, 'Paulus in der Apostelgeschichte', *Th.Lit.* 100 (1975), col. 881–95 (890); M. Dumais, *Le langage de l'évangélisation: l'annonce missionnaire en milieu juif (Actes 13.16–41)* (*Recherches* 16), Tournai-Montréal 1976, pp. 244–51; E. Kränkl, 'Paulus und die Auferweckungszeugen nach der Apostelgeschichte', *Kirche im Werden: Studien zum Thema Amt und Gemeinde im Neuen Testament*, ed. J. Hainz, Paderborn 1976, pp. 205–14; E. Nellessen, *Zeugnis für Jesus und das Wort: Exegetische Untersuchungen zum lukanischen Zeugnisbegriff*, BBB 43, Köln-Bonn 1976, pp. 76–246; A. A. Trites, *The New Testament Concept of Witness*, SNTSMS 31, Cambridge 1977, pp. 128–55; C. Burchard, 'Formen der Vermittlung christlichen Glaubens im Neuen Testament: Beobachtungen anhand von kerygma, martyria und verwandten Wörtern, *EvTh* 38 (1978), pp. 313–40 (324s.); R. J. Dillon, *From Eye-Witnesses to Ministers of the Word. Tradition and Composition in Luke 24*, AnBib 82, Rome 1978, pp. 212–18; 279–96; M. Dömer, *Das Heil Gottes: Studien zur Theologie des lukanischen Doppelwerkes*, BBB 51, Köln-Bonn 1978, pp. 134–6; R. F. O'Toole, *Acts 26: the Christological climax of Paul's defense (Acts 22.1—26.32)*, AnBib 78, Rome 1978, pp. 69; 102–4; H. J. Hauser, *Strukturen der Abschlusserzählung der Apostelgeschichte (Apg. 28.16–31)*, AnBib 86, Rome 1979, pp. 126–30; J. Lambrecht, 'Paul's Farewell-Address at Miletus (Acts 20.17–38), *Les Actes des Apôtres: traditions, rédaction, théologie*, ed. J. Kremer, BETL 48, Gembloux-Leuven 1979, pp. 307–37 (p. 333, n. 94).

6 C'est l'aspect sous lequel nous nous sommes occupé de cest textes dans notre étude sur 'La portée christologique de l'évangélisation des nations d'après Luc 24.47', *Neues Testament und Kirche. Für R. Schnackenburg*, ed. J. Gnilka, Freiburg i.B. 1974, pp. 125–43. Voir aussi M. Dömer, *Das Heil Gottes*, pp. 203–6.

7 Voir notre étude 'La conclusion des Actes et son rapport à l'ensemble de

l'ouvrage de Luc', *Les Actes des Apôtres: traditions, rédaction, théologie*, ed. J. Kremer, BETL 48, Gembloux-Leuven 1979, pp. 359–404 (380–83).

8   Lucien, *Hist. conscr.*, 55 (64). Voir à ce propos notre article 'La question du plan des Actes des Apôtres à la lumière d'un texte de Lucien de Samosate', *NT* 21 (1979), pp. 220–31.

9   Rappel de Deut. 1.1.

10 Sur cette expression voir la note récente de J. Plevnik, ' "The Eleven and those with them" according to Luke', *CBQ* 40 (1978), p. 205–211.

11 Nous avons dit ailleurs (*Th.Rev.* 73 (1977), col. 279s.)notre désaccord avec la manière dont E. Nellessen élargit le groupe des témoins; nous nous trouvons en même temps d'accord, notamment, avec R. J. Dillon, *From Eye-Witnesses*, pp. 218; M. Dömer, *Das Heil Gottes*, p. 134.

12 On reconnaît dans ce v. 7 une variante du logion de Marc 13.32.

13 Noter le lien étroit que la particule τε assure entre la mention de Jérusalem et celle de ces deux régions, et le fait que celles-ci sont regroupées sous un seul article.

14 L'expression rappelle naturellement celle de Luc 1.2, qui désignait les Apôtres.

ENGLISH SUMMARY

One of the points of disagreement between the Pauline letters and Acts is the way in which Paul claims the title of 'apostle' which is denied to him in Acts. Luke nevertheless attributes a unique role to Paul. This study compares the passage in Acts where Paul's mission is most clearly set out, namely in the third and final description of his call on the Damascus road (Acts 26.16–23), with the final instructions of Jesus to his disciples (Luke 24.44–9, cf. Acts 1.8).

The passage in Paul's speech in Acts 26 falls into three sections: (i) the task which awaits Paul, vv. 16–18 (ii) his fulfilment of this mission, vv. 19–20 (iii) the message which he preached, vv. 21–3. In each of these three sections we notice the following points: (A) Paul is given a heavenly vision or divine aid, vv. 16 (referring back to 14); 19; 22. (B) The call is to be a 'minister and witness', and to 'declare' the message entrusted to him, vv. 16; 20; 22. (C) Those to whom Paul is sent are 'the people' (beginning in Damascus, Jerusalem and Judaea) and the Gentiles, vv. 17; 20; 23. (D) The task entrusted to Paul is to bring men and women to the light, and to offer them forgiveness of sins, in other words to preach the gospel which is the fulfilment of the Scriptures. This fourfold scheme thus appears three times in this passage.

Luke carefully joined his two books together with overlapping sections, in both of which Jesus entrusts the apostles with their mission. In each case, the words are introduced by reference to an appearance of the risen Christ (Lk. 24.36–43, Acts 1.3). Luke 24 contains two separate sayings. In the first (v. 44), the gospel is presented as the fulfilment of scripture. In the second (vv. 46–9), the content of that gospel is spelled out and the apostles are appointed its witnesses and promised divine assistance. In Acts, the apostles are named (vv. 3, 13) and promised divine power to be Jesus' witnesses throughout the world.

A comparison of these two accounts of the mission entrusted to the apostles with the three-fold summary of Paul's mission in Acts 26 shows interesting similarities. The apostles are unable to undertake their mission until invested with heavenly power (A). They are appointed by the risen Jesus to be his witnesses (B). The recipients of the message are members of all nations, beginning from Jerusalem, Judaea and Samaria (C). The message, which concerns the death and resurrection of Christ, is the fulfilment of scripture, calls for repentance, and offers forgiveness of sins (D).

This comparison suggests that Luke applied to the mission of Paul the same model as that which he used for the mission of the apostles. According to Acts, it is in fact Paul who carries out the mission entrusted to the apostles, and does so in virtue of the commission received directly from Christ.

25

A Reconsideration of Ephesians 1.10b in the Light of Irenaeus

John McHugh

It is by no means easy to determine the precise meaning of the phrase ἀνακεφαλαιώσασθαι τὰ πάντα ἐν τῷ Χριστῷ in Eph. 1.10b, as even the most cursory survey of the better-known English versions reveals. The Authorized or King James Version gives 'that he might gather together in one all things in Christ'; the Revised Version of 1881, 'to sum up all things in Christ'; the Revised Standard Version, 'to unite all things in him'; the New English Bible, 'that the universe might be brought into a unity in Christ'. The Jerusalem Bible reads 'that he would bring everything together under Christ, the head', thus placing at least equal, if not more, emphasis on Christ's headship than on the unification of creation; and the New International Version is for all practical purposes the same, 'to bring all things together under one head, even Christ'. Individual translators offer an equally wide range of wordings.

Enigmatic as the Greek may be, it can hardly be said that any of these English renderings would by itself be sufficient to unveil to the average reader the thought underlying the word in the mind of the original author. Some commentary or further elucidation is needed. But when one turns to the major Greek lexicons, they are (with two exceptions) equally frustrating. Liddell-Scott-Jones restricts itself to the original meaning of the root in rhetoric, 'to sum up the argument', and gives only five lines to the cognate verb, noun, adjective and adverb, mentioning Rom. 13.9, but quite unaccountably omitting even a reference to Eph. 1.10 (a defect unremedied in the *Supplement*). The old Grimm-Thayer is slightly more helpful than others when it writes: 'In Eph. 1.10 God is said ... to bring together again for himself (note the mid.) all things and beings (hitherto disunited by sin) into one combined state of fellowship in Christ, the universal bond.'[1] Moulton-Milligan tersely comments that the verb 'naturally does not figure in our non-literary sources', and even Bauer-Arndt-Gingrich simply gives 'to bring everything together in Christ'.

Lampe's *Patristic Greek Lexicon* is much more helpful, devoting a full column to the noun and verb. There we read that Origen sought to explain Eph. 1.10 by reference to banking and similar businesses, so that the meaning would be 'to balance accounts'.[2] Chrysostom gives two meanings, not mutually exclusive, one of which affirms that God brought history to its culminating point, the other that he restored unity to heaven and earth by placing both angels and men under one new head, namely Christ.[3] Other patristic references call for the translation 'recapitulate, restore', and of these we shall speak later.

But incomparably the most informative entry in a Greek lexicon is the article by Heinrich Schlier in the *TWNT* iii. 680–1. Yet even here, after a long list of classical, hellenistic and patristic texts in the preliminary small print, the author feels compelled to conclude: 'In Eph. 1.10 it is difficult to choose between these various possible senses of ἀνακεφαλαιοῦσθαι. This may be seen from the variations in translations and commentaries. The ἀνακεφαλαιοῦσθαι τὰ πάντα ἐν τῷ Χριστῷ obviously consists in the διδόναι αὐτὸν κεφαλὴν ὑπὲρ πάντα τῇ ἐκκλησίᾳ (1.22). The summing up of the totality takes place in its subjection to the Head. The subjection of the totality to the Head takes place in the co-ordinating of the Head and the Church. As the Church receives its Head the totality receives its κεφάλαιον, its definitive, comprehensive and (in the Head) self-repeating summation. In the Head, in Christ, the totality is comprehended afresh as in its sum.[4] To be sure, ἀνακεφαλαιοῦσθαι is to be derived from κεφάλαιον rather than κεφαλή. But it is most likely that what is meant by the designation of Christ as κεφαλή led the author of Eph. to choose this relatively infrequent but rich and varied term which agrees so well with his intention.'[5]

Schlier's dense and philosophical prose will throw little light on the meaning of ἀνακεφαλαιοῦσθαι except for those who already know what is meant by a 'self-repeating summation' and 'comprehended afresh as in its sum'. And if such abstract terminology is not readily comprehensible to English-speaking readers, it is reasonable to wonder whether the citizens of first-century Ephesus would have felt any more at home amid so many abstract nouns. Yet the text of Ephesians must have carried some meaning intelligible to its first readers, and I suggest that Irenaeus supplies the key to a most lucid and satisfactory interpretation.

Jerome points in the same direction too, when he comments on this verse: 'Pro *recapitulare* in Latinis codicibus scriptum est *instaurare*.'[6] We

303

shall return to the implications of the two Latin renderings, *restaurare* and *instaurare*, at the end; let it suffice here to note that both these verbs connote renewal rather than unification, so that the sense attributed to Eph. 1.10 in the Latin versions may be said to differ significantly from the sense given by the English versions in the first paragraph of this article. Jerome, however, is surely on good ground in choosing to put the verb into Latin as *recapitulare*, which is etymologically the obvious choice. Similarly in English, the rendering 'to recapitulate' would have the great advantage of recapturing exactly the original sense, in oratory, of ἀνακεφαλαιοῦσθαι; but like Jerome's *recapitulare*, it would still leave to be answered the question, 'What does "recapitulation" here mean?' (And perhaps, in a volume offered to Professor Barrett, one may be permitted to mention here the curious but interesting fact that the first English theologian to introduce it as a technical theological term was the former Master of Pembroke, Cambridge, Lancelot Andrewes.[7] But it has never become common currency.)

Now any theologian, when he hears the word ἀνακεφαλαίωσις or 'recapitulation', instinctively thinks of Irenaeus of Lyons. Unfortunately, when one asks what he understood by the term, modern scholars proffer a bewildering variety of divergent answers.[8] Yet perhaps this fact itself should dissuade us from trying to find in Irenaeus a single well-pitched note where he himself intended a euphonious harmony. One can hardly appreciate a Palestrina Mass or a Bach chorale by concentrating on the tune alone, and Irenaeus himself invites us to listen for harmony in the Bible rather than to think of it as a series of solo voices singing different arias.

In two remarkable passages, both of which contain in the original Greek the noun οἰκονομία and the verb ἀνακεφαλαιοῦσθαι, he calls attention to the coherence of God's salvific design. The first occurs in the opening sentence of the second part of Book I of the *Adversus Haereses*, where he is setting out the *regula fidei* of the Church. The Church has received from the apostles its faith '. . . in the Holy Spirit who proclaimed through the prophets the "economies" and the coming and the birth from the Virgin and the suffering and the resurrection from the dead and the bodily ascension into the heavens of the beloved Christ Jesus our Lord and his Parousia from the heavens in the glory of the Father ἐπὶ τὸ ἀνακεφαλαιώσασθαι τὰ πάντα and to raise up all flesh of all mankind.'[9] Here it is easy to perceive that for Irenaeus the whole sweep of salvation history, from the earliest days to the final Parousia, is one great design – οἰκονομία. The second text occurs in Book III, where he writes: 'Four covenants were given to the human race: one before the Flood, under Adam; a second after the Flood, under Noah; a third – the giving of the Law – under Moses; and the fourth, which renews man and recapitulates in itself everything, which is through the gospel, lifting men up and carrying them on wings into the heavenly kingdom.'[10] Again, it requires but a moment's reflection to discern the connection between the four covenants. The divine covenant with Adam was wrecked through man's disobedience, as was Noah's, and that of Moses too. Only the gospel covenant, because it was not external but internal, that is, because it brought with it the gift of the Spirit, could 'carry men on wings into the heavenly kingdom'.

Now if Irenaeus wants us, when we hear the word ἀνακεφαλαίωσις, to think not of one precisely defined concept, but of several interrelated notions, we must ask what these several notions are. If we hear a chord instead of a single note, it is still true that to understand the chord we must consider the individual notes which form it. And it would seem that Irenaeus' idea of recapitulation is constituted by four major themes, each of which is for him an essential aspect of 'redemptive incarnation'. Between them, they cover the whole span of the historical incarnation.

The first aspect of recapitulation is to be found in the conception of Jesus by a virgin mother. The importance Irenaeus attaches to this doctrine is well known, as is the use he makes of it to draw a parallel between Adam and Jesus Christ; and it will be sufficient to cite one passage not to justify these statements but rather to direct the reader's attention to the number of times the term 'recapitulation' occurs in this context of the virginal conception. 'Just as that first-formed Adam received his substance from earth that was untilled and as yet virgin [soil] . . . so he who existed as Word, recapitulating Adam in himself, rightly took from Mary when she was still a virgin that manner of generation which would be a recapitulation of Adam' (and the root 'recapitulation' recurs twice more in the four subsequent sentences).[11]

'Another way of expounding *Recapitulation* . . . was to show that Christ shared successively every part of human experience.'[12] 'For He came to save all by means of Himself . . . He therefore passed through every age, becoming an infant for infants, thus sanctifying infants; a child for children, thus sanctifying those who are of this age . . . Then at last he came on to death itself.'[13] In particular, by resisting temptation and following his God-given destiny even to the cross, he *recapitulated* the destiny God had designed for every man. And if that sounds obscure, Newman has expressed the identical notion with unforgettable lucidity:

> O wisest love! that flesh and blood
>   Which did in Adam fail,
> Should strive afresh against their foe,
>   Should strive and should prevail.[14]

The terms 'economy' and 'recapitulation' are found also in contexts which speak directly of Christ's victory over death by his resurrection and ascension, notably in *Adversus Haereses* III. 18, at the beginning and end of the chapter,[15] but one of the clearest texts connecting recapitulation with the resurrection is in Book V. 21, 1. The Lord 'recapitulating in himself that primeval Man, calls himself Son of Man ... so that as our race went down to death by the conquest of a man, so we should rise again to life through the victory of a man; and just as death triumphed over us through a man, so we in turn should triumph over death through a man.'[16]

The fourth and final element in the concept is not so easily expressed by one English word, but let us for convenience here label it the Parousia, taking the word as including every aspect of Christ's second coming in glory, to raise the dead to life, and to establish and to manifest his lordship over all that exists, in heaven and on earth. For Irenaeus, this too is comprised in the ἀνακεφαλαίωσις. 'The only-begotten Word of God, the self-same is Jesus Christ our Lord, who suffered for us and rose for our sakes and shall come again in the glory of the Father to raise up all flesh, and to make salvation manifest and to extend the rule of righteous judgement to all who are under him. There is therefore but one God the Father, as we have shown, and one Christ Jesus, our Lord, who in every dispensation was coming and who has recapitulated all things in himself.[17] "All things" includes also man, the handiwork of God. That is why he recapitulated in himself man too, becoming visible where before he had been invisible, comprehensible where before he had been incomprehensible, capable of suffering where before he had been incapable of it. Thus when the Word became man, he gathered everything to himself (*universa in semetipsum recapitulans*), so that just as the Word of God is first in rank among those beings which are above the heavens and of a spiritual nature, and among invisible beings, so he should have the primacy among beings that are visible and of a material nature. By appropriating this primacy to himself and setting up himself as head of the Church, he thus draws everything to himself at the due time.'[18] The reader will recall that this affirmation of a Parousia in glory ἐπὶ τὸ ἀνακεφαλαιώσασθαι τὰ πάντα was contained also in the *regula fidei* cited earlier, from Book I.[19]

There are then four senses or references for the word ἀνακεφαλαίωσις in Irenaeus, and if we keep in mind the fact that the term originated in rhetorical circles, to indicate that the speaker was now going to summarize and recapitulate his argument from the beginning to the end, in order to close his oration, it may be possible to discern one fundamental meaning, akin to that used by public orators, which applies to all the four 'mysteries of salvation' just described. As applied to the virginal conception of Jesus, the term means 'giving humanity a fresh start by creating a New Man, a Second Adam, in one sense "out of" the Old (*ex Maria*) but in another sense (far more weighty) not out of the Old since it was by direct creation'. Applied to the earthly life of Jesus, the term means 'giving humanity a fresh start by re-enacting the drama of Everyman, only this time successfully'. The third reference, to the resurrection, carries above all the sense of restoring to mankind the immortality lost by Adam; and the fourth refers to the inauguration of a New World where Christ is King of earth and heaven. Thus all four references contain the idea of starting afresh, of making a new beginning, yet in each of the four contexts we meet a different aspect of one great design. It is indeed inaugurated by the virginal conception, worked out during the earthly life, completed in principle at the resurrection, but consummated in fact only by the Parousia. The four aspects certainly constitute a most harmonious chord; and if we change the metaphor, and think of them as God's final statement on human history, we may say that in these four ideas taken together, he has 'recapitulated' all that he ever said to mankind.

If this is the meaning in Irenaeus, it remains to inquire whether it is also the sense to be found in Eph. 1.10, and I suggest that *in its broad outlines* it is, and that it fits the context excellently. Indeed, this understanding of the Greek would seem to underlie the Old Latin version, *restaurare omnia in Christo*; but perhaps the (Vulgate?) reviser showed deeper insight when he altered this to *instaurare omnia in Christo*. For *restaurare* means 'restoring things to what they were before', and would therefore not include (indeed, would apparently exclude) the future Parousia. *Instaurare*, by contrast, would be in this context entirely forward-looking, and could be glossed as 'to establish and to inaugurate a wholly new world in Christ'.

If this idea is even approximately correct, then all the English translations given in the first paragraph of this essay miss the main point of the phrase, as does Schlier's comment. Yet the interpretation set out here can claim the support of Theodoret of Cyrrhus,[20] and especially of John of Damascus, who speaks here of ἀνανέωσις and equiparates ἀνακεφαλαιώσασθαι with ἀνανέωσαι.[21] Perhaps only the German language could condense all the thought into one nominal phrase, as Rudolf Haubst does in the *Lexicon für Theologie und Kirche*, when, basing himself on Irenaeus, he speaks of 'eine sich endzeitlich vollendende Anakephalaiosis des Alls durch Christus als "das alles überragende Haupt der Kirche" (1.22) heilsgeschichtlich vorbereitet'.[22] It is not so easy to express all that in simple English, so perhaps we ought to settle for 'to make everything new, in Christ'.

NOTES

1 *A Greek-English Lexicon of the New Testament* (4th edn Edinburgh 1896).

2 The text is quoted fairly fully in Lampe from Origen's *Fragmenta ex commentariis in Eph.* as published by J. A. F. Gregg in *JTS* 3 (1902), p. 241.

3 *Hom. in Eph.* 1.4 (*PG* 62. 16).

4 This sentence, spaced out in the original (but not in the American translation) to indicate the kernel of the paragraph, reads in the German: 'Im Haupte, in Christus, wird das All als in seiner Summe neu zusammengefasst'.

5 Translation from *TDNT* iii, p. 682.

6 *In Epistulam ad Eph.* 1.1 (*PL* 26. 483D). Migne adds: 'Alii, *restaurare*'.

7 See the *Oxford English Dictionary* under 'Recapitulation'.

8 There is a splendid summary of the differing views in John Lawson, *The Biblical Theology of Saint Irenaeus* (London 1948), on pp. 140–3, followed by a discussion of the term on pp. 143–54.

9 *Adv. Haer.* I. 10, 1, translated from the Greek as given in *Sources Chrétiennes* 264 (Paris 1979), pp. 155–7.

10 ibid. III. 11, 8, translated from the Latin as given in *Sources Chrétiennes* 211 (Paris 1974). The justification for here following the Latin text rather than the Greek may be found in the accompanying volume of *Sources Chrétiennes* (210) on p. 286. The final clause of the quotation reads in Latin: 'quartum vero quod renovat hominem et recapitulat in se omnia, quod est per Evangelium, elevans et pennigerans homines in caeleste regnum.' (In this passage, the word οἰκονομία occurs six lines later, in 11.9.)

11 ibid. III. 21, 10, on pp. 428–30.

12 Lawson, p. 153.

13   *Adv. Haer.* II. 22, 4, cited by Lawson, loc. cit.

14   Indeed, these lines of Newman could be taken as a summary of *Adv. Haer.* V. 21; for other texts containing the same idea see the footnotes in Lawson, pp. 148–9.

15   'Quando incarnatus et homo factus, longam hominum expositionem in seipso recapitulavit' (18,1); 'dispensationem consummans salutis nostrae' (18,2); and (18,7) 'Deus hominis antiquam plasmationem in se recapitulans, ut occideret quidem peccatum, evacuaret autem mortem et vivificaret hominem.'

16   Translated from the Latin as given in *Sources Chrétiennes* 153, p. 264.

17   'Veniens per universam dispositionem et omnia in semetipsum recapitulans.' The sense is that the Word manifested himself at every stage of the economy, by his multiple appearances and interventions in the Old Testament, and 'summed them all up' by coming on earth in person, at the end of time, through the incarnation. Thus the note on this text in *Sources Chrétiennes* 210, p. 323.

18   *Adv. Haer.* III. 16, 6, translated from the Latin as given in *Sources Chrétiennes* 211, pp. 312–4.

19   See above, p. 304 and n.9.

20   *In Eph.* 1.10 (*PG* 82. 512).

21   *In Eph.* 1.10 (*PG* 95. 824–5).

22   I. 466 (Freiburg-im-Breisgau 1957).

26

Some Issues of Church and Society in the Light of Paul's Eschatology

M. E. Glasswell

It is now over twenty years since, in the Michaelmas Term of 1958, I climbed Princes Street, Durham, every week to read my essays on Paul to Charles Kingsley Barrett. This was the start of my theological development and those essays gave me my first orientation in New Testament studies. They laid the foundation for my conviction about the continued relevance of the New Testament to the life and work of the Church today and caused for me a radical realignment, which, though differently understood today, established in me both a critical and confessional stance, the combination of which has never left me. In this I have remained a pupil of C.K.B., since I see it as an endorsement of both his unreservedly critical approach and his deep commitment to the Bible as a book of faith. The idea that what criticism can now reveal of the Bible simply expresses in another way the essentials of the same original faith is something I think both of us also owe to Rudolf Bultmann.

This conviction of the unity between modern criticism and the faith of the Church over the centuries was never more needed than today, when a blind scepticism and a naive faith are often juxtaposed as if they were the only alternatives, even in works of scholars. We need to rediscover what Paul has to say to us today in what he said when he first despatched his letters to his churches. This involves both a serious piece of historical research and a serious effort at interpretation. The two go together. I am sure I still share this conviction with C.K.B.

Against this there is a tendency today to relativize the words of Scripture historically and also sociologically, and even culturally, and then to ignore things which are theologically fundamental, or even to deny their existence. This is true of both churchmen and scholars. It is a sign of a failure of nerve in western Christianity. In this essay I wish to pick out some strands in Paul's thought in 1 Corinthians which are fundamentally theological and to point out the error of taking them sociologically or culturally, without ignoring those dimensions completely. It is the eschatological basis of Paul's thought – something rightly recognized by C. K. Barrett as fundamental to the whole New Testament[1] – which makes it impossible to take the passages I shall discuss in any culturally relative sense and which freed Paul from the possibility of any such danger.

In 1 Corinthians Paul was concerned with issues in one of his churches which can be summarized under the problem of the present implications of a salvation in Christ which is to be understood eschatologically.[2] In this context Paul discusses problems which concern the relationship between Church and society. Chapters 5 and 6 of 1 Corinthians sufficiently illustrate this in the way Paul probably both corrects the Corinthians' misunderstanding of his earlier letter and modifies his own earlier views, or at least the way he had expressed them. But it is chapter 7 that takes up the first specific question addressed to him by the Corinthians, that about marriage and sexual relations. In the course of his reply Paul asserts an eschatological principle of wider application to the whole relationship between the Christian and the world around – see vv. 17–24. This principle at one and the same time renders all external relationships relative whilst making them the prior conditions of one's vocation and of its continued exercise.

To take the first example, the significance of the question of circumcision or uncircumcision had been raised and discussed with regard to particular controversies elsewhere, probably already in Galatia, and would be further expounded in Romans in wider terms. It was probably not an issue in Corinth, but it is mentioned with reference to the eschatological context of salvation as a recognizable illustration of the principle Paul wished to demonstrate. Circumcision is taken as a sign of an external relationship or as merely a contingent factor in our previous fleshly condition which has no further significance. It is at most the condition in which one became a Christian and then receives what significance it has from that fact alone. As in Paul's discussion elsewhere,[3] it can only signify something else of which it is a sign, but which does not depend upon it and can be separate from it, and which is more important than either circumcision or uncircumcision (v. 19). Both are immaterial but either condition can be a means of fulfilling one's calling and *must be* the means of fulfilling it. This point had already been established by Paul generally but it is now used to illustrate the same principle which he had enunciated with regard to marriage and goes on to enunciate with regard to slavery and freedom (vv. 21–3). Here one can best see how this relates to issues of Church and society.

There is a problem of translation in v. 21 of chapter 7 which is amply discussed in the commentaries,[4] but whether we take it as implying remaining a slave or getting one's freedom does not affect the points Paul wishes to make or the consistency of what he says. On the surface the first is more consistent, but the latter is not inconsistent because Paul is not concerned with either condition as such. They are as immaterial in themselves as circumcision or uncircumcision, Jew or Gentile. Paul could therefore in this instance accept an external change or improvement in one's condition in society without this having any ultimate significance or importance. The change would be in itself within the realm of the contingent or relative, whilst having some value within the context of this world. A concession on this point here and there would not affect Paul's basic principle. How then does his basic principle affect the question of the relation between Church and society?

Paul sees the relationships of this world as being of limited significance as far as final salvation is concerned. If keeping the commandments of God is what matters in one's behaviour (see 1 Cor. 7.19), then being a slave or a free man does not have any effect on one's ability to keep them. This is not because of an inner ἀπάθεια such as the Stoic Epictetus spoke of, but because of a higher service which relativizes both conditions (v. 22). Each, however, can be dangerous for the Christian and needs to be used in a specifically Christian direction if it is not to pervert the Christian's calling. There is the danger of the slave becoming actually subject to men rather than to God (v. 23), but this is also a danger for the freed man. The Christian's true freedom from men and service of God needs guarding in either condition. Thus there are more implications to Paul's basic principle than appear at first sight.

It is important to point out that this view, which depends on an eschatological view of salvation, does not depend for its validity on the *nearness* of the end because the nature of salvation itself is the controlling factor. Salvation for Paul cannot be expressed fully or finally in the here and now, but only in the future Reign of God.[5]

It is also important to note that Paul is not concerned in this passage with the issues of slavery and freedom themselves as parts of a particular social order in this world, or with their rightness or wrongness in social terms. If the second meaning of v. 21 is accepted Paul might even acknowledge that there is an answer in this world's terms to the question what is good or bad, without this affecting his basic conviction about the irrelevance of present social conditions for eternal salvation. That conviction cannot be faulted whatever view one takes about present conditions in themselves. Nor is Paul avoiding the issue of the rightness or wrongness of present conditions by his assertion that being a slave is no disqualification for salvation. Paul is concerned in this passage with the individual's response to his situation – which may for him be unalterable and need not be altered for him to be a Christian, even though it might be altered without necessarily influencing his commitment. The alteration of his situation should not be seen as essential for that commitment to succeed. The issue of the structure of society itself is a different one, but Paul never envisaged changes in society itself as a precondition for the Kingdom of God to come, nor as a substitute for that Kingdom. He never even envisaged a Christian society, not because of shortage of time or because of the circumstances of his day, but because it is probably an illegitimate concept and certainly cannot be an ultimate aim.

Nonetheless there are implications for society at large if individual Christians behave in sufficient numbers in the ways implied by Paul in this passage. The existence of a Christian master with a Christian slave would strain the fabric of a society structured in that way. This would not of itself bring in the Kingdom of God, but it might involve a more radical change than a Marxist revolution could achieve because it would lead to a society ready to be transformed into God's Kingdom, whenever that might come. The world itself would be transformed if a Christian slave or oppressed person, even though remaining outwardly a slave, behaved as the servant of God alone, even though he suffered in the process. Suffering is after all part of the Christian's calling. On the other hand, to seek simply external freedom could involve a failure to fulfil one's true vocation and as an end in itself it would lack the character of Christian discipleship.

The Christian response to a situation of oppression must on Paul's terms therefore be more radical than that of the revolutionary. Mere external freedom from oppression would not be adequate enough even for society. But, in terms of the individual's own attitudes, the man who has been set free from oppression still has to face the issue of his vocation in society. Paul is not guilty of the distortion that it does not matter what happens to the body if the soul is saved, because in any case he *is* concerned with the full implications of being a Christian in society. The moral issues involved in this are not relativized by Paul, but rather the external circumstances in which one's calling may have to be exercised.[6] Paul does not thereby give those external conditions either validity or permanence. He simply recognizes their existence as aspects of this world. Paul is being more radical than he is often given credit for. The Roman Empire did not distort his vision because there will always be comparable situations. He was in fact being realistic about the response needed, whilst not ruling out secular programmes for change. Paul was right neither to secularize the gospel nor sacralize the world.[7] But the world is seen as the proper sphere, however constituted, of Christian obedience.

The same issues of the present implications of eschatological salvation and the same contemporary doubts about Paul's sociological conditioning arise in chapter 11.2–16. Chapter 7 had discussed the issue of marriage; this discusses one aspect of that of women in the Church. I will not enter here into contemporary debates about women and the ministry nor the exegesis of difficult verses,[8] but simply discuss the implications of the passage for the theme of this essay. Paul is not talking anyway here about relations between men and women in marriage, women and the ministry or women in society, but women as such with respect to their place in creation and in Christ, both in the Church now[9] and with regard to eschatological salvation.[10] A similar issue arises here as in the former passage about a confusion at Corinth between the here and now and the Kingdom of God.[11] The difference here is that Paul introduces the concept of the Church itself standing over against society and representing the Kingdom of God, yet not being that Kingdom and still existing within present society in this world. The now and not yet of the salvation process comes here into view. Redemption is achieved but salvation is not yet finally realized. The Corinthians seemed to think that more was already realized of future salvation in the Church and this led them to be off their guard with regard to moral pressures they thought no longer affected them. Against this Paul emphasizes the continuing validity of the natural order protected by natural law without regard for social pressures or any particular existing social pattern. The Church can only to an extent mirror the future Kingdom of God and in the meantime the same principle applies as in chapter 7 – 'each in his own calling'.[12] Difference of function, not inferiority, is what is implied by Paul's argument here, and this is to be distinguished from the ultimate, and in principle already valid, equality between man and woman. There is no discussion here about society itself.[13]

The question now arises how these passages fit with the attitudes of Paul expressed elsewhere, particularly in Gal. 3.28 where the same three areas covered above are mentioned. It has to be borne in mind that that passage is not a summary of Paul's total view, existing as the passage does in its own particular context, and that the three pairs do not have precisely the same significance if one looks at other places where Paul discusses them separately. The differences within each pair are seen as being overcome in Christ but not abolished completely, though this is true of each pair differently.

The first pair – Jew and Greek – corresponds to circumcision and uncircumcision elsewhere, for instance in Gal. 5.6. Without going into the whole issue it must be pointed out that Paul does not think there is no difference at all between Jew and Greek; there is no difference in the basis for inclusion in Christ and for justification, or for ultimate salvation, but there is a historical difference within the *Heilsgeschichte* itself, without this difference implying any superiority of one over the other. There is also a priority and advantage of the Jew and of circumcision, even if this points to the same principle of inclusion, i.e. faith. Eschatologically there is also for Paul the necessary inclusion of Israel in the final outcome, not for ethnic reasons but because of the nature of God.

With regard to the second pair we have already seen that the distinction between slave and free does not *have* to be done away externally in order to become a Christian, even if secular reasons may themselves demand it. Neither does it correspond to Christian truth about humanity. This truth must be expressed in individual behaviour and may also be mirrored in society. The issue for Paul is not slavery or freedom as such but being in Christ, and *both* are rendered irrelevant by that norm.

'Maleness' and 'Femaleness' (neuter) are likewise not distinct, understood eschatologically in Christ, yet the difference between them is not abolished, but retained within the created order. Paul is not concerned here with social distinctions, which, like those between slave and free, are just irrelevant. The difference between this pair and the others theologically, though not culturally or sociologically (together with his experiences in Corinth), may have led to its omission in Col. 3.11.[14] As we have seen, it had introduced issues about the present and future of salvation and the status of the Church between the times

315

which the others did not. With regard to society there is, of course, an analogy with the relationship between slave and free insofar as society might in some respects mirror in advance the Kingdom of God, but equally there are dangers in identifying present relationships with those of the Kingdom of God. For both pairs what matters for the present, as far as Paul is concerned, is one's Christian obedience. In the case of male and female this must remain within the peculiar vocation of each, with modifications arising from the structure of society itself. Even within the Church the situation of the old man still impinges. But the created order, which under God is the means of ministering to his glory, is expressed and witnessed to by some external distinction. There is never any question for Paul of woman's inferiority to man. On this issue too, however, the Church is not simply a pointer to changes in society, though these may occur, but to ultimate salvation in the Kingdom of God. This is at present expressed in terms of one's present calling as man or woman. To see the issue in social or cultural terms is to distort Paul's argument and leads to false applications of Paul's principles.

What view of the relation between Church and society can be discerned in these passages? This cannot be derived from Gal. 3.28 since Paul is not there talking about society, nor even about the Church in this world order, but about the eschatological significance of being in Christ. In 1 Corinthians the Church is seen as distinct from society but it is not yet the Kingdom of God. That Kingdom will in the future include the whole world and not just the Church. The Church witnesses at present to the future transformation of the world whilst being still composed of men and women of this present age who are on the way to salvation but who must demonstrate in Church and world their freedom in Christ as well as their responsibility with regard to their present calling. This calling must be within their present condition, racially, sexually and socially. Each of these different areas of life, which have their own separate historical, biological or political significances, can and must be vehicles of service and obedience without being given absolute or ultimate significance in themselves – that significance is reserved for our being in Christ. All distinctions are seen as absorbed into that status without being finally abolished as long as this world exists. Something of this relativizing of distinctions may well be reflected in society before the end with a concomitant transformation of some relationships, especially between Christians, as in the case of Philemon and Onesimus. But society itself is not the place where the ultimate transformation will come about. Any changes in society will in fact be legitimized only by the Church's continuing witness to the true basis of any change, i.e. Christ, and, in the case of male and female, be built upon the theological status of woman as the glory of man. It is this glory which should be reflected in her role in the Church. Creation itself, not social convention, and not just biological difference, prevents a total abolishing of any difference yet. Society is not the starting-point of Paul's argument, nor can it be decisive for issues in the Church, whether society exists as a place of subjugation or of liberation.

Since society is not the starting-point of Paul's argument, the difference between male and female is not the same as other distinctions but it shows most clearly the basis of Paul's argument for those other distinctions as well. For Paul it is only being in Christ that renders these existing distinctions ultimately meaningless because they cannot affect one's call. In society or the world that call must take these distinctions into account where they exist because they cannot be ignored as areas of service and obedience. In the Church they are to be seen as equal opportunities of fulfilling one's vocation and the differences between them can be ignored with regard to the future Kingdom of God. The tension between now and not yet however forces the Church at present to preserve a difference without a distinction between man and woman in a more fundamental way than in the case of the other divisions because of Creation itself.[15]

I hope I have been faithful to the approach of C.K.B. in claiming that the Bible is independent of cultural relativism whilst not treating it in a fundamentalist way – unlike the so-called radicals who still use a text like Gal. 3.28 out of context.[16] I would also not go beyond what the New Testament can teach us whilst seeing it as central to a continuous church tradition rather than being fossilized in the past. *Ad multos annos*!

NOTES

1 See the subject of C. K. Barrett's Inaugural Lecture in the University of Durham, *Yesterday, Today and For Ever: The New Testament Problem* (University of Durham 1959).

2 cf. D. J. Doughty, 'The Presence and Future of Salvation in Corinth', *ZNW* 66 (1975), pp. 61–90.

3 See M. E. Glasswell, 'Circumcision', *ET* 85 (1974), pp. 328–32, especially p. 329.

4 As in C. K. Barrett, *1 Corinthians* (London 1968), p. 170, who accepts the implications of the context as decisive; cf. also H. Conzelmann, *1 Corinthians* (Hermeneia, Philadelphia, 1975), p. 127, for the application of the eschatological factor as against culturally orientated attitudes or considerations of a civil nature (German edn Göttingen 1969, pp. 152f).

5 I am conceding here that the idea of the *nearness* of the end may be an incidental factor arising from Paul's contemporary religious environment but asserting that the *future* aspect of salvation, which I would take to be the fundamental eschatological element in Paul's thought, is both decisive and fundamental to his whole message, and indeed to that of the New Testament itself.

6 This is the truth of E. Norman's position in *Christianity and the World Order*, printed version of the 1978 Reith Lectures (OUP 1979). See his conclusions to chapter 6, 'The Indwelling Christ', about what he calls 'historical relativism', especially pp. 83–5. Despite the sometimes shallow and unthinking reaction, Norman's differentiation between political stances and solutions, which must be judged as such, and Christianity fits Paul's viewpoint. One must distinguish between the areas of validity in respect of worldly answers to problems and the ultimate solution of Christianity. I myself have tried to express this in terms of a false dichotomy between the vertical and the horizontal, or a false choice between two opposing views of Christianity which is being forced on the Church by a politicizing of Christianity. This militates against both the proper autonomy of the political realm and the proper Christian perspective. That perspective does not confuse or separate the areas of Christian obedience but leaves the Christian free to operate in the political realm as such. It is not true that the only right way to understand Christianity is political or that the only correct political stance is one identified with Christianity. To accept such ideas would be a strange return to earlier attempts, now rejected, to make Christianity an absolute force in this world and one seeking to control the political realm!

7 cf. M. Bonino, *Doing Theology in a Revolutionary Situation* (Philadelphia 1975), pp. 161–4 (Eng. edn, *Revolutionary Theology Comes of Age*, London 1975). The Church and the world must be autonomous to avoid confusing the ultimate salvation of the Christian with the aims of revolution. This is both a theological and a political necessity.

8 See, e.g., M. D. Hooker, 'Authority on her Head: an examination of 1 Cor. xiv. 10', *NTS* 10 (1964), pp. 410–16; A. Jaubert, 'Le voile des femmes (1 Cor. xi. 2–16).' *NTS* 18 (1972), pp. 422–4.

9 See H. Conzelmann, op. cit., p. 184 (German edn, p. 216f), esp. n34 and the statement to which it refers.

10 ibid., p. 185 (German edn, p. 218) n41; and p. 188 (German edn, p. 222), on vv. 8f.

11 ibid., p. 191 (German edn, p. 225), 'At bottom the summons is a critical one: not to confuse a direct desecularization that is carried on by ourselves with the eschatological desecularization brought about by Christ.'

12 ibid., p. 191 (German edn, p. 226).

13 1 Cor. 14.33b–36 is left out of account as not affecting the meaning of chapter 11 and as being irrelevant to the issues presented here. It is either an interpolation or concerned with something else such as the relation between wives and husbands or the teaching office in the Church.

14 See N. A. Dahl, 'Nations in the New Testament', *New Testament Christianity for Africa and the World*, Essays in honour of Harry Sawyerr, ed. M. E. Glasswell and E. W. Fasholé-Luke (SPCK 1974), p. 63.

15 This is important for current discussion about the validity of the ordination of women to the priesthood. This discussion has often assumed an identity between the questions of the status of women and the status of slaves in the Church on the basis of their status in society at different times in history and has seen Paul's argument in 1 Cor. 11 as being affected by this. But Paul could not have treated slaves in the way he treats women in that chapter because temporary social or cultural factors are not what he has in mind. There are other factors affecting women which do not affect slaves, or for that matter Gentiles. In the latter case it is the process of the *Heilsgeschichte* which is the issue, whilst Creation is the fundamental one with regard to women.

16 Its meaning is much more like the statement of E. Norman, (op. cit.) about cultural relativism. What Paul is saying is that in Christ there is no such thing as racial or class superiority, oppression or liberation, masculinity or feminism; to be in Christ transcends all opposites and renders relative all worldly relationships and values as the one thing that matters. The result is that in Christ each has his/her proper sphere and his/her fulfilment, whatever his/her social condition might be. This paraphrase of Paul is intended to take into account both the collective and individual aspects of Paul's statement.

27

The Significance of 'Paulinism'

Robert Morgan

When shortly before the First War a prominent theologian from County Durham remarked that 'Paulinism' was 'a figment of the Teutonic brain',[1] he was not wishing to recommend either the concept or its source. The word had come into the English language through the discussion of F. C. Baur's 'antithesis of Petrinism and Paulinism'[2] in primitive Christianity, and implied a denial of the doctrinal unity of the New Testament. Nowadays the 'diversity' revealed by historical analysis is taken for granted, and perhaps exaggerated. But the victory of this approach within biblical scholarship has not rehabilitated the word 'Paulinism'. An '-ism' refers to 'a system of theory or practice' (OED) and 'system', with its scholastic overtones, scarcely seems appropriate in discussing early Christianity. Professor Barrett, however, while repeating the customary warning that 'Paul was not a systematic theologian',[3] is willing to talk of 'Paulinism', and even (on occasion) of Paul's 'doctrinal system'.[4]

He also confesses in a preface that for him personally, 'if Christianity is true it is truest *in the form it took* with Paul, and after him with such interpreters of his as Augustine, Luther, Calvin, Barth.'[5] This theological confession implies a distinction between what Christians consider the gospel event of God encountering and giving himself to men, and the various historically conditioned theologies in which this has found or may find expression. The distinction is not a separation, because the gospel can be heard only as mediated in some form of theological expression. But it implies that some of these are more and some less adequate to the alleged divine reality that they seek to express.

This raises the question of criteria, and one of the burning questions in modern theology concerns the contribution of the New Testament *historian* to making *theological* judgements about the adequacy of particular theological expressions of Christianity. The fire is in the New Testament scholar's own house when the adequacy of the theological statements of the New Testament authors themselves is discussed, as it must be if their claim to truth is to be taken seriously and they are no longer declared immune from criticism. Any such judgements will involve one's understanding of Christianity, because it is only on appeal to this that a modern theologian can be convinced about the adequacy of any theological formulation of the truth of the gospel. But then it is not a historical judgement, however inescapably its justification will involve appeals to history; and the fascination of New Testament *theology* as a Christian theological enterprise and not simply an exercise in the history of ideas, lies in the interaction between the Christian's personal theological appropriation of the texts and the historical analysis to which the biblical scholar is professionally committed. It is a two-way affair in which one's theological convictions may well affect one's perception of the history, and historical conclusions will influence theological convictions. Instead of vainly trying to banish theological interests from biblical scholarship it is necessary to define the relationship in a way that does justice to both sides.[6] For Professor Barrett himself the theological dimension of New Testament historical scholarship is sufficiently important to encourage a grateful student to take this opportunity to probe it from the perspective afforded by a once fashionable abbreviation for the distinctively Pauline theology.

I

In addition to the distinction between the Christian 'thing itself' and its various theological manifestations, Professor Barrett's confession implies that he himself finds in Paul, or rather in an interpretation of the epistles which emphasizes the dialectic between law and grace, the religious and theological heart of Christianity.

It is reasonable to suspect some connection between this 'theological appropriation' of the epistles and the readiness to systematize Paul's thought. Some systematization, or the construction of a provisional 'model' of Paul's theology, is necessary before the Christian theologian can see in the epistles a 'form of Christianity' which may be recognized as corresponding to or differing from his own understanding of their subject-matter. The systematic arrangement of Paul's concepts not only clarifies how these form an organic whole, but also enables the interpreter who so wishes, to relate this whole to his own understanding of Christianity.

321

If this is right, part of the significance of the modern abstraction 'Paulinism' lies in its capacity to focus for the Christian reader the theological illumination which he receives from these texts. New Testament theology is not a 'purely historical' discipline if that phrase is meant to repudiate theological interests. The historical reconstruction of early Christian thought is often inspired by a contemporary theological interest in understanding the texts which tell of the God acknowledged in the community that uses them as holy Scripture.

This Christian presupposition, implied in the notions of Scripture and 'New Testament', as well as the God word 'theology' is not the historian's concern. 'No New Testament writing was born with the predicate "canonical" attached.'[7]

Wrede's attempt to keep theological interests to a minimum in biblical scholarship, and to transform New Testament *theology* into the *history* of early Christian religion and theology, retains its validity as a plea for the integrity of historical study. But presenting an author's understanding of God, man and the world involves the interpreter's own pre-understanding, and provided that he does not impose this upon his author, but is ready to recognize possible differences, it need not distort his analysis.[8] Despite the danger (which besets all interpretation) of 'reading into' a text what we expect to find, a Christian's sense of sharing Paul's view of his subject-matter may inform his understanding of this ancient author. His interpretation will be subject to critical historical evaluation; the believer has neither privileged access to these texts nor sole rights on historical imagination. But while remaining within the bounds of what is historically cogent his interpretation of Paul may communicate something of his own theological convictions. As such, New Testament theology or interpretation fulfils a theological as well as a historical function: It expresses Christian faith today, albeit in a form which is constrained by the historian's first loyalty to these early Christian texts.

Both historians and theologians are nowadays suspicious of such abstractions as 'Paulinism'. Systematizations of Paul's theology do inadequate justice to the tensions, developments and possible inconsistencies in his thought; to the differences between the epistles, and to the character of these occasional writings. It is wrong, for example, to assume that Romans and Galatians reflect identical views on the Law, and quite probable that Paul's opinions changed as his language varied under pressure of argument, and as he came to doubt that he would live to see the (still imminent) Parousia.

More important than these legitimate historical warnings is the theological consideration that many modern Christians understand their faith as mediated in life and historical experience rather than in pure ideas, preached words or traditional doctrinal concepts. This partly accounts for the new interest in sociology within biblical research and will no doubt lead to a new style of New Testament theology. But that desideratum is better served by sympathetic understanding than by ill-informed criticism of the discipline as practised for nearly two hundred years.

As currently stated the historians' objections to 'Paulinism' often evade the central issue of the basic coherence and consistency of Paul's understanding of Christianity in all its varied expression. One may affirm or deny this, but neither judgement is possible without some reference to one's own understanding of Christianity. This wider theological dimension in the interpretation of Paul is evaded when his thought is presented, whether systematically or not, without reference to the 'central thrust' of his understanding of Christianity. It is this which was at stake in such phrases as 'the essence of Paulinism', and in the claim of Schlatter and Bultmann that the justification terminology of Romans, Galatians and Philippians 3 contains an understanding of the gospel which explains the theological stance which Paul expressed in different language against the gnostic tendencies apparently confronting him in Corinth. One may dispute that their 'centre' provides the best reading of Paul, but they were surely right both to look for some inner consistency in Paul's thought, and also to seek to relate this to their own understanding of Christianity.

The search for a 'central thrust' presupposes a modern critical view of theology which no longer identifies Paul's doctrinal concepts with the gospel itself. It is not a total inventory of Paul's theological opinions which is aimed at (some of these are of no more than passing interest and none of them can be assimilated uncritically today), but a presentation of the data which clarifies what he was talking about. While not drawing a ready-made systematic theology from the epistles we need to systematize in order to understand, as can be seen from the past masters of the art.

Wrede's main objection to Holtzmann's New Testament theology was that it failed to draw the full methodological consequences of its author's own distinction between 'religion' and 'theology'. His brilliant critique of orienting New Testament theology on dogmatic *loci* (op. cit., pp. 73–84) rests as much upon a theological judgement locating the Christian 'thing itself' in 'religion' as upon his historical sensitivity. He saw that it made 'some sense' to 'work out a "doctrinal scheme" or sketch of the theological viewpoint' of the 'Christian thinker' Paul, and a few years later published his own systematization of one whose 'theology is his religion'.[9] He recognized (*Task and Methods*, p. 83) that his strictures on the older 'orthodox' style of biblical theology did not apply to the greatest systematizer of all, F. C. Baur. They do not apply, either, to Bultmann's systematic presentation of Pauline theology which distinguishes between the believer's new self-understanding and the concepts through which this is unfolded. Like Wrede and Holtzmann, Baur and Bultmann knew that what they were finally looking for lay 'behind' the concepts in which it had found expression. These are a mere 'glass' on which the pre-critical or undiscerning man 'may stay his eye', but through which the New Testament theologian may 'pass, And then the heaven espy'.

The spatial metaphor clarifies the distinction between text and subject-matter, but is not quite satisfactory because the subject-matter is perceived (Baur) or heard (Bultmann) only in and through the interpreter's reflection on or confrontation with the texts. Wrede's orientation was more historical than theological and his insistence upon 'the normative and dominant, and hence the characteristic and indicative' concepts, the 'main lines', the 'essentials', the 'historically important and typical aspects' of a New Testament author (p. 77), was directed towards achieving a more sensitive grasp of the historical Paul. But his purpose in studying the history of religion was to understand what he considered its transcendent subject-matter. There is theological pathos as well as historical passion in his protest against an approach to the New Testament in which 'the main things are obscured', the subject is made 'arid and boring' and 'the thought of the New Testament is not reaching us in the living freshness which belongs to it' (p. 78). The theological interests of the original 'history of religions school' should not be obscured by the dialectical theology's unfortunate hostility to the notion of 'religion', nor by the more value-free way in which that concept is used today.

Another example of concealed theological interests in a historical attack upon modern systematizations of Paul's thought is provided by Adolf Deissmann's spirited polemic against 'the paper Paul of our Western libraries, the Germanized, dogmatized, modernized, stilted Paul'.[10] The warm Christ-mysticism of Deissmann's Paul was just as modern (and just as German) as what he considered the 'bloodless, timeless paragraphs of the "doctrine" or the "theology" of Paul' (p. 47). Whether this liberal Protestant penetrated any more deeply into Paul's subject-matter than his predecessors with their 'vacuum of a purely christological conceptuality' (p. 189) need not be decided here. Both orthodox protestant presentations of Paul's theology and also Baur's 'considering the Pauline doctrine as a connected and organic system in which one idea rose logically out of the other till the whole stood before us',[11] had come to sound intolerably intellectualistic. The 'Paulinism' of Pfleiderer[12] and Holtzmann[13] had begun to look more like an empty dogmatic shell than the living religious and theological organism that these authors had intended. Deissmann's attempt to rescue Paul from 'the paper bondage of "Paulinism"' (p. x) and recover 'a living complex of inner polarities which refuse to be parcelled out' (ibid.) was thus as much a theological act intended to appropriate and communicate Paul's 'inner' theological subject-matter, as was Barth's explicitly theological commentary on Romans a few years later, or the ideas-oriented presentation of Baur two generations earlier, or the structuring of Pauline thought on the model of a dogmatic text book by orthodox theologians.

In all these cases modern theological interpreters expressed their conviction that Paul was talking of the God they, too, acknowledged. They did so by constructing Paul's thought in ways which corresponded to their own understandings of God and Christianity. The liberals' opposing of 'theology' (i.e. orthodox dogmatics) with 'religion' was only a bid to replace an outmoded style of theology with one better suited to the new climate in the modern philosophy and history of religion. Like all theology, the theological interpretation of the New Testament is directed to a particular social and intellectual milieu and must be judged in terms of its response to that as well as its faithfulness to the historical Paul. Given the German philosophical climate of 1845 Baur's presentation made it clearer for some people that Paul was talking about God, or the reality that determines everything, that determines our existence. Its attempt 'to apprehend the person of Christ in its highest, its absolute significance' (p. 311) and discover 'the deep inward foundation of the apostle's doctrine' in 'the moral consciousness of man' (p. 182) remains exemplary long after its exegetical basis in Baur's interpretation of 'spirit' in Paul has been superannuated by subsequent historical criticism.[14] That construction was falsified and new ones had to be attempted, but the task of theological interpretation remains.

Deissmann's Paul corresponded better than Baur's to the later liberals' impatience with ideas and their sense for the historically concrete, as well as to the exegetical advances made possible by the newer history of religions research. But after the First World War other theological interpreters rejected the liberal theology and some of the exegesis on which it was based. In their 'dialectical theology', 'religion' became a bogey word, together with 'idealism', 'mysticism', 'metaphysics' and even 'experience'. Paul's subject-matter was expressed afresh in terms which the new men found meaningful, a modernized (post-Kantian) form of Luther's theology of the Word. The '-ism' in 'Paulinism' never lived down its associations with German idealist system-building, but systematizing Pauline theology once again became respectable.

The theological reaction against liberalism was justified both by the change of cultural climate and by the sheer philosophical and theological naiveté of such great historians and linguists as Deissmann. It is impossible to interpret the New Testament theologically without laying philosophical foundations, as Baur and Bultmann did. Nevertheless, Deissmann's protest against Baur's relative isolation of Paul's ideas from their social and religious context continues to challenge more recent Pauline theologies. The older liberals' interest in religious experience and ethics is therefore being taken up with the greater sophistication made possible by subsequent scientific study of religion, in the new 'religious studies of the New Testament'. It provides a fresh means of theological appropriation – or may be pursued independently of any such aim and interest.

This indirect approach to Paul's theology contextualizes and avoids objectifying his ideas, but it cannot avoid analysing them and showing how they are interrelated. It inevitably gives a systematic presentation which reflects something of the interpreter's own pre-understanding. The danger of this is not so much that the historical contours will be petrified through being cast in a static mould, but that as the theological interpreter penetrates into the heart of Paul's subject-matter, aspects of the apostle's thought which do not echo in his own apprehension of Christianity may be ignored or suppressed. The danger of uncontrolled hypotheses is especially acute if the interpreter judges that in some places Paul is being influenced by the language of his opponents, or fails to maintain his own best understanding of the gospel. Baur saw it his constructive theological task 'to separate the essential and the universal from the less essential, the fortuitous, and

326

that which has reference only to the special circumstances of his time' (op. cit., p. 115). The intuitive element in this cannot be denied. The dangers of subjectivism can only be minimized by the on-going debate between interpreters holding different standpoints. The checks provided by other historians are particularly important on matters where satisfying interpretations often reflect personal engagement. Implausible interpretations can be discredited, and replaced by interpretations which do better justice to the theological witness of these texts.

The main objection to the concept 'Paulinism' is not that it systematizes Paul's theology but that its *content* is indeterminate. The word inevitably presupposes a particular interpretation of Paul – and this is contested. The difficulty is evident in C. H. Dodd's *mot* that whether or not Paul wrote Ephesians 'certainly its thought is the crown of Paulinism'.[15] The implied content of the word must be different here from the more typical orientation to law and grace. If, on the other hand, Marcion's 'exaggerated Paulinism',[16] and above all Luther, have all but captured the term for that particular line of interpretation, this is unsatisfactory. It canonizes one particular reading of texts whose value resides partly in their capacity to illuminate very different generations and situations. There is no finally correct interpretation of these classical writings.

Both the necessity and the dangers of systematizing Paul become clearer in considering the secondary meaning of 'Paulinism' which refers to Pauline influence in the post-apostolic (once called more evaluatively 'sub-apostolic') period. This now seems less pervasive than Baur and his followers thought, but the existence of Acts and a Pauline pseudepigrapha still compels the historian to describe and assess the appeal to Paul in second- and third-generation Christianity.

II

It is possible to detect a bifurcation in the Pauline 'school', with the trend represented by Colossians (if this is deutero-Pauline) pointing in some ways towards the Christian Gnosticism of the second century, and the Pastorals clearly foreshadowing catholic orthodoxy.[17] The problem already noted of varying content in the word Paulinism is therefore even more acute in its secondary reference to diverging trends in the post-Pauline period. Its value in this context is likely to be found less in its usefulness for historical analysis than at the level of

327

theological evaluation and appropriation. These overtones were present at the beginning (for Baur Paulinism was the purest expression of the gospel), and are still potent, despite some attempts to use the word in a value-free way.

The term had made historical sense, granted Baur's bi-linear reconstruction of early Christian history as the gradual reconciliation of the Petrine and the Pauline parties. It designated one of the two 'trajectories' (the word is modern, but not the thought); and granted Baur's chronology, which placed each document on one or other trajectory at the point suggested by its theological tendency, the result was an account of the differences between the various 'Pauline' writings, which penetrated to the heart of their conceptions of Christianity.

But early Christian history was less tidy, and influenced by more factors, than Baur considered. His bi-linear model with its elongated chronology was soon abandoned, and this evacuated the concept of its explanatory power. 'Paulinism' continued to indicate an 'external' historical relationship to Paul among writers who echoed Pauline tradition and used his name, but it no longer interpreted or defined an inner theological relationship between these different New Testament writings. The question which had earlier made it theologically significant, i.e. how far certain authors shared a common understanding of Christianity, began to recede as the historical interest outweighed the theological.

The inadequacy of the concept for describing historically the development after Paul became especially clear in the disagreements between Overbeck and Hilgenfeld over the characterization of Acts and of Justin.[18] Overbeck retained the word for the sake of clarifying his challenge to the view of Acts pioneered by Baur and Zeller and defended by Hilgenfeld. But his qualification of this 'Paulinism' as 'impure' or 'degenerate' in effect denies the applicability of the word to Acts. Overbeck's opinion of Acts has deeply influenced both historical and theological evaluations of Luke in the past generation, and so provides a way into our problem of the relationship of these, as focused in the secondary use of the word Paulinism. Although Overbeck was more scrupulous than most of his contemporaries in keeping his theological judgements separate from his history, he did not abjure them. His savage theological criticism of Luke for confusing religion and history reflected the sharp separation which he personally made. This criticism has more recently been taken up from the standpoint of a different shade of theological aversion to history. New Testament theologians such as Käsemann, Vielhauer, Haenchen and Conzelmann, were mostly influenced by the Luther and Kierkegaard inspired 'Paulinism' of the dialectical theology; they felt as little sympathy as Overbeck for Luke's history of salvation.[19]

The slogan 'early Catholicism' by which Käsemann highlighted the theological differences between Paul and third-generation Christianity has not won general acceptance.[20] But as discussed by Protestant theologians who evidently find Paul more congenial, or as taken up in Hans Küng's discussion with Käsemann on the canon,[21] it underlines the modern theological interests present in this debate. Behind the historical question of the differences between Paul and Acts is implicit the theological question: which of them represents a more adequate understanding of Christianity? Comparisons between thinkers often elicit the interpreter's personal opinions about their subject-matter – in this case, what is authentically Christian.

The question of authentic Christianity, or what Paul would call 'the truth of the gospel', is posed by the theological diversity apparent in the New Testament, and especially by the apparent bifurcations in the Pauline and Johannine schools. Even if all these different trends be judged defensible in their time and place, and the genius of Christianity be to contain both trends in tension, the divisions of the second century invite the historical theologian to say where an imbalance has occurred; and his judgement here will reflect something of his own conception of what Christianity essentially is or ought to be. The New Testament scholar cannot settle these questions by historical argument but his work raises theological questions and the different ways in which different historians read the evidence may reflect among other things their theological preferences. It is this borderland between contemporary Christian theology and modern historical study which becomes visible in concepts such as 'Paulinism' and 'early Catholicism'.

In his celebrated essay on 'The Paulinism of Acts'[22] Philipp Vielhauer asked whether Paul and the author of Acts 'belong together theologically' (p. 33). His conclusion that there is a 'material' (i.e. theological) distance between them may imply a theological evaluation, but this is not made explicit. Vielhauer remains in the realm of historical judgements which can be rationally argued on the basis of public evidence. He does not advance to the more private realm of personal theological preferences, though had he done so and even

329

conceded that these may have affected his perception of the data, his case would still be open to inspection on the basis of public evidence. No doubt disagreements in interpreting the evidence occasionally hinge on the conflicting religious commitments of interpreters; truth is then best served by making these explicit. In recognizing the relativity of his own position and arguing rationally about the data, an interpreter may be led to modify his theological standpoint.

This delicate question of the relation between historical study and theological interest in the subject-matter of the New Testament is illuminated by Professor Barrett's own probings of the 'Paulinism' of Acts and the Pastoral Epistles. His personal theological preference for Paul has been noted, as has his debt to the dialectical theology – though this never extended to its dualist aversion to history, which has sometimes hindered a sympathetic judgement on Acts. But the cool historian does not allow his own theology to obtrude in his exegesis. The texts must be heard so far as possible in their own terms, however different their backgrounds and concerns may be from those of the exegete. In his popular commentary on *The Pastoral Epistles*.[23] Barrett calls them not 'somewhat faded Paulinism' (Bultmann) but simply and non-evaluatively 'developed Paulinism'. Admittedly, the 'splendour of these letters' is 'sometimes hidden' (p. 34), but the commentator accepts them 'as one element in the apostolic testimony that God has caused to be borne to his Son' (p. 33), and evidently respects the attempt of 'those who held fast to the doctrine they had received from their master . . . to represent in their own generations the genuine Pauline voice' (p. 17).

The theological pre-judgement contained in this reference to the canon suggests that Barrett the theologian stands closer to Calvin and Barth on this issue than to the 'canon criticism' of Luther (occasionally), Bultmann and Käsemann. Whether or not this theological interest has influenced either his assumption that these epistles understand Paul better than the gnostic Christians did, or his defence of Luke against modern theological critics, the latter case is carried by historical argument. Luke is 'not so much a theologian as a pastor'[24] who is not 'sufficiently interested in theology (beyond basic Christian convictions) to be called a *theologus* of any colour'.[25] He did not fully understand 'the depths of his own christocentric theology' (*New Testament Essays*, p. 83; subsequent page numbers given also refer to this book). In other words, Luke had a theology, as every Christian has one, whether or not he makes it explicit. But he was not a self-conscious theologian and it is unreasonable to expect of him the coherence and consistency one might look for in Paul.

This historical evaluation of Luke protects the evangelist from being judged by an inappropriate standard, and in thus rescuing him from the verdict of those who would anathematize him it also rescues the New Testament canon as such, while leaving room for the interpreter's actual theological preference for Paul. But such a corrective to the historically improbable and theologically damaging judgement which places Luke and his hero in an antithetical relationship modelled on the modern western opposition of Catholicism and Protestantism does not answer all the historian's questions, much less settle the theological question of the adequacy of Luke's conception of Christianity. To say that Luke is a 'Paulinist' in the sense that 'he admired Paul, perhaps defended him; he imitated his theology and (so far as he understood it) reproduced it' (p. 92, cf. p. 82), only sharpens the question how successfully he imitated and how well he understood Paul's theology.

That looks like a historical question about Luke's relation to Paul. But if the subject-matter of Paul's theology, the Christian gospel, lies behind the theological language in which it is expressed, and if it may (in principle) be distinguished from this, then the question of Luke's Paulinism gains a further dimension. We are now more interested to know how far Luke grasped the central thrust of Paul's conception of Christianity, rather than how far he reproduced his theological concepts. This requires an intuitive grasp of Luke's understanding of Christianity, which Luke himself scarcely articulated in a reflected way, as well as a similar grasp of Paul's theology. And if these interpretative ventures draw upon the interpreter's own understanding of Christianity, this involvement becomes even more prominent in the evaluation made when comparing them. Some fruitful comparisons can be made without leaving the historical plane, but the more deeply the question of Paulinism is probed the more the interpreter is drawn towards making a theological judgement which frankly involves his own view of what Christianity is and ought to be.[26]

The problem of the New Testament theologian here is that his historical methods do not yield normative theological judgements. His commitments cannot therefore be made explicit in his historical presentation. He may advance to the brink of theological evaluation but will lose his licence if he oversteps it. This brinkmanship is evident in Barrett's argument that Luke lacked Paul's 'theological profundity', and failed to understand his hero's theology 'at its full depth' (p. 82, cf.

p. 86). Any historian of religion with some grasp of his subject-matter can see that Paul is more 'profound' than Luke. It does not necessarily follow that his understanding of the gospel is more true, which would be a theological judgement, because profound theologians can be profoundly wrong, however technically brilliant. Nevertheless, there is a clear implication that Paul's christocentric theology of the cross is the more adequate understanding of Christianity.

Barrett's solution is historically attractive. Luke probably intended 'no more than a development and application of [Paul's theology] to a new historical situation' (p. 91). He and the Pastor were probably more interested in 'holding fast to the doctrine they had received from their master' than in developing an alternative theology. Barrett's judgement therefore does better justice to the authors' intentions than do the harsh theological judgements passed by the modern opponents of 'early catholicism'. But this historical judgement would only contribute to the modern theological debate about authentic Christianity if the Christian gospel could be identified with Paul's theological conceptuality. It would then be possible to think of Luke 'applying' this and having no special theology of his own. But once a distinction is made between the Christian gospel and any particular theology, including Paul's, it is necessary to recognize that every pastor has his own theology, or overall understanding of Christianity, however poorly this is articulated. Even to repeat Paul's theology in a new situation is to adopt a new theological position, and nobody who is concerned about the truth of the gospel can evade the question of its adequacy. The epigone, like Paul himself, deserves to be judged according to his intentions to express the gospel. The significance of 'theological comparisons' is to be found as much in their contribution to theological as to historical clarification. They not only sharpen the historical contours of each author's thought, but also draw the interpreter's own understanding of Christianity into the evaluation. This is what gives them theological 'bite'.

Barrett's remarks on the Pastorals and Luke imply a common view of theology as secondary reflection and critical sifting of doctrinal statements received as tradition, and this is confirmed by his lecture on 'Theology in the World of Learning' (pp. 144–56). Credal or Pauline statements may be more or less profoundly thought about. This, however, is a rather different view of theology from the 'understanding of faith' which Bultmann and Käsemann for example have in mind in writing of a New Testament author's theology. Their more radical conception of the theological task involves evaluating an author's conception of Christianity by looking behind his theological statements towards the reality these claim to be expressing. That requires both a systematic grasp of the author's theology as a whole (individual 'doctrines' or statements cannot be treated in isolation as in the older form of theological comparisons) and also a theology of one's own through which one perceives the reality to which the author points. 'Theological comparisons' sharpen the theological as well as the historical focus. The question of Luke's 'Paulinism' may illuminate the 'central thrust' of his understanding of Christianity and also assist theological evaluation of this by reference to one's own understanding of the gospel – which in the case of many Protestants (and others) owes more to Paul than to anyone. A negative verdict on Luke's conception of Christianity need not prevent Christians from using his valuable material, but may encourage a more critical reception of his witness than has been common among Christians. The effort to assess his theology – and the modern discussion of his 'Paulinism' is more concerned with this than with his historical relationship to Paul – is a necessary element in the critical theological appropriation of the New Testament.

The interpreter's own view of Christianity will influence both his constructions of these models (or abstractions) of a New Testament author's theology and also his evaluation of them. The former operation lies within the scope of historical procedures, provided that all such hypotheses are tested by reference to the evidence. The latter task goes beyond historical evaluation, but is necessary for anyone wishing to do justice to Luke's intention to communicate Christianity as well as defend Paul, in his effort to 'maintain Pauline Christianity'.[27] Barrett recognizes that evaluation is necessary when he writes that 'the real problem of the Paulinism of Acts' lies in the question whether Luke's theology, admittedly different from Paul's 'constitutes a *corruption* of Pauline theology, or is no more than a *development* and application of it to a new historical situation' (p. 91, my italics). 'Corruption' contrasted with the more neutral word 'development' implies (in this context of the German debate) a theological evaluation of Luke's conception of Christianity, not simply a historical evaluation of his presentation of Paul. That is an inner necessity for the Christian theologian; his engagement with the material draws from him an evaluation of its truth, or its adequacy to the gospel which it seeks to express, and which he too seeks to understand. But since this goes beyond the bounds of historical reason the New Testament theologian who wishes to remain on the ground of rational appeal to public evidence can only hint at his opinion here.

Professor Barrett's historico-theological brinkmanship becomes most clear when he advances to a substantive theological judgement and shows that his ambiguous phrase 'theological profundity' in fact refers to the depth of Paul's (true) insight into the Christian mystery, not simply to his technical ability. The theological dimension implicit in the 'comparative method' by which he aims 'to bring out the special characteristics of Acts by means of historical and theological comparisons' with Paul (p. 101) emerges when he goes beyond sympathetic understanding of Luke to a critical assessment. Luke 'intended to apply [Paul's theology], but . . . he made the application without Paul's critical insight' (p. 115). Barrett admires the first Christian generation not because it was harmonious and ecumenical (as Luke claims), but because it was creative; 'and Paul was a creative theologian not in spite of his conflicts but because of them' (p. 115).

This preference for Paul's argumentative style over Luke's smoother 'narrative' theology should not be allowed to obscure what Luke's parables make plain, that even narrative can have critical edge. But it presupposes a theological conviction, a 'Pauline' understanding of Christian faith, learned from Luther: the gospel is best communicated in and through the dialectic with 'law', or by means of *critical* interpretation of the dominant religious tradition. Christian theology, and indeed the gospel itself, is necessarily critical and dialectical, and a theologian is someone who can distinguish between law and gospel. The historical Paul understood Christianity better (i.e. more truly) than Luke did in his back-handed apologia for him. Luke's conception of apostleship can be criticized for its historical inaccuracy (p. 83). Critical historians fulfil a theological function in exposing ideological distortions of history. But the main reason why Barrett the theologian rejects Luke's conception is not the historical flaw in its title-deeds, but its disagreement with Paul's conception. We are not told how he 'knows' Paul is right. Paul's theology corresponds to his own understanding of the gospel and the justification of this would involve much more than rational (including historical) argument.

The relationship of this Lutheran Paulinism to the Eastern Orthodox ideal of the theologian as one whose prayer is true cannot be discussed here, but if the truth of the gospel of freedom emerges from a critical approach to received traditions it requires a strong religious tradition with which to interact. That it has done so is implied in Harnack's famous comment that 'Paulinism has proved to be a ferment in the history of dogma; a basis it has never been'.[28] This quotation also underlines our contention that the main significance of the concept itself is to be found in its contributions to the modern theological appropriation, the *Rezeptionsgeschichte* and the *Wirkungsgeschichte* of the New Testament in the Christian Church.

It belongs on the borderland where the constructive imaginative element characteristic of all creative historical work carries the willing interpreter into the field of theological judgements. Constructing historical models of a religious thinker draws from the sympathetic interpreter some degree of identification with his author. Without prejudice to the historian's integrity it may serve a theological purpose by involving his prior understanding of what the author is trying to express. H. J. Schoeps rightly observes that the Christian theologian 'is able to interpret the apostle's articulation of his faith on the basis of that Christian profession which he holds in common with him',[29] but wrongly contrasts this with the supposedly superior insight of the historian of religion. The historical theologian's convictions remain unspoken and his history is open to inspection like anyone else's. His actual identification with the author may be indistinguishable from the sympathetic historian's pretended identification as both try to do better justice to the author than their rationalist predecessors, both orthodox and atheist, did.

'Theological comparisons', are a particularly effective means of drawing into the discussion the interpreter's own estimate of his authors' subject-matter and thus generating what is best called 'theological interpretation'. The historical comparison of other men's thoughts on any subject stimulates our own present thoughts about the subject as well as sharpening our historical picture of these past thinkers. But the personal theological dimension remains implicit, and intuiting the 'shape' of an author's theology can only propose a hypothesis for interpreting the text; the argument itself is carried on by historical appeal to public evidence.

The special role of 'Paulinism' in this historical theology or theological history of the New Testament is summed up in Professor Barrett's statement that 'Pauline theology is the heart of New Testament theology as a whole' and will function as 'an historical and a theological norm' (p. 101). Paul is 'the one absolutely fixed point in early Christian history'.[30] In the same breath, 'as a man and a

335

theologian', Barrett reaffirms Luther's theological judgement that the
Epistle to the Romans is 'the plainest gospel of all'. Comparing other
New Testament writers with Paul not only clarifies the historical
picture but implies or makes possible a normative theological
judgement. This is only possible if the epistles can be seen to provide a
'form of Christianity' (cf. n5 above). Paul was 'not a systematic
theologian, but he laid the foundations for systematic theology . . . As
such a theologian he conceives a picture of God's dealings with
humanity as a whole'.[31]

Paul's theological formulations combine variety with self-consis-
tency in a way that enables modern readers to find in them
correspondences with their own different understandings of Christianity. The resultant New Testament theologies provide no definitive
answer as to what Christianity is. They simply reflect the different
ways in which the New Testament has informed and strengthened
Christians' understandings of their faith. These different historical
constructions contain a kind of 'implicit theology' wherever a
theological interpreter presents the history in ways which reveal its
compatibility or incompatibility with his own understanding of the
gospel. The relationship which emerges from the 'fusion of horizons'
(Gadamer) between text and interpreter may be made visible without
being made explicit. The interpreter's own convictions remain
unspoken (or restricted to prefaces); his conclusions stand or fall on
their historical and exegetical merits. The question of theological truth
is bracketed off from historical work, but the theological interests
which every Christian brings to his reading of the New Testament are
tested by reference to the texts to which they in part appeal, and this
rational historical activity is a part of the wider experiential verifica-
tion to which theological claims are subject. Conversely, the historian
with theological interests cannot 'as a man and a theologian' for ever
bracket off the question of truth. If his attempt to understand these
first-century documents makes any progress it will draw him on to (at
least silent) assent or dissent. Historical theology, including New
Testament theology, describes other men's talk of God. But if it is
indeed *theology* as well as history it will include critical assessment,
because theology is the attempt to speak truthfully of God. For the
Christian that means the attempt adequately to express the revelation
of God in Christ. If God is the reality which determines everything this
must result in coherent systems of thought. All such theological
systems, including those inspired largely by Paul, are provisional.

They are open to criticism on exegetical, philosophical and theological grounds. But they are necessary conceptual underpinning for anyone who wishes to say with Paul: I am not ashamed of the gospel.

NOTES

1   A. C. Headlam in *Church Quarterly Review* vol. lxxvi (1913), p. 167.

2   Mark Pattison, 'Present State of Theology in Germany' (1857), reprinted in *Essays*, vol. ii, ed. H. Nettleship (Oxford 1889), p. 234.

3   *From First Adam to Last* (London 1962), p. 3; cf. Wrede, *The Task and Methods of 'New Testament Theology'* (ET London 1973), p. 76; also Bultmann, *Theology of the New Testament*, vol. i (ET London 1952), p. 190; Bornkamm, *Paul* (ET London 1971), pp. 117f, etc.

4   *Luke the Historian in Recent Study* (London 1961; Philadelphia, 1970), p. 70, quoted in *The Signs of an Apostle* (London 1970), p. 125; cf. 'The Pauline system', in *From First Adam to Last*, p. 4.

5   A Commentary on *The Second Epistle to the Corinthians* (BNTC 1973), p. vii, my italics; cf. *The Epistle to the Romans* (BNTC 1957), p. vi; *From First Adam to Last*, p. 2.

6   cf. Karl Barth, *The Epistle to the Romans* (ET Oxford 1933), p. 7; and Barrett's appreciation of this work in *Romans*, p. vi. This essay also owes a debt to Barth's Preface to the Second Edition.

7   W. Wrede, op. cit., p. 70.

8   A. C. Thiselton, *The Two Horizons* (Exeter, 1980), provides the best English statement of this case.

9   *Paul* (1904; ET London 1907), p. 76.

10 *Paul: A Study in Social and Religious History* (1911; ET of 2nd edn London 1926).

11 *Paul the Apostle of Jesus Christ* (1845; ET of 2nd edn 2 vols. London 1873–5).

12 *Paulinism* (1873; ET 2 vols. London 1877).

13 *Lehrbuch der neutestamentlichen Theologie*, vol. ii (2nd edn Tübingen 1911).

14 Notably by Gunkel, *The Influence of the Holy Spirit* (1888; ET Philadelphia, 1979).

15 *The Abingdon Bible* (1929), p. 1225. Similarly, F. F. Bruce borrows A. S. Peake's phrase, 'the quintessence of Paulinism' and applies it to Ephesians which he interprets as 'an exposition of dominant themes of Paul's ministry'. *Paul: Apostle of the Free Spirit* (Exeter, 1977), p. 427.

16 Professor Barrett's phrase. *The Signs of an Apostle*, p. 127.

17 cf. U. Luz, 'Erwägungen zur Entstehung des "Frühkatholizismus". Eine Skizze', *ZNW* LXV (1974), pp. 88–111.

18 *Zeitschrift für wissenschaftliche Theologie* XIV–XV (1871–2), discussed by

J. C. Emmelius, *Tendenzkritik und Formengeschichte* (Göttingen, 1975), pp. 129–35.

19 cf. U. Wilckens, 'Interpreting Luke–Acts in a Period of Existentialist Theology', *Studies in Luke-Acts*, ed. L. E. Keck and J. L. Martyn (London 1968), pp. 60–83; W. G. Kümmel 'Lukas in der Anklage der heutigen Theologie', *ZNW* LXIII (1972), pp. 149–65.

20 The reservations of Conzelmann, *An Outline of the Theology of the New Testament* (ET London 1969), pp. xvi, 289, gain additional force in the light of the dangers in the slogan exemplified by S. Schulz, *Die Mitte der Schrift* (Stuttgart, 1976). They also gain support from A. Lindemann, *Paulus im ältesten Christentum* (Tübingen 1979).

21 H. Küng, 'Der Frühkatholizismus im Neuen Testament als kontroverstheologisches Problem' (1962), reprinted in E. Käsemann, ed., *Das Neue Testament als Kanon* (Göttingen, 1970), pp. 175–204.

22 1950; ET in Keck and Martyn, *Studies in Luke-Acts*, pp. 33–50.

23 New Clarendon Bible (Oxford 1963).

24 *New Testament Essays* (London 1972), p. 86.

25 'Theologia Crucis – in Acts', in *Theologia Crucis-Signum Crucis*, ed. C. Andresen and G. Klein (Tübingen, 1979), p. 84.

26 cf. *New Testament Essays*, pp. 142f. A 'literary and historical' case is here adduced in support of a theological judgement which Barrett shares with Jeremias and Käsemann.

27 cf. 'Paul's address to the Ephesian Elders' in *God's Christ and his People*, ed. J. Jervell and W. A. Meeks (Oslo 1977), p. 119.

28 *History of Dogma*, vol. i (New York, 1961), p. 136.

29 *Paul. The Theology of the Apostle in the Light of Jewish History* (London 1961), p. xi, cf. p. 50.

30 *From First Adam to Last*, pp. 2f.

31 ibid, p. 3.

28

Paul and Religion

S. G. Wilson

'The word religion to me is like a red rag to a bull. It is religion which Paul, as I understand him, energetically attacks.' Spoken by C. K. Barrett in conversation a few years ago, these words have an unmistakable Barthian ring. A cursory glance at his commentary on Romans indicates the connection. In his comments on Rom. 1—3 Barrett uses the term 'religion' pejoratively to describe that Jewish and Gentile piety which Paul declared to have been radically negated by the gospel. The following is typical:

> Only when human achievement in religion had reached its highest point could its absolute negation in the universality of human guilt and the freedom of God be proclaimed.[1]

In the commentary itself there are no direct references to Barth in this connection, but the preface reveals his indebtedness:

> Barth's commentary I read as an undergraduate. If in those days, and since, I remained and have continued to be a Christian, I owe the fact in large part to that book and to those in Cambridge who introduced it to me.[2]

My aim is to explore and reflect upon this Barthian interpretation of Rom. 1—3. I shall begin, as Barth and Barrett do, and as the title of this volume obliges me, with Paul.

I   *Romans 1.18—3.20*

My purpose here is simply to recover the gist of Paul's critique of Gentile and Jewish religion, not only to discover what he concludes – about which there seems little room for dispute – but how and why he does so.

It is essential to begin with the immediate context, namely 1.16–17 and 3.21f. It is widely agreed that the 'revelation of God's wrath'

(v. 18) is an appropriate description of what follows but less clear, in terms of both syntax and content, how it relates to the revelation of righteousness in the gospel (vv. 16–17). The precise formulation will vary,[3] but clearly the revelation of wrath is both simultaneous with (ἀποκαλύπτεται in vv. 16 and 17) and intimately related to (the repeated γάρ in vv. 16–18) the revelation of righteousness in the gospel, and both are eschatological pronouncements on the present. If so, then two observations can immediately be made. First, it would be a mistake to read 1.19f as a neutral or comprehensive assessment of Jewish and Gentile piety; it is rather an impassioned, selective, even tendentious critique from the perspective of the gospel. Secondly, we are immediately alerted to the apocalyptic texture of Paul's thought, which accounts for much of the tone and some of the content of what follows – not least his penchant for making sweeping judgements.[4]

The triumphant announcement of the new revelation of God's righteousness in Jesus Christ (3.21f) is clearly the conclusion towards which Paul is driving from 1.16, and is made in the context of his bleak vision of the universality of human sin (3.9f; 3.23). Rom. 3.21f, however, must be read in the light of Rom. 1.16–18, and we should not be misled by the structure of these chapters to suppose that Paul, observing the universality of sin, concludes from this that a new revelation of God's righteousness is required. Quite the contrary, it is the presence of a new revelation which leads to the conclusions about universal sin. The revelation of God's wrath (1.18–3.20) can only be understood in the light of the revelation of God's righteousness (1.16–17; 3.21f). Or, putting it a little more forcefully, 3.21f is to 1.18f as premise is to conclusion and not the reverse.[5]

What arguments does Paul marshal? From 1.18–32 two things are transparently clear: that God has revealed his 'eternal power and deity' in the natural order of creation (vv. 19–20), but that mankind has wilfully and consistently ignored him. Both assertions are crucial for Paul's argument. The revelation in creation was universally available but universally rejected. In place of the humble gratitude with which creature should worship creator, men, in their vanity and folly, substitute idolatry – the worship of created beings and, ultimately, themselves (vv. 21–5). God abandons them to every form of immorality and vice (vv. 24–32), allowing Paul to conclude: they are without excuse (v. 20).

Paul's indictment of the Gentiles echoes Stoic and popular philosophy and hellenistic-Jewish apologetics, but with subversive intent. He radically alters both the tone and the intention of those he echoes,[6] intending neither to create a natural theology nor to establish a point of contact. For Paul, knowledge of God was available in theory but in practice ignored, and his exposé of pagan idolatry is not designed to enlighten or entice, but to condemn.

He then turns his attention to the Jews (2.1f).[7] The transition is obscure (to what does διό refer and is it to be given its full force?) but the intention is not. It is radically to challenge their sense of security and privilege, to show that this does not exempt them from God's judgement any more than ignorance exempts the Gentiles. That the privilege is real Paul does not wish to deny – and the tangled rhetoric of 3.1f is his none too successful attempt to show this[8] – but far from preserving them, it merely compounds their guilt. The gist of Paul's accusation is simple enough: despite privileged access to God's will in the Law, they do not obey it. This accusation is doubly reinforced. On the one hand, they have arrogated the role of judge but do not judge themselves (vv. 1–5); indeed, they transgress the very prohibitions which they proclaim to the Gentile world (vv. 17–24). On the other hand, Paul observes, adding insult to injury, there are Gentiles who keep the commands of the Law while being ignorant of its written form (vv. 14–15, 26–9 and perhaps vv. 6–7). The existence of obedient Gentiles serves to accuse the disobedient Jews and is the last nail in the coffin of Jewish privilege. For while disobedience can nullify the advantage of the Jew, obedience can nullify the disadvantage of the Gentile. As Paul borrowed from Judaism to indict the Gentiles, so now he uses Gentiles to indict the Jews.[9]

Three interesting issues emerge from the manner in which Paul conducts his argument. First, how realistic is his account of Gentile religion in ch. 1? Second, who are the exemplary Gentiles of ch. 2 and do they not contradict both the general tenor of 1.18f and the specific conclusion of 3.9f? Third, is there any way of showing that the accusations in 2.17f are not evidence of cheap polemics?

Doubtless there was much in Paul's world to confirm his view of Gentile religion, especially as viewed by a Jew, but it is clearly a selective and unsympathetic account. The impact might be reduced by referring to 2.14–15 or by supposing that Paul was ignorant of the higher philosophies,[10] but a more significant observation is that it is a prophetic judgement which is different from, and cannot be used as evidence for, the scientific study of religion. It is, as we observed above, a judgement made from the privileged perspective of the gospel.

To suppose that Paul has Gentile Christians in mind in ch. 2, or perhaps only in 2.29,[11] resolves some of the tensions but creates others. It contradicts both the detailed description and the general tenor of ch. 2 and anticipates the theme which Paul appears to pick up only in 3.21f. Many commentators who rightly draw the conclusion that they are ordinary Gentiles then hedge it about with qualifications, as their comments on 2.14–16, for example, show. Thus while it is probably true that not all Gentiles, and individuals rather than nations, are in mind, and the general intent is certainly to accuse the Jews and not to praise the Gentiles,[12] it seems unlikely that the 'things of the law' (v. 14) refers to 'obedient faith' or to a few demands of the Law occasionally performed,[13] that the conscience of the Gentiles confirms their guilt at the judgement day,[14] or that the whole argument is hypothetical.[15]

In the end the tension remains and the exegetical ploys used to remove it are not persuasive. It is understandable that this is attempted since, while minor contradictions in Paul's thought may be conceded, this one would undercut one of the central themes of his gospel.[16] And while for some 'belief in his muddleheadedness is not a sound hermeneutical principle',[17] for others it may be a necessary exegetical conclusion. Paul, it seems, in the course of his prophetic denunciation of the Jews, and leaning on the familiar notions of Stoic and popular philosophy, cannot resist ramming his point home with the example of Gentiles who do keep the Law.

The third problem, less discussed but equally serious, concerns the charges made in 2.17–24: the Jews rightly teach the Gentiles to deplore theft, adultery and robbery, but do not realize that they too are thieves, adulterers and temple-robbers. Can Paul be suggesting that all Jews stand so accused? If so, the charges are palpably absurd, and scarcely less so if Jewish propagandists[18] alone are in mind. Rabbinic parallels are interesting, but do not prove Paul's charge.[19] To see occasional crimes as adding vividness to a profounder understanding of the charges[20] does not appear to be Paul's point, and the suggestion that he had in mind the Jews' murder of Jesus and persecution of his apostles is an unhappy fancy.[21]

If Paul's intention is to suggest that as some Jews commit these crimes so all Jews contradict their nominal status by their actual behaviour,[22] or to emphasize the paradigmatic rather than the typical,[23] it must be said that he chooses a strange way to make his point and that the charges cannot be empirically justified for Jews as a whole. Paul's polemics may have roots in earlier conflicts with the synagogues, may have been affected by the failure of the Jewish mission, and certainly were designed to convert and not simply to condemn the Jews. It is also important to note that he sees himself as a Jew addressing his fellow-Jews. Such observations may help us to explain, but not necessarily to condone, Paul's argument. His judgement on Judaism is based ultimately on his Christian convictions and not on empirical facts, but he could not resist the polemicist's impulse to confuse the two.

The content of Paul's argument thus confirms what we learned from its framework (1.16–17; 3.21f). His central conviction is that God has brought man a new redemption based on grace and to be received by faith, exclusively mediated in Christ but universal in scope. Paul was therefore obliged to show that the old modes of redemption, Jewish or Gentile, had failed. His purpose is clear even though the coherence and justice of some of his arguments are not.

II *Barth and Religion*

In his vivid and eccentric commentary on Romans Barth first gives expression to his views on religion.[24] A great deal of its passion is directed against the use of the concept 'religion' in liberal theology rather than against non-Christian religions as such.[25] It is clear, however, from passing comments and from the subsequent discussion in *Church Dogmatics*, that Barth does include non-Christians in the term as well.

The tone is set in a comment on Rom. 1.16: 'The gospel is not a truth among other truths. Rather it sets a question mark against all truths' (p. 25). The gospel is a scandal, a contradiction which does not expound, recommend or negotiate but shatters all human perceptions – the most insidious of which is 'the criminal arrogance of religion' (p. 37). In his reflections on Rom. 1.18–32 Barth repeats the core of Paul's argument: knowledge of God was available, but suppressed (pp. 46–7). Underlying religion, even forms of Christian piety, is man's attempt to possess and patronize God, to bring him down to his own level. Ignoring the paradoxical revelation of God, man prefers the familiarity of that which he likes to call God, worshipping images of himself and his world. The divinities man creates proliferate and, in the end, succeed in dominating their creators (pp. 50–1, alluding to Indian polytheism and hellenistic mystery deities).

343

Turning to Rom. 2.1f he asks, 'Are there no saints, no prophets who elude the common fate of man?' – but his answer is unclear. On the one hand he sees the whole of 2.1f as an attack on human perceptions of piety, devotion and religion. Faith, he declares, is 'pure, absolute, vertical miracle' (p. 60) and radically independent of human achievement. Dressed in religious garb – as mysticism, ecstasy, awe, or even the 'submissive behaviour of the biblical man' (p. 56) – human achievement is deceptive; but it is finally exposed in the judgement of God which is neither accessible to nor in conformity with human expectation (pp. 62–3). The place for saints and prophets looks unpromising. Yet in commenting on 2.14–16, described as 'strangely obscure and provocative information', he notes that there may be simple, godly, unpretentious men, known only to God, who achieve justification (pp. 65–6). Here, in contrast to his later writings, he does not identify them as Christians.[26]

The accusations against the Jews in Rom. 2.17f, 'a disturbing and surprising piece of information from the invisibility of the other side' (p. 70), confirm that in God's new dealings with men all privilege and piety, however worthy and real, are irrelevant. Human righteousness is shaken to the roots when those in the very home of righteousness are shown to be vulnerable (pp. 71–5). The Jews may have the oracles of God, but the oracles themselves confirm that they share the common fate of sinful man.

Rom. 3.21f reveals that 'the righteousness of God is the meaning of all religion' (p. 95). It exposes man's illusions and protects God from 'every intimate companionship and from all the arrogance of religion' (p. 98), even that most subtle and dangerous form, the religion of humility:

> There is no limit to the possibilities of the righteousness of men: it may run not only to self-glorification, but also to self-annihilation, as it does in Buddhism, mysticism and pietism. The latter is a more terrible misunderstanding than the former, because it lies so near to the righteousness of God, and it too is excluded – at the last moment (p. 109).

In *Church Dogmatics* 1/2, Barth returns to the same themes in a more systematic way.[27] Most of the major themes are adumbrated in the commentary and it clearly had a profound effect on his later reflections even though the language of the later work is more cautious and restrained. The section is paradoxically entitled 'The Revelation of

God as the Abolition/Exaltation (*Aufhebung*) of Religion'.[28] The emphasis is more on abolition than exaltation and the latter applies exclusively to the revelation in Christ, which stands over and against most forms of Christianity as well as all non-Christian religions. Christianity is only the true religion, paradoxically, insofar as it is not 'religion' in the usual pejorative Barthian sense.

The first section ('The Problem of Religion and Theology', pp. 280–96) sets the scene with a stark contrast between revelation and religion, arguing that the error of neo-Protestantism was to place revelation and religion on a par, to concern itself with the revelation of religion rather than the religion of revelation. As it abandoned the Reformation insight into the centrality of Christ, so it declined into religionism and unbelief. The second unit ('Religion as Unbelief', pp. 297–325) opens with a reminder of the need for caution, charity and tolerance in the assessment of other religions, and yet insists that they are to be viewed in terms of the revelation in Christ which is God's judgement on all religion. The outcome is predictable and unambiguous: all religion is unbelief.

> This judgement can be explained and expounded, but it cannot be derived from any principle higher than revelation, nor can it be proved by any phenomenology or history of religion (p. 300).

From the viewpoint of faith religion is the attempt to usurp the unique role of revelation. The biblical evidence confirms that it is only from the privileged viewpoint of revelation that religion can be seen for what it is: idolatry, self-righteousness and unbelief (pp. 303–7). Internal critiques of religion in terms of atheism or mysticism (defined as 'esoteric atheism') confirm the judgement of revelation on religion, but revelation alone provides the death-blow (pp. 314–25).

In the final and most intriguing section ('True Religion', pp. 326–61) Barth makes two important moves: he directs the critique of religion against Christianity and compares it with other religions of grace, in particular, Amida Buddhism – and it is perhaps no coincidence that his argument is here at its most tortuous and unconvincing. As a human phenomenon Christianity is frequently indistinguishable from, and as likely to be riddled with idolatry and self-righteousness as, any other religion – as a brief survey of western Christendom all too easily shows (pp. 326–39). The fate of Israel warns us that revelation may overturn even the religion of revelation, which contradicts the grace and revelation of God no less when it claims these as its 'peculiar

345

and most sacred treasures'. As a religion of revelation it is also unbelief, a contradiction of grace, and it becomes the true religion only insofar as grace contradicts this contradiction (pp. 337–8).

The existence of Amida Buddhism, Barth somewhat perversely declares, is a 'providential disposition' because, as a religion of grace and in its popular form, it is remarkably similar to Lutheranism.[29] There are of course differences, of which Barth gives a somewhat tendentious account, but even if there were not, Amida Buddhism would still be unmistakably erroneous, a religion of unbelief, for it lacks the one essential possession – the name of Jesus Christ. Christianity is true not because it is a religion of grace but because it has the name of Jesus Christ. It has been elected as the true religion by the gracious act of an inscrutable God and this can be demonstrated only in the fact that 'the Church listens to Jesus Christ and to no one else as grace and truth' (p. 344).

Is Barth a faithful interpreter of Paul? In important matters I think he is. His commentary can be faulted on exegetical details, to which he at any rate pays scant attention. His suggestion, for example, that Jewish legalism inevitably led to false piety subtly alters Paul's accusation which is simply that they did not keep the Law, though he is neither the first nor the last to give a 'Lutheran' interpretation to Rom. 2. It may be justifiable elsewhere in Paul, but not here. Turning the critique of religion on Christianity itself extends Paul's argument, but Paul, I am sure, would have approved (cf. 1 Cor. 10). The term 'revelation' is more central to Barth than to Paul and the dialectic with religion exaggerated. Indeed there is no equivalent to the term 'religion' in Romans which applies to both Gentiles and Jews. Yet there can be little doubt that it is the religion of Gentiles and Jews which Paul attacks and that 'Gentile and Jew' is his way of speaking about all mankind. Above all, however, Barth concurs with Paul at the crucial point. His exposé of religion and religions rests finally not on empirical or intuitive observation but on a theological *a priori*. Outside of the revelation of God in Christ all religion is by definition false. It may be higher or lower, a religion of grace or works, aniconic or idolatrous, with its saints or its sinners, but without Christ it is nothing. The sense of an exclusive *a priori* is certainly heightened in Barth, but it merely makes Paul's view more explicit. Essentially he begins where Paul begins and, though travelling a somewhat different route, ends where Paul ends. Barth's critique of religion is recognizably and essentially that of Paul and both he and Barrett, insofar as he follows

Barth on this matter, can legitimately be counted among the ranks of true and faithful interpreters of Paul.

III *Critical Reflections*

Rom. 1—3 has been the basis for a seemingly endless debate over the role of natural theology, though the connection with what Paul says is frequently far from obvious. Its significance for the problem of religion is, however, far more pressing at present, and it is to Barth's credit that he sees this. The central issue can be simply stated: Is Paul's critique of religion adequate as a basis for reflecting upon the claims, and living with adherents, of non-Christian faiths? I believe it is not. This conviction, while it is a response to empirical evidence and to living with those of other faiths, is itself finally an act of faith. It would be inappropriate at this point, and in the last resort perhaps impossible, to justify this viewpoint further. More important than any individual view, however, is the problem itself. The challenge which other faiths pose to one's own tradition, long familiar to missionaries and historians of religion, is increasingly a problem for the average believer and can no longer be ignored by biblical scholars. The issue is eloquently stated by W. C. Smith:

> The time will come when a theologian who attempts to work out his position unaware that he does so as a member of a world society in which other theologians equally intelligent, equally devout, equally moral, are Hindus, Buddhists, Muslims, and unaware that his readers are likely to be Buddhists or to have Muslim husbands or Hindu colleagues, such a theologian is as out of date as is one who attempts to construct an intellectual position unaware that . . . the earth is a minor planet in a galaxy that is vast only by technical standards.[30]

What is incumbent upon a theologian in Smith's view is, I believe, incumbent upon biblical scholars too. With this in mind, what then do we make of Paul?

1   Smith himself thinks that an important step is to remove the term 'religion' from the discussion altogether, and not just in its pejorative Barthian sense.[31] Both 'religion' and the terms we use for particular religions (Buddhism, Hinduism, etc) are, he argues, recent, culture-bound coinages which give a misleadingly simple impression of

complex matters. This is an important warning and might well lead to greater clarity, but it would not resolve the problem for Paul, or, indeed, in many another instance. Call it what we will, and Smith suggests the dual terms 'cumulative tradition' and 'faith', it is the relationship of men to their god(s) which Paul attacks and this aspect cannot be defined away.

2   Another tack would be to concentrate on the weaknesses in Paul's argument. It could be maintained that his account of Gentile piety is unsympathetic, selective and unduly affected by his horror of idols. The assault on Judaism could likewise be seen as misleading and unscrupulously selective since it conveniently overlooks important aspects of Jewish practice and belief (e.g. repentance and forgiveness). It clearly would be a mistake to use Paul as a comprehensive and reliable source for first-century Jewish and Gentile religion; and there is no doubt that the balance could and should be redressed, in part from Paul himself (Rom. 9—11). Obviously, too, the admitted existence of unnamed pious Gentiles is an embarrassment to Paul's intended conclusion. It might thus be conceded that there is a need to cool his passion, tone down his polemics and straighten his logic, and in the process it would be legitimate to observe that Rom 1—3 is a prophetic judgement and not a dispassionate report and that we should not expect the detail and accuracy from the one as we do from the other – though it would also be necessary to consider at what point the notion of a prophetic judgement ceases to be an excuse for misrepresentation.

All such observations may be more or less accurate, more or less illuminating, but in the end they miss the crucial point. For there is no reason to suppose that if Paul had been more sympathetic towards Gentile religion or forced to reckon with deeply pious and godly Jews he would have changed his stance. Likewise, familiarity with another major religion apart from Judaism, for example Buddhism, would have made little difference. Greater knowledge and different circumstances might have changed his tone, as is suggested by the analogy of Barth's treatment of Buddhism, but his fundamental christological premise would have led him, like Barth, to insist on the privileged status of Christianity over all other traditions and faiths. Paul's conviction about the revelation of God's righteousness in Christ is absolute and exclusive, and from this all else flows.

3   Why did Paul think this way? It is probable that the tradition of

Jewish exclusivism contributed since he does at times seem to think of Christianity as the true Judaism. As with the material in Rom. 2, however, his views on this matter cannot be wholly explained from within Judaism, despite the variety of beliefs and practices in his day. The sectarian mentality of early Christianity, engendered partly by its struggle with Judaism, may have enhanced Paul's exclusivism, for it is in the nature of sects to create a stark contrast between insiders and outsiders as a form of psychological and social self-protection.[32] But it is ultimately Paul's own religious experience, beginning with his call on the Damascus road, which lies at the root of his exclusivism. Experience of the Absolute frequently leads to absolutizing of the experience. It is what Troeltsch calls 'naive absolutism', common in religious as in many other experiences: 'All religions are born absolute, for without reflecting on the matter they simply obey a divine compulsion and proclaim a reality that demands acknowledgement and belief.'[33]

4   The responses considered above concern both the tone and the substance of Paul's argument. Useful as they are, however, in the end we must face squarely the central, obstinate fact of his christological exclusivism. If we leave this untouched then we shall, like Barth, remain essentially faithful to Paul. For many, however, his exclusivism has to be abandoned and his absolutism relativized. And Paul, of course, does not stand alone. The rest of the New Testament and most forms of Christianity since share essentially the same view. I am fully aware that, for many New Testament scholars, to tamper with Paul's conviction that Christ is the new and exclusive revelation of God's righteousness is to tamper with 'the canon within the canon', 'the article on which the Church stands or falls'. We are engaged, therefore, in no mean undertaking but can at least take comfort in the thought that we are dealing with *the* central issue. For if the challenge of other religions affected only the peripheral parts of Christian tradition, belief in the virgin birth for example, the problem could readily be resolved at least for those who are already satisfied that they can be reinterpreted or jettisoned without loss. We are dealing now, however, with the heart of Paul's gospel and, at the same time, with the crucial theme in all Christian attempts to devise a 'theology of religion'.

There is perhaps a partial and a radical way of relativizing. The former might be illustrated by the common nineteenth-century missionary strategy of conceding that all religions possess a greater or

349

lesser degree of the truth but insisting that Christianity is the ultimate goal and fulfilment of them all.[34] This is not dissimilar to Luke's view in Acts 17. It does allow for a charitable assessment of other religions, but in the last resort must also consider them defective. P. Althaus perhaps best exemplifies those who attempt to give systematic expression to this and similar views. While his intention is to provide a positive evaluation of other religions the result is, typically, a negative judgement based ultimately on the principle of *solus Christos*.[35]

A more radical approach, responding to the considerable evidence for the relativity of all human experience, including religious experiences,[36] would be to argue for a more thorough levelling in which Christians forgo their claim to absolute truth and recognize both that they have but one truth among many and that they have an important, but not necessarily decisive, contribution to make in the dialogue between religions. It is the view which Troeltsch finally arrived at and, until recent years, perhaps no other major Christian thinker has struggled so persistently to come to terms with both the historical developments of Christianity and the existence of a plurality of autonomous religious traditions. In his earlier work, while admitting to an irreducible element of personal conviction, he maintained that historical evidence could be used to demonstrate the supremacy of Christianity as the culmination of the main tendencies in the various religions. By the end of his career, however, he had abandoned this view in favour of a more radical acceptance of the relativity of all truths.[37] The consequences for Christian thought remained undeveloped, since Troeltsch died in his prime and his work was rapidly eclipsed by the neo-orthodox movement initiated by Barth. One cannot, of course, revive Troeltsch without further ado. Even so, and despite the temporary decline of interest in his work, the questions he addressed with such clarity and honesty have arguably become more rather than less urgent; and for some, at least, he provides a more viable starting point than do those who believed they had once and for all laid him, and the liberal theology which he represents, to rest.

Attempts to explore the effects of such an approach on specific Christian beliefs have scarcely begun.[38] It does not, of course, mean the wholesale abandoning of Pauline or other Christian insights, but rather that we should set them in a broader context and without polemical intent. Thus, for example, reverting to Barthian terminology for a moment, we might apply the revelation/religion distinction internally to all religions (as Barth does to Christianity) – not, however, from the conviction that it is an absolute truth or that it provides a privileged status for one religion, but because it is a powerful prophetic insight into man's relationship to God.

I imagine that my mentor, to whom this volume is dedicated, will be happier with my understanding of Paul and Barth than with my reaction to them. It is no small compliment to him, however, that by his own example and constant encouragement he taught his students to think for themselves, however different their conclusions turned out to be from his own.

NOTES

1   C. K. Barrett, *A Commentary on the Epistle to the Romans* (London 1957), p. 29; cf. pp. 59, 83.

2   ibid., p. vi.

3   See especially G. Bornkamm, 'The Revelation of God's Wrath', in *Early Christian Experience* (London 1969), pp. 47–9, 61–4. E. Käsemann, *An die Römer* (Tübingen 1974), pp. 31–2, reviews the options and strains for a precision that goes beyond Paul.

4   O. Michel, *Der Brief an die Römer* (Göttingen 1966), p. 62; U. Wilckens, *Der Brief an die Römer* (Vluyn, Zurich, Cologne, 1978), vol. i; and Käsemann, *Römer*, throughout. See too S. Schulz, 'Die Anklage in Röm. 1.18–32', *TZ*, 14 (1958), pp. 161–73; cf. Baruch 54.17f, 1 Enoch 1—5; 91.7–9.

5   For this tendency in Paul see E. P. Sanders, *Paul and Palestinian Judaism* (London 1977), pp. 442f. Käsemann, *Römer*, p. 32, comments in a similar vein that 'the reality and the necessity of salvation go together'.

6   For the parallels see Bornkamm, *Early Christian Experience*, pp. 50f. The parallel with Wisd. 13—15 is especially striking and is clearly set out in W. Sanday and A. C. Headlam, *The Epistle to the Romans* (Edinburgh 1905), pp. 51–2.

7   Barrett, *Romans*, p. 43, thinks that Gentiles are included in 2.1–16.

8   C. H. Dodd, *The Epistle of Paul to the Romans* (Fontana, London, 1959), p. 70, calls the argument 'obscure and feeble'.

9   Bornkamm, *Experience*, p. 61.

10   The former is common, the latter is suggested by Dodd, *Romans*, p. 53.

11   For the former see K. Barth, *A Shorter Commentary on Romans* (London 1954), p. 36; C. E. B. Cranfield, *A Critical and Exegetical Commentary on the Epistle to the Romans* (Edinburgh 1975), vol. i, pp. 155–6; M. Barth, 'Speaking of Sin: some interpretative notes on Rom. 1.18—3.20', *SJT* 8 (1955), pp. 288f. For the latter see Käsemann, *Römer*, pp. 71–2, and Wilckens, *Römer*, pp. 157–8, who thinks 2.29 refers to all Christians, Jewish or Gentile. In view of the spirit/letter contrast in 2.29 there is more to be said for the latter view. Some would include 2.6–7 on the grounds

that they otherwise contradict Paul's view of justification by faith. Wilckens, *Römer*, pp. 142–5 is a balanced discussion. The history of the interpretation of 2.14–16 can be found in J. Riedl, *Das Heil der Heiden nach Röm. 2.14–16, 27* (Vienna 1965).

12 See variously M. Black, *Romans* (London 1973), p. 57; Sanday and Headlam, *Romans*, p. 59; Käsemann, *Römer*, p. 58; Wilckens, *Römer*, pp. 132–3; A. Nygren, *Commentary on Romans* (Philadelphia 1949), pp. 127–8. Note especially ἔθνη without the article and ὅταν instead of ἐάν in v. 14. An interesting analogy can be found in F. Rahman's reference to the attempts by Muslim exegetes to explain away the positive references to Jews, Christians and Sabaeans in the Koran (Sura II.62, V. 69): *Christian Faith in a Religiously Plural World*, ed. D. G. Dawe and J. B. Carman (New York 1978), pp. 73–4.

13 For the former see Barrett, *Romans*, p. 51; and the latter, Nygren, *Romans*, pp. 123–4.

14 Nygren, *Romans*, pp. 123–4; Käsemann, *Römer*, pp. 59–60. The connection of v. 16 to what precedes it is notoriously obscure. The 'thoughts' (v. 15), which may be part of the 'conscience', excuse as well as accuse.

15 H. Lietzmann, *An die Römer* (Tübingen 1971), pp. 40–1.

16 Käsemann, *Römer*, pp. 53–4; Cranfield, *Romans*, pp. 151–2. The issue is most pointed in 2.14–16, and for the sake of brevity discussion of vv. 6–7, 25f has been omitted.

17 M. Barth, 'Speaking of Sin', *SJT* 8 (1955) p. 290.

18 Lietzmann, *Römer*, p. 43; cf. Cranfield, *Romans*, p. 166; and Käsemann, *Römer*, pp. 65–6.

19 T. *Sot.* 14.1f; cf. Strack-Billerbeck, III, pp. 106–15. The Rabbis see them as aberrations that do not affect Israel's status.

20 Barrett, *Romans*, pp. 56–7, referring to Matt. 5, and to various OT passages.

21 K. Barth, *A Shorter Commentary on Romans*, pp. 37–8.

22 P. Althaus, *Der Brief an die Römer* (Göttingen 1970), p. 27.

23 Wilckens, *Römer*, pp. 151–3, is the best discussion. He also mentions the explanations in the sentence which follows but comes to a similar conclusion.

24 K. Barth, *The Epistle to the Romans* (Oxford 1933). Page numbers in parenthesis refer to this edition.

25 J. Hagaard, 'Revelation and Religion', *ST* 14 (1960) pp. 148f. He suggests that 'liberal theology' could often be substituted for 'religion' (158 n1). The opening section on religion in *Church Dogmatics* 1/2 shows why.

26 K. Barth, *A Shorter Commentary on Romans*, p. 36, and *Church Dogmatics* 1/2 (Edinburgh 1956), p. 304.

27 See previous note. Page numbers in parenthesis refer to this edition. That the verdict on religions expressed here remains essentially unchanged in later volumes of *Church Dogmatics* is persuasively argued by Hagaard,

'Revelation and Religion', *ST* 14 (1960) pp. 166f, and P. Knitter, *Towards a Protestant Theology of Religions* (Marburg 1974), pp. 32f.

28 The English translation removes the ambiguity by translating *Aufhebung* as 'abolition', but in view of the sub-section called 'True Religion' the ambiguity should probably be retained.

29 Francis Xavier, the first Christian missionary to Japan, described it as 'a brand of that Lutheran heresy'. Barth considers the Indian Bhakti movement a less viable parallel but in this, as in his judgement on Amida Buddhism, his knowledge is superficial.

30 W. C. Smith, *Religious Diversity*, ed. W. Oxtoby (New York 1976) p. 9.

31 W. C. Smith, *The Meaning and End of Religion* (New York 1962). See also the essays by J. Hick and N. Smart, in *Truth and Dialogue: the Relationship Between World Religions*, ed. J. Hick (London 1974).

32 J. Gager, *Kingdom and Community* (New Jersey 1975), pp. 19f.

33 E. Troeltsch, *The Absoluteness of Christianity and the History of Religions* (Richmond 1971), pp. 131f., here 138. He also discusses the institutionalizing and rationalizing of absolutism in the Christian West, pp. 148f.

34 E. J. Sharpe, *Faith Meets Faith* (London 1977), gives a fascinating account of this (pp. 19f) and other attitudes developed as a result of the meeting of Christianity and Hinduism. It is no accident that some of the most sensitive and provocative explorations have come from those (often missionaries) with first-hand experience of non-Christian cultures. It is interesting to compare Barth's response in 1935 when questioned about his view that religion is unbelief. Having admitted that he thought Hinduism was unbelief, but also that he had never met a Hindu, he was asked by D. T. Niles *how* he knew. '*A priori*' was the unhesitating reply. Quoted by G. H. Anderson in *Christian Faith* (see n13 above), p. 114 n1.

35 P. Althaus, *Römer*, pp. 17f, and *Die Christliche Wahrheit* (Gütersloh 1966), pp. 36f. Althaus deliberately attempted to mediate between the views of Troeltsch and Barth and this led him to be obscure and inconsistent – see Knitter, *Towards a Protestant Theology of Religions*, which is a valuable case-study of Althaus. He also believed (mistakenly, I think) that the more positive side of his evaluation of religions accurately reflected the views of various NT writers, including Paul.

36 A few examples are B. L. Whorff, *Language Thought and Reality* (Cambridge, Mass., 1957); L. Wittgenstein, *On Certainty* (New York 1972); B. Wilson, ed., *Rationality* (London 1974); G. D. Kaufmann, *Relativism, Knowledge and Faith* (Chicago 1960); see the recent reaction by R. Trigg, *Reason and Commitment* (Cambridge 1973); and S. Toulmin, *Human Understanding*, vol. i (Oxford 1972).

37 Contrast Troeltsch, *Absoluteness*, pp. 112f, and *Christian Thought* (London 1923), pp. 1f; cf. B. A. Gerrish in *E. Troeltsch and the Future of Theology*, ed. J. P. Clayton (Cambridge 1976), pp. 134–5. Relativism raises complex philosophical and moral problems and perhaps especially when applied to the sensitive topic of religious beliefs. The scope of this essay allows no more than a few sketchy hints. The problem is, of course, familiar to many

theologians and historians of religion, though I suspect less so to many biblical scholars. My concern is simply to hint at the consequences when one aspect of Pauline belief is considered in this light. I might add that I do not believe that relativism necessarily leads to pessimism and indifference. Intellectually, the relativity of all truths implies a relative truth in them all. Experientially, it is consistent with relativism to remain committed to that tradition which is personally and culturally most familiar. Religious experience, such as an experience of faith, will tend to function as an absolute, but the absolutism can be confined to the experiential level and need not be apologetically developed as it was by Paul. See R. Morgan in *Troeltsch*, ed. Clayton, pp. 59–60.

38 See the interesting explorations of G. Rupp, *Christologies and Cultures* (The Hague/Paris 1974).

29

Shame Culture in Luke

David Daube

To be allowed to contribute to a *Festschrift* for Charles Kingsley Barrett, to whose work – *aere perennius* – students of the New Testament are indebted for a wealth of learned information, for profound new insights and for what can only be called inspiration, is an inestimable honour. It is also, for me, a source of deep, personal joy; for what he and Margaret have given me, generously, unfailingly, in times good and bad, has been among the great blessings of my life. I am sorry I cannot at the moment think of anything worth-while in the Pauline field on which this volume focuses. But in view of the dedicatee's important A. S. Peake Memorial Lecture, my topic may not be quite out of place.[1]

Ruth Benedict's *The Chrysanthemum and the Sword*, of 1946, was an outstanding achievement, spiritually and academically. It drew a respectful, sympathetic picture of Japan at a time when feelings against that country were running high; and it familiarized scholars with the dichotomy between eastern shame culture and western guilt culture. Of course, both traits, attentiveness to appearances and attentiveness to the inner voice, play some part in every society, class and individual (except in California, which seems to be doing without either). Yet more often than not one or the other distinctly prevails. Ceremonial harakiri contrasts with our solitary suicide. Of two budding executives, one may have a liaison beneath his station for a few years and be thoroughly happy so long as there is no scandal, indeed, the memory of it will be a solace to him in old age;[2] while the other will be tortured for the rest of his life by a single night's lapse which cannot possibly ever become known.

It is almost two decades since I noticed that Deuteronomy is considerably more shame-oriented than the remaining four Books of Moses.[3] For example, the army must have a spot outside the camp where to relieve oneself, in order that God should see no immodest mark among his protégés; a bastinado inflicted on a wrong-doer may

355

not be excessive, lest he become contemptible; the punishment of one who breaks faith with a dead brother is public degradation, the dead man's widow spitting at him in front of the elders; God himself is anxious about his reputation – he spares the sinful Israelites because their enemies would assign the credit for their downfall to themselves instead of to him.[4] To account for it, I referred to Deuteronomy's affiliation with Wisdom, whose ideal, reaching outward, is to find favour and avoid disgrace.[5] Some three years ago it struck me that, just as Deuteronomy stands out for shame-cultural emphasis in the Pentateuch, so does Luke among the Synoptics. More than that: basically, the explanation is very similar.

Here is the material, some two dozen excerpts with a shame-cultural flavour – and Wisdom elements in most of them. I shall follow the order in which we find them. I start with the parables, looking first at three the Gospel shares with Mark or Matthew so that its particular note is clearly revealed.

I   *The Watchmen*   In Luke,[6] if they are vigilant, the returning master will wait on them: a choice of symbol reflecting a fair interest in table etiquette. It is met neither in the corresponding Marcan section nor in the Matthean,[7] but we shall come across it in yet another exclusively Lucan formulation outside the parables.[8] It depicts, of course, a tremendous reversal of the norm – which latter itself, significantly, figures in a parable offered by Luke only.[9]

2   *The Great Supper*   In Matthew,[10] the invitees simply 'did not want to come'; even when pressed, they simply 'paid no heed and went off, one to his farm and another to his business'. In Luke,[11] they send their regrets: a piece of land or a number of oxen just bought must be inspected, a newly-wed pleads that event. We are in the Berkeley hills. Lady Troubridge recommends 'owing to a previous engagement'; and if you can specify an urgent one – 'I have already undertaken to conduct the youth orchestra' – all the better. These apologies are perfect. A purchaser of land or oxen might incur serious loss by letting the term set for examination expire;[12] the phrasing, 'I have necessarily to inspect the land', makes the point. A recent marriage – not mentioned in Mark and Matthew – exempts from otherwise inescapable obligation in Deuteronomy as well as Lydio-Greek saga.[13]

Moreover, the form is no less impeccable than the substance. Both the buyer of land and that of oxen end their messages with the polite, lengthy 'I beg you, hold me excused'. The newly-wed says: 'Therefore I cannot come'. 'I cannot' obviously does not envisage either physical or legal impossibility. However, in many languages, ancient and modern, 'I cannot', 'you cannot' etc. may mean 'cannot in deference to a belief, standard, convention which it would be improper to breach'. A behind-the-times father to his son: 'You cannot remain seated when a lady enters the room.' A professor offered a fortnight at the Villa Serbelloni: 'I cannot in all decency ask for special leave here, having joined the faculty only two months ago.' It is this shame-cultural usage that we have before us; and we shall indeed encounter a second instance in a parable peculiar to Luke.[14] What is intriguing is that, of all the codes in the Pentateuch, Deuteronomy alone employs the expression. The king ought to be a Hebrew, 'you cannot put a foreigner over yourself'. If a divorcee has remarried, then after dissolution of her second marriage, 'her former husband cannot come back to take her to wife'.[15] It is always treated as interchangeable with 'you shall not', 'he shall not'. But whereas the latter is the prophetic injunction or ban of guilt culture,[16] the former implies: that would be out of tune with the model order here designed, in so wonderful a set-up surely that will be out of the question – something of this nature.

3   *The Lost Sheep*   In Matthew,[17] the owner, having it back, simply rejoices. In Luke,[18] he rejoices and collects his acquaintances to rejoice with him. An eager sharing of happiness suits a demonstrative, display-geared ethos. Deuteronomy, it should be recalled, sets much store by communal merry-making on the festivals of pilgrimage.[19] How important such gatherings are for the Third Gospel is shown by their recurrence in two more parables, to be adduced among the next category, parables not paralleled elsewhere.[20]

I proceed, then, to this group.

1   *The Importunate Friend*[21]   Permeated with shame considerations. The neighbour called out at midnight submits an excuse, like the Lucan invitees to a feast. Matthew might have written, 'He did not want to get up.' It is a good excuse: 'The door is shut and my children are with me in bed.' No mention of his own comfort; that would not do. He is prevented by his position as *paterfamilias*. Hence, not 'I shall, or will, not rise' but 'I cannot rise': the 'cannot in view of the superior pattern to which we conform'. 'Considering my responsibilities here, it would be the wrong thing to rise.'

357

So there is he, his children and the bed – *koite* in Greek, often signifying 'marriage-bed'. As far as I am aware, no commentator has asked: where is the wife? If the scene were laid in this State, there would indeed be no cause for wonder: there has been a divorce and, as he is the more mothering of the two and she has a career, he got custody. But it is Luke. She is omitted from squeamishness: one does not announce, 'I am lying with my wife.' In this case, as the man stands for God, her inclusion would be doubly offensive. Conceivably, in some version she did figure while the children did not. The closed door sounds like a symbol of the privacy of the marital night which it is indelicate to breach, be it intruding from outside, be it emerging from within.

In the end, he is stirred up into compliance 'because of his shamelessness': a straight shame term. It may have regard to the supplicant's insolent stubbornness;[22] or to his own ill-fame if he dismisses a friend in need.[23] Sirach attaches much weight to old friendship; and he lists the turning away of a friend among conduct 'to be ashamed of'.[24] Or to his debasement by being involved in an unpleasant scene or, simply, by watching the caller carry on in a pitiful condition. In analysing a cluster of Deuteronomic directions 'not to hide yourself' (one of them 'you cannot hide yourself'), I pointed out that, in this milieu, shame may be experienced not only on being discovered in an undignified state but also on discovering somebody else in it.[25] Of the Three Monkeys at Nikko, only one portrays abstention from unbecoming action, 'speak no evil', while two portray abstention from unbecoming reception, 'see no evil', 'hear no evil'. Quite likely, we have to reckon with a mixture of the various aspects outlined.

The petitioner, too, is enveloped in embarrassment. He has no victuals in store; and though his guest arrives unannounced and after dark, it would be discreditable to give him nothing to eat. Hospitality to a wanderer at night is an old Wisdom value.[26] What to do? One would never, at this hour, disturb anyone on one's own behalf. But his concern for his good name as a host can be represented as dutifulness to the traveller – just as his neighbour, we saw, makes play with what is owing to his children. Indeed, he is justified in persisting despite his neighbour's initial reluctance. In general, as illustrated by Proverbs and Horace,[27] that would be impudent. But there are exceptions: the Rabbis encourage the penitent sinner to pray and pray – 'the impudent one overcomes the All-Good one'.[28] At the same time, he scrupulously keeps within the limits of good taste, requesting only the minimum sufficient for a meal. Gentility at this point almost gets the better of the parable's lesson, which is that we ought to ask, seek, knock for mercy – not reticence. In turn, the neighbour, once responding at all, knows what is expected in such circumstances and supplies everything needed. I am reminded of the well-bred games in the old-fashioned Freiburg of my youth. One student to another after class: 'I have an appointment with my dentist but left my money in another suit. Can you lend me 5 Pfennige for a tram-ride?' 'Oh, but you must have lunch also. Here are 2 Marks.'

2   *Humility*[29]   To this piece, it is true, the Western Matthew offers a parallel,[30] so it does not, perhaps, belong here. At any rate, it urges that if, invited to a wedding feast, you place yourself near the head of the table, you will incur 'shame' should the host evict you in favour of somebody 'more esteemed'; whereas if you choose a lowly spot, you have a good chance of being publicly singled out as 'Friend' and promoted, winning 'honour in front of all'. Straight shame vocabulary again.

Jesus gives this instruction in a distinguished Pharisee's home, as he and his fellow-guests are about to sit down to a Sabbath dinner, the others trying to come out as high as possible. Seating-order is a popular topic of refined hellenistic table talk; and needless to say, the motif of homage and slight plays an enormous part.[31] The main idea, as is well known, already occurs in Proverbs:[32] 'Put not forth yourself in the presence of the king. For better it is said unto you, Come up hither, than that you should be put lower in the presence of the prince whom your eyes have seen.'

3   *The Cost of Discipleship*[33]   Two similes. First, a man begins building a tower he has not the means to complete; everybody now 'mocks' him. For the immediate purpose of the admonition – think twice, the risks of this undertaking are heavy – the latter result is not needed, stark failure is enough. But in a shame environment, it is the ridicule ensuing that hurts most.

Second, a king embarks on a war with vastly inferior forces. He will not simply lose, he will become a joke: long before even sighting the enemy, he must sue for peace. Again, the stress lies on the humiliation.

The advisability of knowing one's limitations and looking before leaping is an established Wisdom theme, and in Proverbs we learn that 'any purpose is established by counsel, and with good advice make war'.[34] The builder ought to have 'sat and calculated the cost', the king 'sat and taken counsel'. To this day, 'to sit' characterizes a person or body deliberating; the only other New Testament passage with 'to calculate' contemplates extraordinary sagacity;[35] and 'to take counsel' speaks for itself.

4   *The Lost Coin*[36]   Like the owner of the lost sheep, the woman wants everybody around to celebrate the successful outcome of the search with her.

5   *The Prodigal Son*[37]   He is charged, not with any specific sins, but with wasting his goods. This is shameful and foolish, Wisdom warns us,[38] doubly so when it is done in pursuit of whores. What happens to him is predicted in Proverbs:[39] 'Strangers will be filled with your wealth and your labour will be in the house of a stranger, and you will mourn at the last, How have I despised reproof.' His abject situation as a dependent of a citizen in a foreign country chimes with descriptions by hellenistic philosophers: you might have to eat dog-fashion at your protector's feet what he tosses to you.[40] Finally he returns to his father and declares himself 'no longer worthy to be called his son': language that in both Greek and Semitic expresses deep shame. 'I am not worthy' no doubt also occurs in formal self-deprecation. But even here we have to do with shame culture; and there are countless nuances between the formal and the genuine, some of which we shall meet below.[41] So degraded was his recent life that he will gladly occupy the position of a paid hireling – lower than that of an unpaid family member.[42] An even subtler differentiation in status is introduced at the end: a steady, reliable son ranks above one to celebrate whose homecoming after straying the fatted calf is killed.

As for the father, he is not satisfied with intimate happiness but arranges a festivity with music and dance. Furthermore, his first step, in preparation, is to have the boy clad in gorgeous attire: a spectacular restoration.

6   *The Unjust Steward*[43]   About to be dismissed, he ponders his future. 'To dig I am not strong enough': possibly a bit contemptuous of the labouring class who, as Sirach puts it,[44] 'shall not be inquired of for public counsel and in the assembly enjoy no precedence'. The proverbial Greek, 'I cannot dig', seems to have this overtone.[45] Anyhow, shame is the explicit ground for rejecting the second

alternative: 'To beg I am ashamed'. This assessment of begging is commonplace in Wisdom.[46]

What he does is make sure by means of unusual benefactions that there will be people around to take care of him when he is out of office. That you should prepare in good times for hard ones is one of the hoariest Wisdom slogans all over the globe. The ant stores up food in summer for the winter,[47] Joseph laid in corn in the seven plentiful years for the seven lean ones,[48] 'Remember the time of famine in the time of fulness', we are warned by Sirach.[49] Jesus lauds such foresight; and the opening of his response virtually proclaims its Wisdom contact – 'he had done wisely', 'the children of this world are wiser than the children of the light'.

7 *The Servant's Reward*[50]   An appeal to meal etiquette in a well-regulated household. The slave, however hard he has worked all day, may not sup before serving his master, nor is he to be specially thanked for it. It may be recalled that, in the eyes of punctilious traditionalists, overmuch affability on the part of a superior is despicable.[51] At certain formal parties – and not only in Britain – the personnel are still to be treated as non-persons.

8 *The Unjust Judge*[52]   He is, *au fond*, incorrigible yet does end by listening to the widow who would not be shaken off. As has long been seen, in quite a few societies, ancient and not-so-ancient, obligations – a promise, a Nabob's duty to an aged retainer – are apt to be fulfilled mainly in order to get rid of embarrassing protestations of the claimant.[53] Shame culture. There are striking examples from the judicial sphere. 'Opposite the entrance of the court sat the Cadi', relates a nineteenth-century traveller. 'The front-hall was crowded with people, each demanding that his case should be heard first. In the meanwhile, a poor woman broke through the orderly proceedings with loud cries for justice. She was sternly bidden to be quiet and reproachfully told that she came every day. "And so will I do", she loudly exclaimed, "until the Cadi hears my case." Her story was soon told, the case was quickly decided and her patience was rewarded.'[54] I have a feeling that the report is influenced by Luke: the author was an ardent divine. Even so it is, on the whole, a dependable parallel.

The reflection prompting the judge to yield deserves examination: *hina me hypopiaze me*. I would take it as it stands: 'lest she strike me in the face'. A blow in the face is the archetypal shaming insult among

Hebrews, Greeks and Romans.[55] In the New Testament, it figures several times: Jesus charges his followers to bear it meekly,[56] and while he himself does so,[57] Paul is less patient when similarly tested.[58] What the fellow is dreading is a desperate assault that would lower him in public esteem. It is widely argued[59] that considerations of Greek grammar militate against one final outbreak, so we ought to assume a mitigated, metaphorical sense: 'lest she cause me grave trouble'. I suspect the advocates of this interpretation are themselves a little offended by the crudeness of the literal alternative: contemporary shame reflex. However, even on their basis, the essential point would remain. Surely, the 'grave trouble' must be an escalation comparable to a slap, her visits will have that disgracing effect.

Commentators on the parable call attention to Sirach's trust in God as the rescuer of widows neglected by judges.[60] Equally relevant is his advice to avoid noisy quarrels,[61] which the judge prudently follows. Wisdom accounts, too, for the latter's characterization, given twice: when he is introduced as one who 'feared not God nor regarded man', and at the turning-point when he himself subscribes to this por-trayal – I must give in 'though I fear not God nor regard man'. The sage of Proverbs 'will find favour in the eyes of God and man'.[62] Nor is this vision confined to the Hebrews. In fact, a very close approximation to the Lucan summing-up of the anti-hero is found in Dionysius of Halicarnassus: a gang of Roman conspirators are stigmatized as 'neither fearing the wrath of the gods nor regarding the indignation of men'.[63]

We must not overlook the widow's shame dilemma, already adverted to in connection with the Importunate Friend: as a rule, forwardness is frowned on, and yet now and then it is in order.

9 *The Pharisee and the Publican*[64] The former 'stands up' visibly to pray: arrogance. We shall see, however, that there can be in this culture a commendable standing up.[65] The latter 'stands afar', in the typical position of shame. Nor does he dare to look up. Enoch is asked by the fallen angels to intercede for them, 'for they could not lift up their eyes to heaven for shame of their sins'.[66] An eighteenth-century variety: 'Fixing his eyes on Clara, who modestly dejected hers'.[67]

So much for the parables; now for the rest.

1   The barren Elisabeth, miraculously conceiving in old age, like the

Rachel of Genesis, thanks God – not for the pregnancy but – for taking away 'her reproach among men'.[68] The disgrace resulting from childlessness is treated as almost worse than the deprivation itself.

2 During pregnancy she hides herself[69] – plainly shame. No need to enquire here into the exact nuance: was she bashful generally or apprehensive that people might laugh because of her and her husband's age?[70] From the garden of Eden on, shame avoids sight;[71] and above I touched on 'hiding oneself' in Deuteronomy.[72] The sexual domain is indeed shame's birthplace and forever and everywhere remains its *point d'appui*.[73] Ordinarily, moreover, its presence in this field is looked on as, *au fond*, a blessing. Elsewhere I have argued[74] that the Genesis myth, like the Greek one of the acquisition of fire, commemorates man's rise, notwithstanding its pious reinterpretation as concerned with his fall; and the acquisition of shame, for this Wisdom narrator, is the most desirable achievement, actually represents the basis of all civilization. To be without it is to be animal-like, unenlightened, pitiable.

It has been suggested that Elisabeth's retirement is dictated by the plot: the news of her pregnancy is not to reach Mary just yet.[75] I am not excluding this explanation. Even if we proceed from it, her conduct must make sense to the readers, and it does so in a shame milieu.

3 The aspersions non-believers doubtless heaped on Mary are countered with the utmost delicacy. There is no express reference to them. Yet, as I have shown previously, an effective refutation is furnished in the annunciation scene by depicting her as a second Ruth.[76] The latter, the Rabbis insist, despite her pre-marital, nocturnal visit to Boaz, at first sight highly dubious, was the purest of all women.

Matthew is more direct: he does mention Joseph's initial, unworthy suspicions.[77] Here, too, by the way, the shame aspect plays a major role: Joseph generously refrains from 'making her a public example'. As just noted, where sexual matters are involved, the tendency for shame to come to the fore is pretty universal.

4 The child Jesus 'grew and became strong, filled with wisdom, and the grace of God was upon him'; the adolescent Jesus 'advanced in wisdom and stature and grace with God and men'.[78] Similarly – as has long been observed[79] – the young Samuel 'went on and was good

both with God and with men'.[80] The ideal progress of Wisdom's
votary: he enjoys the favour of, is in good standing with, not only
heaven but also this world. The repeated Lucan insertion of the
concept 'Wisdom' is significant.

In fact, a measure of importance is attached to bodily appeal: 'he
became strong', 'he advanced in stature'. Saul was handsome and
'higher than any of the people'.[81] There is an old and persistent
Wisdom strand with esteem for beauty male as well as female: Joseph,
David and Daniel belong here.[82] This does not mean that good looks
cannot be inadequate (David's eldest brother)[83] or misused (Absalom
and Adonijah)[84] or that the blemish of their lack cannot be
compensated by weightier qualities: we shall find a possible allusion to
this in the Third Gospel itself.[85]

5   At Nazareth, the audience wonder at Jesus' 'words of grace':[86] the
same key term as in the verses just cited. The remark does not figure in
Mark or Matthew.[87]

6   Immediately after, he guesses that they will confront him with 'this
proverb, Physician, heal yourself'.[88] Not in the other Synoptics. It is a
common tag in the ancient world: 'Physician, heal your own limp', 'A
physician of others, himself covered with festering boils',[89] holding up
its target to derision. The word *parabole*, by the way, when denoting
'proverb', seems usually to refer to exposure: 'byword of reproach'.[90]
Of course, proverbs belong to wisdom.

7   Whereas in Matthew,[91] the centurion with a sick slave approaches
Jesus in person, in Luke,[92] he despatches Jewish elders who explain
that in view of what he has done for the Jews 'he is worthy' of special
attention. In both accounts, he professes that 'he is not worthy' to have
Jesus enter under his roof. But in Matthew, he continues speaking to
him directly; in Luke, once again, he sends friends to tell him so, as he is
approaching his house. There is evidently a certain degree of shame
culture even in Matthew: I remarked on 'unworthiness' above, in
commenting on the Prodigal Son. But the Third Gospel has superim-
posed a most elaborate etiquette.

Quite likely, this version is designed to allude to later gentile
converts who never met Jesus in the flesh.[93] Even so, the man's doings
cannot be absurd – else the evangelist's public would be put off. They
are perfectly sound in an environment keen on decorum.

8   For the story of the woman with an issue of blood, we also have another Synoptic as a foil. In Mark,[94] she fears only Jesus' reaction to her daring. In Luke,[95] the stress lies on her exposure: 'she saw that she was not hidden'. In Mark, she confesses to Jesus. In Luke, 'she declared in front of all people'. As a result, the praise she received from him is represented as private in Mark, as public in Luke.

9   'Go not from house to house',[96] the seventy are advised – without parallel in Mark and Matthew.[97] Such conduct offends the refined sensibilities. Sirach speaks of 'the reproach of wandering' and deems it 'an evil life to go from house to house'.[98] The 'shamelessness' of an uninvited guest is censured in hellenistic literature,[99] and Horace sketches 'a parasite at large with no fixed stable'.[100]

10   Jesus' opponents, shown up as treating their cattle better than their sick, 'are ashamed'.[101] Whether or not this effect implies a harking back to Isaiah,[102] neither Mark nor Matthew has it in comparable situations. Who knows?, when the *pericope de adultera* was assigned by some to the Third Gospel,[103] one of the considerations may have been the similar experience of the accusers there.[104] I shall presently come back to this.

11   Possibly, the tiny Zacchaeus who has to climb a tree to see Jesus[105] stands for (among other things) those unfortunates who, because of the lack of normal, visible endowments, are apt to be laughed at. That this Gospel is interested in stature, we saw above. Plato thinks an undersized person deserves pity,[106] but that is not all he commonly gets.[107] Randy Newman's splendid song springs from a sensitivity rare even today.[108]

12   The apocalyptic discourse culminates in the exhortation to the disciples so to apply themselves that they can 'stand up before the Son of man'.[109] Not in Mark and Matthew.[110] It may mean 'remain undestroyed'.[111] On the other hand, it may be shame-oriented. A sinner like the publican, conscious of his shortcomings, will not 'stand up'. A self-righteous sinner like the Pharisee will, all the worse for him. The fragment before us may envisage a state in which you have nothing to be ashamed of and are, therefore, able to 'stand up' genuinely. Whoever placed the *pericope de adultera* after this chapter perhaps thought along such lines.

13　As Jesus eats with his disciples for the last time, he teaches that while, in general, the diner is greater than he who serves him, he is serving them.[112] An allied saying in Mark and Matthew[113] neither speaks of a waiting at table nor is presented as table talk at the Last – or any other – Supper. In Luke, the choice of symbol we met in the parable of the Watchmen, focusing on the meal conventions of the élite, surfaces again on this solemn occasion.

For a thorough evaluation of the phenomenon here demonstrated, we should have to examine the precise varieties of shame and Wisdom represented in these quotations. Thus, as for Wisdom, we would discover in the parables of the Importunate Friend, Unjust Steward and Unjust Judge traces of a wide-ranging debate whether a good deed remains good even if performed for one's own benefit and at little cost. The Importunate's neighbour and the Judge oblige not from affection or highmindedness but in order to avoid loss of face; and the Steward reduces the debtors' burdens not from kindness but in order to win supporters. Pragmatic and purist ethicists of antiquity fight over the problem. Among the Rabbinic cases are extra courtesy to your lender, a small gift to a poor man which will just bring him up to a total excluding him from such privileges as gleaning in your field, abstention from work as the Sabbath approaches from indolence rather than devotion.[114] Notions like '*aram* and *piqqeah*, 'subtle', 'clever', reminiscent of *phronimos* in the parable of the Unjust Steward, occur in this context.[115] In the early third century A.D., Rabh bridged the gulf between the two camps by pleading that, once you get into the habit of doing good, then, even if to begin with you are out for yourself, you will finish up with the right motivation.[116] His argument has become a canon in Jewish moral instruction. The difficulty theologians have with the three parables[117] would be greatly mitigated if the Wisdom input were appreciated.

However, it would lead too far afield here to pursue this investigation. One reason relatively little has been done in this area by New Testament scholars no doubt lies in Wisdom's concentration on how to succeed on earth with, *prima facie*, scarce thought for things divine. But, in actual fact, for Hebrew Wisdom – and much Gentile Wisdom as well – the latter are an absolute *sine qua non*. The first member in 'to find favour in the eyes of God and man'[118] is meant very seriously indeed. Still, I must not enlarge,[119] and shall be brief even on the question of whether the Lucan data are to be linked to hellenization.

Hellenization, it is by now agreed, was ubiquitous at the time. But there were degrees – just as in West Germany, there is a difference in intensity of Americanization between Heidelberg and Konstanz or a psychoanalyst and a coalminer. Now by itself, preoccupation with shame and Wisdom is no clue since it has a long, uninterrupted history in Judea as well as Greece. Nevertheless, Jewish shame and Wisdom and Greek shame and Wisdom, so long as not fully amalgamated, are distinct in many respects. It may well be that, on careful probing, the material here collected would come out nearer to Heidelberg. I can remember no Midrash addressing a class where to thank a servant counts as not *comme il faut*; 'I cannot dig', we saw, is Greek cliché; and 'to fear not God nor regard man' may be derived – directly or indirectly – from Dionysius of Halicarnassus, to whose *Roman Antiquities* Josephus opposed his *Jewish Antiquities*.[120] It may be added that the parables of the Rich Fool and the Cost of Discipleship and a section about inheritance – all peculiar to Luke – contain ideas and rare words met in Dionysius and Josephus.[121] Enough.

It remains to ask to whom the extraordinary shame component is due. It is certainly post-Jesuanic. This needs no proof for statements about him; but even with regard to statements put in his mouth, a glance at the major commentaries will show that, on one ground or another, the feature in question is pronounced secondary. Neither, however, is it chiefly the evangelist's work. For one thing, a parable quite similar to that about Humility is included in the Western Matthew.[122] Admittedly, a weak argument: this version may be dependent on Luke. A far stronger one is that, here and there, the evangelist tones down an excessive leaning towards pragmatism, most conspicuously in the parable of the Unjust Steward. The man doing good from selfishness and with somebody else's money is greatly praised to begin with, but then follows denunciation after denunciation of such dishonesty – anticipating the concern of many a later reader. What decides me is that, with one or two possible minor exceptions (such as the fear of those who hear of a capital punishment, *à la* Deuteronomy),[123] I can detect no particular interest of the sort discussed in Acts.

It follows that, on the whole, he found it in his sources, oral or written. It is in any case likely that he was in touch with more sophisticated circles than Mark and Matthew: this legacy is a consequence. He took it over from faithfulness to tradition: its absence from Acts is evidence that his own world view was not deeply affected.

It is a complicated situation, but not so hard to grasp. Somebody today might write a life of the founder of Hasidism. This might be distinctly influenced by Martin Buber's tales of him – which, needless to say, comprise much theology alien to eighteenth-century Lithuania: analogous to shame and Wisdom emphasis. The same writer, if going on to describe the revival of Hasidism in the States – Acts – might display hardly any vestiges of Buber's thought.

This is not to maintain that not one of the illustrations I have listed can be owing to Luke. I like to think that 'Physician, heal yourself' comes from him. Alas, one indication making it plausible is that it is out of place:[124] it is never alleged by Jesus' opponents that he is himself suffering from the ills he sets out to cure.

NOTES

1 Said a Fellow of Boalt: 'I've a block/against writing on Paul and his flock./Any mention of law/leaves my nerve-endings raw./It's high time that I turned to a Doc.'

2 Paradoxically (as he likes it), Heine in his early twenties publicizes his participation in this kind of thing:
> *Blamier' mich nicht, mein schönes Kind,*
> *und grüss' mich nicht unter den Linden.*
> *Wenn wir nachher zu Hause sind*
> *wird sich schon alles finden.*

3 I outlined my thesis in No. 2 of my Edinburgh Gifford Lectures 1963, on Law and Wisdom in the Bible, taped but as yet unpublished. An address, with extensive documentation, which I had delivered before the Institute of Jewish Studies, University College, London, and the Oxford Society of Historical Theology, appeared in *Orita*, vol. 3 (1969), pp. 27ff. My connection with this journal I owe to my friend E. Bolaji Idowu whom, like Charles Kingsley, I first met when he studied at Wesley House, Cambridge. The transfer of a Deuteronomic shame-cultural provision to an international setting in the First Book of Kings will be discussed in the forthcoming issue of the *Juridical Review*.

4 Deuteronomy 23.13ff; 25.1ff; 25.5ff; 32.26f.

5 Proverbs 3.4, 34f.

6 Luke 12.37.

7 Mark 13.33ff, Matthew 24.45ff.

8 See below, p. 366, on Luke 22.27.

9 See below, p. 361, on Luke 17.7ff.

10 Matthew 22.1ff.

11 Luke 14.16ff.

12 Shades of *de modo agri, displicentia, ad gustum* and so forth.

13 Deuteronomy 20.7; 24.5; Herodotus 1.36. See J. M. Creed, *The Gospel according to St. Luke* (1930), p. 192.

14 See below, p. 357f, on Luke 11.5ff.

15 Deuteronomy 17.15; 24.4. See *Orita*, pp. 41ff; also *Studies in Honour of Matthew Black* (1968), p. 236; *Studi in onore di Edoardo Volterra* (1969), vol. 2, pp. 1ff; and *Journal of Biblical Literature*, vol. 90 (1971), pp. 480f.

16 See my forthcoming *Ancient Jewish Law* (1981), part III, 'The Form is the Message' pp. 74ff.

17 Matthew 18.12ff.

18 Luke 15.3ff.

19 e.g. Deuteronomy 12.12. See *Orita*, p. 41.

20 See below, p. 360, on Luke 15.8ff.; and 15.11ff.

21 Luke 11.5ff.

22 This is how it is usually taken.

23 A. Fridrichsen's interpretation, *Symbolae Osloenses*, vol. 13 (1934), pp. 40ff, quoted by J. Jeremias, *Die Gleichnisse Jesu* 6th edn (1962), p. 157.

24 Ecclus. 9.10; 41.21 belonging with 41.16ff.

25 Deuteronomy 22.1, 3, 4. See *Orita*, pp. 29f.

26 Job 31.32.

27 Proverbs 25.17; Horace, *Satires* 1.9.

28 Palestinian *Taanith* 65b.

29 Luke 14.7ff.

30 At Matthew 20.28. See below, p. 367.

31 Plutarch, *Moralia* 148E ff; 615C ff; 644C. See my essay in *Gesellschaft, Kultur, Literatur* – Beiträge Luitpold Wallach Gewidmet (1975), p. 206.

32 Proverbs 25.6f. See J. M. Creed, op. cit., p. 190.

33 Luke 14.28ff.

34 Ecclus. 32.19, the anonymous *quidquid agis prudenter agas et respice finem*; Prov. 20.18, similarly 24.6.

35 Revelation 13.18.

36 Luke 15.8ff.

37 Luke 15.11ff.

38 Proverbs 5.10ff; 12.11; 17.2; 21.17; 23.19ff.

39 Proverbs 5.10ff.

40 Athenaeus, *Deipnosophists* 4.152F f, quoting Posidonius.

41 See below, p. 364, on Luke 7.1ff.

42 Something of an early precedent is discussed by Reuven Yaron and me in *Journal of Semitic Studies*, vol. 1 (1956), pp. 60ff.

43 Luke 16.1ff.

44 Ecclus. 38.33.

45 Aristophanes, *Birds* 1432.

46 Ecclus. 40.28ff with, in the Greek, the same word for 'to beg' as in Luke.

47 Proverbs 6.6ff; 30.25; Babrius, *Fable* 140.

48 Genesis 41.

49 Ecclus. 18.25.

50 Luke 17.7ff.

51 Plutarch, *Aemilius Paulus* 38.3; Cicero, *Letters to Atticus* 1.12, confesses that the loss of his charming young reader affects him more than a slave's death should. See W. Kroll, *Die Kultur der Ciceronischen Zeit* (1933), vol. 2, pp. 86, 114.

52 Luke 18.1ff.

53 See R. C. Thurnwald, art. Recht, in *Reallexikon der Vorgeschichte*, vol. 11 (1927/8), p. 60.

54 See H. B. Tristram, *Eastern Customs in Bible Lands* (1894), p. 228, quoted by B. T. D. Smith, *The Parables of the Synoptic Gospels* (1937), p. 150; and J. Jeremias, op. cit., p. 154.

55 Isaiah 50.6. See my *The New Testament and Rabbinic Judaism* (1956, repr. 1973), pp. 259ff.

56 Matthew 5.39; Luke 6.29.

57 Mark 14.65; 15.19; Matthew 26.67f; 27.30; Luke 22.63f; John 18.22; 19.3.

58 Acts 23.2ff. See my *Sin, Ignorance and Forgiveness in the Bible* (1960), p. 13.

59 See J. M. Creed, op. cit., p. 223. K. H. Rengstorf, *Das Evangelium nach Lukas*, 9th edn (1962), p. 205, gives a fairly literal rendering: *damit sie nicht mir ins Gesicht fährt*.

60 Ecclus. 35.14. See J. M. Creed, op. cit., p. 222; K. H. Rengstorf, op. cit., p.206.

61 Ecclus. 8.3.

62 Proverbs 3.4.

63 Dionysius of Halicarnassus, *Roman Antiquities* 10.10.7. See J. M. Creed, op. cit., pp. 222f.

64 Luke 18.9ff.

65 See below, p. 365, on Luke 21.36.

66 1 Enoch 13.5.

67 *The Woman of Honour* (1768), III 26.

68 Luke 1.25; Genesis 30.23.

69 Luke 1.24.

70 cf. Genesis 17.17; 18.12ff; 21.6.

71 Genesis 3.8, 10.

72 Not, however, in the Greek.

73 See *Orita*, pp. 33, 40.

74 See my *Civil Disobedience in Antiquity* (1972), p. 61.

75 See J. M. Creed, op. cit., pp. 12f.

76 Luke 1.35, 38. See *The New Testament and Rabbinic Judaism*, pp. 27ff.

77 Matthew 1.19ff.

78 Luke 2.40, 52.

79 See J. M. Creed, op. cit., p. 46.

80 1 Samuel 2.26.

81 1 Samuel 9.2, 10.23.

82 Genesis 39.6; 1 Samuel 16.12; 17.42; Daniel 1.4, 15.

83 1 Samuel 16.7.

84 2 Samuel 14.25; 1 Kings 1.6.

85 See below, p. 365, on Luke 19.1ff.

86 Luke 4.22.

87 Mark 6.2, Matthew 13.54.

88 Luke 4.23.

89 *Genesis Rabba* 23, on 4.23; Euripides, Fragment 1071, in A. Nauck, *Tragicorum Graecorum Fragmenta*, 2nd edn (1889). See J. M. Creed, op. cit., p. 68.

90 Wisdom of Solomon 5.3; cf. Ezekiel 18.2; Psalms 44.14, in LXX 43.14.

91 Matthew 8.5ff.

92 Luke 7.1ff.

93 See J. M. Creed, op. cit., p. 100.

94 Mark 5.24ff.

95 Luke 8.47ff.

96 Luke 10.7.

97 Mark 6.10; Matthew 10.11.

98 Ecclus. 29.23f.

99 Athenaeus, *Deipnosophists* 1.8B, quoting Archilochos.

100 Horace, *Epistles* 1.15.28. Maenius, to be sure, has a certain grandeur, having gone through a large inheritance with supreme indifference.

101 Luke 13.17.

102 Isaiah 45.16. See J. M. Creed, op. cit., p. 183.

103 After Luke 21.38.

104 Now John 8.9. No shame term, however.

105 Luke 19.1ff.

106 Plato, *Protagoras* 323D. Crito seems not too happy that his elder son is a bit short for his age: *Euthydemus* 271B. (He also worries about his education: 306D.)

107 Aristophanes, *Frogs* 709.

108 I am sorry for him. Over here, many people are so literal-minded that they mistook his satire on the brutes for an attack on their victims. Hard to believe but true.

109   Luke 21.36.

110   Mark 13; Matthew 24.

111   cf. Revelation 6.17.

112   Luke 22.27.

113   Mark 10.43ff; Matthew 20.26ff.

114   Babylonian *Baba Metzia* 75b; *Sotah* 21b; *Pesahim* 50b.

115   Babylonian *Sotah* 20a.

116   Babylonian *Pesahim* 50b.

117   Or such difficulty as remains even on the basis of J. D. M. Derrett's interpretation, *Law in the New Testament* (1970), pp. 48ff.

118   Proverbs 3.4. Cf. the clause from Dionysius of Halicarnassus adduced above.

119   I have penned the first draft of an *Encomium Prudentiae*.

120   See my 'Typologie im Werk des Flavius Josephus', No. 6 of *Sitzungsberichte der Bayerischen Akademie der Wissenschaften* (1977), pp. 28f, ET *Journal of Jewish Studies*, vol. 31 (1980), pp. 35f.

121   Luke 12.16ff; 14.28ff (discussed above); 12.13ff. See J. M. Creed, op. cit., pp. 173, 194, and my article in *Zeitschrift der Savigny-Stiftung*, vol. 72 (1955), Roman. Abt., pp. 326ff.

122   At Matthew 20.28, as already mentioned.

123   Acts 5.5, 11 (cf. 19.17); Deut. 13.12; 17.13; 19.20; 21.21; see *Orita*, p. 40. The 'church' of Acts 5.11 may correspond to 'Israel' or 'the people' of Deut. 13.12; 17.13.

124   See J. M. Creed, op. cit., p. 68.

C. K. BARRETT
Bibliography of Published Works 1942–80

1942
'κατέλαβεν in John 1.5', *ET* liii (June 1942), p. 297.

1943
'Questions about Reformed Theology: (6) Does it ignore Modern Scholarship?', *The Presbyter* (ns 1 June), pp. 8, 9, 16.
'Q: a Re-examination', *ET* liv (September) pp. 320–3.

1947
Review: J. Levie, *Sous les yeux de l'incroyant* (Bruxelles 1946), in *Erasmus* i (Feb.), pp. 129–31.
'The OT in the Fourth Gospel', *JTS* xlviii (July–Oct.) pp. 155–69.
The Holy Spirit and the Gospel Tradition (SPCK, London), pp. viii + 176.

1948
'The Imperatival Participle' *ET* lix (March), pp. 165f.
'The place of Eschatology in the Fourth Gospel', *ET* lix (August), pp. 302–5.

1949
Review: A. C. Headlam, *The Fourth Gospel as History* (Oxford 1948), *JTS* l (Jan.–Apr.), pp. 82–4.

1950
Review: T. Innitzer, *Leidens-ü. Verklarüngsgeschichte Jesu* (Wien 1948), *Erasmus* iii (June), pp. 361–4.
Review: A. Schweitzer, *The Psychiatric Study of Jesus* (Boston 1948), *Erasmus* iii (Apr.), pp. 197f.
Review: J. Maritain, *La Pensée de Saint Paul* (Paris 1947), *Erasmus* iii (May), pp. 255f.
'The Holy Spirit in the Fourth Gospel', *JTS* ns i (Apr.), pp. 1–15.
'New Testament Chronicle', *JTS* ns i (Oct.), pp. 247–56.

1951
Review: S. G. F. Brandon, *The Fall of Jerusalem and the Christian Church* (London 1951), *View Review* ii (July), 8.
'New Testament Chronicle', *JTS* ns ii (Oct.), pp. 245–56.

1952
'New Testament Chronicle', *JTS* ns iii (Oct.), pp. 312–20.

1953
Review: C. T. Chapman, *The Conflict of the Kingdoms* (London 1951), *Erasmus* vi (June), pp. 391–3.

'New Testament Chronicle', *JTS* ns iv (Oct.), pp. 311–20.
'New Testament Eschatology I', *SJT* vi (June), pp. 136–55.
'New Testament Eschatology II', *SJT* vi (Sept.), pp. 225–43.
'Paul and the "Pillar" Apostles', in *Studia Paulina in honorem J. de Zwaan*, ed.
  J. N. Sevenster and W. C. van Unnik (Haarlem), pp. 1–19.
Review: S. L. Greenslade, *Studies in the Early Church* (London 1953), *Durham University Journal* xlvi (ns xv) (Dec.), pp. 30f.

1954
'New Testament Commentaries: I Classical Commentaries', *ET* lxv (Jan.),
  pp. 109–11.
'New Testament Commentaries: II Gospels and Acts', *ET* lxv (Feb.),
  pp. 143–6.
'New Testament Commentaries: III Epistles and Revelation', *ET* lxv
  (March), pp. 177–80.
'Important and Influential Foreign Books: Cullmann's "Christ and Time"',
  ET lxv (Sept.), pp. 369–72.
Review: H.v. Campenhausen, *Kirchliches Amt und Geistliche Vollmacht*
  (Tübingen 1953), *Erasmus* vii (Oct.), pp. 586–90.
Reviews: *JTS* ns v (Oct.) as follows:
  C. F. D. Moule, *An Idiom Book of New Testament Greek* (CUP 1953), pp. 243f.
  E. Percy, *Die Botschaft Jesu* (Lund 1953), pp. 252f.
  G. Dix, *Jew and Greek* (London 1953), pp. 256f.
  H. W. Bartsch, ed., *Kerygma and Myth* (London 1953), pp. 257f.
  C. H. Dodd, *New Testament Studies* (Manchester 1953), pp. 258ff.
  R. Bultmann, *Theologie des Neuen Testaments* (iii) (Tübingen 1953), pp. 260ff.
  A. R. George, *Communion with God in the New Testament* (London 1953), pp.
    262f.
  E. Fascher, *Textgeschichte als Hermeneutisches Problem* (Halle 1953), p. 315.
  E. Smalley, *Towards an Understanding of the Gospels* (London 1953), p. 316.
  R. Koh, *The Writings of St. Luke* (Hong Kong 1953), p. 316.
  R. Dunkerley, *The Hope of Jesus* (London 1953), p. 317.
  J. N. Geldenhuys, *Supreme Authority* (London 1953), pp. 317f.
  G. Lindeskog, *Studien zum Neutestamentlichen Schöpfungsgedanken* (Uppsala
    1952), p. 318.
  M. Barnett, *The Living Flame* (London 1953), p. 318.
The Holy Spirit and the Gospel Tradition (SPCK, London), corrected impression,
  see 1947.
'Zweck des vierten Evangeliums', *ZST* xxii (1953–4), pp. 257–73.

1955
Review: *Rabbinische Texte: Die Tosefta* (Stuttgart) *Erasmus*, viii (Oct.), pp.
  593–5.
'The Lamb of God', *NTS* i (Feb.), pp. 210–18.
Review: *Neutestamentliche Studien für R. Bultmann*, ed. W. Eltester (Berlin 1954),
  JTS ns vi (Oct.), pp. 267–70.
The Gospel According to St John (SPCK, London), pp. xii + 531.
The Fourth Gospel in Recent Criticism and Interpretation, by W. F. Howard, rev. edn
  (SPCK, London), pp. xiv + 327.

1956
'Important Hypotheses Reconsidered: V. The Holy Spirit and the Gospel Tradition', *ET* lxvii (Feb.), pp. 142–5.
Review: A. Farrer, *St. Matthew and St. Mark* (London 1954), *JTS* ns vii (Apr.), pp. 107–10.
Review: L. Morris, *The Apostolic Preaching of the Cross* (London 1955), *JTS* vii (Oct.), p. 347.
The New Testament Background: Selected Documents (SPCK, London), pp. xxiv + 276.
'The Methodist Church and Episcopacy', *London Quarterly and Holborn Review*.
Review: C. L. Mitton, *The Formation of the Pauline Corpus* (London 1955), *LQR*.
'The Eschatology of the Epistle to the Hebrews', in *The Background of the New Testament and its Eschatology*: Studies in honour of C. H. Dodd, ed. W. D. Davies and D. Daube (Cambridge).

1957
Biblical Preaching and Biblical Scholarship (Epworth Press, London), pp. 18.
'Papyrus Bodmer II: A Preliminary Report', *ET* lxviii (March), pp. 174–7.
The Epistle to the Romans (A. & C. Black, London), pp. viii + 294.
Review: E. Repo, *Der Begriff 'Rhema' im Biblisch-Griechen* (Helsinki 1954), *JTS* ns viii (April), p. 143.
Review: R. Bultmann, *Theology of the New Testament* (ET London 1955), *JTS* ns viii, p. 221.
Review: H. Schneider, *Der Text der Gutenbergbibel* (Bern 1954), *Erasmus* x (Feb.), pp. 83ff.
'Myth and the New Testament I', *ET* lxviii (Aug.), pp. 345–8.
'Myth and the New Testament II', *ET* lxviii (Sept.), pp. 359–62.
Review: R. Bultmann, *Primitive Christianity in its Contemporary Setting* (London 1956), *JTS* ns viii (Oct.), pp. 313ff.
Various articles in *The Oxford Dictionary of the Christian Church*, ed. F. L. Cross (Oxford).
'The Apostles in and after the New Testament', *Svensk Exegetisk Årsbok* xxi, pp. 30–49.
Review: *Studies in the Fourth Gospel*, ed. F. L. Cross (London 1957), *Mowbray's Journal* 65 (Autumn 1957), pp. 9f.
Review: H. Becker, *Die Reden des Johannesevangelium und der Stil der gnostischen Offenbarungsrede* (Göttingen 1956), *Th.Lit.* no. 12 (1957), pp. 911f.
'The Gospel of Truth', *ET* lxix (March), pp. 167–70.
The Epistle to the Romans (Harper, New York), pp. viii + 294. See 1957.
Review: R. M. Grant, *The Letter and the Spirit* (London 1957), *ET* lxix (Apr.), pp. 204f.
Review: N. Q. Hamilton, *The Holy Spirit and Eschatology in Paul* (Edinburgh 1957), *ET* lxx (Oct.), pp. 8f.
'Lk 22.15: To eat the Passover', *JTS* ns ix (Oct.), pp. 305–7.
Review: O. Cullmann, *The Early Church* (London 1956), *Th. Lit.* no. 7 (1958), pp. 520ff.
'Books on the Gospels', *View Review* ix (Nov.), p. 6.

375

1959

'Professor Bultmann', *ET* lxx (Jan.), pp. 125f.

'New Testament Books', *View Review* x (Feb.), p. 8.

'Apostolic Succession', *ET* lxx (Apr.), pp. 200–2.

Westcott as Commentator, Westcott Memorial Lecture 1958 (CUP), pp. 26.

Die Umwelt des Neuen Testaments, Wissenschaftliche Untersuchungen zum Neuen Testament 4, tr. Dr C. Colpe (J. C. B. Mohr (Paul Siebeck) Tübingen), pp. xii + 290.

'The Background of Mark 10.45', in *New Testament Essays*, Studies in Memory of T. W. Manson, ed. A. J. B. Higgins (Manchester UP), pp. 1–18.

'Apostolic Succession Again', *ET* (Aug.), pp. 330f.

Yesterday, Today, and For Ever: The New Testament Problem (Durham University), pp. 20.

Review: W. Wilkens, *Die Entstehungsgeschichte des vierten Evangeliums* (Zollikon 1958), *Th. Lit.* no. 11, pp. 828f.

Review: E. E. Ellis, *Paul's use of the Old Testament* (Oliver & Boyd 1957), Society for Old Testament Studies *Book List* 26.

1960

Review: M. F. Wiles, *The Spiritual Gospel* (Cambridge 1960), *ET* lxxi (June), p. 263.

Review: K. Grobel, *The Gospel of Truth* (A. & C. Black 1960), *ET* lxxii (Dec.), p. 76.

Review: B. Gärtner, *Die rätselhapfen Termini Nazoräer und Iskariot* (C. W. K. Gleerup 1957), *JTS* ns xi pp. 135f..

'Four Books on the NT', *View Review* xi (Nov.), p. 9.

1961

Review: R. McL. Wilson, *Studies in the Gospel of Thomas* (Mowbray 1960), *ET* lxxii (May), p. 233.

Review: J. N. Birdsall, *The Bodmer Papyrus of the Gospel of John* (Tyndale Press 1960), *ET* lxxii (June), p. 267.

Review: A. Guilding, *The Fourth Gospel and Jewish Worship* (Clarendon Press 1960), SOTS *Book List* 64.

Luke the Historian in Recent Study, A. S. Peake Memorial Lecture No. 6 (Epworth Press, London), pp. 76.

'Recent Biblical Theologies: I. Ethelbert Stauffer's Theology of the New Testament', *ET* lxxii (Sept.), pp. 356–60.

Review: B. Gärtner, *The Theology of the Gospel of Thomas* (London 1961), *ET* lxxiii (Oct.), pp. 12f.

Review: T. F. Glasson, *Greek Influence in Jewish Eschatology* (London 1961), *ET* lxxiii (Nov.), p. 40.

Review: R. M. Grant, *The Earliest Lives of Jesus* (London 1961), *ET* lxxiii (Dec.), p. 72.

1962

Review: H. J. Schoeps, *Paulus* (Tübingen 1959), *JTS* ns xii (Oct. 1961 publ. Jan. 1962), pp. 324–7.

The Book that Makes Men Free (Epworth Press, London), pp. 15.

'John', *Peake's Commentary on the Bible*, ed. M. Black and H. H. Rowley (Nelson), pp. 844–69.

'The Theological Vocabulary of the Fourth Gospel and the Gospel of Truth', in *Current Issues in New Testament Interpretation*; Essays in honour of Otto A. Piper, ed. W. Klassen and G. F. Snyder (London), pp. 210–23, 297–8.

'1662 and 1962', *ET* lxxiii (July), pp. 291–5.

'Recent Trends in New Testament Scholarship', *The Fraternal* No. 126 (Oct.), pp. 7–11.

From First Adam to Last: A Study in Pauline Theology (A. & C. Black, London), pp. x + 124.

1963

The Pastoral Epistles in the New English Bible, With Introduction and Commentary (Clarendon Press, Oxford), pp. viii + 151.

'The Bible in the New Testament Period', in *The Church's Use of the Bible Past and Present*, ed. D. E. Nineham (SPCK, London), pp. 1–24.

Review: R. McL. Wilson, *The Gospel of Philip* (Mowbray 1962), *ET* lxxiv (March), pp. 171f.

'Cephas and Corinth', in *Abraham unser Vater*, Festschrift für Otto Michel, ed. O. Betz, M. Hengel, P. Schmidt (Leiden), pp. 1–12.

Reading through Romans (Epworth Press, London), pp. 94.

1964

Biblical Problems and Biblical Preaching, Facet Books, Biblical Series 6 (Fortress Press, Philadelphia), pp. xii + 52. Reprint of *Yesterday, Today, and For Ever* (see 1959) and *Biblical Preaching and Biblical Scholarship* (see 1957).

'Christianity at Corinth', Manson Memorial Lecture 1963, *BJRL* 46 (March), pp. 269–97.

'John xvii: An Exposition of the Prayer for Unity', *Faith and Unity* VIII, 3 (May), pp. 43f.

'The Ministry in the New Testament', in *The Doctrine of the Church*, ed. D. Kirkpatrick (Epworth Press, London), pp. 39–63.

Review: J. N. D. Kelly, *The Pastoral Epistles* (London 1963), *JTS* ns xv (Oct.), pp. 375ff.

'Stephen and the Son of Man', in *Apophoreta*; Festschrift für Ernst Haenchen, ed. W. Eltester (Berlin), pp. 32–8.

Review: C. F. D. Moule, *The Birth of the New Testament* (London 1962), *Th. Lit.* 89 (June), pp. 429ff.

1965

'Immortality and Resurrection', *LQR* (April), pp. 91–102.

Reviews: *LQR* (April), pp. 161f.

  H.Q. Morton and G. H. Macgregor, *The Structure of Luke and Acts* (London, 1964).

  M. D. Goulder, *Type and History in Acts* (SPCK, London, 1964).

  F. V. Filson, *Three Crucial Decades* (Epworth Press, London, 1964).

'Things Sacrificed to Idols', *NTS* xi (Jan.), pp. 138–53.

1966

Review: D. M. Smith, *The Composition and Order of the Fourth Gospel* (New Haven/London 1965), *JTS* ns xvii (Oct.), pp. 438–41.

Notice: W. G. Kümmel, *Heilsgeschehen und Geschichte* (Marburg 1965), *JTS* ns xvii (Oct.), p. 557.

Notice: A. Farrer, *St. Matthew and St. Mark* (London 1966), *JTS* ns xvii (Oct.), p. 557.

1967

History and Faith: The Study of the Passion (BBC publication), pp. 40.

Review: R. E. Brown, Anchor Bible: *The Gospel According to John* (i–xii) (New York 1966), *JBL*, pp. 481–4.

Jesus and the Gospel Tradition (SPCK, London), pp. xii + 116.

1968

Jesus and the Gospel Tradition (Fortress Press, Philadelphia) American edn; see 1967.

The First Epistle to the Corinthians (A. & C. Black, London), pp. xii + 410.

The First Epistle to the Corinthians (Harper & Row, New York and Evanston).

Review: R. McL. Wilson, *Gnosis and the New Testament* (Oxford 1968), *ET* lxxix (Sept.), pp. 363f.

'Anglican-Methodist Union: A Symposium, 5', *Church Quarterly* i (Oct.), pp. 114–19.

Review: L. E. Keck and J. L. Martyn, *Studies in Luke-Acts* (London 1968), *CQ* i (Oct.), pp. 163f.

'Anglican-Methodist Relations', *The Churchman* 82.4 (Winter), pp. 262–77.

Review: S. Freyne, *The Twelve: Disciples and Apostles* (London 1968), *CQ* (Jan. 1969, publ. 1968), pp. 237f.

1969

Review: H. von Campenhausen, *Die Entstehung der christlichen Bibel* (Tübingen 1968), *Erasmus* xxi (June), pp. 332ff.

Review: J. Morgenstern, *Some Significant Antecedents of Christianity* (Leiden 1966), *JTS* ns xx (April), pp. 271f.

'Titus', in *Neotestamentica et Semitica*; Studies in honour of Matthew Black, ed. E. E. Ellis and M. Wilcox (Edinburgh), pp. 1–14.

'Theology in the World of Learning', *Australian Biblical Review* xvii (Oct.), pp. 9–20.

1970

Review: *Regensburger Neues Testament*, ed. O. Kuss, 7.2 (Brox 1969); 8.2 (Michel 1968); 10 (Richter 1962), *Erasmus* xxii (March), pp. 204–7.

'Ο 'ΑΔΙΚΗΣΑΣ (2 Cor. 7.12)', in *Verborum Veritas*; Festschrift für Gustav Stählin, ed. O. Böcher and K. Haacker (Theologischer Verlag Rolf Brockhaus, Wuppertal).

'The Interpretation of the Old Testament in the New', in *Cambridge History of the Bible*: I, From the Beginnings to Jerome, ed. P. R. Ackroyd and C. F. Evans (Cambridge), pp. 377–411.

'ψευδαπόστολοι (2 Cor. 11.13)', in *Mélanges Bibliques* en hommage au R. P. Beda Rigaux, ed. A. Deschamps and A. de. Halleux (Gembloux), pp. 377–96.

The Signs of an Apostle (Epworth Press, London), pp. 143.

Das Johannesevangelium und das Judentum: Franz Delitzsch Vorlesungen 1967 (Verlag W. Kohlhammer, Stuttgart), pp. 79.

'I am not ashamed of the Gospel', *Foi et Salut selon S. Paul (Épître aux Romains 1.16)*, Analecta Biblica 42 (Rome), pp. 19–50.

'The Holy Spirit', *ABR* xviii (Oct.), pp. 1–9.

1971

The Prologue of St John's Gospel: The Ethel M. Wood Lecture of 1970 (Athlone Press, University of London), pp. 28.

'Paul's Opponents in 2 Cor.', *NTS* xvii (April), pp. 233–54.

'Christianity and History', *Theological Review*, pp. 19f.

Reviews in *CQ* 3.4 (April), pp. 329f:

    G. Johnston, *The Spirit-Paraclete in the Gospel of John* (Cambridge 1970).

    T. E. Pollard, *Johannine Christology and the Early Church* (Cambridge 1970).

1972

'Vincent Taylor', *Proceedings of the British Academy* LVI, pp. 283–92.

'Joseph Barber Lightfoot', *DUJ* lxiv (xxxiii) 3 (June), pp. 193–204.

New Testament Essays (SPCK, London), pp. viii + 159.

Review: R. Bultmann, *The Gospel of John – A Commentary* (Oxford 1971), *ET* lxxxiii (Mar.), p. 185.

1973

The Second Epistle to the Corinthians (A. & C. Black, London), pp. xvi + 354.

'Conversion and Conformity: The Freedom of the Spirit and the Institutional Church', *Christ and Spirit in the New Testament*, Studies in honour of C. F. D. Moule, ed. B. Lindars and S. S. Smalley (Cambridge), pp. 359–81.

Review: H. W. Hoehner, *Herod Antipas* (Cambridge 1972), *DUJ* lxv (xxxiv) 3 (June), pp. 316f.

Review: M. Dibelius and H. Conzelmann, *The Pastoral Epistles* (Philadelphia 1972), *ET* lxxxv (Oct.), p. 23.

1974

'What to Teach', *Epworth Review* i.1 (Jan.), pp. 95–108.

'The Father is greater than I' (John 14.28): Subordinationist Christology in the New Testament', in *Neues Testament und Kirche*, für Rudolf Schnackenburg, ed. J. Gnilka (Freiburg), pp. 144–59.

'Pauline Controversies in the Post-Pauline Period', *NTS* xx (Apr.), pp. 229–45.

'John and the Synoptic Gospels', *ET* lxxxv (May), pp. 228–33.

'Paul's Speech in the Areopagus', in *New Testament Christianity for Africa and the World*, Essays in honour of Harry Sawyerr, ed. M. E. Glasswell and E. W. Fasholé-Luke (SPCK, London), pp. 69–77.

Review: E. Lohse, *Die Einheit des Neuen Testaments* (Göttingen 1973), *Göttingische Gelehrte Anzeigen* 226, pp. 179–86.

1975
Review: S. Scott Bartchy, ΜΑΛΛΟΝ ΧΡΗΣΑΙ: *First-Century Slavery and the Interpretation of 1 Cor. 7.21* (Missoula 1973), *JTS* xxvi (Apr.), pp. 173f.
'The House of Prayer and the Den of Thieves', in *Jesus und Paulus*; Festschrift für W. G. Kümmel, ed. E. E. Ellis and E. Grässer (Göttingen), pp. 13–20.
'Unity Sermon', *Ushaw Magazine* 245 (June), pp. 39–42.
The Gospel of John and Judaism (SPCK, London), pp. x + 101. See 1970.
Review: B. A. Pearson, *The pneumatikos-psychikos Terminology in 1 Cor.* (Missoula 1973), *JTS* xxvi (Oct.), p. 458.
'Albert Schweitzer and the New Testament', *ET* lxxxvii (Oct.), pp. 4–10.

1976
'Das Fleisch des Menschensohnes (John 6.53)', in *Jesus und der Menschensohn*, Festschrift für Anton Vögtle, ed. R. Pesch, R. Schnackenburg, and O. A. Kaiser (Freiburg), pp. 342–54.
'The Allegory of Abraham, Sarah, and Hagar in the Argument of Galatians', in *Rechtfertigung*, Festschrift für Ernst Käsemann, ed. J. Friedrich, W. Pöhlmann and P. Stuhlmacher (Göttingen), pp. 1–16.
'Christocentric or Theocentric? Observations on the Theological Method of the Fourth Gospel', in *La Notion biblique de Dieu*, Bibliotheca Ephemeridum Theologicarum Lovaniensium XLI, ed. J. Coppens, pp. 361–76.
'Acts and the Pauline Corpus', *ET* lxxxviii (Oct.), pp. 2–5.
'Jews and Judaizers in the Epistles of Ignatius', in *Jews, Greeks and Christians*; Essays in honour of W. D. Davies, ed. R. Hammerton-Kelly and R. Scroggs (Leiden), pp. 220–44.

1977
'Fall and Responsibility of Israel', in *Die Israelfrage nach Röm. 9–11*, Monographische Reihe von *Benedictina*, Biblisch-ökumenische Abteilung 3, ed. Lorenzo De Lorenzi (Rome), pp. 99–121.

1978
'Paul's Address to the Ephesian Elders', in *God's Christ and His People*; Studies in honour of N. A. Dahl, ed. J. Jervell and W. A. Meeks (Oslo), pp. 107–21.
'Gestanten zu 1 Kor. 15.1–11', in *Erbe und Auftrag* 54 (Feb.), pp. 73–6.
'Shaliah and Apostle' in *Donum Gentilicium*; New Testament Studies in honour of David Daube, ed. C. K. Barrett, E. Bammel and W. D. Davies (OUP), pp. x + 342, pp. 88–102.
The Gospel According to St John (2nd edn, SPCK, London), pp. xvi + 638.
'Biblical Classics IV: J. H. Moulton, *A Grammar of New Testament Greek: Prolegomena*', *ET* xc (Dec.), pp. 68–71.

1979
'Is there a theological tendency in Codex Bezae?', in *Text and Interpretation: Studies in the New Testament presented to Matthew Black*, ed. E. Best and R. McL. Wilson (Cambridge), pp. 15–27.
'Light on the Holy Spirit from Simon Magus (Acts 8.4–25)', in *Les Actes des Apôtres: Tradition, redaction, théologie*, Bibliotheca Ephemeridum Theologicarum Lovaniensium XLVIII, ed. J. Kremer, pp. 281–95.

'Theologia Crucis – in Acts', in *Theologia Crucis – Signum Crucis*: Festschrift für Erich Dinkler zum 70. Geburtstag, ed. C. Andresen and G. Klein (Tübingen), pp. 73–84.

'Immortality and Resurrection', in *Resurrection and Immortality*, ed. C. S. Duthie (London), pp. 68–88. See 1965.

Reviews: *ET* xci (Oct.), p. 25:

W. A. Meeks and R. R. Wilken, *Jews and Christians in Antioch* (Missoula).

E. Richard, *Acts 6.1—8.4: The Author's Method of Composition* (Missoula).

'Ethics and Eschatology: A Resumé', in *Dimensions de la vie chrétienne* (Rom. 12—13); Série Monographique de *Benedictina*, Section Biblica-Oecuménique 4, ed. Lorenzo De Lorenzi (Rome), pp. 221–35.

1980

'Il Simbolismo nel IV Evangelo', in *Protestantesimo* XXXV (2/1980), pp. 65–80.

Review of M. Hengel, *Acts and the History of Earliest Christianity*, in *New Blackfriars* 61 (May 1980), pp. 246f.

'Che cos' è la Teologia del Nuovo Testamento?', in *Protestantesimo* XXXV (4/1980), pp. 207–29.

INDEX OF NAMES AND SUBJECTS

INDEX OF BIBLICAL REFERENCES

Habakkuk

2.4	21, 29, 128

Zechariah

14.4–5	126
14.5	87–8

Malachi

3.23–4	130

Matthew

1.—28.—	356–7, 359, 363–7
4.1	209
5.39, 43	11
13.41	88
16.18	265, 268
16.27	88
22.15–22	11
23.15	46
24.8	58
24.30–1	88
27.52	96
28.20	116

Mark

1.—16.—	356, 364–7
1.12	209
8.38	87
9.41	136
10.45	115
12.35–7	150
13. *passim*	57–8
14.62	74–5, 150
15.26–32	147

Luke

1.—24.—	355–72
2.30	70
4.1	209
6.13–16	295
7.35	116
9.26	87
10.24	70
11.49–51	116

22. *passim*	292
24. *passim*	294–7
24.44–9	290–1, 293–301

John

1.3, 4, 10	163
1.14, 18	118
3.13	116, 118
3.14–16	123
3.16–17	118
5.17–19	164
6.51, 53, 62	115
20.28	170

Acts

1.—28.—	368
1. *passim*	295
1.2, 4–8	294
1.8	290–301
2.4–6, 13, 15	244
2.36	124
5.51	124
6.9, 11, 14	17
8.21	84
9.13, 32, 41	86
10.1, 11, 18	297
10.22	87
11.19–21	18
11.26	124
12.17	297
13.33	124
13.47	295
16.3	37
17	350
20.18–35	290
20.32	88, 99
21.17–19	297
26. *passim*	295–7
26.10	86
26.16–23	290–301
26.18	99
28.17–22, 25–8	291

389

INDEX OF MODERN AUTHORS

WILLIAM V. CROCKETT

Paul and Paulinism